MATH | for Business and Life

John Webber

Executive Editor	Carol Rose
Editorial/Marketing Consultant	Richard T. Hercher, Jr.
Development and Research	Craig Beytien
Cover	Gary Bandfield
Interior Design	Design Type Service
Color Design	Stephanie Staheli
Chapter Opening Illustrations	Liz Ence
Composition	Jason Hintze
Accuracy Checking	Jina Severinsen
Web Design	Jac Koeman
Online Assessment Tools	John Travis Webber
Instructor Resources	Josh Mendenhall

Photo Credits

Chapter 1: Burger King, courtesy of Jack Richard Berry III; *Chapter 5:* UPS airplane, courtesy of United Parcel Service; *Chapter 7:* Bank lobby, courtesy of Zions Bank; *Chapter 8:* U.S. Congress, courtesy of Congressman Tom Barrett; *Chapter 10:* Bank vault, courtesy of Zions Bank, Car assembly line; courtesy of Scott Klett, Ford Motor Company; *Chapters 11 and 17:* Anne Scheiber, AP/Wide World Photos; *Chapter 12:* Casino, courtesy of Peppermill Resort*Spa*Casino (Reno, Nevada); *Chapter 16:* American Stock Exchange trading floor, courtesy of American Stock Exchange; *Chapter 22:* Firemen, courtesy of Gina Bell, Salt Lake City Fire Department. *All other photos:* Posh Photography/Marla Lofgreen.

Cartoon Credits

Chapter 1: Welcome to Hell's Library, Kent Minson; *Chapter 3:* Roundtable, Kent Minson; *Chapter 16* Fun Corner, Tara Webber. *All other Fun Corner cartoons:* Kent Minson.

Article Credits

Ann Landers: permission granted by Ann Landers and Creators Syndicate. *Dear Abby:* Reprinted with permission from Dear Abby column by Abigail and Jeanne Phillips—© Universal Press Syndicate, all rights reserved. *Ask Marilyn:* Reprinted with permission—© Parade and Marilyn vos Savant. Several sources from Dave Barry, humor columnist for the *Miami Herald:* (1) *Dave Barry's Greatest Hits:* Copyright © 1988 by Dave Barry, used with permission of Crown Publishers, a division of Random House, Inc; (2) *Dave Barry's Homes and Other Black Holes:* Copyright © 1988 by Dave Barry, illustrations copyright © 1988 by Jeff MacNelly; used with permission of Fawcett Books, a division of Random House, Inc.; (3) Dave Barry articles: © Tribune Media Services, Inc, all rights reserved, reprinted with permission. John Papanikolas, former writer, *Salt Lake Tribune*.

Fun Corner Contributions

Dan Engler (San Antonio, TX), Jay Hirschi (Chicago, IL), Orson Porter (SLC, UT), Sandra Streitenberger (Tipp City, OH), and Sara Au (Orville, OH).

Copyright © 2016, Olympus Publishing Company. All rights reserved. No part of this publication may be reproduced or distributed in any form or by any means, or stored in a data base or retrieval system, without the prior written permission of Olympus Publishing Company, including, but not limited to, in any network or other electronic storage or transmission, or broadcast for distance learning.

To place an order: orders@olympuspub.com OR 800-844-1856

General questions: info@olympuspub.com

Student hotline: studentsupport@olympuspub.com

Faculty support: facultysupport@olympuspub.com

Author: jwebber@olympuspub.com OR 800-6WEBBER

Website: www.webbertext.com

A Note to Students

Guide to Success

Many people consider math to be a logical, fun subject. To others, "math" is a four-letter word! If you are one of those, don't be scared. The text is written in a friendly conversational way, in a logical sequence, and with straight-forward language. To get the most out of this book and other aids

Step 1   **Read the introductory page of each chapter.** This page gives the big picture. Taking a moment to read it will get you going in the right direction.

Step 2   **Each chapter is divided into units; read one unit at a time.**

How can I tell if the stuff has sunk in?

- Do the U-Try-It questions at the end of each unit. Answers are shown below the questions.
- If you get a different asnwer, look at the step-by-step solutions in Appendix A.
- Go on to the next unit.

Step 3   **Review the "Chapter in a Nutshell" at the end of the chapter.** This short reference guide summarizes the chapter.

Step 4   **Do the Chapter Review Problems at the end of the chapter.** Some students make the mistake of skipping review problems because problems done in class (with an instructor's help) seem so easy; then later (like at test time), a similar problem looks like a foreign language!

How can I tell if I get the right answer?

- Answers to every problem are in Appendix B.
- If you get a different answer, step-by-step solutions are provided, free of charge, on our website. Go to **www.webbertext.com** and click Step-by-Step Solutions.

What if I'm still stumped?

- Contact us through the Student Hotline. Go to our website, click I Need Help!, explain your dilemma, and click Submit.

What if I need more practice?

- Student Tutorials (free of charge on our website) are a fun way to sharpen your skills even more.

Step 5   **Do the Practice Test at the end of the chapter before taking the real one in class.** Answers are in Appendix B. Solutions are on our website.

I hope this book helps you in your endeavors. Have an enjoyable, successful course, and much success in your business and personal ventures.

                                                                                                                                John Webber

Special Features

Math for Business and Life was written to provide up-to-date ways of solving business problems—not only for the business person—but also for the consumer and investor. The text deals with realistic, down-to-earth situations and will continue to be a good reference book even after you have finished school. Hopefully, you will join thousands of others by concluding, This is stuff I can really use! Here are a few features of the text that make learning easier:

Objectives These are the goals of the chapter. They are summarized on the introductory page of each chapter and referenced throughout the chapter.

Boxes Three kinds of boxes are used to highlight important information.

  How-To Boxes Include easy-to-follow steps or guidelines.

  Formula Boxes Contain formulas.

TIP **Tip Boxes** Provide shortcuts, memory aids, mistakes to avoid, and real-world suggestions.

Examples Each chapter contains lots of examples, with step-by-step solutions.

Word Problem Guide This easy guide is like a map, to get from Point A (the question) to Point B (the answer).

Activities

  THINK activities are designed to provoke thought and to help see the big picture.

  EXPLORE activities allow you to use the Internet and spreadsheet programs to increase real-world awareness and skills.

  APPLY activities provide the opportunity to apply concepts in the real world and to meet businesspeople who use the concepts each day in their work.

Fun Corner Appearing at the beginning of each chapter, this has tidbits of fun, related stuff.

Calculators We provide calculator keystrokes sparingly, for unique situations. If you are using the HP 10BII+ or TI BAII PLUS, a few keystrokes are provided in Appendix C to get you started. If you are using another calculator, chances are we have a set of keystrokes for your calculator; you can send a request for customized keystrokes to *studentsupport@olympuspub.com*.

TVM Methods Most books rely on tables to solve time-value-of-money (TVM) problems. Because *tables are not used in the real world* (for good reason), we are saying NO! to tables. Instead, we cover TVM topics with formulas (Ch 10, 11), financial calculators (Ch 12, 13, 17), and Excel (Appendix E); this innovative approach allows instructors to use their favorite method(s).

Web Visit our site at **www.webbertext.com**. The site contains step-by-step solutions to Chapter Review Problems and Practice Tests, a Pre-Quiz (so you can measure your knowledge at the start of the course), study tips, Student Tutorials, calculator videos, auto-graded homework assignments, plus many other useful things.

Contributing Authors

I extend my special thanks to the following individuals who have authored material that is used in the text and ancillary materials. *Math for Business and Life* is a much better product because of your expertise and willingness to share. Thanks so much!

Marylynne Abbott—Ozarks Technical Community College
Sara Au—North Central State College
Emily Asher—Bates Technical College
Jesse Cecil—College of the Siskiyous
Jim Ellis—Central Oregon Community College
Rosemary Fajgier—Burlington County Community College
Betsie Moore—Edison Community College
Stephanie Morgan—Alaska Pacific University
Joe Polidoro—Berkshire Community College
Teresa A. Sept—College of Southern Idaho
Sandra Streitenberger—Edison Community College

Acknowledgments

This book reflects the efforts of many people. I extend my thanks:

- To the thousands of instructors who responded to our questionnaires. This is a better book as a result of your input.

- To users of previous editions for your insightful comments and suggestions.

- To the following reviewers, proof readers, and accuracy checkers for your valuable feedback.

Diana Arn	Dave DeBruyne	Kent Harfst	Nick Lang	Sandra Robertson
Robert Avakian	Rachelle Duncan	Cristy Hediger	Jason Malozzi	Dawn Stevens
Amber Ballard	Karen Emerson	Tish Holleman	Sheila Mclendon	Terry Stokes
Jill Bandfield	Paula Emerson-Glade	Juanita Irvin Fraley	Terry Moore	JoAnne Strickland
Yvonne Block	Larry Epperson	Jan Jordan	Nora Niece	Cara Thompson
Carolyn Chapel	Dorvin Froseth	Elizabeth Katz	Sue Norris	Leslie Thompson
Ann Clifton	Kristin Hagins	R.W. Kennedy	Richard Paradiso	Jimmie A. VanAlphen
Pat Cunningham	Karen Halpern	Jan Kraft	Tatyana Pashnyak	Jennifer Weeks

- To individuals outside the academic community for providing valuable suggestions in your area of expertise.

    Mark R. Duffin, CPA—Income tax topics
    Mark E. Papanikolas, CPA—Accounting topics
    Ben K. Blake—Stocks, bonds, and mutual funds
    Wayne F. Gledhill, CLU—Life insurance
    Jim A. Webber, Foothill Oriental Rugs—Merchandising and international business
    Bill Pizza, Cottonwood Insurance—Casualty insurance
    Ron Baker, State Farm Insurance—Auto insurance
    Landon Ward, Zions Bank—Banking
    The staff at Hewlett Packard
    The staff at Texas Instruments
    The many governmental officials, too numerous to mention

- To my many students over the years, for their valuable feedback and suggestions.

- To our partners in research and development—The Grandview Group—for your creative guidance and advice.

- To the entire Olympus Team for putting your hearts and talents into this edition. You have made this a top-quality product. The key members of the team are listed on the copyright page.

- And last, to my family and friends, who have been major cheerleaders—especially to my cute wife Debbie and my children Wendy, Robin, Toni, Tara, and Casey.

Our Lineup of Products for the 5th Edition

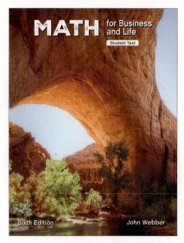

Student Text
Softback version: ISBN 978-0-9848032-4-8
Hardback version: ISBN 978-0-9848032-6-2

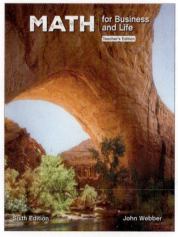

Teacher's Edition
ISBN 978-0-9848032-5-5

Homework Booklet
ISBN 978-0-9848032-8-6

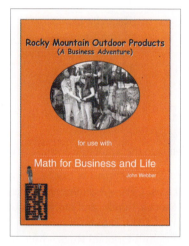

Comprehensive Exercise
ISBN 978-0-9716809-4-4

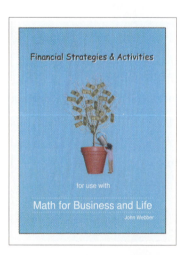

Financial Strategies Booklet
ISBN 978-0-9769930-0-1

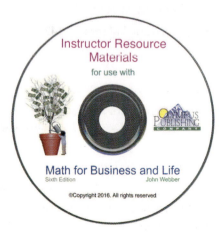

Instructor Resource Materials CD

Contents

Chapter 1 Whole Numbers and Decimals 2
- 1.1 **Reading, writing, and rounding numbers** 4
- 1.2 **Working with whole numbers** 7
- 1.3 **Strategy for solving word problems** 12
- 1.4 **Working with decimal numbers** 15

Chapter 2 Fractions 28
- 2.1 **Types of fractions and modifying fractions** 30
- 2.2 **Working with fractions and mixed numbers** 33
- 2.3 **Fraction/decimal conversions** 38

Chapter 3 Equations: A Guide to Finding the Unknown 48
- 3.1 **Mathematical symbols and expressions** 50
- 3.2 **Equations: Solving for the unknown** 54
- 3.3 **Guideline for solving word problems** 58

Chapter 4 Percents 72
- 4.1 **Percent conversions** 74
- 4.2 **The percent formulas** 76
- 4.3 **Increase and decrease problems** 80

Chapter 5 Trade and Cash Discounts 96
- 5.1 **Trade discounts** 98
- 5.2 **Cash discounts** 102

Chapter 6 Markup and Markdown 116
- 6.1 **Markup** 118
- 6.2 **Percent markup** 121
- 6.3 **Markdown** 123
- 6.4 **Break-even analysis** 127

Chapter 7 Checking Accounts 140
- 7.1 **Checking account balance** 142

Chapter 8 Payroll 156
- 8.1 **Gross pay: Wages and incentive plans** 158
- 8.2 **Payroll deductions for employees** 161
- 8.3 **Employer taxes and settling up with the IRS** 165

Chapter 9 Simple and Compound Interest 178
- 9.1 **Computing simple interest and maturity value** 180
- 9.2 **Solving for principal, rate, and time** 185
- 9.3 **Compound interest** 189

Contents

Chapter 10 Future Value and Present Value: Using Formulas 204
- 10.1 Time-value-of-money terminology 206
- 10.2 Future value 207
- 10.3 Present value 213

Chapter 11 Sinking Funds, Annuities, and More: Using Formulas 226
- 11.1 Sinking funds 228
- 11.2 Annuities 230
- 11.3 Loan payments 232
- 11.4 Solving for rate (i) 234

Chapter 12 Future Value and Present Value: Using Financial Calculators 248
- 12.1 Time-value-of-money terminology 250
- 12.2 Financial calculators 252
- 12.3 Future value 255
- 12.4 Present value 260

Chapter 13 Sinking Funds, Annuities, and More: Using Financial Calculators 272
- 13.1 Sinking funds 274
- 13.2 Annuities 276
- 13.3 Loan payments 278

Chapter 14 Installment Loans and Open-End Credit 290
- 14.1 Cost of installment buying 292
- 14.2 Paying off an installment loan 295
- 14.3 Open-end credit 298

Chapter 15 Home Ownership and Mortgage Loans 310
- 15.1 Home ownership and mortgage payments 312
- 15.2 Paying off a mortgage loan and increasing equity 318
- 15.3 Amortization with a financial calculator 321
- 15.4 Repayment variations and loan charges 324

Chapter 16 Stocks, Bonds, and Mutual Funds 340
- 16.1 Stocks 342
- 16.2 Bonds 346
- 16.3 Mutual funds 349

Chapter 17 Additional Applications Using Financial Calculators 358
- 17.1 Solving for interest rate paid 360
- 17.2 Growth rates 366
- 17.3 Solving for interest rate earned 367
- 17.4 Cash flow problems 370

Contents

Chapter 18 Financial Statements: How to Read and Interpret 386
- 18.1 **Income statements** 388
- 18.2 **Balance sheets** 392
- 18.3 **Trend and ratio analysis** 395

Chapter 19 Inventory and Overhead 410
- 19.1 **Inventory methods: Assigning a cost to ending inventory** 412
- 19.2 **Overhead: Spreading expenses to departments** 416

Chapter 20 Depreciation 424
- 20.1 **Depreciation for financial accounting** 426
- 20.2 **Depreciation for federal income taxes (MACRS)** 431

Chapter 21 Taxes: Income, Sales, and Property 444
- 21.1 **Federal income tax** 446
- 21.2 **Sales tax** 451
- 21.3 **Property tax** 453

Chapter 22 Insurance 464
- 22.1 **Property insurance** 466
- 22.2 **Life insurance** 471

Chapter 23 Measurements: Real-World Applications 482
- 23.1 **Length, area, and volume: Applications** 484
- 23.2 **Unit costs and converting measurements (U.S. to U.S.)** 490

Chapter 24 International Business: Exchange Rates and Metrics 502
- 24.1 **Monetary exchange rates: Significance in international business** 504
- 24.2 **Metric system: Significance in international business** 506

Chapter 25 Statistics: An Introduction 518
- 25.1 **The three Ms: Mean, median, and mode** 520
- 25.2 **Graphs: Presenting data so it is easy to understand** 523
- 25.3 **Measures of dispersion** 527

Appendix A Step-by-Step Solutions: U-Try-It Exercises A-1
Appendix B Answers: Review Problems and Practice Tests B-1
Appendix C Calculator—Quick Start C-1
Appendix D Day-of-the-Year Calendar D-1
Appendix E Excel: Solving TVM Problems E-1
Appendix F Formulas: Concepts in Using Compound Interest Formulas F-1
  Glossary G-1
  Index I-1

MATH | for Business and Life

FUN CORNER

Close Not Enough

PHOENIX, AZ. (AP) — Albert Pujols won his first baseball batting title, edging out Todd Helton in the closest race in National League history.

On the final day of the 2003 season, Pujols went 2-for-5. At the same time, Helton went 2-for-4. Pujols ended the season with 212 hits out of 591 at-bats, for a batting average of .35871 while Helton finished with 209 hits out of 583 at-bats for an average of .35849. On his final at-bat, Helton was intentionally walked; if he had gotten a hit, he would have won the batting title with an average of .35959.

Large Numbers

Zeros	U.S. Title	Zeros	U.S. Title
6	million	18	quintillion
9	billion	21	sextillion
12	trillion	24	septillion
15	quadrillion	27	octillion

Observation

If 61 is pronounced sixty-one and 71 is pronounced seventy-one, why isn't 11 pronounced onety-one?

Math Magic

Grab a calculator and try this. Put in the number that represents the month you were born (Jan. = 1, Feb. = 2, etc.). Multiply by 20, then add 3 and multiply that by 5. Add the date of the month you were born (like 17 for the 17th). Multiply by 20 again, add 3, then multiply by 5. Now add the year you were born (00 through 99), and subtract 1515. You'll be left with your birthdate—month, day, year.

What a great deal—a hamburger for less than a penny (.89¢ means 89 hundredths of a penny). This sign brought lots of business until they painted over the decimal point!

Brainteasers

Here are a few arithmetic problems you might have fun with. Try answering all of the questions before looking at the answers below. If you have fun, give the problems to some friends.

1. A farmer had 17 sheep. All but 9 died. How many did he have left?
2. Ten birds are on a flat roof. You throw a rock that hits and kills one of the birds. How many birds are left on the roof?
3. Take two apples from three apples and what do you have?
4. I have two U.S. coins in my pocket and together they total 55 cents in value, but one of them is not a nickel. What are the two coins?
5. How many outs in an inning of baseball?

Answers: 1. 9   2. 1 (the dead one; the rest fly away)   3. 2 apples   4. Half dollar and nickel (one of them is not a nickel)   5. 6

"I have a seven figure salary, too. Unfortunately, there's a decimal point involved with mine."

Whole Numbers and Decimals

Being able to work with whole numbers and decimals is essential for solving problems encountered in business and everyday life. In this chapter, we will review how to read, write, and round numbers, as well as how to perform basic arithmetic calculations (add, subtract, multiply, and divide). Along the way, we will develop a strategy to solve "word problems." I can hear some of you groaning! But as you will see, word problems become easier with practice and can actually be fun.

While calculators are used to perform basic arithmetic operations, calculators have limitations. First, calculators are not always available or may not operate. Second, a person not understanding the basic concepts may use a calculator improperly. And most instructors do not allow students to use calculators on exams covering material in this chapter! So, this chapter uses noncalculator methods.

UNIT OBJECTIVES

Unit 1.1 Reading, writing, and rounding numbers

- **a** Reading and writing numbers
- **b** Rounding numbers

Unit 1.2 Working with whole numbers

- **a** Adding whole numbers
- **b** Subtracting whole numbers
- **c** Multiplying whole numbers
- **d** Dividing whole numbers

Unit 1.3 Strategy for solving word problems

- **a** Using a systematic approach to solve word problems
- **b** Estimating

Unit 1.4 Working with decimal numbers

- **a** Adding and subtracting decimals
- **b** Multiplying and dividing decimals

Unit 1.1 Reading, writing, and rounding numbers

Our decimal system uses the digits 0, 1, 2, 3, 4, 5, 6, 7, 8, and 9. The position of each digit affects the value, as shown in the chart below.

The value 237, for example, means 2 hundreds, 3 tens, and 7 units; in terms of money, which might be easier to visualize, if we had $237 we would have the equivalent of 2 hundred dollar bills, 3 ten dollar bills, and 7 one dollar bills. This is the basis for adding, subtracting, multiplying, and dividing.

Dollars and cents are based on the decimal system. The numbers to the left of the decimal represent the whole number (dollars) and the numbers to the right represent the decimal part of the number (cents).

trillions			billions			millions			thousands						decimal point	decimal part				
hundreds	tens	units	hundreds	tens	units	hundreds	tens	units	hundreds	tens	units	hundreds	tens	units		tenths	hundredths	thousandths	ten-thousandths	hundred-thousandths	millionths
1	2	3	4	5	6	7	8	9	0	1	2	3	4	5	.	6	7	8	9	0	1

a Reading and writing numbers

The decimal point is the center of the decimal system, with the **whole number** located to the left of the decimal point and the decimal part located to the right of the decimal point. Here are a few guidelines for changing numbers to words.

changing numbers to words

Step 1 Break the number into two parts—the whole number and the decimal part.

Step 2 Beginning at the decimal point and proceeding to the left, the whole number is separated by commas into groups of three digits. To read and write in words, begin at the left and read each group of three digits by itself, adding the group name (like *million*).

Step 3 The whole number and decimal part are separated by the word "and."

Step 4 To read and write the decimal part in words, read it as a whole number except that the "decimal word" (like "hundredths") is added; the decimal word is the word appearing in the column in which the last digit is located.

rules for expressing numbers as words

Group Name Rule. The whole number group name is read at each comma. Don't read or name a group that is all zeros (like the three zeros in 86,000,123). Group names are in the singular: 48,000 is forty-eight *thousand*, not forty-eight *thousands*. The rightmost two digits do not have a group name: 18 is read only as eighteen.

"And" Rule. Don't use the word "and" in the whole number or in the decimal part; it is used only to separate the whole number from the decimal part.

"ths" Rule. Decimal part words always end in "*ths*": .35 is read as thirty-five hundred*ths*.

Hyphen Rule. The numbers 21 through 99 (except those ending in zero, like 30) are written with a hyphen: 37 is written as *thirty-seven*, not *thirty seven*.

Dollar Amount Rule. Read dollar amounts as dollars and cents: $30.42 is read as *thirty dollars and forty-two cents*, not thirty and forty-two hundredths dollars.

Example 1 Change the following numbers to words: **a.** 1,578 **b.** 3,567,234,789,123 **c.** 123.037

a. One thousand, five hundred seventy-eight
b. Three trillion, five hundred sixty-seven billion, two hundred thirty-four million, seven hundred eighty-nine thousand, one hundred twenty-three
c. One hundred twenty-three and thirty-seven thousandths

In Example 1, we changed numbers to words. In Example 2, we will change words to numbers.

Example 2 Change the following words to numbers:
a. Two hundred twenty-six thousand
b. Two hundred twenty-six thousandths
c. Two hundred and twenty-six thousandths

a. 226,000   *Notice that the final word is "thousand."*
b. .226   *Notice that the final word is "thousandths," not "thousand."*
c. 200.026   *Notice that the word "and" separates the whole number from the decimal part.*

In the newspaper article on the right, Boeing got an order for $2.3 billion. Notice, the amount is two billion plus three-tenths of another billion. Let's review how to change numbers like these to regular numbers.

Boeing gets a $2.3 billion order from leasing company for 737s

SEATTLE (Bloomberg) — Boeing Co., the world's biggest planemaker, confirmed it won an order valued at $2.3 billion for another 50 of its 737 jetliners from International Lease Finance Corp., an aircraft leasing company,

changing parts of a million, billion, trillion, etc., to a regular number

Step 1 Replace the decimal point with a comma.

Step 2 Add enough zeros after the last given digit so that the leftmost digit represents the word-name it was assigned. Remember to add commas where needed.

Example 3 Change 2.3 billion to a regular number.

Step 1 2.3 billion
           ↓
           2,3   *Replace decimal point with comma.*

Step 2 2,300,000,000   *Add zeros and commas so that the "2" ends up in the "billions" place.*

Unit 1.1   Reading, writing, and rounding numbers   5

b Rounding numbers

Often, numbers are rounded—for example, to the nearest whole number (first digit to the left of the decimal point), to the nearest thousand (fourth digit to the left of the decimal point), or to the nearest tenth (first digit to the right of the decimal point). Instead, we may be asked to express a value with a certain number of *decimal places*. For example, if we are asked to round a number to two decimal places, the number is rounded to the nearest hundredth (two digits will appear to the right of the decimal point).

> **rounding numbers**
>
> **Step 1** Underline the digit you want to round.
>
> **Step 2** If the digit to the right of the underlined digit is a 4 or less, do not change the underlined digit. If the digit to the right of the underlined digit is 5 or more, increase the underlined digit by 1.
>
> **Step 3** Change all digits to the right of the underlined digit to zeros.

Example 4   Round 18,724 to the nearest thousand.

Step 1   18,724   *The digit in the thousands place (the 8) is underlined.*

Step 2   19,724   *The digit to the right of the underlined digit is 5 or greater (it is a 7), so 8 becomes 9.*

Step 3   19,000   *Change digits to the right of the underlined digit to zeros.*

18,724 rounded to the nearest thousand is 19,000. Notice 18,724 is between 18,000 and 19,000 but is closer to our answer of 19,000.

> **how do we increase a 9?**
>
> If the underlined digit is a 9 and is to be increased (because the digit to its right is 5 or more), we are supposed to change the 9 to a 10. But we cannot change the 9 to a two-digit number, so instead we change the 9 to a zero and increase the digit to the left by one.

Example 5   Round $12,954 to the nearest hundred dollars.

Step 1 $12,954   *The digit in the hundreds place (the 9) is underlined.*

Step 2 $13,054   *The digit to the right of the underlined digit is 5 or greater (it is a 5), so the 9 must be increased; it becomes a zero and we increase the digit to the left.*

Step 3 $13,000   *Change digits to the right of the underlined digit to zeros.*

$12,954 rounded to the nearest hundred dollars is $13,000. Notice $12,954 is between $12,900 and $13,000 but is closer to our answer of $13,000.

> **extra step for rounding decimal numbers**
>
> **Step 4** If the underlined digit is to the right of the decimal point, drop all zeros to the right of the underlined digit (these are known as *trailing zeros*, and dropping trailing zeros does not affect the value). If the underlined digit is left of the decimal point, drop all zeros to the right of the decimal point and eliminate the decimal point.

Example 6 Round 523.6847 to two decimal places.

Step 1   523.6847   *The digit two places to the right of the decimal point is underlined.*

Step 2   523.6847   *The digit to the right of the underlined digit is less than 5 (it is a 4), so the 8 remains unchanged.*

Step 3   523.6800   *Change digits to the right of the underlined digit to zeros.*

Step 4   523.68   *Drop trailing zeros.*

523.6847 rounded to two decimal places is 523.68.

> **what if we aren't told where to round?**
>
> While there are no hard-and-fast rules for rounding without instructions, here are a few generally accepted guidelines.
> - Unless otherwise indicated, round only the final answer; don't round intermediate results.
> - Unless otherwise indicated, round dollar amounts to the nearest penny.

Congratulations on finishing the first unit of the text. Only 12,322 units left! (Just kidding.) Let's test our understanding of this unit by completing the U-Try-It exercises.

U-Try-It (Unit 1.1)

1. Change to words: **a.** 72,168   **b.** 32.084
2. Change to numbers:
   a. Three hundred twenty-eight thousand, six hundred eight
   b. Five hundred and fourteen thousandths   **c.** 48.2 million
3. Round as indicated:
   a. 12,448 to the nearest thousand   **b.** 12.86513 to the nearest hundredth
   c. 72,971 to the nearest hundred

Answers: (If you have a different answer, check the solution in Appendix A.)
1a. Seventy-two thousand, one hundred sixty-eight   **1b.** Thirty-two and eighty-four thousandths
2a. 328,608   **2b.** 500.014   **2c.** 48,200,000   **3a.** 12,000   **3b.** 12.87   **3c.** 73,000

Unit 1.2 Working with whole numbers

In this unit, we will review the basic arithmetic functions: adding, subtracting, multiplying, and dividing.

a Adding whole numbers

Numbers being added are called **addends**, and the answer is called the **sum**, or total.

```
  7   addend
 +5   addend
 12   sum
```

> **adding whole numbers**
>
> Step 1   Arrange the numbers in columns with units above units, tens above tens, and so on.
> Step 2   Add the units column. Write the sum at the bottom of the column; if the sum is greater than 9, write the units digit and carry the tens digit.
> Step 3   Move to the left, repeating Step 2 until all columns are added.

To check an addition answer, add from bottom to top.

Example 1 Add: 5,497 + 683 + 7,438. Then check your answer.

$$\begin{array}{r} \overset{1\ 2\ 1}{5{,}497} \\ 683 \\ +\ 7{,}438 \\ \hline 13{,}618 \end{array}$$

Add, top to bottom. ↓   Check bottom to top: 8 + 3 + 7 = 18, etc.

Some business reports—such as payroll, production reports, and employee time records—require that numbers be added down (vertically) as well as across (horizontally). While many companies use computer spreadsheets, other businesses find the totals manually, as shown in Illustration 1-1.

> **TIP** — **stay in groups whenever possible**
>
> Adding is made easier by finding groups of numbers that add to 10, 20, 30, and so on. For example, add: 13 + 7 + 5 + 8 + 6 + 22 = ?
>
> ⑬ + ⑦ + 5 + ⑧ + 6 + ㉒
>   ⤷20⤶   ⤷30⤶
>
> *Think: 20, 50, 55, 61*

b Subtracting whole numbers

Subtraction is used to find the difference between two numbers. In subtraction, the top number is called the **minuend**, the number being subtracted is called the **subtrahend**, and the answer is called the **difference**.

$$\begin{array}{rl} 28 & minuend \\ -5 & subtrahend \\ \hline 23 & difference \end{array}$$

> **subtracting whole numbers**
>
> **Step 1** Arrange the minuend and subtrahend with units above units, tens above tens, and so on.
>
> **Step 2** Start subtraction in the units column. Write the difference at the bottom of the column. If the units digit in the subtrahend is larger than that of the minuend, borrow 1 from the tens digit in the minuend; remember, 1 tens digit equals 10 units.
>
> **Step 3** Move to the left, repeating Step 2 until subtraction in all columns is complete.

To check a subtraction answer, we add the bottom two numbers; we should get the top number. In doing this, there is no need to rewrite the numbers.

Illustration 1-1   Spreadsheet with Vertical and Horizontal Addition

Employee time sheet summary: Hours worked					
Employee	Week 1	Week 2	Week 3	Week 4	Total
Neal	40	38	40	40	*158*
Michelle	40	42	40	45	*167*
Cory	36	24	20	30	*110*
Totals	*116*	*104*	*100*	*115*	**435**

1. Add totals down to get grand total.

2. Add totals across to check grand total.

Chapter 1   Whole Numbers and Decimals

Example 2 Subtract 1,531 from 3,712.

	Problem	Check	
minuend	3 7̶ 1̶ 2 (6 11)	3 7 1 2	
subtrahend	-1 5 3 1	+ 1 5 3 1	*Add up: 1 + 1 = 2, etc.*
difference	2 1 8 1	2 1 8 1	

Notice that when we try to subtract 3 from 1 in the tens column, we cannot do it. The minuend needs more tens, so we borrow 10 tens from the hundreds column. Now we have 11 tens in the minuend, but only 6 hundreds instead of 7 (remember, we borrowed 10 tens, which is the same as 1 hundred, from the hundreds column). We show this by crossing out the 7 and writing 6 above it and then crossing out the 1 and writing 11 above it.

C Multiplying whole numbers

Suppose on a nice sunny day, we go to a neighborhood yard sale and buy four used books at $5 each. To find the total price, we could add $5 four times: $5 + 5 + 5 + 5 = 20$. Or we could use multiplication, which is a shortcut for addition: $5 \times 4 = 20$. In multiplication, the number being multiplied is called the **multiplicand** and the number doing the multiplying is the **multiplier**. These two numbers are also referred to as **factors**. The answer is called the **product**.

$$
\begin{array}{rl}
5 & \text{multiplicand} \\
\times 4 & \text{multiplier} \\
\hline
20 & \text{product}
\end{array} \Big\} \text{factors}
$$

When the multiplier has more than one digit, we multiply each digit of the multiplier by the multiplicand, resulting in a **partial product** for each digit of the multiplier; if, for example, the multiplier has three digits, there will be three partial products.

multiplying whole numbers

Step 1 Write the multiplier below the multiplicand; align both numbers at the right.

Step 2 Multiply the right digit of the multiplier with each digit of the multiplicand, starting with the right digit. Move left through the multiplier one digit at a time, multiplying by each digit of the multiplicand. The right digit of each partial product is written directly below the digit doing the multiplying.

Step 3 Add the partial products.

Example 3 Multiply 418 by 124.

418	multiplicand
× 124	multiplier
1 672	first partial product: $4 \times 418 = 1672$; write 2 directly below 4 of multiplier
8 36	second partial product: $2 \times 418 = 836$; write 6 directly below 2 of multiplier
4 1 8	third partial product: $1 \times 418 = 418$; write 8 directly below 1 of multiplier
51,832	product: found by adding the partial products

Notice in Example 3 that the second partial product of 836 is found by multiplying 418×2. What we are really doing is multiplying 418×20, since the 2 is in the tens place of the multiplier: $418 \times 20 = 8,360$. By writing the partial product of 836 one place to the left we are, in effect, writing 8,360. The same principal applies to the third partial product: $418 \times 100 = 41,800$; writing 418 two places to the left is the same as writing 41,800.

> **TIP** — the alignment error
>
> Don't make the common mistake of aligning all partial products on the right. Here is what Example 3 would look like if we fell into this trap:
>
> ```
>    418
>  × 124
>   1672
>    836
>    418
>   2926   ← WRONG
> ```

> 🔑 **multiplication shortcut if numbers end in zero**
>
> **Step 1** If the factors have one or more zeros at the end (like the number 230), pretend the zeros are not there and multiply.
>
> **Step 2** Count how many zeros were disregarded in Step 1; attach that number of zeros to the end of the product.

Example 4 Multiply 2300 × 110.

```
  2300   pretend       23        2 zeros disregarded
  ×110      →         ×11      + 1 zero disregarded
                       23        3
                       23
                      253   — attach 3 zeros →  253,000
```

> **TIP** — pick and choose
>
> In multiplying, if one of the factors has fewer digits than the other, it is easier to use that number as the multiplier (bottom number). Doing this will result in less partial products. For example, 12 × 225:
>
> | **Easier way** | **Harder way** |
> |---|---|
> | 225 | 12 |
> | × 12 | × 225 |
> | 450 ⎫ | 60 ⎫ |
> | 225 ⎬ 2 partial products | 24 ⎬ 3 partial products |
> | 2700 ⎭ | 24 ⎭ |
> | | 2700 |

ⓓ Dividing whole numbers

Just as subtraction is the opposite of addition, division is the opposite of multiplication. Suppose we want to divide 18 juicy apples evenly among 6 people. This is a division problem and could be stated "what number must we multiply by 6 to get 18?" The answer is, of course, that each person gets 3 apples. We say "18 divided by 6 is 3." In division, one number (the **dividend**) is divided by another number (the **divisor**) to get the answer (the **quotient**). Division is shown by a variety of symbols. For example, "18 divided by 6" could be shown as **(a)** $18 \div 6$, **(b)** $6\overline{)18}$, or **(c)** $\frac{18}{6}$.

a. $\overset{\text{divisor}}{\underset{\downarrow}{}}$
$18 \div 6 = 3$
$ \underset{\downarrow}{} \underset{\downarrow}{}$
dividend quotient

b. divisor ← $6\overline{)18}$ → dividend, with 3 → quotient above

c. $\overset{\text{dividend}}{\underset{\text{divisor}}{}} \leftarrow \dfrac{18}{6} = 3 \to$ quotient

In the apple problem, each person got 3 apples. If we were dividing 19 apples evenly among 6 people (without cutting the apples), each person would get 3 apples and we would have 1 left over (a **remainder**). The following example shows the process of division. Notice how we check the answer using multiplication.

Example 5   What is $547 \div 16$?

Another way of stating this problem is "What number must we multiply by 16 to get 547?" One way to find the answer is to try some numbers until one works. Another way is to use the standard division setup (as you have probably guessed, that is what we will do).

```
         34  R3              Check answer
   16)547                 16    divisor
      48↓                × 34   quotient (whole number part)
       67                 64
       64                 48
        3   remainder    544
                        + 3    remainder
                        547    dividend
```

Notice that there are three 16s in 54, with a remainder of 6. We bring the 7 down, giving 67. There are four 16s in 67, with a remainder of 3.

In real-world applications, we do not express division answers with remainders (like 34, R3); instead we show the answer as either a decimal number (like 34.1875) or a mixed number (like $34\frac{3}{16}$). We will review these procedures later in the text.

> **TIP**   where to start writing the quotient
>
> In the above example, 16 will not divide into 5 but will divide into 54. So, we wrote the first digit of the quotient (3) above the 4 of the dividend. The most common error in division problems is to write the first digit of the quotient in the wrong spot.
>
> | Correct start | Wrong start | Wrong start |
> |:---:|:---:|:---:|
> | 3 | 3 | 3 |
> | 16)547 | 16)547 | 16)547 |

Well, how are you doing? Does all the terminology (minuend, multiplicand, dividend, etc.) confuse you? If so, you aren't alone. Remember, understanding the procedures is more important than memorizing terms. Now it's time for another set of U-Try-It questions.

U-Try-It (Unit 1.2)

1. Add: $3{,}172 + 283 + 1{,}765$
2. Subtract and check your answer: $1{,}283 - 718$
3. Multiply: **a.** $48 \times 4{,}721$ **b.** $34{,}000 \times 140$
4. Divide 813 by 28.

Answers: (If you have a different answer, check the solution in Appendix A.)
1. 5,220   2. 565   3a. 226,608   3b. 4,760,000   4. 29, R1

Unit 1.3 Strategy for solving word problems

In the drawing on the side, *Hell's Library* is filled to the brim with books of "Word Problems." Well, that is the way some people feel about word problems—they are punishment.

Remember that most math problems we encounter in the real world are word problems; we are given some numbers and must figure out what to do with them. In this unit, we will develop a strategy for solving word problems; it should help, especially if word problems scare you.

a Using a systematic approach to solve word problems

To help solve many of the word problems in the text, we will use a *word problem guide*. Let's do a problem.

Example 1 You buy a car for $21,200 and the dealer gives you a $3,600 trade-in on your old car. What is the net amount you owe the dealer, after the trade-in is deducted?

word problem guide

1. Solving for	Net amount due dealer
2. Known facts	New car costs $21,200 Trade-in value of old car is $3,600
3. Procedure	We are asked to find the *difference* between two numbers; therefore, this is a subtraction problem. $21,200 price of new car − 3,600 trade-in value of old car $17,600 difference (amount due dealer)

You must pay the dealer $17,600.

> **TIP**   the two helpers: experimentation and reason
>
> The most difficult part of doing word problems is deciding what to do with the numbers. In Example 1, we were given two numbers and had to figure out what to do with them. We could have added the numbers: $21,200 + $3,600 = $24,800. But you probably wouldn't be too excited about paying the dealer $24,800. We could have multiplied or divided the numbers, but the answers would be even more unreasonable. This illustrates two important points in solving word problems: (1) if we have trouble deciding what to do, we can experiment with the numbers until we figure out which operation results in a reasonable answer, and (2) when we get an answer, we should always decide if the answer seems reasonable.

Some problems use words that suggest addition, subtraction, multiplication, or division. The following table shows a few *key words* to look for.

> ## key words
>
> | If we are asked to solve for | The last operation is |
> |---|---|
> | a sum | addition |
> | a difference, remainder, or net amount | subtraction |
> | an equal share or average | division |
> | a total | addition or multiplication |
> | ____ per ____ (like cost per pound) | division |
>
> *Caution:* Not all problems include key words, but when included, they are helpful in deciding which operation to use. Some problems include more than one operation; operations shown here are for the last step.

Example 2 Laurie owns a 12-unit apartment building. If the apartments are rented for $825 each, what is the total monthly rent Laurie can collect?

word problem guide

1. Solving for	Total monthly rent
2. Known facts	$825 for each apartment 12 apartments
3. Procedure	We are asked to find *total* monthly rent. The word *total* suggests either *addition* or *multiplication*. We could solve this problem by adding $825 twelve times. Instead, let's use multiplication as a shortcut for addition.

$$\begin{array}{r} \$\,825 \\ \times 12 \\ \hline 1650 \\ 825 \\ \hline \$9900 \end{array}$$

Total monthly rent is $9,900.

Example 3 Ben Link has a fence business and is trying to figure the cost per foot for a certain type of fence. For 240 feet of fence, materials will cost $1,920 and labor will be $720. What is the cost per foot?

word problem guide

1. Solving for	Cost per foot of fencing
2. Known facts	Materials cost $1,920 Labor is $720 240 feet of fence
3. Procedure	This is a two-step problem. In the first step we must figure the *total* cost (an addition problem). The second step is a division problem (the words "*per* foot" suggest division). In fact, cost *per* foot means "cost *divided by* number of feet."

Step 1 $1,920   *materials*
          + 720   *labor*
          $2,640 *total cost*

Step 2 cost per foot = cost ÷ number of feet

$$\text{number of feet} \rightarrow 240\overline{)2640} \leftarrow \text{cost}$$
with quotient 11, 240 subtracted, 240 remaining, 240 subtracted.

This fencing job will cost $11 per foot.

If you feel a bit intimidated by word problems, don't worry. You will have lots of opportunities to sharpen your skills because many of the upcoming problems are word problems. Is that good news or bad news? We will continue using the word problem guide for problems that are unique.

b Estimating

Estimating is a valuable tool that serves two main purposes. First, estimating an answer saves time and energy when all we need is an approximate answer; we can often do the calculations in our head. Second, estimating an answer before or after calculating a precise answer is a good way to insure that our answer is reasonable. Estimating uses rounding, as shown in the next example.

Example 4 You are thinking about buying three pieces of furniture for your new family room. Prices are $1,238, $785, and $1,812. Approximately, what is the total price?

To approximate this total, we could round each amount to the nearest ten dollars, nearest hundred dollars, or nearest thousand dollars. To give some degree of accuracy, let's round to the nearest hundred dollars.

```
                Rounded
$1,238 ⎫       $1,200
   785 ⎬  →       800
 1,812 ⎭       +1,800
               $3,800    Think: 12 + 8 = 20; +18 = 38; then attach the two zeros.
```

The total price is approximately $3,800.

Front-end rounding is a form of rounding in which the first digit (left digit) is rounded and all other digits become zero. In the next example, we will use front-end rounding to estimate an answer.

Example 5 Suppose you own a furniture store. During June, sales were $842,586 for week 1; $1,123,448 for week 2; $793,286 for week 3; and $912,484 for week 4. Use front-end rounding to estimate sales for the entire month.

```
                  Rounded
$  842,586 ⎫    $  800,000
 1,123,448 ⎬      1,000,000
   793,286 ⎭  →    800,000
   912,484 ⎭    + 900,000
                $3,500,000    Think: 8 + 10 = 18; + 8 = 26; + 9 = 35; attach five zeros.
```

Monthly sales are approximately $3,500,000.

Rounding can also be used for subtraction, multiplication, and division.

Example 6 Jeb Maddox is thinking about buying a 6-unit apartment building. Rents are $825, $810, $795, $790, $805, and $810. What is the approximate monthly income from the apartments?

Rents average about $800, rounded to the nearest hundred dollars. Let's multiply the average rounded rent by the number of units:

$800 × 6 = $4,800

Monthly income is approximately $4,800.

As mentioned, estimating is a valuable tool in deciding if an answer is reasonable. Suppose Jeb, from Example 6, had incorrectly added the six rents to get $8,835. If he purchases the apartments, he will be very disappointed when the rent checks arrive, totaling only $4,835. By taking the time to estimate monthly rents ($4,800), Jeb will discover his addition error and can avoid a costly mistake.

Remember that estimating doesn't replace calculating actual answers, but can be helpful in making decisions. Hope you're doing okay. Let's find out by doing the U-Try-It exercises.

U-Try-It (Unit 1.3)

1. You buy a 6-unit apartment building. Two of the units are rented for $750 each and the other four units are rented for $770 each. Complete a word problem guide to find the total monthly rents.
2. On a vacation, you traveled 756 miles and used 42 gallons of gasoline. Complete a word problem guide to find your average miles per gallon.
3. You are thinking about buying a computer system. The computer costs $1,329, the monitor is $598, and the printer is $379.
   a. Estimate the price by rounding to the nearest hundred dollars.
   b. Estimate the price by using front-end rounding.
   c. Calculate the actual price.
   d. Determine which estimate is closer to the actual price.

Answers: (If you have a different answer, check the solution in Appendix A.)
1. $4,580   2. 18 miles per gallon (mpg)   3a. $2,300   3b. $2,000   3c. $2,306   3d. Rounding to the nearest $100 ($2,300)

Unit 1.4 Working with decimal numbers

In this unit, we will review how to add, subtract, multiply, and divide decimal numbers (rather than whole numbers). A *decimal number* is one that has digits to the right of the decimal point.

a Adding and subtracting decimals

To add or subtract decimals, we place the numbers in a column with the decimal points lined up. When lining up numbers that have a different number of digits to the right of the decimal point, attach trailing zeros so that all numbers have the same number of digits to the right of the decimal point. By aligning numbers at the decimal point and attaching trailing zeros, thousandths are combined with thousandths, hundredths with hundredths, tenths with tenths, digits with digits, tens with tens, hundreds with hundreds, and so forth.

> **adding and subtracting decimals**
>
> **Step 1** Write the numbers in a column with the decimal points lined up.
>
> **Step 2** Attach trailing zeros so that all numbers have the same number of digits to the right of the decimal point.
>
> **Step 3** Add or subtract the digits starting at the right and moving to the left. Place the decimal point in the answer so that it is directly under the decimal points.

Example 1 You own four adjoining parcels of land: 234 acres, 125.789 acres, 11.1 acres, and .37 acre. What is the total acreage?

This is an addition problem, as we need to find the *total* of four numbers.

Step 1 (line up decimals)	Step 2 (attach zeros)	Step 3 (add)
234.	234.000	234.000
125.789	125.789	125.789
11.1	11.100	11.100
.37	.370	+ .370
		371.259

The four parcels contain a total of 371.259 acres.

> **TIP** — out of alignment?
>
> The most common error in adding and subtracting decimals is to forget to line up decimal points.
>
> | Correct setup | Incorrect setup |
> |---|---|
> | 234. | 23 4 |
> | 125.789 | 125.78 9 |
> | 11.1 | 11.1 |
> | .37 | .3 7 |
> | 371.259 | 12617 1 ← WRONG |

Example 2 You go into a grocery store with $100. You come out with a small bag of groceries and $3.47 in change. How much did you spend?

This is a subtraction problem. We need to find the *difference* of the two amounts.

Step 1 (line up decimals)	Step 2 (attach zeros)	Step 3 (subtract)
$100.	$100.00	$100.00
- 3.47	- 3.47	- 3.47
		$ 96.53

You spent $96.53.

b Multiplying and dividing decimals

Decimals are multiplied just like whole numbers, but we have to determine where to place the decimal point in the product.

> **multiplying decimals**
>
> **Step 1** Multiply the numbers as though they are whole numbers; ignore the decimal points.
>
> **Step 2** Count the total number of decimal places in the factors.
>
> **Step 3** Starting at the right of the product, move the decimal point left the number of places we counted in Step 2. If necessary, attach zeros on the left of the product so that the decimal point can be moved the correct number of places.

> **TIP** — to align or not to align, that is the question
>
> Unlike addition and subtraction, we do *not* align decimal points in multiplication. Instead, we line up factors on the right.
>
> | Correct setup | Incorrect setup |
> |---|---|
> | 123.658 | 123.658 |
> | × 1.8 | × 1.8 |

16   Chapter 1   Whole Numbers and Decimals

Example 3 Bob Toombs owns a carpet business. If a certain carpet costs $28.35 per square yard, what should Bob charge for 62.5 square yards?

Each square yard of carpeting costs $28.35, and there are 62.5 square yards, so finding the total cost is a multiplication problem.

Step 1 (multiply)	Step 2 (count decimal places)	Step 3 (move decimal)
$28.35	2	$1771.875
× 62.5	+1	
14175	3	
5670		
17010		
1771875		

Bob should charge $1,771.88 (rounded to the nearest penny).

Example 4 Multiply: 3.1 × .012

Step 1 (multiply)	Step 2 (count decimal places)	Step 3 (move decimal)
3.1	1	.0372
× .012	+3	
62	4	↑
31		added a zero
372		

To divide decimals, we first make the divisor a whole number by moving the decimal point to the far right. To keep things in balance, we move the decimal point an equal number of places in the dividend.

dividing decimals

Step 1 Move the decimal point to the far right of the divisor so it becomes a whole number. Move the decimal point right an equal number of places in the dividend; trailing zeros can be added to the dividend if needed.

Step 2 Divide and bring the decimal point straight up into the answer.

If the divisor is a whole number we, of course, do not have to move the decimal point. Also, if the quotient has a remainder, we can continue the division process by adding trailing zeros to the dividend until (1) there is no remainder or (2) the quotient has one more digit than the desired precision for rounding.

One common application of using decimal numbers is in figuring our gas mileage (referred to as miles per gallon, or mpg).

Example 5 On a vacation, you drove 803.4 miles and used 41.2 gallons of gasoline. Calculate the average miles per gallon.

This is a division problem. Remember, miles *per* gallon means miles *divided by* gallons.

Step 1 (move decimal points) **Step 2 (divide and place decimal)**

$$41.2\overline{)803.4}$$

move decimal point to far right   *move decimal point an equal number of places (1)*

$$\begin{array}{r} 19.5 \\ 412\overline{)8034.0} \\ \underline{412} \\ 391 \\ \underline{370 8} \\ 206\ 0 \\ \underline{206\ 0} \end{array}$$ ← *trailing zero added*

You got 19.5 miles per gallon (mpg) on the trip.

In Example 5, we were supposed to divide 803.4 by 41.2, but instead we divided 8,034 by 412 (a whole number). Either way, the answer is 19.5.

The following box provides a shortcut for multiplication if one of the factors is a multiple of 10 (like 10, 100, or 1000) or for division if the divisor is a multiple of 10.

"1 followed by zeros" shortcut

Multiplication
Step 1 If one of the factors is a multiple of 10 (like 10, 100, 1000), count the number of zeros.

Step 2 Move the decimal point in the other number the same number of places to the *right* that we counted in Step 1. Attach zeros if needed. This is the answer.

Division
Step 1 If the divisor is a multiple of 10 (like 10, 100, 1000), count the number of zeros.

Step 2 Move the decimal point in the dividend the same number of places to the *left* that we counted in Step 1. Attach zeros to the left of the dividend if needed. This is the answer.

Remember, if we are multiplying a number by a multiple of 10, the answer will be *larger*, so we move the decimal to the *right*. If we are dividing a number by a multiple of 10, the answer will be *smaller*, so we move the decimal to the *left*. The above shortcut works with whole numbers and decimals.

Example 6 Find the product: **a.** 135.235 × 100   **b.** 23 × 1,000

	Step 1 (count zeros)	**Step 2 (move decimal)**	
a. 135.235 × 100	100	135.235 →	13,523.5
	(2 zeros)	(2 places right)	
b. 23 × 1,000	1,000	23.000 →	23,000
	(3 zeros)	(3 places right, need 3 zeros)	

TIP **using our heads**

Here is a tip for multiplying numbers in our heads: Multiply in steps, using 10s, 100s, etc. To multiply 12 × 13, first multiply 10 × 13, getting 130. Then add two more 13s (or 26), getting 156.

Example 7 Find the quotient: **a.** 12,453 ÷ 10   **b.** 1.23 ÷ 1,000

	Step 1 (count zeros)	Step 2 (move decimal)
a. 12,453 ÷ 10	10 (1 zero)	12,453 → 1,245.3 (1 place left)
b. 1.23 ÷ 1,000	1,000 (3 zeros)	001.23 → .00123 (3 places left, need 2 zeros)

> **TIP** — writing cell formulas for computer spreadsheets
>
> Computer spreadsheets, such as Excel, enable us to perform certain arithmetic operations. Multiplication is shown with an asterisk (*); division is show with a forward slash (/). While there is a large variety of formulas, here are a few basic examples:
>
> 1. Suppose we want to find the total of 48 numbers listed in column B of a speadsheet, rows 1 through 48, and want the result shown in column B, row 49. We type the following formula in cell B49: =SUM(B1:B48); for other spreadsheet programs, we type: @SUM(B1..B48)
>
> 2. Suppose we want to multiply the value in cell A50 by .40 and put the result in cell A51. We type the following formula in cell A51: =A50*.40; for other programs, we type: +A50*.40
>
> 3. Suppose we want to divide the value in cell D25 by 3 and put the result in cell D26. We type the following formula in cell D26: =D25/3; for other programs, we type: +D25/3

Well, that concludes this final unit of Chapter 1. Give yourself a big pat on the back! Now, let's test our knowledge by completing the U-Try-It problems.

U-Try-It (Unit 1.4)

Do the following problems without a calculator. You can use a calculator to check your answers, if you want.
1. Add: 45 + 4.76 + 12.8652
2. Your checking account balance was $385.21 before writing a check for $48.17. What is your new balance?
3. Multiply: **a.** 12.64 × 32.1   **b.** 12.63 × 1,000
4. Divide: **a.** 791.01 ÷ 42.3   **b.** 1.67 ÷ 100

Answers: (If you have a different answer, check the solution in Appendix A.)
1. 62.6252   2. $337.04   3a. 405.744   3b. 12,630   4a. 18.7   4b. .0167

Chapter in a Nutshell

Objectives	Examples
Unit 1.1 Reading, writing, and rounding numbers	
a Reading and writing numbers	726.023 → Seven hundred twenty-six and twenty-three thousandths
	Three hundred twelve and eight tenths → 312.8
	9.7 billion → 9,7 → 9,700,000,000
b Rounding numbers	762 to nearest hundred → 762 → 800
	11.324 to nearest hundredth → 11.324 → 11.32

Chapter in a Nutshell (continued)

Objectives	Examples

Unit 1.2 Working with whole numbers

a Adding whole numbers

$$\begin{array}{r} \overset{1\ 1}{768} \\ +\ \ 87 \\ \hline 855 \end{array}$$ Check by adding up.

b Subtracting whole numbers

$$\begin{array}{r} \overset{4\ 12}{5\cancel{2}8} \\ -\ 41 \\ \hline 487 \end{array} \qquad \begin{array}{r} 528 \\ +\ 41 \\ \hline 487 \end{array}$$ Check by adding up.

c Multiplying whole numbers

$$\begin{array}{r} 341 \\ \times\ 13 \\ \hline 1023 \\ 341 \\ \hline 4433 \end{array}$$

$$\begin{array}{r} 3100 \\ \times\ 40 \end{array} \longrightarrow \begin{array}{r} 31 \\ \times 4 \\ \hline 124 \end{array} \quad \begin{array}{l} 2\ \text{zeros disregarded} \\ +1\ \text{zero disregarded} \\ \ 3\ \text{zeros} \longrightarrow 124{,}000 \end{array}$$

d Dividing whole numbers

$$\begin{array}{r} 65\ \text{R2} \\ 12\overline{)782} \\ \underline{72} \\ 62 \\ \underline{60} \\ 2 \end{array}$$

Unit 1.3 Strategy for solving word problems

a Using a systematic approach to solve word problems

On a vacation, you drove 726 miles and used 33 gallons of gas. Find your average miles per gallon (mpg).

word problem guide

1. Solving for	Average mpg
2. Known facts	Drove 726 miles Used 33 gallons of gas
3. Procedure	This is a division problem; notice key word "per."

$$\begin{array}{r} 22 \\ 33\overline{)726} \\ \underline{66} \\ 66 \\ \underline{66} \end{array}$$ You got **22 mpg**

b Estimating

Find the approximate sum of $722 and $1,276 by rounding to the nearest hundred dollars.

$$\left.\begin{array}{r} \$\ \ 722 \\ +1276 \end{array}\right\} \longrightarrow \begin{array}{r} \$\ 700 \\ +1300 \\ \hline \$2000 \end{array}$$ Think: 7 + 13 = 20; then attach the 2 zeros

Objectives	Examples

Chapter in a Nutshell (concluded)

Unit 1.4 Working with decimal numbers

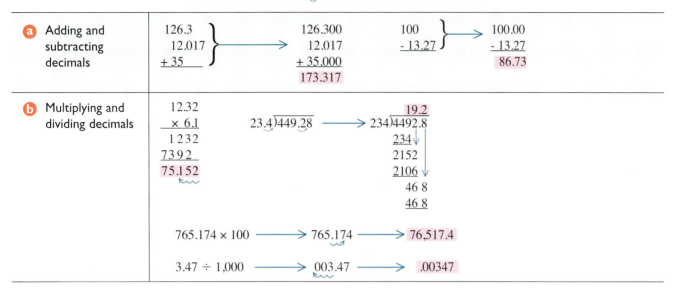

a. Adding and subtracting decimals

b. Multiplying and dividing decimals

Enrichment Topics

The following Enrichment Topics, which go a bit beyond what is in the text, are available for this chapter:

Scientific Notation
Binary Number System

If your instructor doesn't cover these topics in class and you would like to dig deeper on your own, please send a request to *studentsupport@olympuspub.com*.

Think

1. Addition and subtraction are opposite operations. Find the missing value and then write the problem as a subtraction problem: $22.3 + ? = 37.8$
2. Multiplication is a shortcut for addition. Find the sum and then write the problem as a multiplication problem: $18 + 18 + 18 + 18 = ?$
3. Multiplication and division are opposite operations. Find the missing value and then write the problem as a division problem: $24 \times ? = 96$
4. Suppose you go to the supermarket. Describe a situation that would require adding decimal numbers.
5. Describe a situation that would require multiplying decimal numbers at the supermarket.
6. Describe how you might be required to subtract decimal numbers at the checkout counter of the supermarket.
7. Suppose you are trying to multiply 123,000,000,000 by 4,000 on your calculator but your calculator will not accept all of the digits. How could you solve the problem on your calculator?

Activities 21

Explore

1. Search on the Internet for a history of the decimal number system. Write a short report about how the decimal number system was developed.
2. Use a Microsoft® Excel spreadsheet to solve the following problems; each problem is a continuation. *Tip:* If ###### appears in a cell, the cell must be widened to accommodate all of the digits.

    Addition. To add numbers in, say, cells B5, B6, and B7, in cell B8 we would type =B5+B6+B7 or =SUM(B5:B7).

    Problem. Enter 122.1, 28, 29.753, and 45.6 in Cells A1 through A4. In Cell A5, type a formula to find their sum. Set the decimal so all significant digits are shown.

    Subtraction. Use a minus sign (-) for subtraction.

    Problem. Enter 42.1 in cell A6. Type a formula in cell A7 that will subtract 42.1 from the value in cell A5. Set the decimal so all significant digits are shown.

    Multiplication. Use an asterisk (*) to denote multiplication.

    Problem. Type a formula in cell A8 to multiply the value in cell A7 by 12.1. Set the decimal so all significant digits are shown.

    Division. Use a forward slash (/) to denote division.

    Problem. Type a formula in cell A9 to divide the value in cell A8 by 3. Set the decimal at 8 places.

Apply

1. **Real-Life Word Problems.** Write word problems that you encounter in real life: (a) an addition problem involving decimal numbers, (b) a subtraction problem involving decimal numbers, (c) a multiplication problem involving decimal numbers, and (d) a division problem involving decimal numbers. Then, solve each problem. Show all of your work, including the answer. If you cannot think of problems on your own, visit with people in various occupations to get ideas.
2. **Math in Business.** List at least three different ways that the concepts of this chapter are used in each of the following businesses: (a) a restaurant, (b) a gas station, and (c) a movie theater.

Chapter Review Problems

Unit 1.1 Reading, writing, and rounding numbers

Change these numbers to words:

1. 317
2. 8,257,116
3. 2.1
4. 12.0012

Change these words to numbers:

5. Four hundred twenty-six thousand
6. Four hundred twenty-six thousandths
7. Four hundred and twenty-six thousandths
8. Fourteen million, seven hundred twenty-six thousand, one hundred eleven and two tenths
9. 4.8 trillion

Round each number.

10. 76.12506 to the nearest hundredth
11. 123,678,499 to the nearest thousand
12. 23,467.5000001 to the nearest whole number
13. 45,951 to the nearest hundred

Unit 1.2 Working with whole numbers

Find the sum of each group of numbers. Remember, do not use a calculator.

14. 123 + 456 + 54 + 8
15. 76 + 7 + 341 + 25,018
16. 15,000 + 2,111 + 7,085 + 12,448

Subtract. Remember, do not use a calculator.

17. 127 - 12
18. 1,171 - 489
19. 12,762 - 1,134

Multiply. Do not use a calculator.

20. 123 × 45
21. 45 × 1,832
22. 120 × 1,800

1 *Divide. Indicate any remainder.*

23. 48 ÷ 3   **24.** 3,528 ÷ 24   **25.** 8,724 ÷ 41

Unit 1.3 Strategy for solving word problems

26. You buy a car for $24,300 and the dealer gives you a $5,275 trade-in on your old car. What is the net amount you owe the dealer after the trade-in is deducted?

27. A movie theater has 40 seats in each row. If there are a total of 53 rows, what is the total number of seats?

28. Your golf scores on 9 holes were 4, 5, 3, 4, 7, 6, 4, 2, and 5. If par is 36 for the 9 holes, how many strokes over par did you shoot?

29. You are ordering soda pop for your company picnic. There are 96 people coming to the picnic and you think each person will drink about 3 cans of soda pop. How many cans of soda pop should you order?

30. Refer to Problem 29. How many 24-can cases do you need?

31. You are thinking about buying a computer system. The computer costs $980, the monitor is $425, and the printer is $310. Estimate the total price by rounding each amount to the nearest hundred dollars.

Unit 1.4 Working with decimal numbers

Find the result.

32. 123 + 456.1 + 548.179 + 1.23   **33.** 76.52 + 83.71 + 41.68 + 250   **34.** 15,000 + 2,111.1 + 7,086.2764 + 1.12

35. 123.46 - 1.23   **36.** 11.71 - 4.89   **37.** 12,762 - 113.468

38. 112.45 × 2.1   **39.** 12.79 × 2.19   **40.** 48.1 × 2.3844

41. 122.85 ÷ 27   **42.** 108.9044 ÷ 2.12   **43.** 148 ÷ 12.5

44. 47 × 1,000   **45.** 4.68 ÷ 100

46. During the last week, you wrote checks for $77.85, $32, $450, and $92.16. What is the total amount of checks written during the week?

47. You have $745.26 in your checking account before writing a check for $110.78. What is your new balance?

48. You own 3 adjoining parcels of land containing 22 acres, 105.643 acres, and .92 acres. What is the total acreage?

49. You go into an office supply store with a $50 bill. You buy some office supplies and come out of the store with $8.52 in change. How much did you spend?

50. Luciano Montoya owns a tile business. Luciano charges $9.50 a square foot (sq ft) for a certain tile. How much should Luciano charge a customer for 322 square feet of tile?

51. You are thinking about buying a watermelon. If the melon weighs 18.5 pounds (lb) and sells for 39 cents a pound, how much will the melon cost (rounded to the nearest penny)?

52. Howard Sadler is a traveling salesman. His employer reimburses employees for car mileage at 55 cents per mile. If Howard drove 1,872.4 miles during June, how much will he receive from his employer?

53. A company has 295.75 square feet (sq ft) of leather from which it makes baseball gloves. If each glove requires 3.5 square feet of leather, how many full gloves can be made from the 295.75 square feet of leather?

Challenge problems

For Problems 54–56, we will figure your gas mileage. Your auto mileage at the beginning of a vacation is 23,578.9. You filled your gas tank prior to leaving town by putting in 15.4 gallons of gas, and bought gas as follows during the trip: 14.6 gallons, 17.4 gallons, 11.7 gallons, 15.6 gallons, 17.1 gallons, and 9.4 gallons to fill the tank when you got home. Your mileage at the end of your vacation was 26,007.4.

54. How many miles did you travel on the trip?

55. How many gallons (gal) of gas did you use? (*Tip*: When calculating the gallons used, start with a full tank and end with a full tank; ignore the gallons used for the initial fill-up.)

56. Calculate your average miles per gallon (mpg), to the nearest tenth, for the trip.

57. Suppose you rent a moving truck for 2 days. You are charged $49 per day plus 24 cents per mile. If the mileage was 34,122.8 when you picked up the truck and 34,428.3 when you returned the truck, what is the total amount you will owe for the 2 days?

58. Assuming the average heartbeat is 73 beats per minute, how many beats are there in **(a)** 1 hour, **(b)** 1 day, **(c)** 1 year (assume an average of 365.25 days per year), and **(d)** a 70-year life?

59. A warehouse rents for $3,450 per month. Calculate the annual rent (i.e., how much rent is paid each year).

60. Refer to Problem 59. Assuming that the warehouse contains 9,720 square feet, calculate the annual rent per square foot. Round your answer to the nearest penny.

61. Jewell Koga weighed 151 pounds 3 months ago and now weighs 124 pounds. How many pounds did Jewell lose?

62. Refer to Problem 61. On average, how many pounds per month did she lose?

63. You are thinking about buying a 16-unit apartment building. Ten of the units are rented for $700 per month, four are rented for $725, and two are rented for $750. What is the total annual (yearly) rent?

64. Refer to Problem 63. You anticipate expenses of $41,000 per year (for property taxes, insurance, repairs, utilities, etc.) and your monthly mortgage payment is $7,730. What amount should you have left over at the end of the year after depositing rents and paying expenses and mortgage payments?

65. The Yang family is planning a vacation. They will be gone 15 days. They estimate that lodging will cost an average of $85 per night (they will need lodging for only 14 nights, since they will get back home on the fifteenth day). Meals will average $24 per person per day (there are four people in the family). They will drive about 3,300 miles. Their vehicle gets about 22 miles per gallon, and they estimate gas will cost an average of $4.19 per gallon. They want to allow $60 per day for entertainment. What total amount should they budget for their trip?

66. You can buy copy paper from Staples for $33.50 per case. Central Supply charges $46.89 per case but gives 1 case free if you buy 3 cases. If you need 4 cases, which is the better deal?

67. Maria Verde is about to get a cell phone and is considering two plans. The basic plan includes 500 minutes a month and costs $43.95 a month; Maria would pay 40¢ a minute for each minute over 500 minutes and would pay 20¢ for each text message sent or received. The upgrade plan includes 900 minutes a month plus 250 text messages a month, and costs $74.95 a month. Maria figures that she would not exceed the 500 minutes a month. How many text messages could Maria send or receive each month under the basic plan until her cost equals that of the upgrade plan?

Practice Test

1. Change the number "87,022.35" to words.
2. Change "three hundred and eighty-four thousandths" to a number.
3. Change 26.1 billion to a regular number.
4. Round 618.7665 to the nearest hundredth.
5. Round $28,958 to the nearest hundred dollars.
6. Find the sum: 2,384 + 818 + 73
7. Find the difference: 155 - 29
8. Multiply: 2,300 × 140
9. Divide: 2,841.02 ÷ 22.3
10. You are buying some treats at the baseball game: a hot dog for $3.75, peanuts for $4.75, and a soda for $2.25. Estimate the total by rounding each amount to the nearest dollar.
11. You buy a car for $22,400 and the dealer gives you a $4,200 trade-in on your old car. You must pay sales tax of $1,228.50 and a registration fee of $135. What amount will you owe the dealer?
12. You own three adjoining parcels of land: 112 acres, 84.625 acres, and .82 acres. What is the total acreage?
13. If carpet costs $21.25 per square yard, pad costs $4.65 per square yard, and installation costs $4 per square yard, what is the total cost of 182.5 square yards?

14. Your auto mileage was 12,852.6 at the beginning of a trip and 13,904.2 at the end of the trip. You used 53.82 gallons of gas. Use the following word problem guide to determine how many miles per gallon (mpg), rounded to the nearest tenth, you got on the trip.

    word problem guide
    1. Solving for
    2. Known facts
    3. Procedure

FUN CORNER

Youngest College Graduates

Michael Kearney became the world's youngest college graduate in June 1994, when at the age of 10 years, 4 months, he obtained a B.A. in anthropology from the University of South Alabama. He started college when he was 6 years old.

– Source: Guinness World Records

Math Around the World

Recently, 76 countries participated in a math and science test of 15-year olds. Here are the top 15 countries.

1. Singapore
2. Hong Kong-China
3. South Korea
4. Japan
5. Taiwan
6. Finland
7. Estonia
8. Switzerland
9. Netherlands
10. Canada
11. Poland
12. Vietnam
13. Germany
14. Australia
15. Ireland
  ⋮
28. United States

Source: Organization for Economic Cooperation and Development (OECD)

Math Magic

Grab a calculator. Key in the first three digits of your phone number (not the area code). Multiply by 80, then add 1. Multiply by 250. Add the last 4 digits of your phone number. Add the last 4 digits of your phone number again. Subtract 250, then divide by 2. You'll be left with your phone number.

Brainteasers

1. You have $4\frac{1}{4}$, $5\frac{1}{2}$, and $3\frac{5}{8}$ haystacks and you put them all together. How many haystacks do you then have?
2. How far can a dog run into the woods?

Answers: 1. 1 big haystack 2. Halfway; then the dog is running out of the woods.

"Why are we having such trouble balancing our budget."

Fractions

Fractions have a variety of business applications. For example, interest rates are quoted in fractions, like $3\frac{7}{8}\%$. Architects, real estate appraisers, graphic designers, merchants, contractors, and accountants work regularly with fractions.

If fractions scare you, this chapter should alleviate those fears (you're saying "I've heard that story before," aren't you?). We will start off by reviewing different ways fractions can be written. Then we will do some calculations involving fractions and mixed numbers. We will finish the chapter by changing decimals to fractions and fractions to decimals.

UNIT OBJECTIVES

Unit 2.1 Types of fractions and modifying fractions
- **a** Changing a mixed number to an improper fraction
- **b** Changing an improper fraction to a whole or mixed number
- **c** Writing equivalent fractions

Unit 2.2 Working with fractions and mixed numbers
- **a** Adding and subtracting fractions
- **b** Multiplying and dividing fractions
- **c** Adding and subtracting mixed numbers
- **d** Multiplying and dividing mixed numbers

Unit 2.3 Fraction/decimal conversions
- **a** Changing a decimal to a fraction
- **b** Changing a fraction to a decimal

Unit 2.1 Types of fractions and modifying fractions

Numbers such as $\frac{1}{2}$ (read as one-half), $\frac{2}{3}$ (two-thirds), and $\frac{3}{4}$ (three-fourths) are fractions. A **fraction** is a mathematical way of expressing part of a whole thing. Each fraction is composed of a **numerator** (the top number) and a **denominator** (the bottom number).

$$\frac{3}{8} \begin{matrix}\leftarrow \text{numerator} \\ \leftarrow \text{denominator}\end{matrix}$$

The denominator indicates how many parts the whole was divided into, and the numerator indicates how many of those parts are included. For example, if an apple pie is cut into 8 equal pieces and you get 3 pieces, you get $\frac{3}{8}$ of the pie.

Apple pie cut into 8 pieces $\frac{3}{8}$ (total number of pieces you get) / (total number of pieces in pie)

A **proper fraction** is a fraction in which the numerator is smaller than the denominator, such as $\frac{3}{8}$. **An improper fraction** is a fraction in which the numerator is equal to or greater than the denominator, such as $\frac{5}{4}$. A **mixed number** includes a whole number together with a proper fraction, such as $1\frac{1}{4}$.

A common visual aid for fractions is the good, old-fashioned, apple pie.

a Changing a mixed number to an improper fraction

There are times when we must change a mixed number to an improper fraction. For example, we may need to write $3\frac{1}{4}$ as an improper fraction. Let's take a look, using tasty apple pies cut into fourths.

1 full pie   +   1 full pie   +   1 full pie   +   1 fourth of a pie   = $3\frac{1}{4}$ pies

4 fourths   +   4 fourths   +   4 fourths   +   1 fourth   = 13 fourths ($\frac{13}{4}$)

We can see from the pie illustration that $3\frac{1}{4}$ is the same value as $\frac{13}{4}$. While drawing pies is a sure-fire method for changing a mixed number to an improper fraction, it can be time-consuming. Here is a quicker method:

🔑 changing a mixed number to an improper fraction

Step 1 Find the numerator by multiplying the whole number by the denominator of the fraction and then add the result to the original numerator of the fraction.

Step 2 The denominator is the same as the denominator of the original fraction.

Example 1   Change $2\frac{3}{5}$ to an improper fraction.

Step 1 (find numerator)

$2\frac{3}{5} = \frac{(2 \times 5) + 3}{?} = \frac{13}{?}$

Step 2 (write denominator)

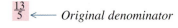

$\frac{13}{5}$ ⟵ Original denominator

If we used the pie-drawing approach to do Example 1 and cut the full pies into 5 pieces each, we would have 2 full pies × 5 pieces + 3 extra pieces, totaling 13 pieces ($\frac{13}{5}$). The step-approach of Example 1 is based on the same procedure.

b Changing an improper fraction to a whole or mixed number

A fraction is a way of indicating division. For example, the fraction $\frac{17}{3}$ means 17 ÷ 3. An improper fraction can be changed to a mixed number by performing division.

> **changing an improper fraction to a whole or mixed number**
>
> **Step 1** Divide the numerator by the denominator.
>
> **Step 2** Observe the remainder.
>   **a.** If we have no remainder, the answer is a whole number.
>   **b.** If we have a remainder, the answer is a mixed number. We write the fractional part of the mixed number by placing the remainder over the divisor.

Example 2 Change $\frac{17}{3}$ to a mixed number.

Step 1 (divide numerator by denominator)

$$\begin{array}{r} 5 \\ 3\overline{)17} \\ \underline{15} \\ 2 \end{array}$$

Step 2 (remainder becomes numerator)

$$5\tfrac{2}{3} \begin{array}{l}\text{(remainder)}\\\text{(divisar)}\end{array}$$

$$\begin{array}{r} 3\overline{)17} \\ \underline{15} \\ 2 \end{array}$$

> **TIP   should answers be written as improper fractions or as mixed numbers?**
>
> The general rule is that a final answer should be expressed as an improper fraction. Here are the exceptions:
>
> 1. Express the answer as a mixed number if instructed to do so.
>
> 2. Express the answer as a mixed number if the problem started with one or more mixed numbers, like finding the sum of $1\frac{3}{4} + 2\frac{1}{2}$.
>
> 3. If the answer represents units of something (like miles, hours, or pies), we should state the answer as a mixed number: "$5\frac{2}{3}$ miles" sounds okay but "$\frac{17}{3}$ miles" sounds goofy!

c Writing equivalent fractions

Different fractions can have an identical value. For example, if a pie is cut into 8 pieces and Bob gets 4 pieces, he gets $\frac{4}{8}$ of the pie. If a second pie is cut into 4 pieces and Alice gets 2 pieces, she gets $\frac{2}{4}$ of the pie. If a third pie is cut into 2 pieces and Ned gets 1 piece, he gets $\frac{1}{2}$ of the pie.

Bob gets $\frac{4}{8}$

Alice gets $\frac{2}{4}$

Ned gets $\frac{1}{2}$

Each person gets the equivalent of half of a pie, making it apparent that $\frac{4}{8}, \frac{2}{4}$, and $\frac{1}{2}$ are equivalent values. Multiplying or dividing both the numerator and the denominator of a fraction by the same number, except zero, gives a fraction of equal value. The two fractions are referred to as **equivalent fractions**.

If a fraction is rewritten with a larger denominator, the numerator must be increased proportionately.

> **rewriting a fraction with a larger denominator**
>
> **Step 1** Figure out what the old denominator was multiplied by to become the new denominator; if you have trouble determining the multiplier, it is "the new denominator divided by the old denominator."
>
> **Step 2** Multiply the old numerator by the same amount.

Example 3 Find the new numerator so that the fractions are equivalent: $\frac{2}{3} = \frac{?}{12}$

Step 1 (find multiplier for denominator)

$$\frac{2}{3} = \frac{?}{12} \quad (\times 4)$$

Step 2 (apply multiplier to numerator)

$$\frac{2}{3} = \frac{8}{12} \quad (\times 4)$$

Notice the fractions $\frac{2}{3}$ and $\frac{8}{12}$ are equivalent.

Some fractions can be rewritten so that the fraction has a lower denominator. For example $\frac{21}{28}$ can be rewritten as $\frac{3}{4}$ by dividing both the numerator and the denominator by 7. This is known as **reducing the fraction.** A fraction with a smaller denominator is easier to understand. For example, if you told a friend you had eaten $\frac{21}{28}$ of a pie, your friend might look a little puzzled. On the other hand, if you told your friend you had eaten $\frac{3}{4}$ of a pie, your friend would probably give you a strange look (because of your large appetite) but would understand how much pie you had eaten. Since fractions in reduced form are easier to understand, *fractions are always reduced to lowest terms*. This is accomplished by dividing the numerator and denominator by the largest value (called the **greatest common divisor,** or **GCD**) that can be evenly divided into both.

> **reducing a fraction**
>
> To reduce a fraction, divide the numerator and denominator by the largest value that can be divided evenly into both.

Some fractions can be reduced by inspection.

Example 4 Reduce the following fractions: **a.** $\frac{6}{9}$ **b.** $\frac{20}{16}$ **c.** $\frac{3}{7}$

a. $\frac{6}{9} = \frac{6 \div 3}{9 \div 3} = \frac{2}{3}$ **b.** $\frac{20}{16} = \frac{20 \div 4}{16 \div 4} = \frac{5}{4}$

c. The largest number that will divide evenly into both 3 and 7 is 1, so $\frac{3}{7}$ cannot be reduced.

In Example 4, $\frac{6}{9}$ was reduced to $\frac{2}{3}$; the fractions $\frac{6}{9}$ and $\frac{2}{3}$ have the same value. And $\frac{20}{16}$ was reduced to $\frac{5}{4}$; the two fractions have the same value.

> **TIP — reducing, but not all the way**
>
> If, after reducing a fraction, another number (other than 1) will divide evenly into both the numerator and denominator, we know that we did not select the "greatest" common divisor. In this case, we continue reducing until no number (other than 1) will divide evenly into both the numerator and denominator.
>
> **Reduce but not all the way**   **Continue reducing**
>
> $\frac{12}{54} = \frac{12 \div 2}{54 \div 2} = \frac{6}{27}$ $\frac{6}{27} = \frac{6 \div 3}{27 \div 3} = \frac{2}{9}$
>
> We could have avoided the multistep process by selecting the GCD of 6: $\frac{12}{54} = \frac{12 \div 6}{54 \div 6} = \frac{2}{9}$

Some fractions (like $\frac{119}{391}$) are not easily reduced by inspection. In this case, we can use another approach to find the greatest common divisor.

> **finding the greatest common divisor (GCD)**
>
> **Step 1** Divide the larger number by the smaller number.
>
> **Step 2** Divide the previous divisor by the previous remainder. Continue this process until there is no remainder. The last divisor used is the GCD.

Example 5 Reduce the fraction $\frac{119}{391}$.

The last divisor (17) is the GCD, so: $\frac{119}{391} = \frac{119 \div 17}{391 \div 17} = \boxed{\frac{7}{23}}$

Well, that finishes this unit. Let's check our understanding by doing the U-Try-It exercises.

U-Try-It (Unit 2.1)

1. Change $4\frac{3}{8}$ to an improper fraction.
2. Change $\frac{11}{3}$ to a mixed number.
3. Find the new numerator so that the fractions are equivalent: **a.** $\frac{3}{4} = \frac{?}{16}$ **b.** $\frac{8}{3} = \frac{?}{24}$
4. Reduce: **a.** $\frac{14}{21}$ **b.** $\frac{52}{195}$

Answers: (If you have a different answer, check the solution in Appendix A.)

1. $\frac{35}{8}$ 2. $3\frac{2}{3}$ 3a. $\frac{12}{16}$ 3b. $\frac{64}{24}$ 4a. $\frac{2}{3}$ 4b. $\frac{4}{15}$

Unit 2.2 Working with fractions and mixed numbers

a Adding and subtracting fractions

The following illustrations show the concept of adding and subtracting fractions.

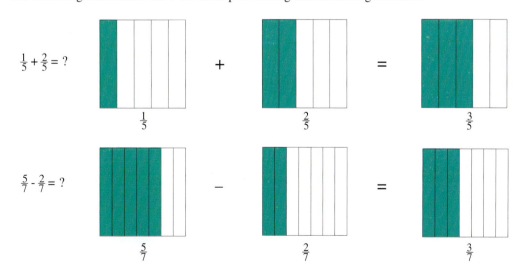

🔑 adding and subtracting fractions with the same denominator

To add or subtract fractions that have the same denominator, add or subtract the numerators and keep the denominator.

Example 1 Find the result: **a.** $\frac{1}{5} + \frac{2}{5}$ **b.** $\frac{5}{7} - \frac{2}{7}$ **c.** $\frac{5}{8} + \frac{7}{8} - \frac{3}{8}$

a. $\frac{1}{5} + \frac{2}{5} = \frac{1+2}{5} = \boxed{\frac{3}{5}}$ **b.** $\frac{5}{7} - \frac{2}{7} = \frac{5-2}{7} = \boxed{\frac{3}{7}}$ **c.** $\frac{5}{8} + \frac{7}{8} - \frac{3}{8} = \frac{5+7-3}{8} = \boxed{\frac{9}{8}}$

The next illustration shows what happens when we try to add or subtract fractions that have different denominators.

$\frac{4}{5} + \frac{3}{4} - \frac{3}{10} = ?$

$\frac{4}{5} \quad + \quad \frac{3}{4} \quad - \quad \frac{3}{10} \quad = \quad ?$

We cannot combine these fractions the way they are written because the denominators are different.

🔑 adding and subtracting fractions with different denominators

Step 1 Find the **lowest common denominator (LCD)**. Often we can determine the LCD by inspection. For more difficult problems, here is one way to find the LCD: Multiply the largest denominator by 1, 2, 3, 4, and so forth, until the product can be divided evenly by all other denominators; that product is the LCD.

Step 2 Rewrite each fraction with the new denominator (as shown in Unit 2.1, Example 3). Combine the numerators; use the new denominator.

Example 2 Find the result: $\frac{4}{5} + \frac{3}{4} - \frac{3}{10}$

Step 1 Find the lowest common denominator. We can find the LCD by multiplying the largest of the denominators (10) by 1, 2, 3, 4, and so on, until the product can be divided evenly by the other denominators (4, 5).

$10 \times 1 = 10$; 10 cannot be divided evenly by 4.
$10 \times 2 = 20$; 20 can be divided evenly by 4 and 5, so 20 is the LCD.

Step 2 $\frac{4}{5} + \frac{3}{4} - \frac{3}{10}$
↓ ↓ ↓
$\frac{16}{20} + \frac{15}{20} - \frac{6}{20} = \frac{16+15-6}{20} = \frac{25}{20} = \boxed{\frac{5}{4}}$ *(reduced)*

ⓑ Multiplying and dividing fractions

The following diagram illustrates the concept of multiplying fractions.

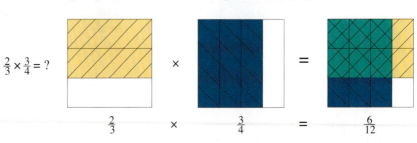

$\frac{2}{3} \times \frac{3}{4} = ?$

$\frac{2}{3} \quad \times \quad \frac{3}{4} \quad = \quad \frac{6}{12}$

Since 6 of the 12 sections are double-hatched, it appears the answer is: $\frac{6}{12}$ or $\frac{1}{2}$

34 Chapter 2 Fractions

Multiplying and dividing fractions is generally easier than adding and subtracting fractions because we don't have to worry about common denominators.

> **multiplying fractions**
>
> To multiply fractions, multiply the numerators and multiply the denominators. As always, remember to reduce the final answer.

Example 3 Multiply: $\frac{2}{3} \times \frac{3}{4}$

$$\frac{2}{3} \times \frac{3}{4} = \frac{2 \times 3}{3 \times 4} = \frac{6}{12} = \boxed{\frac{1}{2}}$$

> **TIP** — **timesaver: cross-canceling**
>
> **Cross-canceling** is based on switching denominators and reducing fractions before multiplying. Switching denominators does not affect the answer, since we still multiply all denominators together.
>
> **Actually switch denominators**
>
> $\frac{2}{3} \times \frac{3}{4} = \frac{2}{4} \times \frac{3}{3} = \frac{1}{2} \times \frac{1}{1} = \frac{1 \times 1}{2 \times 1} = \frac{1}{2}$
>
> ↑ Switch denominators   ↑ Reduce
>
> **Cross-canceling**
> (we *pretend* to switch denominators)
>
>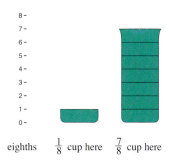
>
> Think: $\frac{2}{4}$ is like $\frac{1}{2}$ and $\frac{3}{3}$ is like $\frac{1}{1}$

Suppose we want to divide $\frac{7}{8}$ by $\frac{1}{8}$. The expression $\frac{7}{8} \div \frac{1}{8}$ means, How many times will $\frac{1}{8}$ fit into $\frac{7}{8}$? The following diagram uses cups to illustrate the concept of dividing fractions.

Since there are a total of 7 one-eighth cups on the right, it takes 7 of the one-eighth cups on the left to fill the portion on the right. So $\frac{7}{8} \div \frac{1}{8} = 7$.

eighths $\frac{1}{8}$ cup here $\frac{7}{8}$ cup here

To divide fractions, we multiply the first fraction by the reciprocal of the second. The **reciprocal** of a number is the value by which the original number must be multiplied to get a result of exactly 1. Put simply, the reciprocal of a number is found by switching the numerator and denominator. For example, the reciprocal of $\frac{1}{8}$ is $\frac{8}{1}$; the reciprocal of $\frac{3}{2}$ is $\frac{2}{3}$; and the reciprocal of 4 (or $\frac{4}{1}$) is $\frac{1}{4}$.

> **dividing fractions**
>
> To divide fractions, multiply the first fraction by the reciprocal of the second fraction.

Example 4 Divide: **a.** $\frac{7}{8} \div \frac{1}{8}$ **b.** $\frac{14}{3} \div \frac{5}{6}$

a. $\frac{7}{8} \div \frac{1}{8} = \frac{7}{{}_1\cancel{8}} \times \frac{\cancel{8}^1}{1} = \frac{7}{1} = \boxed{7}$ **b.** $\frac{14}{3} \div \frac{5}{6} = \frac{14}{{}_1\cancel{3}} \times \frac{\cancel{6}^2}{5} = \boxed{\frac{28}{5}}$

Unit 2.2 Working with fractions and mixed numbers

C Adding and subtracting mixed numbers

Builders must measure building materials by using fractions.

Adding mixed numbers is a bit more complex than adding regular fractions.

> **adding mixed numbers**
>
> **Step 1** Add the whole numbers.
>
> **Step 2** Add the fraction parts (we may need to get a common denominator first).
>
> **Step 3** Combine the results of Steps 1 and 2. If Step 2 results in an improper fraction, change it to a whole or mixed number and add the whole number part to the whole number result of Step 1.

Example 5 Bill McMurrin, an architect, is designing a home and needs to know the thickness of the exterior walls. The brick measures $3\frac{1}{4}$ inches deep. Behind the brick are metal ties and air space, $\frac{1}{2}$ inch deep; wood studs, $3\frac{1}{2}$ inches deep; and finally the interior sheetrock, $\frac{5}{8}$ inch deep. Help Bill determine the total thickness of the wall.

$$
\begin{array}{rcl}
3\frac{1}{4} & \longrightarrow & 3\frac{2}{8} \\
\frac{1}{2} & \longrightarrow & \frac{4}{8} \\
3\frac{1}{2} & \longrightarrow & 3\frac{4}{8} \\
+\frac{5}{8} & \longrightarrow & +\frac{5}{8} \\
\text{Need} & & 6\frac{15}{8} = 6 + \frac{15}{8} = 6 + 1\frac{7}{8} = \boxed{7\frac{7}{8}} \\
\text{LCD} & & \text{Step 1 Step 2 (the LCD is 8)}
\end{array}
$$

The wall is $7\frac{7}{8}$ inches thick.

In subtracting mixed numbers, sometimes borrowing is needed (like it is when subtracting whole numbers).

> **subtracting mixed numbers**
>
> **When borrowing is not needed**
> **Step 1** Subtract the fraction parts (we may need to get a common denominator first).
> **Step 2** Subtract the whole numbers.
>
> **When borrowing is needed**
> **Step 1** Rewrite fraction parts with a common denominator, if necessary.
> **Step 2** Borrow from the whole number of the minuend (top whole number).
> **Step 3** Subtract the fraction parts and the whole numbers.

Example 6 Subtract: **a.** $3\frac{5}{8} - 1\frac{1}{4}$ **b.** $5\frac{1}{3} - 2\frac{5}{6}$

a. (borrowing is not needed)

$$
\begin{array}{rcl}
3\frac{5}{8} & \longrightarrow & 3\frac{5}{8} \\
-1\frac{1}{4} & \longrightarrow & -1\frac{2}{8} \\
\text{Need} & & \boxed{2\frac{3}{8}} \\
\text{LCD} &
\end{array}
$$

b. (borrowing is needed)

$$
\begin{array}{rcccl}
5\frac{1}{3} & \longrightarrow & 5\frac{2}{6} & \longrightarrow & 4\frac{8}{6} \quad (\frac{6}{6} + \frac{2}{6}) \\
-2\frac{5}{6} & \longrightarrow & -2\frac{5}{6} & \longrightarrow & -2\frac{5}{6} \\
\text{Need} & & \text{Must} & & 2\frac{3}{6} = \boxed{2\frac{1}{2}} \\
\text{LCD} & & \text{borrow} &
\end{array}
$$

d Multiplying and dividing mixed numbers

To multiply mixed numbers, we start off by converting the mixed numbers to improper fractions.

> **multiplying mixed numbers**
>
> **Step 1** Convert any mixed numbers to improper fractions.
>
> **Step 2** Multiply the numerators and multiply the denominators. Use cross-canceling, if desired.

Example 7 A recipe calls for $1\frac{1}{3}$ cups of flour. If you want to make $2\frac{1}{2}$ times the normal amount, how much flour should you use?

This is a multiplication problem; we want to make $2\frac{1}{2}$ *times* the normal amount, suggesting multiplication.

$$1\frac{1}{3} \times 2\frac{1}{2} = \frac{\cancel{4}^{\,2}}{3} \times \frac{5}{\cancel{2}_{\,1}} = \frac{10}{3} = \boxed{3\frac{1}{3} \text{ cups}}$$

You should use $3\frac{1}{3}$ cups of flour.

To divide mixed numbers, we also convert the mixed numbers to improper fractions first.

> **dividing mixed numbers**
>
> **Step 1** Convert any mixed numbers to improper fractions.
>
> **Step 2** Multiply the first fraction by the reciprocal of the second.

Example 8 A bread recipe calls for $\frac{1}{8}$ cup of sugar. A baker has $2\frac{3}{4}$ cups of sugar on hand. How many loaves of bread can be made?

As you might have guessed, this is a division problem (after all, this example does follow the guidelines for dividing mixed numbers). Let's use a word problem guide to help.

word problem guide

1. Solving for	Number of loaves of bread that can be made
2. Known facts	$2\frac{3}{4}$ cups of sugar on hand
	$\frac{1}{8}$ cup of sugar needed for each loaf of bread
3. Procedure	If we have a measuring cup that holds $\frac{1}{8}$ cup (for each loaf of bread), how many of these can we fill from the entire $2\frac{3}{4}$ cups of sugar that we have to work with? To find out, we'll divide $2\frac{3}{4}$ by $\frac{1}{8}$.

$$2\frac{3}{4} \div \frac{1}{8} = \frac{11}{4} \div \frac{1}{8} = \frac{11}{\cancel{4}_{\,1}} \times \frac{\cancel{8}^{\,2}}{1} = \frac{22}{1} = \boxed{22 \text{ loaves}}$$

The baker can make 22 loaves of bread.

Are you ready for another set of U-Try-It exercises?

U-Try-It (Unit 2.2)

Reduce all answers.

1. Find the result. a. $\frac{5}{12} + \frac{11}{12} - \frac{7}{12}$ b. $\frac{3}{4} + \frac{1}{2} - \frac{1}{6}$ c. $\frac{7}{8} \times \frac{1}{4}$ d. $\frac{4}{3} \div \frac{1}{2}$
2. Add: $2\frac{2}{3} + \frac{3}{4} + 1\frac{1}{2}$
3. Subtract: a. $4\frac{1}{2} - 1\frac{1}{4}$ b. $3\frac{1}{6} - 1\frac{2}{3}$
4. A cookie recipe calls for $1\frac{1}{2}$ cups of flour, $\frac{1}{3}$ cup of chocolate chips, $\frac{1}{4}$ cup of butter, and 4 eggs. If you want to make $2\frac{1}{2}$ times the normal amount, how much of each ingredient should you add?
5. What is $5\frac{1}{3} \div 1\frac{1}{2}$?

Answers: (If you have a different answer, check the solution in Appendix A.)
1a. $\frac{3}{4}$ 1b. $\frac{13}{12}$ 1c. $\frac{7}{32}$ 1d. $\frac{8}{3}$ 2. $4\frac{11}{12}$ 3a. $3\frac{1}{4}$ 3b. $1\frac{1}{2}$
4. Flour: $3\frac{3}{4}$ cups; chocolate chips: $\frac{5}{6}$ cup; butter: $\frac{5}{8}$ cup; eggs: 10   5. $3\frac{5}{9}$

Unit 2.3 Fraction/decimal conversions

Business calculations often require converting a fraction to a decimal or a decimal to a fraction. Let's start by reviewing procedures for changing decimals to fractions.

ⓐ Changing a decimal to a fraction

Decimal numbers usually have two parts: the whole number part and the decimal part. For example, the number 12.34 consists of the whole number (12) and the decimal part (.34). The number, read as "twelve and thirty-four hundredths," can be written as $12\frac{34}{100}$. This is the basis of changing decimals to fractions.

> 🔑 **changing a decimal to a fraction or mixed number**
>
> **Step 1** State the decimal number in words, using "tenths," "hundredths," "thousandths," etc.
> **Step 2** Write the number as a fraction or mixed number and reduce.

Example 1 Change these decimals to fractions or mixed numbers: a. 12.34   b. .4   c. .125

		Step 1 (state in words)	**Step 2 (write as fraction and reduce)**
a.	12.34	twelve and thirty-four hundredths	$12\frac{34}{100} = 12\frac{17}{50}$ (GCD = 2)
b.	.4	four tenths	$\frac{4}{10} = \frac{2}{5}$ (GCD = 2)
c.	.125	one hundred twenty-five thousandths	$\frac{125}{1000} = \frac{1}{8}$ (GCD = 125)

> **TIP** optional method for changing a decimal to a fraction
>
> If you had trouble with the approach of Example 1, here is an alternate method for finding the numerator and denominator of the fraction.
>
> *numerator:* The numerator is the group of digits to the right of the decimal point.
> *denominator:* The denominator is a "1" followed by zeros; the number of zeros is the total digits in the numerator.
>
> .125: numerator is "125"; denominator is "1" followed by 3 zeros (3 digits in numerator): $\frac{125}{1000}$

38   Chapter 2   Fractions

ⓑ Changing a fraction to a decimal

Now we will review how to change a fraction to a decimal number. As mentioned, a fraction bar indicates division. For example, $\frac{3}{16}$ means $3 \div 16$. To change a fraction to a decimal, we divide the numerator by the denominator.

> **changing a fraction to a decimal**
>
> To change a fraction to a decimal, divide the numerator by the denominator. In doing so, place a decimal point at the right of the numerator and attach zeros as needed; keep dividing until there is no remainder or until the desired precision is reached.

Example 2 Convert $\frac{3}{16}$ to a decimal.

```
      .1875
16)3.0000
   1 6
   1 40
   1 28
     120
     112
      80
      80
```

Keep dividing until there is no remainder or until the desired precision is reached.

The decimal equivalent of $\frac{3}{16}$ is .1875.

In the next example we will use a calculator to find the decimal equivalent of some fractions. Before doing the example, make sure you understand how to change the decimal setting on your calculator. If you have the HP 10BII+ or TI BAII PLUS, refer to Appendix C. If you are using the HP 10B, HP 10BII, HP 12C, HP 17BII, HP 39gs, TI 30XIIS, TI 83+, TI 84+, Casio 9750G PLUS, or LeWorld FIN, you can request keystrokes at *studentsupport@olympuspub.com*.

Example 3 Use a calculator to find the decimal equivalent; set your decimal at 8 places: **a.** $\frac{7}{8}$ **b.** $\frac{1}{3}$ **c.** $\frac{3}{11}$

Keystrokes (for most calculators)	
7 ÷ 8 =	0.87500000
1 ÷ 3 =	0.33333333
3 ÷ 11 =	0.27272727

Notice in Example 3 that the decimal equivalent of $\frac{7}{8}$ is .875, followed by a bunch of zeros; the zeros are *trailing zeros* and do not affect the value. Decimal numbers with trailing zeros (like .875) are known as **terminating decimals.** The decimal equivalent of $\frac{1}{3}$ is .33333333, with the "3s" continuing forever; and the decimal equivalent of $\frac{3}{11}$ is .27272727, with "27s" continuing forever. Decimal numbers with repeating digits are known as **repeating decimals.** When we write repeating decimals, we don't have to continue writing the repeating digits forever (that's a relief, isn't it?); instead, it is customary to place a bar over (or under) the repeating digits. So the decimal equivalent of $\frac{1}{3}$ is written as $.\overline{3}$ (or $.\overline{33}$), and the decimal equivalent of $\frac{3}{11}$ is written as $.\overline{27}$. Some common fractions and their decimal equivalents are shown in Illustration 2-1; you might want to check these with a calculator.

Illustration 2-1 A Few Common Fractions and Their Decimal Equivalents

Fraction	Decimal Equivalent	Fraction	Decimal Equivalent	Fraction	Decimal Equivalent	Fraction	Decimal Equivalent
$\frac{1}{2}$	.5	$\frac{3}{4}$	.75	$\frac{4}{5}$	.8	$\frac{3}{8}$	.375
$\frac{1}{3}$	$.\overline{33}$	$\frac{1}{5}$	.2	$\frac{1}{6}$	$.1\overline{6}$	$\frac{5}{8}$	.625
$\frac{2}{3}$	$.\overline{66}$	$\frac{2}{5}$	.4	$\frac{5}{6}$	$.8\overline{3}$	$\frac{7}{8}$	.875
$\frac{1}{4}$	.25	$\frac{3}{5}$	.6	$\frac{1}{8}$	.125	$\frac{1}{10}$	.1

TIP   beware of repeating decimals

When doing calculations, avoid using a repeating decimal if a precise answer is desired. For example, it is okay to use .25 rather than $\frac{1}{4}$ in a calculation because $\frac{1}{4}$ is *exactly* .25; but do not use .33 rather than $\frac{1}{3}$, because $\frac{1}{3}$ is not *exactly* .33.

Example 4   Your rich uncle dies and leaves an inheritance of $13,476,211. If you receive one-third of the amount, what will you receive? First figure the amount by multiplying $13,476,211 by the fraction $\frac{1}{3}$. Then figure the amount by multiplying $13,476,211 by .33.

Multiply by $\frac{1}{3}$: $13,476,211 × $\frac{1}{3}$ = $\frac{\$13,476,211}{1}$ × $\frac{1}{3}$ = $\frac{\$13,476,211}{3}$ = **$4,492,070.33**

Multiply by .33: $13,476,211 × .33 = **$4,447,149.63**

As you can see from Example 4, using the approximate decimal equivalent of a repeating decimal can result in a dramatic difference. In Example 4, using .33 as the decimal equivalent of $\frac{1}{3}$ would result in a loss of $44,920.70—an expensive math error!

Converting a mixed number to a decimal is similar to converting a fraction to a decimal, except we combine the whole number with the result.

changing a mixed number to a decimal

Step 1   Change the fraction part to a decimal by dividing the numerator by the denominator.
Step 2   Add the whole number part to the result of Step 1.

Example 5   Change $4\frac{1}{5}$ to a decimal.

Step 1   Step 2
$5\overline{)1.0}^{\,.2}$ + 4 = **4.2**
$\underline{1\,0}$

Some problems state one or more numbers in decimal form and the remaining numbers as fractions, in which case we must convert all of the numbers to one form.

Example 6   Beth and Harry jointly own a parcel of land containing .73 acre. If they each take $\frac{1}{2}$ of the land, how many acres will each get? Express the answer as a decimal.

$\frac{1}{2}$ × .73 = .5 × .73 = **.365**

Each person will get .365 acres.

Congratulations! You've finished the last unit of this chapter. That wasn't too bad, was it? Let's do another set of U-Try-It exercises.

U-Try-It
(Unit 2.3)

When the answer is a fraction, reduce.

1. Change to a fraction or mixed number: **a.** 15.76   **b.** .6
2. Convert $\frac{5}{12}$ to a decimal.
3. Use a calculator to determine if each decimal equivalent is a *terminating decimal* or *repeating decimal*.   **a.** $\frac{7}{12}$ **b.** $\frac{3}{16}$ **c.** $\frac{5}{9}$
4. Change $61\frac{7}{8}$ to a decimal number.

Answers: (If you have a different answer, check the solution in Appendix A.)

1a. $15\frac{19}{25}$ **1b.** $\frac{3}{5}$ **2.** $.41\overline{6}$ **3a.** $.58\overline{3}$ (repeating)   **3b.** .1875 (terminating)   **3c.** $.\overline{55}$ (repeating)   **4.** 61.875

Chapter in a Nutshell

Objectives	Examples

Unit 2.1 Types of fractions and modifying fractions

a Changing a mixed number to an improper fraction	$4\frac{1}{6} = \frac{(4 \times 6) + 1}{6} = \frac{25}{6}$	
b Changing an improper fraction to a whole or mixed number	$\frac{11}{4} \rightarrow 4\overline{)11}\ \ \frac{2}{\ \ 8}\ \ \frac{}{3} \rightarrow 4\overline{)11}\ \ \frac{2\frac{3}{4}}{\ \ 8}\ \ \frac{}{3}$	
c Writing equivalent fractions	**Finding new numerator** $\frac{3}{7} = \frac{?}{28} \rightarrow \frac{3}{7}(\times 4) = \frac{?}{28} \rightarrow \frac{3}{7}(\times 4) = \frac{12}{28}$	**Reducing** $\frac{9}{15} = \frac{9 \div 3}{15 \div 3} = \frac{3}{5}$
	$\frac{92}{207} = \frac{92 \div ?}{207 \div ?} \rightarrow 92\overline{)207}\ \frac{2}{184}\ \frac{}{23} \rightarrow 23\overline{)92}\ \frac{4}{92}\ \frac{}{0} \leftarrow$ no remainder	**Reducing** $\frac{92}{207} = \frac{92 \div 23}{207 \div 23} = \frac{4}{9}$

Unit 2.2 Working with fractions and mixed numbers

a Adding and subtracting fractions	$\frac{1}{7} + \frac{4}{7} - \frac{2}{7} = \frac{1+4-2}{7} = \frac{3}{7}$
	$\frac{2}{3} + \frac{3}{4} - \frac{1}{6} = \frac{?}{12} + \frac{?}{12} - \frac{?}{12} = \frac{8}{12} + \frac{9}{12} - \frac{2}{12} = \frac{8+9-2}{12} = \frac{15}{12} = \frac{5}{4}$
b Multiplying and dividing fractions	$\frac{3}{4} \times \frac{5}{6} = \frac{1\ 3}{4} \times \frac{5}{6_2} = \frac{1 \times 5}{4 \times 2} = \frac{5}{8}$ $\frac{3}{5} \div \frac{1}{3} = \frac{3}{5} \times \frac{3}{1} = \frac{9}{5}$
c Adding and subtracting mixed numbers	$3\frac{1}{2} \rightarrow 3\frac{3}{6}$
	$+1\frac{2}{3} \rightarrow +1\frac{4}{6}$
	$\underset{\text{Need LCD}}{\ }\ \ 4\frac{7}{6} = 4 + \frac{7}{6} = 4 + 1\frac{1}{6} = 5\frac{1}{6}$
	No borrowing **Borrowing needed**
	$2\frac{3}{4} \rightarrow 2\frac{3}{4}$ $12\frac{1}{3} \rightarrow 12\frac{4}{12} \rightarrow 11\frac{16}{12}\ \ \left(\frac{12}{12} + \frac{4}{12}\right)$
	$-1\frac{1}{2} \rightarrow -1\frac{2}{4}$ $-4\frac{3}{4} \rightarrow -4\frac{9}{12} \rightarrow -4\frac{9}{12}$
	$\underset{\text{Need LCD}}{\ }\ \ 1\frac{1}{4}$ $\underset{\text{Need LCD}}{\ }\ \underset{\text{Must borrow}}{\ }\ \ 7\frac{7}{12}$

Chapter in a Nutshell

Chapter in a Nutshell (concluded)

Objectives	Examples
(d) Multiplying and dividing mixed numbers	$1\frac{2}{3} \times 3\frac{1}{2} = \frac{5}{3} \times \frac{7}{2} = \frac{35}{6} = 5\frac{5}{6}$ $\qquad$ $\frac{3}{4} \div 2\frac{1}{2} = \frac{3}{4} \div \frac{5}{2} = \frac{3}{\cancel{4}_2} \times \frac{\cancel{2}^1}{5} = \frac{3}{10}$

Unit 2.3 Fraction/decimal conversions

(a) Changing a decimal to a fraction	$.6 = \frac{6}{10} = \frac{3}{5}$	$15.72 = 15\frac{72}{100} = 15\frac{18}{25}$
(b) Changing a fraction to a decimal	$\frac{5}{12} \rightarrow$ $12\overline{)5.000}$ gives $.416 \rightarrow .41\overline{6}$ (subtractions: 48, 20, 12, 80, 72, 8 repeating)	$7\frac{1}{8} \rightarrow 8\overline{)1.000}$ gives $.125$; $.125 + 7 = 7.125$ (subtractions: 8, 20, 16, 40, 40, 0)

Think

1. What do we get if we multiply a fraction by its reciprocal? Give an example to verify your answer.
2. Give an example of (a) a proper fraction, (b) an improper fraction, and (c) a fraction that has a value equal to 1.
3. We must often express a given quantity as a fractional part of something else. 5 months is what fractional part of a year? 4 inches is what fractional part of a foot?
4. If we multiply a proper fraction by another proper fraction, will the result be (a) a proper fraction or (b) an improper fraction? Explain why.
5. If we divide an improper fraction by a proper fraction, will the result be a proper fraction? Explain why.

Explore

1. Using Microsoft® Excel, find the decimal equivalents of these fractions: $\frac{1}{4}, \frac{3}{8}, \frac{5}{32}$, and $\frac{1}{7}$. Type 3 column headings in row 1: Numerator, Denominator, and Decimal Equivalent. Enter each numerator and denominator in rows 2 through 5. Type a formula in cell C2 to determine the decimal equivalent for the fraction $\frac{1}{4}$. Then copy the formulas to cells C3 through C5. Determine if each decimal equivalent is a terminating decimal or a repeating decimal by using as many decimal places as needed.

Apply

1. **Fractions in the Real World.** Write word problems that you encounter in real life: (a) an addition problem involving fractions, (b) a subtraction problem involving fractions, (c) a multiplication problem involving fractions, and (d) a division problem involving fractions. If you cannot think of problems on your own, visit with people in various professions to get ideas.
2. **Fractions in Business.** Investigate how fractions are used in the following things. Write a problem for each: (a) bonds, (b) stocks, (c) architecture, (d) building construction, (e) cooking, (f) medicine or pharmacy, (g) manufacturing. Then solve each problem. Show all of your work.

Chapter Review Problems

Unit 2.1 Types of fractions and modifying fractions

1. In the fraction $\frac{3}{4}$, identify the numerator and denominator.

Classify each fraction as a proper fraction, improper fraction, or mixed number.

2. $\frac{3}{4}$
3. $1\frac{1}{2}$
4. $\frac{5}{2}$
5. $\frac{4}{4}$

Change these mixed numbers to improper fractions.

6. $5\frac{3}{4}$
7. $2\frac{7}{8}$
8. $2\frac{5}{6}$

Change these improper fractions to whole or mixed numbers.

9. $\frac{3}{2}$
10. $\frac{8}{3}$

Find the new numerator so that the fractions are equivalent.

11. $\frac{3}{4} = \frac{?}{12}$
12. $\frac{7}{6} = \frac{?}{30}$

Reduce.

13. $\frac{8}{12}$
14. $\frac{76}{437}$

Unit 2.2 Working with fractions and mixed numbers

Find the result. Reduce.

15. $\frac{2}{7} + \frac{3}{7}$
16. $\frac{3}{5} - \frac{1}{5}$
17. $\frac{2}{11} + \frac{5}{11} - \frac{1}{11}$
18. $\frac{2}{3} + \frac{1}{4}$
19. $\frac{4}{3} - \frac{1}{5}$
20. $\frac{3}{8} + \frac{1}{4} - \frac{1}{6}$
21. $\frac{2}{3} \times \frac{3}{5}$
22. $\frac{4}{5} \times \frac{3}{8}$
23. $\frac{4}{3} \times \frac{2}{5}$
24. $\frac{3}{5} \div \frac{4}{3}$
25. $4\frac{1}{4} + 2\frac{1}{3}$
26. $2\frac{3}{4} + 2\frac{2}{3}$
27. $4\frac{3}{4} - 2\frac{1}{2}$
28. $4\frac{1}{4} - 2\frac{1}{3}$
29. $4\frac{1}{4} \times 2\frac{1}{3}$
30. $4\frac{1}{4} \div 2\frac{1}{3}$

31. Duane Murray, a builder, is trying to figure out the thickness of a floor. The floor joists are $9\frac{1}{2}$ inches thick. On top of the floor joists are a $\frac{3}{4}$ inch subfloor and $\frac{1}{2}$ inch tile. What is the total thickness?

32. A bread recipe calls for $\frac{1}{3}$ cup of flour. A baker has $3\frac{2}{3}$ cups of flour on hand. How many loaves of bread can be made?

33. A farmer owns 7 acres of land. If the farmer gives $\frac{1}{5}$ of the land to his daughter, how many acres of land does the daughter get?

34. You buy a home for $250,000. If a bank will loan you $\frac{4}{5}$ of that amount, what amount is needed for a down payment?

35. A package of dental floss contains 150 feet of floss. If you use $1\frac{1}{4}$ feet each day, how many days should the floss last?

36. Flame Firewood Company charges $120 per cord of firewood. If you order $2\frac{1}{2}$ cords, what will your total cost be?

37. Tim, Jessie, and Daniel buy a rental property together. Tim has enough cash to buy a $\frac{1}{5}$ interest and Jessie has enough to buy a $\frac{1}{3}$ interest. Daniel agrees to buy the remainder. What portion will Daniel own?

38. Todd Holmes is paid $14 per hour but time and one-half for Saturdays. If he works 5 hours on Saturday, how much does he earn?

39. A set of house plans has a scale of $\frac{1}{4}$ inch equals 1 foot. If a kitchen wall measures $2\frac{3}{4}$ inches on the plans, what is the actual length of the wall?

40. During its annual sale, Nifty Department Store offers $\frac{1}{4}$ off all clothing. You find a colorful shirt you like, regularly priced at $44. What is the sale price?

41. A shirt requires $2\frac{1}{3}$ yards of fabric. How many whole shirts can be made from 85 yards of fabric?

Unit 2.3 Fraction/decimal conversions

Change these decimals to fractions or mixed numbers (remember to reduce):

42. 15.22

43. .3

44. .375

Change to a decimal:

45. $\frac{5}{16}$

46. $\frac{2}{3}$

47. $\frac{5}{11}$

48. $3\frac{4}{5}$

49. Look at Problems 45–48. Which answers are terminating decimals and which are repeating decimals?

50. Jamie and Shad jointly own .57 acre of land. If they each take half of the land, how many acres will each get?

51. Your rich uncle dies, leaving an inheritance of $12,320,000. If you get $\frac{1}{7}$, how much will you get?

52. Suppose you are asked to add $\frac{1}{4} + \frac{1}{5}$. Can you get a precise answer if you first convert each fraction to a decimal number? Explain why or why not?

53. Suppose you are asked to add $\frac{2}{5} + \frac{1}{3}$. Can you get a precise answer if you first convert each fraction to a decimal number? Explain why or why not?

Challenge problems

54. You are installing a wood fence. The fence is 118 feet long. Each wood slat, to be installed vertically, is $3\frac{3}{4}$ inches wide. What is the total cost of the wood slats if each slat costs $1.25? *Hint: 1 foot = 12 inches.*

55. A cookie recipe calls for $1\frac{2}{3}$ cups flour, $\frac{1}{3}$ cup peanut butter, and 2 eggs. If you want to make $3\frac{1}{2}$ times the normal amount, how much of each ingredient should you use?

56. A family has an annual income of $68,400, of which $\frac{1}{4}$ is budgeted for housing, $\frac{1}{5}$ for food, and $\frac{1}{8}$ for transportation. What fraction is left for other things?

57. Refer to Problem 56. Determine the dollar amount that is budgeted for each: Housing, Food, Transportation, Other Things.

For Problems 58–60, assume your company buys a parcel of land containing 252 acres.

58. If $\frac{1}{3}$ of the land must be used for streets, how much is available for homesites?

59. If each homesite is to contain $\frac{3}{8}$ of an acre, how many homesites will there be?

60. The land costs $30,000,000 and you have additional costs of $12,000,000 (for streets, utilities, engineering, and fees). If you can sell the lots for $125,000 each, what is your projected profit?

For Problems 61–64, help Sadie Heron, a tailor, determine how much she should charge customers for a suit.

61. Sadie makes men's suits. Pants require $2\frac{1}{4}$ yards of material, vests $1\frac{3}{8}$ yards, and jackets $4\frac{1}{2}$ yards. How many yards of material are required for each suit?

62. If Sadie buys fabric in rolls containing 195 yards, how many suits can she make from each roll?

63. If each roll of material costs $3,000, what is the cost of material per suit?

64. If Sadie adds $120 to the cost of each suit to cover labor and costs of operation and another $75 for profit, how much should she charge customers for a suit?

65. Tom Stevens, a contractor, is building a storage shed for a homeowner. Tom is leveling the ground prior to installing the forms and pouring the concrete floor. To help insure that the floor is level, Tom uses a builder's level to determine ground *elevations* at each corner. (*Note:* A builder's level sits on a tripod, about five feet above the ground, ans swivels so it can be aimed in any direction.) Tom records the following elevations:

Corner A is $59\frac{1}{2}$ inches below the builder's level

Corner B is $60\frac{3}{8}$ inches below the builder's level

Corner C is $58\frac{3}{16}$ inches below the builder's level

Corner D is $59\frac{11}{16}$ inches below the builder's level

First, determine which point has the lowest elevation. Then, calculate how much higher the ground is at the other corners.

Practice Test

Note: If the answer is a fraction, reduce.

1. Change $3\frac{5}{8}$ to an improper fraction.
2. Change $\frac{13}{3}$ to a mixed number.
3. Reduce $\frac{21}{27}$
4. Reduce $\frac{153}{198}$

5. Find the result: $\frac{2}{5} + \frac{2}{3} - \frac{1}{4}$
6. Find the result: $1\frac{2}{3} \times \frac{5}{4}$
7. Find the result: $2\frac{1}{4} \div \frac{5}{7}$
8. Find the result: $3\frac{2}{3} - 1\frac{3}{4}$

9. Change the decimal .625 to a fraction.
10. Convert $4\frac{11}{16}$ to a decimal number.

11. Find the thickness of an interior wall with a $3\frac{1}{2}$ inch stud and a piece of $\frac{5}{8}$ inch sheetrock on each side of the stud.

12. You are installing a wood fence. The fence is 155 feet long. Each wood slat, to be installed vertically, is $3\frac{3}{4}$ inches wide. What is the total cost of the wood slats if each slat costs $1.45?

FUN CORNER

Who Invented This Algebra Stuff Anyway?

Algebra is a branch of mathematics that uses numbers, variables, and symbols to solve problems. You may wonder who came up with the idea of algebra. Okay, so you don't want to know! But, aren't you just a bit curious?

Here's a crash course in the origination of algebra. Algebra started in Arabia. The Arabic word shei stands for "the unknown." Translated into English, shei became "xei," later abbreviated as the letter x representing the unknown value.

Records indicate that algebra has been used for many years. For example, in the Rhind papyrus, dated about 1650 B.C., a problem asks for the value of a "heap" if the heap and a seventh of a heap is 19. (What is a heap, anyway?) Today, we would write:

$$H + \frac{1}{7}H = 19$$

Using Equation-Solving Skills to Buy a Home

*From Homes and Other Black Holes
by Dave Barry*

In deciding which house to buy, the first thing to do is determine your Price Range, using this simple formula:

1. Take your total annual family income, including coins that have fallen behind the bureau.
2. Count up the number of children you have and note how many of them are named Joshua or Ashley. That many? Really? Don't you feel this trend toward giving children designer names has gone far enough? Don't you think we should go back to the old system of naming children after beloved uncles and aunts, even if we in fact hate our beloved uncles and aunts and they have comical names such as Lester? Can you imagine having an aunt named Lester? These questions are not directly related to your Price Range. I'm just curious how you feel.
3. Now take these figures (No! I'm not going to tell you again which ones! Pay attention!) and multiply them by six; which will tell you, in thousands of yards, roughly how far away the lightning bolt was. No! Wait! Sorry! Wrong formula! You want to take these figures and multiply them by something other than six. This should give you a very strong idea of what your Price Range is, although it doesn't matter because there are no homes in it anyway.

Business Math Teachers

There are three kinds of business math teachers:

1. Those who can count.
2. Those who can't count.

Quotable Quip

When you are dissatisfied and would like to go back to youth, think of Algebra.
— Will Rogers

Brainteaser

An electric locomotive is traveling north at the rate of 40 miles per hour. It is being chased from the south by a wind blowing at 80 miles per hour. Will the smoke from the locomotive be blown ahead of the train at the rate of 40 miles per hour?

Answer: No (electric locomotives have no smoke).

"Ha! And they said we couldn't avoid using math in real life!"

Equations: A Guide to Finding the Unknown

3

In this chapter we will develop a strategy for finding unknown values in equations. You may wonder why this chapter is important. First, we will be using lots of formulas throughout the text, like the simple interest formula ($I = PRT$) and present value formula $PV = \frac{FV}{(1+i)^n}$. Without a basic understanding of how equations work, we might pull some hair out when we encounter a formula! Second, the best way to solve many real-life problems is to first write the problem as an equation and then solve. Next, by understanding how to solve equations, our overworked brains won't have to memorize as many formulas. Finally, an understanding of these concepts is essential in working with many computer software packages. So, are you ready for the adventure into equation-solving?

UNIT OBJECTIVES

Unit 3.1 Mathematical symbols and expressions

ⓐ Understanding symbols and exponents
ⓑ Using the order of operations
ⓒ Working with positive and negative numbers
ⓓ Using the distributive rule and combining terms

Unit 3.2 Equations: Solving for the unknown

ⓐ Understanding how equations work: The balance principle
ⓑ Solving equations
ⓒ Working with formulas

Unit 3.3 Guideline for solving word problems

ⓐ Writing phrases using symbols
ⓑ Solving word problems with a "word problem guide"

Unit 3.1 Mathematical symbols and expressions

In the expression "$2m + 8$," 8 is a **constant** (the value is known) and m is a **variable** (the value of m is unknown). The 2 is a **coefficient** and means *2 times m*. In this chapter, we will work with constants, variables, coefficients, and a variety of mathematical symbols.

a Understanding symbols and exponents

Let's review some common mathematical symbols.

---

mathematical symbols

Equality and inequality symbols
- $=$ means "equals": $2 + 3 = 5$
- $\neq$ means "is not equal to": $y \neq 5$ means that y is not equal to 5
- $\approx$ means "is approximately equal to": $\frac{1}{3} \approx .33$
- $<$ means "is less than": $m < 4$ means m is less than 4
- $>$ means "is greater than": $p > 8$ means p is greater than 8
- $\leq$ means "is less than or equal to": $b \leq 12$ means b either is less than 12 or is 12
- $\geq$ means "is greater than or equal to": $q \geq 5$ means q either is greater than 5 or is 5

Operator symbols
Addition is shown by the symbol +
Subtraction is shown by the symbol -
Multiplication is shown by a variety of symbols. All of the following indicate multiplication:

$3 \times 4 \qquad 3 \cdot 4 \qquad 3(4) \qquad (3)(4)$

$4A \qquad 4 \cdot A \qquad 4(A) \qquad (4)(A)$

The multiplication symbol "×" should be avoided wherever it can be confused with the variable "x." For example, does "4×A" mean "4 times A" or "4 times x times A"?

Division is shown in several ways; for example, 6 divided by 2 can be shown as $6 \div 2$, $\frac{6}{2}$, 6/2, or $2\overline{)6}$.

We can find the product of (2)(2)(2)(2) by multiplying 2 four times: (2)(2) = 4; multiplying that result by 2 gives 8; and multiplying that result by 2 gives 16. So, (2)(2)(2)(2) = 16. To save space, repeated values are written with an **exponent**. For example, (2)(2)(2)(2) can be written as 2^4 (read as "two to the fourth power"); (3)(3) can be written as 3^2 (read as "three to the second power" or "three squared"); and (5)(5)(5) can be written as 5^3 (read as "five to the third power" or "five cubed").

Example 1 Write (4)(4)(4)(4)(4) using exponents.

Since the value 4 appears five times, the expression can be written as 4^5.

Example 2 Find the value of **(a)** 23^2 and **(b)** 4^5.

a. $23^2 = (23)(23) = 529$ b. $4^5 = (4)(4)(4)(4)(4) = 1{,}024$

Most calculators have exponent keys: [x^2] to square a number, and a power key, such as [y^x] or [∧] to raise a number to any power. While keystrokes vary from calculator to calculator, here are some general keystrokes: (1) to find the value of 23^2, we press 23 followed by [x^2]—the result of 529 will appear; (2) to find the value of 4^5 we press 4, then the power key, followed by 5, then the equal key—the result 1,024 will appear.

> **TIP** — **spreadsheet operator symbols**
>
> Computer spreadsheets use certain operator symbols. An asterisk (*) is used for multiplication, the symbol ^ is used for exponents, and a forward slash (/) is used for division. For Excel:
> 1. To multiply the value in cell B49 by 8: =B49*8
> 2. To raise the value in cell A25 to the fourth power: =A25^4
> 3. To divide the value in cell D10 by 3: =D10/3

b Using the order of operations

Back in the "old days," mathematicians probably got different answers to simple problems, depending on the order in which they performed the operations. Look at the following mathematical expression:

$$2 + 3 \times 4$$

Some mathematicians probably added 2 and 3, getting 5, and then multiplied by 4, getting *20*. Others might have multiplied 3 times 4, getting 12, and then added 2, getting *14*. This must have created lots of confusion at math conventions! At one of their math conventions, mathematicians must have decided to vote on a universal "order of operations" so that everyone would get identical answers to problems like this one. Here is the order of operations currently used.

> **order of operations**
>
> **Step 1** Perform calculations inside of parentheses.
>
> **Step 2** Apply exponents.
>
> **Step 3** Perform multiplication and division, at the same time, from left to right.
>
> **Step 4** Perform addition and subtraction, at the same time, from left to right.
>
> *Note:* If there are no parentheses, ignore Step 1. If there are parentheses, perform calculations inside of parentheses using Steps 2 through 4, in order; then use Steps 2 through 4 outside of parentheses.

> **TIP** — **Please Excuse My Dear Aunt Sally**
>
> Some people remember the order of operations by thinking "**P**lease **E**xcuse **M**y **D**ear **A**unt **S**ally."
>
> | Please | Excuse | My | Dear | Aunt | Sally |
> |---|---|---|---|---|---|
> | ↓ | ↓ | ↓ | ↓ | ↓ | ↓ |
> | **P**arentheses | **E**xponents | **M**ultiplication | **D**ivision | **A**ddition | **S**ubtraction |

Combine terms using the order of operations: **a.** $2 + 3 \times 4$ **b.** $4 + 2(2 + 3^2)$

a. $2 + 3 \times 4 = 2 + 12 = \boxed{14}$
b. $4 + 2(2 + 3^2) = 4 + 2(2 + 9) = 4 + 2(11) = 4 + 22 = \boxed{26}$

In Example 3, we found that $2 + 3 \times 4$ is 14 and $4 + 2(2 + 3^2)$ is 26. "14" and "26" are easier to understand than the original expressions; we refer to this process as **simplifying an expression.**

Some expressions contain more than one set of parentheses, in which case we use parentheses ( ), brackets [ ], and braces { } to distinguish each set. *We always do calculations within the innermost set first.*

Unit 3.1 Mathematical symbols and expressions 51

Example 4 Simplify: 2[3 + 2(5 - 2)]

2[3 + 2(5 - 2)] = 2[3 + 2(3)] = 2[3 + 6] = 2[9] = 18

C Working with positive and negative numbers

Some expressions, such as 2 + 7 - 4, are easily simplified. One easy way to simplify expressions like this one is to think in terms of playing poker: in the first hand you won $2, in the second hand you won $7, and in the third hand you lost $4. After three hands, you are ahead $5. Or, if you don't relate to poker, think in terms of taking steps forward and backward: you took 2 steps forward, then 7 steps forward, followed by 4 steps backward. The net result is 5 steps forward. Either way, 2 + 7 - 4 = 5. Not all expressions are as easy to simplify. Look at this one:

$$2 + (6 - 2) + (3 - 4) - (7 - 4) - (2 - 6)$$

In Example 5, we will simplify this expression, but first let's review guidelines for adding and subtracting signed numbers (positives and negatives).

guidelines for adding and subtracting signed numbers

Operation	Example	Is like	Think	Result
Adding a positive	+ (+4)	Adding	Getting something good is *good* (so add)	+4
Adding a negative	+ (- 1)	Subtracting	Getting something bad is *bad* (so subtract)	-1
Subtracting a positive	- (+3)	Subtracting	Getting rid of something good is *bad* (so subtract)	-3
Subtracting a negative	- (- 4)	Adding	Getting rid of something bad is *good* (so add)	+4

Example 5 Simplify: 2 + (6 - 2) + (3 - 4) - (7 - 4) - (2 - 6)

2 + (6 - 2) + (3 - 4) - (7 - 4) - (2 - 6)	*Original expression*
= 2 + (+4) + (-1) - (+3) - (-4)	*Simplify inside parentheses*
= 2 +4 - 1 - 3 +4	*Remove parentheses, using guidelines*
= 6	*Combine numbers by adding and subtracting*

Some expressions involving multiplication or division are easy to simplify. For example, (2)(3) is 6. However, multiplication and division with negative numbers takes a bit more effort.

When multiplying or dividing two numbers with the same sign (both positive or both negative), the result is positive. When multiplying or dividing two numbers with different signs (one positive and one negative), the result is negative.

Example 6 Find the value: **a.** (-2)(3)   **b.** $\frac{-6}{-2}$ **c.** (3)(-4)(-2)

a. A negative value times a positive value is a negative, so: (-2)(3) = -6

b. A negative value divided by a negative value is a positive, so: $\frac{-6}{-2}$ = 3

c. A positive 3 times a negative 4 = -12; the negative 12 times a negative 2 = 24

TIP operation pitfall

Don't be tricked into adding and subtracting when multiplication is called for:

| this is an addition and subtraction problem: | - 2 + 4 - 5 | *(answer is -3)* |
| this is a multiplication problem: | (-2)(+4)(-5) | *(answer is 40)* |

Chapter 3 Equations: A Guide to Finding the Unknown

d Using the distributive rule and combining terms

To simplify an expression like 2(3 + 5), we can add 3 and 5, getting 8, and then multiply the result by 2, getting 16. Another choice is to use the **distributive rule.**

> **distributive rule**
>
> The distributive rule says we can multiply a value outside parentheses (like 2) by each individual value inside the parentheses and then add the products.

Example 7 Evaluate 2(3 + 5) two ways: (a) simplifying inside parentheses and (b) using the distributive rule.

a. $2(3 + 5) = 2(8) = 16$
b. $2(3 + 5) = 2(3) + 2(5) = 6 + 10 = 16$

Notice, the results are the same. The distributive rule must be okay to use!

I know what you are thinking: Why should we worry about the distributive rule if we can simplify inside parentheses first? Here is the answer: not all expressions inside of parentheses can be simplified first, like $2(a + 5)$. In this case, the distributive rule is the only choice we have.

> **TIP   paper bag with objects inside**
>
> In the expression $2(a + 5)$, the letter a is a variable. Some people like to think of variables in terms of objects; for example, the a could represent apples. Imagine the parentheses as a paper bag, each containing an apple and $5. The 2 indicates that we have 2 paper bags. If we dump the contents of each bag on a table, we have a total of 2 apples and $10.

Example 8 Simplify: $4(3b + 2)$

$$4(3b + 2) = 4(3b) + 4(2) = 12b + 8$$

If you have trouble, think: there are 4 paper bags and each contains 3 bananas and $2. Altogether, there are 12 bananas and $8.

In the expression $2 + 3$, we can combine terms to get a total of 5. Likewise, in the expression $3m + 4m$, we have 3 ms plus 4 ms, for a total of 7 ms. Combining constants (like 2 and 3) and variables represented by the same letter and exponent (like $3m$ and $4m$) is known as **combining like terms.**

> **combining like terms**
>
> | Start with | Okay to combine terms? | End up with |
> |---|---|---|
> | $4 + 8 - 2$ | Yes. Can combine numbers with numbers. | 10 |
> | $7 + 3m$ | No. Cannot combine numbers (7) with variables (m). | $7 + 3m$ |
> | $6m + 3m - 2m$ | Yes. Can combine the ms: 6 of them + 3 more - 2 of them = 7 ms. | $7m$ |
> | $5a + 2b$ | No. Cannot combine different variables. | $5a + 2b$ |
> | $4p + 10 + 3p - 6$ | Yes. Can combine variables: $4p + 3p = 7p$
Can combine numbers: $10 - 6 = 4$ | $7p + 4$ |
> | $2x^2 + 3x$ | No. Exponents are different. | $2x^2 + 3x$ |

Example 9 Simplify: **a.** $3(4m - 2) - 5m$ **b.** $3y - (y - 4)$

a. $3(4m - 2) - 5m = 3(4m) + 3(-2) - 5m = 12m - 6 - 5m = 7m - 6$
b. $3y - (y - 4) = 3y - (y) - (-4) = 3y - y + 4 = 2y + 4$

Part (b) was a bit tricky. We were asked to subtract (y - 4). This means to subtract y and also subtract a negative 4. Subtracting a positive y results in a negative y. Subtracting a negative 4 results in a positive 4. Another approach (if it makes more sense) is to insert a 1 in front of the parenthesis, since we were asked to subtract 1 of that quantity:

$$3y - (y - 4) = 3y - 1(y - 4) = 3y - 1(y) - 1(-4) = 3y - y + 4 = 2y + 4$$

That's all for this unit. Let's check our progress by doing the U-Try-It exercises.

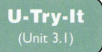
U-Try-It
(Unit 3.1)

1. Show four different ways to indicate "3 times y."
2. Write (3)(3)(3)(3) using exponents.
3. Find the value of 18^3.
4. Combine terms using the order of operations: **a.** $3 + 2(5 + 3)^2$ **b.** $2[4 + 3(5 - 2)]$
5. Simplify: $3 + (5 - 3) + (2 - 3) - (4 - 2) - (1 - 6)$
6. Find the value: **a.** $(-2)(-4)$ **b.** $\frac{-8}{2}$
7. Simplify: $2(3a + 2) - 1 + 2a$

Answers: (If you have a different answer, check the solution in Appendix A.)
1. $3y$, $3 \cdot y$, $3(y)$, $(3)(y)$ 2. 3^4 3. 5,832   4a. 131   4b. 26   5. 7   6a. 8   6b. -4   7. $8a + 3$

Unit 3.2 Equations: Solving for the unknown

In Unit 3.1, we focused on *simplifying expressions*. In this unit, we will study **equations**. *An equation consists of two expressions separated by an equal sign.*

Mathematical expression
$8x - 3x + 2$

Equation
$x + 3 = 26$

This has no equal sign. We can simplify $8x - 3x + 2$ to $5x + 2$ but cannot find a value for x because we do not know what $8x - 3x + 2$ is equal to.

This is a mathematical expression.   *This is a mathematical expression.*

The two expressions are separated by an equal sign. We can find a value for x that makes the equation true.

To solve an equation, we find all values of the variable that make the statement true. In the preceding equation, $x + 3 = 26$, we are asked, "What value, when added to 3, equals 26?" Since 23 is the value that must be added to 3 to get 26, $x = 23$. Some equations, like this one, can be solved intuitively. That is, we can "see" what the answer is. For many equations, however, it is hard to "see" the answer. So, we will establish a procedure for solving all types of equations.

ⓐ Understanding how equations work: The balance principle

An equation is similar to the balancing scale shown in Illustration 3-1. The equal sign (=) is like the center post of the scale, and the two sides of the equation balance each other like the two pans of the scale.

Illustration 3-1 Balancing Scale

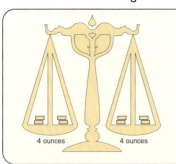
4 ounces   4 ounces

Start with 4 ounces (oz) on each side

If we add 2 oz to each side, each side will have 6 oz; scales still balance.

If, instead, we subtract 1 oz from each side, each side will have 3 oz; scales still balance.

If, instead, we double the weight on each side (multiply each side by 2), each side will have 8 oz; scales still balance.

If, instead, we cut each weight in half (divide each side by 2), each side will have 2 oz; scales still balance.

Illustration 3-1 demonstrates that, *as long as we do the same thing to each side of an equation, balance is maintained.*

> **Golden Rule of Equation Solving**
>
> *Do unto one side as you do unto the other*

b Solving equations

The goal in solving an equation is to *get the variable all by itself on one side of the equation;* whatever is on the other side is the solution. To get the variable all by itself, we manipulate the equation by adding, subtracting, multiplying, or dividing. *Manipulating equations is one of the most powerful problem-solving tools in mathematics.*

> **"do the opposite" rule**
>
> To manipulate equations, perform an operation that is the opposite of how the variable is affected.
> - If the variable is affected by *subtraction* (like $x - 7 = 4$), *add* that value (7) to both sides.
> - If the variable is affected by *addition* (like $m + 3 = 22$), *subtract* that value (3) from both sides.
> - If the variable is affected by *multiplication* (like $2b = 16$), *divide* both sides by the coefficient (2).
> - If the variable is affected by *division* (like $\frac{P}{3} = 7$), *multiply* both sides by the divisor (3).

Let's do some problems.

Example 1 Solve: $x - 7 = 4$

$$\begin{array}{rl} x - 7 = & 4 \\ +7 & +7 \\ \hline x = & 11 \end{array}$$ Do the same thing to both sides

We can check our answer to Example 1 by substituting the answer (11) for the variable into the original equation. If, after substituting, the equation is in balance, the answer is correct.

> **TIP** what's inside
>
> To begin the substitution process, think of the variable as a surprise package, with the answer inside. For example, in checking the answer to Example 1, when we open the package representing x, guess what we find inside: 11.

Example 2 Check the solution to Example 1.

$$\boxed{x} - 7 = 4$$
$$\downarrow$$
$$11 - 7 = 4$$
$$4 = 4$$

Example 3 Solve: $m + 3 = 22$

$$m + 3 = 22$$
$$\underline{-3 \quad -3}$$
$$m = 19$$

Check by substituting

$\boxed{m} + 3 = 22$
$19 + 3 = 22$
$22 = 22$

Example 4 Solve: $2b = 16$

$$2b = 16$$
$$\frac{2b}{2} = \frac{16}{2}$$
$$b = 8$$

← Divide both sides by 2

Check by substituting

$2b$ means 2 times b → $2\boxed{b} = 16$
$2(8) = 16$
$16 = 16$

Example 5 Solve: $\frac{P}{3} = 7$

$$\frac{P}{3} = 7$$
$$3\left(\frac{P}{3}\right) = 3(7)$$
$$P = 21$$

Multiply both sides by 3

Check by substituting

$\frac{\boxed{P}}{3} = 7$
$\frac{21}{3} = 7$
$7 = 7$

If the coefficient of the variable is a fraction, we multiply both sides of the equation by the **reciprocal** of the coefficient. The reciprocal is found by switching the numerator and denominator. For example, the reciprocal of $\frac{23}{17}$ is $\frac{17}{23}$.

Example 6 Solve: $\frac{4}{5}t = 16$

$$\frac{4}{5}t = 16$$
$$\frac{5}{4}\left(\frac{4}{5}\right)t = \frac{5}{4}\left(\frac{16}{1}\right)$$
$$t = 20$$

Multiply both sides by the reciprocal $\left(\frac{5}{4}\right)$

Check by substituting

$\frac{4}{5}\boxed{t} = 16$
$\frac{4}{5}\left(\frac{20}{1}\right) = 16$
$16 = 16$

In Example 6, we multiplied both sides of the equation by $\frac{5}{4}$. We could have instead used a two-step process: first multiplied both sides by 5, getting $4t = 80$; then divided both sides by 4, getting $t = 20$. Use the approach that you find easier. The upcoming examples require more than one step.

> **TIP** — attack constant before attacking coefficient
>
> The goal in solving an equation is to get the variable all by itself on one side of the equation; whatever is on the other side is the solution. Some equations require more than one step. For example, in the equation "$2a - 7 = 5$" we must get rid of the 2 (the coefficient) and the 7 (the constant). Here is a suggestion: It is easier if we attack the constant (the 7) before attacking the coefficient (the 2). Stated another way, perform addition or subtraction first, then multiplication or division.

Example 7 Solve for a: $2a - 7 = 5$

$$2a - 7 = 5$$
$$\underline{+7 = +7}$$
$$2a = 12$$
$$\frac{2a}{2} = \frac{12}{2}$$
$$a = 6$$

Check by substituting

$2\boxed{a} - 7 = 5$
$2(6) - 7 = 5$
$12 - 7 = 5$
$5 = 5$

You might wonder if, in Example 7, we could attack the coefficient (the 2) before attacking the constant (the 7). The answer is yes. We would end up with the same answer ($a = 6$), but the procedure would be more difficult. Try it, if you would like; remember in the first step to divide *everything* on both sides (2a, 7, and 5) by 2.

Some equations, like the one in the next example, require even more steps. Here are some guidelines.

procedure for multiple operations

Step 1 Simplify each side of the equation.

Step 2 If the variable is on both sides of the equation, use addition or subtraction to get the variable on one side; do it so that the resulting coefficient is *positive*.

Step 3 Get the variable all by itself; do addition or subtraction before doing multiplication or division (in other words, attack the constant before attacking the coefficient).

Example 8 Solve for y: $6(2y + 1) + 5 = 7(3y - 2) + 7$

$$6(2y + 1) + 5 = 7(3y - 2) + 7$$

Step 1
$$12y + 6 + 5 = 21y - 14 + 7$$
$$12y + 11 = 21y - 7$$

Step 2
$$\underline{-12y \qquad\qquad -12y}$$
$$11 = 9y - 7$$

Step 3
$$\underline{+7 \qquad\qquad +7}$$
$$18 = 9y$$
$$\frac{18}{9} = \frac{9y}{9}$$
$$\boxed{2} = y$$

C Working with formulas

A **formula** is a *rule or principle expressed as an equation*. For example, the simple interest formula "$I = PRT$" is used to find the dollar amount of interest (I) for a simple interest loan. "P" is the principal (loan amount), "R" is the interest rate, and "T" is the amount of time, in years. Assume you borrow $2,000 for 4 months at 6% interest. If you want to find the amount of interest you will owe in 4 months, simply substitute the known values for the variables in the formula: $P = \$2{,}000$; $R = 6\%$, or .06; $T = \frac{4}{12}$ of a year.

$$I = PRT = \$2{,}000 \times .06 \times \frac{4}{12} = \frac{\$2{,}000 \times .06 \times 4}{12} = \$40$$

You will owe $40 interest. You must pay a total of $2,040 (the $2,000 principal + $40 interest).

The simple interest formula $(I = PRT)$ is designed to solve for I (the dollar amount of interest). There are lots of situations in which we must calculate the interest rate (R); doing so would be easier if we had a formula designed to solve for "R" instead of "I." In the next example, we will use the Golden Rule of Equation Solving *(Do unto one side as you do unto the other)* to create a formula that is designed to solve for R.

Example 9 Use the simple interest formula $(I = PRT)$ to create a formula designed to solve for "R."

$I = PRT$ The simple interest formula

$\frac{I}{PT} = R$ Divide both sides by PT

$\boxed{R = \frac{I}{PT}}$ Rearrange so "R" is on the left

We now have a formula that is designed to solve for "R." We will use this formula extensively in Unit 9.2. Using the procedure of Example 9, we can manipulate any formula so it is designed for a different variable; we will do this a number of times in the text.

Unit 3.2 Equations: Solving for the unknown

Well, that wraps up Unit 3.2. Let's do the U-Try-It questions to see if it sunk in!

U-Try-It (Unit 3.2)

1. Solve for the variable:
   a. $m - 3 = 5$ b. $a + 6 = -2$ c. $4b = 5$ d. $\frac{x}{4} = 3$ e. $\frac{2}{3}y = 10$ f. $2(p + 6) - 4 = 3(2p - 2) + 3p$
2. The formula "$V = \pi r^2 h$" is used to find the volume of a cylinder (like a grain silo or gasoline storage tank). Rewrite the formula so it is designed to solve for "h."

Answers: (If you have a different answer, check the solution in Appendix A.)
1a. $m = 8$ **1b.** $a = -8$ **1c.** $b = \frac{5}{4}$ **1d.** $x = 12$ **1e.** $y = 15$ **1f.** $p = 2$ **2.** $h = \frac{V}{\pi r^2}$

Unit 3.3 Guideline for solving word problems

Many people shudder when they hear the term "word problem." The most difficult part of solving word (story) problems is translating the words into an equation. In fact, once that is done, we are about 90% finished; then we can "crank out" the answer by applying the previous concepts of this chapter. Some people prefer having a tooth pulled to doing word problems. However, most people lose their fear of word problems after some practice; some people even start to enjoy them. Rather than start out solving problems, we will begin slowly and then "build to a mild roar."

Equation-solving skills can be used in real-life situations, like figuring how much homeowner's insurance we need to meet a lender's requirements.

ⓐ Writing phrases using symbols

Let's start off writing some simple phrases using symbols.

Example 1   Write the following phrases using symbols:
  a. 6 times d
  b. 4 more than t
  c. 15 less than r
  d. The sum of x, y, and z
  e. Twice the sum of m and n

  a. The word "times" suggests multiplication: $6d$
  b. The word "more" suggests addition: $t + 4$
  c. The word "less" suggests subtraction: $r - 15$
  d. The word "sum" suggests addition: $x + y + z$
  e. We must first find the sum and then multiply by 2: $2(m + n)$

> **TIP — is it okay to reverse the values?**
>
> When adding two numbers, it is okay to reverse the order; but when subtracting one number from another, it is *not* okay to reverse the order. For example, $5 + 2 = 7$ and $2 + 5 = 7$. However, $5 - 2 = 3$ but $2 - 5 = -3$. In Example 1, part b, it would be okay to write $4 + t$ instead of $t + 4$, but in part c, it would not be okay to write $15 - r$ instead of $r - 15$.

Next, let's change some phrases to equations.

Example 2   Change the following phrases to equations:
  a. x equals 3 more than y
  b. m is 4 times n
  c. t plus 3 totals 6 less than r

  a. The word "equals" can be replaced with an equal sign: $x = y + 3$
  b. The word "is" can be replaced with an equal sign: $m = 4n$
  c. The word "totals" can be replaced with an equal sign: $t + 3 = r - 6$

b Solving word problems with a "word problem guide"

Now, we'll get to the fun part: changing word problems into equations. While getting the answer is important, so is developing a strategy for solving the problems.

strategy for solving word problems

Step 1 Read the problem carefully. Ask, What am I supposed to find?
Step 2 Write the problem as an equation.
Step 3 Substitute what is known.
Step 4 Solve for the unknown.
Step 5 Make sure the solution answers the question that was asked. Then, check the answer.

TIP — the tough part

Step 2 (writing the problem as an equation) is the tough part of solving word problems. In word problems, we are given a sum, difference, product, or quotient that helps describe the "big picture." A good place to start is to write that number on the right side of the equal sign (=). Then ask, What is it that equals that number? For example, if an auto dealer is going to order a total of 152 cars and trucks, we could start by writing:

$$? = 152$$

and then fill in the left side: $C + T = 152$

In the next example, we will use a word problem guide. Notice that in Step 2 we write an equation and in Step 5 we check the answer.

Example 3 I. M. Rich is about to open a car dealership. His property can accommodate a total inventory of 152 vehicles. The auto manufacturer told I. M. that he should have three times as many cars as trucks. How many of each should he order?

word problem guide

1. Solving for	Number of cars (C) and trucks (T)	
2. Write equation	$? = 152$	*Something equals 152*
	$C + T = 152$	*Cars + trucks = 152*
3. Substitute known facts	$3T + T = 152$	*We were told (in words) that $C = 3T$*
4. Solve for unknown	$4T = 152$	*Combine terms on left*
	$\frac{4T}{4} = \frac{152}{4}$	*Divide both sides by 4*
	$T = 38$	*Number of trucks*
	$\times 3$	*We also need to find number of cars*
	$C = 114$	*Number of cars*
5. Check answer	Cars 114	
	Trucks 38	
	152	*Total (152) is correct*

I. M. should order 114 cars and 38 trucks.

Unit 3.3 Guideline for solving word problems

> **TIP** — the clue game
>
> For word problems, there is one clue per variable. In Example 3, there were two variables (cars and trucks), and we were given two bits of information: (1) total of 152 vehicles and (2) three times as many cars as trucks. We changed the two clues into equations: (1) $C + T = 152$ and (2) $C = 3T$. You might have been tempted to start with the second equation. We should *always* start with the equation that describes the "big picture" ($C + T = 152$). The other equation ($C = 3T$) merely describes the "relationship between the variables" and is used to substitute for one of the variables.
>
> Here is a common mistake: Some people in Step 3 treat the relationship between cars and trucks as $T = 3C$ instead of $C = 3T$. With $T = 3C$ we are saying, if I know how many cars there are (C) and multiply by 3, that gives the number of trucks (T). That is not true, since that means there are more trucks than cars. With $C = 3T$ we are saying, if I know how many trucks there are (T) and multiply by 3, that gives me the number of cars (C); this is correct.

For upcoming examples, we will show *results* for each step *without showing calculations;* this should reduce clutter and make steps easier to follow.

Example 4 Suppose you just bought a home and your lender requires that you have $242,000 of property insurance. The policy will insure the home for a certain amount and automatically covers additional structures (like decks, carports, sheds, fences) for $\frac{1}{10}$ of the home coverage. The more coverage you have, the greater the fee, so find the minimum amount of coverage required on the home so that the total coverage (home plus additional structures) is $242,000.

word problem guide

1. Solving for	Home coverage (H)	
2. Write equation	$? = \$242{,}000$	*Something* = $242,000
	$H + A = \$242{,}000$	Home coverage + additional coverage = $242,000
	↓	
3. Substitute known facts	$H + \frac{1}{10}H = \$242{,}000$	Substitute: $A = \frac{1}{10}H$
4. Solve for unknown	$1\frac{1}{10}H = \$242{,}000$	Combine terms on left
	$\frac{11}{10}H = \$242{,}000$	Change mixed number to improper fraction
	$\frac{10}{11}\left(\frac{11}{10}\right)H = \frac{10}{11}(\$242{,}000)$	Multiply both sides by reciprocal of coefficient $\left(\frac{10}{11}\right)$
	$H = \boxed{\$220{,}000}$	Coverage for home
5. Check answer	Home $\quad \$220{,}000$	
	Additional $\underline{+\ 22{,}000}$	$\frac{1}{10}(\$220{,}000) = \$22{,}000$
	Total $\quad \$242{,}000$	Answer ($242,000) is correct

By insuring the home for $220,000, you will have total coverage of $242,000.

> **TIP** — impulse solving
>
> Your first impulse in solving Example 4 may have been to find $\frac{1}{10}$ of $242,000 ($24,200) and subtract that amount from $242,000, giving $217,800; but you would have total coverage of only $239,580 ($217,800 + $21,780), which is not enough to satisfy the lender. Another impulse may have been to add $\frac{1}{10}$ of $242,000 ($24,200) to $242,000, giving $266,200; but you don't need that much coverage.
>
> So, what's the point? Don't solve word problems on impulse. Write equations carefully. Stand back and see if the equations make sense. Then, after solving, check your answer.
>
> *Here's a suggestion you may find helpful.* If you have trouble writing an equation for a problem, try a *Guess and Check* approach. Guess an answer and check it. If that guess does not work, try other guesses until one works. For instance, with Example 4 you might have first guessed $230,000 coverage on the home: $230,000 + $23,000 = $253,000 (too high). Try $220,000: $220,000 + $22,000 = $242,000 (correct).

Example 5 Reagan Paisley sells jewelry and rents a booth at the local fair. She is required to collect sales tax on all sales and, at the end of the fair, send the sales tax to the government. The sales tax is .065 of the price. If, for example, Reagan sold a necklace for $45 she would collect an additional $2.93 in sales tax ($45 × .065 = $2.93), so the customer would pay a total of $47.93. Reagan decides to sell items for whole dollar amounts that includee sales tax (like $48 for a necklace); this will make it easier for her and her customers who pay with cash. During the fair, she collects a total of $8,570. How much sales tax must Reagan send to the government?

We can't figure the sales tax until we know the price of the goods. Let's solve for the price of the goods.

word problem guide

1. Solving for	Price of goods (P)	
2. Write equation	? = $8,570	*Something = $8,570*
	P + T = $8,570	*Price of goods + sales tax = $8,570*
3. Substitute known facts	P + (.065 P) = $8,570	*Substitute: T = .065 P*
4. Solve for unknown	1.065 P = $8,570	*1.000 P + .065 P = 1.065 P*
	$P = \frac{\$8,570}{1.065}$	*Divide both sides by 1.065*
	P = $8,046.95	*Price of goods*

Because the sales tax is .065 times the price of the goods, sales tax is: $8,046.95 × .065 = **$523.05**

5. Check answer

Price of goods	$8,046.95
Sales tax	+ 523.05
Total collected	$8,570.00

Reagan collected $8,570; she must send $523.05 to the government, leaving her with the price of the goods ($8,046.95).

In Example 5, you may have been tempted to figure the sales tax by multiplying $8,570 by the tax rate: $8,570 × .065 = $557.05. But Reagan would be paying $34 too much.

We're now finished with Chapter 3. Way to go! Now, let's sharpen our skills in solving word problems by doing a few more in the U-Try-It set.

U-Try-It (Unit 3.3)

1. Write phrases using symbols:
   a. 4 times m b. 3 more than a c. 8 less than b d. The sum of p, q, and r
2. Change the phrase "b is 5 more than a" to an equation.
3. An investment company has $4,500,000 to invest in stocks, bonds, and mutual funds. The company decides to invest $1,200,000 in bonds and twice as much in stocks as they invest in mutual funds. How much money should they invest in each? Use a *word problem guide*, and check your answer.

Answers: (If you have a different answer, check the solution in Appendix A.)
1a. $4m$ 1b. $a + 3$ (or $3 + a$)   1c. $b - 8$ 1d. $p + q + r$ 2. $b = a + 5$ (or $b = 5 + a$)   3. stocks: $2,200,000; bonds: $1,200,000; mutual funds: $1,100,000

Chapter in a Nutshell

Objectives	Examples

Unit 3.1 Mathematical symbols and expressions

a Understanding symbols and exponents

a. $\neq$ means "not equal to"   b. $\approx$ means "approximately equal to"
c. $m < 2$ means "m is less than 2"   d. $p \geq 5$ means "p either is greater than 5 or is 5"
e. 4 times R: $4R$, $4 \cdot R$, $4(R)$, $(4)(R)$ f. $\frac{6}{3}$ means $6 \div 3$
g. $(3)(3)(3)(3)$ can be written as 3^4 h. $6^3 = (6)(6)(6) = 216$

b Using the order of operations

Please → Parentheses
Excuse → Exponents
My → Multiplication
Dear → Division
Aunt → Addition
Sally → Subtraction

a. $3 + 2(3 + 2^2) = 3 + 2(3 + 4) = 3 + 2(7) = 3 + 14 = 17$
b. $5 + 3[2(3^2 + 1)] = 5 + 3[2(9 + 1)] = 5 + 3[2(10)] = 5 + 3[20] = 5 + 60 = 65$

c Working with positive and negative numbers

a. $4 + (5 - 2) + (2 - 6) - (6 - 4) - (1 - 5)$
   $= 4 + (+3) + (-4) - (+2) - (-4)$
   $= 4 + +3 \quad -4 \quad -2 \quad +4$
   $= 5$

b. $(-3)(5) = -15$ c. $(-2)(-6) = 12$ d. $\frac{10}{-2} = -5$

d Using the distributive rule and combining terms

a. $4(2m + 6) = 4(2m) + 4(6) = 8m + 24$
b. $5(3p - 2) + 6p = 5(3p) + 5(-2) + 6p = 15p - 10 + 6p = 21p - 10$

Unit 3.2 Equations: Solving for the unknown

a Understanding how equations work: The balance principle

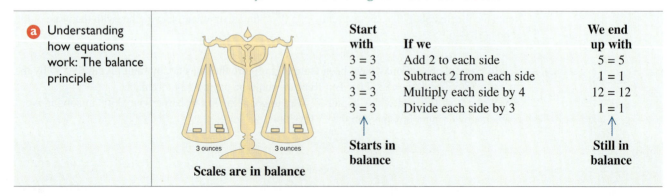

3 ounces   3 ounces
Scales are in balance

Start with	If we	We end up with
3 = 3	Add 2 to each side	5 = 5
3 = 3	Subtract 2 from each side	1 = 1
3 = 3	Multiply each side by 4	12 = 12
3 = 3	Divide each side by 3	1 = 1
↑ Starts in balance		↑ Still in balance

62   Chapter 3   Equations: A Guide to Finding the Unknown

Chapter in a Nutshell (concluded)

Objectives	Examples
b Solving equations	**a.** $x - 3 = 8$ $\quad +3 \quad +3$ $\quad x = 11$ **b.** $b + 2 = 6$ $\quad -2 \quad -2$ $\quad b = 4$ **c.** $3a = 12$ $\quad \frac{3a}{3} = \frac{12}{3}$ $\quad a = 4$ **d.** $\frac{m}{3} = 2$ $\quad \frac{3}{1}\left(\frac{m}{3}\right) = 3(2)$ $\quad m = 6$ **e.** $\frac{2}{3}p = 8$ $\quad \frac{3}{2} \cdot \frac{2}{3}p = \frac{3}{2}\left(\frac{8}{1}\right)$ $\quad p = 12$ **f.** $4(3c - 2) + 2c = 7c + 6$ $\quad 12c - 8 + 2c = 7c + 6$ $\quad 14c - 8 = 7c + 6$ $\quad -7c \quad\quad = -7c$ $\quad 7c - 8 = 6$ $\quad +8 \quad +8$ $\quad 7c = 14$ $\quad \frac{7c}{7} = \frac{14}{7}$ $\quad c = 2$
c Working with formulas	The formula "$P = B \times R$" is used to find the portion (P) in percentage problems. Use that formula to create one designed to solve for "B." $P = B \times R \;\longrightarrow\; \frac{P}{R} = B \;\longrightarrow\; B = \frac{P}{R}$

Unit 3.3 Guideline for solving word problems

a Writing phrases using symbols	**a.** 6 times p: $6p$ **b.** 2 more than b: $b + 2$ **c.** 8 less than m: $m - 8$ **d.** Sum of a, b, and c: $a + b + c$ **e.** m is 3 times r: $m = 3r$
b Solving word problems with a "word problem guide"	A corporation decides to acquire some money by selling 450,000 shares of stock. They want to sell 8 shares of common stock for each share of preferred stock. How many shares of each should they sell? *word problem guide*

1. Solving for	Common Stock (C) and preferred stock (P)	
2. Write equation	? = 450,000 shares $C + P$ = 450,000 shares	*Something* = 450,000 shares $C + P$ = 450,000 shares
3. Substitute known facts	$8P + P$ = 450,000 shares	$C = 8P$
4. Solve for unknown	$9P$ = 450,000 shares P = 50,000 shares $\times 8$ C = 400,000 shares	*Combine terms on left* *Divide both sides by 9*
5. Check answer	Common stock 400,000 shares Preferred stock 50,000 shares 450,000 shares	

Enrichment Topics

The following Enrichment Topics, which go a bit beyond what is in the text, are available for this chapter:

Roots
Formulas: The Hows and Whys of Using and Modifying Them

If your instructor doesn't cover these topics in class and you would like to dig in deeper on your own, please send a request to *studentsupport@olympuspub.com*.

Think

1. If $m > 4$ can m be 4? Explain.
2. Why is 4 - (-3) the same as 4 + 3?
3. Why is it important to have a universal order of operations?
4. In the expression $4b^2 + 8$, what are the variable, coefficient, exponent, and constant? Explain what a variable, coefficient, exponent, and constant are. Then, find the value of $4b^2 + 8$, assuming that b is 3.
5. Using the distributive rule, we find that $3(a + 5)$ is the same as $3a + 15$. Prove that the distributive rule works by substituting a value (like 2) for a in both expressions.
6. In solving the equation $4m + 9 = 33$ we are advised to subtract 9 from both sides before dividing both sides by 4. Solve for m using this approach. Then, rework the problem by doing division *before* subtraction. (*Hint:* Remember to divide "everything" on both sides by 4.) Do we get the same answer, and why? Which approach is easier, and why?
7. A *Guess and Check* approach is mentioned in the Tip box just after Example 4 of Unit 3.3. Explain how you could use the Guess and Check approach to solve word problems (use Chapter Review Problem 41 to illustrate).

Explore

1. Use Microsoft® Excel to solve Chapter Review Problem 53. Widen column A to 15, then in row 1, type Customers; in row 2, type Fixed Costs; in row 3, type Variable Costs; in row 4, type Total Costs; and in row 5, type Revenues. If you need to review Excel arithmetic symbols, refer to Explore activity 2 of Chapter 1. In rows 2 through 5 of column B, type what you know; for example, in cell B3: =B1*8. Then, enter a guess in cell B1 for the number of customers. If total revenues (B5) is less than total costs (B4), increase the number of customers; if B5 is greater than B4, reduce the number of customers; keep adjusting the number of customers until the total costs (B4) = total revenues (B5).

Apply

1. **In Your Own Words.** Write six "real-life" word problems. Solve each problem using a *word problem guide*. Show all of your work, together with the answer. Finally, prove your answer.
2. **Equation-Solving in Business.** Interview someone from at least two of the following professions. Get some examples of how they use equation-solving skills in their profession. Show the equations, together with solutions.
   A. Construction   B. Graphic design   C. Architecture
   D. Real Estate   E. Medicine   F. Banking

64 Chapter 3 Equations: A Guide to Finding the Unknown

Chapter Review Problems

Unit 3.1 Mathematical symbols and expressions

1. The symbol ≠ means "approximately equal to." (T or F)
2. Show three different ways to indicate "7 times 12."
3. $\frac{17}{13}$ means 13 divided by 17. (T or F)
4. If $m \geq 4$, can m be
   a. 13? (yes or no)
   b. 2? (yes or no)
   c. 4? (yes or no)
5. Write 7·7·7·7·7 using exponents.
6. What is the value of 3^5?

For Problems 7–15, simplify.

7. $4 + 2 \cdot 5$
8. $(8 + 3)^2$
9. $8 + 3^2$
10. $5[2 + 3(4 - 2) - 5] + 3$
11. $3 + (3 + 2) + (2 - 4) - (7 - 5) - (2 - 8)$
12. $(4)(3)$
13. $-4 - 3$
14. $(2)(-3)(2)(4)(-3)(-2)$
15. $\frac{-18}{-3}$

For Problems 16–20, simplify each expression using the distributive rule and/or combining terms.

16. $2(m + n)$
17. $5(3a + 2b)$
18. $2y - (y - 2)$
19. $3m + 2(2m + 1) - 3m + 6$
20. $2x + 2y$

Unit 3.2 Equations: Solving for the unknown

21. Which of these are equations?   a. $3x - 2y + 2$ b. $x - 2 = 16$ c. $3a + 2$

For Problems 22–30, solve for the variable.

22. $x - 8 = 27$
23. $y + 17 = 23$
24. $3a = 15$
25. $\frac{t}{8} = 3$
26. $\frac{2}{7}y = 3$
27. $2b + 7 = 43$

28. $3m - (m - 4) = 14$ **29.** $2p - 4 = 5p + 8$ **30.** $3(3x + 5) - 19 = 2(x + 5)$

31. Prove your answer to Problem 30 by substituting your answer for the variable.

32. The formula "$FV = PV(1 + i)^n$" is used to find what an amount will grow to if earning compound interest. Assume you deposit $500 ($PV = \$500$) for 5 years ($n = 5$) earning 4% interest ($i = .04$). Determine the amount the money will grow to (FV).

33. Refer to Problem 32. Use the compound interest formula "$FV = PV(1 + i)^n$" to create a formula designed to solve for "PV."

Unit 3.3 Guideline for solving word problems

For Problems 34–37, write phrases using symbols.

34. 4 times m

35. 12 more than x

36. 8 less than a

37. Twice the sum of x, y, and z

For Problems 38–40, change the phrase to an equation.

38. y equals 4 more than x

39. r plus 2 totals 4 more than t

40. A number divided by 3 is 18 (use n as the variable)

41. Britney and Megan decide to open an accounting business. They will need a total of $65,000 to get the business started. Britney has spent a lot of time getting the business set up, so Megan agrees to contribute $8,000 more than Britney. How much money should each contribute?

42. Nathan White is thinking about leasing a new building with 6,100 square feet (sq ft). If Nathan needs 1,300 sq ft for offices and twice as much warehouse space as showroom space, what size (in sq ft) should the warehouse and showroom be?

43. Samantha and Brandon Bassett are thinking about buying a vacant lot so they can build their dream home. They want to limit their total investment to $280,000. They are told that in this area the cost of the home (without land) should be about two and one-half times the cost of the land. What is the maximum price Samantha and Brandon can pay for the land?

44. Clayton Holt dies intestate (without a will), leaving an estate of $350,000. Clayton's heirs consist of his wife and two adult children. His state requires that, in the absence of a will, each child is to receive two-thirds as much as a spouse. How much will each receive?

45. Ginny O'Neil is about to open a car dealership. Her property can accommodate a total inventory of 238 vehicles. The auto manufacturer told Ginny that she should have six times as many cars as trucks. How many of each should she order?

46. You paid $58 for a coat. If the coat was on a rack marked $\frac{1}{3}$ off, what was the original price?

Challenge problems

47. Craig Dean owns a ready-mix concrete company. Craig receives an order for 1.5 cubic yards of concrete. This mixture of concrete contains sand, cement, gravel, and water; for each pound (lb) of water, there are 5 lb of sand, 2 lb of cement, and 7 lb of gravel. Find **(a)** the total *weight* of the order (in pounds), assuming a cubic yard of concrete weighs 4,000 lb, and **(b)** how many pounds of each ingredient must be used.

48. Eddie and June just bought a home and the lender requires that they have $198,000 of property insurance. The policy will insure the home for a certain amount, and automatically covers additional structures for $\frac{1}{10}$ of the home coverage. Use the Guess and Check approach to find the minimum amount of coverage required on the home so that the total coverage (home plus additional structures) is $198,000. Start with a guess of $190,000 coverage on the home.

49. Evaluate the guess used in Problem 48. Then explain a Guess and Check strategy that will provide the answer.

50. Maria Martinez sells jewelry and rents a booth at the annual city fair. She is required to collect sales tax on all sales and, at the end of the fair, send the sales tax to the government. The sales tax is .07 of the price. Maria decides to sell items for whole dollar amounts that include sales tax; this will make it easier for her and her customers who pay with cash. During the fair, she collects a total of $3,590. How much sales tax must Maria send to the government.

51. A certain mixture of nuts contains cashews, almonds, and macadamia nuts. Each container must include three times as many almonds as cashews and twice as many cashews as macadamia nuts. If there is a total of 18 ounces (oz) in each container, how many ounces of each nut must be included?

52. You want to get a home loan that nets you $180,000 after paying a fee to your lender of .0225 of the loan amount and additional fees of $3,200 (for an appraisal, title fees, etc.). What does the loan amount have to be so your net proceeds will be $180,000?

53. You are thinking about opening an oil change shop. Your fixed costs will be $13,000 per month. You will charge customers $28 for a lube-oil-filter. The cost of materials is in addition to your fixed costs and is estimated at $8 per customer. How many customers must you have each month in order to break even? *Hint:* "Break even" means revenues equal expenses, so we could say "Fixed Costs + Variable Costs = Revenues."

54. Refer to Problem 53. If your shop is open an average of 25 days each month, how many customers do you need each day to break even?

Practice Test

1. $\frac{5}{8}$ means 8 divided by 5. (T or F)
2. What is the value of 4^3?
3. Simplify: $2 + 8 \times 4$
4. Simplify: $2 + 3(7 - 2^2)^2$
5. Simplify: $\frac{(2)(-3)(-2)}{-4}$
6. Simplify: $5 - 2(3a - 4) + 3a$
7. Solve: $m - 12 = 28$
8. Solve: $\frac{4}{5}y = 28$
9. Solve: $3p + 5 = 17$
10. Solve: $2(4p - 2) - (3p - 4) = 2p + 5$

11. Change the phrase "*m* plus 4 totals 3 more than n" to an equation.

12. Brandy and Carlos need a total of $30,000 to start an engineering business. Brandy has spent a lot of time getting the business set up, so Carlos agrees to contribute $5,000 more than Brandy. How much money should each contribute?

13. You are thinking about opening a copy center. Your fixed costs are $4,800 per month. You will charge customers 6 cents ($0.06) per copy. The cost of materials is in addition to your fixed costs and is estimated at 1.5 cents ($0.015) per copy. How many copies must you make each month in order to break even? Round your answer to the nearest whole number.

Classroom Notes

FUN CORNER

Business Math Student Finds Costly Error

A mathematical error on a Christian County, Missouri, ballot resulted in a $215,657.12 error. The ballot, created to raise money for senior citizen projects, asked voters "Shall Christian County levy a tax of .05 cents for each $100 of assessed value?" The county meant to ask for 5 cents ($0.05), not .05 cents (which is 5% of a penny).

The ballot passed, and when the county started collecting 5 cents per $100 of value, an alert business math student at Ozarks Technical Community College brought the error to the county's attention. According to the official ballot, the county was able to collect only $2,178.35 instead of the $217,835.47 they were counting on.

Sports Averages

Sports averages are generally written in decimal form with three decimal places. For example, a football team with a winning percentage of .750 has won 75% of their games. A basketball player with a free throw percentage of .912 has made 91.2% of free throws. A baseball player with a batting average of .297 has gotten a hit in 29.7% of at-bats.

Quotable Quip

Baseball is 90% mental. The other 50% is physical.
—Yogi Berra
Baseball Hall of Famer

How Do We Spend Our Money?

Percents are often used to show portions of a whole. Here are the top expenditures in the U.S. for the year 2014, as a percent of total expenditures.

Housing	33.27%
Transportation	16.96%
Insurance/Retirement	14.05%
Food	12.63%
Health Care	8.02%
Entertainment	5.10%
Clothing	3.34%
Miscellaneous	6.63%
Total	100.00%

Source: U.S. Department of Labor

Worth Repeating

Kip Keatings had never done well in school, but made millions of dollars as a wholesaler of Gadgets.

One day, Kip paid a visit to his old business math teacher. His teacher congratulated Kip on his successful business career. Kip responded that he owed his success to the things he learned in his business math class. When his teacher asked what he meant, Kip responded, "Well, the lesson on percents must have sunk in. I bought Gadgets for $1 and sold them for $5, and a 4% profit ain't bad."

Brainteaser

Christi got 70% on a test. Antone says his score was 40% higher than Christi's. How can that be, knowing that the highest possible score is 100%?

Answer: Antone got a score of 98%; .70 × 1.40 = .98

Percents

4

Percents are commonly used in business and everyday life. Consider the following statements, for example:

I got 91.7% on the exam.

Our administrative expenses were 12.2% of net sales.

This year's property taxes are 15.5% higher than last year's.

The unemployment rate is 5.5%.

While many of us have a basic understanding of percents, we may not understand their many applications. Since percents will be used throughout the text, an understanding of percents is vital. So, take your time absorbing the concepts of this chapter. Are you ready to give it *110%*?

Unit Objectives

Unit 4.1 Percent conversions
- **a** Converting decimals to percents and percents to decimals
- **b** Converting fractions to percents and percents to fractions

Unit 4.2 The percent formulas
- **a** Solving for portion
- **b** Solving for base
- **c** Solving for rate

Unit 4.3 Increase and decrease problems
- **a** Solving percentage increase problems
- **b** Solving percentage decrease problems
- **c** Finding rate of increase or decrease

Unit 4.1 Percent conversions

Fractions and decimal numbers are used to show parts of a whole. Percents are another way of showing parts of a whole.

Percent, denoted by the sign %, means "hundredths." So, 75% means 75 parts out of 100, or 75 hundredths. As you may recall, 75 hundredths can be written in decimal form as .75 or in fraction form as $\frac{75}{100}$. So, 75%, .75, and $\frac{75}{100}$ all have the same value. Often, we must convert from one form to another. Let's start off by reviewing how to change a decimal to a percent and vice versa.

A baseball player with a batting average of .328 means the player got a hit in 32.8% of at-bats.

a Converting decimals to percents and percents to decimals

converting decimals to percents

Step 1 Move the decimal point two places to the right (or multiply by 100). Add trailing zeros (to the right), if needed.

Step 2 Attach the % sign at the right of the number.

Example 1 Convert these decimals to percents: **a.** .73   **b.** .007   **c.** 1.2

a. .73 = .73 = 73%   **b.** .007 = .007 = .7%   **c.** 1.2 = 1.20 = 120%

Notice, in part (b) of Example 1, the answer is .7%, which is less than 1%. In part (c), the answer is 120%, which is more than a whole (100%). Now, we'll convert percents to decimals.

converting percents to decimals

Step 1 Move the decimal point two places to the left (or divide by 100). Attach zeros on the left, if needed. If the value preceding the % sign is a fraction or mixed number (as in $122\frac{1}{2}$%), convert to a decimal first. As you may recall, to change a fraction to a decimal, divide the numerator by the denominator (for example, $\frac{1}{2}$ means 1 ÷ 2, resulting in .5).

Step 2 Discard the % sign.

Example 2 Convert these percents to decimals: **a.** 48.3%   **b.** 6.1%   **c.** $112\frac{1}{2}$%   **d.** $\frac{3}{8}$%

a. 48.3% = 48.3% = .483   **b.** 6.1% = 06.1% = .061
c. $112\frac{1}{2}$% = 112.5% = 1.125   **d.** $\frac{3}{8}$% = 00.375% = .00375

TIP   show me the money

Some people like to think of percents and decimals in terms of dollars. For example, 83¢, written as $0.83, is 83% of a dollar; 9¢, written as $0.09, is 9% of a dollar. Likewise, 45% of a dollar is written as $0.45; 154% of a dollar is written as $1.54.

74   Chapter 4   Percents

b Converting fractions to percents and percents to fractions

To convert a fraction to a percent, we first convert the fraction to a decimal number; then we convert the decimal to a percent.

> **converting fractions to percents**
>
> **Step 1** Convert the fraction to a decimal number by dividing the numerator by the denominator.
> **Step 2** Move the decimal point two places to the right (or multiply by 100).
> **Step 3** Attach the % sign.

Example 3 Convert these fractions to percents: **a.** $\frac{3}{4}$ **b.** $\frac{5}{8}$

a. $\frac{3}{4} = .75 = 75\%$ **b.** $\frac{5}{8} = .625 = 62.5\%$

> **converting percents to fractions**
>
> **Step 1** Discard the % sign.
> **Step 2** Multiply by $\frac{1}{100}$. As with all fractions, reduce if possible.
>
> *Note:* For a mixed number percent (like $37\frac{1}{2}\%$), first change the mixed number to an improper fraction ($\frac{75}{2}\%$). For a decimal percent (like 87.5%), first change to a mixed number percent (like $87\frac{1}{2}\%$); then change the mixed number percent to an improper fraction (like $\frac{175}{2}\%$).

Example 4 Convert these percents to fractions: **a.** 48% **b.** $37\frac{1}{2}\%$ **c.** 87.5%

a. $48\% = 48 \times \frac{1}{100} = \frac{48}{100} = \frac{12}{25}$

b. $37\frac{1}{2}\% = \frac{75}{2}\% = \frac{75}{2} \times \frac{1}{100} = \frac{75}{200} = \frac{3}{8}$

c. $87.5\% = 87\frac{1}{2}\% = \frac{175}{2}\% = \frac{175}{2} \times \frac{1}{100} = \frac{175}{200} = \frac{7}{8}$

Are you doing okay? Let's find out by doing the U-Try-It questions.

U-Try-It (Unit 4.1)

Convert these decimals to percents:
1. .62   *62%*
2. .003   *.3%*
3. 3.4   *340%*

Convert these percents to decimals:
4. 37.2%   *.372*
5. 2.8%   *.028*
6. $132\frac{1}{4}\%$ *132.25 1.3225*
7. $\frac{1}{8}\%$ *$\frac{1}{100}$ $\frac{1}{800}$ .00125*

Convert these fractions to percents:
8. $\frac{1}{4}$ *.25 25*
9. $\frac{7}{8}$ *.875 87.5*

Convert these percents to fractions:
10. 36%   *$\frac{36}{100}$ $\frac{9}{25}$*
11. $62\frac{1}{2}\%$ *$\frac{125}{2} \times \frac{1}{100}$ $\frac{125}{200}$ $\frac{5}{8}$*
12. 18.75%   *$18\frac{3}{4}$ $\frac{75}{4} \cdot \frac{1}{100}$ $\frac{75}{400}$ $\frac{3}{16}$*

Answers: (If you have a different answer, check the solution in Appendix A.)
1. 62% 2. .3% 3. 340% 4. .372 5. .028 6. 1.3225 7. .00125 8. 25% 9. 87.5% 10. $\frac{9}{25}$
11. $\frac{5}{8}$ 12. $\frac{3}{16}$

Unit 4.2 The percent formulas

In every percent problem, there are three elements: base, rate, and portion. To illustrate, let's multiply 200 by 10%:

$$200 \times 10\% = 200 \times .10 = 20$$

In this problem, base, rate, and portion are represented:

$$\underset{base}{200} \times \underset{rate}{10\%} = \underset{portion}{20}$$

Before we proceed, let's make sure we understand the meaning of each of the three elements.

definitions: base, rate, portion

Base This is the value to which the percent is applied.

Rate This is the percent that is applied to the base.

Portion This is the product obtained by multiplying the base by the rate.

A **formula** is a rule or principle expressed as an equation. Formulas provide an easy way to find the value for one element if we know the other values. As you might know, formulas are written with the unknown element on the left side of the equation. The relationship among base, rate, and portion leads to the formula Portion = Base × Rate. We can use equation-solving procedures to modify the formula so we end up with a formula designed to solve for either base or rate. For example, by dividing both sides of the preceding formula by Rate we get $\frac{Portion}{Rate}$ = Base; by dividing both sides by Base we get $\frac{Portion}{Base}$ = Rate. We now have three formulas instead of one.

the percent formulas

Portion = Base × Rate   Base = $\frac{Portion}{Rate}$ Rate = $\frac{Portion}{Base}$

TIP memory aid

As a way to remember each of these three formulas, some people like to place the three elements in a circle, with *portion* at the top. We will use this circle as an aid throughout the text. To help, the element for which we are solving will appear shaded; the unshaded areas represent the known elements. To help remember which formula to use, put your finger on the unknown element (shaded area). If the unshaded areas are side-by-side, we *multiply* the two; if the unshaded areas are one above the other, we *divide* the top number by the bottom number. Notice that doing so results in the percent formulas.

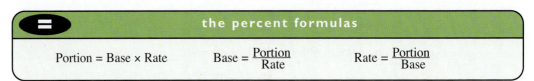

Portion = Base × Rate   Base = $\frac{Portion}{Rate}$ Rate = $\frac{Portion}{Base}$

Identifying the variables (base, rate, and portion) is the key to solving percent problems. The rate is not difficult to identify because it has a percent sign (%). Remember, the base is the value to which the percent is applied, and the portion is the result. Let's see if we can identify the variables in these situations. While we are at it we will solve for the unknown variable by using the appropriate formula.

Situation 1. What number is 22% of $500? *Identifying the variables.* The rate is 22%. $500 is the number we multiply by 22%, so $500 is the base. The portion is the unknown (the value we are looking for).

$$\text{Portion} = \text{Base} \times \text{Rate} = \$500 \times 22\% = \$500 \times .22 = \$110$$

Situation 2. 15% of what number is $120? *Identifying the variables.* The rate is 15%. If we multiply a number by 15%, we get $120. So, $120 is the portion (the result of the multiplication). The base is the unknown (the value we are looking for).

$$\text{Base} = \frac{\text{Portion}}{\text{Rate}} = \frac{\$120}{15\%} = \frac{\$120}{.15} = \$800$$

Check answer: Portion = Base × Rate = $800 × 15% = $800 × .15 = $120

Situation 3. 102 is what percent of 120? *Identifying the variables.* We do not know the rate. If we multiply 120 by a certain percent, we get 102. So, 120 is the base; 102 is the portion (the result of the multiplication).

$$\text{Rate} = \frac{\text{Portion}}{\text{Base}} = \frac{102}{120} = .8500 = 85\%$$

Check answer: Portion = Base × Rate = 120 × 85% = 120 × .85 = 102

Now we will do some word problems. We will use a word problem guide that is specially designed for working with formulas.

a Solving for portion

Example 1 Wendy's International, Inc., oversees Wendy's Old Fashioned Hamburger restaurants. Some of the locations are company-owned, and others are operated by individual owners (under a franchise agreement). If there are a total of 5,600 restaurants and 70% are franchised, how many locations are franchised?

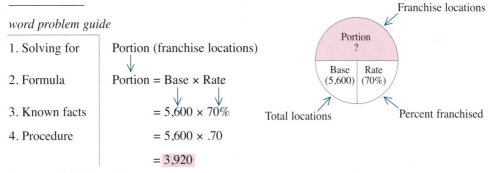

word problem guide

1. Solving for	Portion (franchise locations)
2. Formula	Portion = Base × Rate
3. Known facts	= 5,600 × 70%
4. Procedure	= 5,600 × .70
	= **3,920**

There are 3,920 franchise locations.

Notice the steps of Example 1. In Step 1, we wrote what we were solving for (portion). So, in Step 2, we used the formula for portion. In Step 3, we substituted known values for base and rate. In Step 4, we merely cranked out the answer by doing the arithmetic. That is the procedure we will follow over and over again in using the word problem guide.

With a calculator, we can do the Example 1 arithmetic in one of two ways: multiply by a decimal (.70) or by a percent (70%):

Keystrokes (for most calculators)	
5,600 × .70 =	3,920.00
5,600 × 70 % =	3,920.00

Unit 4.2 The percent formulas

b Solving for base

Example 2 Wendy's has 1,680 company-owned locations. If 30% of all locations are company-owned, how many locations are there altogether?

word problem guide

1. Solving for   Base (total locations)
2. Formula   Base = Portion/Rate
3. Known facts   = 1,680/30%
4. Procedure   = 1,680/.30
    = **5,600**

Wendy's has a total of 5,600 locations.

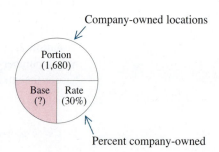

Using calculators, we can do the Example 2 arithmetic in one of two ways: divide by a decimal (.30) or by a percent (30%).

Keystrokes (for most calculators)	
1,680 ÷ .30 =	5,600.00
1,680 ÷ 30 % =	5,600.00

c Solving for rate

Example 3 Wendy's has 5,600 locations, of which 3,920 are franchised. What percent of Wendy's locations are company-owned?

word problem guide

1. Solving for   Rate (percent company-owned)
2. Formula   Rate = Portion/Base
3. Known facts   = 1,680/5,600
4. Procedure   = .30
    = **30%**

30% of Wendy's locations are company-owned.

TIP — don't mix and match

A common error is to use the stated numbers instead of matching the rate with its portion. Don't be tricked: make sure that the rate and portion refer to the same part of the base. In Example 3:

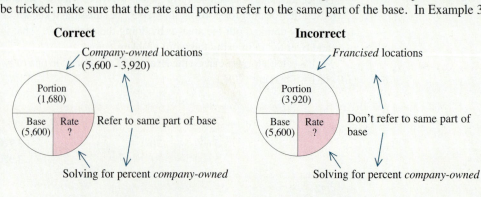

78   Chapter 4   Percents

Here is a summary of Wendy's locations to help us visualize the preceding examples.

Total Locations (5,600)	
Company-Owned 1,680 30%	**Franchised** 3,920 70%

In the next example, we will be asked to round a percent.

> 🔑 **rounding percents**
>
> When asked to round a percent, write the answer as a percent *before* rounding.

Example 4

Suppose on an exam, you got 34 questions correct out of 38. What is your score, rounded to the nearest tenth of a percent?

word problem guide

1. Solving for — Rate (percent correct)
2. Formula — Rate = $\frac{\text{Portion}}{\text{Base}}$
3. Known facts — = $\frac{34}{38}$
4. Procedure
   - ≈ .8947368
   - ≈ 89.47368%
   - ≈ **89.5%** ← Notice, we changed to a percent *before* rounding.

The symbol ≈ is used where the value is not precise.

Portion correct → Portion (34)
Base (38) | Rate (?)
Total questions → Percent correct
Refer to same part of base

Your score is 89.5%, rounded to the nearest tenth of a percent.

Take your time with the U-Try-It questions. Be careful in identifying the base, rate, and portion. Review the definitions, if needed.

U-Try-It (Unit 4.2)

Solve for Portion:
1. 27% of $370
2. 74% of 1,200

Solve for Base:
3. 33 is 20% of _____
4. $1,470 is 70% of _____

Solve for Rate, rounded to the nearest tenth of a percent:
5. 210 is _____ % of 870
6. $45 is _____ % of $600

7. Katherine, Rachel, and Meghan are partners in an accounting business. Katherine gets 40% of the profits, Rachel 35%, and Meghan 25%. If this year's profits were $82,300, how much should each receive?
8. You take an exam with 35 questions and miss 4. What is your score, as a percent? Use one decimal place in your answer.
9. You own a restaurant. Ingredients for a prime rib dinner cost you $7.70. If ingredient costs should be 40% of the retail price of the meal, what should you charge customers?

Answers: (If you have a different answer, check the solution in Appendix A.)
1. $99.90 2. 888 3. 165 4. $2,100 5. 24.1% 6. 7.5% 7. Katherine: $32,920; Rachel: $28,805; Meghan: $20,575
8. 88.6% 9. $19.25

Unit 4.3 Increase and decrease problems

a Solving percentage increase problems

Many situations involve increasing a number. For example, if your current salary is $30,000 a year and you get a 10% increase in pay, you will get a raise of $3,000 ($30,000 × 10%). That will result in a new salary of $33,000. We can summarize the problem this way:

New Salary ($33,000)	
Original salary	Increase
$30,000	$3,000
100%	10%

Notice, the 10% increase is "based" on the original salary, so the original salary is the base. The new salary is a portion, even though it is greater than the base (it is 110% of the original salary).

things to remember about percentage increase problems

1. Base, rate, and portion have the same definitions we used in Unit 4.2:

   Base is the value to which the percent is applied.
   Rate is the percent that is applied to the base.
   Portion is the product obtained by multiplying the base by the rate.

2. The original amount is always the base and is 100%.

3. There are two portions: (a) the amount of increase and (b) the new amount. The new amount will be greater than 100% of the base.

The next two examples involve sales tax being added to a price; this is one type of increase problem. We will continue using the percent formulas.

Example 1 You buy a TV for $350. You must also pay sales tax of 6%. First find the amount of sales tax. Then, determine the total amount you must pay.

word problem guide

1. Solving for	Portion (sales tax)
2. Formula	Portion = Base × Rate
3. Known facts	= $350 × 6%
4. Procedure	= $350 × .06
	= $21

Total amount: $350 (price of TV) + $21 (sales tax) = $371

Sales tax is $21, resulting in a total amount due of $371.

We can do the Example 1 arithmetic with a calculator, as shown below.

Keystrokes (for most calculators)	
350	350
+ 6 %	21.00
=	**371.00**

In Example 1, if we were asked only to find the total amount due (and not the sales tax), we could have found the amount in one step, instead of two, like this:

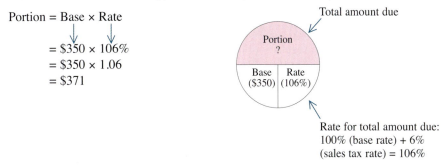

Portion = Base × Rate
= $350 × 106%
= $350 × 1.06
= $371

Rate for total amount due:
100% (base rate) + 6% (sales tax rate) = 106%

Example 2 Six months ago, you bought a TV. You cannot remember the price of the TV, so you look through your checkbook. You find that the check amount was $371, which included 6% sales tax. What was the price of the TV, exclusive of sales tax?

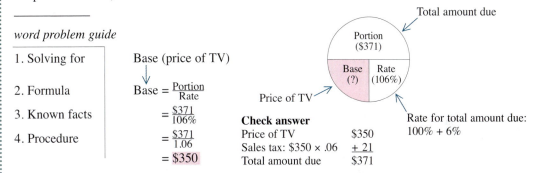

word problem guide

1. Solving for — Base (price of TV)
2. Formula — Base = Portion/Rate
3. Known facts — = $371/106%
4. Procedure — = $371/1.06
= **$350**

Price of TV

Check answer
Price of TV $350
Sales tax: $350 × .06   + 21
Total amount due $371

Rate for total amount due:
100% + 6%

The price of the TV was $350.

TIP — jumping to conclusions

Many people would try to solve Example 2 by subtracting 6% of $371 from $371:

Faulty calculations		**Check answer**	
Beginning amount	$371.00	Price of TV	$348.74
Less: 371 × .06	−22.26	Sales tax: 348.74 × .06	+20.92
Price of TV	$348.74	Total amount due	$369.66 (wrong)

The total amount due is supposed to be $371 (not $369.66). The error resulted from "basing" sales tax on total amount due rather than on price.

TIP — portion or base?

This makes two tips in a row (it must be your lucky day!). For most people, solving for base is more difficult than solving for portion or rate, especially on percentage increase problems. Remember, the base is the value that we multiply by the rate. In Example 2, for instance, the 6% sales tax rate is multiplied by the price of the TV, so the price is the base. We were asked to find the price of the TV (the base).

Here is a summary of the TV examples:

Total ($371)		
	Price	**Tax**
	$350	$21
	100%	6%

Unit 4.3 Increase and decrease problems

b Solving percentage decrease problems

Some situations involve decreasing a number. For example, assume your golf game is bad and you decide to buy a new set of golf clubs (it can't be your swing that is bad, can it?) You find a nice set of clubs, regularly priced at $800, but you get 25% off. Your discount will be $200, resulting in a net price of $600. We can summarize the problem this way:

←	Original Price ($800)	→
Discount $200 25%		**Net amount due** $600 75%

The next two examples involve selling a home and paying a commission to a real estate agent.

Example 3 You retain a real estate agent to help sell your home. The home sells for $200,000, and you have agreed to pay your real estate agent a 7% commission. First find the commission. Then, determine the net amount you will receive after the commission.

word problem guide

1. Solving for — Portion (commission)
2. Formula — Portion = Base × Rate
3. Known facts — = $200,000 × 7%
4. Procedure — = $200,000 × .07
   = $14,000

Net amount: $200,000 (price) - $14,000 (commission) = $186,000

The commission is $14,000. You will get $186,000 after the commission is paid.

We can do the Example 3 arithmetic with a calculator, as shown below.

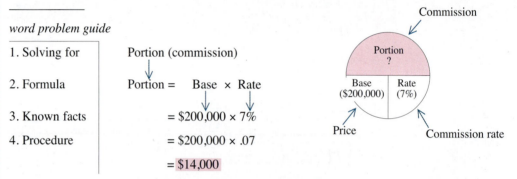

Keystrokes (for most calculators)	
200,000	200,000
- 7 %	14,000.00
=	**186,000.00**

Example 4 You retain a real estate agent to help sell your home. If the agent's commission is 6% of the price and you want to net $235,000 after the commission, what should the price be?

word problem guide

1. Solving for — Base (selling price)
2. Formula — Base = Portion / Rate
3. Known facts — = $235,000 / 94%
4. Procedure — = $235,000 / .94
   = $250,000

Check answer
Price $250,000
Commission: $250,000 × .06   - 15,000
Net amount due $235,000

Rate for net amount: 100% (base rate) - 6% (commission rate) = 94%

The price should be $250,000.

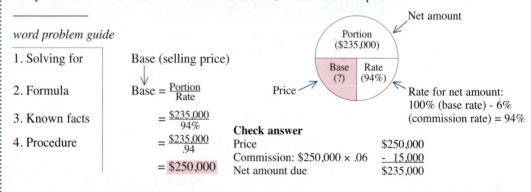

> **TIP** money down the drain
>
> Many people would try to solve Example 4 by adding 6% of $235,000 to $235,000:
>
> | **Faulty calculations** | | **Check answer** | |
> |---|---|---|---|
> | Beginning amount | $235,000 | Price | $249,100 |
> | Plus: $235,000 × .06 | +14,100 | Commission: $249,000 × .06 | - 14,946 |
> | Price | $249,100 | Net amount | $ 234,154 (Wrong) |
>
> The net amount is supposed to be $235,000 (not $234,154). The error resulted from "basing" the commission on the net amount rather than on the selling price. This math error would be a costly one ($846 down the drain).

C Finding rate of increase or decrease

Costs and other numbers continually change. For example, tuition changes from year to year ("changes" most likely means "goes up," doesn't it?). To find a percent increase (or decrease), we divide the amount of increase (or decrease) by the *original* amount. The following formula is like the formula for rate: Rate = $\frac{Portion}{Base}$.

Lots of numbers are expressed as a percent increase or decrease. For example, tuition at your school may have increased 62% over the last 3 years.

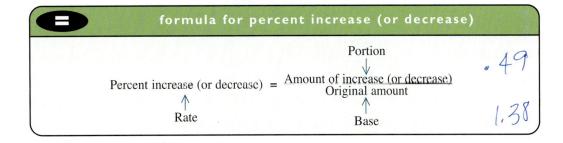

= formula for percent increase (or decrease)

Percent increase (or decrease) = $\frac{\text{Amount of increase (or decrease)}}{\text{Original amount}}$

↑ Rate   ↑ Portion   ↑ Base

.49

1.38

Unit 4.3 Increase and decrease problems   83

Example 5 Tuition at a college has been increased from $2,820 per year to $3,435 per year. What is the percent increase? Show your answer with two decimal places.

word problem guide

1. Solving for — Rate (percent increase)
2. Formula — Percent increase = $\frac{\text{Amount of increase}}{\text{Original amount}}$
3. Known facts — $= \frac{\$615}{\$2,820}$
4. Procedure — $\approx .218085$
   $\approx 21.8085\%$
   $\approx 21.81\%$

Amount of increase ($3,435 - $2,820)

Portion ($615)
Base ($2,820)
Rate (?)

Original amount   Percent increase

Change to a percent *before* rounding.

Tuition has increased 21.81%.

Example 6 In a certain state, highway deaths decreased from 231 last year to 212 this year. Calculate the percent decrease. Show two decimal places in your answer.

word problem guide

1. Solving for — Rate (percent decrease)
2. Formula — Percent decrease = $\frac{\text{Amount of decrease}}{\text{Original amount}}$
3. Known facts — $= \frac{19}{231}$
4. Procedure — $\approx .082251$
   $\approx 8.2251\%$
   $\approx 8.23\%$

Amount of decrease (231 - 212)

Portion (19)
Base (231)
Rate (?)

Original amount   Percent decrease

Highway deaths decreased 8.23%.

Well, we made it through Chapter 4! Let's see how much we remember from Unit 4.3 by doing the U-Try-It exercises.

U-Try-It (Unit 4.3)

1. Your annual salary is $40,000. You have been doing a great job at work and get a 15% raise. What is your new annual salary?
2. Three months ago you bought a computer. You cannot remember the price of the computer so you look through your checkbook. You find the check was written for $1,381.79 which included $6\frac{3}{8}\%$ sales tax. What was the price of the computer, exclusive of sales tax?
3. You buy a tent at a 40% off sale. If the reduced price is $312, what was the original retail price?
4. Your property taxes last year were $2,135. This year they are $2,417. Find the percent increase, to the nearest tenth of a percent.
5. During a year, the population of a small town decreased from 518 to 497. What is the percent decrease, to the nearest hundredth of a percent?

Answers: (If you have a different answer, check the solution in Appendix A.)
1. $46,000   2. $1,298.98   3. $520   4. 13.2%   5. 4.05%

84 Chapter 4 Percents

Chapter in a Nutshell

Objectives	Examples

Unit 4.1 Percent conversions

a Converting decimals to percents and percents to decimals

$.64 = .64 = 64\%$ $.005 = .005 = .5\%$ $41.7\% = 41.7\% = .417$

$6.8\% = 06.8\% = .068$ $34\frac{1}{4}\% = 34.25\% = .3425$ $\frac{5}{16}\% = 00.3125\% = .003125$

b Converting fractions to percents and percents to fractions

$\frac{3}{5} = .60 = 60\%$ $\frac{3}{8} = .375 = 37.5\%$ $56\% = 56 \times \frac{1}{100} = \frac{56}{100} = \frac{14}{25}$

$12\frac{1}{2}\% = \frac{25}{2}\% = \frac{25}{2} \times \frac{1}{100} = \frac{25}{200} = \frac{1}{8}$ $31.25\% = 31\frac{1}{4}\% = \frac{125}{4}\% = \frac{125}{4} \times \frac{1}{100} = \frac{125}{400} = \frac{5}{16}$

Unit 4.2 The percent formulas

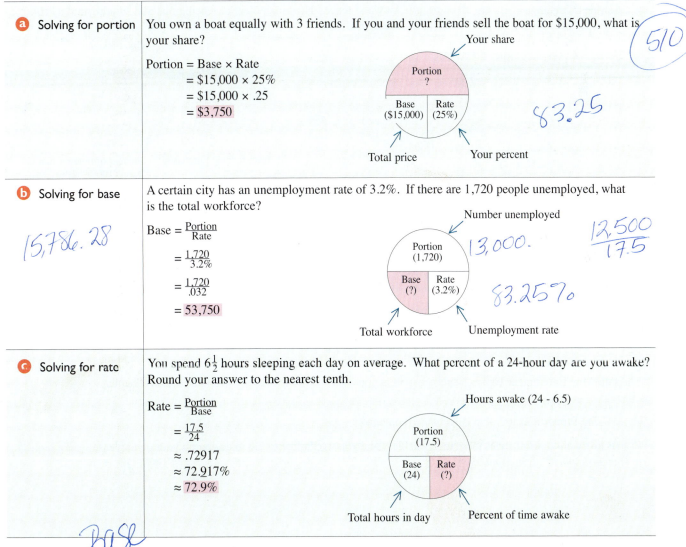

a Solving for portion

You own a boat equally with 3 friends. If you and your friends sell the boat for $15,000, what is your share?

Portion = Base × Rate
= $15,000 × 25%
= $15,000 × .25
= $3,750

(handwritten: 510, 83.25)

b Solving for base

(handwritten: 15,786.28)

A certain city has an unemployment rate of 3.2%. If there are 1,720 people unemployed, what is the total workforce?

Base = $\frac{\text{Portion}}{\text{Rate}}$
= $\frac{1,720}{3.2\%}$
= $\frac{1,720}{.032}$
= 53,750

(handwritten: 13,000, 12,500/17.5, 83.25%)

c Solving for rate

You spend $6\frac{1}{2}$ hours sleeping each day on average. What percent of a 24-hour day are you awake? Round your answer to the nearest tenth.

Rate = $\frac{\text{Portion}}{\text{Base}}$
= $\frac{17.5}{24}$
≈ .72917
≈ 72.917%
≈ 72.9%

*(handwritten at bottom:
Base
Total
original amt
whole amt
% of Base)*

Chapter in a Nutshell (concluded)

Objectives	Examples

Unit 4.3 Increase and decrease problems

a Solving percentage increase problems

You buy a new, red Jeep Wrangler. The price is $24,500 plus sales tax of $6\frac{1}{8}\%$. What is the total amount, including sales tax?

Portion = Base × Rate
= $24,500 × 106.125%
= $24,500 × 1.06125
= $26,000.63

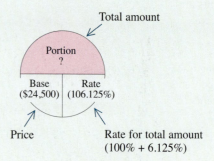

Total amount → Portion ?
Base ($24,500) — Price
Rate (106.125%) — Rate for total amount (100% + 6.125%)

b Solving percentage decrease problems

You are about to install a wood fence. How many feet of fencing material should you buy if you need 315 feet of fencing and 10% of the material purchased will be wasted?

Base = $\frac{\text{Portion}}{\text{Rate}}$

= $\frac{315}{90\%}$

= $\frac{315}{.90}$

= 350

Check answer
Total purchased 350
Bad: 350 × 10%   - 35
Good   315

Good fencing → Portion (315)
Base (?) — Total fencing purchased
Rate (90%) — Percent of fencing that is good (100% − 10%)

c Finding rate of increase or decrease

Your landlord raises your rent from $850 to $925. What is the percent increase to the nearest tenth of a percent?

Percent increase = $\frac{\text{Amount of increase}}{\text{Original amount}}$ = $\frac{\$925 - \$850}{\$850}$ = $\frac{\$75}{\$850}$ ≈ .08824 ≈ 8.824% ≈ 8.8%

You bought a new car 4 years ago for $22,000. It is now worth $9,700. What is the percent decrease, to the nearest tenth of a percent?

Percent decrease = $\frac{\text{Amount of decrease}}{\text{Original amount}}$ = $\frac{\$22,000 - \$9,700}{\$22,000}$ = $\frac{\$12,300}{\$22,000}$ ≈ .55909 ≈ 55.909% ≈ 55.9%

Enrichment Topics

The following Enrichment Topics, which go a bit beyond what is in the text, are available for this chapter:

Ratios and Proportions
Using Proportions to Solve Percentage Problems

If your instructor doesn't cover these topics in class and you would like to dig in deeper on your own, please send a request to *studentsupport@olympuspub.com*.

Think

1. Molly, Matt, and Margo all play softball. Molly's coach tells her she has 45 hits out of 120 at-bats. Matt's coach tells him he has a batting average of .348. Margo's coach tells her she gets hits 35% of the time. Explain what is required to determine which person has the best batting average. Then decide who has the best batting average.
2. For which type of percentage problem is the portion greater than the base? Explain how this happens.
3. Give a real-world example of a percentage increase problem. Then solve the problem.
4. Give a real-world example of a percentage decrease problem. Then solve the problem.
5. Open a bag of M&Ms® or Skittles®. Separate the colors and count the number of each. Then, figure the percent for each color.

Explore

1. Create a Microsoft® Excel spreadsheet to solve percent problems. In cell A1, type Portion; in cell B1, type Base; in cell C1, type Rate. Leave row 2 for typing variables. In Row 3, type formulas for Portion, Base, and Rate in columns A, B, and C (for example in cell A3, type =B2*C2). Test your spreadsheet by solving Chapter Review Problems for Unit 4.2. Type the 2 known values in appropriate cells of row 2; type "?" in the other cell. The answer will appear in the appropriate cell of row 3. *Note:* "#VALUE!" will appear in the other 2 cells of row 3.
2. Create a Microsoft® Excel spreadsheet to determine the percentage increase (or decrease) for Chapter Review Problems 32-39. Type 5 column headings in row 1: Problem Number, Original Amount, New Amount, Amount of Increase (or Decrease), and % Increase (or Decrease). Put problem numbers in column A (32 in A2, 33 in A3, etc.). Type formulas in cells D2 and E2, then copy to remaining cells of columns D and E. Enter given values in columns B and C. The correct answers should appear in columns D and E.
3. Assume that you are considering buying a 12-unit apartment building for $900,000. Five of the units rent for $650 per month each, 4 rent for $680 per month each, and 3 rent for $700 per month each. Using a Microsoft® Excel spreadsheet, determine (a) total monthly rent (Gross Monthly Rent), (b) annual rent (Potential Rental Income), (c) dollar amount of vacancy, based on a 5% vacancy rate, (d) Effective Rental Income (Potential Rental Income - Vacancy), (e) estimated annual expenses, based on expenses being 35% of Potential Rental Income, and (f) Net Operating Income (Effective Rental Income - Expenses). Then find (h) the price per unit, (i) Monthly Gross Rent Multiplier (price ÷ by gross monthly rent), and (j) capitalization rate (Net Operating Income ÷ by price). Round dollar amounts to the nearest dollar; express Gross Rent Multiplier with two decimal places; express the capitalization rate as a percent, with two decimal places in the percent.

Apply

1. **Truth in Advertising?** Find five advertisements or articles from newspapers or magazines that deal with percents. Determine whether the ads or articles are stating facts correctly. Apply the concepts of this chapter and show all work and conclusions. Submit all articles.
2. **Sports & Percents.** Choose a sport. Then, determine at least five ways that decimal numbers or percents are used to reflect how well a team or player is doing. Include a printed newspaper or magazine copy of the statistics you are using. Show how you arrived at the numbers and what the results mean.

Chapter Review Problems

Unit 4.1 Percent conversions

Convert these decimals to percents.

1. .079   7.9%
2. 1.35   135%

Convert these percents to decimals.

3. 52.1%   .521
4. 8.3%   .083
5. $137\frac{1}{2}$%   137.5   1.375
6. $\frac{5}{8}$%   .625   .00625

Convert these fractions to percents.

7. $\frac{7}{8}$ 87 1/2%   87.5%
8. $1\frac{1}{4}$ 125%

Convert these percents to fractions.

9. 36%   36/100   9/25
10. 62.5%   62.5/100   62 1/2%   125/2 · 1/100   125/200   5/8

For all remaining problems, if the answer is a percent, round to the nearest tenth of a percent.

Unit 4.2 The percent formulas

Solve for portion: Portion = Base × Rate

11. 8% of $500
12. 35% of 250

Solve for base: Base = $\frac{\text{Portion}}{\text{Rate}}$

13. 60 is 40% of what number?
14. 240 is 75% of what number?

Solve for rate: Rate = $\frac{\text{Portion}}{\text{Base}}$

15. 25 is what percent of 50?
16. 117 is what percent of 90?

17. You, as a real estate agent, sell a property for $230,000. If you earn a 5% commission, what is your commission?

18. You take an exam with 18 questions and miss 2. What is your score as a percent?

19. Matt and Robbie are partners in a restaurant. Matt is to receive 60% of the profits and Robbie is to receive the remainder. If this year's profits were $42,700, how much should each receive?

20. A "B" grade on a certain test is 85%. How many questions can you miss on a 35-question exam to get a B?

21. You own a small restaurant. You are trying to determine what price you should charge for your meals. If ingredient costs should be 25% of the retail price of the meal and the ingredients for a grilled cheese sandwich cost 70¢, what should you charge customers for a grilled cheese sandwich?

22. You borrow $700 for 1 year at 9% interest. How much interest will you owe?

23. Joe, an antiques dealer, is thinking about buying a 60-year-old rocking chair. He customarily sells antiques for 350% of cost. What price should Joe pay for the rocking chair if he thinks it will sell for $300.

24. You want to buy a home. You can borrow 95% of the purchase price. Assuming you can make a down payment of $24,000, what price home can you afford?

25. The population of the largest county in a state is 3,450,000, while the population for the entire state is 6,010,000. What percent of the state's population resides in the largest county?

Unit 4.3 Increase and decrease problems

26. You are about to buy a refrigerator priced at $970. You must pay 6.75% sales tax. First, find the dollar amount of sales tax. Then, find the total amount you must pay including sales tax.

27. A local utility company declares that utility rates for this year will be 3% less than last year's rates. If your utility costs were $872 last year, what can you expect to pay this year?

28. Your boss promises you a 10% pay raise in 2 months. If you currently earn $13.70 an hour, what will your hourly rate be in 2 months?

29. A customer orders 75,000 car batteries. If experience has shown that 8% of batteries produced will be defective, how many batteries must be produced to ensure production of 75,000 good ones?

30. You receive your weekly paycheck in the amount of $344.50. If approximately 35% of wages goes to federal and state taxes, what is your weekly gross pay?

31. What amount of wallpaper should you purchase if you need to cover 384 square feet of wall area and 15% of the material purchased will be wasted? Round to the nearest square foot.

32. The population of a town increased from 13,577 last year to 14,817 this year. What is the percent increase?

33. A year ago, your uncle purchased a set of golf clubs for $429. You want to buy the same set but the retailer's price has increased to $479. What is the percent increase?

34. During a year, the population for a small town decreased from 433 to 402. What is the percent decrease?

35. Your landlord raises your rent from $675 to $750. What is the percent increase?

36. During a 1-year period, the Dow Jones Industrial Average increased from 10,242.53 to 11,844.22. What is the percent increase?

37. If your gross pay is $2,200 per month and your take-home pay is $1,477, what percent of your gross pay is withheld?

38. In the following news article is the information stated correctly? Explain your answer.

> Dollar volume for all United Bank offices has increased 26.7% percent from $31.9 million in loans for the first quarter of last year to $43.5 million in the same period this year.

39. In the following ad, what is the percent discount?

Challenge problems

40. You are a real estate agent with ABC Real Estate Company. You help sell a home for $235,000. The total commission is 7%. Your company is to receive 60% of the total commission; you will receive 70% of that amount. What is your personal share of the commission?

For Problems 41–43, answer questions about a Keogh retirement plan.

41. You, as the owner of a small business, have a Keogh retirement plan. Suppose your plan allows annual contributions up to 13% of net income (profit). If your net income was $42,378, what is your maximum allowable contribution?

42. If, for a particular year, you made a contribution of $2,000 and had net income of $28,000, what percent contribution was made?

43. You cannot remember what your net income was 5 years ago, but you know you made a maximum allowable contribution to your Keogh plan. If your contribution was $8,718.45, what must your net income have been?

44. You and your dining partner are thinking about ordering the "romantic dinner for two" costing $55. If the sales tax rate is 7% and you want to leave a 15% tip (based on the total cost of the meal, including sales tax), should you order the $55 meal if you have only $65?

For Problems 45 and 46, answer questions about a fund-raising campaign.

45. Wanting to help those in need, students of Edison Community College in Ohio have made donations to an organization for many years. Last year they donated $1,250. This year their goal is to raise 20% more than they did last year. How much must they raise to reach their goal?

46. If at the end of the fund-raising drive students have raised $2,450, what percent of the goal have they reached?

47. The annual net income on a neighborhood shopping center is $422,500. Richard Martinez is interested in buying the property and wants to earn 9.5% on his investment. What price, rounded to the nearest thousand dollars, should he pay for the property?

48. You work for a manufacturing company that decides to introduce a new product. If your company offers retailers a 30% discount off list price, what should the list price be to ensure that your company nets $1,200?

49. In the chair ad, confirm that the reduced price is really 64% off.

50. Refer to the newspaper article. Confirm the 17.88% decrease in net income.

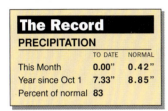

First Security 2nd-Quarter Income Declined 17.88%

In what will likely be its last quarterly report before being acquired by Wells Fargo, First Security reported second-quarter net income of $56.5 million, down from $68.8 million for the same period last year.

51. In the news report, precipitation through October 1 is 7.33 inches, while the normal is 8.85 inches. Confirm that this year's precipitation is actually 83% of normal.

The Record
PRECIPITATION

	TO DATE	NORMAL
This Month	0.00"	0.42"
Year since Oct 1	7.33"	8.85"
Percent of normal	83	

52. Write an essay answer to the "Ask Marilyn" question.

BY MARILYN VOS SAVANT

Ask Marilyn

On Dec. 1, Mr. Ely decides to buy a hot stock from a commission-free brokerage house. His purchase price of Volatile Inc. is $1000, and he is pleased to see the stock soar 20% the same day he buys it. The next day, however, Volatile plunges 20%. On Dec. 3, the stock is back up 20%; but on Dec. 4, it's back down 20%.

Volatile continues its yo-yo trip throughout the month, rising 20% on the odd days and falling 20% on the even days. On Dec. 31, after the 20% gain, Ely sells his stock. He is shocked to receive less than his original investment. How much did he receive, and how could this be?

—Jim Low, American Fork, Utah

Practice Test

1. Convert .065 to a percent.
2. Convert $87\frac{1}{2}\%$ to a decimal number.
3. Convert $\frac{5}{16}$ to a percent.
4. Convert 12.5% to a fraction.
5. If you buy a home for $210,000 and need 20% for a down payment, what is the dollar amount of the down payment?

6. Ed, a used car dealer, is thinking about buying a 3-year-old vehicle. He customarily sells the cars for 120% of his cost. What price should Ed pay for the car if he thinks he can resell it for $10,800?

7. You take an exam with 24 questions and miss 3. What is your score, to the nearest tenth of a percent?

8. You buy a TV for $750. You must also pay sales tax of 7%. What is the total amount you must pay?

9. A customer orders 21,000 tires. If experience has shown that 4% of tires produced will be defective, how many tires must be produced to ensure production of 21,000 good ones?

10. The population of a town decreased from 8,422 to 8,318. What is the percent decrease, to the nearest tenth of a percent?

Classroom Notes

3.855
385.570

.7380 95238
73.81

162 1/2 %   162.5   1.625

324
325 325
— ———
2   100 200

1625

7.6

12.5870

.51634798
51.63

.483146067
.88%

.064798
4.47
4.5

.625

25.75

56.25%

48.31

.0.4.4875

FUN CORNER

Worth Repeating

A retailer had ordered a large quantity of merchandise from his supplier. He received a telegram, "Cannot ship until you pay your last bill." The retailer sent a return message, "Unable to wait that long; cancel the order."

Appliances Will Be Smarter Than Their Owners

by Dave Barry

Recently the Washington Post printed an article explaining how the appliance manufacturers plan to drive consumers insane.

Of course they don't SAY they want to drive us insane. What they SAY they want to do is have us live in homes where "all appliances are on the Internet, sharing information" and appliances will be "smarter than most of their owners." For example, the article states, you would have a home where the dishwasher "can be turned on from the office" and the refrigerator "knows when it's out of milk."

Did they ever stop to ask themselves WHY a consumer, after loading a dishwasher, would go to the office to start it? Would there be some kind of career benefit?

YOUR BOSS: What are you doing?

YOU (tapping your computer keyboard): I'm starting my dishwasher!

YOUR BOSS: That's the kind of productivity we need around here!

YOU: Now I'm flushing my toilet.

Likewise, we don't need a refrigerator that knows when it's out of milk. We already have a foolproof system for determining if we're out of milk: We ask our wife.

Is this the kind of future you want, consumers? Do you want appliances that are smarter than you? Of course not. Your appliances should be DUMBER than you, just like your furniture, your pets and your representatives in Congress. So I am urging you to let the appliance industry know, by phone, letter, fax and e-mail, that when it comes to "smart" appliances, you vote NO. You need to act quickly. Because while you're reading this, your microwave oven is voting YES.

Extended Warranties

When you buy an appliance, such as a refrigerator, you generally get a warranty that covers the appliance for a certain period of time, like 5 years. Often, the store offers an extended warranty that covers the appliance for an additional period of time. Be cautious of extended warranties. Because of administrative costs, consumers often get back far less from the extended warranty than they pay for it.

Quotable Quip

Money is like manure. You have to spread it around or it smells.
– J. Paul Getty

Brainteaser

Some months have 30 days, some have 31 days. How many have 28 days?

Answer: All of them

"We need to spend as little as possible, honey, so let's get the fridge that's 40 percent off!"

Trade and Cash Discounts

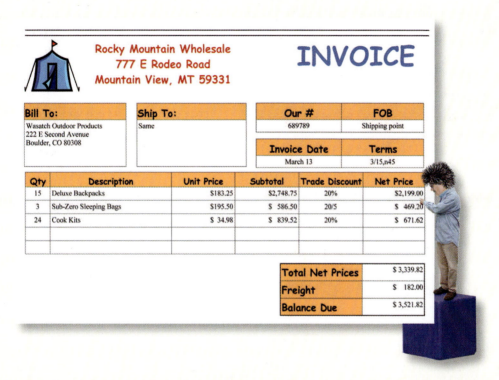

Providing goods to consumers is a multistep process. **Manufacturers** buy raw materials and assemble them into products that can be sold to other manufacturers or to **wholesalers.** Wholesalers, after buying from manufacturers or other wholesalers, sell to **retailers,** who then sell to **consumers.** Several sales take place in this process, each involving a seller and a buyer. Sellers often extend a price discount, called a **trade discount,** to buyers, and may extend a second type of discount, called a **cash discount.** Trade discounts and cash discounts differ in the following way: trade discounts are given as an incentive to *buy products*, while cash discounts are given as an incentive to *pay the seller promptly*. In this chapter, we will study both types of discounts.

Unit Objectives

Unit 5.1 Trade discounts
  a Finding net price for a single trade discount
  b Finding net price for a series trade discount
  c Finding an equivalent single discount rate

Unit 5.2 Cash discounts
  a Calculating cash discount and net amount due
  b Counting days
  c Understanding discount terminology
  d Determining amount credited for a partial payment
  e Measuring the benefit of cash discounts

Unit 5.1 Trade discounts

Wholesalers and retailers generally receive a discount (called a trade discount) on the merchandise they buy. They can pass this savings on to the company or person they sell to.

Sellers frequently state a price as a **list price**; this may be an arbitrary figure, or it may be the manufacturer's suggested retail price. Buyers are often given a discount (called a trade discount) off the list price. The result, after deducting the trade discount from list price, is known as **net price**.

Trade discounts often vary from customer to customer depending on the volume of goods purchased, the importance of the customer in distributing goods in a certain geographical area, and competition. Trade discounts may differ from product to product and may vary from time to time depending on seasonal goods, special promotions, and available inventory. By using trade discounts, sellers can publish a single catalog or price sheet, and still end up with different net prices.

a Finding net price for a single trade discount

Often, trade discounts are stated as a single rate (such as 40%). In this case, the **trade discount amount** is found by multiplying the list price by the **trade discount rate.**

---

trade discount amount formula

Trade discount amount = List price × Trade discount rate

In a few of the upcoming examples, we will use a word problem guide and a circle aid from Unit 4.2.

Example 1 Suppose you are an electronics dealer. A-1 Company, a wholesale supplier, will sell you a Hewlett Packard printer for a list price of $550 with a 40% trade discount. What is the trade discount amount?

word problem guide

1. Solving for   Trade discount amount

2. Formula   Trade discount amount = List price × Trade discount rate

3. Known facts   = $550   ×   40%

4. Procedure   = $550   ×   .40

    = $220

You will get a $220 trade discount.

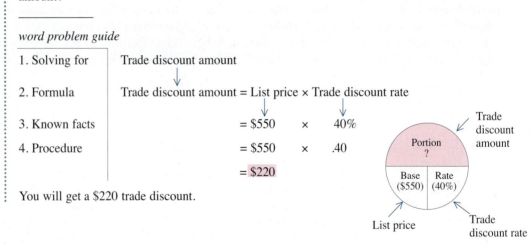

We find the net price by subtracting the trade discount amount from the list price.

Chapter 5 Trade and Cash Discounts

net price formula

Net price = List price - Trade discount amount

Example 2 Refer to Example 1. Find your net price.

word problem guide

1. Solving for	Net price
2. Formula	Net price = List price - Trade discount amount
3. Known facts	= $550 - $220
4. Procedure	= $330

The arithmetic of Examples 1 and 2 can be combined using a calculator, as follows:

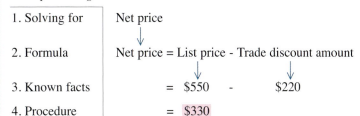

Keystrokes (for most calculators)	
550	550
- 40 %	220.00
=	**330.00**

In Examples 1 and 2, the 40% trade discount rate represents the percent of list price you do not pay; you save 40 cents on the dollar. Stated another way, you *do* pay 60% of list price (60 cents on the dollar). The two rates (40% and 60%) are **complements** of each other because they add up to 100%. Another way to find the net price is to multiply the list price by the complement of the trade discount rate.

finding net price using complement of trade discount rate

Step 1 Determine the complement of the trade discount rate by subtracting the trade discount rate from 100%.

Step 2 Multiply the list price by the complement (found in Step 1).

Example 3 The list price of a Hewlett Packard printer is $550. You get a 40% trade discount. Find your net price using the complement of the trade discount rate.

Step 1 Determine complement: 100% - 40% = 60%
Step 2 Net price = List price × Complement
= $550 × 60%
= $550 × .60
= $330

Notice that the answer in Example 3 ($330) is the same answer that we got in the two-step approach of Examples 1 and 2. The results of the preceding examples can be summarized as follows:

List price	100%	$550
Trade discount	- 40%	-220
Net price	60%	$330

Unit 5.1 Trade discounts

b Finding net price for a series trade discount

A **series discount** (sometimes referred to as a **chain discount**) is two or more discounts *taken one after the other.* A series discount of 30/15/5 is read "thirty, fifteen, five" and is illustrated in the next example.

Example 4 Before buying the Hewlett Packard printer from A-1 Company, you check with another supplier, B-2 Company. Their list price is also $550, but they will give you a series discount of 30/15/5. What is your net price from B-2 Company?

List price	$550.00
Less first discount: $550 × 30%	-165.00
Price after first discount	$385.00
Less second discount: $385 × 15%	- 57.75
Price after second discount	$327.25
Less third discount: $327.25 × 5%	- 16.36
Net price	$310.89

Your net price from B-2 Company is $310.89. You will save $19.11 by buying from B-2 instead of from A-1 (net price of $330).

The arithmetic of Example 4 can be done with a calculator, as shown below.

Keystrokes (for most calculators)

550	550
- 30 %	165.00
=	385.00
- 15 %	57.75
=	327.25
- 5 %	16.36
=	**310.89**

TIP mix and match

We can write a series discount in any order and still get the same net price. In Example 4, we would get the same net price if the 30/15/5 discount were written as 30/5/15 (or in any other order). Test it yourself. While the order of the series does not matter, series discounts are generally written with the larger discounts first.

TIP doesn't add up!

Don't make the common mistake of adding the individual discounts. For example, a 30/15/5 series discount is not the same as a 50% single discount, even though 30 + 15 + 5 = 50. By making this mistake, Example 4 would have been solved incorrectly as follows:

List price	$550
Less trade discount: $550 × 50% =	-275
Net price	$275

} wrong approach

The $275 net price is wrong (it should be $310.89). Here's why: When done correctly, each successive discount is applied to a *reduced* amount, not to the original list price.

Chapter 5 Trade and Cash Discounts

C Finding an equivalent single discount rate

As part of the previous "Tip," it was stated that a 30/15/5 series discount is not equivalent to a 50% single discount. You may wonder, What is a 30/15/5 series discount equivalent to, in terms of a single trade discount? Even if you don't want to know, you will soon find out! Notice the steps to find an **equivalent single discount rate.**

finding equivalent single discount rate

Step 1 Determine the complement for each rate in the series discount.

Step 2 Multiply the complements. This is the percent of list price that *is* paid.

Step 3 Determine the complement of the result of Step 2. This is the equivalent single discount rate (the percent of the list price that is *not* paid).

Example 5

For the last 22 years, B-2 Company has been giving you a 30/15/5 series discount on all products. Find the equivalent single discount rate.

Step 1 (complements)	Step 2 (multiply complements)	Step 3 (complement of Step 2)
30% 15% 5%	70% × 85% × 95%	100.000%
↓ ↓ ↓	= .70 × .85 × .95	- 56.525%
70% 85% 95%	= .56525	43.475%
	= 56.525%	

A 30/15/5 series discount is identical to a 43.475% single trade discount.

In Example 5, we found that a 30/15/5 series discount is identical to a 43.475% single trade discount. For any products purchased from B-2 Company in the future, you could calculate net price by using a single trade discount rate of 43.475%. In Example 4, we found the net price on the $550 printer is $310.89, after applying the 30/15/5 series discount. Let's see if we get the same net price by using a single discount of 43.475%:

List price	$550.00
Less trade discount: $550 × 43.475%	-239.11
Net price	$310.89 *(Same answer as using a 30/15/5 series discount)*

TIP — rounding equivalent single discount rate

Don't be tempted to round the equivalent single discount rate. In Example 5, if we had rounded the rate to 43%, we would have incorrectly calculated the net price to be $313.50 (should be $310.89).

That does it for this unit. You're saying, Thank goodness, aren't you? Let's try some U-Try-It problems to see how we're doing.

U-Try-It (Unit 5.1)

1. A computer has a list price of $1,300 with a 30% trade discount. First, find the trade discount amount. Then, find the net price.
2. A bedroom dresser has a list price of $800 with a 20% trade discount. Find the net price using complements.
3. A refrigerator has a list price of $995 with a 25/15 series discount. Find the net price.
4. Find the single equivalent discount rate for a 25/10 series discount.

Answers: (If you have a different answer, check the solution in Appendix A.)
1. $390; $910   2. $640   3. $634.31   4. 32.5%

Unit 5.2 Cash discounts

Shipping costs are sometimes paid by the seller (FOB destination), and sometimes paid by the buyer (FOB shipping point).

A buyer may be required to pay for goods when they are received, known as **COD** (cash on delivery). Generally, however, buyers are given a certain period of time to pay. Sales are recorded on an **invoice,** which lists the merchandise, prices, and terms of payment (an invoice is shown on the chapter-opening page). Policy differs with respect to how prices are stated: some invoices show list price and trade discount, while others show only net price.

Trade discounts are earned when the goods are purchased and do not depend on how promptly the invoice is paid. Cash discounts, on the other hand, are offered to encourage prompt payment. Invoices, if prepared correctly, define (a) the **credit period,** which is the total amount of time the buyer has to pay the invoice before it is declared overdue and subject to late charges; (b) the **discount period,** which is the first part of the credit period, during which the buyer is entitled to a cash discount; and (c) the **cash discount rate,** which is the percent of the discount (such as 4%) the buyer gets if the invoice is paid within the discount period.

When goods are shipped from a seller to a buyer, freight costs are either an expense of the seller, referred to as **FOB destination** (FOB stands for "free on board"), or an expense of the buyer, referred to as **FOB shipping point.** Where freight is the expense of the buyer, the seller may, as a service to the buyer, prepay the freight company and add the freight charges to the amount of the invoice. If goods are defective, the buyer may return the defective part of the shipment.

a Calculating cash discount and net amount due

Buyers are entitled to a cash discount *only on the net price of the goods*. Returned goods, trade discounts, and freight charges that have been added to the invoice amount must be subtracted before the cash discount is calculated. We calculate the cash discount by multiplying the net price by the cash discount rate.

> **cash discount formula**
>
> Cash discount = Net price × Cash discount rate
>
> *Note:* Deduct returned goods, trade discounts, and freight charges before figuring cash discount.

After the cash discount is deducted, freight paid by the seller on behalf of the buyer is added back to find the **net amount due.**

Example 1 You purchase goods with a list price of $500. You return goods that are defective, having a list price of $30. You are entitled to a trade discount of 25%. The seller paid $20 in freight on your behalf and added the amount to the invoice. You are offered a 4% cash discount if you pay the invoice within 15 days. What is the net amount you should pay the supplier if you pay within the discount period?

List price	$500.00
Less returned goods	- 30.00
Price of goods after returns	$470.00
Less trade discount: $470 × 25%	- 117.50
Net price	$352.50
Less cash discount: $352.50 × 4%	- 14.10
Net price, less cash discount	$338.40
Add freight	+ 20.00
Net amount due	$358.40

102   Chapter 5   Trade and Cash Discounts

b Counting days

In order to determine the **last day of the discount period** and the **last day of the credit period,** we must know how to count days from one date to another. One method is to look at a regular calendar and start counting: the day *after* the invoice date is day 1, and so on. This method can be time-consuming, and it is easy to make a mistake along the way. We will rely on two other methods, described below.

Method 1 (If the later date is in the same calendar month)
We simply add the number of days to the invoice date. For example, 10 days past October 12 is October 22 (12 + 10 = 22).

Method 2 (If the later date is in another month)
We will use a **day-of-the-year calendar,** shown in Appendix D. Each day is numbered (for example, November 19 is the 323rd day of the year). Pay special attention to the exciting footnote regarding leap years. The next example shows how to use a day-of-the-year calendar.

Example 2 Find **(a)** 10 days past November 19, **(b)** 20 days past November 19, and **(c)** 75 days past November 19.

a. Nov. 19 + 10 = Nov. 29

b. The date occurs in a later month, so we will use a day-of-the-year calendar.

   Nov. 19 → Day 323
   + 20
   Dec. 9 ← 343   *The 343rd day of the year is Dec. 9*

c. The date occurs in the next year; we will use a day-of-the-year calendar.

   Nov. 19 → Day 323
   + 75
   398   *This is greater than 365, so we must subtract 365*
   -365
   Feb. 2 ← 33

An optional method for counting days is known as the *days-in-a-month method*. With this method, we remember how many days there are in each month; the method is shown in Appendix D, page D-2. While a day-of-the-year calendar is often easier to use, understanding the days-in-a-month method is important because we may not always have a day-of-the-year calendar with us. Here is how we could do Example 2, part (c), using the days-in-a-month method:

Days left in November: 30 - 19 =	11	*November has 30 days; not charged for first 19 days*
Days in December:	+31	
Subtotal	42	
Days in January	+31	
Subtotal	73	
Days in February	+ 2	*We need 2 more days to total 75*
Total	75	

Date is **February 2**

c Understanding discount terminology

The credit period, discount period, and cash discount rate appear on an invoice as a sort of "code." The most common credit terms are *ordinary dating, sliding scale, receipt of goods (ROG), end of month (EOM),* and *extra dating.* We will review these one at a time.

Ordinary dating method. This does not refer to spending a night on the town with an average, everyday person. It merely refers to a boring invoice. This is the most common cash discount terminology, in which an invoice states terms such as "2/10, n/30," read "two, ten, net thirty." This means that the buyer will receive a 2% discount for payment within 10 days of the invoice date, but if not paid within 10 days, the entire amount must be paid no later than 30 days after the invoice date.

Example 3   You purchase goods with a net price of $740. The invoice is dated September 5 with terms of "2/10, n/45." Determine (a) the cash discount, (b) the net amount due if paid within the discount period, (c) the last day of the discount period, and (d) the last day of the credit period.

a. cash discount: $740 × 2% = $14.80
b. net amount due: $740 - $14.80 = $725.20
c. last day of discount period: Sep. 5 + 10 = Sep. 15
d. last day of credit period: Sep. 5 is day 248; 248 + 45 = 293. Day 293 is Oct. 20.

If you pay the invoice no later than September 15, you can pay $725.20. If you fail to pay by September 15, you must pay $740 no later than October 20.

Here is a timeline for Example 3.

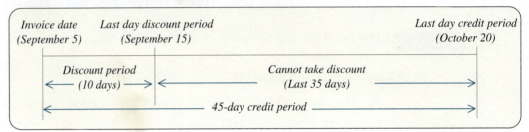

Sliding scale discount. This is a variation of the ordinary dating method, in which an invoice states terms such as "4/10, 2/30, n/60," meaning the buyer may deduct 4% if paid within the first 10 days of the credit period and may deduct 2% if paid between the 11th and 30th days of the credit period but must pay the full invoice amount if paid after the 30th day of the credit period. The credit period ends 60 days after the invoice date.

Example 4   You purchase goods with a net price of $58.50 and terms of 4/10, 2/20, n/60. Assuming an invoice date of October 3, calculate (a) the last day of the first discount period, (b) the last day of the second discount period, and (c) the last day of the credit period. Calculate the net amount due in each case.

a. Last day of first discount period: Oct. 3 + 10 = Oct. 13. You will pay $56.16 ($58.50 - $2.34) if you pay by Oct. 13.

b. Last day of second discount period: Oct. 3 + 20 = Oct. 23. You will pay $57.33 ($58.50 - $1.17) if you pay between October 14 and October 23.

c. Last day of credit period: Oct. 3 is day 276; 276 + 60 = 336; day 336 is Dec. 2. If you do not pay the invoice by October 23, you must pay $58.50 no later than December 2.

Here is a timeline for Example 4.

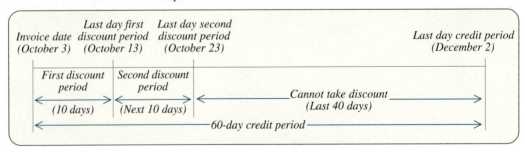

Receipt of goods (ROG). When a long period of time is required to transport goods to the buyer, terms such as "2/10, n/30 ROG" may be used, which means that the credit period begins the date goods are received, *not* the date of the invoice.

Example 5 You purchase goods on an invoice dated June 28 with terms of 3/15, n/60 ROG. If you receive the goods on July 18, calculate **(a)** the last day of the discount period and **(b)** the last day of the credit period.

────────

a. Last day of discount period: The credit period begins on July 18, the date the goods were received. July 18 is day 199: 199 + 15 = 214; day 214, Aug. 2 , is the last day of the discount period.

b. Last day of credit period: 199 + 60 = 259; day 259, Sep. 16 , is the last day of the credit period.

Here is a timeline for Example 5.

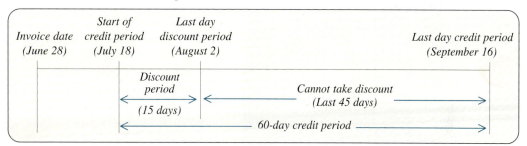

Before reviewing the next type of credit terminology, it should be mentioned that some invoices identify the end of the discount period but fail to identify the end of the credit period. In this case, the normally accepted practice is to assume that the credit period ends 20 days after the last discount period.

> **what if invoice does not state end of credit period?**
>
> If an invoice identifies the end of the discount period but fails to identify the end of the credit period, the normally accepted practice is to assume that the credit period ends 20 days after the last discount period.

End of month (EOM). When the EOM code (sometimes referred to as **prox**) is used, the discount period does not start until the end of the month in which the invoice is dated. An EOM invoice allows a buyer extra time to pay; the earlier in the month the invoice is dated, the more time the buyer has to pay. Because invoices dated near the end of the month do not give the buyer much benefit, most suppliers stipulate that on invoices dated after the 25th of the month, the discount period does not begin until the end of the following month.

Example 6 You purchase goods on an invoice dated March 13, with terms of 2/15 EOM. Determine: **(a)** the last day of the discount period and **(b)** the last day of the credit period.

────────

a. Last day of discount period: The discount period does not start until the last day of March. The last day of the discount period is 15 days beyond March 31, which is Apr. 15 .

b. Last day of credit period: The invoice does not specify when the credit period ends. Assuming that the supplier uses the customary policy of extending the credit period 20 days past the last day of the discount period, the last day of the credit period is May 5 .

Example 7   You purchase goods on an invoice dated March 26, with terms of 3/10, n/30 EOM. Determine **(a)** the last day of the discount period and **(b)** the last day of the credit period.

a. Last day of discount period: The discount period does not begin until the last day of April (because the invoice is dated after the 25th of the month). The last day of the discount period is 10 days beyond April 30, which is May 10.

b. Last day of credit period: The last day of the credit period is 30 days beyond April 30, which is May 30.

Extra. The "extra" code, also referred to as **ex** or **X**, is often used for seasonal goods. For example, a manufacturer of ski jackets may offer terms of "3/10-80 extra," which means that the discount period ends 90 (10 + 80 extra) days after the invoice date. These terms might be offered during the summer months to induce sporting goods stores to make their purchases prior to the winter season. This helps the sporting goods stores by allowing a delay in payment until the winter season is underway and helps the manufacturer by spreading sales over a longer period of time as well as reducing storage space needs. Although 3/10-80 extra provides a 90-day cash discount period, it is not written "3/90" because doing so would imply that a 90-day cash discount period is the usual policy.

Often, seasonal goods such as ski equipment are sold with "Extra" terms allowing the retailer some extra time to pay for the goods.

Example 8   You purchase goods on an invoice dated January 18 of a leap year, with terms of 4/10-60X. Calculate the last day of the discount period.

The discount period ends 70 days (10 + 60 = 70) after the date of the invoice. January 18 is day 18. The last day of the discount period is day 88 (18 + 70 = 88). Day 88 is March 28 (remember, because the year is a leap year, 1 must be added to each day after February 28; therefore, March 29 is day 89 and March 28 is day 88).

d Determining amount credited for a partial payment

In some cases a buyer does not have sufficient funds to make a full payment within the discount period. Most suppliers allow a cash discount for partial payments, in which case the buyer gets credit for the amount paid *plus some additional credit for paying part of the invoice within the discount period*. To determine the amount credited for a partial payment, we can use the following formula:

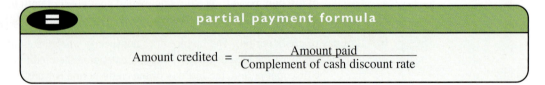

partial payment formula

$$\text{Amount credited} = \frac{\text{Amount paid}}{\text{Complement of cash discount rate}}$$

Chapter 5   Trade and Cash Discounts

Example 9 You receive an invoice for $45,600 with terms of 2/15, n/60. If the supplier has a policy of allowing a cash discount for partial payments and you pay $20,000 within the discount period, calculate the amount of credit you will receive for the payment.

$$\text{Amount credited} = \frac{\text{Amount paid}}{\text{Complement of cash discount rate}}$$

$$= \frac{\$20,000}{100\% - 2\%} = \frac{\$20,000}{98\%} = \frac{\$20,000}{.98} = \$20,408.16$$

By making a $20,000 payment, you will receive credit for $20,408.16. After making the payment, you will still owe $25,191.84 ($45,600 - $20,408.16).

You may wonder why in the world the total amount credited in Example 9 is $20,408.16 when only $20,000 is paid. Here is the logic. Pretend you had asked the seller to send you two separate invoices, totaling $45,600: one for $20,408.16 and the other for the remainder ($25,191.84). Then, you pay the $20,408.16 invoice. Because you pay within the discount period, you get a 2% discount, amounting to $408.16 ($20,408.16 × 2%), so you pay only $20,000. You still owe the other invoice for $25,191.84.

TIP — are you getting enough credit?

A common mistake is to figure the discount on the amount of the payment rather than using the formula. Here is the result of doing Example 9 incorrectly.

Amount of payment	$20,000
Extra credit for paying within discount period: $20,000 × 2%	+ 400
Total credit	$20,400 ← Wrong

The actual amount of credit, as calculated in Example 9, is $20,408.16. You would lose $8.16 by not figuring the discount correctly. I'll bet there is more than one person out there who says using the formula is not worth the $8.16! Most business owners, however, agree that when the pennies are watched, the dollars take care of themselves.

e Measuring the benefit of cash discounts

When we have an invoice that provides for a cash discount, we must decide whether to make payment within the discount period. If we fail to pay an invoice within the discount period, we must pay the supplier a larger amount at the end of the credit period than we would have paid at the end of the discount period. We are, in effect, borrowing money from the supplier (the amount we would have paid at the end of the discount period) and repaying that amount together with interest (the lost discount) at the end of the credit period. We can use the following formula to determine the rate of interest we are paying to the supplier.

interest rate formula for lost discounts

$$\text{Rate} = \frac{\text{Cash discount rate}}{\text{Complement of cash discount rate}} \times \frac{365}{\text{Days in credit period - Days in discount period}}$$

Note: Cash discount rate and complement can be shown without a percent sign.

Example 10 For each set of terms, determine the annual rate you pay the supplier if you fail to pay the invoice at the end of the discount period: **(a)** 2/10, n/30; **(b)** 8/10, n/45.

a. $\frac{2}{98} \times \frac{365}{30 - 10} = \frac{2}{98} \times \frac{365}{20} = \frac{2 \times 365}{98 \times 20} = \frac{730}{1,960} \approx .3724 \approx 37.24\%$

b. $\frac{8}{92} \times \frac{365}{45 - 10} = \frac{8}{92} \times \frac{365}{35} = \frac{8 \times 365}{92 \times 35} = \frac{2,920}{3,220} \approx .9068 \approx 90.68\%$

The symbol ≈ means "approximately equal to"

Once we know the annual rate we pay suppliers when discounts are lost, we can make several well-informed decisions. For example, assume you don't have funds to pay either invoice of Example 10, but you can borrow money from your bank at 11.5%. You would be wise to borrow the money and pay both suppliers because you will then be paying only 11.5% instead of the higher rates to the suppliers. Here's another example. Suppose you cannot borrow money from your bank and have funds to pay only one of the invoices. By failing to pay the first invoice you pay the supplier an interest rate of 37.24%; by failing to pay the second invoice you pay the supplier an interest rate of 90.68%, so you should pay the second invoice rather than the first.

When buyers fail to pay within the discount period, they may be paying the supplier an extremely high rate of interest. You may wonder if the supplier, who gets the high interest rate, secretly hopes the buyer will not pay within the discount period. On the contrary, suppliers offer cash discounts and encourage early payment to avoid cash flow problems and minimize bad debt losses.

> **TIP**   how was your date?
>
> Most accounts payable departments file invoices under the payment date. If an invoice is to be paid within the discount period, it is filed under the last day of the discount period; and if the invoice is not to be paid within the discount period, it is filed under the last day of the credit period. By following this procedure, businesses can avoid losing worthwhile discounts without paying invoices sooner than necessary. If the payment date is on a Sunday or a holiday, the next business day is used. In determining whether payments are timely, some suppliers use the date payment is *received by them,* while some accept the *postmark date.* Buyers must be familiar with the policy of each supplier and pay invoices accordingly.

How is it going? Should we find out by doing the U-Try-It exercises? Answering the last question "No" is a good indication you need to be extra careful doing the exercises!

U-Try-It (Unit 5.2)

1. You purchase goods with a list price of $850. You return goods that are defective, having a list price of $45. You get a trade discount of 30% and a cash discount of 6% if you pay the invoice within 10 days. The seller paid $73 in freight on your behalf and added the amount to the invoice. What is the net amount you should pay the supplier if you pay within the discount period?

For Problems 2–4 find each date.
2. 15 days past April 4
3. 45 days past July 28
4. 90 days past November 12

For Problems 5–7 find the last day of the discount period and the last day of the credit period.
5. On an invoice dated July 18 with terms of 3/10, n/60
6. On an invoice dated March 2 with terms of 6/15, n/45 ROG. Goods are received March 17.
7. On an invoice dated May 27 with terms of 4/15 EOM.
8. Find the last day of the discount period on an invoice dated October 19 with terms of 3/10-80X.
9. You receive an invoice for $12,400 with terms of 5/15, n/60. If the supplier has a policy of allowing a cash discount for partial payments, calculate the amount of credit you will receive for a payment of $5,000 within the discount period.
10. For terms of 5/10, n/60 determine the annual rate you pay the supplier if you fail to pay the invoice at the end of the discount period.

Answers: (If you have a different answer, check the solution in Appendix A.)
1. $602.69   **2.** Apr. 19   **3.** Sep. 11   **4.** Feb. 10   **5.** July 28, Sep. 16   **6.** Apr. 1, May 1   **7.** July 15, Aug. 4
8. Jan. 17   **9.** $5,263.16   **10.** 38.42%

Chapter in a Nutshell

Objectives	Examples

Unit 5.1 Trade discounts

a Finding net price for a single trade discount

$1,450 list price, 25% trade discount. Net price?

Method 1
Trade discount amount = List price × Trade discount rate = $1,450 × 25% = $362.50
Net price = List price - Trade discount amount = $1,450 - $362.50 = $1,087.50

Method 2
$1,450 × 75% = $1,087.50

b Finding net price for a series trade discount

$75 list price, series discount of 20/5. Net price?

List price	$75.00
Less first discount: $75 × 20%	-15.00
Price after first discount	$60.00
Less second discount: $60 × 5%	- 3.00
Net price	$57.00

c Finding an equivalent single discount rate

What is equivalent single discount rate for a 40/10/5 series discount?

Step 1 (complements)	Step 2 (multiply)	Step 3 (complement of Step 2)
40% 10% 5%	60% × 90% × 95%	100.0%
↓ ↓ ↓	= .60 × .90 × .95	- 51.3%
60% 90% 95%	= .513	48.7%
	= 51.3%	

Unit 5.2 Cash discounts

a Calculating cash discount and net amount due

$1,600 list price, 30% trade discount, $60 freight, 3% cash discount. Net amount if paid in discount period?

List price	$1,600.00
Less trade discount: $1,600 × 30%	- 480.00
Net price	$1,120.00
Less cash discount: $1,120 × 3%	- 33.60
Net price, less cash discount	$1,086.40
Add freight	+ 60.00
Net amount due	$1,146.40

b Counting days

15 days past May 12
May 12 + 15 → May 27

45 days past July 23
July 23 → Day 204
　　　　　　　+ 45
Sep. 6 ←　　 249

60 days past Dec. 13
Dec. 13 → Day 347
　　　　　　　+ 60
　　　　　　　 407
　　　　　　　-365
Feb. 11 ←　　 42

Chapter in a Nutshell (concluded)

Objectives	Examples
c Understanding discount terminology	**Ordinary dating:** invoice for $600 dated May 3; 2/10, n/60. Discount period ends: May 3 + 10 → **May 13** Net amount due: $600 − $12 (2% of $600) = **$588** Credit period ends: May 3 → Day 123 $\qquad\qquad\qquad\qquad\qquad\quad +60$ $\qquad\qquad$ **July 2** ← 183 **Receipt of goods (ROG):** dated Aug. 14; goods received Sep. 8; 6/15, n/45 Discount period ends: Sep. 8 + 15 → **Sep. 23** Credit period ends: Sep. 8 → Day 251 $\qquad\qquad\qquad\qquad\qquad\quad +45$ $\qquad\qquad$ **Oct. 23** ← 296 **End of month (EOM):** invoice dated July 27; 4/10 EOM. Discount period ends: 10 days past Aug. 31 → **Sep. 10** *(get extra month because invoice dated after 25th)* Credit period ends: Sep. 10 + 20 → **Sep. 30** *(add 20 days because credit period not defined)* **Extra:** invoice dated Apr. 23; 5/10-90X. Discount period ends: Apr. 23 → Day 113 $\qquad\qquad\qquad\qquad\qquad\quad +100$ *(10 + 90 extra)* $\qquad\qquad$ **Aug. 1** ← 213
d Determining amount credited for a partial payment	$13,500 invoice; 6/15, n/30. You pay $8,000 within discount period. Amount credited? $$\text{Amount credited} = \frac{\text{Amount Paid}}{\text{Complement of cash discount rate}} = \frac{\$8{,}000}{100\% - 6\%} = \frac{\$8{,}000}{94\%} = \frac{\$8{,}000}{.94} = \$8{,}510.64$$
e Measuring the benefit of cash discounts	4/10, n/45. Annual rate paid supplier if discount lost? $$\frac{4}{96} \times \frac{365}{45-10} = \frac{4}{96} \times \frac{365}{35} = \frac{4 \times 365}{96 \times 35} = \frac{1{,}460}{3{,}360} \approx .4345 \approx \mathbf{43.45\%}$$

Think

1. Golden Robbins buys some goods at a list price of $300 with a 20% trade discount and gets a 7% cash discount for paying the invoice within 15 days. Golden decides to take a total 27% discount (20% + 7% = 27%). Is Golden's reasoning correct? Who would be hurt by using this approach?
2. Bobbi Thornton buys some goods at a list price of $500 with a 30/20/5 series discount. Does it matter what order the discounts are taken? Prove your answer by taking the discounts in at least three different orders.
3. For a 30% trade discount rate, the complement is 70%. What does the 70% represent?
4. What is the difference between a trade discount and a cash discount?
5. What is the difference between a discount period and a credit period?
6. Suppose a company does not have enough money to pay all invoices within the discount period. How should the company decide which invoices to pay within the discount period?

Explore

1. Create a spreadsheet to determine the net amount due on an invoice that has a 3-part series trade discount and a cash discount. Create these headings in Column A: row 1, List Price; row 2, Trade Disc (%) #1; row 3, Price After Disc #1; row 4, Trade Disc (%) #2; row 5, Price After Disc #2; row 6, Trade Disc (%) #3; row 7, Price After Disc #3; row 8, Cash Discount(%); row 9, Net Amount Due. Enter formulas in cells B3, B5, B7, and B9 to solve for the resulting prices. *Tip:* A possible formula for cell B3: =B1*(1-B2). Use two decimal places in cells B1, B3, B5, B7 and B9. You may want to color-code the cells that need amounts entered (B1, B2, B4, B6 and B8.) Save the file (maybe as Trade & Cash Discounts). Then, test your formulas by entering a list price in cell B1, and percent discounts in cells B2, B4, B6, and B8 (like 25%, 15%, 10%, 2%); is your net amount due (cell B9) correct?

Apply

1. **The Retailer/Wholesaler Problem.** Contact a retailer or wholesaler who buys a variety of goods and ask for help with this school project. Get copies of five purchase invoices, each from a different supplier (your contact may want to block out information like the name of the supplier and description of goods). On each invoice, identify the invoice date, trade discount, terms of sale, last day of the discount and credit periods, net amount due, etc. Include an accompanying report about the company's procedure, taking into account the following questions:
   A. Are all cash discounts taken advantage of, or does the company carefully select which invoices to pay within the discount period?
   B. How are invoices filed so that cash discounts are not lost and late fees are not incurred?
   C. Do sellers of goods allow cash discounts on the basis of postmark or on the basis of when the check is received?
   D. How many people are involved in the payment of these invoices, and what are their individual responsibilities?

Chapter Review Problems

For all problems, do not round dollar amounts to the nearest penny until the final answer is obtained.

Unit 5.1 Trade discounts

For Problems 1 and 2 determine the trade discount amount and the net price.

	Product	List price	Trade discount rate	Trade discount amount	Net price
1.	Computer	$1,200	30%		
2.	Copy machine	$700	25%		

For Problems 3 and 4 find the net price using the complement of the trade discount rate.

	Product	List price	Trade discount rate	Complement of rate	Net price
3.	Computer	$1,200	30%		
4.	Copy machine	$700	25%		

5. Compare net prices: Problem 1 with Problem 3, and Problem 2 with Problem 4.

6. Santiago Gonzalez, an appliance dealer, can buy a big-screen TV at a list price of $6,400 with a 25/10/10 series discount. Find the net price by calculating the price after each discount.

7. Refer to Problem 6. Determine the equivalent single discount rate.

8. Refer to Problem 7. What is the significance of the equivalent single discount rate?

9. Refer to Problems 6 and 7. Find the net price using the equivalent single discount rate from Problem 7.

Unit 5.2 Cash discounts

10. You buy goods with a list price of $800. You return goods that are defective, having a list price of $50. You are entitled to a trade discount of 20%. The seller paid $20 in freight on your behalf and added the amount to the invoice. You are offered a 4% cash discount if you pay the invoice within 15 days. What is the net amount you should pay the supplier if you pay within the discount period?

11. You purchase goods with a net price of $240. The invoice is dated October 7 with terms of 3/20, n/45. Determine (a) the cash discount, (b) the net amount due if paid within the discount period, (c) the last day of the discount period, and (d) the last day of the credit period.

12. An invoice for $75.20 has terms of 3/10, 1/30, n/60. If you make payment 25 days after the invoice date, what amount should you pay?

13. You purchase goods on an invoice dated July 5 with terms of 4/15, n/45 ROG. If you receive the goods on July 23, calculate (a) the last day of the discount period, and (b) the last day of the credit period.

14. You purchase goods on an invoice dated July 27 with terms of 3/10 EOM. Determine (a) the last day of the discount period, and (b) the last day of the credit period.

15. You purchase goods on an invoice dated February 5 of a leap year, with terms of 5/10-90X. Calculate the last day of the discount period.

16. You receive an invoice for $18,300 with terms of 3/15, n/60. If the supplier has a policy of allowing a cash discount for partial payments and you pay $10,000 within the discount period, calculate the amount of credit you will receive for this payment.

17. For terms of 6/10, n/30, what annual rate do you pay the supplier if you fail to pay the invoice at the end of the discount period?

Challenge problems

18. Which type of discount (trade discount or cash discount) is given as an incentive to pay the seller promptly?

19. Series discounts are a form of trade discount. (T or F)

20. Trade discounts are given only if the invoice is paid during the discount period. (T or F)

21. You can buy a product from one of three companies. Company A for $3,200 with a trade discount of 30%, Company B for $2,900 with a trade discount of 20/10, or Company C for $3,450 with a trade discount of 20/15/5. Which company has the lowest net price?

For Problems 22–24 calculate the net price and net amount due (assuming the invoice is paid within the discount period).

	Product	List price	Trade discount rate	Net price	Cash discount	Net amount due
22.	Tent	$600	30%		2%	
23	Backpack	$400	30/10		8%	
24.	Sleeping bag	$500	25/15/5		4%	

For Problems 25–29 assume that you purchase goods with a list price of $455 and a trade discount of 25%. The invoice is dated October 3 with terms of 3/15, n/45.

25. What is the net price after trade discount?

26. What is the last day you can take a cash discount?

27. What is the net amount due if you pay within the discount period?

28. If you do not pay within the discount period, what is the final date to pay the invoice?

29. If you do not pay within the discount period, what annual interest rate are you, in effect, paying the supplier? Express the rate with two decimal places.

For Problems 30–34, refer to the invoice on the chapter-opening page.

30. Confirm each of the Subtotal amounts on the invoice.

31. Are each of the Net Price amounts correct?

32. What is the balance due?

33. Determine **(a)** the last day of the discount period, and **(b)** the last day of the credit period.

34. What is the net amount due if paid within the discount period?

35. Your business just produced a new mousetrap that you want to sell for a net price (after trade discount) of $8.78 per dozen. If you currently offer a trade discount of 30%, what should the list price be?

36. Show that the list price you found in Problem 35 results in the desired net price of $8.78.

Practice Test

1. Amber is an appliance dealer. She can buy a freezer for a list price of $820 with a 25% trade discount. What is Amber's net price?

2. Sean is a carpet retailer. He can buy carpet from a wholesaler for a list price of $22 per yard. If Sean receives a series discount of 20/10, what is his net price?

3. For the last 15 years, Tina has been receiving a 20/15/5 series discount. Find the equivalent single discount rate.

4. You buy goods on an invoice dated October 28, with terms of 2/20, n/45. What is the last day of the discount period?

5. You buy goods at a list price of $820. If you receive a trade discount of 25% and terms are "2/15, n/30," what amount must you pay if you pay within the discount period?

6. You receive an invoice for $18,300 with terms of 5/15, n/60. If the supplier has a policy of allowing a cash discount for partial payments and you pay $11,500 within the discount period, calculate the amount of credit you will receive for this payment.

7. For terms of 8/10, n/60 determine the annual rate you, in effect, pay the supplier if you fail to pay the invoice at the end of the discount period. Express the rate with 2 decimal places.

Top 5 U.S. Restaurants 2014 Sales

1. McDonald's $35,447,000,000
2. Starbucks $12,688,900,000
3. Subway $11,900,000,000
4. Burger King $8,640,100,000
5. Wendy's $8,512,800,000

Source: QSR Magazine

Quotable Quip
Advertising is legalized lying.
– H. G. Wells

Quotable Quip
There is only one boss. The customer. And he can fire everybody in the company from the chairman on down, simply by spending his money somewhere else.
— Sam Walton, Founder of Wal-Mart

Top 5 General Merchandisers in the U.S., 2014 Sales

1. Wal-Mart $485,651,000,000
2. Target $74,520,000,000
3. Sears $31,198,000,000
4. Macy's $28,105,000,000
5. Kohls $19,023,000,000

Source: Fortune Magazine

Save Some Money
If you paid full price for a product and it later goes on sale, many stores will give you a refund if you have purchased the item within 30 days of the sale. You will need to provide your receipt to get the difference between the price you paid and the sale price.

How to Sell Women's Clothing Like Crazy
by Dave Barry

The other day my wife, Michelle, was in a terrific mood, and you know why? Because she had successfully put on a size 6 outfit. She said this made her feel wonderful. She said, and this is a direct quote: "I wouldn't care if these pants were this big (here she held her arms far apart) as long as they have a '6' on them."

Here's how you could get rich: Start a women's clothing store called "Size 2," in which all garments, including those that were originally intended to be restaurant awnings, had labels with the words "Size 2." I bet you'd sell clothes like crazy.

"Yeah, they cost us fifty bucks each, but we'll make up the difference in high-volume sales!"

Markup and Markdown

6

In this chapter, we will examine the process of selling goods. Some businesses, in an attempt to make lots of money, charge customers too much for goods; these businesses are doomed to fail because potential customers do business elsewhere where prices are more reasonable. Other businesses, in an attempt to attract lots of customers, charge too little; these businesses are doomed to fail because revenues do not cover expenses. In order for a business to succeed, the selling price must be low enough to attract customers, yet high enough to cover expenses and provide a profit.

In this chapter, we will examine **markup,** which is the difference, in dollars, between cost and selling price. Occasionally, a business reduces the original asking price; this is known as a **markdown.**

Consider this little jingle:

To ignore what's in this chapter, a merchant must be bold,
It's like strolling through a jungle, wearing a blindfold.
While some may be lucky, and actually survive,
Most, after a while, will be eaten alive!

As you can tell, I am not a poet! But, the message is true. Many businesses fail because the principles of markup and markdown are ignored.

UNIT OBJECTIVES

Unit 6.1 Markup
- **a** Understanding the markup formula
- **b** Making calculations when markup is a percent of cost
- **c** Making calculations when markup is a percent of selling price

Unit 6.2 Percent markup
- **a** Calculating percent markup
- **b** Converting percent markups

Unit 6.3 Markdown
- **a** Calculating markdown and percent markdown
- **b** Pricing products for which a markdown is anticipated

Unit 6.4 Break-even analysis
- **a** Understanding the effect of markdowns
- **b** Calculating break-even volume

Unit 6.1 Markup

As mentioned, markup (sometimes referred to as *mark-on,* or *margin*) is the difference, in dollars, between cost and selling price. Let's start off by examining the relationship between cost, markup, and selling price.

a Understanding the markup formula

Because markup is the difference between cost and selling price, we can establish the selling price of merchandise by adding the dollar amount of markup to the cost.

> **markup formula**
>
> Selling price (S) = Cost (C) + Dollar amount of markup (M)

Example 1 Max Nez is a furniture retailer. He buys a sofa from a wholesaler for $500 (this is Max's cost after deducting trade and cash discounts and adding freight paid by Max). If Max wants a markup of $300, for what price should he sell the sofa?

$S = C + M = \$500 + \$300 = \boxed{\$800}$

The $300 markup is used to help cover Max's operating expenses (like rent, utilities, advertising, and wages) and provide for some profit.

Some of the problems of this unit are pretty simple; others are a bit tricky. This is one chapter in which problems are, for most people, easier to solve if we use equation-solving skills. By using equation-solving skills, we can avoid having to memorize a whole bunch of formulas and procedures. For each problem in this unit, we will start with the markup formula: $S = C + M$. Then we will substitute known values. Finally, we will solve for the unknown using the Golden Rule of Equation Solving: *Do unto one side as you do unto the other.* To help make the job easier, we will use a word problem guide.

In Example 1, markup was expressed as a dollar amount. Most businesses, however, calculate markup as a *percent of cost* or as a *percent of selling price*. Manufacturers generally establish markup as a *percent of cost* because cost figures are easily obtained. Wholesalers and retailers, on the other hand, often calculate markup as a *percent of selling price,* because income and expenses are often compared to sales revenues. Let's first examine markup as a percent of cost.

> **LA CAILLE**
> Little Cottonwood Canyon
>
> *Ahi Tuna*
> A unique presentation of Ahi Tuna rolled with nori and wasabi. Prepared rare with ginger and chinois sauce
> Seventy-Five
>
> *Carré d' Agneau*
> Rack of New Zealand Lamb with a Grand Marnier glaze and mint pesto
> Could a million coyotes be wrong?
> Eighty-Two

Some retailers, in order to project a superior image, price their products as a whole number, such as $200. Most retailers, however, want to project a low price, and therefore price their goods just below a whole number, such as $199.95; in theory, a price of $199.95 is considered to be much lower than $200.

b Making calculations when markup is a percent of cost

When markup is figured as a percent of cost, the rate of markup is referred to as **percent markup on cost.** To find the dollar amount of markup, we multiply cost by the percent markup on cost. For example, if cost is $300 and there is a 60% markup on cost, the dollar amount of markup is $180 ($300 × 60%).

If we know the percent markup on cost, we can establish (1) a selling price, based on a certain cost, or (2) cost to pay, based on a projected selling price. Let's start off by finding selling price.

Situation 1: Know cost, find selling price

Example 2 Sybil McGuire, an antiques dealer, buys a 70-year-old lamp for $300. If Sybil wants to maintain a 60% markup on cost, at what price should she resell the lamp?

word problem guide

1. Solving for	Selling price	
2. Formula	$S = C + M$	*Markup formula*
3. Known facts	$S = C + 60\%(C)$	$M = 60\%$ of cost
	$S = \$300 + 60\%(\$300)$	$C = \$300$
4. Procedure	$S = \$300 + \$180$	$60\%(\$300) = \$180$
	$S = \$480$	$\$300 + \$180 = \$480$

Situation 2: Know selling price, find cost

Example 3 Sybil has the chance to buy an antique rocking chair that she figures she can sell for $1,500. If she wants to maintain a 60% markup on cost, what price should she pay for the rocking chair?

word problem guide

1. Solving for	Cost	
2. Formula	$S = C + M$	*Markup formula*
3. Known facts	$\$1,500 = 100\%C + (60\%C)$	"C" = means "$100\%C$"; $M = 60\%$ of cost
4. Procedure	$\$1,500 = 160\%C$	*Combine terms:* $100\%C + 60\%C = 160\%C$
	$\$1,500 = 1.60C$	*Convert "160%" to a decimal number*
	$\dfrac{\$1,500}{1.60} = \dfrac{1.60}{1.60}C$	*Divide both sides of the equation by 1.60*
	$\$937.50 = C$	*Simplify*

> **TIP** what makes example 3 trickier than example 2?
>
> In Example 2, we were able to calculate the dollar amount of markup because we knew cost and the percent markup on cost: $300 cost × 60% = $180 markup. In Example 3, we were not able to find the dollar amount of markup because we did not know cost. As a result, a few extra steps were involved. Checking an answer may be helpful in visualizing the process (given facts are shown in bold).
>
> | Check answer, Example 2 | | Check answer, Example 3 | |
> |---|---|---|---|
> | C | $300 | C | $ 937.50 |
> | $+ M$: **$300 (cost) × 60%** | +180 | $+ M$: $937.50 (cost) × **60%** | + 562.50 |
> | S | $480 | S | **$1,500.00** |

C Making calculations when markup is a percent of selling price

When markup is figured as a percent of selling price, the rate of markup is referred to as **percent markup on selling price.** To find the dollar amount of markup, we multiply selling price by the percent markup on selling price. For example, if selling price is $900 and there is a 40% markup on selling price, the dollar amount of markup is $360 ($900 × 40%).

If we know the percent markup on selling price, we can establish (1) cost to pay, based on a projected selling price, or (2) selling price when we know cost. Let's start off finding cost.

Situation 1: Know selling price, find cost

Example 4   Larry Pino sells musical instruments. Larry has the chance to buy a used accordion that he figures he can resell for $900. He sells instruments based on a 40% markup on selling price. What should Larry pay for the accordion?

word problem guide

1. Solving for	Cost
2. Formula	$S = C + M$ *Markup formula*
3. Known facts	$S = C + 40\%(S)$ $M = 40\%$ of selling price
	$\$900 = C + 40\%(\$900)$ $S = \$900$
4. Procedure	$\$900 = C + \$360$ $40\%(\$900) = \$360$
	$\$540 = C$ *Subtract $360 from both sides of the equation*

Situation 2: Know cost, find selling price

Example 5   Larry buys a guitar for $450. If Larry wants to maintain a 40% markup on selling price, what price should he resell the guitar for?

word problem guide

1. Solving for	Selling price
2. Formula	$S = C + M$ *Markup formula*
3. Known facts	$100\%S = \$450 + 40\%S$ "S" = means "100%S"; M = 40% of selling price
4. Procedure	$60\%S = \$450$ *Subtract 40%S from both sides*
	$.60S = \$450$ *Convert 60% to a decimal number*
	$\frac{.60}{.60} S = \frac{\$450}{.60}$ *Divide both sides of the equation by .60*
	$S = \$750$ *Simplify*

> **TIP**   **example 4 vs example 5**
>
> In Example 4, we were able to calculate the dollar amount of markup because we knew the selling price and the percent markup on selling price: $900 selling price × 40% = $360 markup. In Example 5, we were not able to find the dollar amount of markup because we did not know the selling price, so a few extra steps were required. Let's check the answers (given facts are shown in bold).
>
> | Check answer, Example 4 | | Check answer, Example 5 | |
> |---|---|---|---|
> | C | $540 | C | $450 |
> | + M: **$900** (selling price) × **40%** | +360 | + M: $750 (selling price) × **40%** | +300 |
> | S | $900 | S | $750 |

The preceding examples have focused on buying products and reselling them. The same concepts also apply to pricing services. For example, a plumbing repair company may pay employees $20 per hour to make repairs for customers but charge the customers $35 per hour; the markup ($15 per hour) is used to cover expenses such as payroll taxes, vehicle costs, insurance, and rent, and provide for some profit. We will solve a problem involving "markup on services" in the U-Try-It exercises. Are you ready?

1. Tosh Shibata owns a car dealership. Tosh's cost on a sports car is $38,500. If he wants a markup of at least $2,150, what is the minimum price he can sell the vehicle for?
2. Francisco Ramirez owns a plumbing repair business. Francisco pays employees $25 per hour to do plumbing repairs for customers. If Francisco wants to maintain an 80% markup on employees' pay, what hourly rate should he bill customers?
3. Felicity Searle owns an art studio. She just purchased a sculpture for $550. If Felicity wants to maintain a 60% markup on selling price, what price should she resell the sculpture for?

Answers: (If you have a different answer, check the solution in Appendix A.)
1. $40,650   **2.** $45   **3.** $1,375

Unit 6.2 Percent markup

In this unit, we will calculate the percent markup on cost and the percent markup on selling price. We will also explore the relationship between these two rates.

a Calculating percent markup

As mentioned, markup is the difference, in dollars, between cost and selling price. If a product is purchased at a certain cost and then resold at another price, we can determine the rate of markup (either as a percent of cost or as a percent of selling price).

markup formulas

Dollar amount of markup (M) = Selling price (S) - Cost (C)

Percent markup on cost = $\dfrac{M}{C}$

Percent markup on selling price = $\dfrac{M}{S}$

Example 1 Jim Alfred, a rug dealer, paid $2,625 for an oriental rug. Jim later sold the rug for $4,200. Find: **(a)** dollar amount of markup, **(b)** percent markup on cost, and **(c)** percent markup on selling price.

a. $M = S - C = \$4{,}200 - \$2{,}625 = \$1{,}575$

b. Percent markup on cost = $\dfrac{M}{C} = \dfrac{\$1{,}575}{\$2{,}625} = .6000 = 60\%$

c. Percent markup on selling price = $\dfrac{M}{S} = \dfrac{\$1{,}575}{\$4{,}200} = .3750 = 37.5\%$

The $1,575 markup is 60% of cost and 37.5% of selling price.

The results of Example 1 can be summarized in a chart:

		Markup		
Cost	Percent of cost	Dollar amount	Percent of selling price	Selling price
$2,625	60%	$1,575	37.5%	$4,200

From Example 1, we can conclude that a 60% markup on cost is *identical* to a 37.5% markup on selling price. You may wonder how a 60% markup could be identical to a 37.5% markup. Well, the rates are applied to different amounts—the 60% is applied to cost (the small number), while the 37.5% is applied to selling price (the large number). Both result in the same dollar amount of markup:

$2,625 × 60% = $1,575 $4,200 × 37.5% = $1,575

b Converting percent markups

Occasionally, a company may want to compare percent markup on cost with percent markup on selling price or vice versa. Let's start off by converting a percent markup on cost to find the *equivalent percent markup on selling price*.

= equivalent percent markup on selling price

$$\text{Equivalent percent markup on selling price} = \frac{\text{Percent markup on cost}}{100\% + \text{Percent markup on cost}}$$

Example 2 Diane Nessen sells used cars. For the last 12 years, she has used a 60% markup on cost. Diane decides it makes more sense to base her markup on selling price (in this way it will be easier for her to determine what price to pay for a used car, based on what she thinks she can resell the car for). Help Diane calculate the equivalent percent markup on selling price.

$$\text{Equivalent percent markup on selling price} = \frac{\text{Percent markup on cost}}{100\% + \text{Percent markup on cost}}$$
$$= \frac{60\%}{100\% + 60\%} = \frac{60\%}{160\%} = \frac{.60}{1.60} = .375 = \boxed{37.5\%}$$

Diane can instead use a 37.5% markup on selling price.

Again, we see that a 60% markup on cost is identical to a 37.5% markup on selling price. Next, we will convert a percent markup on selling price to find the *equivalent percent markup on cost*.

= equivalent percent markup on cost

$$\text{Equivalent percent markup on cost} = \frac{\text{Percent markup on selling price}}{100\% - \text{Percent markup on selling price}}$$

Example 3 Judd Wilcox builds doghouses. His markup is 20% of the selling price. Judd decides it would be easier to establish markup as a percent of cost (because his cost figures are readily available). Help Judd calculate the equivalent percent markup on cost.

$$\text{Equivalent percent markup on cost} = \frac{\text{Percent markup on selling price}}{100\% - \text{Percent markup on selling price}}$$
$$= \frac{20\%}{100\% - 20\%} = \frac{20\%}{80\%} = \frac{.20}{.80} = .25 = \boxed{25\%}$$

Judd can instead use a 25% markup on cost.

TIP — is answer reasonable?

You may have noticed that the percent markup on cost is always larger than the percent markup on selling price. This is because cost is less than selling price, and in order to get the same dollar amount of markup, we must multiply the cost by a larger percent than we multiply the selling price by. If, when converting a percent markup, our percent markup on cost ends up being *smaller* than the percent markup on selling price, we know we have done something wrong!

Now let's do a few more U-Try-It problems.

U-Try-It (Unit 6.2)

1. Sean McGregor owns a sporting goods store. Sean buys a canoe for $1,800 and sells it for $2,070. Determine: **(a)** dollar amount of markup, **(b)** percent markup on cost, and **(c)** percent markup on selling price.
2. Yoko Ung prices goods on the basis of a 30% markup on cost. She hears that a competitor uses a 25% markup on selling price. Find Yoko's equivalent percent markup on selling price to determine if Yoko's markup is greater or less than her competitor's.

Answers: (If you have a different answer, check the solution in Appendix A.)
1a. $270 **1b.** 15% **1c.** 13.04% **2.** 23.08% (less than her competitor)

Unit 6.3 Markdown

We will begin this unit by studying markdowns. Later, we will look at how businesses price products for which a markdown is anticipated.

a Calculating markdown and percent markdown

Markdowns are used to increase sales or to get rid of excess or damaged merchandise.

Not all merchandise is sold at its **original marked price.** A reduction in price is known as a *markdown*. Businesses reduce prices to get rid of merchandise that is damaged or unpopular, to attract customers, to meet or beat the competition, and so on.

Markdown is sometimes expressed as a **dollar markdown.** For example, if a retailer sells $195 tennis rackets at $50 off, the **reduced price** is $145. In other cases, markdown is expressed as a percent of the original marked price; to find the dollar markdown, we multiply the original marked price by the **percent markdown.**

```
13 000.00
10,822.50
―――――――
 2,177.50
```

Example 1

An appliance dealer advertises a refrigerator at a 20% discount, based on an original marked price of $875. A second dealer advertises the same refrigerator at a 15% discount, based on an original marked price of $810. Which dealer offers the lower reduced price?

Dealer 1		Dealer 2	
Original marked price	$875.00	Original marked price	$810.00
Dollar markdown: $875 × 20%	- 175.00	Dollar markdown: $810 × 15%	- 121.50
Reduced price	$700.00	Reduced price	$688.50

Even though the first dealer offers a larger percent markdown (20% compared with 15%), the second dealer's reduced price is lower.

Often, merchants use a series of markdowns; the markdowns are taken one after the other. In this case, we calculate each markdown on the previous reduced price.

Example 2

A sporting goods store priced a tent at $475. New models were coming in, so the store reduced the price 20%. Eight weeks later, as the camping season was coming to a close, the store reduced the price an additional 15%. Calculate the reduced price after the second markdown.

Original marked price	$ 475
Markdown 1: $475 × 20%	- 95
Reduced price, after markdown 1	$ 380
Markdown 2: $380 × 15%	- 57
Reduced price, after markdown 2	$ 323

> **TIP** — **resist temptation**
>
> You may be tempted to combine discounts for a series of markdowns. Don't do it! In Example 2, doing so would result in a combined discount of 35% (20% + 15% = 35%) and we would get a wrong answer:
>
> | | |
> |---|---|
> | Original marked price | $475.00 |
> | Total markdown: $475 × 35% | - 166.25 |
> | Reduced price | $308.75 ←—WRONG! |

In the next example, we will find the percent markdown. Notice the similarity to the rate formula from Chapter 4: Rate = $\frac{\text{Portion}}{\text{Base}}$.

> **finding percent markdown**
>
> **Step 1** Find dollar markdown, if not given:
>
> Dollar markdown = Original marked price - Reduced price
>
> **Step 2** Find percent markdown:
>
> Percent markdown = $\frac{\text{Dollar markdown}}{\text{Original marked price}}$
>
> Original marked price
> (Markdown is "based" on original marked price, so original marked price is the base.)

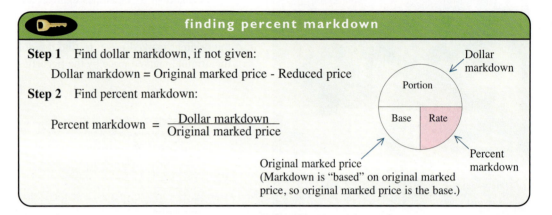

Example 3 A TV originally priced at $495 is marked down to $346.50. What is the percent markdown?

Step 1 Find dollar markdown

Dollar markdown = Original marked price - Reduced price = $495 - $346.50 = $148.50

Step 2 Find percent markdown

Percent markdown = $\frac{\text{Dollar markdown}}{\text{Original marked price}}$ = $\frac{\$148.50}{\$495}$ = .3000 = **30%**

The TV was marked down 30%.

b Pricing products for which a markdown is anticipated

Some products lose their value over time. For example, products such as produce, bakery items, meat, and dairy items have a relatively short shelf life. Not all of these goods will sell at regular prices; some may be sold at a reduced price, and some may be discarded. Other products, such as clothing and sporting equipment, are seasonal and may have to be sold at a reduced price as the season for which they were designed comes to an end. Maybe you have seen this sign before:

Well, this advice definitely applies to pricing goods for which some of the goods will be marked down or discarded. *With advance planning, the combined selling prices will provide the markup required for the entire stock.*

 finding original marked price when markdown is anticipated

Step 1 Determine the desired sales proceeds from entire stock.

Step 2 Deduct the projected proceeds from discounted products; the result is the proceeds required from products projected to be sold at the original marked price.

Step 3 Find the original marked price by dividing the result of Step 2 by the quantity expected to be sold at the original marked price. Always round *up*.

Some products, like pineapples, have a short shelf life. Some may be sold at a reduced price and some may be discarded. With advance planning, the combined prices will provide enough markup for the entire stock.

Example 4 A grocer bought 300 pineapples at $2.39 each. Experience at the store indicates that, as a result of aging, 20% of the pineapples will be sold at cost, and 20% will be discarded. Find the original marked price that will produce a 20% markup on cost.

Step 1 Determine desired sales proceeds from entire stock (refer to Unit 6.1, if needed)

word problem guide

1. Solving for	Sales proceeds from entire stock	
2. Formula	$S = C + M$	*Markup formula*
3. Known facts	$S = C + 20\%(C)$	$M = 20\%$ *of cost*
	$S = \$717 + 20\%(\$717)$	$C = 300 \times \$2.39 = \$717$
4. Procedure	$S = \$717 + \$143.40$	$20\%(\$717) = \$143.40$
	$S = \mathbf{\$860.40}$	$\$717 + \$143.40 = \$860.40$

[handwritten: X = 88.75 + 87.5(88.75) 7,765.625]

The grocer must get a total of $860.40. If all of the pineapples were sold at the same price, the price could be $2.87 each ($860.40 ÷ 300 pineapples ≈ $2.87). But 60 of the pineapples (300 × 20%) will be sold at cost and 60 pineapples (300 × 20%) will be discarded. Therefore, 180 pineapples must be sold for more than $2.87 each. We will find the required price in the next two steps.

Step 2 Deduct proceeds from products sold at a discount

Desired sales proceeds (from Step 1)	$860.40
Less proceeds from 60 pineapples sold at cost: 60 × $2.39	- 143.40
Proceeds required from top-quality pineapples	**$717.00**

Step 3 Find original marked price

180 will sell at original marked price, so: $717 ÷ 180 ≈ $3.9833 ≈ $3.99 each (*rounded up*)

The pineapples should originally be priced at $3.99 each.

Unit 6.3 Markdown

In Example 4, we found that the original marked price should be $3.99 per pineapple. Let's see if the grocer will, in fact, receive at least $860.40 from the 300 pineapples:

180 pineapples at full price: 180 × $3.99	$718.20
60 pineapples at cost: 60 × $2.39	143.40
+ 60 pineapples discarded	0.00
300	$861.60

Total sales proceeds are slightly more than the desired $860.40 because we *rounded up* the original marked price from $3.9833 to $3.99.

Once the relationship between selling price ($3.99) and cost ($2.39) is determined, the grocer can use this relationship (referred to as a **price/cost ratio**) to establish the original marked price of pineapples purchased later. A price/cost ratio is found by dividing selling price by cost.

price/cost ratio formula

$$\text{Price/Cost ratio} = \frac{\text{Selling price}}{\text{Cost}}$$

Example 5 Refer to Example 4. Determine the price/cost ratio. Then, assuming the next bunch of pineapples is purchased at a cost of $2.45 each, determine the original marked price that should produce a 20% markup on cost.

$$\text{Price/Cost ratio} = \frac{\text{Selling price}}{\text{Cost}} = \frac{\$3.99}{\$2.39} \approx 1.67$$

This means that pricing pineapples at 1.67 times cost should produce a 20% markup on cost. For all future purchases of pineapples, the grocer can price them at 1.67 times cost: *Always round up*

Price for next bunch of pineapples: $2.45 cost × 1.67 ≈ $4.0915 = **$4.10 each**

Using a price/cost ratio is a real time-saver. Instead of using the three-step process of Example 4 to price products for which a markdown is anticipated, we can use the price/cost ratio as we did in Example 5.

That completes this chapter. Let's do the U-Try-It exercises to check our understanding of this last unit.

U-Try-It (Unit 6.3)

Jennifer Tyler is a computer retailer. Let's help Jennifer figure a few things.

1. Jennifer prices a certain model computer at $1,500. After 6 months, one of these computers is unsold. Because a newer model is now available, Jennifer decides to reduce the price 25%. After 3 weeks, the computer is still not sold, so she reduces the price another 10%. The computer still does not sell, so Jennifer reduces the price another 20% and finally sells the darn thing. What is the final reduced price?
2. Based on the original marked price of $1,500 and the final reduced price found in Problem 1, what is the overall percent markdown?
3. Jennifer decides that in the future she will price products based on anticipated markdowns. Her experience indicates that, as a result of new models being introduced, 20% of her computers must be sold at 70% of her cost. Jennifer buys 30 computers at a cost of $1,200 each. Find the original marked price that will produce a 25% markup on cost.
4. Using a price/cost ratio, determine the original marked price for the next shipment of computers that cost $1,175 each.

Answers: (If you have a different answer, check the solution in Appendix A.)
1. $810.00   2. 46%   3. $1,665 each   4. $1,630.32 each

126   Chapter 6   Markup and Markdown

Unit 6.4 Break-even analysis

Some businesses, when pricing goods or services, fail to consider whether the pricing strategy will result in a profit or loss for the business.

a Understanding the effect of markdowns

Let's start by reviewing how to determine cost and original marked price.

Example 1

Emmett Leonard, the owner of an office supply store, buys calculators at a list price of $72 with a 40% trade discount. He prices the calculators using a 50% markup on cost. Determine the cost per calculator and the original marked price.

List price	$72.00
Trade discount: $72 × 40%	- 28.80
Cost	$43.20
Markup: $43.20 × 50%	+21.60
Original marked price	$64.80

When prices are reduced (marked down), special consideration must be given to profitability. Here are the four possibilities:

- The actual selling price is less than cost. The result is called an **absolute loss**, or **gross loss**.
- The actual price is greater than the cost, but not enough to cover operating expenses. The result is called an **operating loss**.
- The actual selling price covers cost and operating expenses, but provides no profit. That *precise* selling price is called the **break-even price**.
- The actual selling price is greater than the break-even price, providing some **profit**.

In the next example, we will determine the price needed to cover operating expenses (like rent, insurance, salaries, utilities, etc.).

Example 2

Refer to Example 1. Emmett needs 20% above cost to cover operating expenses. What is the break-even price on the calculators.

Cost (from Example 1)	$43.20
Amount to cover operating expenses: $43.20 × 20%	+ 8.64
Break-even price	$51.84

A price of $51.84 will cover operating expenses, but will provide no profit.

Example 3

Refer to Examples 1 and 2. Emmett sold most of the calculators at the original marked price ($64.80). During a weekend sale, he sold some calculators at his break-even price of $51.84. Two weeks later, a new model calculator was introduced and he sold most of the remaining calculators for $47.80 each. A few days later, he sold the few remaining calculators at a "clearance price" of $41.95 each. For each price, determine the outcome.

First batch (price of $64.80). $64.80 - $51.84 break-even price = $12.96 profit.

Second batch (price of $51.84). This is the break-even price, producing no profit and no loss.

Third batch (price of $47.80). This is greater than the cost ($43.20), but less than the break-even price ($51.84): $51.84 - $47.80 = $4.04 operating loss.

Final batch price (price of $41.95). This is less than the cost ($43.20): $43.20 - $41.95 = $1.25 absolute loss.

Here are the results of Examples 1-3 in graphic form:

b Calculating break-even volume

Businesses have two kinds of expenses:

Fixed costs. These are costs that are not affected by sales; fixed costs include rent, insurance, utilities, a business licenses, labor, etc. A business must pay these even if they have no sales.

Variable costs. These costs are affected by sales; variable costs include the cost of goods, sales commissions, etc. For example, an oil change shop would incur costs for oil and oil filters for each oil change. A copy center would incur costs for paper, toner, and wear and tear on copy machines for each copy made for a customer. A company that sells flashlights would incur the cost of a flashlight for each flashlight sold.

We can use the following formula to determine the number of sales needed to break even (pay for fixed and variable costs):

break-even formula

$$\text{Number of units needed to break even} = \frac{\text{Fixed costs}}{\text{Selling price per unit - Variable cost per unit}}$$

Example 4 You are thinking about opening an oil change shop. Your fixed costs will be $15,600 per month. You will charge customers $38 for a lube-oil-filter. The cost of materials is in addition to your fixed costs and is estimated at $14 per customer. How many oil changes must you do each month to break even?

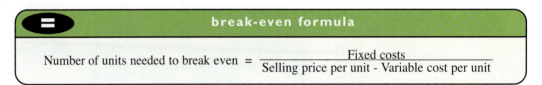

Proof: Revenues: 650 oil changes × $38 $24,700
         Less fixed costs   - 15,600
         Less variable costs: 650 oil changes × $14   - 9,100
         Profit $ 0

If you do 650 oil changes you will break even for the month. If you do more than 650 oil changes you will earn a profit. If you do fewer than 650 oil changes you will have a loss.

In Example 4, you need to do 650 oil changes a month to break even. Assuming you are open 25 days a month for an average of 11 hours a day, you will be open 275 hours a month (25 × 11 = 275). You will need to do an average of 2.36 oil changes an hour (650 oil changes ÷ 275 hours ≈ 2.36) to break even. Before opening your oil change shop it would be wise to survey some of your competitor's locations (perhaps parked across the street, counting customers) at varous times of the week to see if 2.36 oil changes per hour is reasonable.

For a business that sells a variety of products, we can determine the number of units that must be sold by allocating fixed expenses among the various products; to see how to make the allocations, go to Unit 19.2 of the text. Problem 3 of the following U-Try-It exercises asks how many units of a certain product must be sold for a company that sells more than one product.

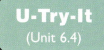

U-Try-It (Unit 6.4)

1. Olivia Lauren has a retail business that sells phones. She buys a particular smart phone from a supplier at a price of $92.80 with a trade discount of 20%. She establishes a retail price, based on a 35% markup on cost (20% to cover operating expenses and 15% to provide some profit). Determine (a) cost, (b) original marked price, (c) break-even price.
2. Refer to Problem 1. Olivia sold most of the smart phones at the original marked price. She sold a second batch for $85 each, and a third batch at a "clearance price" of $70 each. For each batch of sales, determine the amount of profit, operating loss, or absolute loss.
3. Outdoor Products manufactures tents and sleeping bags. They have fixed costs of $17,920 per month. Because 60% of the space and 60% of the labor is used to manufacture tents, the company decides to allocate 60% of the fixed costs to tents and 40% to sleeping bags. If they sell tents for $180 each and the variable cost per tent is $52, how many tents must they sell each month to cover the tent share of fixed costs?

Answers: (If you have a different answer, check the solution in Appendix A.)
1a. $74.24 **1b.** $100.22 **1c.** $89.09 **2.** Batch 1: Profit of $11.13; Batch 2: Operating loss of $4.09; Batch 3: Absolute loss of $4.24
3. 84 tents

Chapter in a Nutshell

Objectives	Examples

Unit 6.1 Markup

a Understanding the markup formula	Fernando Montoya is a car dealer. He buys a car for $24,200 and wants a $2,100 markup. Selling price? $S = C + M = \$24{,}200 + \$2{,}100 = \$26{,}300$	
b Making calculations when markup is a percent of cost	**Situation 1:** Know cost ($300) and percent markup on cost (40%); find selling price. $$\begin{aligned} S &= C + M & \text{Markup formula} \\ S &= \$300 + 40\%(\$300) & \text{Known values: } C = \$300; M = 40\% \text{ of cost} \\ S &= \$300 + \$120 & 40\%(\$300) = \$120 \\ S &= \$420 & \$300 + \$120 = \$420 \end{aligned}$$ **Situation 2:** Know selling price ($420) and percent markup on cost (40%); find cost. $$\begin{aligned} S &= C + M & \text{Markup formula} \\ \$420 &= 100\%C + 40\%C & \text{Known values: } S = \$420; \text{"C" means "}100\%C\text{"}; M = 40\% \text{ of cost} \\ \$420 &= 140\%C & 100\%C + 40\%C = 140\%C \\ \$420 &= 1.40C & \text{Convert 140\% to 1.40} \\ \tfrac{\$420}{1.40} &= \tfrac{1.40}{1.40}C & \text{Divide both sides of the equation by 1.40} \\ \$300 &= C & \text{Simplify} \end{aligned}$$	*S = 88.75 + 87.5%* *S = 88.75+* *77.66*
c Making calculations when markup is a percent of selling price	**Situation 1:** Know selling price ($300) and percent markup on selling price (40%); find cost. $$\begin{aligned} S &= C + M & \text{Markup formula} \\ \$300 &= C + 40\%(\$300) & \text{Known values: } S = \$300; M = 40\% \text{ of selling price} \\ \$300 &= C + \$120 & 40\%(\$300) = \$120 \\ \$180 &= C & \text{Subtract \$120 from both sides of the equation} \end{aligned}$$ **Situation 2:** Know cost ($180) and percent markup on selling price (40%); find selling price. $$\begin{aligned} S &= C + M & \text{Markup formula} \\ 100\%S &= \$180 + 40\%S & \text{Known values: "S" means "}100\%S\text{"}; C = \$180; M = 40\%S \\ 60\%S &= \$180 & \text{Subtract 40\%S from both sides of the equation} \\ .60S &= \$180 & \text{Convert 60\% to .60} \\ \tfrac{.60}{.60}S &= \tfrac{\$180}{.60} & \text{Divide both sides of the equation by .60} \\ S &= \$300 & \text{Simplify} \end{aligned}$$	

Chapter in a Nutshell   129

Chapter in a Nutshell (continued)

Objectives	Examples

Unit 6.2 Percent markup

a Calculating percent markup

Cost = $1,500; Selling price = $1,800.

a. Dollar amount of markup: $M = S - C = \$1,800 - \$1,500 = \$300$

b. Percent markup on cost = $\frac{M}{C} = \frac{\$300}{\$1,500} = .2000 = 20\%$

c. Percent markup on selling price = $\frac{M}{S} = \frac{\$300}{\$1,800} \approx .1667 \approx 16.67\%$

b Converting percent markups

Situation 1: Know percent markup on cost (25%); find equivalent percent markup on selling price

Equivalent percent markup on selling price = $\frac{\text{Percent markup on cost}}{100\% + \text{Percent markup on cost}}$

$= \frac{25\%}{100\% + 25\%} = \frac{25\%}{125\%} = \frac{.25}{1.25} = .20 = 20\%$

Situation 2: Know percent markup on selling price (20%); find equivalent percent markup on cost

Equivalent percent markup on cost = $\frac{\text{Percent markup on selling price}}{100\% - \text{Percent markup on selling price}}$

$= \frac{20\%}{100\% - 20\%} = \frac{20\%}{80\%} = \frac{.20}{.80} = .25 = 25\%$

Unit 6.3 Markdown

a Calculating markdown and percent markdown

A TV had an original marked price of $800. To make room for new models, the dealer marked it down twice: first 15%, then 10%. **(a)** Reduced price, after second markdown? **(b)** Overall percent markdown?

a.
Original marked price	$800
Markdown 1: $800 × 15%	- 120
Reduced price, after markdown 1	$680
Markdown 2: $680 × 10%	- 68
Reduced price, after markdown 2	$612

b. Total dollar markdown = Original marked price - Final reduced price = $800 - $612 = $188

Percent markdown = $\frac{\text{Dollar markdown}}{\text{Original marked price}} = \frac{\$188}{\$800} = .2350 = 23.5\%$

Chapter 6 Markup and Markdown

Chapter in a Nutshell (concluded)

Objectives	Examples
b Pricing products for which a markdown is anticipated	Grocer buys 500 pumpkins for $0.40 each. Grocer expects, as a result of aging, 20% of the pumpkins will be sold for $0.20 each and an additional 10% of the pumpkins will be discarded. Find the original marked price that will produce a 20% markup on cost.

(Handwritten note: S = 775 + 31.25(775))

Step 1 (desired sales proceeds)

S	$=$	$C + M$		Markup formula
S	$=$	$\$200 + 20\%(\$200)$		$C = 500 \times \$0.40 = \$200$; $M = 20\%$ of cost
S	$=$	$\$200 + \$40$		$20\%(\$200) = \$40$
S	$=$	**\$240**		$\$200 + \$40 = \$240$

Step 2 Deduct proceeds from pumpkins sold at a discount

100 pumpkins (500 pumpkins × 20%) will be sold at $0.20 each, so:

Desired sales proceeds (from Step 1)	$ 240
Less proceeds from pumpkins sold at discount: 100 × $0.20	- 20
Proceeds required from pumpkins sold at original marked price	**$ 220**

Step 3 Find original marked price

500 total pumpkins - 100 sold at discount (500 × 20%) - 50 discarded (500 × 10%) = 350 at original marked price, so:

$\$220 \div 350 \approx \$0.6286 \approx$ **\$0.63 each**

Check answer:

350 pumpkins × $0.63	$220.50		Slightly more than desired sales proceeds of $240, because price per pumpkin was *rounded up* from $0.6286 to $0.63
100 pumpkins × $0.20	20.00		
+50 pumpkins discarded	+ 0.00		
500	$240.50		

Price/Cost ratio = $\dfrac{\text{Selling price}}{\text{Cost}} = \dfrac{\$0.63}{\$0.40} =$ **1.575**

If the next purchase is at a cost of $0.35 per pumpkin, the original marked price should be:

$\$0.35 \times 1.575 =$ **$0.56 each**   ← Always round *up*

Unit 6.4 Break-even analysis

Objectives	Examples
a Understanding the effect of markdowns	Product purchased from supplier for $220 with 20% trade discount. Markup on cost = 35%.

Cost: $220 - 20%($220) = **$176**   Original marked price: $176 + 35%($176) = **$237.60**

Need 20% to cover operating expenses. Break-even price? $176 + 20%($176) = **$211.20**

Result, if sold for $237.60?   Greater than break-even price, so there is a *profit*:

$237.60 - $211.20 (break-even price) = **$26.40 profit**

Result, if sold for $211.20. Sold for break-even price, so **there is no prifit and no loss**

Result, if sold for $200? Less than break-even price, but greater than cost, so there is an *operating loss*:

$211.20 (break-even price) - $200 = **$11.20 operating loss**

Result, if sold for $170? Less than cost, so there is an *absolute loss*:

$176 (cost) - $170 = **$6 absolute loss**

Objectives	Examples
b Calculating break-even volume	You are thinking about opening a copy center. Fixed costs = $5,490 a month. You will charge customers 7 cents ($0.07) per copy; each copy will cost you 2.5 cents ($0.025). How many copies are needed each month to break even?

$$\text{Number of units needed} = \dfrac{\text{Fixed costs}}{\text{Selling price per unit - Variable cost per unit}} = \dfrac{\$5{,}490}{\$0.07 - \$0.025} = \dfrac{\$5{,}490}{\$0.045} = \textbf{122,000 copies}$$

Think

1. Many companies discount the price of some merchandise. Others don't discount prices—instead, they offer everyday low prices on all merchandise. Which strategy do you think is best, and why?
2. Some businesses, in an attempt to make lots of money, charge customers a very high price. Other businesses, in an attempt to attract lots of customers, sell at lower prices. What are the dangers of each approach? What approach do you think a business should use in pricing its products?
3. A 25% markup on cost is identical to a 20% markup on selling price. Prove this with a real price (cost or selling price).
4. Woo Kim owns a clothing store. She buys a dress from a supplier at a net price of $100 and marks it up 50% on cost. After 6 months, as the summer season is coming to a close, she reduces the price 50%. What is the reduced price? Why, if the dress was first marked up 50% and then marked down 50%, is the reduced price lower than the $100 cost?

Explore

1. Search on the Internet for *retail pricing strateies*. Review at least 3 of the sites you find. Based on the information on the sites, write a report about pricing strategies you think a specific retailer or wholesaler should consider.

Apply

1. **Merchandising Interview.** Meet personally with the managers or owners of at least two merchandising companies. Determine how they price their products (markup on cost or markup on selling price; if some other method is used, explain the method in detail). Determine how they monitor profitability on products that are marked down. Submit your findings, together with the company names and the people you met with. Those you meet may be reluctant to provide you with the exact percent markup; that is not required in your report.
2. **The Shopping Spree.** Find at least two advertisements in which merchandise is marked down at retail stores in your area. Personally visit the two stores. Answer the following questions.
   A. Are the numbers in the ad stated correctly? If necessary, determine something that is *not* stated in the ad (original marked price, dollar markdown, or reduced price).
   B. What kind of signs or other displays are used to identify the marked-down merchandise?
   C. Is the merchandise marked the same as in the ads?
   D. How could the store have done a better job of advertising the "sale" items?
   E. What are your conclusions from this experience?

Chapter Review Problems

For all answers that are percents, express the answer to the nearest tenth of a percent.

Unit 6.1 Markup

For Problems 1–4, find the missing amount.

	Cost	Markup($)	Selling price
1.	$2,450	$800	
2.	$1.57	$0.50	
3.	$100		$170
4.		$200	$500

5. You, as the owner of a shoe store, discount the price of a certain pair of shoes to $72. If your cost is $72, what is the dollar amount of markup?

6. Markup can be used only for products, not for pricing services. (T or F)

7. Ben Bower owns a computer store. Ben pays $700 for a computer and uses a 20% markup on cost. At what price should Ben resell the computer?

8. Ben has the chance to buy a used computer that he thinks he can resell for $360. If Ben needs a 20% markup on cost, what price should Ben pay?

9. Grace Frandsen owns an appliance store. Grace has the chance to buy a used refrigerator that she thinks she can resell for $250. If Grace needs a 30% markup on selling price, what price can she pay?

10. Grace buys a new microwave for $168. If she needs a 30% markup on selling price, at what price should she resell the microwave?

11. A property management company furnishes skilled help to maintain apartment complexes. If it pays employees $18 per hour and wishes to maintain a 20% markup based on the employees' hourly pay, what hourly rate should it bill property owners?

12. Refer to Problem 11. If the property owners expect to be charged $21 per hour, what hourly rate must the property management company pay its employees in order to maintain a 20% markup, based on the employees' hourly pay?

Unit 6.2 Percent markup

13. A clothing retailer paid $48 for a jacket. The retailer later sold the jacket for $72. Find: **(a)** dollar amount of markup, **(b)** percent markup on cost, and **(c)** percent markup on selling price.

For Problems 14–17, find the missing amount.

	Percent markup on cost	Percent markup on selling price
14.	40%	
15.	25%	
16.		30%
17.		25%

For Problems 18–21, answer questions about Jacob Marchant's business. Jacob builds birdhouses. His markup is 60% on cost.

18. What is the dollar amount of markup on a birdhouse that costs $40?

19. What should the selling price be?

20. What is the equivalent percent markup on selling price?

21. Using the preceding numbers, show that a 37.5% markup on selling price is identical to a 60% markup on cost.

Unit 6.3 Markdown

22. Merchandising companies often have markdowns on products that are in high demand. (T or F)

23. If a retailer sells a $250 TV at $50 off, what is the reduced price?

For Problems 24–26, answer questions about the price of a refrigerator.

24. Dependable Appliance Company advertises a refrigerator at a 15% discount, based on an original marked price of $900. What is the reduced price?

25. True Appliance Company advertises the same refrigerator at a 10% discount, based on an original marked price of $870. What is the reduced price?

26. Which company has the lowest reduced price?

27. A ski shop priced a snowboard at $500. New models were coming in, so the store reduced the price 25%. Eight weeks later, as the ski season was coming to a close, the store reduced the price an additional 20%. Calculate the reduced price, after the second markdown.

28. A hot tub, originally priced at $9,500 is marked down to $8,250. What is the percent markdown?

For Problems 29–32, answer questions about pricing mangos.

29. A grocer bought 200 mangos at $0.60 each. Experience has shown that, as a result of aging, 15% of the mangos will be sold at cost and 20% will be discarded. Find the original marked price per mango that will result in a 25% markup on cost.

30. Prove that the total proceeds are equal to (or slightly more than) the desired proceeds.

31. Find the price/cost ratio.

32. Assuming the next bunch of mangos costs $0.70 each, use the price/cost ratio to find the original marked price.

Unit 6.4 Break-even analysis

For Problems 33–38, answer questions about a furniture business owned by Eli Marvin.

33. Eli buys a dining table from a supplier at a list price of $620 with a 20% trade discount. Determine Eli's cost, after the trade discount.

34. Eli prices dining tables using a 45% markup on cost. Determine the original marked price.

35. Eli needs 28% above cost to cover operating expenses. What is the break-even price?

36. If Eli sells the table for $710, determine if he has (a) a profit, (b) an operating loss, or (c) an absolute loss, and the dollar amount of profit or loss.

37. What if he sells the table for $615?

38. What if he sells the table for $440?

39. Ryder Sterling makes kitchen cutting boards. Ryder's fixed costs are $5,300 a month. The materials and labor for each cutting board cost $26.75. If Ryder sells the cutting boards for $68.50 each, how many must Ryder sell each month to break even?

40. Refer to Problem 39. If Ryder sells 282 cutting boards, what is his projected profit?

Challenge problems

For Problems 41–47, fill in the blanks.

	Cost	Markup % of cost	Markup Dollar amount	Markup % of selling price	Selling price
41.	$1,300	40%		—	
42.	$180				$355
43.		—		25%	$3,400
44.	$28.50	—	—	30%	
45.		15%			$4,500
46.	—	20%		—	—
47.	—		—	60%	—

For Problems 48–55, answer questions about a winter coat.

48. A retailer purchased a winter coat for $95. If the coat is priced at $165, what is the dollar amount of markup?

49. What is the percent markup on cost?

50. What is the percent markup on selling price?

51. Because the winter season was coming to a close, the price was reduced 20%. After 3 weeks, the price was reduced an additional 15%. After the price was reduced an additional 10%, the coat sold. What is the reduced price after the third markdown?

52. What is the net markup in dollars?

53. Based on the reduced price, what is the percent markup on cost?

54. What is the total dollar amount of markdown?

55. What is the markdown as a percent of the original marked price?

56. A certain bank pays interest on savings accounts of 1.25% interest. They use this same money to make car loans at 4.9%. What is the percent markup on cost?

57. Write a short answer to the "Ask Marilyn" question.

ASK MARILYN
BY MARILYN VOS SAVANT

A wholesaler sells a dress for $20. The store marks it up to $40—a markup of 100%. But the dress doesn't sell by the end of the holiday season, and the store discounts it to 50% off. The price is now back to $20. How can a 100% markup and a 50% reduction result in the same figure?

—Judy and Greg Winski, Lakeland, Fla

58. A manufacturer produces a mattress at a cost of $192.45, then sells to a wholesaler based on a 30% markup on cost, a 15% trade discount, and terms of 1/20, n/60. The wholesaler sells to a retailer based on a 35% markup on cost, a 10% trade discount, and terms of 2/15, n/45. The retailer prices the product based on a 30% markup on selling price. The wholesaler and retailer each pay within the cash discount period, and base markup on net amount due (after cash discount). Four weeks after the retailer prices the mattress, a new model is introduced so the retailer marks down the mattress 25%. Determine the reduced price.

Practice Test

1. Tai Chow has an art gallery. He pays $525 for a painting and uses a 60% markup on cost. At what price should Tai resell the painting?

2. An automotive repair shop employs automotive technicians to work on customers' cars. The prevailing billing rate for other repair shops is $45 per hour. If the repair shop decides to charge customers the prevailing rate, what hourly rate can the technicians be paid in order to maintain a 125% markup on employees' pay?

3. Kermit Shaw owns an appliance store. He has the chance to buy a used refrigerator that he thinks he can resell for $200. If Kermit needs a 40% markup on selling price, what price can he pay?

4. Delma Swint owns a shoe store. Delma paid $55 for a pair of shoes and later sold the shoes for $77. What is the percent markup on cost?

5. A computer retailer uses a 40% markup on cost. What is the equivalent percent markup on selling price (to the nearest tenth of a percent)?

6. Brad Hayes, a snowmobile retailer, priced a snowmobile at $5,500. New models were coming in, so Brad reduced the price 10%. Eight weeks later, as the winter season was coming to a close, he reduced the price an additional 10%. Calculate the reduced price, after the second markdown.

7. A desk, originally priced at $1,200, is marked down to $780. What is the percent markdown?

8. A grocer bought 300 pounds of bananas at 32¢ per pound. Experience indicates that, as a result of aging, 25% of the bananas are sold at 75% of cost and another 15% are discarded. Find the original marked price that will produce a 25% markup on cost.

9. If selling price is $157.50 and cost is $90, what is the price/cost ratio?

10. A retailer buys a product from a supplier for a price of $22. The retailer needs a 25% markup on cost to cover operating expenses. If the product is sold at a price of $24, is there a (a) profit, (b) operating loss, or (c) absolute loss?

11. You are thinking about opening a copy center. Fixed costs = $4,910 a month. You will charge customers 6 cents ($0.06) per copy; each copy will cost you 2 cents ($0.02). How many copies do you need to make each month to break even?

FUN CORNER

Can You Guess?

Ben Counter is a bank teller. Bill Gates, the richest person in the U.S. (as of the writing of this text) brings all of his wealth, $56 billion, to deposit at Ben's bank. The deposit is in $1 bills. If Ben can count 80 bills a minute, approximately how long will it take (with no breaks) to count the entire deposit?

    A. 130 days   B. 130 months
    C. 130 years   D. 1,300 years

Answer: D. It will take 1,331 years! $56,000,000,000 ÷ 80 per minute = 700,000,000 min = 11,666,667 hrs ≈ 486,111 days. 486,111 days ÷ 365.25 average days per year ≈ 1,331 years.

Avoid Identity Theft

- Don't provide financial information over the phone unless you initiated the call and know the person.
- Destroy financial solicitations that are mailed; otherwise, thieves can get them from your garbage and assume your identity.
- Don't put outgoing mail in your mailbox; thieves can take it to get your account numbers.
- Guard ATM transactions so others cannot see your account number.
- Don't respond to "phishing" e-mails or phone calls that ask for personal information, even if they appear to be from a company you know.
- Consider buying an Identity Theft Protection program; most providers notify you of any suspicious activity under your name, and reimburse (up to a certain limit) for financial loss due to identity theft.
- You can get a free credit report each year from each of the three bureaus (Experian, Equifax, and TransUnion); many people get one every four months, alternating bureaus.

Worth Retelling

A man loved his money a lot. Just before he died he asked his wife to put all of his money in his casket at his funeral; that way, he could take his money to the afterlife.

At his funeral, a friend observed the wife putting a package in the casket, and afterwards asked the wife if she was crazy enough to put all of the money in the casket. The wife said, "I had to; I promised. I got all of his money together, put it in my account, and wrote him a check for every cent of it."

Check-Writing Tips

Some people out there alter checks to their advantage. Here are a few ideas to consider when writing a check.

- Checks should be typed or clearly written. Don't use pencil.
- Follow the name of the payee with asterisks or a line—to avoid someone inserting his or her own name after the payee's name. For example, "Tom Bell" could become "Tom Bell or Suzie Smith."
- Even though banks are supposed to rely on the word-form of a dollar amount, some banks process checks based on the number-form. So, write numbers carefully. When writing the check amount in numbers, keep the left digit close to the $ sign, or precede the left digit with asterisks; this prevents someone from adding extra digits to the left: 28.45 could become 9,928.45. Follow the last digit with asterisks or a line; this prevents someone from changing a decimal point to a comma and adding extra digits: 28.45 could become 28,450.00.

"How can our account be out of money? We still have a whole box of checks!"

7

Checking Accounts

A **check** is a note instructing a bank to pay a certain sum of money to someone. The person to receive the money is known as the **payee**, and the person issuing the check is known as the **payor** or **maker**.

When a check is written without enough money in the checking account and the bank does not pay the check, the check is referred to as a **nonsufficient funds check, bad check**, or **bounced check**. While a few people knowingly write bad checks, most bad checks are a result of not managing a checking account properly. Some people forget to record checks and therefore think that their balance is greater than it really is. Others don't add and subtract accurately, giving an incorrect balance. Many don't take the time to reconcile their bank statement each month. Have you ever been guilty of any of these things? In this chapter, we will review how to keep track of a checking account balance.

UNIT OBJECTIVES

Unit 7.1 Checking account balance

- **a** Keeping track of a checking account balance
- **b** Reconciling the bank statement
- **c** Adjusting a checking account balance after the reconciliation

Unit 7.1 Checking account balance

If a checking account balance is not known at all times, the possibility exists for writing a bad check, resulting in embarrassment, bad credit, returned check fees, and additional bookkeeping time.

a Keeping track of a checking account balance

Checking accounts are offered by a variety of financial institutions.

In this chapter, we will help Bob Green with his checking account. Bob, a surveyor, just started his own business. One of the first things Bob had to do was open a checking account for his business. Checking accounts are offered by banks, credit unions, savings and loans, stock brokerage firms, and through the Internet. Each institution may offer a variety of accounts and services.

Most banks provide customers with a **debit card**. A debit card looks like a credit card, but the similarity ends there. Using a debit card is like writing a check; money is deducted from the customer's account *immediately*. When a debit card is used to make purchases, the customer must enter a **personal identification number (PIN)**; with some debit cards, the customer can instead treat the debit card transaction as a credit card transaction and provide a signature instead of entering a PIN, but the transaction is still treated as a debit card transaction, in which the money is taken out of the customer's checking account (generally within a day or two). Most institutions provide **automatic teller machines (ATMs)** that allow customers to withdraw cash using their debit card, 24 hours a day, provided the customer has enough money in the account.

Most banking institutions will, upon request of the customer, transfer funds into or out of the account in what is known as an **electronic funds transfer (EFT)**—a computerized transaction without the use of paper checks or deposits. For example, your bank may withdraw money from your account each month to make your car payment, or it may deposit your paycheck into your account each month.

Most institutions provide **online banking** services, in which customers can pay bills, transfer funds, review balances, and view bank statements through the Internet. In some cases, customers can use cell phones to review balances, pay bills, and transfer funds. Some people are able to make payments with specially equipped cell phones; for example, in some places people can pay for a commuter train simply by holding their cell phone as they walk through the turnstile. Watch for more creative banking applications as technology changes.

> **TIP — where and what type?**
>
> It is a good idea to "shop around" before opening a checking account. Here are a few things to consider: monthly service charges, interest earned on the account, minimum balance requirement, check printing charges, overdraft protection and fees, ATM availability and fees, debit card fees, online banking options, and any additional fees. Also determine whether you will get preferred rates on safety boxes, loans, cashier's checks, notary service, and traveler's checks.

Here are some methods people use to keep track of their checking account balance:

- **Check register method**. Each transaction is recorded on a separate line of the register; a running balance is kept in the right-hand column.

- **Check stub method.** There are three checks to a page, with stubs on the left. When a check is written or a deposit is made, the information—as well as a running balance—is recorded on the stub.
- **Computer method.** Check and deposit information is entered into a computer, and the computer maintains the balance. Some people do this by creating their own spreadsheet (using a program like Excel®). Other people get a software program designed specifically for managing personal or business finances (like Quicken®, QuickBooks®, and Peachtree®).
- **Online banking method.** Some people who use online banking rely on the balance shown online. Doing this can create problems if the customer does not allow for "pending" checks (those that are to be paid at a later date); once those checks are paid, the balance will decrease and may result in a negative balance (and overdraft/bad check fees).

Throughout this chapter, we will use the check register method. The procedure used to keep track of a checking account balance is the same no matter what method is used: *the account balance is found by adding deposits and deducting checks*. Besides adjusting a checking account balance because of deposits and checks, banks may add or deduct funds for:

- **Bank fees.** Your bank may charge you check printing fees, monthly service fees, returned check fees, non-sufficient funds fees, and wire transfer fees.
- **Interest.** Some banks pay interest on checking accounts, based on the average daily balance.
- **Reverse entries for bad checks.** If you deposit someone else's check and his or her bank refuses to pay the check (usually because the account does not have sufficient funds), the check is returned to your bank unpaid and your account balance is reduced accordingly.
- **ATM and debit card transactions.** When you make an ATM withdrawal or use your debit card, money is taken from your account.
- **Electronic fund transfers.** Funds electronically transferred into your account (like your payroll check each pay period) are added to your account balance. Funds electronically transferred from your account (like your car payment each month or checks authorized via online banking) are subtracted from your account balance.
- **Errors in deposits.** If you prepare a deposit ticket with an incorrect total, your bank will make the correction and adjust your account balance accordingly.

Banks send a memo for some of the preceding items. The memo is referred to as a **debit memo** if the bank *reduces* the balance and as a **credit memo** if the bank *increases* the balance. Generally, banks do not send memos for monthly service fees, interest earned, ATM withdrawals, debit card transactions, and electronic fund transfers; we see these items on the monthly bank statement. Illustration 7-1 is a debit memo for check printing charges. *When we get a debit or credit memo, we should immediately make an entry in our checking account records to adjust the balance.*

Illustration 7-1 Debit Memo

Example 1 Bob opened a checking account. Here is a list of his transactions.

Oct. 1	Deposited $2,000 to open his account
Oct. 7	Wrote check 1001 to American Plaza for last 25 days Oct. rent; $403.25
Oct. 7	Wrote check 1002 to John Smith for survey equipment; $678
Oct. 7	Wrote check 1003 to York Office Supply for office supplies; $75.82
Oct. 8	Deposited money received from Jack Jones survey; $350
Oct. 12	Received debit memo (Illustration 7-1); $73.25
Oct. 14	Wrote check 1004 to DeSign Co for sign; $175
Oct. 31	Deposited money received from Steve Sims survey; $3,000
Oct. 31	Wrote check 1005 to U.S. Telephone for phone bill; $185
Nov. 1	Wrote check 1006 to American Plaza for Nov. rent; $500

Record these transactions in a check register. Show the account balance after each transaction. Use register headings, like the ones shown below.

Check Number	Date	Description of Transaction	(−) Payment/Debit	(+) Deposit/Credit	Balance

Check Number	Date	Description of Transaction	(−) Payment/Debit	(+) Deposit/Credit	Balance
	10-1	Open account		2,000.00	2,000.00
1001	10-7	American Plaza; 25 days Oct. rent	403.25		1,596.75
1002	10-7	John Smith; survey equipment	678.00		918.75
1003	10-7	York Office Supply; office supplies	75.82		842.93
	10-8	Jack Jones survey		350.00	1,192.93
	10-12	Debit memo; ck printing charges	73.25		1,119.68
1004	10-14	DeSign Co; sign	175.00		944.68
	10-31	Steve Sims survey		3,000.00	3,944.68
1005	10-31	U.S. Telephone; phone bill	185.00		3,759.68
1006	11-1	American Plaza; Nov. rent	500.00		3,259.68

> **TIP** balance goes down even if we don't record a transaction
>
> Don't make the mistake of forgetting to enter debit card transactions, ATM withdrawals, and electronic fund payments in your check register. If you do forget, your checking account balance will be less than what you think it is, opening the door for bounced checks, embarrassment, and extra fees. And don't forget to add electronic fund deposits so you know how much money is in your account.

b Reconciling the bank statement

Banks provide monthly summaries, known as **bank statements**, to checking account customers. Bank statements for businesses are generally for a *calendar-month*, while those for individuals may cover a monthly period *other than a calendar-month*. Bank statements include beginning balance; additions to the account, referred to as *credits* by the bank; deductions from the account, referred to as *debits* by the bank; and ending balance. Refer to Illustration 7-2, which is Bob's October 31 bank statement.

Illustration 7-2 Bank Statement

UTAH BANK & TRUST

Bob Green Engineering Company
1234 Anywhere Street
Yourtown, USA 54321

STATEMENT DATE
October 31, 20xx

ACCOUNT NUMBER	ACCOUNT TYPE	Y-T-D INTEREST	PREVIOUS BALANCE	DEPOSITS NO.	AMOUNT	REGULAR CHECKS NO.	AMOUNT	OTHER DEBITS NO.	AMOUNT	CURRENT BALANCE
12-34567-8	Check	6.13	0.00	3	2,356.13	3	1,139.07	1	73.25	1,143.81

DEPOSITS AND OTHER CREDITS TO NOW ACCOUNT

DESCRIPTION	DATE	AMOUNT	DESCRIPTION	DATE	AMOUNT
Deposit	10/01	2,000.00			
Deposit	10/07	350.00			
Interest	10/31	6.13			

REGULAR CHECKS

DATE	CHECK	AMOUNT	DATE	CHECK	AMOUNT	DATE	CHECK	AMOUNT	DATE	CHECK	AMOUNT
10/08	1001	403.25									
10/12	1002	678.00									
10/10	1003	57.82									

OTHER DEBITS

| 10/10 | Check printing charge | 73.25 |

Notice for Illustration 7-2, the previous balance is zero because the account was opened in October. When October deposits (totaling $2,356.13) are added and October checks (totaling $1,139.07) and other debits ($73.25) are deducted, the result is the October 31 bank balance of $1,143.81.

Bank tellers (those who receive deposits from customers) must balance their cash drawers at the end of each business day. Depending on how the bank records teller transactions, this can be time-consuming, so some banks close each day's work in mid-afternoon. If we make a deposit late in the afternoon, or on a weekend, it may be dated the following business day by the bank. Banks provide customers with a **deposit receipt**; the date of the deposit is indicated on the receipt. In Illustration 7-2, the date for each check is the date the check is paid by the bank, *not* the date of the check. Usually the checkbook balance does not agree with the bank statement balance. In Example 1, the checkbook balance after the final October entry (check 1005) is $3,759.68, while the bank statement balance in Illustration 7-2 is $1,143.81, a difference of $2,615.87! You may think Bob should immediately march into his bank saying, *You've cheated me!* But first, Bob should do a **bank reconciliation** to find out if there is a mistake, and if there is, who made it (the bank or Bob). Most banks provide a reconciliation form on the back of the bank statement.

Notice that the bank statement does not show the October 31 deposit; the deposit was apparently made late in the afternoon and dated the next business day. This deposit is referred to as an **outstanding deposit**, since it was not recorded on the bank's records during the statement period. Also, the bank statement does not show check numbers 1004 and 1005; these checks have not yet been presented for payment. Checks not paid by the bank as of the date of the bank statement are referred to as **outstanding checks**.

Reconciling a bank statement can be a bit tricky. To make it less painful, we can follow certain steps:

reconciling a bank statement

Step 1 Notice the date of the bank statement. Determine the checkbook balance *as of that date*. It is helpful to draw a line under this balance; we will compare everything *above* this line with what is on the bank statement. Write this balance on the *checkbook balance* side (the left side of the reconciliation form).

Step 2 Write the bank statement balance on the *bank statement* side (the right side).

If these two balances are not the same, continue.

Step 3 Make adjustments to the *checkbook balance* side, if necessary, by entering things that appear on the bank statement that are not recorded in the checking account records, such as interest earned (this amount will be added) and bank charges (this amount will be deducted).

Step 4 Make adjustments to the *bank statement* side by entering things that appear in the checking account records (*above* the hand-drawn line from Step 1) that do not appear on the bank statement, such as outstanding deposits (these will be added) and outstanding checks (these will be deducted). *Note*: Remember to consider outstanding checks from the previous reconciliation.

If the adjusted balances are not the same, continue.

Step 5 Check for arithmetic errors on the reconciliation form.

Step 6 Review the bank statement to make sure all items that appear on the bank statement are either entered in the checking account records or are shown as adjustments in Step 3.

Step 7 Check for arithmetic errors in your checking account records.

Step 8 Compare check amounts and deposit amounts with those shown on the bank statement. If the bank made an error, make an adjustment on the *bank statement* side and request that the bank make a correction. If you made an error, make an adjustment on the *checkbook balance* side; for example, you may have forgotten to record a check or deposit, or you may have recorded an amount incorrectly.

TIP — who didn't know?

To decide which balance (the checkbook or the bank) gets adjusted, ask, *Who didn't know?* For example, if the bank didn't know about a deposit (outstanding deposit), the bank statement side should be adjusted. If the checking account records didn't know about a service charge, the checkbook side should be adjusted. *Add* the adjustments that would have increased the balance, and *subtract* those that would have decreased the balance.

Example 2 Refer to Example 1 (Bob's check register) and Illustration 7-2 (bank statement). Help Bob prepare a bank reconciliation. Assume that the amounts on the bank statement are correct.

Reconciliation Period Ending October 31, 20xx

CHECKBOOK BALANCE	
1. Ending balance in your check register	$3,759.68
2. Add:	
October interest	6.13
ck 1003 error	18.00
3. Subtotal	$3,783.81
4. Subtract:	
5. TOTAL	$3,783.81

BANK STATEMENT	
1. Ending balance on bank statement	$1,143.81
2. Add: Outstanding deposits	
October 31	3,000.00
3. Subtotal	$4,143.81
4. Subtract:	
ck 1004	175.00
ck 1005	185.00
5. TOTAL	$3,783.81

These two totals are the same

Notes on the left side of reconciliation
- Bob's checking account balance after the last entry in October is $3,759.68; the October 31 date is used because that is the bank statement date.
- October interest of $6.13 is shown on the bank statement but is not yet entered in Bob's October records. If it had been entered, Bob's balance would have been $6.13 more.
- Check 1003 was recorded as $75.82 in Bob's records but was actually written for $57.82. The error was not discovered until the bank statement arrived. If the check had been properly recorded, Bob's checkbook balance would be $18 more.

Notes on the right side of reconciliation
- Bob deposited $3,000 on October 31 but apparently too late in the day to be entered on that day's bank records. If the bank had shown the deposit during October, the bank balance would be $3,000 more.
- Checks 1004 for $175 and 1005 for $185 did not reach the bank for payment during October. If they had, the bank balance would be less.

In Example 2, the adjusted balances ($3,783.81) are the same, so the reconciliation is complete. We now know that Bob's records and the bank's records are accurate (through October 31, at least). Good thing Bob didn't storm into the bank accusing them of cheating him!

Some banks provide a reconciliation form that resembles only the *bank statement* side. These banks assume the customer will adjust his or her checking account balance (because of interest earned, bank charges, etc.) before completing the reconciliation form.

Because doing a bank reconciliation requires some concentration, many people don't take the time to do one. By not doing bank reconciliations, errors (our own and those of the bank) will not be caught.

C Adjusting a checking account balance after the reconciliation

Once a reconciliation is complete, there may be follow-up work to do.

follow-up to the reconciliation
Step 1 Verify that outstanding deposits have now been credited to the account.
Step 2 If a check has been outstanding for too long, check the status; a replacement check might be necessary.
Step 3 Adjustments on the checkbook balance side of the reconciliation form need to be entered in the checkbook records.

Example 3 Refer to Bob's bank reconciliation of Example 2. What items need to done as a follow-up to the reconciliation?

Step 1 (review outstanding deposits): Bob should determine whether the October 31 deposit ($3,000) has been credited to his account. He can do this by inspecting his deposit receipt (it will have a *November* date) or calling his bank.

Step 2 (review outstanding checks): Check 1004 was written quite a while ago (October 14). Bob should check the status.

Step 3 (enter adjustments): There are two adjustments on the left side of the reconciliation form. These must be entered in the check register: October interest ($6.13) must be added to the balance, and $18 must be added to the balance to correct the error in recording check 1003.

If Bob forgets to make the adjustments (from Step 3), his checkbook balance will be wrong and Bob will go through a lot of grief when he does the next bank reconciliation! The adjustments could be made after the last entry (check 1006, dated November 1). Instead, Bob could have left space after the last entry for that bank statement period (between checks 1005 and 1006). Then, the October interest ($6.13) and correction to check 1003 ($18) could be made in *October's* section of the register, ahead of check 1006; remember, however, to change the balances to reflect the entries.

Some people use computer software to do a bank reconciliation. Even with computers, however, it is important to understand how to do a reconciliation and the follow-up stuff manually.

Now, let's *check* our understanding of checking accounts by doing the U-Try-It exercises.

U-Try-It (Unit 7.1)

1. Assume you open a checking account on September 5 by depositing $1,700. You wrote checks and made deposits as shown in the check register. Determine the balance after each transaction.

Check Number	Date	Description of Transaction	(-) Payment/Debit	(+) Deposit/Credit	Balance
	9-5	Open account		1,700.00	
101	9-7	ABC Grocery	275.00		
102	9-12	Car Specialists; car repair	283.00		
	9-15	Paycheck		2,800.00	
103	9-15	Homestead Mortgage; mortgage payment	958.00		
104	9-23	ABC Grocery	173.25		
105	9-30	Electricity bill	98.32		

2. Refer to the bank statement. Confirm the current balance of $2,968.60.

BANK STATEMENT								Statement Date:	September 25, 20xx
Previous Balance:	$0.00	Total Deposits:	$4,507.85	Total Checks:	$1,516.00	Other Debits:	$23.25	Current Balance:	$2,968.60

Deposits and other credits:
    Deposit   9-5   1,700.00
    Deposit   9-13   2,800.00
    Interest   9-25   7.85
Checks:
    101   9-9   275.00
    102   9-13   283.00
    103   9-19   958.00
Other debits:
    Ck printing   23.25

3. Refer to Problems 1 and 2. Complete a bank reconciliation.

Reconciliation Period Ending _____

CHECKBOOK BALANCE	
1. Ending balance in your check register	
2. Add:	
3. Subtotal	
4. Subtract:	
5. **TOTAL**	

BANK STATEMENT	
1. Ending balance on bank statement	
2. Add: Outstanding deposits	
3. Subtotal	
4. Subtract: Outstanding checks	
5. **TOTAL**	

4. What follow-up items, if any, need to be completed? _____

Answers: (If you have a different answer, check the solution in Appendix A.)
1. Ending balance: $2,712.43 **2.** $2,968.60 **3.** Totals: $2,795.35 **4.** Add Sep. interest ($7.85); subtract check printing charges ($23.25)

Chapter in a Nutshell

Objectives | **Examples**

Unit 7.1 Checking account balance

a Keeping track of a checking account balance

Check Number	Date	Description of Transaction	(−) Payment/Debit	(+) Deposit/Credit	Balance
	3-31	Previous balance			1,544.32
182	4-2	Rent	825.00		719.32
	4-15	Paycheck		1,700.00	2,419.32
183	4-23	Groceries	253.00		2,166.32
184	4-29	Electric bill	82.33		2,083.99

b Reconciling the bank statement

BANK STATEMENT Statement Date: April 25, 20xx

Previous Balance: $1,544.32 | Total Deposits: $1,700.00 | Total Checks: $825.00 | Other Debits: $7.25 | Current Balance: $2,412.07

Deposits and other credits:
    Deposit   4-15   1,700.00
Checks:
    182   4-5   825.00
Other debits:
    Monthly fee   7.25

Reconciliation Period Ending __April 25, 20xx__

CHECKBOOK BALANCE	
1. Ending balance in your check register	$2,166.32
2. Add:	
3. Subtotal	$2,166.32
4. Subtract: Monthly fee	7.25
5. **TOTAL**	**$2,159.07**

BANK STATEMENT	
1. Ending balance on bank statement	$2,412.07
2. Add: Outstanding deposits	
3. Subtotal	$2,412.07
4. Subtract: Outstanding checks ck 183	253.00
5. **TOTAL**	**$2,159.07**

Chapter in a Nutshell (concluded)

Objectives	Examples
C Adjusting a checking account balance after the reconciliation	**Step 1** (review outstanding deposits): There are none. **Step 2** (review outstanding checks): Check 183 was written fairly recently (Apr. 23), so no need to check on status. **Step 3** (enter adjustments): The only item on left side of reconciliation form is the $7.25 monthly fee; subtract this in the check register.

Enrichment Topics

The following Enrichment Topic, which goes a bit beyond what is in the text, is available for this chapter:

    Checks

If your Instructor doesn't cover this topic in class and you would like to dig in deeper on your own, please send a request to *studentsupport@olympuspub.com*.

Think

1. What things can you do to avoid writing a bad check? If you do write a bad check, what are the repercussions?
2. What are some things you should consider before opening a checking account?
3. Name some situations in which the bank statement balance is greater than the checkbook balance. Name some situations in which the bank statement balance is less than the checkbook balance.
4. If you reverse two adjacent digits in your check register, your register balance will be off by a number divisible by 9. Give an example, and show that the difference in the balance is divisible by 9.
5. Suppose you are doing a bank reconciliation and the adjusted balance for the left side of the reconciliation (checkbook balance side) is $84 more than the adjusted balance for the right side. To help find the error, you divide the $84 difference by 2, getting $42. You notice a check written for $42. What error did you likely make?

Explore

1. Review the check register from Example 1 of Unit 7.1. Create a similar check register on a spreadsheet, with column headings in Columns A through F. Create formulas for column F that will show the checking account balance after a check or deposit is made. *Tip:* You can copy and paste formulas from cell to cell, rather than retyping. Use 2 decimal places for values in columns D through F. Save the file (perhaps as *Check Register*). Then test your spreadsheet by entering the checks and deposits from Example 1 of Unit 7.1.

Apply

1. **The Checking Account Process.** Submit the following checking account items. You can use your own checking account or that of a friend or relative. To maintain confidentiality, black out the name and account number on all documents.
    A. Copy of the most recent bank statement.
    B. Copy of the check stubs, check register, or computer printout, showing all checking account transactions for the period of time covered by the bank statement.
    C. Copies of all debit and credit memos issued by the bank during the period of time covered by the bank statement.
    D. The bank reconciliation for the *previous* period.
    E. A bank reconciliation completed by you for the *current* period.

   Highlight (in color) the items entered in the checking account records as a follow-up to the bank reconciliation.

2. **Shopping for a Checking Account.** Contact a local bank and credit union and ask for their help with this school project. Determine what kinds of checking accounts are available. For each institution, write a report, answering the following questions for each type of account.
    A. What size of checks are available? Do checks have duplicate copies?
    B. Are (1) stubs or (2) registers provided for recording transactions?
    C. What are the check-printing fees?
    D. Is a minimum balance required for the account? If so, how much?
    E. Is interest paid? If so, how is the amount calculated?
    F. What kinds of fees are charged? Are the fees based on the number of checks written or on something else?
    G. Is overdraft protection automatically provided? What are overdraft fees?
    H. How often are bank statements provided? Are they mailed? Provided on-line?
    I. Are checks and deposit tickets returned with the bank statement?
    J. Is your account insured? If so, by what agency? How good is the insurance?

   Write a concluding paragraph stating which type of account best meets your needs and why.

Chapter Review Problems

Unit 7.1 Checking account balance

1. A debit memo decreases your account balance. (T or F)

For Problems 2–5, indicate whether you will likely (a) receive a debit memo, (b) receive a credit memo, or (c) find out only when the bank statement is received.

2. Your monthly service charge is $10.
3. You deposited a customer's check. Your customer's bank returned the check unpaid to your bank.
4. Your account earned monthly interest of $18.22.
5. You prepared a deposit, indicating a total of $162.38. The bank determined that the correct amount of the deposit was $168.38.
6. A customer's bank statement balance at the end of June was $2,450. During July, the bank received deposits totaling $18,422 and paid checks totaling $17,948. Assuming there were no other charges or credits, calculate the bank statement balance at the end of July.
7. A deposit taken to your bank on July 31 will, for sure, be credited to your account on July 31. (T or F)
8. You take a deposit to the bank on July 31 and get a deposit receipt dated August 1. Assuming bank statements are provided for each calendar month, will the deposit appear on the **(a)** July or **(b)** August bank statement?

For Problems 9–19, indicate by each where they appear on your September 30 bank reconciliation. Here are the choices:

   (C+) Add to checkbook balance side   (B+) Add to bank balance side
   (C-) Subtract from checkbook balance side (B-) Subtract from bank balance side
                (None) No adjustment necessary

9. Check 474 was written on September 28 and was outstanding on September 30.

10. A service charge appeared on your September bank statement.

11. The bank withdraws $225 each month to make your car payment, but you forgot to record the September withdrawal in your checkbook.

12. You made a $100 cash withdrawal on September 9 but forgot to enter the transaction in your checkbook.

13. You incorrectly recorded a deposit as $875. The bank sent a credit memo for $50 because the deposit was determined to be $925. You received the memo on September 23 and immediately adjusted your checking account balance to reflect the additional $50.

14. A deposit prepared on August 31 appeared on the September bank statement.

15. Check 457 was written on August 24 and was still outstanding on September 30.

16. A deposit prepared on September 30 did not appear on the September bank statement.

17. A debit memo, together with a customer's returned check, was mailed to you on September 29 by the bank but was not entered in your checkbook records.

18. Interest earned on the account appeared on the September bank statement.

19. Check 424 was recorded incorrectly as $137 in the checkbook register but appeared correctly on the bank statement as $173.

20. Keystone Company receives a bank statement dated June 30 that shows a balance of $13,556.25. Keystone's checkbook balance as of June 30 is $12,434.74. The bank has not processed check 583 for $220 or check 585 for $1,851. A $900 deposit made on June 30 does not appear on the bank statement. The bank statement shows a few items that Keystone is unaware of: check printing charges of $82 and interest earned of $12.51. Keystone recorded check 579 incorrectly as $220; the bank statement shows the check correctly as $200. Find the reconciled balance by completing a bank reconciliation.

Reconciliation Period Ending _____

CHECKBOOK BALANCE	
1. Ending balance in your check register	
2. Add:	
3. Subtotal	
4. Subtract:	
5. **TOTAL**	

BANK STATEMENT	
1. Ending balance on bank statement	
2. Add: Outstanding deposits	
3. Subtotal	
4. Subtract: Outstanding checks	
5. **TOTAL**	

21. Capital Cleaners receives a bank statement dated October 31 that shows a balance of $18,443.18. Capital's checkbook balance as of October 31 is $18,837.00. The following checks have not cleared the bank: check 844 for $180 and check 863 for $778. A $1,400 deposit made on October 31 does not appear on the bank statement. The bank statement shows interest earned of $32.18. Capital received a debit memo dated October 18 for $11 but forgot to record the amount in the checking account. Capital recorded check 858 incorrectly as $952; the bank processed the check correctly during October as $925. Find the reconciled balance by completing a bank reconciliation.

Reconciliation Period Ending _____

CHECKBOOK BALANCE	
1. Ending balance in your check register	
2. Add:	
3. Subtotal	
4. Subtract:	
5. **TOTAL**	

BANK STATEMENT	
1. Ending balance on bank statement	
2. Add: Outstanding deposits	
3. Subtotal	
4. Subtract: Outstanding checks	
5. **TOTAL**	

Challenge problems

For Problems 22–26, we will keep track of a checking account balance.

22. Assume you open a checking account on October 5 by depositing $700. You wrote checks and made deposits as shown in the check register. Determine the balance after each transaction.

Check Number	Date	Description of Transaction	(−) Payment/Debit	(+) Deposit/Credit	Balance
	10-5	Open account		700.00	
101	10-8	Friendly Grocery	150.00		
102	10-14	The Car Doctor; car repair	176.00		
	10-15	Paycheck		1,800.00	
103	10-15	Security Mortgage Co; mortgage payment	1,322.00		
104	10-29	Friendly Grocery	327.25		
	10-31	Paycheck		1,800.00	

23. Refer to the bank statement. Confirm the current balance of $843.57 by **(a)** adding deposits to the previous balance and **(b)** subtracting checks and other debits.

BANK STATEMENT Statement Date: October 31, 20xx

| Previous Balance: $0.00 | Total Deposits: $2,511.32 | Total Checks: $1,639.00 | Other Debits: $28.75 | Current Balance: $843.57 |

Deposits and other credits:
- Deposit   10-5   700.00
- Deposit   10-15   1,800.00
- Interest 10-31   11.32

Checks:
- 101   10-9   150.00
- 102   10-17   167.00
- 103   10-19   1,322.00

Other debits:
- Ck printing   28.75

24. Refer to Problems 22 and 23. Complete a bank reconciliation. If there are any differences between amounts on the check register and those on the bank statement, assume that the amounts on the bank statement are correct.

Reconciliation Period Ending _____

CHECKBOOK BALANCE	
1. Ending balance in your check register	
2. Add:	
3. Subtotal	
4. Subtract:	
5. **TOTAL**	

BANK STATEMENT	
1. Ending balance on bank statement	
2. Add: Outstanding deposits	
3. Subtotal	
4. Subtract: Outstanding checks	
5. **TOTAL**	

25. What follow-up items, if any, need to be completed?

26. What will your checking account balance be after you enter the items in Problem 25?

Practice Test

1. Suppose you incorrectly recorded a deposit as $465. The bank discovered the correct amount was $455. Will the bank send (a) a debit memo or (b) a credit memo to inform you of the error?

2. Your checking account balance, after completing a July 31 bank reconciliation, is $482.33. During August you made deposits of $700, $145.45, and $1,200. You wrote checks of $228, $145.22, $950, and $45. What is your August 31 checkbook balance?

3. Pinnacle Company receives a bank statement dated April 30 that shows a balance of $5,466.35. Pinnacle's checkbook balance, as of April 30, is $5,545.90. The bank has not processed check 928 for $320 or check 930 for $510. A $650 deposit made on April 30 does not appear on the bank statement. The bank statement shows a few items that Pinnacle is unaware of: check printing charges of $78 and interest earned of $18.45. Pinnacle forgot to record a $200 cash withdrawal made on April 22. Find the reconciled balance by completing the bank reconciliation.

   Reconciliation Period Ending _____

CHECKBOOK BALANCE	
1. Ending balance in your check register	
2. Add:	
3. Subtotal	
4. Subtract:	
5. TOTAL	

BANK STATEMENT	
1. Ending balance on bank statement	
2. Add: Outstanding deposits	
3. Subtotal	
4. Subtract: Outstanding checks	
5. TOTAL	

4. You made an addition error in your check register. You will most likely never discover the error, even if you complete a bank reconciliation. (T or F)

5. A bank reconciliation is shown. Upon completion of the bank reconciliation, what needs to be entered in your checking account records?

Checkbook balance		Bank statement	
Checkbook balance	$1,152.72	Bank statement balance	$1,458.69
Add: March interest	+ 9.22	Add:	+ 0.00
Subtotal	$1,161.94	Subtotal	$1,458.69
Subtract: Ck printing	− 48.25	Subtract: Ck 121	− 345.00
Total	$1,113.69	Total	$1,113.69

FUN CORNER

Is School Worth It?

In the middle of a school term, you may wonder whether all of this studying is worth it. Maybe this will help. Here is the average (median) annual earnings, by educational level.

Not a high school graduate	$20,241
High school graduate	$30,627
Some college, no degree	$32,295
Associates degree	$39,771
Bachelor's degree	$56,665
Master's degree	$73,738
Doctorate	$103,054

Source: Bureau of the Census, U.S. Dept of Commerce, 2012

Quotable Quip

I love work. It fascinates me.
I can sit and watch it for hours.
– Author unknown

Quotable Quip

The longer the title, the less important the job.
– George McGovern,
U.S. Presidential candidate

Bring Home the Bacon

This saying refers to bringing home a paycheck. Are you curious where the saying comes from? Well, here goes, anyway.

The saying goes back to a custom that was recorded as early as 1362 in Dunmow, England, in which a side of bacon was awarded annually to any married couple who swore they had lived harmoniously during the past year.

Where Does Social Security Money Go?

by Dave Barry

Many Americans believe that Social Security works this way: The government takes money out of your paycheck, keeps it for you in a safe place such as a giant federal mattress, then, when you retire, starts giving it back to you. If that's how you think it works, then let me quote the famous French economist Francois Quesnay (1694–1774): "Ding Dong, you're wrong."

What actually happens is, the government takes your money out of your paycheck and immediately gives it to a retired person (in your particular case, this person is Mrs. Edwina P. Loogersnapper of Yeasting Springs, Vermont; she says 'hi').

What is Your Degree Worth?

Here are a few average starting salaries for specific bachelor of science (B.S.) degrees, 2015.

Petroleum Engineering	$101,000
Chemical Engineering	$69,500
Computer Science	$69,100
Nuclear Engineering	$68,200
Aeronautical Engineering	$65,100
Actuarial Mathematics	$58,800
Statistics	$55,200
Accounting and Finance	$51,200
Business and Marketing	$44,800

Source: www.payscale.com

"How come my bills are always plus taxes and my paycheck is always minus taxes?"

Payroll

8

Most businesses hire people to help operate the business. A person who is employed is called an **employee,** while the business or owner is referred to as an **employer.** Employees are paid in a variety of ways. Some are paid by the hour (wage), some by the pay period (salary), some by production (piecework), and others by sales volume (commission).

Many employees, upon receiving their first paycheck, say "Where is the rest of my pay?" Well, it went to pay taxes. Employers are also required to pay taxes on wages. Nobody escapes the "tax man." In this chapter, we will focus on calculating the amount employees earn and the resulting taxes.

Unit Objectives

Unit 8.1 Gross pay: Wages and incentive plans
- **a** Calculating gross pay from wages
- **b** Comparing gross pay for different pay periods
- **c** Calculating gross pay from piecework
- **d** Calculating gross pay from commissions

Unit 8.2 Payroll deductions for employees
- **a** Calculating FICA withholding
- **b** Calculating federal income tax withholding
- **c** Calculating net pay

Unit 8.3 Employer taxes and settling up with the IRS
- **a** Calculating payroll taxes for an employer
- **b** Calculating self-employment FICA tax
- **c** Determining overpayment or underpayment to the IRS

Unit 8.1 Gross pay: Wages and incentive plans

Gross pay, or **gross earnings,** is the total amount of compensation received by an employee before any deductions are made. Employees may be paid (a) a wage, (b) a salary, (c) piecework, or (d) a commission. We will review these different methods one at a time.

a Calculating gross pay from wages

Some companies use time clocks to keep track of employees' hours.

The federal **Fair Labor Standards Act** prescribes a minimum hourly wage and overtime pay for employees of companies covered by the law.

> ### Fair Labor Standards Act
>
> As of the writing of this text, the minimum hourly wage is $7.25. Employees working for an hourly rate are entitled to time and a half for hours over their regular 40-hour week. Some states have minimum wage and overtime pay requirements that exceed those of the Fair Labor Standards Act, and some counties and cities have requirements that exceed those of their states. Many employees are exempt from this law, including many managers and seasonal workers.

> ### calculating gross pay: hourly wage
>
> **Step 1** Multiply the first 40 hours by the regular hourly rate.
> **Step 2** Multiply the overtime hours by the overtime rate.
> **Step 3** Add the results of Steps 1 and 2.

Example 1 You are paid weekly at a rate of $8.75 per hour. Calculate your gross pay for the week, assuming you worked 47.25 hours and you receive time and a half after the first 40 hours.

Overtime hours: 47.25 total hours - 40 regular hours = 7.25 overtime hours
Overtime rate: $8.75 regular rate × 1.5 = $13.125 (*Note:* we don't round this amount.)

Pay for regular hours: 40 hours × $8.75	$350.00
Pay for overtime hours: 7.25 hours × $13.125	+ 95.16
Total gross pay for week	$445.16

Some companies provide overtime pay that is superior to that required by the Fair Labor Standards Act. Some pay **double time** for Sundays and holidays. Some employers pay overtime when an employee works more than 8 hours in a single day, even if the hours per week do not exceed 40. Some employers pay overtime pay for working less desirable hours, such as a **swing shift** (4:00 P.M. to midnight) or a **graveyard shift** (midnight to 8:00 A.M.).

b Comparing gross pay for different pay periods

Some employees are paid a **salary,** which is a certain dollar amount per pay period rather than a certain dollar amount per hour. Common pay periods are *weekly, biweekly* (every second week, such as every other Friday), *semimonthly* (twice a month, such as on the 1st and 16th of each month), and *monthly.* Some employees prefer to get paid more often because it spreads their pay more evenly; others prefer to get paid less often so that they won't be tempted to spend money on unnecessary items (now, who would ever do that?). In the next example, we will compare pay for different pay periods.

> **TIP** — **how many pay periods in a year?**
>
> If we are paid monthly, we will receive 12 paychecks in a year. If we are paid semimonthly (twice a month), we will receive 24 paychecks in a year. A biweekly pay period (once every two weeks) is *not* the same as a semimonthly pay period. To find the number of biweekly pay periods in a year, we divide the number of days in a year (365) by the number of days in each pay period (14), getting about 26.07 pay periods. (*Note:* For most years, we would receive 26 paychecks, but for some years we would receive 27 paychecks; the *average* number of paychecks per year over a long period of time is 26.07.) To find the number of weekly pay periods in a year, we divide 365 by 7, getting about 52.14 pay periods. (*Note:* This is the *average* number of paychecks per year over a long period of time.)
>
> | If paid | Pay periods per year |
> |---|---|
> | Monthly | 12 |
> | Semimonthly | 24 |
> | Biweekly | 26.07 |
> | Weekly | 52.14 |

Example 2   Suppose you just graduated from college with your accounting degree. Accounting firms are knocking down your door to hire you. You have five offers: Company A will pay you $3,700 a month; Company B, $1,830 semimonthly; Company C, $1,700 biweekly; Company D, $860 a week; and Company E, $21 per hour. Which company is offering the greatest gross pay?

A: $3,700 a month × 12 months $44,400.00
B: $1,830 semimonthly × 24 semimonthly pay periods $43,920.00
C: $1,700 biweekly × 26.07 biweekly pay periods $44,319.00
D: $860 a week × 52.14 weeks $44,840.40
E: $21 per hour × 40 hours per week × 52.14 weeks per year $43,797.60

Company D has the greatest gross pay.

Example 2 is not meant to infer that gross pay is the only consideration in selecting a job. Besides the emotional concerns of job environment, satisfaction, and working hours, for example, there are lots of financial considerations, including: medical coverage, retirement plan benefits, vacation pay, sick pay, and opportunity for advancement. The approach of Example 2 is a good starting place in evaluating job opportunities.

C Calculating gross pay from piecework

Some companies, such as manufacturers, pay employees on the basis of how much each employee produces. This is known as a **piecework rate.**

> **gross pay from piecework**
>
> Gross pay = Number of units produced × Rate per unit

Example 3   Bob Gant sews canvas tents. He is paid $70 per tent. What is Bob's gross pay for a 2-week period, based on sewing 17 tents?

Gross pay = Number of units produced × Rate per unit = 17 × $70 = **$1,190**

In some cases, employees are paid a base salary plus a piecework rate.

Unit 8.1 Gross pay: Wages and incentive plans 159

Example 4 Margaret Harlin sews insignias on shirts. She is paid $7.00 per hour plus 65¢ per insignia. During the last week, she worked 40 hours and completed 103 insignias. Calculate her gross pay.

Base salary: 40 hours × $7	$280.00
Piecework: 103 insignias × $0.65	+ 66.95
Total gross pay	$346.95

Another variation of the piecework rate is the **differential piece rate,** in which the rate per item increases as production increases.

Example 5 Slicer, Inc., pays employees a weekly piecework rate for assembling paper cutters:

The first 100:	$2.10 per paper cutter
The next 50:	$2.50 per paper cutter
Thereafter:	$2.75 per paper cutter

Brad Jones assembled 162 paper cutters during the week. Calculate his gross pay.

100 × $2.10	$210.00
50 × $2.50	125.00
+12 × $2.75	+ 33.00
162	$368.00

d Calculating gross pay from commissions

Piecework is based on production. **Commissions** are similar but are based on sales. Some commissions are based on a fixed amount per item sold. Most, however, are figured as a percent of the dollar amount of sales. Some salespeople receive a **draw** (often called an **advance**); a draw is deducted from commission payments.

Example 6 Phil Berry works in a shoe store and receives a $600 semimonthly draw. Phil is paid a 7% commission on net sales (net sales are total sales less sales returns). During August, Phil sold $34,124 of merchandise; his share of sales returns was $819. Calculate Phil's final commission payment for August.

Net sales: $34,124 - $819 = $33,305

Commission: $33,305 × 7%	$2,331.35
Less draw: 2 draws × $600	-1,200.00
Commission still due	$1,131.35

You may wonder what happens if an employee's draws exceed the commission. Some businesses pay the employee the greater of the two, while others require the employee to reimburse the employer if the draws exceed the commission.

Some companies pay salespeople a salary (not a draw) plus a commission. And some companies use a **sliding scale** (or **variable commission**) plan, in which the commission rate increases as sales volume increases.

That concludes this unit. Now let's do the U-Try-It exercises.

U-Try-It (Unit 8.1)

1. You are paid weekly at a rate of $9.25 per hour. Calculate your gross pay for the week, assuming you worked 46.5 hours and you are paid time and a half for overtime hours.
2. You have five job offers: $3,000 a month, $1,450 semimonthly, $1,375 biweekly, $700 a week, and $17 per hour. Which offer results in the greatest gross pay?
3. Chairs-To-Stow pays employees $6 per hour plus the following piecework rate for assembling folding chairs: 30¢ per chair for the first 400, 40¢ per chair for the next 200, and 50¢ per chair thereafter. During the week, Ian McGregor worked 38 hours and assembled 944 chairs. Calculate his gross pay.

4. Suzie Que is a salesperson for a computer store. She is paid a semimonthly salary of $600 plus 3% of monthly net sales over $60,000. Suzie's sales during October were $97,300. Her share of returns was $5,800. Determine Suzie's gross pay for October.

Answers: (If you have a different answer, check the solution in Appendix A.)
1. $460.19   2. Weekly ($36,498)   3. $600   4. $2,145

Unit 8.2 Payroll deductions for employees

When employees receive paychecks, certain items are deducted from gross pay. We'll start out by discussing FICA withholdings.

a Calculating FICA withholding

The **Federal Insurance Contributions Act (FICA)** provides old-age benefits, Medicare, and other forms of social insurance. For 2015, FICA tax consists of: (1) Social Security tax, (2) Medicare tax, and (3) Additional Medicare tax. Employers are required to withhold tax from employees' pay, based on rates and limits in the following table. For Social Security tax and Medicare tax, the amounts withheld are periodically remitted by the employer to the Internal Revenue Service, and that is the end of the story.

For Additional Medicare tax, the story is a bit more complicated. The actual tax is *not determined until the employee files a tax return*, and the tax is calculated *per household*: 0.9% of combined household earned income that exceeds a certain threshold, outlined below. Employers are required to withhold based on employee earnings, *regardless of household earned income or filing status*. The amount of Additional Medicare tax that employers must withhold is 0.9% of all annual wages over $200,000; taxpayers are given credit for amounts withheld by employers in computing their overall tax liability or refund.

2015 FICA rates

Tax	Employers must withhold
Social Security	6.2% on the first $118,500 of annual wages
Medicare	1.45% on all wages (no limit)
Additional Medicare	0.9% on all wages over $200,000

Filing Status	Actual Additional Medicare tax
Married filing joint	0.9% of combined earned income over $250,000
Married filing separately	0.9% of earned income over $125,000
All others (including single)	0.9% of earned income over $200,000

Note: FICA rates and dollar limits change from year to year; for up-to-date amounts, visit www.irs.gov.

Example 1 David Fairbanks had 2015 wages of $240,000. His wife, Ellen, had 2015 wages of $32,000. Determine the amount each of their employers withholds for Social Security tax, Medicare tax, and Additional Medicare tax. Then, assuming they file their income tax return jointly, calculate the actual Additional Medicare tax.

	David	**Ellen**
Social Security tax	$118,500 × 6.2% = **$7,347**	$32,000 × 6.2% = **$1,984**
Medicare tax	$240,000 × 1.45% = **$3,480**	$32,000 × 1.45% = **$464**
Additional Medicare tax	$40,000 × 0.9% = **$360**	None (because below $200,000)

Actual Additional Medicare tax:

Household earned income: $240,000 + $32,000 = $272,000
Amount subject to Additional Medicare tax: $272,000 − $250,000 (threshold) = $22,000
Tax: $22,000 × 0.9% = $198

Their actual Additional Medicare tax is $198; they will get credit for the $360 withheld by David's employer in computing their tax liability or refund.

Unit 8.2 Payroll deductions for employees   161

In the upcoming examples, we will examine the payroll of Creative Architecture Company. They have three employees. Toni Nilson, an architect, is one of the employees.

Example 2 — Toni Nilson is an architect working for Creative Architecture Company. Her gross pay for the last week of December 2015 is $1,375. Her calendar-year gross pay *prior* to this pay period is $70,125. Based on the FICA rates shown above, calculate the amount Creative should withhold from her paycheck for FICA tax.

Social Security tax: $1,375 × 6.2%	$ 85.25
Medicare tax: $1,375 × 1.45%	19.94
Additional Medicare tax: None (wages less than $200,000)	+ 0.00
Total FICA tax withheld from Toni's pay	**$105.19**

ⓑ Calculating federal income tax withholding

Federal income tax, like FICA tax, is collected on a "pay-as-you-go" basis. Employers are required to withhold federal income tax from employees' pay and periodically remit the money to the IRS. *The amount withheld is applied against the actual tax liability.*

You may wonder how an employer determines how much to withhold. Here's how it works. Employers require employees to complete a **Form W-4 (Employee's Withholding Allowance Certificate)** stating the number of **withholding allowances** (exemptions) the employee claims. Toni's W-4 is shown as Illustration 8-1. Determining the number of allowances can be simple in many cases but can be somewhat complex for married couples when both spouses work, for a taxpayer who holds more than one job at a time, for a taxpayer who has nonwage income (such as interest income or self-employment income) or when a job is seasonal. A worksheet, which accompanies Form W-4, helps determine the proper number of allowances.

> **TIP — how many exemptions should we claim on Form W-4?**
>
> Remember, the number of exemptions claimed on Form W-4 does not affect actual federal income tax liability, only the amount of federal income tax withheld by an employer. Each allowance claimed on Form W-4 lowers the amount withheld. Many people prefer to have a little extra withheld from their pay so that they can get a tax refund; this is accomplished by claiming fewer exemptions on Form W-4 than they are entitled to on the tax return or by requesting the employer withhold an additional amount (see line 6, Form W-4). The drawback of this is that the government has use of the money, and guess what: they pay no interest. While there is some flexibility in the number of allowances claimed on Form W-4, *exemptions on an income tax return must be accurate*.

Illustration 8-1 Form W-4

162 Chapter 8 Payroll

Illustration 8-2 Percentage Method (2015), Part 1

Payroll Period	One Withholding Allowance
Weekly	$ 76.90
Biweekly	153.80
Semimonthly	166.70
Monthly	333.30

Based on Form W-4, employers determine how much federal income tax to withhold. The two most popular methods are the wage-bracket method and the percentage method. With the **wage-bracket method**, we find the table for the appropriate pay period (weekly, bi-weekly, semi-monthly, monthly, etc.) and marital status (single or married), and then find the amount to withhold depending on the gross pay. Up-to-date wage-bracket tables can be found in IRS Publication 15, Circular E (on **www.irs.gov**). Because the wage-bracket tables are so lengthy and are not used by most large employers, we will rely on the percentage method.

The **percentage method** is well-suited for companies with computerized payrolls. This method requires the use of two tables. The first table is shown as Illustration 8-2. Then, based on the result of using that table, we use a second set of tables, shown as Illustration 8-3.

Illustration 8-3 Percentage Method (2015), Part 2

Percentage Method Tables for Income Tax Withholding
(For Wages Paid in 2015)

TABLE 1—WEEKLY Payroll Period

(a) SINGLE person (including head of household)—
If the amount of wages (after subtracting withholding allowances) is:
Not over $44 . . . . $0

Over—	But not over—	The amount of income tax to withhold is:	of excess over—
$44	—$222	$0.00 plus 10%	—$44
$222	—$764	$17.80 plus 15%	—$222
$764	—$1,789	$99.10 plus 25%	—$764
$1,789	—$3,685	$355.35 plus 28%	—$1,789
$3,685	—$7,958	$886.23 plus 33%	—$3,685
$7,958	—$7,990	$2,296.32 plus 35%	—$7,958
$7,990		$2,307.52 plus 39.6%	—$7,990

(b) MARRIED person—
If the amount of wages (after subtracting withholding allowances) is:
Not over $165 . . . . $0

Over—	But not over—	The amount of income tax to withhold is:	of excess over—
$165	—$520	$0.00 plus 10%	—$165
$520	—$1,606	$35.50 plus 15%	—$520
$1,606	—$3,073	$198.40 plus 25%	—$1,606
$3,073	—$4,597	$565.15 plus 28%	—$3,073
$4,597	—$8,079	$991.87 plus 33%	—$4,597
$8,079	—$9,105	$2,140.93 plus 35%	—$8,079
$9,105		$2,500.03 plus 39.6%	—$9,105

TABLE 2—BIWEEKLY Payroll Period

(a) SINGLE person (including head of household)—
If the amount of wages (after subtracting withholding allowances) is:
Not over $88 . . . . $0

Over—	But not over—	The amount of income tax to withhold is:	of excess over—
$88	—$443	$0.00 plus 10%	—$88
$443	—$1,529	$35.50 plus 15%	—$443
$1,529	—$3,579	$198.40 plus 25%	—$1,529
$3,579	—$7,369	$710.90 plus 28%	—$3,579
$7,369	—$15,915	$1,772.10 plus 33%	—$7,369
$15,915	—$15,981	$4,592.28 plus 35%	—$15,915
$15,981		$4,615.38 plus 39.6%	—$15,981

(b) MARRIED person—
If the amount of wages (after subtracting withholding allowances) is:
Not over $331 . . . . $0

Over—	But not over—	The amount of income tax to withhold is:	of excess over—
$331	—$1,040	$0.00 plus 10%	—$331
$1,040	—$3,212	$70.90 plus 15%	—$1,040
$3,212	—$6,146	$396.70 plus 25%	—$3,212
$6,146	—$9,194	$1,130.20 plus 28%	—$6,146
$9,194	—$16,158	$1,983.64 plus 33%	—$9,194
$16,158	—$18,210	$4,281.76 plus 35%	—$16,158
$18,210		$4,999.96 plus 39.6%	—$18,210

TABLE 3—SEMIMONTHLY Payroll Period

(a) SINGLE person (including head of household)—
If the amount of wages (after subtracting withholding allowances) is:
Not over $96 . . . . $0

Over—	But not over—	The amount of income tax to withhold is:	of excess over—
$96	—$480	$0.00 plus 10%	—$96
$480	—$1,656	$38.40 plus 15%	—$480
$1,656	—$3,877	$214.80 plus 25%	—$1,656
$3,877	—$7,983	$770.05 plus 28%	—$3,877
$7,983	—$17,242	$1,919.73 plus 33%	—$7,983
$17,242	—$17,313	$4,975.20 plus 35%	—$17,242
$17,313		$5,000.05 plus 39.6%	—$17,313

(b) MARRIED person—
If the amount of wages (after subtracting withholding allowances) is:
Not over $358 . . . . $0

Over—	But not over—	The amount of income tax to withhold is:	of excess over—
$358	—$1,127	$0.00 plus 10%	—$358
$1,127	—$3,479	$76.90 plus 15%	—$1,127
$3,479	—$6,658	$429.70 plus 25%	—$3,479
$6,658	—$9,960	$1,224.45 plus 28%	—$6,658
$9,960	—$17,504	$2,149.01 plus 33%	—$9,960
$17,504	—$19,727	$4,638.53 plus 35%	—$17,504
$19,727		$5,416.58 plus 39.6%	—$19,727

TABLE 4—MONTHLY Payroll Period

(a) SINGLE person (including head of household)—
If the amount of wages (after subtracting withholding allowances) is:
Not over $192 . . . . $0

Over—	But not over—	The amount of income tax to withhold is:	of excess over—
$192	—$960	$0.00 plus 10%	—$192
$960	—$3,313	$76.80 plus 15%	—$960
$3,313	—$7,754	$429.75 plus 25%	—$3,313
$7,754	—$15,967	$1,540.00 plus 28%	—$7,754
$15,967	—$34,483	$3,839.64 plus 33%	—$15,967
$34,483	—$34,625	$9,949.92 plus 35%	—$34,483
$34,625		$9,999.62 plus 39.6%	—$34,625

(b) MARRIED person—
If the amount of wages (after subtracting withholding allowances) is:
Not over $717 . . . . $0

Over—	But not over—	The amount of income tax to withhold is:	of excess over—
$717	—$2,254	$0.00 plus 10%	—$717
$2,254	—$6,958	$153.70 plus 15%	—$2,254
$6,958	—$13,317	$859.30 plus 25%	—$6,958
$13,317	—$19,921	$2,449.05 plus 28%	—$13,317
$19,921	—$35,008	$4,298.17 plus 33%	—$19,921
$35,008	—$39,454	$9,276.88 plus 35%	—$35,008
$39,454		$10,832.98 plus 39.6%	—$39,454

Example 3 — Toni Nilson's W-4 indicated she is married and claims 2 exemptions. Toni's gross pay for the last week of December is $1,375. Using the percentage method, determine the amount Toni's employer should withhold for federal income tax.

Step 1 Using Illustration 8-2, locate the weekly amount for 1 withholding allowance. Multiply by the number of allowances: $76.90 × 2 allowances = $153.80

Step 2 Subtract the result of Step 1 from Toni's gross pay: $1,375.00 - $153.80 = $1,221.20

Step 3 Using Illustration 8-3, Table 1 (weekly), married persons, find the range that includes the result of Step 2 ($1,221.20). Use the range labeled "over $520 but not over $1,606." The amount to be withheld is $35.50 plus 15% of the excess over $520:

$$\begin{aligned}\text{Amount} &= \$35.50 + 15\%(\$1{,}221.20 - \$520.00) \\ &= \$35.50 + 15\%(\$701.20) \\ &= \$35.50 + \$105.18 \\ &= \$140.68\end{aligned}$$

If Toni's employer uses the percentage method, $140.68 of federal income tax should be withheld from Toni's pay.

Arithmetic for Step 3 of Example 3 can be done with a calculator, as follows:

Keystrokes (for most calculators)	
1,221.20 [-] 520 [=]	701.20
[×] 15 [%] [=]	105.18
[+] 35.50	35.50
[=]	**140.68**

C Calculating net pay

In addition to making deductions for Social Security tax, Medicare tax, and federal income tax, employers may also make a deduction for state income tax. All but a few states have state income tax. Because state income tax rates are different from state to state, we will not attempt to cover state income tax withholdings.

Employees may authorize other deductions, such as union dues, contributions for a savings or retirement plan, insurance premiums, and car payments. In some cases, a court requires that money be withheld from a person's pay to cover child support, alimony, or obligations to creditors; the employee's wages are said to be *garnished*.

Gross pay minus deductions is called **net pay**; this is the dollar amount of the paycheck. The next example shows how we calculate Toni's net pay.

Example 4 — Toni Nilson's gross weekly pay is $1,375. Toni's employer withholds $85.25 for Social Security tax and $19.94 for Medicare tax (see Example 2) plus $140.68 for federal income tax (see Example 3). In addition, Creative withholds 5% of gross pay for state income tax ($68.75) and a $50 contribution into a savings plan. What is Toni's net pay?

Net pay = $1,375 - $85.25 - $19.94 - $140.68 - $68.75 - $50 = **$1,010.38**

A **payroll register** is used to record payroll deductions and net pay for each employee. Many businesses use computer spreadsheets to do payroll registers. Illustration 8-4 is a payroll register for Creative Architecture's three employees. Toni Nilson is one of the employees. You may want to check the withholding amounts for Tom and Amy using the same rates we used for Toni; most of you, I'm betting, will just trust my calculations!

Illustration 8-4

CREATIVE ARCHITECTURE
Payroll Register
December 31, 2015

Employee	W-4 form	Prior YTD earnings	Gross pay this period	Gross pay this period subject to		Deductions from employee's pay						Total	Net pay
				SS	MED	SS	MED	FIT	SIT	Other	Explain		
Toni Nilson	M-2	70,125	1,375	1,375	1,375	85.25	19.94	140.68	68.75	50.00	Savings	364.62	1,010.38
Tom Hess	M-3	14,400	1,250	1,250	1,250	77.50	18.13	110.40	62.50			268.53	981.47
Amy Salk	S-1	6,600	750	750	750	46.50	10.88	85.47	37.50			180.35	569.65
Totals	—	91,125	3,375	3,375	3,375	209.25	48.95	336.55	168.75	50.00	—	813.50	2,561.50

We're finished with Unit 8.2. Let's do the U-Try-It exercises to see how we're doing.

U-Try-It (Unit 8.2)

Tanya Sargent is a college professor. She is paid monthly. Her gross pay for this pay period is $10,500. Prior year-to-date gross pay is $115,500.

1. Based on the FICA rates given in Unit 8.2, how much Social Security tax and Medicare tax should be withheld?
2. Tanya is married and claims 3 exemptions on Form W-4. Using the percentage method, figure out federal income tax withholding.
3. The college also withholds state income tax at 5.5% of Tanya's gross pay. What is Tanya's net pay?

Answers: (If you have a different answer, check the solution in Appendix A.)
1. Social Security: $186; Medicare: $152.25   2. $1,494.83   3. $8,089.42

Unit 8.3 Employer taxes and settling up with the IRS

In addition to withholding taxes from employee's gross pay, employers incur several of their own payroll taxes. In this unit, we will study taxes for employers and self-employed individuals; then we will review the all-important concept of determining if we get a refund from the Internal Revenue Service (IRS).

a Calculating payroll taxes for an employer

Some employers provide health insurance, sick pay, and even vacation pay to their employees.

Employers must pay their own FICA tax, federal unemployment tax, and state unemployment tax. In many states, employers also must either contribute to a workers' compensation fund or provide private workers' compensation. Employers often pay health, life, or disability insurance for employees. Some companies make contributions into an employees' retirement plan. We will limit our study to employers' FICA tax and unemployment tax.

For 2015, employers pay Social Security tax of 6.2% on the first $118,500 of annual wages paid to each employee plus 1.45% on all wages (no limit). Employers are *not* subject to Additional Medicare tax (the 0.9% tax on earnings over $200,000). So, employers match the employee amounts for Social Security tax and Medicare tax, but do not match employee withholding for Additional Medicare tax.

Example 1 Refer to the payroll register of Illustration 8-4. What is Creative's share of FICA tax?

Employees' share of Social Security tax:	$209.25
Employees' share of Medicare tax:	+ 48.95
Total, to be matched by Creative	$258.20

In Example 1, Creative withheld $258.20 from employees for Social Security tax and Medicare tax. Creative must pay an additional $258.20 to the federal government as their share.

The federal government participates with the states in an unemployment insurance program. The **federal unemployment tax** (FUT), paid by employers, is theoretically 6% of the first $7,000 paid each employee (per calendar-year). However, federal law allows a maximum credit of 5.4% to employers in a state that has a federally approved program. Since all states currently have federally approved programs, the *net federal unemployment tax is .6%* (6.0 - 5.4 = .6). The money is used to cover administrative expenses only, not to pay benefits; benefits are paid by the state plans.

State unemployment tax (SUT), also paid by employers, is based on a **merit-rating system.** Companies with a good history of stable employment pay a lower rate than companies with a history of high unemployment. Each state has its own rates (often ranging from about .4% to about 8%) and dollar ceilings (not necessarily the $7,000 federal ceiling).

Note that the FUT and SUT are imposed on employers only; employees pay nothing.

Example 2 Refer to the payroll register of Illustration 8-4. Calculate Creative's FUT and SUT. Assume a SUT rate of 3.5% on the first $15,000 paid each employee per year.

Employee	Prior YTD earnings	Gross pay this period	Gross pay this pay period subject to FUT	Gross pay this pay period subject to SUT
Toni Nilson	70,125	1,375	0	0
Tom Hess	14,400	1,250	0	600
Amy Salk	6,600	750	400	750
Total	—	—	400	1,350
Tax rates:			× 0.6%	× 3.5%
Tax			$ 2.40	$ 47.25

Employer payroll expenses (wages, employer's share of FICA tax, FUT, SUT, health insurance premiums, contributions to retirement plans, etc.) are treated as expenses on a company's income statement.

The employer acts as a "middleman" for the employee and the taxing authorities. The amount of FICA tax and federal income tax withheld from employees' pay goes to the IRS. Because the *employer's* FICA tax also goes to the IRS, the employer pays all items at once. Of course, there are lots of forms to fill out, including Form 941 (Employer's Quarterly Federal Tax Return). State income tax withheld and state unemployment tax must be remitted to the appropriate state agency. Like FICA tax and federal income tax, FUT goes to the IRS but is remitted separately. We will not attempt to cover the rules for how often the money for all of these must be sent in; but the general rule is that the more money the employer is holding, the more frequently the money must be remitted.

ⓑ Calculating self-employment FICA tax

People who are **self-employed,** such as owners of a business *are, in effect, both employee and employer.* As a result, they must pay the employee and employer share of Social Security tax and Medicare tax:

	Employee Share	**Employer Share**	**Self-employment total**
Social Security tax	6.2% of first $118,500	Same	12.4% of first $118,500
Medicare tax	1.45% on all earnings	Same	2.9% on all

Stated another way, they must pay a total of 15.3% (12.4% + 2.9% = 15.3%) on the first $118,500 plus 2.9% on the remainder. FICA tax for employers is figured on gross wages; FICA tax for self-employed individuals is figured on **net income** (income minus expenses). Here is a tricky part. Employers deduct their share of FICA tax as a business expense; to allow the same break to self-employed individuals, self-employment FICA tax is charged on only 92.35% (100% - 6.2% - 1.45%) of net income.

> **2015 FICA tax for the self-employed**
>
> **Step 1** Multiply net income by 92.35%.
>
> **Step 2** Evaluate the result of Step 1 and figure the FICA tax
>
> | If the result of Step 1 is | The FICA tax is |
> |---|---|
> | Less than $400 | $0 |
> | $400 or more | 15.3% of first $118,500 + 2.9% of remainder |
>
> 1. Only the first $118,500 of combined wages and self-employment income are subject to Social Security tax; problems in the text assume that the self-employed person has no separate wage income.
> 2. The self-employment tax, shown above, does not include Additional Medicare tax. The Additional Medicare tax is calculated *per household* when the taxpayer's income tax return is filed. The tax is 0.9% on earned income (wages plus self-employment income) that exceeds certain thresholds. The thresholds are outlined on page 161.

Example 3 Shane Nilson, Toni's husband, owns his own accounting business. Shane's net income during 2015 was $128,700. Calculate Shane's 2015 self-employment FICA tax. Round amounts to the nearest dollar (doing this is customary on tax returns).

Step 1 $128,700 × 92.35% = $118,854 (rounded)

Step 2 FICA tax on first $118,500: $118,500 × 15.3% $18,130.50
 FICA tax on remainder: 2.9%($118,854 - $118,500)   +   10.27
 Total, rounded $18,141.00

C Determining overpayment or underpayment to the IRS

By January 31, employers must provide employees with a **Form W-2** for the previous calendar-year, showing gross wages and withholdings. Form W-2 for Toni Nilson is shown as Illustration 8-5. A copy of Form W-2 is sent to the IRS (and, where required, to the state tax commission).

Employees who have not had a sufficient amount of federal income tax withheld will owe a balance and could be subject to a penalty for not paying enough through withholdings; if too much tax is withheld, the taxpayer will receive a refund from the IRS within about 6 weeks of filing the tax return. About 4:00 P.M. on April 15, millions of Americans remember that they forgot something: to file their income tax return for the previous calendar-year. Perhaps you, like myself, have been part of the excitement at the post office on April 15!

Illustration 8-5 Form W-2

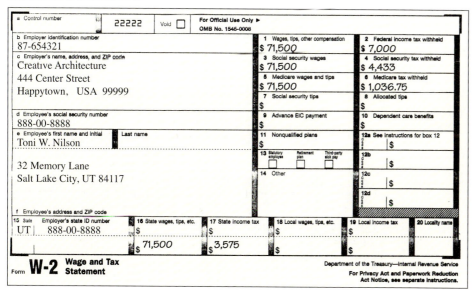

Unit 8.3 Employer taxes and settling up with the IRS

Self-employed individuals don't have an employer to withhold federal income tax and FICA tax. When April 15 rolls around, they may find they owe a substantial amount of tax (and an underpayment penalty). People with nonwage income (like interest income and rental income), for which no one is withholding federal income tax, can be in a similar situation on April 15. To avoid this, taxpayers can make direct payments (called **estimated payments**) to the IRS. Estimated payments are based on *projected income and deductions;* actual income and deductions are not established until the end of the year. Due dates for quarterly estimated payments are: April 15, June 15, September 15, and January 15 (of the following year). The estimated payments apply to actual tax liability.

Example 4

Toni and Shane filed their 2015 income tax return in March 2016. They listed Toni's wages of $71,500, Shane's business net income of $128,700, and exemptions and deductions they were entitled to. Their federal income tax liability came to $22,488 (not including Shane's self-employment FICA tax of $18,141 from Example 3). They made quarterly estimated payments of $9,000 per payment. Based on additional information found on Toni's W-2 Form (Illustration 8-5), calculate the Nilson's overpayment or underpayment.

Amounts owed to IRS		Amounts already paid to IRS	
Income tax liability	$22,488	Federal income tax w/h Toni's pay	$ 7,000
Self-employment FICA (Example 3)	+18,141	Estimated payments: 4 × $9,000	+36,000
Total tax liability	$40,629	Total already paid to IRS	$43,000

Toni and Shane paid a bit too much to the IRS; they will get a refund of $2,371 ($43,000 - $40,629).

TIP — **is it a tax or an estimate of tax?**

In doing Example 4, you may have wondered which amounts apply against the federal income tax liability. Well, here is a summary using Toni's W-2 of Illustration 8-5:

These are other taxes; *don't* apply to federal income tax liability
- Social Security tax withheld ($4,433) is the actual amount; gone when withheld.
- Medicare tax withheld ($1,036.75) is the actual amount; gone when withheld.

These are estimates only; *apply* toward federal income tax liability
- Federal income tax withheld ($7,000)
- Quarterly estimated payments ($36,000)

State income tax ($3,575) is an estimate but applies against the state income tax liability.

We're done with this chapter. Congratulations! Are you ready for another set of U-Try-It exercises?

U-Try-It (Unit 8.3)

Bennion Insurance Agency has 2 employees. Bennion's semimonthly payroll register for the first half of May is shown. (In case you're checking the numbers, Bennion withholds 6% of gross pay for state income tax.)

Employee	W-4 Form	Prior YTD Earnings	Gross pay this period	Subject to: SS	Subject to: MED	Deductions SS	Deductions MED	Deductions FIT	Deductions SIT	Total	Net pay
Tina Roe	S-1	6,400	800	800	800	49.60	11.60	61.40	48.00	170.60	629.40
Andy Sly	M-4	11,200	1,400	1,400	1,400	86.80	20.30	37.52	84.00	228.62	1,171.38
Totals	—	17,600	2,200	2,200	2,200	136.40	31.90	98.92	132.00	399.22	1,800.78

1. What is Bennion's share of FICA tax for this pay period?
2. Calculate Bennion's FUT and SUT; assume the SUT is 2.5% of the first $12,000 paid each employee per year.
3. Ed Bennion, owner of Bennion Insurance Agency, had 2015 net income of $97,400. Calculate Ed's self-employment FICA tax. Round amounts to the nearest dollar.
4. In addition to Ed's self-employment FICA tax, Ed and his wife Marilyn have a federal income

tax liability of $23,382. During the tax year, Marilyn's employer withheld $2,976 for Social Security tax, $696 for Medicare tax, $6,122 for federal income tax, and $2,855 for state income tax. Ed and Marilyn made quarterly estimated payments of $7,000 per payment. Determine if Ed and Marilyn overpaid or underpaid their federal income tax and by what amount.

Answers: (If you have a different answer, check the solution in Appendix A.)
1. $168.30   **2.** FUT: $3.60, SUT: $40   **3.** $13,762   **4.** They owe an additional $3,022

Chapter in a Nutshell

Objectives	Examples

Unit 8.1 Gross pay: Wages and incentive plans

a Calculating gross pay from wages

Regular pay rate = $7.65 per hour; 52 hours for the week. Gross pay?

Overtime hours: 52 hrs - 40 hrs = 12 hrs; Overtime rate: $7.65 × 1.5 = $11.475

Pay for regular hours: 40 × $7.65	$306.00
Pay for overtime hours: 12 × $11.475	+137.70
Total gross pay	$443.70

b Comparing gross pay for different pay periods

Which is greater: $800 per week or $3,400 per month?

$800 per week × 52.14 weeks = $41,712 per year
$3,400 per month × 12 months = $40,800 per year

c Calculating gross pay from piecework

495 units produced; $1.80 per unit for first 300; $2.00 per unit thereafter; gross pay?

300 × $1.80	$540.00
195 × $2.00	+390.00
495	$930.00

d Calculating gross pay from commissions

$58,300 sales; $3,100 sales returns; 4.5% commission on net sales; commission?

($58,300 - $3,100) × 4.5% = $55,200 × 4.5% = $2,484

Unit 8.2 Payroll deductions for employees

a Calculating FICA withholding

Gertrude earned $125,000 during 2015; Social Security and Medicare withholdings?

Social Security: $118,500 ceiling × 6.2% = $7,347.00
Medicare: $125,000 × 1.45% = $1,812.50

b Calculating federal income tax withholding

Buck is married, 4 exemptions; paid $2,300 biweekly; federal income tax withholding using percentage method?

Step 1 Illustration 8-2, biweekly: $153.80 × 4 = $615.20
Step 2 $2,300 - $615.20 = $1,684.80
Step 3 Illustration 8-3, Table 2 (biweekly), married, over $1,040 but not over $3,212:

$70.90 + 15%($1,684.80 - $1,040) = $70.90 + 15%($644.80) = $70.90 + $96.72 = $167.62

c Calculating net pay

$2,200 gross pay; withholdings: $136.40 Social Security, $31.90 Medicare, $340 federal income tax, and $118 state income tax; net pay?

$2,200 - $136.40 - $31.90 - $340 - $118 = $1,573.70

Chapter in a Nutshell (concluded)

Objectives	Examples

Unit 8.3 Employer taxes and settling up with the IRS

ⓐ	Calculating payroll taxes for an employer	Bob is the only employee; $6,340 prior year-to-date earnings; $800 gross pay this pay period. Find employer FUT and SUT, assuming 4% SUT rate on first $15,000 earnings per year. FUT: $7,000 limit - $6,340 prior earnings = $660; $660 × 0.6% = **$3.96** SUT: $800 × 4% = **$32**
ⓑ	Calculating self-employment FICA tax	$130,000 net income for 2015; self-employment FICA tax? **Step 1** $130,000 × 92.35% = $120,055 **Step 2** Tax on first $118,500: $118,500 × 15.3% $18,130.50 Tax on remainder: 2.9%($120,055 - $118,500) + 45.10 Total, rounded **$18,176.00**
ⓒ	Determining overpayment or underpayment to the IRS	Matt and Cheri complete their federal income tax return. Matt owes $8,422 self-employment FICA tax, plus Matt and Cheri's federal income tax liability is $12,444. Cheri's employer withheld $9,143 federal income tax during the year, and Matt and Cheri made quarterly estimated payments of $3,000 per payment. Amount of underpayment or overpayment? Amounts owed to IRS: $8,422 + $12,444 $20,866 Amounts already paid to IRS: $9,143 + (4 × $3,000) $21,143 **Overpaid $277** ($21,143 - $20,866)

Enrichment Topics

The following Enrichment Topic, which goes a bit beyond what is in the text, is available for this chapter:

Overtime for Salaried Employees

If your instructor doesn't cover this topic in class and you would like to dig in deeper on your own, please send a request to *studentsupport@olympuspub.com*.

Think

1. What is the difference between semimonthly and biweekly? Who gets more paychecks each year—a person paid semimonthly or a person paid biweekly?
2. Tariq and Kate work for a clothing retailer. Tariq is paid a 7% commission with a $700 semimonthly salary. Kate is paid a 7% commission with a $700 semimonthly draw. Which person has the better deal? Explain why.
3. For the FICA rates shown in Unit 8.2, are there any situations in which an employee could end up paying more Medicare tax than Social Security tax for the year? Be specific.
4. Some people prefer to have their employer deduct more federal income tax than they will owe. Others prefer to have their employer deduct as little as possible. What are the advantages and disadvantages of each approach? Which approach do you prefer?
5. Which payroll taxes are a cost to an employee, and which are a cost to the employer?
6. When a person files a federal income tax return, which payroll taxes that have been deducted from gross pay are not applied against tax liability, and why?
7. Suppose your company has a special project that will last 4 months and will require extra help from employees for that 4 months. You are considering three possible ways of getting the help: (1) asking current employees to put in lots of overtime, (2) using a temp agency to supply the help, or (3) hiring new people for the 4 months (requiring laying them off at the end of the 4-month period). What are the advantages and disadvantages of each approach? Which approach do you prefer, and why?

Explore

1. Search on the Internet for FICA rates, typing in the current year (such as *2016 FICA rates*). Submit a short report on how Social Security and Medicare tax are computed.
2. Go to **www.irs.gov**. Find Publication 15, Circular E for the current year. Locate the wage-bracket tables and percentage method tables. Refer to Example 2 from Unit 8.2. Using the tables for the current year, determine the amount Toni's employer should withhold for federal income tax using the (1) wage-bracket tables, and (2) percentage method tables. Compare the results of each.
3. Review the payroll register of Illustration 8-4. Create that same payroll register on a spreadsheet. Enter formulas in appropriate cells. Assume that none of the employees will exceed the $118,500 ceiling during the year for Social Security tax. Assume SIT withholdings of 5% of gross pay. Don't worry about entering formulas for FIT withholdings; instead just enter the amounts shown in Illustration 8-4. You may need to round values to the nearest penny, so the total in that column will equal the sum of the displayed values. To round a value in, say, Cell J3 (for state income tax, which is 5% of cell D3), type =ROUND((D3*5%),2). To verify that your formulas are correct, compare the amounts on your spreadsheet (including totals and Net Pay) with those of Illustration 8-4. Save the file as *Payroll Register*.

Apply

1. **Interview Earners.** Interview an individual who makes each type of pay:
   A. Hourly rate of pay   B. Straight salary   C. Piecework   D. Commission
   Submit a report on your findings. In your report, include (1) the names of the individuals you interviewed, (2) the names of the companies they work for, (3) the overtime policies of the companies, and (4) how their gross pay is established.
2. **Real Payroll.** Submit a payroll register for an actual company having at least 5 employees. Company and employee names may be deleted. Your report should include (1) *current* rates for all taxes, (2) calculations for employee Social Security and Medicare tax, (3) the method and calculations for federal income tax withholdings, (4) the method and calculations for state income tax withholdings (use rates and rules for your state), (5) calculations for federal unemployment tax, (6) calculations for state unemployment tax, and (7) calculations for all other employee and employer taxes.

Chapter Review Problems

Unit 8.1 Gross pay: Wages and incentive plans

1. The Fair Labor Standards Act applies to all employees. (T or F)

2. Some employers provide overtime pay that is superior to what the Fair Labor Standards Act requires. (T or F)

3. The employees of Sunshine Outdoor Products are paid time and a half after 40 hours per week. Compute each employee's gross pay.

Name	M	T	W	Th	F	S	Total hours	Regular hours	Overtime hours	Reg. rate per hour	Overtime rate	Regular pay	Overtime pay	Gross pay
Don Day	8	8	8	10	8	4.5				8.00				
Joy Erb	8	8	8	8	8	8				8.25				
Bo Hart	8	8	8	8	8	0				7.25				
Thu Ho	8	8	8	10	4	0				8.25				

4. You and three classmates work for different companies. Your gross pay is $1,295 a month. Betty earns $640 semimonthly, Brad earns $310 a week, and Meg earns $600 biweekly. Who has the greatest gross pay?

5. Jay Hirschi sold eight new cars during the week. If he earns $150 per sale, what is his gross pay for the week?

6. Tom Judkins sews sleeping bags. He is paid $5.50 per hour plus $1.50 per sleeping bag. During the week, Tom worked 40 hours and sewed 32 sleeping bags. What is Tom's gross pay for the week?

7. Brock Snyder assembles chairs. During the pay period, Brock assembled 344 chairs. Determine his gross pay, based upon these piecework rates:

   The first 100: $1.75 per chair
   The next 100: $2.00 per chair
   Thereafter: $2.25 per chair

8. Blanche Baker is a salesperson in a computer store and receives a $1,200 semimonthly draw. Blanche is paid a 3% commission on net sales. During October, Blanche sold $125,800 of merchandise; her share of sales returns was $2,592. Calculate Blanche's final commission payment for October.

9. Alfonso Gallegos is a salesperson for a furniture store. He is paid a semimonthly salary of $800 plus 3% of monthly net sales over $80,000. Alfonso's sales during November were $128,300. His share of returns were $3,400. Determine his gross pay for November.

Unit 8.2 Payroll deductions for employees

10. Which statement is true?

    a. Social Security consists of (1) FICA and (2) Medicare.
    b. FICA consists of (1) Social Security and (2) Medicare.
    c. Medicare consists of (1) FICA and (2) Social Security.

11. The number of allowances claimed on Form W-4 must match the number of exemptions claimed on the federal income tax return. (T or F)

12. American Pharmacy has three employees. Complete American's weekly payroll register. Use: **(a)** FICA tax rates shown in Unit 8.2, **(b)** the percentage method shown in Illustrations 8-2 and 8-3, and **(c)** a 5% rate for withholding state income tax.

AMERICAN PHARMACY
Payroll Register
December 15, 2015

Employee	W-4 form	Prior YTD earnings	Gross pay this period	Gross pay this period subject to: SS	MED	Deductions from employee's pay SS	MED	FIT	SIT	Other	Explain	Total	Net pay
Dan Bevan	M-1	63,750	1,275							50.00	Savings		
Ashlie Dobbs	S-1	14,580	810							—	—		
Ian Rice	M-3	6,500	1,140							—	—		
Totals	—										—		

13. Dario Garcia had 2015 wages of $230,000. His wife Maria had wages of $48,000. Determine (1) how much Additional Medicare tax each of their employers had to withhold from their paychecks, and (2) the actual Additional Medicare tax for their household, assuming they file their tax return jointly.

14. Cliff Garton works for West Engineering Company. His gross pay during 2015 for week 46 is $2,600. Prior year-to-date earnings are $117,000. Using FICA tax rates shown in Unit 8.2, determine how much Social Security tax and Medicare tax should be withheld from Cliff's pay.

Unit 8.3 Employer taxes and settling up with the IRS

15. Employers withhold Social Security tax and Medicare tax from employees' pay. Based on rates shown in Units 8.2 and 8.3, employers must pay matching amounts. (T or F)

16. FUT and SUT are withheld from employees' pay. (T or F)

For Problems 17–20, refer to Problem 12.

17. Determine American Pharmacy's share of Social Security tax.

18. Determine American's share of Medicare tax.

19. Calculate American's FUT and SUT. Assume a SUT rate of 2.5% on the first $15,000 paid each employee each year.

Employee	Prior YTD Earnings	Gross pay this period	Gross pay this pay period subject to	
			FUT	SUT
Dan Bevan	63,750	1,275		
Ashlie Dobbs	14,580	810		
Ian Rice	6,500	1,140		
Total	—	3,225		

20. American incurs these additional payroll expenses: (a) health insurance of $100 per employee and (b) a contribution to employees' retirement plans at 8% of gross pay. What is American's total payroll expense for this pay period (including wages)?

21. To avoid an underpayment penalty on federal income tax, a taxpayer can make estimated payments of sufficient amount. (T or F)

22. Estimated payments are a guess, based on projected income and deductions. (T or F)

For Problems 23–25, consider the tax situation of Lee Albert, a self-employed artist. Lee's 2015 net income is $140,000.

23. Based on rates shown in Unit 8.3, calculate Lee's self-employment FICA tax, to the nearest dollar.

24. When Lee prepares his 2015 federal income tax return, his federal income tax is figured at $17,211 (not including self-employment FICA tax). What is Lee's total tax liability?

25. If Lee made quarterly estimated tax payments of $9,000 per payment, calculate the dollar amount of refund or balance due.

Challenge problems

For Problems 26 and 27, consider the situation of Janele Stratton. Janele assembles tents. She is paid $8.50 per hour plus $2.50 per tent.

26. During the week, Janele worked 40 hours and completed 48 tents. What is her gross pay for the week?

27. Calculate Janele's average hourly wage for the week.

For Problems 28–30, consider the paycheck of Taryn Olds, who works for National Technologies. During 2015, Taryn earns $2,500 semi-monthly. Her prior year-to-date earnings are $5,000. She is married and claims 2 withholding allowances.

28. Calculate Taryn's payroll deductions for this pay period: **(a)** Social Security tax; **(b)** Medicare tax; **(c)** federal income tax (using the percentage method); and **(d)** state income tax (figured as 6.5% of gross pay).

29. Taryn has National withhold $75 each paycheck for a savings plan. What is the amount of Taryn's paycheck?

30. Determine National's payroll expenses, as a result of Taryn's wages: **(a)** Social Security tax; **(b)** Medicare tax; **(c)** FUT; and **(d)** SUT (assume that National pays 2% on the first $10,000).

31. Galey and Connie Colosimo filed their 2015 income tax return in April 2016. They listed Galey's wages of $38,000, Connie's business net income of $53,000, and exemptions and deductions they were entitled to. Their federal income tax liability came to $16,378 and Connie's self-employment FICA tax was $7,489. Galey's employer withheld $2,356 for Social Security; $551 for Medicare; $4,940 for federal income tax; and $2,100 for state income tax. Galey and Connie paid quarterly estimates of $4,500 per payment. Calculate their overpayment or underpayment.

Practice Test

1. Tan Ho is paid weekly at a rate of $9.75 per hour. Calculate Tan's gross pay for the week, assuming he worked 44 hours and receives time and a half after the first 40 hours.

2. You have two job offers: $3,500 a month, and $820 weekly. Which offer results in the greatest gross pay?

3. Geraldine Upton sews coats. She is paid $7.50 per hour plus $2.50 per coat. During the week, she worked 40 hours and sewed 63 coats. What is Geraldine's gross pay for the week?

4. Gilbert Wilcox works for Gardner Engineering Company. Gilbert earns $2,500 a week during 2015 and has prior year-to-date earnings of $117,500. Using rates shown in Unit 8.2, what amount should Gardner withhold for FICA tax?

5. Irving Fox works for Green Landscaping Company. Irving's weekly gross pay during 2015 is $800. Irving is single and claims 1 exemption. What amount of federal income tax should Green withhold, assuming Green uses the percentage method?

6. Employers pay no FICA tax; they simply withhold FICA tax from employees' pay. (T or F)

7. Mindy Lowe works for Founders Hospital. She is paid $1,600 for the month of May 2015. Her prior year-to-date earnings are $6,400. Calculate Founder's FUT on Mindy's pay.

8. Clint Perry is a self-employed accountant. Clint's net income during 2015 was $105,200. Using the self-employment FICA rates shown in Unit 8.3, calculate Clint's 2015 self-employment FICA tax.

9. Terry and Margie Anderson filed their 2015 income tax return in March 2016. They listed Margie's wages, Terry's business net income, and exemptions and deductions they were entitled to. Their federal income tax liability came to $13,280, and Terry's self-employment FICA tax was $4,192. Margie's employer withheld $1,860 for Social Security, $435 for Medicare, $7,970 for federal income tax, and $1,625 for state income tax. Terry and Margie made quarterly estimates of $2,500 per payment. Calculate their overpayment or underpayment.

FUN CORNER

No-Interest Plans
Have you seen advertisements for products, like a $2,000 TV, with no interest for 12 months? Here's a tip. If you have the $2,000, don't pay it. Instead, buy the TV with the 12-month, no-interest plan and keep your $2,000 in an interest-bearing account. Pay the store just before the no-interest period expires. Assuming that your $2,000 earns 5% ($100), the TV will, in effect, cost you only $1,900.

Where Did Calendars Come From?
Our current calendar goes back to Julius Caesar, in 46 B.C. To get the calendar year to equal the astronomical year, Caesar ordered the calendar to have 365 days. He wanted the calendar to have 12 months, so days were added to various months to bring the total to 365. Because seasons do not repeat every 365 days, but actually 365 days, 5 hours, 48 minutes, and 46 seconds, the calendar ended about one-quarter of a day early. After every fourth year, it would have been a full day in error.

To make up for this difference, every fourth year had an extra day added to February. It was decided that any year evenly divisible by 4 was a leap year, which made the average length of the calendar exactly 365.25 days. However, that correction made the year 11 minutes, 14 seconds too long; after 128 years, the calendar was ending a full day later than the astronomical year.

In 1582, Pope Gregory XII stepped in and ordered yet another correction to the calendar. This change resulted in the Gregorian calendar. The change stated that century years not evenly divisible by 400 would not be leap years. Thus, 1900 was not a leap year, but 2000 was. This made the average length of the calendar 365.244 days and reduced the calendar error to only 1 day in 3,322 years.

To obtain still greater accuracy, another change was made. Years evenly divisible by 4,000 are non-leap years. With this modification the Gregorian calendar's accuracy improves even more—our calendar will lose only a single day over a time span of 20,000 years.

Quotable Quip
A banker is a fellow who lends you his umbrella when the sun is shining and wants it back the minute is starts to rain.
— Mark Twain

Quotable Quip
Compound interest is the eighth wonder of the world.
— Albert Einstein

Brainteaser
Suppose someone agrees to pay you 1¢ today, 2¢ tomorrow, 4¢ the third day, and keeps doubling the amount each day. How much would you receive on day 40?

Answer: $5,497,558,138.88

"Linda, my interest in you is compounding daily!"

Simple and Compound Interest

9

Interest is the fee paid for borrowed money. We *receive* interest when we let others use our money (for example, by depositing money in a savings account or making a loan). We *pay* interest when we use other people's money (such as when we borrow from a bank or a friend). Are you a "receiver" or a "payer"?

In this chapter we will study simple and compound interest. **Simple interest** is interest that is calculated on the balance owed but not on previous interest. **Compound interest**, on the other hand, is interest calculated on any balance owed including previous interest. Interest for loans is generally calculated using simple interest, while interest for savings accounts is generally calculated using compound interest.

The concepts of this chapter are used in many upcoming topics of the text. So hopefully you have *interest* in mastering the stuff in this chapter.

Unit Objectives

Unit 9.1 Computing simple interest and maturity value

- **a** Computing simple interest and maturity value—loans stated in months or years
- **b** Counting days and determining maturity date—loans stated in days
- **c** Computing simple interest—loans stated in days

Unit 9.2 Solving for principal, rate, and time

- **a** Solving for *P* (principal) and *T* (time)
- **b** Solving for *R* (rate)

Unit 9.3 Compound interest

- **a** Understanding how compound interest differs from simple interest
- **b** Computing compound interest for different compounding periods
- **c** Calculating annual percentage yield (APY)

Unit 9.1 Computing simple interest and maturity value

Wendy Chapman just graduated from college with a degree in accounting and decided to open her own accounting office (she can finally start earning money instead of spending it on college). On July 10, 2015, Wendy borrowed $12,000 from her Aunt Nelda for office furniture and other start-up costs. She agreed to repay Aunt Nelda in 1 year, together with interest at 9%.

The original amount Wendy borrowed—$12,000—is the **principal**. The percent that Wendy pays for the use of the money—9%—is the **rate of interest** (or simply the interest rate). The length of time—1 year—is called the **time** or **term**. The date on which the loan is to be repaid—July 10, 2016—is called the **due date** or **maturity date**. The total amount Wendy must repay (which we will calculate later) consists of principal ($12,000) and **interest** ($1,080); the total amount ($13,080) is called the **maturity value**.

Banks provide a valuable service as money brokers. They borrow from some people (through savings accounts, etc.) and loan that same money to others (at a higher rate). Some of these loans are simple interest loans.

a Computing simple interest and maturity value—loans stated in months or years

To calculate interest, we first multiply the principal by the annual rate of interest; this gives us interest per year. We then multiply the result by time (in years).

---

simple interest formula

$$I = PRT$$

I = Dollar amount of interest P = Principal R = Annual rate of interest T = Time (in years)

TIP — what is PRT?

Remember, when symbols are written side by side, it means to multiply, so PRT means $P \times R \times T$. Also, don't forget R, the interest rate, is the *annual* rate; and T is expressed in *years* (or a fraction of a year).

Example 1 On July 10, 2015, Wendy Chapman borrowed $12,000 from her Aunt Nelda. If Wendy agreed to pay a 9% annual rate of interest, calculate the dollar amount of interest she must pay if the loan is for **(a)** 1 year, **(b)** 5 months, and **(c)** 15 months.

a. 1 year: $I = PRT = \$12{,}000 \times 9\% \times 1 = \$1{,}080$
b. 5 months: $I = PRT = \$12{,}000 \times 9\% \times \frac{5}{12} = \$450$
c. 15 months: $I = PRT = \$12{,}000 \times 9\% \times \frac{15}{12} = \$1{,}350$

We can do the arithmetic of Example 1 with a calculator:

Keystrokes (for most calculators)	
12,000 × 9 % =	1,080.00
12,000 × 9 % × 5 ÷ 12 =	450.00
12,000 × 9 % × 15 ÷ 12 =	1,350.00

To find the maturity value, we simply add interest to the principal.

> **maturity value formula**
>
> $$M = P + I$$
>
> M = Maturity value P = Principal I = Dollar amount of interest

Example 2 Refer to Example 1. Calculate the maturity value if the 9% $12,000 loan is for **(a)** 1 year, **(b)** 5 months, and **(c)** 15 months.

a. 1 year: $M = P + I = \$12{,}000 + \$1{,}080 = \$13{,}080$
b. 5 months: $M = P + I = \$12{,}000 + \$450 = \$12{,}450$
c. 15 months: $M = P + I = \$12{,}000 + \$1{,}350 = \$13{,}350$

Wendy must pay a total of $13,080 if the loan is repaid in 1 year (July 10, 2016), $12,450 if the loan is repaid in 5 months (December 10, 2015), and $13,350 if the loan is repaid in 15 months (October 10, 2016).

b Counting days and determining maturity date—loans stated in days

In Examples 1 and 2, the term was stated in months or years. Short-term bank loans often have a term stated in days (such as 90 or 180 days) rather than months. Before calculating the amount of interest for these loans, we must know how to count days. One method is to look at a regular calendar and start counting: the day *after* the date of the loan is day 1, and so on. However, that method can be time-consuming and it is easy to make a mistake along the way. We will, instead, use a **day-of-the-year calendar**, shown in Appendix D. In the day-of-the-year calendar, each day is numbered; for example, July 10 is day 191 (it is the 191st day of the year). The next example shows how to use a day-of-the-year calendar.

Example 3 Find **(a)** 90 days from September 10, 2013; **(b)** 180 days from September 10, 2013; and **(c)** 180 days from September 10, 2015.

a. Sep. 10 → Day 253
                       +90
    Dec. 9 ←   343

b. Sep. 10 → Day 253
                       +180
                       433   *(This is greater than 365, so we must subtract 365)*
                       -365
    Mar. 9 ←   68

c. Sep. 10 → Day 253
                       +180
                       433   *(This is greater than 365, so we must subtract 365)*
                       -365
    Mar. 8 ←   68   *(Because this is a leap year, March 8 is day 68)*

In parts (b) and (c) of Example 3, we found that the final date was the 68th day of the year. For a *non-leap year*, the 68th day is March 9. With a *leap year*, like 2016, there is an extra day in February so March 9 is day 69; March 8 is day 68.

An optional method for counting days is known as the *days-in-a-month method*. With this method, we remember how many days there are in each month; the method is shown in Appendix D, page D-2. While a day-of-the-year calendar is often easier to use, understanding the days-in-a-month method is important because we may not always have a day-of-the-year calendar with us. Here is how we could do Example 3, part (c), using the days-in-a-month method:

180 days from September 10, 2015?

Days left in September: 30 - 10 =	20	*September has 30 days; not charged interest for first 10 days*
Days in October	+ 31	
Subtotal	51	
Days in November	+ 30	
Subtotal	81	
Days in December	+ 31	
Subtotal	112	
Days in January	+ 31	
Subtotal	143	
Days in February (leap year)	+ 29	
Subtotal	172	
Days in March	+ 8	*We need 8 more days to total 180*
Total	180	

Date is **March 8**

In the next example, we'll figure out how many days between two dates. For some of us, there are quite a few days between dates (oops, wrong kind of date).

Example 4 Find the number of days between each set of dates: **(a)** July 24 to November 22, **(b)** July 24 to March 13 of the following year (non-leap year), and **(c)** July 24 to March 13 (leap year).

a. Nov. 22 → Day   326   (*Last day is minuend, on top*)
       July 24 → Day -205
                        121 days

b. Number of days left in first year: 365 - 205 (day number for July 24)   160
       Number of days in next year: Mar. 13 →   +72
                                                                               232 days

c. Number of days left in first year: 365 - 205 (day number for July 24)   160
       Number of days in next year: Mar. 13 → 72 + 1 (for leap year) →   +73
                                                                               233 days

In part (b) of Example 4 (non-leap year), March 13 is day 72. But with a leap year in part (c), there is an extra day in February, making March 13 day 73, not day 72.

Here is how we could do Example 4, part (c), using the days-in-a-month method:

Days between July 24 and March 13 (a leap year)?

Days in July: 31 - 24 =	7	*July has 31 days; not charged interest for first 24 days*
Days in August	31	
Days in September	30	
Days in October	31	
Days in November	30	
Days in December	31	
Days in January	31	
Days in February (leap year)	29	
Days in March	+ 13	
Total	**233 days**	

C Computing simple interest—loans stated in days

The **Truth in Lending Act**, also known as **Regulation Z**, applies to **consumer loans**. The regulation does *not* set maximum interest rates; however many states set limits. It does require lenders to notify the borrower of two things: how much extra money the borrower is paying (known as **finance charges**) as a result of borrowing the money and the **annual percentage rate (APR)** the borrower is paying, accurate to $\frac{1}{8}$ of 1%. The law does not apply to business loans, loans over $25,000 (unless they are secured by real estate), most public utility fees, and student loan programs. Apparently, the government figures that businesspeople and students are bright enough to figure their own APR (and they are right!).

Prior to 1969, when the Truth in Lending Act became effective, lenders generally used a 360-day year for calculating interest. Without calculators and computers, calculations were easier using a 360-day year than a 365-day year. In calculating an APR for Truth in Lending purposes, lenders are required to use a 365-day year. Many lenders use a 360-day year for business loans (remember, business loans are exempt from the Truth in Lending Act).

Although we will not emphasize the following terminology, some people and some textbooks refer to interest based on a 360-day year as **ordinary interest** (or **banker's interest**) and interest based on a 365-day year as **exact interest**.

Example 5 Calculate interest on a 90-day $5,000 loan at 11%, using **(a)** a 360-day year and **(b)** a 365-day year.

a. 360-day year: $I = PRT = \$5{,}000 \times 11\% \times \frac{90}{360} = \$137.50$

b. 365-day year: $I = PRT = \$5{,}000 \times 11\% \times \frac{90}{365} = \$135.62$

As you can see from Example 5, a 360-day year benefits the lender and a 365-day year benefits the borrower.

> **TIP** use estimating to determine if an answer is reasonable
>
> It is easy to make a mistake when lengthy calculations are involved (none of us ever makes mistakes though, do we?). Estimating can be helpful in detecting errors. Using a rate of 10% and a term of 1 year provides a good reference point to estimate interest. In Example 5, $5,000 × 10% interest for 1 year is $500 (we simply move the decimal point one place to the left). The loan of Example 5 is for about $\frac{1}{4}$ of a year; $\frac{1}{4}$ of $500 is $125. And the rate is 11%, not 10%, so the amount would be slightly greater than $125. The two answers of Example 5, $137.50 and $135.62, seem reasonable.

While some loan agreements require the borrower to pay a **prepayment penalty** if the loan is paid off early, most loans give the borrower the right to prepay part or all of the loan without penalty. Most lenders rely on what is called the **U.S. Rule** to calculate interest. With the U.S. Rule, interest is calculated to the date payment is received and on the basis of a 365-day year.

Example 6 Refer to Example 5, in which you get a 90-day $5,000 loan at 11%. You are able to pay the loan off early, in 65 days. Calculate interest using the U.S. Rule.

$I = PRT = \$5{,}000 \times 11\% \times \frac{65}{365} = \$97.95$

Interest is $97.95. You saved $37.67 ($135.62 - $97.95) by paying off the loan early.

When a borrower elects to repay a single-payment loan with **partial payments**, interest is calculated first; the remainder of each partial payment is treated as principal and reduces the loan balance.

> **partial payments: calculating interest, principal, and remaining balance**
>
> **Step 1** Calculate interest: $I = PRT$
>
> **Step 2** The remainder of the payment is principal: Principal = Total paid - Interest portion
>
> **Step 3** New balance = Previous balance - Principal portion of payment
>
> *Note:* For the final payment, principal is the previous balance (so the balance will end up zero).

Example 7 Refer to Example 6, in which you get a 90-day $5,000 loan at 11% interest. Suppose you have some extra cash and pay $2,000 on day 21 (21 days after getting the loan); on day 65 (65 days after getting the loan) you pay off the loan. Calculate the amount of interest and principal for each payment as well as the total amount of your final payment.

Day number	Total payment	Interest	Principal	Balance
0	—	—	—	$5,000.00
21	$2,000.00	$31.64	$1,968.36	$3,031.64
65	$3,071.84	$40.20	$3,031.64	$ 0.00
Totals	$5,071.84	$71.84	$5,000.00	—

Procedure for payment on day 21
$I = PRT = \$5{,}000.00 \times 11\% \times \frac{21}{365} = \$31.64$
Principal = $2,000.00 - $31.64 = $1,968.36
Balance = $5,000.00 - $1,968.36 = $3,031.64

Procedure for payment on day 65
$I = PRT = \$3{,}031.64 \times 11\% \times \frac{44}{365} = \$40.20$ *(65 days - 21 days = 44 days)*
Principal = $3,031.64 (previous balance, so balance will be $0.00)
Total payment = $40.20 interest + $3,031.64 principal = $3,071.84

> **TIP** **double the interest**
>
> In Example 7, when calculating interest for the payment on day 65, you may have been tempted to calculate interest for 65 days. Remember, however, we calculated interest for the first 21 days as part of the first payment; you don't want to be charged interest again for the first 21 days (once is enough!).

Notice that in Example 7 you paid total interest of $71.84 compared to interest of $97.95 in Example 6. You may wonder why you saved some interest since both loans were paid off on day 65. The reason is that by paying $2,000 on day 21, the balance decreased, and interest for the last 44 days was figured on that reduced balance.

Well, that does it for this unit. Let's do the U-Try-It exercises to see if you understand the *principal* points of this unit. Take your *time*; do the problems at your own *rate*.

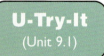

1. Suppose you borrow $8,000 for 18 months at 11% simple interest. Find: **(a)** interest and **(b)** maturity value.
2. Find 180 days from August 5.
3. How many days are there between May 22 and October 14?
4. You get a 90-day $15,000 business loan from your bank at 9.25% interest. Calculate interest assuming the bank uses **(a)** a 365-day year and **(b)** a 360-day year.

5. You get a 180-day $20,000 loan from your credit union at 10.5% interest. You have some extra cash and pay $8,000 on day 40 (40 days after getting the loan); on day 115 (115 days after getting the loan) you pay off the loan. Find the missing numbers (use a 365-day year).

Day number	Total payment	Interest	Principal	Balance
0	—	—	—	$20,000.00
40	$8,000.00			
115				
Totals				—

Answers: (If you have a different answer, check the solution in Appendix A.)
1a. $1,320 **1b.** $9,320 **2.** Feb. 1 **3.** 145 days **4a.** $342.12 **4b.** $346.88 **5.** Payment on day 40: $230.14, $7,769.86, $12,230.14. Payment on day 115: $12,494.01, $263.87, $12,230.14, $0.00 Totals: $20,494.01, $494.01, $20,000.00

Unit 9.2 Solving for principal, rate, and time

In Unit 8.1, we used the simple interest formula $I = PRT$ to solve for I. We can also solve for the other variables (P, R, and T). It will be easier if we have a formula especially designed for the variable in question. We can create separate formulas by using the Golden Rule of Equation Solving: *Do unto one side as you do unto the other.* For example, to find P, we can divide both sides of the formula $I = PRT$ by RT, getting $\frac{I}{RT} = P$. Or, we can use the following memory aid:

> **TIP**   **memory aid**
>
> As a memory aid, some people like to place the symbols I, P, R, and T in a circle (notice that the I is alone at the top). The formula for each of the variables is found by covering the appropriate letter. Covering P with your finger, for example, shows I over RT.
>
>
>
> $$I = PRT$$
> $$P = \frac{I}{RT} \qquad R = \frac{I}{PT} \qquad T = \frac{I}{PR}$$
>
> I = Dollar amount of interest P = Principal
> R = Annual rate of interest T = Time (in years)

Now we will solve a few problems for the variables P, R, and T. Because there are many more applications in solving for R than for P and T, we will solve for R last.

ⓐ Solving for P (principal) and T (time)

Example 1 You open a checking account. You are paid 3% interest on the average balance but are charged a $5 monthly charge. Assuming that interest is paid monthly (regardless of the number of days in the month), calculate the average balance you must maintain to offset the $5 monthly charge.

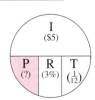

$$P = \frac{I}{RT} = \frac{\$5}{3\% \times \frac{1}{12}} = \frac{\$5}{.03 \times 1 \div 12} = \frac{\$5}{.0025} = \boxed{\$2,000}$$

Check answer: $I = PRT = \$2000 \times 3\% \times \frac{1}{12} = \$5.00$

You must maintain an average balance of $2,000.

Example 2 You decide to pay off an 8% $5,000 loan early. The bank tells you that you owe a total of $82.19 interest. Assuming that the bank uses a 365-day year, for how many days are you being charged interest?

Remember, when we solve for T, we are finding the *portion of a year*, not the number of days.

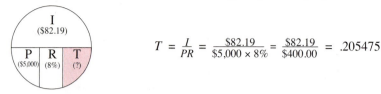

$$T = \frac{I}{PR} = \frac{\$82.19}{\$5,000 \times 8\%} = \frac{\$82.19}{\$400.00} = .205475$$

You are being charged for .205475 of a year. Because there are 365 days in a year:

365 days × .205475 = 75 days.   Check answer: $I = PRT = \$5,000 \times 8\% \times \frac{75}{365} = \$82.19$

You are being charged interest for 75 days.

b Solving for R (rate)

Now we will solve for R. Remember, R can be considered to be an APR (annual percentage rate).

Example 3 You borrow $500 from your uncle and agree to repay the $500 plus $20 interest in 6 months. What interest rate are you paying?

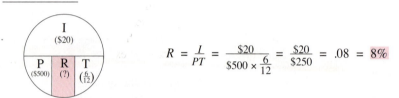

$$R = \frac{I}{PT} = \frac{\$20}{\$500 \times \frac{6}{12}} = \frac{\$20}{\$250} = .08 = 8\%$$

You are paying an annual rate of 8%.

The Truth in Lending Act requires lenders to treat certain loan fees (such as credit report fees or "set-up" fees) as finance charges for purposes of calculating an APR. This is consistent with the concept that an APR considers the "amount and timing of value received and the amount and timing of payments made."

Example 4 You get a 90-day $3,000 consumer loan at 8%. You are required to pay a document preparation fee of $50. Calculate your APR. Express the rate with two decimal places.

The $50 fee is a form of interest, just paid in advance.

- Interest (I) for APR purposes is total finance charges:

    $I = PRT = \$3,000 \times 8\% \times \frac{90}{365} =$ $ 59.18
    Document preparation fee   + 50.00
    Total finance charges $109.18

- You are being charged interest on $3,000, but principal (P) for APR purposes is the amount of money you have use of: $3,000 - $50 fee = $2,950

$$R = \frac{I}{PT} = \frac{\$109.18}{\$2,950 \times \frac{90}{365}} = \frac{\$109.18}{\$727.40} \approx .1501 \approx 15.01\%$$

The symbol ≈ means "approximately equal to"

You are really paying an annual rate (APR) of 15.01%, considerably higher than the 8% stated rate. Because the loan is a consumer loan, the lender must inform you in writing what the APR is before you sign the loan agreement.

Suppose, instead of getting the loan in Example 4, you can get a 12% loan with no fees. You would be better off getting the 12% loan, since the APR is only 12%, while the APR for the loan in Example 4 is 15.01%.

Some lenders use a 360-day year for business loans. In the next example, we will calculate an APR on a loan using a 360-day year.

Example 5

You get a 60-day $2,000 business loan at 10% interest. The lender uses a 360-day year. Calculate your APR.

$$I = PRT = \$2000 \times 10\% \times \frac{60}{360} = \$33.33$$

$$R = \frac{I}{PT} = \frac{\$33.33}{\$2,000 \times \frac{60}{365}} = \frac{\$33.33}{\$328.77} \approx .1014 \approx 10.14\%$$

Even if interest is calculated using a 360-day year, an APR always uses a 365-day year

You must pay $33.33 interest. You are really paying an annual rate (APR) of 10.14%. Because the loan is a business loan (not a consumer loan), the lender is not required to inform you of the APR. But that's no problem because you can calculate your own APR (right?).

Payday loans are designed for people who desperately need money. With this type of loan, borrowers who receive a paycheck get a loan, kind of like an advance on their paycheck, from a payday lender. As you will see, these loans can have an extremely high rate of interest.

Payday loan centers are becoming more and more common. As with all loans, we should determine the APR before getting the loan.

Example 6

You need some money to pay current bills. You go to a local loan center. They agree to make you a payday loan equal to 25% of your net monthly pay. They will charge you $10 per week for each $100 you borrow. Based on net monthly pay of $1,600, determine the maximum amount you can borrow. Then, assuming you borrow the money for 2 weeks, calculate your APR.

You can borrow: $1,600 \times 25\% = \$400$

Interest will be $40 per week × 2 weeks = $80

$$R = \frac{I}{PT} = \frac{\$80}{\$400 \times \frac{14}{365}} \approx \frac{\$80}{\$15.34246575} \approx 5.2143 \approx 521.43\%$$

You will receive $400 and must pay $480 in 2 weeks, resulting in an APR of 521.43%.

High interest rates like the one calculated in Example 6 are not that uncommon. Some states have a **usury law** that sets maximum interest rates. Even in these states, certain loans, like payday loans, may be exempt from usury laws. You may ask, How could a mere $80 interest result in an interest rate of 521.43%? Think of it this way. You pay interest of $80 on $400 and $80 ÷ $400 is 20%. But you are borrowing the money for only 2 weeks. Because there are approximately 26.0714 two-week periods in a year, we multiply the 20% (or .20) by 26.0714: .20 × 26.0714 = 5.2143 = 521.43%!

> **TIP** — **stuff happens**
>
> One reason people get in financial trouble is because "stuff" happens—and when we least expect it. The car breaks down. Our employer goes out of business and we have no job. We end up in the hospital, without health insurance. And the list goes on.
>
> To avoid being desperate for money and forced to get a loan like a payday loan, we should create an emergency fund. An emergency fund of at least 3 months' income, and up to 6 months' income, is recommended. Dip into the fund only for an emergency, and then immediately replenish the fund.

Another way to calculate interest is known as the **discount method** (also referred to as the **bank discount method**). This method, not used as much now as in the past, figures interest on the *maturity value*; the **proceeds** (maturity value minus interest) are given to the borrower, who must repay the maturity value. The bank discount method uses a 360-day year.

> **= bank discount method formulas**
>
> $$D = MRT$$
>
> $$\text{Proceeds} = M - D$$
>
> D = Bank discount (dollar amount of interest) R = Annual rate
> M = Maturity value T = Time, in years (using a 360-day year)

Example 7 You get a loan using the discount method. You sign a note, agreeing to repay $5,000 in 90 days. Assuming a discount rate of 12%, calculate **(a)** interest (discount), **(b)** proceeds you receive, and **(c)** the APR.

a. $D = MRT = \$5{,}000 \times 12\% \times \frac{90}{360} = \$150$

b. Proceeds $= M - D = \$5{,}000 - \$150 = \$4{,}850$

c. APR: $R = \frac{I}{PT} = \frac{\$150}{\$4{,}850 \times \frac{90}{365}} = \frac{\$150}{\$1{,}195.89} \approx .1254 \approx 12.54\%$

↑ This is the amount of money you have use of

You will be given $4,850 and must pay back $5,000 in 90 days, resulting in an APR of 12.54%.

In Example 7, the APR (12.54%) is higher than the discount rate (12%). This is due to two factors: (1) interest for the loan of Example 7 is calculated on the maturity value ($5,000), rather than the amount you have use of ($4,850), and (2) the discount method uses a 360-day year, whereas the APR always uses a 365-day year.

That does it for this unit. Let's try the U-Try-It set to find out if it sunk in!

U-Try-It (Unit 9.2)

1. You pay your bank $157.50 interest for 6 months on a 9% loan. How much did you borrow?
2. You pay your bank $78.90 interest on an 8% $4,000 loan. If the bank uses a 365-day year, for how many days are you being charged interest?
3. You get a $5,000 business loan for 180 days at 10.5% interest. The lender charges you a $150 document preparation fee and uses a 360-day year for calculating interest. What is your APR, to the nearest hundredth of a percent?

Answers: (If you have a different answer, check the solution in Appendix A.)
1. $3,500   **2.** 90 days   **3.** 17.25%

Unit 9.3 Compound interest

a Understanding how compound interest differs from simple interest

Simple interest is interest that's earned only on principal. Compound interest, on the other hand, is interest earned on principal *plus previous interest*. The next example illustrates the difference.

Example 1 Trish and Hannah each have $100. Trish loans her $100 to a friend. Her friend agrees to repay her in 3 years, together with 6% simple interest. Hannah deposits her $100 in a savings account and leaves it there for 3 years to accumulate interest at 6%, compounded annually. Calculate the amount Trish and Hannah will have in 3 years.

Trish's balance at the end of year 3 (simple interest):

$I = PRT = \$100 \times 6\% \times 3 = \$18$ $M = P + I = \$100 + \$18 = \$118$

Hannah's balance at the end of each year (compound interest):

Yr. 1: $I = PRT = \$100 \times 6\% \times 1 = \$6$ $M = P + I = \$100 + \$6 = \$106$
Yr. 2: $I = PRT = \$106 \times 6\% \times 1 = \$6.36$ $M = P + I = \$106 + \$6.36 = \$112.36$
Yr. 3: $I = PRT = \$112.36 \times 6\% \times 1 = \$6.74$ $M = P + I = \$112.36 + \$6.74 = \$119.10$

Trish will end up with $118. Hannah will end up with $119.10. In figuring interest for Hannah, the year 1 ending balance ($106) was used to calculate interest for year 2, and the year 2 ending balance ($112.36) was used to calculate interest for year 3. This is how compound interest works; interest is earned on principal plus previous interest.

When money is invested, earning interest, it grows to a larger sum in the future unless it is stored without earning interest, like in a piggybank.

In Example 1, because of compounding, Hannah ends up with $1.10 more than Trish. The amount may seem fairly insignificant. However, as the time period is extended, the difference becomes substantial. Illustration 9-1 compares simple interest with compound interest over a 100-year period, using a $100 amount at 10% interest. As you can see, compounding makes quite a difference ($1,378,061.23 balance instead of $1,100). Notice that the balance using simple interest is represented by a straight line, while the balance using compound interest is represented by an *accelerated curve* (due to earning interest on interest).

In Example 1, we used a 6% interest rate. You may be saying, Where can I earn a 6% rate these days? Keep in mind that the examples are to illustrate concepts; the interest rates are not as critical as the concepts. But also keep in mind that interest rates can fluctuate dramatically from year to year. In fact, in the 1980s lenders were paying depositors as much as 14% on savings.

Illustration 9-1   Magic of Compound Interest

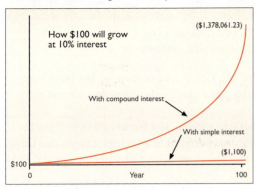

b Computing compound interest for different compounding periods

In Example 1, Hannah earns interest of 6% compounded annually (each year). Interest is often compounded more often than once a year, such as:

- *Semiannually*, where interest is calculated twice a year (each 6 months)
- *Quarterly*, where interest is calculated four times a year (each 3 months)
- *Monthly*, where interest is calculated 12 times a year (each month)
- *Daily*, where interest is calculated each day

In the next example, we will calculate Hannah's balance at the end of 6 months if she earns 6% compounded *semiannually*.

Example 2   Hannah deposits $100 in a savings account earning 6% compounded semiannually. What will her balance be in 6 months?

Let's use the simple interest formula: $I = PRT$. Remember, T is 6 months, or $\frac{1}{2}$ of a year.

$I = PRT = \$100 \times 6\% \times \frac{1}{2} = \$3$ $M = P + I = \$100 + \$3 = \$103$

In 6 months Hannah's balance will be $103.

In Example 2, we found interest by multiplying principal by 6% and then by $\frac{1}{2}$: $100 × 6% × $\frac{1}{2}$ = $3. We would get the same result multiplying principal by $\frac{1}{2}$ of 6%, which is 3%: $100 × 3% = $3. This 3% rate is referred to as the **interest rate per period**, or the **periodic rate.** The periodic rate is found by dividing the annual rate (often called the **nominal rate**) by the number of compounding periods per year.

periodic rate formula

$$\text{Periodic rate} = \frac{\text{Annual Rate}}{\text{Periods per year}}$$

Example 3   Find the periodic rate for **(a)** 6% compounded semiannually, **(b)** 7.5% compounded quarterly, and **(c)** 8.25% compounded monthly.

a. $\frac{6}{2} = 3(\%)$ b. $\frac{7.5}{4} = 1.875(\%)$ c. $\frac{8.25}{12} = 0.6875(\%)$

For an interest rate of 6% compounded semiannually, a person will earn 3% each period (6 months); for 7.5% compounded quarterly, a person will earn 1.875% each period (3 months); and for 8.25% compounded monthly, a person will earn 0.6875% each period (1 month).

> **TIP** — don't round periodic rate
>
> Don't make the common mistake of rounding a preiodic rate. In Example 3(c), the periodic rate for 8.25% compounded monthly is 0.6875%, *not* 0.69%. In some cases the periodic rate may be a repeating decimal. For example, the periodic rate for 7% compounded monthly is 0.583 (with the 3s continuing forever). If the periodic rate is used in calculations, be sure to use as many decimal places for the rate as your calculator will allow (such as 0.58333333%).

In the next example, we will use a periodic rate to find an ending balance. As you will see, it is easier than using the simple interest formula.

Example 4 Hannah deposits $100 in a savings account earning 6% compounded semiannually and leaves it there for 3 years. Find the ending balance using the periodic rate of 3%.

	Interest	Balance
Beginning	—	$100.00
6 months	$100.00 × 3% = $3.00	$103.00
12 months	$103.00 × 3% = $3.09	$106.09
18 months	$106.09 × 3% = $3.18	$109.27
24 months	$109.27 × 3% = $3.28	$112.55
30 months	$112.55 × 3% = $3.38	$115.93
36 months	$115.93 × 3% = $3.48	**$119.41**

Notice, the dollar amount of interest increases each period as the balance increases. That's because of compounding.

The arithmetic of Example 4 can be done on a calculator by increasing the balance 3% each 6 months.

Keystrokes (for most calculators)

100	+	3	%	=	103.00
	+	3	%	=	106.09
	+	3	%	=	109.27
	+	3	%	=	112.55
	+	3	%	=	115.93
	+	3	%	=	**119.41**

Let's compare the results of Examples 1 and 4.

Interest rate	What $100 grows to in 3 years
6% simple interest (Example 1)	$118.00
6% compounded annually (Example 1)	$119.10
6% compounded semiannually (Example 4)	$119.41

As you can see, the more often interest is calculated, the more benefit there is to the person receiving the interest.

C Calculating annual percentage yield (APY)

When we have extra money sitting around (which isn't often enough, is it?), we may decide to deposit it in an interest-bearing account. Suppose we can deposit the money in an account that pays 6% compounded *quarterly* or one that pays 6.10% compounded *annually*. Which is the best choice? The next example shows how we can decide.

Example 5   Your bank pays interest of 6% compounded *quarterly*. Your credit union pays 6.10%, compounded *annually*. Which rate is best?

Let's assume that we deposit $100 in each of the accounts. The balance in 1 year would be:

For 6% compounded quarterly, the periodic rate = $\frac{6}{4}$ = 1.5(%)

Balance in 3 months:	$100 + 1.5% =	$101.50
Balance in 6 months:	+ 1.5% =	$103.02
Balance in 9 months:	+ 1.5% =	$104.57
Balance in 12 months:	+ 1.5% =	$106.14

For 6.10% compounded annually

Balance in 12 months: $100 + 6.10% = $106.10

Because the balance is greater for the rate of 6% compounded quarterly, it appears that 6% compounded quarterly is a better rate than 6.10% compounded annually.

We found that $100 earning 6% compounded quarterly results in an ending balance, after 1 year, of $106.14. To get an identical return we could deposit $100 earning 6.14% compounded annually, because $100 + 6.14% also results in an ending balance of $106.14. In other words, 6% compounded quarterly is *equivalent* to 6.14% compounded annually. The stated annual rate (6%) is called the **nominal rate,** while the rate to which it is equivalent if compounded annually (6.14%) is the **annual percentage yield** or **APY.**

TIP   **rates: nominal vs periodic vs APY**

Nominal rate, periodic rate, and APY are easy to get mixed up. Here is a summary, using a rate of 6% compounded quarterly:

Type of rate	Definition	For 6% compounded quarterly
Nominal rate	Stated annual rate	6%
Periodic rate	Interest rate per period	6% ÷ 4 = 1.5%
APY	Rate compounded annually that provides the same return as the more frequently compounded nominal rate (6%)	6.14%

Special Note: Don't confuse APY with APR of Unit 9.2. An APY is the annual percentage yield *earned* on savings; an APR is the annual percentage rate *paid* on a loan.

We can find an APY by following these steps:

finding APY

Step 1   Find the periodic rate. If it is a repeating decimal, use as many digits as possible.

Step 2   Using the periodic rate, find what $100 will grow to over 1 year (like $106.14 in Example 5). Be sure to use chain calculations (don't round intermediate results).

Step 3   Subtract $100 from the balance; this gives us the dollar amount of interest (like $6.14 in Example 5).

Step 4   Drop the dollar sign and add a percent sign; this is the APY (like 6.14% in Example 5).

> **TIP** — safety
>
> Savings accounts are often insured, in case the savings institution (such as a bank, credit union, or stock brokerage company) experiences financial difficulty. Insurance may be federally regulated, state-regulated, or privately regulated and is only as good as the agency providing the insurance. Before starting a savings plan, don't overemphasize rate; consider the safety factor.

That finishes this chapter. Congratulations! As mentioned, the concepts of this chapter are important to many upcoming topics; we will calculate simple interest and use compounding many times. Hopefully, that excites you. Now, let's make sure we've got the concepts of this last unit mastered by doing the U-Try-It problems.

U-Try-It (Unit 9.3)

1. David Christopher deposits $500 in a savings account earning 5% compounded annually. What will the balance be in 4 years?
2. John Travis deposits $1,200 in a savings account earning 4.5% compounded quarterly. What will the balance be in 1 year?
3. What is the APY for 6.75% compounded quarterly?

Answers: (If you have a different answer, check the solution in Appendix A.)
1. $607.75   2. $1,254.92   3. 6.92%

Chapter in a Nutshell

Objectives | Examples

Unit 9.1 Computing simple interest and maturity value

a Computing simple interest and maturity value—loans stated in months or years

$5,000 at 8% for 18 months:

$$I = PRT = \$5{,}000 \times 8\% \times \frac{18}{12} = \$600$$

$$M = P + I = \$5{,}000 + \$600 = \$5{,}600$$

b Counting days and determining maturity date—loans stated in days

180 days from Apr. 23:

Apr. 23 → Day 113
+180
Oct. 20 ← 293

Days between Mar. 12 and Oct. 28:

Oct. 28 → Day 301
Mar. 12 → Day − 71
230 days

90 days from Nov. 17:

Nov. 17 → Day 321
+ 90
411
− 365
Feb. 15 ← 46

Days between Nov. 13 and Apr. 22 (leap year):

First Year: 365 − 317   48
Next Year: 112 + 1 (leap year)   113
161 days

Chapter in a Nutshell (continued)

Objectives	Examples

(c) Computing simple interest—loans stated in days

$8,000 at 9% for 90 days, using: **(a)** 365-day year and **(b)** 360-day year

a. $I = PRT = \$8{,}000 \times 9\% \times \frac{90}{365} = \$177.53$

b. $I = PRT = \$8{,}000 \times 9\% \times \frac{90}{360} = \$180.00$

$10,000 at 7% for 180 days; $4,800 partial payment on day 52; balance paid on day 115

Day	Total payment	Interest	Principal	Balance
0	—	—	—	$10,000.00
52	$4,800.00	$99.73	$4700.27	$5,299.73
115	$5,363.76	$64.03	$5,299.73	$0.00
Totals	$10,163.76	$163.76	$10,000.00	—

Calculations for payment on day 52
$I = PRT = \$10{,}000 \times 7\% \times \frac{52}{365} = \$99.73$
Principal = $4,800 − $99.73 = $4,700.27
Balance = $10,000 − $4,700.27 = $5,299.73

Calculations for payment on day 115
$I = PRT = \$5{,}299.73 \times 7\% \times \frac{63}{365} = \$64.03$ (115 days − 52 days = 63 days)
Principal = $5,299.73 (previous balance)
Total payment = $64.03 + $5,299.73 = $5,363.76

Unit 9.2 Solving for principal, rate, and time

(a) Solving for P (principal) and T (time)

$3,000 loan for 73 days at 9.75% interest

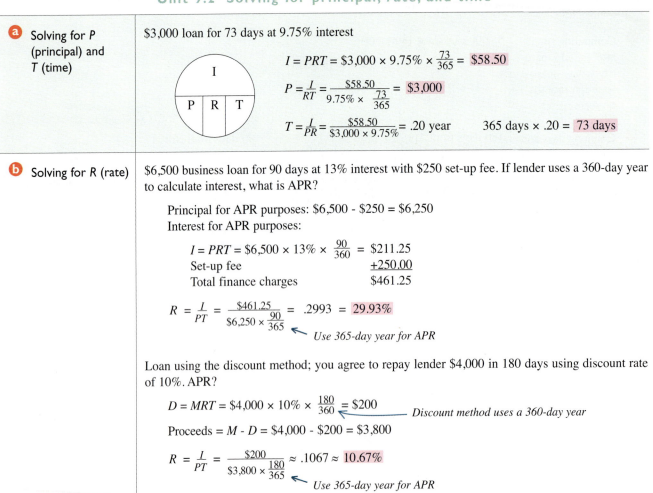

$I = PRT = \$3{,}000 \times 9.75\% \times \frac{73}{365} = \$58.50$

$P = \frac{I}{RT} = \frac{\$58.50}{9.75\% \times \frac{73}{365}} = \$3{,}000$

$T = \frac{I}{PR} = \frac{\$58.50}{\$3{,}000 \times 9.75\%} = .20$ year   365 days × .20 = 73 days

(b) Solving for R (rate)

$6,500 business loan for 90 days at 13% interest with $250 set-up fee. If lender uses a 360-day year to calculate interest, what is APR?

Principal for APR purposes: $6,500 − $250 = $6,250
Interest for APR purposes:

$I = PRT = \$6{,}500 \times 13\% \times \frac{90}{360} = \$211.25$
Set-up fee   +250.00
Total finance charges $461.25

$R = \frac{I}{PT} = \frac{\$461.25}{\$6{,}250 \times \frac{90}{365}} = .2993 = 29.93\%$ ← Use 365-day year for APR

Loan using the discount method; you agree to repay lender $4,000 in 180 days using discount rate of 10%. APR?

$D = MRT = \$4{,}000 \times 10\% \times \frac{180}{360} = \$200$ — Discount method uses a 360-day year

Proceeds = M − D = $4,000 − $200 = $3,800

$R = \frac{I}{PT} = \frac{\$200}{\$3{,}800 \times \frac{180}{365}} \approx .1067 \approx 10.67\%$ ← Use 365-day year for APR

Chapter in a Nutshell (concluded)

Objectives	Examples

Unit 9.3 Compound interest

(a) Understanding how compound interest differs from simple interest

$5,000 for 3 years at 8% using (a) simple interest, and (b) interest compounded annually:

a. $I = PRT = \$5{,}000 \times 8\% \times 3 = \$1{,}200$ $M = P + I = \$5{,}000 + \$1{,}200 = \$6{,}200$

b. Balance
Yr. 1: $I = PRT = \$5{,}000 \times 8\% \times 1 = \$400$ $M = P + I = \$5{,}000 + \$400 = \$5{,}400$
Yr. 2: $I = PRT = \$5{,}400 \times 8\% \times 1 = \$432$ $M = P + I = \$5{,}400 + \$432 = \$5{,}832$
Yr. 3: $I = PRT = \$5{,}832 \times 8\% \times 1 = \$466.56$ $M = P + I = \$5{,}832 + \$466.56 = \$6{,}298.56$

(b) Computing compound interest for different compounding periods

Periodic rate for 2.75% compounded quarterly: $\frac{2.75}{4} = 0.6875(\%)$

Deposit $500 for 1 year at 2.75% compounded quarterly. Ending balance?

	Interest	Balance
Beginning	—	$500.00
3 months	$500.00 × 0.6875% = $3.44	$503.44
6 months	$503.44 × 0.6875% = $3.46	$506.90
9 months	$506.90 × 0.6875% = $3.48	$510.38
12 months	$510.38 × 0.6875% = $3.51	$513.89

(c) Calculating annual percentage yield (APY)

APY for 5.85% compounded semiannually? Periodic rate = $\frac{5.85}{2} = 2.925(\%)$

$100 + 2.925% = $102.93
+ 2.925% = $105.94 → APY = 5.94%

Enrichment Topics

The following Enrichment Topic, which goes a bit beyond what is in the text, is available for this chapter:

Discounting Simple Interest Notes

If your instructor doesn't cover this topic in class and you would like to dig in deeper on your own, please send a request to *studentsupport@olympuspub.com*.

Think

1. Suppose your business borrows some money. Who benefits from calculating interest using a 360-day year—you or the lender—and why?
2. In Unit 9.2, formulas for P, R, and T are derived from the formula $I = PRT$. Using equation-solving skills, show how these three formulas are derived.
3. If you get a loan with a front-end fee, why is the APR greater than the stated annual rate?
4. If you get a loan using the discount method, why is the APR greater than the stated annual rate?
5. Explain why you would rather earn compound interest than simple interest.
6. Explain why you are better off earning 6% interest compounded quarterly than 6% interest compounded semiannually.

Explore

1. Assume that you are thinking about starting up a new business. Visit the site for the Small Business Administration (www.sba.gov). Explore the site and write a report about some of the things you should consider before starting the business.

Apply

1. **It's Pretty Simple.** Find someone who has gotten a single-payment simple interest consumer loan from a bank. Submit copies of the promissory note, payment schedule, and disclosure statement. Confirm that the interest was calculated correctly. Confirm that all items on the disclosure statement were calculated correctly. Show your work.
2. **Shopping for a Savings Account.** Assume that you have an extra $5,000 to deposit. Contact a bank, a credit union, and a stock brokerage firm and ask for their help with this project. Determine what kinds of savings accounts (including CDs and money market accounts) are available. Submit a report for each type of account, including the following information:
   A. What is the minimum deposit, if any?
   B. What are the interest rate and the compounding period? Determine the Annual Percentage Yield (APY).
   C. Can interest be withdrawn at the end of each compounding period, or must the interest be left to accumulate?
   D. How long must the money be left on deposit? What is the penalty for early withdrawal?
   E. Is the account insured? If so, by what agency? How good is the insurance?

   After providing a detailed report about each type of account, write a concluding paragraph stating which type of account best meets your personal situation and why.

Chapter Review Problems

Unit 9.1 Computing simple interest and maturity value

For Problems 1–7, consider a loan of Sterling George. Sterling borrowed $10,000 on October 1, 2017, for 1 year at 8% interest.

1. What is the principal amount?
2. What is the term?
3. What is the maturity date?
4. What is the dollar amount of interest?
5. What is the maturity value?
6. If Sterling borrowed the money for only 8 months, what is the total amount he will owe?
7. If Sterling borrowed the money for 14 months, what is the total amount he will owe?
8. In the simple interest formula $I = PRT$, I stands for the interest rate. (T or F)
9. In the simple interest formula $I = PRT$, T stands for time, in months. (T or F)

For Problems 10–12, calculate the number of days for which interest should be charged.

	Date of loan	Date of payment	Number of days
10.	Jan. 11, 2017	Oct. 28, 2017	
11.	July 13, 2017	Feb. 21, 2018	
12.	Dec. 18, 2015	Mar. 23, 2016 (leap year)	

For Problems 13–15, calculate the maturity date.

	Date of loan	Term	Maturity date
13.	May 15, 2017	60 days	
14.	Aug. 2, 2017	180 days	
15.	Jan. 18, 2016	90 days	

For Problems 16 and 17, we will calculate interest on a 13% 90-day $15,000 loan.

16. Calculate interest, assuming the lender uses a 360-day year.

17. Calculate interest, assuming the lender uses a 365-day year.

18. The Truth in Lending Act sets the maximum interest rate lenders can charge. (T or F)

19. The Truth in Lending Act applies to all loans. (T or F)

20. In calculating an APR for Truth in Lending purposes, lenders are required to use a 365-day year. (T or F)

For Problems 21–24, consider a loan of Mary Patterson. Mary borrowed $25,000 at 11.5% interest for 120 days. The lender uses a 365-day year.

21. How much interest will Mary owe on the maturity date?

22. Assume Mary pays the loan off early, in 89 days. How much interest will she owe?

23. Assume Mary has some extra cash and instead pays $8,000 on day 24 (24 days after getting the loan), then the balance on day 89 (89 days after getting the loan). Fill in the blanks.

Day number	Total payment	Interest	Principal	Balance
0	—	—	—	$25,000.00
24	$8,000.00			
89				$0.00
Totals				—

24. How much interest does Mary pay under each situation: Problem 21, Problem 22, and Problem 23.

Unit 9.2 Solving for principal, rate, and time

For problems in this unit, if the answer is a percent, express the answer to the nearest hundredth of a percent.

25. From memory, or by modifying the formula $I = PRT$, write a formula designed to solve for (a) P, (b) R, and (c) T.

For Problems 26–29, find the missing value.

	I	P	R	T
26.		$5,000	11%	7 months
27.	$63.75		8.5%	2 months
28.	2,964.75	$35,400		6 months
29.	$275	$2,000	11%	

30. You open a checking account. You are paid 3% interest on the average balance but are charged a $7 monthly charge. Assuming that interest is paid monthly (regardless of the number of days in the month), calculate the average daily balance you must maintain to offset the $7 monthly charge.

31. You decide to pay off a 9% $3,000 loan early. The bank tells you that you owe $111.70 interest. Assuming that the bank uses a 365-day year, for how many days are you being charged interest?

32. You borrow $200 from your aunt and agree to repay her $225 ($200 principal + $25 interest) in 18 months. What interest rate are you paying?

33. You get a 180-day $5,000 consumer loan at 9%. You are required to pay a $100 setup fee at the time you get the loan. What is your APR?

34. You get a $3,500 loan for 90 days. Interest of 13% is charged, using a 360-day year. What is the APR?

35. You get a payday loan. The lender charges you $8 per week for each $100 you borrow. Assuming you borrow $500 for 2 weeks, what APR will you be paying?

36. You get a loan using the discount method. You sign a note, agreeing to repay the lender $2,000 in 60 days. Assuming a discount rate of 15%, determine the APR.

Unit 9.3 Compound interest

For Problems 37–39, calculate the periodic rate.

37. 8% compounded semiannually

38. 7% compounded quarterly

39. 7.5% compounded monthly

40. Jessica Gutierrez loans a friend $700 at 5% simple interest for 3 years. What is the maturity value?

41. Glenna Gardner deposits $700 in a savings account. The money is left on deposit for 3 years earning 5% compounded annually. Calculate the account balance at the end of 3 years.

42. George Lavin deposits $700 in a savings account. The money is left on deposit for 3 years earning 5% compounded semiannually. Calculate the account balance at the end of 3 years. Do not round intermediate results, but write amounts to the nearest penny.

43. Refer to Problems 40–42. Each person earned 5% interest. Who ended up with the most money, and why?

44. You just got your income tax refund and have decided to deposit the money in a savings account. Your bank pays 6.125% compounded semiannually, and your credit union pays 6% compounded monthly. Determine which provides the greater return by calculating the APY for each.

45. Refer to the ad to the right. Confirm the annual percentage yield (APY).

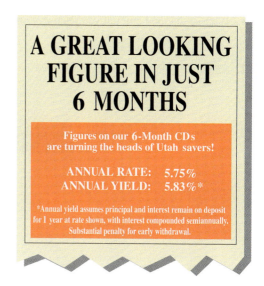

Challenge problems

46. Bob Green purchased merchandise from a supplier and failed to pay the invoice amount ($285) by the last day of the credit period (August 23). Calculate the total amount Bob must pay on October 16 if the supplier charges 18% interest on past-due accounts.

47. Alyce Lee, a sporting goods retailer, purchased ski clothing from a supplier for $2,450. The seller offers a 4% discount if the invoice is paid within 10 days; if not paid within 10 days, the full amount must be paid within 30 days of the invoice date. Use the formula $R = \frac{I}{PT}$ to find the annual rate Alyce, in effect, is paying the supplier if she fails to pay the invoice at the end of the discount period. *Hint*: Alyce is, in effect, borrowing the net amount (amount after deducting the discount) for 20 days and must pay the difference as interest.

48. Babette Lamoreaux needs some money to pay her cell phone bill. She borrows $150 from a pawn shop by giving the pawn shop some jewelry worth about $300. The pawn shop says she can repay the $150 plus 10% interest ($150 × 10% = $15) in 30 days to redeem the jewelry; if she doesn't repay the loan in 30 days, the pawn shop will sell her jewelry. Help Babette calculate the APR.

For Problems 49–52, do some calculations for delinquent property taxes.

49. You fail to pay your annual property taxes on the November 30, 2017, due date. If the tax was $845.23 and you are charged simple interest at 12%, calculate the amount of interest you must pay if you make payment on May 4, 2018.

50. In addition to the 12% simple interest, you are charged a one-time 6% penalty for failing to pay the tax on time. What is the one-time penalty?

51. What is the total amount you must pay on May 4, 2018?

52. Calculate your APR (including the 6% penalty).

53. You are thinking about buying one of two bonds. The first pays 8.35% compounded semiannually; the second pays 8.5% compounded annually. Which provides the greater return?

54. The ad to the right states that $1,000 left on deposit for 5 years earning 8.75% compounded semiannually would result in the same balance as $1,000 earning 10.69% simple interest. Determine if the ad is correct. First, find the maturity value using 10.69% simple interest. Then, find the ending balance for 8.75% compounded semiannually.

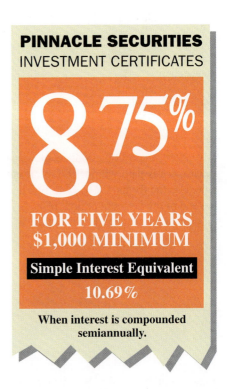

Practice Test

1. In the simple interest formula $I = PRT$, I stands for the interest rate. (T or F)

2. Lynette Read borrowed $12,000 at 9.5% interest for 8 months. What is the maturity value?

3. On June 22, Lo Nguyen borrowed some money for 120 days. What is the maturity date?

4. Buck Tanner gets a 9% $1,500 loan on December 23, 2015, to do some holiday shopping. If Buck repays the money on April 10, 2016 (a leap year), how much interest does he owe? Assume the lender uses a 365-day year.

5. You borrow $15,000 for 90 days at 9% interest. The lender uses a 365-day year. You make a payment of $3,000 on day 22 (22 days after getting the loan). Calculate your balance after the $3,000 payment is applied.

6. You get a 7% 90-day $3,000 loan. The lender uses a 360-day year and charges you a $100 set-up fee at the time you get the loan. What is your APR?

7. You get a loan using the discount method. You sign a note, agreeing to repay the lender $30,000 in 180 days. Assuming a discount rate of 13.5%, determine the APR.

8. Kyle Santini deposits $500 in a savings account. The money is left on deposit earning 6% compounded semiannually. Calculate the account balance at the end of 2 years.

9. Calculate the APY for 7.15% compounded semiannually.

Quotable Quip
I never let my schooling interfere with my education.
– Mark Twain

The Time-Value-of-Money
by John Papanikolas

Sterling G. was one of the most colorful characters I've ever met.

Sterling loved to golf. You would walk down the fairway with him and hear this crackling and popping sound off to the side. Limbs would be shaking and leaves falling off trees. It was Sterling, crunching and crashing through the trees and bushes, looking for golf balls. (Golf was cheaper that way, and his walk down the fairway was more productive.)

If you went to a professional baseball game with Sterling, after the ninth inning everybody would shuffle to the gate. Not Sterling. He would join the clean-up crew. You'd find him bending over picking up stacks of plastic beer cups people left behind that said "St. Louis Cardinal Baseball" on them. "These are good cups," he'd say. "Great to have around the house!"

Don't get me wrong, Sterling could certainly afford golf balls and baseball cups. He was a prosperous real estate investor. He just understood the "time-value" of money a little better than most of us.

"You need to have fun at what you do, or make a lot of money at it," he told young people. "Because if you aren't doing one or the other, you're wasting your time." That is, find something good to do with your "time" — and get a lot of "value" out of it.

The "time-value" of money. Only a few people really do understand it. Sterling was an expert.

Don't Count Your Chickens Before They're Hatched

This proverb suggests that we should not think of money as our own until we actually have it.

The saying is the moral of Aesop's fable about a milkmaid and her pail. She is given a pail of milk by her employer for doing good work, and she knows the doctor will buy it for a shilling. On the way to his house she envisions buying eggs with the shilling; the eggs will hatch into chickens that she can sell for a guinea (21 shillings), with which she can buy a hat and ribbons. Then she spills the milk.

Brainteaser

A standard piece of copy paper is .005 inches thick. If you fold the paper 50 times, how thick will it be?

Answer: 88,849,424 miles (about the distance to the sun)
Fold once: .005 in. x 2
Fold twice: .005 in. x 2 x 2 = .005 in. x 2^2
Fold 50 times: .005 in. x 2^{50} ≈ 5,629,499,530,000 in. ≈ 469,124,961,183 ft ≈ 88,849,424 mi

"You're twenty dollars' late, Simmons!"

Future Value and Present Value: Using Formulas

10

This chapter will introduce time-value-of-money problems. **Time-value-of-money problems** are based on the principle that *money earns interest over time*. For example, if you win a $1,000,000 lottery and the lottery officials give you a choice of receiving the $1,000,000 today or in 10 years, you should take the money today because you can earn interest on the money and end up with considerably more than $1,000,000 in 10 years. So a dollar today is worth more than a dollar received in the future; stated differently, a dollar received in the future is worth less than a dollar received today.

We can solve time-value-of-money problems by using formulas, financial calculators, Excel, or in limited cases with tables. We use formulas in Chapters 10 and 11. We use financial calculators in Chapters 12, 13, and 17. We use Excel in Appendix E. We will not use tables at all. Here's why. Even though using tables gives quick results for a few types of time-value-of-money problems in a *classroom setting*, tables are *not used in the real world*. Tables contain only certain interest rates *(i-values)* and terms *(n-values)*, often not the ones needed. More important, tables cannot be used to solve for *n* and *i*; these problems account for about half of the problems encountered in the real world, such as figuring out how long it will take to accumulate a desired sum or pay off a loan, or calculating an APR on a loan or a yield on a potential investment. *Because the whole premise of this text is to teach real-life skills, we are saying NO! to tables and instead teaching the stuff you'll actually use.*

In this chapter we will calculate how money grows over time and the present value of money to be received in the future.

UNIT OBJECTIVES

Unit 10.1 Time-value-of-money terminology

ⓐ Understanding time-value-of-money terminology

Unit 10.2 Future value

ⓐ Finding what a single deposit will grow to
ⓑ Finding what a series of deposits will grow to

Unit 10.3 Present value

ⓐ Finding the present value of a single sum to be received in the future
ⓑ Finding the present value for a series of payments

Unit 10.1 Time-value-of-money terminology

a Understanding time-value-of-money terminology

The *time-value-of-money* concept states that knowing *when* money is received is just as important as knowing the *amount* of money received. To illustrate, suppose your rich uncle offers you the choice of receiving $10,000 today or $10,300 in 1 year. Your first impulse may be to accept the $10,300, but by doing so you would be ignoring the principal that *money earns interest over time*. Suppose that you accepted the $10,000 today and deposited the money in a savings plan earning 5% compounded annually. You would earn $500 interest ($10,000 × 5% = $500) and end up with $10,500 in 1 year, which is $200 more than your uncle's $10,300 offer.

As you may recall from Unit 9.3 (Compound interest), the frequency of compounding affects how money grows over time. With compound interest, we earn interest not only on amounts deposited, but also on previously earned interest. The period of time between interest calculations is referred to as the **compounding period**, or as just the **period**. For example, if interest is compounded semiannually (twice a year), the compounding period is 6 months, and there are 2 periods per year. If interest is compounded quarterly (four times a year), the compounding period is 3 months, and there are 4 periods per year. With monthly compounding, the compounding period is 1 month, and there are 12 periods per year.

Time-value-of-money (TVM) problems involve 5 variables: n, i, PV, PMT, and FV

	The 5 TVM variables
n	Total number of periods. Stated another way, total number of times interest is calculated.
i	Interest rate per period (or periodic rate).
PV	Present value; a one-time amount that happens at the beginning of the first period.
PMT	Payment, also referred to as periodic payment. Happens once every period.
FV	Future value; a one-time amount that happens at the end of the last period.

To illustrate the TVM variables, suppose that 15 years ago you deposited $500 in a savings plan earning 6% compounded semiannually. Today, you withdrew the entire balance, which has grown to $1,213.63. Here are the values for each variable:

n: 30 (15 years × 2 periods per year = 30)
i: 3% (6% ÷ 2 periods per year = 3%)
PV: $500 (this is the one-time amount that happened at the beginning of the first period)
PMT: None (there is no amount that happens once every period)
FV: $1,213.63 (this is the one-time amount that happened at the end of the last period)

> **TIP**   past, present, and future
>
> In the previous situation, you may have been tempted to treat the $1,213.63 amount as the present value, because it happened today, in the present. Because the $500 happened at the *beginning of the first period*, it is the present value. The $1,213.63, which happened at the *end of the last period*, is the future value.

Let's try to identify the variables in the following examples.

Example 1

Sebastian Xavier is a soda pop "addict" and wonders how much money he could accumulate if he stopped drinking soda pop and deposited the $150 per month he spends on the stuff into a savings plan. Sebastian just turned 20. If his savings plan earns 6% compounded monthly and his first deposit is a month from now, what amount would he have at retirement, 40 years from now? *Don't solve the problem.* Instead, identify the 5 TVM variables.

---

n: 480 (40 years × 12 periods per year = 480)
i: 0.5% (6% ÷ 12 periods per year = 0.5%)
PV: None (There is no one-time, initial deposit at the beginning of the first period)
PMT: $150 (This happens every period)
FV: ? (This is the amount we want to know—the amount at the end of the last period)

You may ask, is it reasonable to expect a 6% return? In today's economy, honestly, no. We may never again see the heyday of the 1980s, where savings rates peaked near 14%, but we'd like to think things will turn around. And, while savings account rates from time to time can be much less, other investments (such as bonds, stocks, real estate, and mutual funds) can over the long haul earn 6% or better.

Example 2

You have the chance to buy a promissory note, in which you would receive 28 quarterly payments of $500, starting 3 months from now. If you buy the note, you will receive a total of $14,000 (28 × $500). If you want to earn 8% compounded quarterly, what price should you pay for the note? *Don't solve the problem.* Instead, identify the 5 TVM variables.

---

n: 28
i: 2% (8% ÷ 4 periods per year = 2%)
PV: ? (This is the amount we want to know—the amount at the beginning of the first period)
PMT: $500 (This happens every period)
FV: None (There is no additional amount you receive or pay at the end of the last period)

In Example 2, you may have been tempted to treat the $14,000 amount as a future value. But you do not receive $14,000 at the end of the last period; instead you receive 28 payments of $500. The $14,000 amount is what we call a "distractor," only there to confuse us!

We will solve Example 1 in Unit 10.2 and Example 2 in Unit 10.3. I'll bet you're excited about that. Meanwhile, let's see if we've mastered the terminology by doing a U-Try-It problem.

U-Try-It (Unit 10.1)

1. You start a savings plan, earning 6% compounded quarterly, by depositing $300. You then deposit $100 at the end of each quarter. You want to know your account balance at the end of 10 years. *Don't solve the problem.* Instead, identify n, i, PV, PMT, and FV.

Answers: (If you have a different answer, check the solution in Appendix A.)
1. $n = 40$; $i = 1.5\%$; PV = $300; PMT = $100; FV = Unknown (this is what we want to know).

Unit 10.2 Future value

If we make deposits into a savings plan, we can calculate the sum to which they will grow if we know the dollar amount of deposits, when the deposits are made, and the interest rate earned. Deposits may consist of one deposit or a series of deposits. Let's start by finding what a single deposit will grow to.

ⓐ Finding what a single deposit will grow to

If we make a deposit into a savings plan, we can calculate the sum to which the money will grow (FV) if we know the dollar amount of the deposit (PV), how long the money is left on deposit (n), and the interest rate earned (i). Let's calculate what a deposit of $400 will grow to if left on deposit for 3 years earning 5% compounded annually. Let's calculate the balance at the end of each year.

Deposit	$400.00
Interest year 1: $I = PRT = \$400 \times 5\% \times 1 =$	+ 20.00
Balance, end of year 1	$420.00
Interest year 2: $I = PRT = \$420 \times 5\% \times 1 =$	+ 21.00
Balance, end of year 2	$441.00
Interest year 3: $I = PRT = \$441 \times 5\% \times 1 =$	+ 22.05
Balance, end of year 3	**$463.05**

Notice that the dollar amount of interest increases each year. That's because of compounding, in which we earn interest not only on the initial deposit but also on previous interest. The arithmetic is fairly easy for this problem, but imagine doing a similar problem if the money were left on deposit for, say, 50 years. The calculations could get a bit tedious! To save time and effort, we can use special formulas, called **compound interest formulas**. A formula for each variable is shown in Illustration 10-1. Notice that the third column of Illustration 10-1 suggests when to use each formula and includes a pictorial showing what we know and what we are solving for. Column 4 will be explained later, when we do Example 5.

Pay special attention to the footnotes of Illustration 10-1. Notice that i stands for the periodic rate (interest rate per period), in decimal form; n stands for the total number of periods. The formulas may look a bit overwhelming at first glance, but don't worry! They are easier to use than they look. In this chapter, we will use Formulas 1A, 1B, 2A, and 2B; we will use the other formulas in Chapter 11.

You may wonder where the compound interest formulas came from. You're probably thinking that someone with a bad sense of humor is responsible, aren't you? Well, actually there is some logic involved in the creation of the formulas. To show the logic of the formulas, let's try the previous problem a different way. The $400 balance is increasing 5% each year, so another way to find the balance is to multiply the balance by 105%, or 1.05:

Balance, end of year 1: $400 × 1.05 =	$420.00
Balance, end of year 2: × 1.05 =	$441.00
Balance, end of year 3: × 1.05 =	**$463.05**

Here's another way of doing the arithmetic:

Balance, end of year 3 = $400(1.05)(1.05)(1.05) = **$463.05**

Because $(1.05)(1.05)(1.05)$ can be written in exponential form as $(1.05)^3$, we could find the ending balance (FV) by multiplying the $400 initial deposit (PV) by $(1.05)^3$.

$$FV = PV(1.05)^3 = \$400(1.05)^3 = \mathbf{\$463.05}$$

What we created above is Formula 1A: $FV = PV(1 + i)^n$, where PV = $400, $i = .05$, and $n = 3$. Once we have Formula 1A, we can derive a formula for PV by dividing each side of the equation by $(1 + i)^n$:

$FV = PV(1 + i)^n$	*Formula 1A*
$\dfrac{FV}{(1 + i)^n} = PV$	*Divide both sides of equation by $(1 + i)^n$*
$PV = \dfrac{FV}{(1 + i)^n}$	*Put PV on left side; this is Formula 2A*

We now have Formulas 1A and 2A. The other formulas were derived by making similar manipulations. *Note:* If you are a glutton for punishment and want to see the derivations, send a request to *studentsupport@olympuspub.com*.

Illustration 10-1 Compound Interest Formulas

	Formula	When to use	If periodic payment is made at the beginning of each period
1A	$FV = PV(1 + i)^n$	Need to know FV; know PV	Not applicable.
1B	$FV = PMT\left[\dfrac{(1 + i)^n - 1}{i}\right]$	Need to know FV; know PMT	Multiply the result by $(1 + i)$.
2A	$PV = \dfrac{FV}{(1 + i)^n}$	Need to know PV; know FV	Not applicable.
2B	$PV = PMT\left[\dfrac{1 - \dfrac{1}{(1 + i)^n}}{i}\right]$	Need to know PV; know PMT	Multiply the result by $(1 + i)$.
3	$i = \left(\dfrac{FV}{PV}\right)^{\frac{1}{n}} - 1$	Need to know interest rate; know PV and FV	Not applicable.
4A	$PMT = \dfrac{FV(i)}{(1 + i)^n - 1}$	Need to know PMT; know FV	Divide the result by $(1 + i)$.
4B	$PMT = \dfrac{PV(i)}{1 - \dfrac{1}{(1 + i)^n}}$	Need to know PMT; know PV	Divide the result by $(1 + i)$.
5*	$n = \dfrac{-\ln\left[\dfrac{PV + \left(\dfrac{PMT}{i}\right)}{\dfrac{PMT}{i} - FV}\right]}{\ln(1 + i)}$	Need to know n; know at least two of these variables: PV, FV, PMT. $n = ?$	$n = \dfrac{-\ln\left[\dfrac{PV + (1 + i)\left(\dfrac{PMT}{i}\right)}{(1 + i)\left(\dfrac{PMT}{i}\right) - FV}\right]}{\ln(1 + i)}$

* Formula 5 is a comprehensive formula that covers quite a few situations. For this formula, use proper sign convention for PV, FV, and PMT. Think of the money from someone's standpoint, and treat each amount accordingly (as a positive if the money is received, or as a negative if the money is paid).

PV = present value; FV = future value; PMT = periodic payment; i = interest rate per period, expressed in decimal form; n = total number of periods. The symbol ln stands for natural logarithm.

Appendix F contains concepts that are important in using the formulas: exponents, order of operations, chain calculations, reciprocals, and logarithms. If you need to brush up on any of these concepts, please review Appendix F now (it is only a few pages long).

When solving time-value-of-money (TVM) problems using formulas, the first step is to figure out which formula to use. Then we substitute known values and do the arithmetic. Let's try some problems, this time using the compound interest formulas. Remember, when changing a percent to a decimal number, we move the decimal point 2 places to the left and discard the % sign.

> **TIP** — **calculator shortcuts**
>
> Most calculators have exponent (power) keys, such as y^x or $\wedge$ to shortcut the arithmetic. If you're using the HP 10BII+ or the TI BAII PLUS, see Appendix C for keystrokes for each of the compound interest formulas (including specific keystrokes for the examples in this chapter marked with a calculator icon in the margin). If you are using the HP 10B, HP 10BII, HP 12C, HP 17BII, HP 39gs, TI 30Xa, TI 30XIIS, TI 83+, TI 84+, Casio 9750G PLUS, or LeWorld FIN, you can request keystrokes at *studentsupport@olympuspub.com*.

Example 1

You get an income tax refund of $1,700 and deposit the money in a savings plan for 6 years, earning 6% compounded quarterly. Find the ending balance using compound interest formulas.

$n = 24$ (6 years × 4 periods per year = 24)
$i = .015$ (6% ÷ 4 periods per year = 1.5% = .015)
PV = $1,700
PMT = None
FV = ?

We want to know FV and we know PV so we use Formula 1A:

$$FV = PV(1 + i)^n = \$1{,}700(1 + .015)^{24} = \$1{,}700(1.015)^{24} = \boxed{\$2{,}430.15}$$

You end up with $2,430.15. You earned $730.15 interest ($2,430.15 - $1,700 initial deposit).

Example 2

Suppose a "wise man" had deposited $1 in a savings account 2,000 years ago and the account earned interest at 2% compounded annually. If the money in the account today were evenly divided among the world's population, how much would each person receive, based on a world population of 7 billion?

We want to know FV and we know PV so we use Formula 1A ($n = 2{,}000$; $i = 2\% = .02$). For this problem, set your decimal at the maximum setting.

Find account balance: $FV = PV(1 + i)^n = \$1(1 + .02)^{2{,}000} = \$1(1.02)^{2{,}000} = 1.58614733 \times 10^{17}$
Amount per person: Account balance (from above) ÷ 7,000,000,000 = $\boxed{\$22{,}659{,}247.54}$

The account balance is too large to fit in a calculator display, so it is written in scientific notation (something like 1.58614733 E17). In simple language, this means to move the decimal 17 places to the right, resulting in an approximate balance of $158,614,733,000,000,000 (read as "One hundred fifty-eight quadrillion, six hundred fourteen trillion, seven hundred thirty-three billion dollars")! Each person would receive $22,659,247.54! Maybe your check is in the mail.

The answer to Example 2 may make your head spin. We would get the same result if we added 2% to the account balance 2,000 times ($1 + 2% + 2% + ⋯). Let friends or relatives solve Example 2 (you will most likely have to help them) and watch the expression on their face when they see the answer.

Example 2 illustrates the power of compounding. By using compound interest, like we did in Example 2, the account balance is $158,614,733,000,000,000. With simple interest, the balance would be:

$$I = PRT = \$1 \times 2\% \times 2{,}000 = \$40$$
$$M = P + I = \$1 + 40 = \mathbf{\$41}$$

So far, we have focused on what a sum of *money* grows to, over time. We can also find how other things (like population of a town, or tuition) will increase over time.

Money earning interest grows over time. Compounding is a powerful tool.

Example 3 Tuition at a local university is currently $4,800 a year. Based on an annual inflation rate of 4%, what will tuition be 15 years from now?

We want to know FV and we know PV so we use Formula 1A ($n = 15$; $i = 4\% = .04$):

$$FV = PV(1 + i)^n = \$4{,}800(1 + .04)^{15} = \$4{,}800(1.04)^{15} = \mathbf{\$8{,}644.53}$$

Based on an annual inflation rate of 4%, tuition will be $8,644.53. We would get the same answer by increasing $4,800 by 4% a total of 15 times: $4{,}800 + 4\% + 4\% + \cdots = \$8{,}644.53$.

ⓑ Finding what a series of deposits will grow to

In Example 1 we made a *single* deposit. We can instead make a series of deposits.

Example 4 You deposit $100 at the end of each year for 4 years, earning 6% compounded annually. Use compound interest formulas to find the balance in 4 years.

We want to know FV and we know PMT so we use Formula 1B ($n = 4$; $i = 6\% = .06$):

$$FV = PMT\left[\frac{(1+i)^n - 1}{i}\right] = \$100\left[\frac{(1.06)^4 - 1}{.06}\right] = \mathbf{\$437.46}$$

Let's check to see if the balance of $437.46 is correct.

	Interest	Deposit	Balance
Balance, end of year 1	None	$100	$100.00
Balance, end of year 2	$I = PRT = \$100 \times 6\% \times 1 = \$6.00$	$100	$206.00
Balance, end of year 3	$I = PRT = \$206 \times 6\% \times 1 = \$12.36$	$100	$318.36
Balance, end of year 4	$I = PRT = \$318.36 \times 6\% \times 1 = \$19.10$	$100	**$437.46**

In Example 4, you deposited $100 at the *end* of each year. How would the balance be affected if the first of your 4 deposits were made immediately (at the beginning of each year)? Because you would start earning interest immediately, your ending balance should be greater than $437.46. Here's what the balance would be:

	Interest	Deposit	Balance
Beginning	None	$100	$100.00
Balance, end of year 1	$I = PRT = \$100 \times 6\% \times 1 = \$6.00$	$100	$206.00
Balance, end of year 2	$I = PRT = \$206 \times 6\% \times 1 = \$12.36$	$100	$318.36
Balance, end of year 3	$I = PRT = \$318.36 \times 6\% \times 1 = \$19.10$	$100	$437.46
Balance, end of year 4	$I = PRT = \$437.46 \times 6\% \times 1 = \$26.25$	None	**$463.71**

The formulas of Illustration 10-1 that involve periodic payments assume that the periodic payments are made at the end of each period. The right-hand column of Illustration 10-1 tells us what to do if periodic payments are made at the *beginning* of each period; notice the pictorials show deposits are made at the *beginning* of each period (left side of payment dashes).

Example 5 Rework Example 4, assuming the deposits are made at the beginning of each year.

The answer from Example 4 ($437.46) is based on deposits being made at the end of each period. The right-hand column for Formula 1B says to multiply the result by $(1 + i)$, so:

$$\$437.46(1 + i) = \$437.46(1 + .06) = \$437.46(1.06) = \$463.71$$

The answer ($463.71) is the same answer we got without using formulas.

Some books use special terminology for a series of payments: if payments are made at the end of each period, the series of payments is referred to as an **ordinary annuity**; if payments are made at the beginning of each period, the series of payments is referred to as an **annuity due**. We will not use that terminology; instead, we will simply state for each problem whether payments are made at the end or beginning of each period.

The next example (the soda pop "addict" problem from Unit 10.1) shows the power of compounding over a long period of time.

Example 6 Sebastian Xavier is a soda pop "addict" and wonders how much money he could accumulate if he stopped drinking soda pop and deposited the $150 per month he spends on the stuff into a savings plan. Sebastian just turned 20. If his savings plan earns 6% compounded monthly and his deposits are made at the end of each month, what amount would he have at retirement, 40 years from now?

We want to know FV and we know PMT, so we will use Formula 1B ($n = 40 \times 12 = 480$; $i = 6\% \div 12 = .5\% = .005$):

$$FV = PMT \left[\frac{(1 + i)^n - 1}{i} \right] = \$150 \left[\frac{(1.005)^{480} - 1}{.005} \right] = \$298{,}723.61$$

Sebastian will end up with $298,723.61! He would earn interest of $226,723.61 ($298,723.61 ending balance - $72,000 deposited).

The next example shows the importance of starting to save as soon as possible.

Example 7 Kristen and Erica are twins. On her 20th birthday, Kristen starts a savings plan by depositing $50 at the beginning of each month. Erica starts a savings plan 25 years later by depositing $100 at the beginning of each month. Both savings plans earn 6% compounded monthly. Find their account balances when they turn 70.

We use Formula 1B ($i = 6\% \div 12 = .5\% = .005$). Because deposits are made at the *beginning* of each month, we must multiply the result by $(1 + i)$, or 1.005.

Kristen. $n = 50 \times 12 = 600$: $FV = PMT\left[\dfrac{(1+i)^n - 1}{i}\right] = \$50\left[\dfrac{(1.005)^{600} - 1}{.005}\right] = \$189,359.55$

Adjustment (deposits are at beginning of each month): $189,359.55 (1.005) = **$190,306.35**

Erica. $n = 25 \times 12 = 300$: $FV = PMT\left[\dfrac{(1+i)^n - 1}{i}\right] = \$100\left[\dfrac{(1.005)^{300} - 1}{.005}\right] = \$69,299.40$

Adjustment (deposits are at beginning of each month): $69,299.40 (1.005) = **$69,645.90***

Note: The answer is $69,645.89 if we do not round 69,299.40 to the nearest penny before multiplying by 1.005.

In Example 7, Kristen ends up with much more than Erica. Notice they both deposited a total of $30,000. Kristen earned interest of $160,306.35 ($190,306.35 - $30,000 deposited) and Erica earned interest of only $39,645.90 ($69,645.90 - $30,000 deposited).

> **TIP** — sooner or later?
>
> Many people delay starting a savings plan because they think a small amount set aside each month will not amount to much later. Perhaps the best investment advice is to "Just Get Started." And the sooner, the better, as pointed out in Example 7.

Let's try a few fun problems in the U-Try-It set. I'll bet you are saying "fun" problems is a contradiction of terms! The two "fun" problems provide a different twist, so be sure to give them a try. In the first "fun" problem, an initial deposit is made into a savings plan and then is followed by a series of deposits. In the second "fun" problem, a series of deposits is made and then the money is left alone, without more deposits, for some additional time.

U-Try-It (Unit 10.2)

1. You start a savings plan by making an initial deposit of $1,250. You then deposit $100 at the end of each quarter for 10 years. What will your balance be in 10 years, assuming you earn 4% compounded quarterly?
2. Sarah Sharp, a 30-year-old insurance broker, decides to start a retirement plan. She figures that her income for the next 25 years will be sufficient to deposit $1,000 at the end of each quarter into her retirement plan. She will let the money sit for another 10 years until she is 65 years old. If Sarah's retirement plan earns 6% compounded quarterly, what amount will she have when she turns 65?

Answers: (If you have a different answer, check the solution in Appendix A.)
1. $6,749.72   2. $415,052.93

Unit 10.3 Present value

In this unit, we will find the value, in today's dollars, of future cash flows. That value is referred to as **present value**. We can find the present value of a single sum to be received in the future, the present value of a series of payments to be received in the future, or the present value of a single sum plus a series of payments. Let's start by finding the present value of a single sum.

a. Finding the present value of a single sum to be received in the future

In Example 1 of Unit 10.2, you got an income tax refund of $1,700 and deposited the money in a savings plan for 6 years, earning 6% compounded quarterly. The money grew to $2,430.15. Let's look at this problem from a different angle. Suppose your aunt says she will give you $2,430.15 in 6 years. Assuming that you can earn 6% compounded quarterly on your money, the real value of her promise, in today's dollars (the present value), is $1,700 because you could invest the $1,700 and end up with $2,430.15. Let's use the compound interest formulas to find the present value of your aunt's promise.

Example 1

Your aunt says she will give you $2,430.15 in 6 years. Assuming that you can earn 6% compounded quarterly, what is the real value of her promise, in today's dollars?

We are solving for PV and we know FV, so we will use Formula 2A (n = 6 years × 4 periods per year = 24; i = 6% ÷ 4 periods per year = 1.5% = .015):

$$PV = \frac{FV}{(1+i)^n} = \frac{\$2{,}430.15}{(1.015)^{24}} = \$1{,}700.00$$

The results of Example 1 are shown graphically in Illustration 10-2. Notice the two-way arrow: with a rate of 6% compounded quarterly, $1,700 will grow to $2,430.15 in 6 years and the present value of $2,430.15 to be received in 6 years is $1,700.

b. Finding the present value for a series of payments

In Example 1, we found the present value of a *single sum* to be received in the future. We can also find the present value of a *series of payments*. For instance, we might want to know the present value of $2,000 to be received at the end of each year for 3 years.

Example 2

You are selling a valuable coin. You have two offers. The first offer is for $5,500 cash. With the second offer, the buyer will pay you $2,000 at the end of each year for 3 years. Assuming that you can earn 8% compounded annually on your money, which offer is better?

Your first reaction may be to accept the second offer because you will receive a total of $6,000. But you would be ignoring the time value of money. Let's calculate the present value of the second offer. We are solving for PV and we know PMT so we use Formula 2B (n = 3; i = 8% = .08):

$$PV = PMT \left[\frac{1 - \frac{1}{(1+i)^n}}{i} \right] = \$2{,}000 \left[\frac{1 - \frac{1}{(1.08)^3}}{.08} \right] = \$5{,}154.19$$

The present value of the second offer is $5,154.19, considerably less than the $5,500 cash offer. You should accept the first offer.

Illustration 10-2 Relationship between Present Value and Future Value

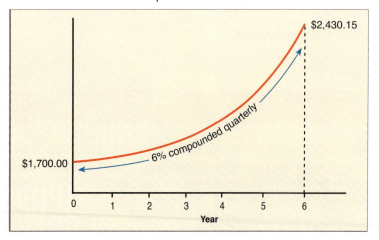

Conclusions
1. $1,700 invested at 6% compounded quarterly will grow to $2,430.15 in 6 years.
2. Assuming that money can earn 6% compounded quarterly, the present value of $2,430.15 to be received in 6 years is $1,700.

There are lots of practical applications for finding the present value of a series of payments. We will explore three common applications: finding the amount to pay for a promissory note (Example 3), determining the value of bonds (Example 4), and finding the value of a long-term project (Example 5).

Finding the amount to pay for a promissory note. Someone who borrows money is generally required to sign a **promissory note**, which spells out the terms of repayment. An owner of a note (a lender) who needs cash may sell the note to a third party. The price is based on the rate of return (referred to as **yield**) the investor demands. As an example, suppose Randy loaned Jinny $15,000 at 6% interest, with quarterly payments of $500. Jinny has been making payments for awhile and the balance is now $11,363.36; Jinny still owes 28 quarterly payments of $500. Randy needs some money for a business venture and asks you to buy the note, in which case you would receive the remaining 28 payments from Jinny. If you are satisfied with the **note rate** of 6%, you would pay the **note balance** of $11,363.36; the note is said to be sold at **par**. If you are satisfied with a rate less than the note rate, you could pay a **premium**. If you require a yield greater than the note rate you would buy the note at a **discount**. Let's find the amount you should pay if you want to earn 8% compounded quarterly (this is Example 2 from Unit 10.1).

Example 3

You have the chance to buy a promissory note, in which you would receive 28 quarterly payments of $500, starting 3 months from now. The note is at 6% interest with an unpaid balance of $11,363.36. If you buy the note, you will receive a total of $14,000 (28 × $500). If you want to earn 8% compounded quarterly, what price should you pay for the note?

You will receive a total of $14,000. If you paid $14,000 for the note, you would earn no interest. In order to earn interest, you must pay less than $14,000. If you paid $11,363.36 you would earn the note rate of 6%. To earn 8% compounded quarterly, you must pay less than $11,363.36. Let's use Formula 2B to find that amount ($n = 28$; $i = 8\% \div 4 = 2\% = .02$):

$$PV = PMT\left[\frac{1 - \frac{1}{(1+i)^n}}{i}\right] = \$500\left[\frac{1 - \frac{1}{(1.02)^{28}}}{.02}\right] = \$10,640.64$$

By paying $10,640.64 you will earn 8% compounded quarterly.

Determining the value of bonds. Corporations, the U.S. government, and local governmental agencies often need large sums of money. They often raise the money by selling bonds to the public. A bond is a written promise to repay the owner of the bond (**bondholder**) a specified amount (**maturity value**) at a future date (**maturity date**). Bondholders also earn interest, generally paid semiannually or annually.

Corporate bonds are generally issued in $1,000 denominations. Many beginning investors think that a $1,000 bond is always worth $1,000. While a $1,000 bond is worth $1,000 at maturity, the same bond may be worth more or less than the $1,000 *prior* to maturity, depending on the prevailing rate for similar bonds. For example, if you own a bond paying 6% and new bonds are paying 8%, investors will buy the 8% bond instead of yours; to attract a buyer you will have to sell it for less than $1,000 (at a *discount*) so that the buyer can earn 8%. On the other hand, if your bond pays 10%, an investor would be willing to pay you more than $1,000 (at a *premium*). In the next example, we will determine the value of a bond.

Example 4 Eight years ago you bought a 20-year 6% $1,000 bond. The bond pays interest each 6 months. You want to sell the bond. You just received the 16th semiannual interest payment, in the amount of $30 ($1,000 × 3% periodic rate = $30). Similar bonds are being issued that pay 8% semiannually. What is your bond worth today?

Let's look at this *from the standpoint of an investor* who might buy your bond. The investor would receive $30 interest checks at the end of each 6 months for the next 12 years plus the $1,000 maturity value in 12 years. Let's find the present value of the interest checks (using Formula 2B), then the present value of the $1,000 maturity value (using Formula 2A), and finally add the two present values. Remember, the investor wants to earn 8% compounded semiannually over the 12-year investment period, so $n = 12$ years × 2 periods per year = 24; $i = 8\% \div 2 = 4\% = .04$.

$$\text{PV of interest checks: PV} = \text{PMT}\left[\frac{1 - \frac{1}{(1+i)^n}}{i}\right] = \$30\left[\frac{1 - \frac{1}{(1.04)^{24}}}{.04}\right] = \$457.41$$

$$\text{PV of maturity value: PV} = \frac{FV}{(1+i)^n} = \frac{\$1,000}{(1.04)^{24}} = \$390.12$$

Total PV $\quad\quad\quad\quad\quad\quad\quad\quad\quad\quad\quad\quad\quad\quad\quad\quad\quad\quad\quad\quad\quad\quad\quad\quad\quad\quad$ **$847.53**

Finding the value of a long-term project. Finding the present value of future cash flows is valuable in deciding whether a business should spend money on a long-term project, like buying machinery or expanding a plant. The evaluation of a long-term project is known as **capital budgeting**.

Businesses often must make capital budgeting decisions—such as whether to expand a plant or purchase a labor-saving device. To help make a decision, the business finds the present value of savings from the venture.

Example 5 You own a manufacturing business and are considering the purchase of a labor-saving device for $100,000. You project that the device will last 15 years and save you $900 per month in labor costs (assume that the savings are realized at the end of each month). At the end of the 15 years, you project you can sell the device for a salvage value of $7,000. Assuming that you can earn 10.25% compounded monthly on your money, find the value of the device. Then decide whether you should buy the device.

You will save a total of $162,000 (180 months × $900). You will also get the $7,000 salvage value, for a total dollar return of $169,000. Let's find the present value of the annual savings (using Formula 2B), the present value of the salvage value (using Formula 2A), and then add the two present values ($n = 15 \times 12 = 180$; $i = 10.25\% \div 12 \approx .8541667\% \approx .008541667$):

$$\text{PV, annual savings: PV} = \text{PMT}\left[\frac{1 - \frac{1}{(1+i)^n}}{i}\right] = \$900\left[\frac{1 - \frac{1}{(1.008541667)^{180}}}{.008541667}\right] = \$82,572.52$$

$$\text{PV, salvage value: PV} = \frac{FV}{(1+i)^n} = \frac{\$7,000}{(1.008541667)^{180}} = \$1,514.28$$

Total PV $\quad\quad\quad\quad\quad\quad\quad\quad\quad\quad\quad\quad\quad\quad\quad\quad\quad\quad\quad\quad\quad\quad\quad\quad\quad\quad$ **$84,086.80**

The device has a value of $84,086.80. Because the value ($84,086.80) is less than the cost of the device ($100,000), you should not buy the device.

> **TIP** — **periodic rate**
>
> In Example 5, the periodic rate is a repeating decimal: .008541666…, with the 6s continuing forever. When using formulas, use as many digits as you can. Don't make the common mistake of rounding a periodic rate to just a few decimal places. By using a periodic rate of, say, .0085 in Example 5, our answer would be off: $84,331.90.

Congratulations on finishing this chapter. Using compound interest formulas provides a straightforward way of solving a variety of time-value-of-money problems. Let's do the U-Try-It exercises to get a little more practice finding the present value of money to be received in the future.

U-Try-It (Unit 10.3)

1. Marcus's rich aunt promises to give him $100,000 on his 25th birthday, 21 years from now. If money is worth 6% compounded annually, what is today's value of her promise?
2. You win a $10,000,000 lottery. When you go to collect your money, you find out the $10,000,000 will be paid with 40 annual payments of $250,000 (totaling $10,000,000). The payments will be made at the end of each year. What is the real value of your prize, in today's dollars, assuming that you can earn 6% compounded annually?
3. You own a manufacturing business and are considering the purchase of a labor-saving device for $100,000. You project that the device will last 15 years and save you $1,500 per month in labor costs (assume that the savings are realized at the end of each month). At the end of the 15 years, you project you can sell the device for a salvage value of $5,500. Assuming that you can earn 12% compounded monthly, find the value of the device.
4. Refer to Problem 3. Should you buy the device?

Answers: (If you have a different answer, check the solution in Appendix A.)
1. $29,415.54   **2.** $3,761,574.22   **3.** $125,899.81   **4.** Yes, because the device is worth more than it costs.

Chapter in a Nutshell

Objectives	Examples
Unit 10.1 Time-value-of-money terminology	
(a) Understanding time-value-of-money terminology	You deposit $500 today and an additional $175 at the end of each 6 months for 5 years. Earn 6% compounded semiannually. TVM variables? $n = 5 \times 2 = 10$ $i = 6\% \div 2 = 3\%$ PV = $500 PMT = $175 FV = Not given
Unit 10.2 Future value	
(a) Finding what a single deposit will grow to	You deposit $125 in a savings plan earning 5% compounded annually. Balance in 30 years? Formula 1A ($n = 30$; $i = 5\% = .05$): $FV = PV(1 + i)^n = \$125(1.05)^{30} = \$540.24$
(b) Finding what a series of deposits will grow to	You deposit $25 at the end of each quarter into a savings plan earning 6% compounded quarterly. Balance in 10 years? Formula 1B ($n = 10 \times 4 = 40$; $i = 6\% \div 4 = 1.5\% = .015$): $FV = PMT\left[\dfrac{(1+i)^n - 1}{i}\right] = \$25\left[\dfrac{(1.015)^{40} - 1}{.015}\right] = \$1,356.70$

Chapter in a Nutshell (concluded)

Objectives	Examples

Unit 10.3 Present value

(a) Finding the present value of a single sum to be received in the future

You win a contest that pays $5,000 in one lump-sum 5 years from now. What is the value of the prize if money is worth 6% compounded annually?

Formula 2A ($n = 5$; $i = 6\% = .06$): $PV = \dfrac{FV}{(1+i)^n} = \dfrac{\$5{,}000}{(1.06)^5} = \$3{,}736.29$

(b) Finding the present value for a series of payments

You invent a product and sell it to a corporation. You will receive $30,000 at the end of each year for 10 years. If money is worth 8% compounded annually, what is the value of your invention?

Formula 2B ($n = 10$; $i = 8\% = .08$):

$$PV = PMT \left[\dfrac{1 - \dfrac{1}{(1+i)^n}}{i}\right] = \$30{,}000 \left[\dfrac{1 - \dfrac{1}{(1.08)^{10}}}{.08}\right] = \$201{,}302.44$$

Think

1. Rosa Ramos bought some IBM stock 15 years ago for $2,000. She sold the stock today for $8,000. Which value—$2,000 or $8,000—is the present value, and why?
2. Suppose you invent a product and sell the patent to a large corporation. The corporation agrees to pay you $5,000 each quarter for 10 years. For each question, select the best choice (choose from $150,000, $200,000, and $270,000). Explain your reasoning. *Note:* For questions (b) and (c), don't do any calculations.
   a. What is the total amount of money you will receive?
   b. If you deposit the $5,000 payments in a savings plan, what will the balance be in 10 years?
   c. What is the value of your invention?
3. Suppose Ted deposits $10,000 in a savings plan earning 5% compounded annually and Tess deposits $10,000 in a savings plan earning 10% compounded annually. Both leave their money on deposit for 40 years. Because Tess's rate is twice as great as Ted's rate, is it true that Tess will earn twice as much interest? Explain why or why not. Then show calculations to support your point of view.

Explore

1. Refer to Appendix E. Review the explanations for using Excel to solve time-value-of-money problems. Then, use Excel to solve each of the U-Try-It problems from Units 10.2 and 10.3.
2. Go to **www.webbertext.com** and click Online Calculator. Using the online calculator and the guidelines shown on that page, solve each of the U-Try-It problems from Units 10.2 and 10.3.
3. Compare the answers using each method (formulas, Excel, and the online calculator). Which answers are different, if any, and why?

Apply

1. **Costs in the Future.** Pick 5 items that you have bought in the last year (like a car, home, gallon of milk, dozen eggs, tuition, gallon of gasoline, etc.) or one that you would like to buy (like a car or home). Based on annual inflation rates of 3%, 5%, and 8%, use Formula 1A to project the cost of each item in 10 years, 20 years, 30 years, and 40 years. *Hint:* Treat the current cost as PV, and the cost later as FV.

Chapter Review Problems

Unit 10.1 Time-value-of-money terminology

For Problems 1-5, assume you deposit $1,000 today in a savings account. You earn 6% compounded quarterly. You deposit an additional $50 each quarter, starting in 3 months. At the end of 3 years, you withdraw the balance of $1,847.68. Identify each value.

1. n?
2. i?
3. PV?
4. PMT?
5. FV?

For Problems 6-8, assume you purchased some corporate stock 8 years ago for $4,000. You received dividends of $50 each quarter; your dividends total $1,600 (32 dividend checks × $50 = $1,600). You sold the stock today for $6,000.

6. The PV is $6,000 because that is the amount you received today (in the present). (T or F)

7. Which variable (PV, PMT, or FV) does $1,600 represent?

8. What is the FV amount?

Unit 10.2 Future value

9. Your great-great-great-great-grandfather lost $42 playing poker at a fur-trading post in Wyoming 170 years ago. If he had not been tempted to get into the poker game and instead had deposited the $42 in a savings account earning 4% compounded annually, how much money would be in the account today?

10. Tammy Brown is 35 years old and deposits $2,000 at the end of each year into an individual retirement account (IRA). If the account earns 8% compounded annually, how much will Tammy have when she retires 30 years later?

11. Jed Redmond just turned 22. He decides to empty the change out of his pocket each day—averaging a dollar a day—and set it aside. Then, at the end of each year, Jed will deposit the $365 in a savings plan earning 2% compounded annually. How much will Jed have when he turns 62, after his final deposit?

12. Jack Green spends $135 a month on cigarettes and is considering kicking the habit. If Jack just turned 19 and deposits the $135 at the end of each month into a savings plan earning 7.5% compounded monthly, how much will he have in his savings plan at age 70?

13. Refer to Problem 12. What if Jack makes deposits at the *beginning* of each month?

220 Chapter 10 Future Value and Present Value: Using Formulas

14. Refer to Problem 13. How much interest will Jack's savings plan earn?

15. Refer to a business magazine article, shown to the right. Assuming that interest is compounded monthly and deposits are made at the end of each month, calculate the *precise* savings plan balance you will have at ages 35, 45, 55, and 65.

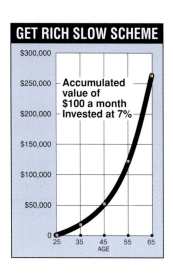

16. The average growth rate for a certain corporate stock over the last 100 years is 12%. If your great-great-grandmother had invested $500 in the stock 100 years ago and received the 12% return, what would her investment be worth today?

17. Tuition at a local college is currently $2,550 per year. You want your newborn daughter to attend when she turns 18. If tuition rates are expected to increase at an annual rate of 5%, what will the annual tuition be at the college 18 years from now?

18. Suppose there are an estimated 4,400 elephants in a certain region. If the elephant population is decreasing 5% per year, what will the elephant population be 40 years from now? *Hint:* The rate is a negative 5%, so i = -5% = -.05, meaning (1 + i) = (1 + (-.05)) = (1 - .05) = .95.

Unit 10.3 Present value

19. Bob's grandfather gives each of his grandchildren $5,000 on their 30th birthday. Bob just turned 20. What is the value of the $5,000 gift, in today's dollars, assuming that Bob can earn 3% compounded annually?

20. Cicily Montague, an author from Paris, sells the movie rights to her book and will receive 600,000 euros at the end of each quarter for the next 4 years. Assuming that money is worth 6% compounded quarterly, what is the value of the movie rights?

For Problems 21-24, assume you own a manufacturing business and are thinking about purchasing a labor-saving device at a cost of $150,000. The device will last 15 years and save you $1,300 per month in labor costs (assume that the savings are realized at the end of each month). You project there will be no salvage value.

21. If you buy the device, what is the total amount of labor costs you will save?

22. Does having the answer to Problem 21 make it possible for you to decide if you should buy the device?

23. Assuming that you need to earn 9% compounded monthly on your money, what is the value of the device?

24. Should you buy the device?

25. You have the chance to buy a promissory note in which you will receive 100 monthly payments of $700, starting a month from now. If you buy the note, what is the total amount you will receive?

26. Refer to Problem 25. If you want to earn 6% compounded monthly, what price should you pay for the note?

27. Seven years ago you bought a 20-year 6% $1,000 bond. The bond pays interest each 6 months. You want to sell the bond. You just received the 14th semiannual interest payment of $30 ($1,000 × 3% periodic rate = $30). Similar bonds are being issued that pay 8% semiannually. What is your bond worth today?

28. Refer to Problem 27. Why is your bond worth less than the $1,000 face value?

29. Some bonds, referred to as *zero-coupon bonds*, pay no periodic interest; instead the bondholder buys the bond at a discount and receives the maturity value on the maturity date. In effect, interest is received in one lump-sum when the bond matures. Suppose a corporation issues 20-year $1,000 zero-coupon bonds. Calculate the price you must pay for one of these bonds based on a prevailing 8% annual rate.

30. You rent an apartment for $700 a month and offer to prepay 6 months' rent. If the landlord can earn 9% compounded monthly, what amount should the landlord accept? *Hint:* Remember, rent is always paid in advance, at the *beginning* of each month (unless the landlord is *exceptionally nice*).

Challenge problems

31. You invest $5,800 today in a savings plan earning 8% compounded semiannually. You then invest $100 each 6 months (starting in 6 months). What will your balance be at the end of 5 years?

For Problems 32-35, consider Social Security and Medicare payroll deductions. As of December, 2015, the federal government requires employees to pay tax of 7.65% on the first $118,500 earned each year plus 1.45% of the remainder. Employers must contribute a matching amount. Assume that an employee earns $45,000 each year during a 40-year working career.

32. Based on these rates, what is the amount withheld from the employee's pay each year?

33. What is the total amount contributed by the employee and employer each year?

34. The money is remitted to the government quarterly. What is the quarterly deposit?

35. Assuming that the deposits were made to a savings plan at the end of each quarter (instead of with the IRS), earning 7% compounded quarterly, how much would the employee have in the savings plan at the end of a 40-year working career?

36. An accomplished pianist lost his right hand in an accident. He successfully sued the party responsible. You, as a member of the jury, are trying to decide what amount the pianist should receive as a settlement. You have determined that the pianist was able to earn $25,000 net income from concerts each month and would have been able to continue earning that amount for another 28 years. Assuming that money is worth 9% compounded monthly and that the $25,000 was received at the end of each month, what is a fair settlement?

37. You leased retail space 5 years ago for $22,000 per month, payable at the beginning of each month. Your lease is for 25 years and allows you to sublease the space. You have outgrown the space and sublease to Smith Furniture Company for the remaining 20 years. Smith will pay you $27,500 at the beginning of each month. What is the value of your position in the lease (referred to as a *leasehold interest*), assuming that money is worth 9% compounded monthly?

38. You win a $5,000,000 lottery. When you go to collect your money, you find out the $5,000,000 will be paid with 10 annual payments of $500,000, starting in 1 year. What is the real value of your prize, in today's dollars, assuming that you can earn 8% compounded annually?

39. Refer to Problem 38. If you invest the lottery payments in a savings plan, earning 8% compounded annually, how much will you end up with in 10 years, after your final deposit?

40. Melvin Maxwell, a 30-year-old real estate broker, decides to start a retirement plan. He figures that his income for the next 25 years will be sufficient to deposit $750 at the end of each quarter into his retirement plan earning 6% compounded quarterly. After 25 years he will let the money sit for another 10 years, without making additional deposits, until he is 65 years old. What amount will Melvin have when he turns 65?

For Problems 41-44, your Aunt Florence decides to sell her office supply business. Ishiro Suma offers to buy the business for $240,000 cash. Michael Gabriel offers to buy the business by paying $6,000 at the end of each quarter for 10 years, followed by $9,000 at the end of each quarter for 5 years.

41. What is the total amount Aunt Florence would receive from Michael?

42. Will having the answer to Problem 43 be all that we need in order to decide which offer Aunt Florence should accept?

43. Help Aunt Florence find the present value of Michael's offer, assuming Aunt Florence can earn 8% compounded quarterly on her money.

44. Which offer should Aunt Florence accept (Ishiro's or Michael's), and why?

Practice Test

1. You deposit $500 today in a savings account that earns 6% compounded quarterly and leave the money there for 5 years. What is the n-value?

2. You deposited $420 in a savings account 13 years ago, earning 5% compounded quarterly. Today, you withdraw the entire balance of $801.29. What is the present value?

3. The average growth rate for a certain stock over the last 50 years is reported to be 12% compounded annually. If your grandmother had invested $500 in the stock 50 years ago, what would her investment be worth today?

4. Maria Martinez is a soda pop "addict" and wonders how much money she could accumulate if she stopped drinking soda pop and deposited the $100 per month she spends on the stuff into a savings plan. If Maria is 20 years old, what amount would she have at retirement, 50 years from now, if she deposited $100 at the end of each month and her savings plan earned 6.75% compounded monthly?

5. Tuition at a local college is currently $3,800 per year. If tuition rates are expected to increase at an annual rate of 4%, what will the annual tuition be 18 years from now?

6. A corporation issues 20-year $1,000 zero-coupon bonds. If you buy one of these bonds you will receive no interest checks during the 20 years, but will receive the $1,000 maturity value in 20 years. Based on a prevailing 8% annual rate, what price must you pay for one of the bonds?

7. You own a manufacturing business and are considering the purchase of a labor-saving device. You project that the device will last 12 years and save you $800 per month in labor costs (assume that the savings are realized at the end of each month). At the end of 12 years, you project you can sell the device for a salvage value of $8,000. Assuming that you can earn 9.75% compounded monthly on your money, what is the value of the device?

FUN CORNER

The 10 Richest People in the World

1. Bill Gates III
   co-founder of Microsoft, U.S. . . . . $79.2 billion
2. Carlos Slim Helu
   telecommunications, Mexico . . . . . $77.1 billion
3. Warren Buffet
   investor, U.S. . . . . $72.7 billion
4. Amancio Orgeta
   Zara (apparel retailer), Spain . . . . $64.5 billion
5. Larry Ellison
   co-founder of Oracle, U.S. . . . . . . $54.3 billion
6. (Tie) Charles Koch
   Koch Industries, U.S. . . . . $42.9 billion
6. (Tie) David Koch
   Koch Industries, U.S. . . . . $42.9 billion
8. Christy Walton
   Wal-Mart, U.S. . . . . $41.7 billion
9. Jim Walton
   Wal-Mart, U.S. . . . . $40.6 billion
10. Liliane Bettencourt
    L'oreal, France . . . . $40.1 billion

Source: *Forbes* magazine, 2015

How Math Professors End up with Small Classes
by Dave Barry

Sir Isaac Newton, the brilliant mathematician, invented calculus, which is defined as "the branch of mathematics that is so scary it causes everybody to stop studying mathematics." That's the whole POINT of calculus. At colleges and universities, on the first day of calculus class, the professors go to the board and write huge incomprehensible "equations" that they make up right on the spot, knowing that this will cause all the students to drop the course and never return to the mathematics building again.

Tuition Increase

When evaluating numbers, many people make the mistake of looking only at the numbers, without considering the time value of money. Here is an example.

In 1900, annual tuition to attend a major university was about $60. One hundred years later, tuition was about $10,000. Sounds like an outrageous increase, doesn't it? While it is a large dollar amount of increase (especially when we are on the paying end), the annual rate of increase is probably less than you thought: 5.25%. Note: If we maintain a 5.25% annual increase, tuition in the year 2100 will be $1,668,055!

Quotable Quip

I wish the buck stopped here, as I could use a few.
– Author unknown

"How much of my $5 weekly allowance will I have to set aside so I can retire at age 17?"

Sinking Funds, Annuities, and More: Using Formulas

11

In Chapter 10, we solved for future value and present value using formulas. If you found that fun, you will enjoy what's to come.

In this chapter, we will figure out how much money we must set aside to reach a goal (this type of problem is known as a *sinking fund* problem). Then we will explore options we have for withdrawing the money that we have saved (this type of problem is known as an *annuity* problem). We will calculate a monthly payment on a car loan and a home loan. And we will calculate rates of return, annual percentage rates (APRs), and growth rates. Sounds exciting, don't you think?

UNIT OBJECTIVES

Unit 11.1 Sinking funds

- ⓐ Finding a one-time deposit to reach a goal
- ⓑ Finding a periodic deposit to reach a goal
- ⓒ Finding the required time to reach a goal
- ⓓ Understanding the effect of rate

Unit 11.2 Annuities

- ⓐ Calculating the periodic withdrawal for an annuity

Unit 11.3 Loan payments

- ⓐ Calculating a payment on an installment loan
- ⓑ Calculating a payment on a mortgage loan
- ⓒ Finding the remaining term (n)

Unit 11.4 Solving for rate (i)

- ⓐ Calculating i when there is no periodic payment
- ⓑ Calculating i when there is a periodic payment

Unit 11.1 Sinking funds

People often save money for a specific purpose, like retirement, a down payment on a home, a wedding, or a college fund. The money set aside is known as a sinking fund.

As mentioned in Chapter 10, the 5 time-value-of-money (TVM) variables are n, i, PV, PMT, and FV. If you have questions about what the variables represent, refer to Unit 10.1. A formula for each of the 5 variables is shown in Illustration 10-1. We used Formulas 1A, 1B, 2A, and 2B in Chapter 10. We will use the other formulas in this chapter. I'll bet you are excited about that, especially about the chance to use Formula 5! (As you will see, even Formula 5 is not as difficult as it may appear.)

Money set aside for a specific purpose is referred to as a **sinking fund.** For example, you might want to establish a college fund for a child, needing $30,000 in 18 years. Or you might need $20,000 in 10 years to replace an apartment building roof.

Corporations use sinking funds to replace worn-out equipment, to repay bondholders the principal portion of the debt, etc. A *sinking fund* is not a fund that is slowly sinking; it is a fund in which we *sink* money.

We can determine the dollar amount of deposits if we know how much money we want to accumulate, when we will need the money, and what interest rate our deposits will earn. Deposits may consist of one lump sum (Example 1) or periodic deposits (Example 2). We can also determine how long it will take to accumulate the desired sum (Example 3).

a Finding a one-time deposit to reach a goal

When a sinking fund is created with a single deposit, we want to know PV (the required one-time deposit) and we know FV (the amount we want the fund to grow to). Therefore, we use Formula 2A.

> **TIP — calculator shortcuts**
>
> Most calculators have exponent (power) keys, such as y^x or $\wedge$ to shortcut the arithmetic. If you're using the HP 10BII+ or the TI BAII PLUS, see Appendix C for keystrokes for each of the compound interest formulas (including specific keystrokes for the examples in this chapter marked with a calculator icon in the margin). If you are using the HP 10B, HP 10BII, HP 12C, HP 17BII, HP 39gs, TI 30Xa, TI 30XIIS, TI 83+, TI 84+, Casio 9750G PLUS, or LeWorld FIN, you can request keystrokes at *studentsupport@olympuspub.com*.

Example 1 You want to accumulate $200,000 for retirement in 40 years. You can earn 6.75% compounded monthly. What amount must you deposit today in one lump sum to have $200,000 in 40 years?

We need to know PV and we know FV, so we use Formula 2A.

FV = $200,000; $n = 40 \times 12 = 480$; $i = 6.75\% \div 12 = .5625\% = .005625$

$$PV = \frac{FV}{(1+i)^n} = \frac{\$200,000}{(1.005625)^{480}} = \$13,543.18$$

By depositing $13,543.18 today, you will have $200,000 in 40 years.

b) Finding a periodic deposit to reach a goal

In Example 1, we made a single deposit to accumulate a certain sum. We can instead fund a plan with regular periodic deposits. We are solving for PMT and we know FV, so we use Formula 4A.

Example 2

Refer to Example 1. Suppose you don't have $13,543.18 to deposit today and instead consider making monthly deposits. What amount must you deposit at the end of each month in order to accumulate $200,000 in 40 years?

Using Formula 4A: $\text{PMT} = \dfrac{FV(i)}{(1+i)^n - 1} = \dfrac{\$200{,}000\,(.005625)}{(1.005625)^{480} - 1} = \$81.71$

Instead, you can deposit $81.71 at the end of each month. You deposit a total of $39,220.80 (480 deposits × $81.71), meaning you earn interest of $160,779.20 ($200,000 you end up with − $39,220.80 deposited)!

c) Finding the required time to reach a goal

If we know the dollar amount of deposits we can afford for a sinking fund, we can determine how long it will take to reach our goal. We are solving for n, so we get to use Formula 5!

Formula 5 is the ugly formula! Notice the footnote in Illustration 10-1; for Formula 5 we must use proper sign convention for PV, PMT, and FV. Think of the money from someone's standpoint, and treat each amount accordingly (as a *positive* amount if the money is received or as a *negative* amount if the money is paid). Before using Formula 5, it may be a good idea to review the concept of logarithms in Appendix F.

Example 3

You want to start a restaurant business and estimate it will take $28,000 to get started. You currently have $3,000 to deposit and can deposit an additional $425 at the end of each month. If your sinking fund will earn 9% compounded monthly, in how many months can you start your business?

n: ?
i: $9\% \div 12 = .75\% = .0075$
PV: −$3,000 (negative amount because you will pay this money into the sinking fund)
PMT: −$425 (negative amount because you will pay this money into the sinking fund)
FV: $28,000 (positive amount because you will receive this money from the fund)

$n = \dfrac{-\ln\left[\dfrac{PV + \left(\frac{PMT}{i}\right)}{\frac{PMT}{i} - FV}\right]}{\ln(1+i)} = \dfrac{-\ln\left[\dfrac{-\$3{,}000 + \left(\frac{-\$425}{.0075}\right)}{\frac{-\$425}{.0075} - \$28{,}000}\right]}{\ln(1.0075)} = 46.83 \text{ months}$

You can start your business in 47 months. The more precise n-value of 46.83 indicates that you must make 46 deposits of $425; the final deposit will be about 83% (or .83) of the regular $425 deposit.

d) Understanding the effect of rate

The interest rate is a significant factor in savings plan problems, as shown in the next example.

Example 4

You want to give your newborn son $1,000,000 for his retirement at age 65. If you establish a savings plan, how much do you need to deposit at the end of each month, provided that the fund earns (a) 3% compounded monthly, (b) 9% compounded monthly, and (c) 15% compounded monthly.

We need to know PMT and we know FV, so we use Formula 4A. $n = 65 \times 12 = 780$.

$$3\% \ (i = 3\% \div 12 = .25\% = .0025): \text{PMT} = \frac{FV(i)}{(1+i)^n - 1} = \frac{\$1,000,000(.0025)}{(1.0025)^{780} - 1} = \$415.86$$

$$9\% \ (i = 9\% \div 12 = .75\% = .0075): \text{PMT} = \frac{FV(i)}{(1+i)^n - 1} = \frac{\$1,000,000(.0075)}{(1.0075)^{780} - 1} = \$22.14$$

$$15\% \ (i = 15\% \div 12 = 1.25\% = .0125): \text{PMT} = \frac{FV(i)}{(1+i)^n - 1} = \frac{\$1,000,000(.0125)}{(1.0125)^{780} - 1} = \$0.77$$

To have $1,000,000 in 65 years, you must make monthly deposits of $415.86, $22.14, or $0.77 (that's right, 77¢), depending on the rate you earn.

As you can see, the rate makes a dramatic difference. You may ask, Is a 9% or 15% rate reasonable? When most people think of savings rates, they limit their thinking to passbook savings accounts, which currently pay very low rates. Rates on passbook savings will likely never rebound to the 14% rates of the 1980s but other investments such as stocks, bonds, real estate, and mutual funds can, over the long haul, provide substantial returns.

Let's try the U-Try-It exercises to find out how much about *sinking funds* has *sunk* in.

U-Try-It (Unit 11.1)

1. While your dentist is filling a cavity in one of your teeth, he is talking with his dental assistant about the new dental equipment he wants to buy in $3\frac{1}{2}$ years for $30,000. He wonders how much money he must deposit today in order to accumulate the $30,000. You get his attention and tell him that if he will quit drilling for a minute you will help him calculate the amount. What amount is required if he can earn 6% compounded quarterly?
2. Refer to Problem 1. If your dentist wants to instead make quarterly deposits, what amount must he deposit at the end of each quarter?

Answers: (If you have a different answer, check the solution in Appendix A.)
1. $24,355.48   2. $1,941.70

Unit 11.2 Annuities

Accumulating savings is the hard part. Spending is the fun part. The money received back from a savings plan is known as an **annuity**. We will refer to an annuity more specifically—as a repetitive, uniform withdrawal of funds. A savings fund could be created slowly by making deposits over a long period of time. Or we could inherit a large sum of money all at once or win the lottery. Once the annuity plan is funded, we can start making withdrawals.

a Calculating the periodic withdrawal for an annuity

A savings plan continues to earn interest during the withdrawal (annuity) stage. If the withdrawals are *identical* to the amount of interest earned, the savings plan balance will remain the same.

Example 1

Suppose you have accumulated $500,000, perhaps from many years of savings or from an inheritance. You put the money in a savings plan earning 6% compounded monthly. If you want to live off the interest without disturbing the $500,000 balance, what amount can you withdraw each month?

———————

Let's use the *simple interest formula* to calculate the monthly interest:

$$I = PRT = \$500{,}000 \times 6\% \times \tfrac{1}{12} = \$2{,}500$$

You can withdraw $2,500 each month forever.

By withdrawing exactly $2,500 at the end of each month, your savings plan balance will remain at $500,000. By withdrawing less than $2,500 each month, your savings plan balance will increase, because withdrawals are less than the interest you earn. By withdrawing more than $2,500 each month the balance will decrease, because withdrawals are more than the interest you earn.

Example 2

Refer to Example 1. You want the plan to last 40 years. How much can you withdraw at the end of each month?

———————

If you earned no interest, you could withdraw $1,041.67 each month ($500,000 ÷ 480 withdrawals). Because you earn interest, you can withdraw more. Let's calculate the amount, using Formula 4B:

$n = 40 \times 12 = 480;\ i = 6\% \div 12 = .5\% = .005;\ PV = \$500{,}000.$

$$PMT = \frac{PV(i)}{1 - \dfrac{1}{(1+i)^n}} = \frac{\$500{,}000\,(.005)}{1 - \dfrac{1}{(1.005)^{480}}} = \$2{,}751.07$$

You can withdraw $2,751.07 at the end of each month for 40 years. Then it's time to go back to work because the savings plan will have no money left in it.

In Example 2, you are able to withdraw a total of $1,320,513.60 (480 × $2,751.07), meaning your savings plan earns $820,513.60 interest ($1,320,513.60 - $500,000 deposited). Your money is at work for you, even though you are gradually depleting the fund.

In Example 2, your withdrawals are made at the *end* of each month. If your withdrawals were to be made at the *beginning* of each month, you would not be able to withdraw as much because your withdrawals start sooner and you would earn less interest. The right-hand column of Illustration 10-1 tells us how to adjust an answer if payments (or withdrawals) are made at the *beginning* of each period. For Formula 4B we divide the answer by (1 + i): $2,751.07 ÷ (1 + i) = $2,751.07 ÷ 1.005 = $2,737.38.

Some books refer to a series of payments in which payments are made at the end of each period as an **ordinary annuity** and to a series of payments in which payments are made at the beginning of each period as an **annuity due**. Instead of using that terminology we will, for each problem, simply state whether payments are made at the end, or beginning, of each period.

Well, that's it for this unit. Let's try some U-Try-It questions.

U-Try-It (Unit 11.2)

Your Aunt Irene has been making deposits to a savings plan for the last 35 years. Her account balance is now $420,000 and her plan earns 8% compounded monthly. Aunt Irene just turned 60 and asks for your advice.

1. What amount can Aunt Irene withdraw at the end of each month so that the plan balance will stay the same?
2. If Aunt Irene wants the plan to last exactly 25 years, what amount can she withdraw at the end of each month?

———————

Answers: (If you have a different answer, check the solution in Appendix A.)
1. $2,800   2. $3,241.63

Unit 11.3 Loan payments

When money is borrowed, it must be repaid. Unless we borrow from a rich, very nice relative, we must pay interest in addition to the amount borrowed. In this unit we will calculate a monthly payment on an installment loan (Example 1) and on a mortgage loan (Example 2). We will also calculate the remaining term of a loan (Example 4).

a Calculating a payment on an installment loan

An **installment loan** is a loan that is paid off with payments of an equal amount. People get installment loans to buy cars, boats, furniture, and other costly items.

People often get installment loans to buy costly items, like cars. Some people prefer buying used cars, but probably not quite this used!

Let's see how an installment loan might work. Assume Casey wants to buy a car and finds one he likes, priced at $13,000. With tax and license fees the total amount comes to $14,200. Suppose Casey has $700 saved up for the car purchase. Where will the remaining $13,500 come from? If he's like most of us, he will borrow the $13,500 from a bank or credit union. Depending on the make and model of the car, as well as his credit history, the lender will decide what interest rate to charge, and the length of the loan. The lender will calculate a monthly payment that will be sufficient to pay back the principal (the $13,500 Casey borrows) plus interest. We can calculate a monthly payment using Formula 4B.

Example 1 Casey gets a 5-year $13,500 car loan at 7.5% interest. Calculate his monthly payment.

If Casey paid no interest, his monthly payment would be $225 ($13,500 ÷ 60 months). Because he must pay interest, his monthly payment will be more. PV = $13,500; $n = 5 \times 12 = 60$; $i = 7.5\% \div 12 = .625\% = .00625$:

$$\text{PMT} = \frac{\text{PV}\,(i)}{1 - \dfrac{1}{(1+i)^n}} = \frac{\$13,500\,(.00625)}{1 - \dfrac{1}{(1.00625)^{60}}} = \$270.51$$

Casey's monthly payment is $270.51. He will pay the lender a total of $16,230.60 (60 payments × $270.51), which means he pays $2,730.60 interest ($16,230.60 repaid - $13,500 principal).

We will explore installment loans more in Chapter 14.

b Calculating a payment on a mortgage loan

Real estate, unlike *personal property*, is immovable. Real estate includes land and buildings. Personal property includes things like cars and furniture. A loan secured by real estate is known as a **mortgage loan.**

Tara has been collecting rent receipts for awhile and has decided to buy a home. After looking at quite a few homes, Tara finds her "dream home," priced at $180,000. She makes an offer of $165,000. The seller is not happy with that price and makes a *counteroffer* of $168,000. Tara accepts the seller's counteroffer.

Tara has saved up some cash but needs to borrow $160,000. Before making an offer to buy the home, Tara visited a lender to get pre-approved for a mortgage loan. The lender has offered two choices: (1) a 30-year loan at 7.75% or (2) a 15-year loan at 7.25%.

Example 2   Tara needs to borrow $160,000 to buy her dream home. She can get a 30-year loan at 7.75% or a 15-year loan at 7.25%. Calculate the monthly payment for each.

If Tara paid no interest, her monthly payment would be $444.44 on the 30-year loan ($160,000 ÷ 360 months) and $888.89 on the 15-year loan ($160,000 ÷ 180 months). Because she pays interest, her monthly payment will be considerably more.

30-year loan. PV = $160,000; $n = 30 \times 12 = 360$; $i = 7.75\% \div 12 \approx .6458333\% \approx .006458333$.

$$\text{PMT} = \frac{PV(i)}{1 - \frac{1}{(1+i)^n}} = \frac{\$160{,}000\,(.006458333)}{1 - \frac{1}{(1.006458333)^{360}}} = \$1{,}146.26$$

15-year loan. PV = $160,000; $n = 15 \times 12 = 180$; $i = 7.25\% \div 12 \approx 0.6041667\% \approx 0.006041667$.

$$\text{PMT} = \frac{PV(i)}{1 - \frac{1}{(1+i)^n}} = \frac{\$160{,}000\,(.006041667)}{1 - \frac{1}{(1.006041667)^{180}}} = \$1{,}460.58$$

> **TIP**   **don't round periodic rate**
>
> In Example 2, the periodic rates are repeating decimals. For the 30-year loan, the periodic rate is 0.6458333...%, with the 3s continuing forever. Don't make the common mistake of rounding the rate to a few decimal places, like 0.65%. Instead, use as many decimal places as your calculator will allow.

Tara's mortgage payment would be $1,146.26 for the 30-year loan, compared to $1,460.58 for the 15-year loan. Her first reaction may be to get the 30-year loan because she could save $314.32 each month. But let's figure the total interest on each loan. *Warning:* The result may take your breath away!

Example 3   Refer to Example 2. What is the total interest for each loan?

30-year loan (total number of payments = 30 years × 12 payments per year = 360)

Total paid: 360 × $1,146.26 =	$412,653.60
Less principal portion (loan amount)	-160,000.00
Interest portion	$252,653.60

15-year loan (total number of payments = 15 years × 12 payments per year = 180)

Total paid: 180 × $1,460.58 =	$262,904.40
Less principal portion (loan amount)	-160,000.00
Interest portion	$102,904.40

The interest is bad enough with the 15-year loan ($102,904.40) but with the 30-year loan, interest is about two and one-half times as much ($252,653.60). Also, notice that the interest on the 30-year loan is more than the $160,000 borrowed!

c) Finding the remaining term (n)

We can find the remaining term of a loan as shown in the next example.

Example 4 Refer to Example 3. Tara likes the idea of the 7.25% 15-year loan but does not feel comfortable *promising* to pay $1,460.58 per month. She is thinking about getting the 7.75% 30-year loan but making payments of $1,460.58. How long would it take to pay off the loan?

The advantage of signing a 30-year mortgage loan is that Tara is obligated to pay only $1,146.26 per month. The disadvantage of signing a 30-year loan is that she is stuck with a higher interest rate (7.75% vs. 7.25%). We can use Formula 5 to solve for n ($i = 7.75\% \div 12 \approx .6458333\% \approx .006548333$; PV = $160,000; PMT = -$1,460.58 [negative because Tara will *pay* this each month]; FV = $0):

$$n = \frac{-\ln\left[\frac{PV + \left(\frac{PMT}{i}\right)}{\frac{PMT}{i} - FV}\right]}{\ln(1+i)} = \frac{-\ln\left[\frac{\$160,000 + \left(\frac{-\$1,460.58}{.006458333}\right)}{\frac{-\$1,460.58}{.006458333} - \$0}\right]}{\ln(1.006458333)} = 190.95 \text{ months}$$

If Tara signs the 15-year mortgage loan it will take 180 months to pay off the loan. By signing the 30-year loan but making monthly payments of a 15-year loan, Tara must make 10.95 extra monthly payments (190.95 - 180 = 10.95). That's because of the higher interest rate (7.75% vs. 7.25%). She would pay approximately $16,000 more interest than if she were to sign the 15-year loan ($1,460.26 × 10.95 months = $15,989.85). Tara is now in a better position to make an informed decision.

We will explore home ownership and mortgage loans more in Chapter 15. Let's try some U-Try-It questions to see how we're doing.

U-Try-It (Unit 11.3)

1. You are thinking about buying a piano. You can get a 6-year $7,000 loan at 9.5% interest from your bank. Calculate your monthly payment.
2. You buy a home for $200,000. If you have $20,000 for a down payment and borrow $180,000 for 30 years at $5\frac{7}{8}\%$ interest, what is your monthly mortgage payment?
3. Refer to Problem 2. How much interest will you pay over the 30 years?
4. Several years ago you got a mortgage loan at 8.5% interest. You just received a mortgage loan statement, showing you owe $105,286.67. Your monthly payment is $922.69. How long until the loan is paid off?

Answers: (If you have a different answer, check the solution in Appendix A.)
1. $127.92   2. $1,064.77   3. $203,317.20   4. 234 months

Unit 11.4 Solving for rate (i)

There are several real-life situations in which we need to solve for *i*. As an example, we might want to know our **rate of return** (often called the yield) on a stock investment. Or, we might want to know the **annual percentage rate (APR)** on a loan. As you will see, solving for *i* is a piece of cake when there is no periodic payment involved. On the other hand, solving for *i* is quite tricky when periodic payments are involved.

a) Calculating i when there is no periodic payment

Many investments consist of investing a sum of money at the beginning of the investment period (PV) and selling the investment at the end of the investment period (FV). We can use Formula 3 to find the rate of return.

Example 1 Dale bought a rare baseball card 3 years ago for $1,500. He just sold the card for $2,000 to get some money for his college tuition. What interest rate, compounded annually, did Dale earn on the investment? For this problem, set your decimal at 6 places.

_____

You may be tempted to treat the $2,000 as a present value because it happened today (in the present). But the $1,500 happened at the beginning of the first period, making it the present value. The $2,000 happened at the end of the last period, making it the future value.

$$i = \left(\frac{FV}{PV}\right)^{\frac{1}{n}} - 1 = \left(\frac{\$2,000}{\$1,500}\right)^{\frac{1}{3}} - 1 = .100642 = 10.0642\%$$

Dale earned 10.0642%, compounded annually. Let's use a calculator to check the accuracy of the answer (we can reset our decimal to 2 places):

Keystrokes (for most calculators)	
1,500 [+] 10.0642 [%] [=]	1,650.96
[+] 10.0642 [%] [=]	1,817.12
[+] 10.0642 [%] [=]	2,000.00

The rate of 10.0642% works, indicating that Formula 3 works!

b Calculating *i* when there is a periodic payment

You may have noticed that there is no compound interest formula that will calculate *i* when a periodic payment is involved. For these problems, we can calculate *i* by using what we call a "Guess and Check Method." With the Guess and Check Method, we can use compound interest formulas of Illustration 10-1, apply an estimated rate, and compare the result against a target figure. If the result is not close enough to the target figure, we use other rates until the result matches (or is sufficiently close to) the target figure.

One real-world application of solving for *i* when periodic payments are involved is in calculating an interest rate on installment loans. Most lenders use the U.S. Rule to calculate interest. With the U.S. Rule, interest is calculated on the unpaid balance to the date payment is received and on the basis of a 365-day year. If a lender uses a different method of calculating interest, or charges front-end loan costs, the real interest rate (called the annual percentage rate, or APR) will be different (usually higher) than the stated annual rate.

One common method that does not comply with the U.S. Rule is the add-on method. With this method, interest is figured in advance using the formula *I = PRT*. The interest is then added to the loan amount; the result is then divided by the number of payments to get the periodic payment. To illustrate, let's assume you buy some furniture for $1,200. The retailer offers an installment plan over 12 months at 10% interest. If the retailer uses the add-on method, here's how your monthly payment is calculated:

Principal amount:	$1,200	
Interest: *I = PRT* = $1,200 × 10% × 1 =	+ 120	
Total	$1,320	÷ 12 payments = $110

Because the retailer is charging you interest on the *entire* loan amount for the 12-month period, you will be paying more interest than you would if the U.S. Rule were used. So, your real interest rate (the APR) will be higher than the 10% stated rate. We will calculate your APR in the next example.

For some loans we may not be told what method is being used to calculate interest. The bottom line is we can calculate the APR if we know (1) the loan amount (PV), (2) the periodic payment (PMT), and (3) the length of the loan (*n*).

Example 2

You buy some furniture for $1,200. The retailer allows you to pay on the installment plan by making 12 monthly payments of $110, starting in 1 month. They tell you they are charging you 10% interest, but you have your suspicions. What interest rate will you be paying if you accept their installment plan?

$$n = 12 \quad i = ? \quad PV = \$1{,}200 \quad PMT = \$110$$

Unfortunately, we cannot solve for *i* using Formula 3 because Formula 3 does not provide for a periodic payment (PMT). So, let's use the Guess and Check Method. Formulas 2B and 4B include the 4 variables involved in this problem, so we can take our pick of which of these two formulas to use. Let's use Formula 4B and guess rates until the PMT answer is sufficiently close to our target figure of $110. Let's start by using a rate of 12% (*i* = 12% ÷ 12 = 1% = .01):

$$PMT = \frac{PV(i)}{1 - \frac{1}{(1+i)^n}} = \frac{\$1{,}200(.01)}{1 - \frac{1}{(1.01)^{12}}} = \$106.62$$

The PMT of $106.62 is quite a bit lower than our target figure of $110. We need to use a much higher rate. Let's try 18% (*i* = 18% ÷ 12 = 1.5% = .015):

$$PMT = \frac{PV(i)}{1 - \frac{1}{(1+i)^n}} = \frac{\$1{,}200(.015)}{1 - \frac{1}{(1.015)^{12}}} = \$110.02$$

The PMT of $110.02 is very close to our target figure of $110. If you elect to accept their financing plan you will be paying an annual rate of approximately 18%. If you can borrow the money at a lower rate elsewhere (like from your bank or credit union, or even with a 15% credit card), that is a better approach.

For some loans we may be charged front-end loan costs. Loan costs are simply interest paid in advance. For these loans we treat the net proceeds (after loan costs are deducted) as the PV amount. We will calculate the APR on a loan with front-end loan costs in the U-Try-It problems.

The Guess and Check Method is a reliable way to calculate an APR. There are several other real-life situations in which we could use the Guess and Check Method to find *i*. Each situation is fairly unique. To get a copy of some additional situations in which the Guess and Check Method is used to solve for *i* (along with suggested solutions), send an e-mail request to *studentsupport@olympuspub.com*.

Instead of using the Guess and Check Method to solve for *i* when a periodic payment is involved, we can use financial calculators (see Chapters 12, 13, and 17), Excel (see Appendix E), or an Online Calculator (on our website).

Congratulations on finishing this chapter. Enjoy solving the variety of TVM problems you will encounter in life! Now, let's try the last set of U-Try-It exercises.

U-Try-It (Unit 11.4)

1. (True story) Anne Scheiber, shown in this passport photo, retired in 1944 after a 23-year career with the Internal Revenue Service. She invested her $5,000 savings in the stock market. When she died in 1995 at the age of 101, her nest egg had grown to $22 million, which she left to Yeshiva University. What average annual rate of return did her investment fund earn over the 51 years?

2. You are thinking about getting a 5-year 7.5% car loan for $12,000 with monthly payments. The lender will withhold a $200 front-end fee, so the net proceeds will be $11,800. What is the APR?

Answers: (If you have a different answer, check the solution in Appendix A.)
1. 17.88%   **2.** Approximately 8.21%

Chapter in a Nutshell

Objectives	Examples

Unit 11.1 Sinking funds

a Finding a one-time deposit to reach a goal

You want to accumulate $200,000 for retirement 25 years from now. You can earn 8% compounded semiannually. What amount must you deposit today in one lump-sum to have $200,000 in 25 years?

Formula 2A ($n = 25 \times 2 = 50$; $i = 8\% \div 2 = 4\% = .04$):

$$PV = \frac{FV}{(1+i)^n} = \frac{\$200{,}000}{(1.04)^{50}} = \$28{,}142.52$$

b Finding a periodic deposit to reach a goal

See above. What amount must you deposit at the end of each 6 months to have $200,000 in 25 years?

Formula 4A ($n = 25 \times 2 = 50$; $i = 8\% \div 2 = 4\% = .04$):

$$PMT = \frac{FV(i)}{(1+i)^n - 1} = \frac{\$200{,}000(.04)}{(1.04)^{50} - 1} = \$1{,}310.04$$

c Finding the required time to reach a goal

See above. How long will it take to accumulate the $200,000 if you deposit $1,500 at the end of each 6 months?

Formula 5 ($i = .04$; PV = $0; PMT = negative $1,500; FV = $200,000):

$$n = \frac{-\ln\left[\dfrac{PV + \left(\frac{PMT}{i}\right)}{\frac{PMT}{i} - FV}\right]}{\ln(1+i)} = \frac{-\ln\left[\dfrac{\$0 + \left(\frac{-\$1{,}500}{.04}\right)}{\frac{-\$1{,}500}{.04} - \$200{,}000}\right]}{\ln(1.04)} = 47.06 \text{ periods}$$

47.06 six-month periods ÷ 2 = about 23.5 years

d Understanding the effect of rate

See above. If you want to accumulate $200,000 in 25 years, what amount must you deposit at the end of each 6 months if you can earn 16% compounded semiannually?

Formula 4A ($n = 25 \times 2 = 50$; $i = 16\% \div 2 = 8\% = .08$):

$$PMT = \frac{FV(i)}{(1+i)^n - 1} = \frac{\$200{,}000(.08)}{(1.08)^{50} - 1} = \$348.57$$

Unit 11.2 Annuities

a Calculating the periodic withdrawal for an annuity

You deposit $42,000, earning 8% compounded monthly. If you want the savings plan to last 40 years, how much can you withdraw at the end of each month?

Formula 4B ($n = 40 \times 12 = 480$; $i = 8\% \div 12 \approx .666667\% \approx .00666667$):

$$PMT = \frac{PV(i)}{1 - \dfrac{1}{(1+i)^n}} = \frac{\$42{,}000(.00666667)}{1 - \dfrac{1}{(1.00666667)^{480}}} = \$292.03$$

Chapter in a Nutshell

Chapter in a Nutshell (concluded)

Objectives	Examples

Unit 11.3 Loan payments

a Calculating a payment on an installment loan

Calculate your monthly payment on a 6-year $15,000 car loan at 9.5% interest.

Formula 4B ($n = 6 \times 12 = 72$; $i = 9.5\% \div 12 \approx .791667\% \approx .00791667$):

$$PMT = \frac{PV(i)}{1 - \frac{1}{(1+i)^n}} = \frac{\$15,000(.00791667)}{1 - \frac{1}{(1.00791667)^{72}}} = \$274.12$$

b Calculating a payment on a mortgage loan

What is the monthly payment on a 30-year 4.75% $250,000 mortgage loan?

Formula 4B ($n = 30 \times 12 = 360$; $i = 4.75\% \div 12 \approx .395833\% \approx .00395833$):

$$PMT = \frac{PV(i)}{1 - \frac{1}{(1+i)^n}} = \frac{\$250,000(.00395833)}{1 - \frac{1}{(1.00395833)^{360}}} = \$1,304.12$$

c Finding the remaining term (*n*)

Mortgage balance = $98,985.19; 9% rate; monthly payment = $1,126.47. How many months left on the loan? Formula 5 ($i = 9\% \div 12 = .75\% = .0075$; PV = $98,985.19; PMT = negative $1,126.47; FV = 0):

$$n = \frac{-\ln\left[\frac{PV + \left(\frac{PMT}{i}\right)}{\frac{PMT}{i} - FV}\right]}{\ln(1+i)} = \frac{-\ln\left[\frac{\$98,985.19 + \left(\frac{-\$1,126.47}{.0075}\right)}{\frac{-\$1,126.47}{.0075} - \$0}\right]}{\ln(1.0075)} = 144 \text{ months}$$

Unit 11.4 Solving for rate (*i*)

a Calculating *i* when there is no periodic payment

You bought a rare postage stamp 8 years ago for $4,200 and just sold it for $12,500. What is your annual rate of return?

Formula 3: $i = \left(\frac{FV}{PV}\right)^{\frac{1}{n}} - 1 = \left(\frac{\$12,500}{\$4,200}\right)^{\frac{1}{8}} - 1 = .1461 = 14.61\%$

b Calculating *i* when there is a periodic payment

Three years ago, you bought some stock for $2,800. You received a $200 dividend at the end of each year. Immediately after getting the third $200 dividend check, you sold the stock for $4,300. Annual rate of return?

There is no formula to solve for *i* when payments are involved. So, we use one of the other formulas, guessing rates until the result is sufficiently close to a target figure.

Think

1. Explain the difference between a future value problem, a sinking fund problem, and an annuity problem. Then, give an example of each type of problem.
2. Suppose you want to accumulate $20,000 in 20 years and can earn 10% compounded annually. Determine the amount you must deposit today in one lump-sum to accumulate the $20,000. Now assume that you can earn only 5% compounded annually. Does it follow that because the interest rate is half as great you must deposit exactly twice as much today to reach your goal? Explain your reasoning. Then show calculations to support your point of view.
3. You may have heard of the Rule of 72. The Rule of 72 is a guideline for *approximating* how long it will take to double money left on deposit. To find the number of years, we divide 72 by the annual rate (without the percent sign). Using the Rule of 72, figure how many years it would take to double money for an annual rate of 9%. Then, use Formula 5 to find the precise time.

Explore

1. Refer to Appendix E. Review the explanations for using Excel to solve time-value-of-money problems. Then use Excel to solve the U-Try-It problems of Unit 11.4. *Tip:* For the "Guess" in the Excel formula, start with an annual rate of 12%.
2. Go to www.webbertext.com and click Online Calculator. Using the online calculator and the guidelines shown on that page, solve the U-Try-It problems of Unit 11.4.
3. Compare the answers using each method (formulas, Excel, and the online calculator). Which answers are different, if any, and why?

Apply

1. **The Car Loan.** Visit a bank or credit union. Ask for their help with this school project. Make a list of available car loans for new vehicles and used vehicles. Show interest rates and resulting monthly payments. What front-end loan fees are there, if any? Do they offer adjustable rate loans and, if so, how do these loans work? How is interest calculated? Are you penalized if you pay off the loan early? How are late fees calculated? Prepare a report on your findings.
2. **The Inflation Factor.** Research the cost of at least 4 products or services that were advertised in newspapers or magazines more than 25 years ago. Then find the current cost. Using Formula 3, calculate the annual rate of increase (or decrease) in prices between the two points in time. Include copies of the articles as well as your solutions. *Note:* To find the old advertisements or articles you can go online or visit a local library.
3. **Retirement.** Figure out a retirement plan for yourself (and spouse, if applicable). Make some assumptions: (1) an interest rate the plan will earn; (2) how much money you need each month to live on today; (3) how much you will need each month during retirement (based on a certain rate of inflation between now and retirement); (4) how much Social Security you will receive each month during retirement; (5) how many years until retirement; and (6) how long you will live. For simplicity, ignore inflation *during* retirement. Assume that for the 10 years before retirement, your earnings will decline and you will not make deposits to the plan. Calculate how much you must deposit at the end of each month into your retirement plan.

Chapter Review Problems

Unit 11.1 Sinking funds

1. Uncle Ted promises to give his niece Beth $50,000 on her 30th birthday, $6\frac{1}{2}$ years from now. Uncle Ted can earn 8% compounded quarterly. What amount could Uncle Ted deposit today in a savings plan so that the plan would have the required $50,000 in $6\frac{1}{2}$ years?

2. Refer to Problem 1. If, instead, Uncle Ted elects to make quarterly deposits into the plan (starting in 3 months), what is the required quarterly deposit?

3. While your dentist is filling a cavity in one of your teeth, he is talking with his dental assistant about the new dental equipment he wants to buy in $4\frac{1}{2}$ years for $40,000. He wonders how much money he must deposit at the end of each quarter to accumulate $40,000. You get his attention and tell him if he will quit drilling for a minute you will help him calculate the amount. What amount is required if he can earn 3% compounded quarterly?

For Problems 4-6, help a British auto manufacturer make calculations on some bonds. The company issues £86,500,000 of 6% 20-year bonds to upgrade its assembly line. Terms of the bond require annual interest payments to bondholders plus annual deposits to a sinking fund for retirement of the bonds when they mature.

4. How much interest must the corporation pay to the bondholders each year?

5. Assuming the corporation can earn 8% compounded annually on its sinking fund, how much must it deposit into the fund at the end of each year?

6. What is the total amount the corporation needs each year to meet its obligations on the bonds?

7. Kristi just turned 28 and can save $180 per month, starting in 1 month. If Kristi can earn 8% compounded monthly, what age will she be when she accumulates $1,000,000?

Unit 11.2 Annuities

For Problems 8-11, pretend you receive an inheritance of $500,000 and deposit it in a savings plan earning 6.75% compounded monthly.

8. If you want to live off the interest without withdrawing any of the $500,000 principal, what amount can you withdraw at the end of each month?

9. How much can you withdraw at the end of each month if you want the plan to last 40 years?

10. How much can you withdraw at the end of each month if you want the plan to last 30 years?

11. Refer to Problem 10. How much can you withdraw if the withdrawals are made at the *beginning* of each month?

12. A wealthy citizen sets up a trust for scholarships at a local community college. The gift is for $4,000,000 and the money is to be distributed at the beginning of each year over the next 150 years. If the trust earns 5.5% compounded annually, how much is available for scholarships each year?

Unit 11.3 Loan payments

13. You are thinking about buying a sports car, priced at $28,500. Your bank will loan you $27,500 at 6.5% for 6 years. Determine your monthly payment.

14. Refer to Problem 13. What is the total amount of interest you will pay over the 6 years?

15. If you purchase a big screen TV for $900 and the store finances the entire amount over 24 months at a monthly rate of 1.75%, what is your monthly payment?

For Problems 16-19, assume you need a $150,000 mortgage loan but are unsure whether to get a 7.25% 15-year loan or a 7.5% 30-year loan.

16. Calculate the monthly payment for each loan.

17. How much more per month will you pay with the 15-year loan?

18. Find the total amount of interest for each loan.

19. How much more interest will you pay with the 30-year loan?

20. Calculate the monthly payment on a 20-year $365,000 mortgage loan at $4\frac{7}{8}$% interest.

21. Several years ago you got a mortgage loan at 8.75% interest. You currently owe $138,743.03 with a monthly payment of $1,180.05. How long until the loan will be paid off?

Unit 11.4 Solving for rate (*i*)

22. Refer to the newspaper article. What is the average annual rate of return?

Ben Franklin is still saving pennies

Birthday gift. Bequest has grown from $4,000 to $520,000 and will be used to help students of trades, crafts and the applied sciences.

PHILADELPHIA (UPI) — The proceeds of Benjamin Franklin's estate will be used to help educate young Philadelphians in the trades and applied sciences, city officials and members of a blue-ribbon panel said Tuesday.

The planned use of the bequest was announced on the 200th anniversary of Franklin's death, the date when Franklin instructed his trust was to be terminated.

The bequest has grown from about $4,000 to $520,000, and the prospect of using his legacy drew more than 300 proposals from various groups. . .

23. (True Story) Clara Patterson and Bill Mayne got married in 1940. A year later, they bought a home in Salt Lake City, Utah, for $2,450. They lived in the home, in romantic bliss, until 2003; the home was worth $165,000. At what average annual rate did the home increase in value?

24. One way of measuring inflation is through the consumer price index (CPI), which tracks the cost of a "basket of goods" (food, housing, medical care, fuel, etc.). The base year of the current index is 1983, when the basket of goods cost $100. The CPI was 9.9 in 1913 (meaning the same basket of goods cost $9.90), 30.6 in 1963, and 238.7 in 2015. Calculate the average annual rate of inflation for the following periods: **(a)** 1913 to 1963, **(b)** 1963 to 1983, **(c)** 1983 to 2015, and **(d)** 1913 to 2015.

25. (True Story) In March, 1986, 15-year-old Jennifer Sanchez, a self-proclaimed "computer geek," invested her $750 life savings into a new stock—Microsoft. 14 years later, her investment turned into $450,000 plus a new Porsche 911 convertible, worth $82,500. Calculate Jennifer's average annual rate of return.

26. Your annual salary 12 years ago was $15,600; it is now $23,000. If the inflation rate over the last 12 years has averaged 3.5% per year, has your salary kept up with inflation?

27. 12 years ago, you bought some corporate stock for $1,200. You received dividends of $50 at the end of each year. Immediately after receiving the final dividend check, you sold the stock for $4,200. What is your rate of return?

Challenge problems

For Problems 28-31, assume that you win $1,000,000 in a lottery. After taxes you are left with $650,000. You deposit the $650,000 in a savings plan that earns 6% compounded monthly.

28. If you want to live off the interest without withdrawing any of the principal, what amount can you withdraw at the end of each month?

29. If you withdraw less than the amount found in Problem 27, what will happen to the savings plan balance?

30. If you make withdrawals of $3,000 at the end of each month, what will the balance be in 40 years?

31. If you want to make withdrawals of $3,500 at the end of each month, how long will the plan last?

For Problems 32-34, assume you want to buy a home in $2\frac{1}{2}$ years. You have some money saved up for part of your down payment but you need to accumulate an additional $8,000.

32. If your savings plan earns 6% compounded monthly, what amount could you deposit today in order to have the $8,000 in $2\frac{1}{2}$ years?

33. You do not have enough money to deposit today, in one lump-sum. If, instead, you make deposits at the end of each month, what is the required monthly deposit?

34. You have $2,400 to deposit today. What additional monthly deposit is required?

35. If gasoline prices increased over a 35-year period from 35.9 cents per gallon to $4.399 per gallon, what is the average annual rate of increase?

36. You can afford a monthly mortgage payment of $1,100 and can get a 30-year 6.75% loan. What is the maximum loan you can get so your payment does not exceed $1,100?

37. Jacob Mullin is 25 years old. Some of Jacob's older relatives have retired, having no income other than Social Security. Jacob does not want to be caught in that situation, so he is thinking about setting up a retirement plan. Jacob wants to retire at age 60, 35 years from now, and wants his retirement plan to provide $2,000 a month for 30 years (until he is 90). His plan can earn 6% compounded monthly. What amount must Jacob deposit at the end of each month for the next 35 years so that he can then start receiving $2,000 at the end of each month for the following 30 years?

38. Refer to Problem 37. How much interest will Jacob's retirement plan earn over the 65 years?

39. In 8 years, Yu Chen's daughter will be entering college and Yu would like to help financially. Tuition is currently $6,000 a year, but is expected to increase at a rate of 4%, compounded annually. Yu decides to create a college fund and make 8 annual deposits, starting in 1 year. In 8 years, he would like his daughter to be able to make 4 annual withdrawals from the fund (at the beginning of each year) that will cover her annual tuition. If the college fund earns 6% compounded annually, how much must Yu deposit at the end of each year? *Note:* Assume that tuition will remain the same for the 4 years of college.

Practice Test

1. You want to accumulate $35,000 in 18 years for your child's education, and you can earn 6% compounded monthly. What amount must you deposit at the beginning of each month to have the $35,000 in 18 years?

2. You want to start an accounting business and estimate it will take $22,000 to get started. You currently have $5,500 and can deposit an additional $400 at the end of each month. If your savings plan will earn 6% compounded monthly, in how many months can you start your business?

3. Your uncle dies and your 62-year-old aunt receives $250,000 life insurance proceeds. She needs monthly income and expects to live for approximately 30 years. If she invests the insurance money, earning 6.5% compounded monthly, how much can she withdraw at the end of each month?

4. Determine your monthly payment on a 4-year $13,500 car loan at 6.5% interest.

5. You are thinking about getting a 30-year $240,000 mortgage loan at 6.75%, with monthly payments. How much interest would you pay over the 30 years?

6. If the average value of homes in your area has increased over the last 10 years from $108,000 to $165,000, what is the average annual rate of increase?

Classroom Notes

FUN CORNER

Savings on the Rebound

Historically, Americans have saved a decent percent of their income. Here are savings, as a percent of disposable income (gross income less taxes):

Year	Savings
1960	7.2%
1970	9.4%
1980	9.8%
1990	6.5%
2000	2.9%
2005	1.6%
2010	5.3%
2014	4.8%

Source: Bureau of Economic Analysis, U.S. Dept. of Commerce

Savings Accounts In The Good Old Days

From Dave Barry's Greatest Hits
by Dave Barry

Back in the old days, if you had any excess money, you put it in a passbook savings account. These were simple, peaceful times.

And then, without warning, they made it legal for consumers to engage in complex monetary acts. Today, there are a whole range of programs in which all that happens is people call up to ask what they should do with their money:

"Hi, Steve? My wife and I listen to you all the time, and we just love your show. Now here is the problem: We're 27 years old, no kids, and we have a combined income of $93,000 and $675,000 in denatured optional treasury instruments of accrual, which will become extremely mature next week."

Now to me, these people do not have a problem. To me what these people need in the way of financial advice is: "Lighten up! Buy yourself a big boat and have parties where people put on funny hats and push the piano into the harbor!" But Mr. Consumer Radio Money Advisor, he tells them complex ways to get even more money and orders them to tune in next week. These shows make me feel tremendously guilty, as a consumer, because I still keep my money in accounts that actually get smaller, and sometimes disappear, like weekend guests in an old murder mystery, because the bank is always taking out a "service charge," as if the tellers have to take my money for walks or something.

Kill the Goose That Lays the Golden Eggs

This saying relates to the time-value-of-money. It refers to destroying (through greed) a source of money or something else of value.

The saying comes from a Greek fable about a farmer who owns a goose that lays eggs of gold. He decides that if he kills the goose, he will get all the eggs at once, instead of only one at a time. Then he will be rich. The killed goose, of course, lays no more eggs.

The farmer ignored the time-value-of-money—that money grows over time; he wanted it all at once.

Quotable Quip

Remember that time is money.
— Benjamin Franklin

"Shh! I'm calculating present value."

Future Value and Present Value: Using Financial Calculators

12

This chapter will introduce time-value-of-money problems. **Time-value-of-money problems** are based on the principle that *money earns interest over time*. For example, if you win a $1,000,000 lottery and the lottery officials give you a choice of receiving the $1,000,000 today or in 10 years, you should take the money today because you can earn interest on the money and end up with considerably more than $1,000,000 in 10 years. So a dollar today is worth more than a dollar received in the future; stated differently, a dollar received in the future is worth less than a dollar received today.

We can solve time-value-of-money problems by using formulas, financial calculators, Excel, or in limited cases with tables. We use formulas in Chapters 10 and 11. We use financial calculators in Chapters 12, 13, and 17. We use Excel in Appendix E. We will not use tables at all. Here's why. Even though using tables gives quick results for a few types of time-value-of-money problems in a *classroom setting*, tables are *not used in the real world*. Tables contain only certain interest rates (*i-values*) and terms (*n-values*), often not the ones needed. More important, tables cannot be used to solve for *n* and *i*; these problems account for about half of the problems encountered in the real world, such as figuring out how long it will take to accumulate a desired sum or pay off a loan, or calculating an APR on a loan or a yield on a potential investment. *Because the whole premise of this text is to teach real-life skills, we are saying NO! to tables and instead teaching the stuff you'll actually use.*

In this chapter we will calculate how money grows over time and the present value of money to be received in the future.

UNIT OBJECTIVES

Unit 12.1 Time-value-of-money terminology
ⓐ Understanding time-value-of-money terminology

Unit 12.2 Financial calculators
ⓐ Understanding the basics of using a financial calculator

Unit 12.3 Future value
ⓐ Finding what a single deposit will grow to
ⓑ Finding what a series of deposits will grow to

Unit 12.4 Present value
ⓐ Finding the present value of a single sum to be received in the future
ⓑ Finding the present value for a series of payments

Unit 12.1 Time-value-of-money terminology

a Understanding time-value-of-money terminology

The *time-value-of-money* concept states that knowing *when* money is received is just as important as knowing the *amount* of money received. To illustrate, suppose your rich uncle offers you the choice of receiving $10,000 today or $10,300 in 1 year. Your first impulse may be to accept the $10,300, but by doing so you would be ignoring the principal that *money earns interest over time*. Suppose that you accepted the $10,000 today and deposited the money in a savings plan earning 5% compounded annually. You would earn $500 interest ($10,000 × 5% = $500) and end up with $10,500 in 1 year, which is $200 more than your uncle's $10,300 offer.

As you may recall from Unit 9.3 (Compound interest), the frequency of compounding affects how money grows over time. With compound interest, we earn interest not only on amounts deposited, but also on previously earned interest. The period of time between interest calculations is referred to as the **compounding period**, or as just the **period**. For example, if interest is compounded semiannually, the compounding period is 6 months, and there are 2 periods per year. If interest is compounded quarterly, the compounding period is 3 months, and there are 4 periods per year. With monthly compounding, the compounding period is 1 month, and there are 12 periods per year.

Time-value-of-money (TVM) problems involve 5 variables: *n*, *i*, PV, PMT, and FV.

The 5 TVM variables	
n	Total number of periods. Stated another way, total number of times interest is calculated.
i	Interest rate per period (or periodic rate).
PV	Present value; a one-time amount that happens at the beginning of the first period.
PMT	Payment, also referred to as periodic payment. Happens once every period.
FV	Future value; a one-time amount that happens at the end of the last period.

To illustrate the TVM variables, suppose that 15 years ago you deposited $500 in a savings plan earning 6% compounded semiannually. Today, you withdraw the entire balance, which has grown to $1,213.63. Here are the values for each variable:

- *n*: 30 (15 years × 2 periods per year = 30)
- *i*: 3% (6% ÷ 2 periods per year = 3%)
- PV: $500 (this is the one-time amount that happened at the beginning of the first period)
- PMT: None (there is no amount that happens once every period)
- FV: $1,213.63 (this is the one-time amount that happened at the end of the last period)

> **TIP** — past, present, and future
>
> In the previous situation, you may have been tempted to treat the $1,213.63 amount as the present value, because it happened today, in the present. Because the $500 happened at the *beginning of the first period*, it is the present value. The $1,213.63, which happened at the *end of the last period*, is the future value.

Let's try to identify the variables in the following examples.

Example 1

Sebastian Xavier is a soda pop "addict" and wonders how much money he could accumulate if he stopped drinking soda pop and deposited the $150 per month he spends on the stuff into a savings plan. Sebastian just turned 20. If his savings plan earns 6% compounded monthly and his first deposit is a month from now, what amount would he have at retirement, 40 years from now? *Don't solve the problem.* Instead, identify the 5 TVM variables.

———————

n	480	(40 years × 12 periods per year = 480)
i	0.5%	(6% ÷ 12 periods per year = 0.5%)
PV	None	(There is no one-time, initial deposit at the beginning of the first period)
PMT	$150	(This happens every period)
FV	?	(This is the amount we want to know—the amount at the end of the last period)

You may ask, Is it reasonable to expect a 6% return? In today's economy, honestly, no. We may never again see the heyday of the 1980s, where savings rates peaked near 14%, but we'd like to think things will turn around. And, while savings account rates from time to time can be much less, other investments (such as bonds, stocks, real estate, and mutual funds) can over the long haul earn 6% or better.

Example 2

You have the chance to buy a promissory note, in which you would receive 28 quarterly payments of $500, starting 3 months from now. If you buy the note, you will receive a total of $14,000 (28 × $500). If you want to earn 8% compounded quarterly, what price should you pay for the note? *Don't solve the problem.* Instead, identify the 5 TVM variables.

———————

n	28	
i	2%	(8% ÷ 4 periods per year = 2%)
PV	?	(This is the amount we want to know—the amount at the beginning of the first period)
PMT	$500	(This happens every period)
FV	None	(There is no additional amount you receive or pay at the end of the last period)

In Example 2, you may have been tempted to treat the $14,000 amount as a future value. But you do not receive $14,000 at the end of the last period; instead you receive 28 payments of $500. The $14,000 amount is what we call a "distractor," only there to confuse us!

We will solve Examples 1 and 2 in the next unit. I'll bet you're excited about that. Meanwhile, let's see if we've mastered the terminology by doing a U-Try-It problem.

U-Try-It (Unit 12.1)

1. You start a savings plan, earning 6% compounded quarterly, by depositing $300. You then deposit $100 at the end of each quarter. You want to know your account balance at the end of 10 years. *Don't solve the problem.* Instead, identify n, i, PV, PMT, and FV.

Answers: (If you have a different answer, check the solution in Appendix A.)
1. n = 40; i = 1.5%; PV = $300; PMT = $100; FV = Unknown (this is what we want to know).

Unit 12.2 Financial calculators

Financial calculators are not magic. They are programmed with the compound interest formulas of Chapter 10. We key in the values for the TVM variables (n, i, PV, PMT, and FV) and the calculators do the arithmetic. Remember, financial calculators do *not* alleviate the need for common sense; they are only a *tool* in solving problems.

Financial calculators are powerful tools. Just as a carpenter must understand how to use a power saw, the operator of a financial calculator must understand how to use the calculator.

TIP — calculator videos

Three calculator videos are available. If you are using the HP 10BII, HP 10BII+, or TI BAII PLUS, please take a few minutes now to watch Video #1 (Getting Started). Go to **www.webbertext.com**, click Calculator Videos, enter the access code provided by your instructor, then click Getting Started for your calculator. In addition to watching Video #1 now, it would be a good idea to review keystrokes on the first two pages of Appendix C.

The ⓠ icon in the text margin later in this chapter and again in Chapter 17 prompts you to watch Videos #2 and #3.

If you are using the HP 10B (not the 10BII or 10BII+), HP 12C, HP 17B, HP 39gs, TI 83+, TI 84+, Casio 9750G PLUS, or LeWorld FIN, you can request keystrokes at *studentsupport@olympuspub.com*.

ⓐ Understanding the basics of using a financial calculator

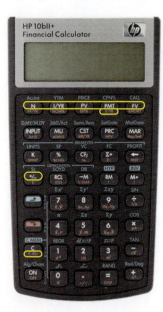

Financial calculators have keys (registers) representing the 5 TVM variables. In this chapter, we show calculator keystrokes for the HP 10BII+ and TI BAII PLUS. For the HP 10BII+, the TVM registers are on the top row; for the TI BAII PLUS, the TVM registers are on the third row from the top. Shortly, we will solve the two examples from Unit 12.1. But first we need to do a few things. The first is to set our calculators so that the interest rate register represents the interest rate *per period*.

initial one-time setup

We want the interest rate register to represent the periodic rate (rather than an annual rate). To accomplish this we need to set our "periods per year" register to 1, and leave it that way for life. Let's do that now.

HP 10BII+	TI BAII PLUS
1 [P/YR] 1.00*	[2ND] [P/Y] 1 [ENTER] [2ND] [QUIT] 0.00*
Note: The P/YR register is located below the PMT key, *not* below the N key.	*Note:* The P/Y register is located above the I/Y key, *not* above the N key.

You may wonder why we did this one-time setup. Here's why. We have two choices for entering the interest rate. With Choice 1, we keep the "periods per year" register at 1 for life, and enter the *periodic rate* in the interest rate register. With Choice 2, we enter the *annual* rate in the interest rate register and change the "periods per year" setting from problem to problem. We will use Choice 1 in the text because (1) having the interest rate register represent the *periodic rate* is conceptually more sound, and (2) it is easy to forget to change the "periods per year" setting from problem to problem (resulting in wrong answers).

The next thing we need to do is review the steps to use when solving TVM problems with a financial calculator.

solving TVM problems with a financial calculator

Step 1   Clear the TVM registers.

For the HP 10BII+, press [C ALL]. For the TI BAII PLUS, press [2ND] [CLR TVM].

Step 2   Enter the given data.

Enter dollar amounts *received* as positive numbers, and dollar amounts *paid* as negative numbers. Suppose we want to enter a negative $300 in the PMT register. We press: 300 [+/-] [PMT].

Step 3   Solve for the unknown.

For the HP 10BII+, press the register representing the unknown. For the TI BAII PLUS, press [CPT] and then the register representing the unknown.

Watch Calculator Video #2 on our website (Solving TVM Problems)

Finally! Now, let's solve the two examples of Unit 12.1 (you're saying, "It's about time," aren't you?).

Example 1   Sebastian Xavier is a soda pop "addict" and wonders how much money he could accumulate if he stopped drinking soda pop and deposited the $150 per month he spends on the stuff into a savings plan. Sebastian just turned 20. If his savings plan earns 6% compounded monthly and his first deposit is a month from now, what amount would he have at retirement, 40 years from now?

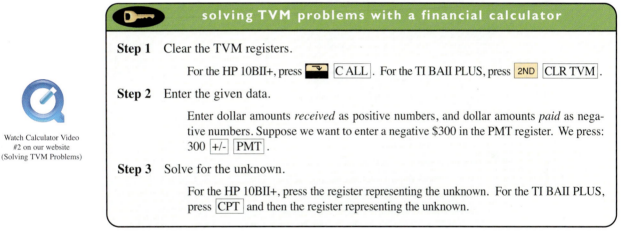

HP 10BII+					TI BAII PLUS				
Step 1: Clear TVM registers					*Step 1: Clear TVM registers*				
[C ALL]				0.00	[2ND] [CLR TVM]				?.??
Step 2: Enter given data					*Step 2: Enter given data*				
150	[+/-]	[PMT]		-150.00	150	[+/-]	[PMT]		-150.00
40	×	12	=	[N] 480.00	40	×	12	=	[N] 480.00
6	÷	12	=	[I/YR] 0.50	6	÷	12	=	[I/Y] 0.50
Step 3: Solve for unknown					*Step 3: Solve for unknown*				
[FV]				298,723.61	[CPT] [FV]				298,723.61

Sebastian will end up with $298,723.61! He would earn interest of $226,723.61 ($298,723.61 ending balance - $72,000 deposited).

Example 2 You have the chance to buy a promissory note in which you would receive 28 quarterly payments of $500, starting 3 months from now. If you buy the note, you would receive a total of $14,000 (28 × $500). If you want to earn 8% compounded quarterly, what price should you pay for the note?

HP 10BII+		TI BAII PLUS	
Step 1: Clear TVM registers		*Step 1: Clear TVM registers*	
▼ C ALL	0.00	2ND CLR TVM	?.??
Step 2: Enter given data		*Step 2: Enter given data*	
500 PMT	500.00	500 PMT	500.00
28 N	28.00	28 N	28.00
8 ÷ 4 = I/YR	2.00	8 ÷ 4 = I/Y	2.00
Step 3: Solve for unknown		*Step 3: Solve for unknown*	
PV	-10,640.64	CPT PV	-10,640.64

By paying $10,640.64 you will earn 8% compounded quarterly.

The answer of Example 2 is a *negative* $10,640.64; it's negative because you will *pay* that amount. You may find it useful to visualize a problem by drawing a *cash flow diagram*. Here are cash flow diagrams for Examples 1 and 2. Notice, *negative cash flows* are shown below the line and *positive cash flows* are shown above the line.

You may wonder if an answer found by using financial calculators can be relied upon. After all, you are not doing the arithmetic, a machine is. One way to feel more comfortable about an answer is to determine if the answer seems reasonable. In Example 2, you will receive a total of $14,000 (28 payments of $500 = $14,000). If you paid $14,000 for the note, you would earn no interest. In order to earn interest, you must pay less than $14,000, so the answer of $10,640.64 seems reasonable.

When using financial calculators to solve TVM problems, the calculator does the arithmetic (using built-in formulas) based on the values we provide. Remember the saying

Garbage In, Garbage Out.

As implied, if we make a mistake with our calculators, the answer will be wrong. Here are a few helpful ideas to use when inputting data into a financial calculator:

> **TIP** — a few ideas to help things go smoothly
>
> **Tip 1** To review values in the TVM registers, press [RCL] [N], [RCL] [PV], etc.
>
> **Tip 2** We are given at least 3 of the 5 variables. For most problems, we are given 3 variables and solve for a 4th. For some, we are given 4 variables and solve for the 5th.
>
> **Tip 3** It doesn't matter what order the given values are entered.
>
> **Tip 4** Remember to enter the *i-value* as a periodic rate. And don't use the % sign; for a periodic rate of 2%, enter the interest rate as "2," *not* "2%" or ".02."
>
> **Tip 5** Remember to enter dollar amounts *received* as positive numbers and dollar amounts *paid* as negative numbers. When entering a negative number, don't use the minus (-) key; instead use the +/- key: 300 [+/-] [PMT].
>
> **Tip 6** For problems in which we know only 3 of the 5 variables, we solve for a 4th variable, meaning there is an unused register. If we forget to clear the TVM registers, a previous value will remain in the unused register, and we will get a wrong answer!
>
> **Tip 7** Instead of clearing the TVM registers we could enter 0 in the unused register.
>
> **Tip 8** If an upcoming problem is merely a *variation* of the preceding problem, there is no need to clear the TVM registers; instead, just enter the values that are different.
>
> *Suggestion:* If you haven't yet watched Calculator Video #2 for the HP 10BII, HP 10BII+, or TI BAII PLUS, you should do so now. Go to www.webbertext.com; click Calculator Videos, and then click Solving TVM Problems for your calculator.

Let's answer a few U-Try-It questions to see how comfortable we are with our TVM registers.

U-Try-It (Unit 12.2)

1. You bought some vacant land 15 years ago for $30,000 and just sold it for $65,000. What is the present value: **(a)** $30,000, **(b)** -$30,000, **(c)** $65,000, or **(d)** -$65,000?
2. Values must be entered in the TVM registers in a certain order. (T or F)
3. By having our "periods per year" register set at 1, we must enter the *periodic* rate in the *i-register*. (T or F)

Answers: (If you have a different answer, check the solution in Appendix A.)
1. (b) -$30,000   **2.** False   **3.** True

Unit 12.3 Future value

If we make deposits into a savings plan, we can calculate the sum to which they will grow if we know the dollar amount of deposits, when the deposits are made, and the interest rate earned. Deposits may consist of one deposit or a series of deposits. Let's start by finding what a single deposit will grow to.

ⓐ Finding what a single deposit will grow to

If we make a deposit into a savings plan, we can calculate the sum to which the money will grow (FV) if we know the dollar amount of the deposit (PV), how long the money is left on deposit (n), and the interest rate earned (i). Let's use arithmetic to calculate what a deposit of $400 will grow to if left on deposit for 3 years earning 5% compounded annually. Let's calculate the balance at the end of each year.

Deposit	$400.00
Interest year 1: $I = PRT = \$400 \times 5\% \times 1 =$	+ 20.00
Balance, end of year 1	$420.00
Interest year 2: $I = PRT = \$420 \times 5\% \times 1 =$	+ 21.00
Balance, end of year 2	$441.00
Interest year 3: $I = PRT = \$441 \times 5\% \times 1 =$	+ 22.05
Balance, end of year 3	**$463.05**

Notice that the dollar amount of interest increases each year. That's because of compounding, in which we earn interest not only on the initial deposit but also on previous interest.

Let's try this problem using our TVM registers. Showing calculator keystrokes can create clutter. So, for upcoming problems, keystrokes will *not* be shown unless the keystrokes are unique. Instead, we will show the values in a TVM format; the answers will be highlighted.

Example 1

You deposit $400 in a savings plan and let the money sit for 3 years earning 5% compounded annually. Find the ending balance.

N	i	PV	PMT	FV
3	5	-400		463.05

Your ending balance will be $463.05, the same answer we got using a longhand approach.

Example 2

Suppose a "wise man" had deposited $1 in a savings account 2,000 years ago and the account earned interest at 2% compounded annually. If the money in the account today were evenly divided among the world's population, how much would each person receive, based on a world population of 7 billion?

For this problem, set your decimal at the maximum setting.

N	i	PV	PMT	FV
2,000	2	-1		1.58614733 17*

Note: The account balance is too large to fit in a standard calculator display and, therefore, is displayed in scientific notation: $1.58614733 \times 10^{17}$. The TI BAII PLUS does not display as many digits (1.586147 17). The "17" means we must move the decimal point 17 places to the right, so the account balance is approximately $158,614,733,000,000,000.

As soon as the answer (1.58614733 17) appears, divide by 7,000,000,000; we get **$22,659,247.54.**

The account balance is approximately $158,614,733,000,000,000 (read as "One hundred fifty-eight quadrillion, six hundred fourteen trillion, seven hundred thirty-three billion dollars")! Each person would receive $22,659,247.54! Maybe your check is in the mail.

The answer to Example 2 may make your head spin. We would get the same result if we added 2% to the account balance 2,000 times ($1 + 2% + 2% + ⋯). Let friends or relatives solve Example 2 (you will most likely have to help them) and watch the expression on their face when they see the answer.

Example 2 illustrates the power of compounding. By using compound interest the account balance is $158,614,733,000,000,000. With simple interest, the balance would be:

$$I = PRT = \$1 \times 2\% \times 2{,}000 = \$40 \qquad M = P + I = \$1 + 40 = \mathbf{\$41}$$

Most time-value-of-money problems involve *receipts and expenditures of money*. Some problems, such as changes over time (like population of a town or tuition), do not.

changes over time not involving receipts and expenditures of money

- The first value to occur (it occurs at the beginning of the first period) is considered the present value; the last to occur (it occurs at the end of the last period) is the future value.
- One of the values—present value or future value—will be positive and the other will be negative; our solutions will show present value as the negative value.

Example 3 Tuition at a local university is currently $4,800 a year. Based on an annual inflation rate of 4%, what will tuition be 15 years from now?

N	i	PV	PMT	FV
15	4	-4,800		8,644.53

Based on an annual inflation rate of 4%, tuition will be $8,644.53. We would get the same answer by increasing $4,800 by 4% a total of 15 times: 4,800 + 4% + 4% + ⋯ = 8,644.53.

b Finding what a series of deposits will grow to

In Example 1 we made a *single* deposit. We can instead make a series of deposits.

Example 4 You deposit $100 at the end of each year for 4 years, earning 6% compounded annually. Find the balance in 4 years.

N	i	PV	PMT	FV
4	6		-100	437.46*

*Note: If you forgot to clear your TVM registers, the PV value from the previous problem (negative 4,800) will still be in the PV register and you will get a wrong answer ($6,497.35).

The balance will be $437.46.

Let's check to see if the balance of $437.46 is correct.

	Interest	Deposit	Balance
Balance, end of year 1	None	$100	$100.00
Balance, end of year 2	I = PRT = $100 × 6% × 1 = $6.00	$100	$206.00
Balance, end of year 3	I = PRT = $206 × 6% × 1 = $12.36	$100	$318.36
Balance, end of year 4	I = PRT = $318.36 × 6% × 1 = $19.10	$100	**$437.46**

The ending balance ($437.46) matches our answer to Example 4, so our calculators must know what they are doing!

In Example 4, you deposited $100 at the *end* of each year. How would the balance be affected if the first of your 4 deposits were made immediately (at the *beginning* of each year)? Because you would start earning interest immediately, your ending balance should be greater than $437.46. Here's what the balance would be:

	Interest	Deposit	Balance
Beginning	None	$100	$100.00
Balance, end of year 1	I = PRT = $100 × 6% × 1 = $6.00	$100	$206.00
Balance, end of year 2	I = PRT = $206 × 6% × 1 = $12.36	$100	$318.36
Balance, end of year 3	I = PRT = $318.36 × 6% × 1 = $19.10	$100	$437.46
Balance, end of year 4	I = PRT = $437.46 × 6% × 1 = $26.25	None	**$463.71**

The known values for this scenario are the same as those of Example 4: $n = 4$, $i = 6$, and PMT = -$100. So what do we do differently with our calculators to indicate that the deposits are made at the *beginning* of each period? Easy! We set our calculators to "begin" mode.

When periodic payments are involved in a TVM problem, we must set our calculators to "begin" mode if payments commence immediately, or to "end" mode if the first payment is made after 1 period has lapsed.

If the HP 10BII+ is in "begin mode," the symbol BEG appears in the display; if it is in "end mode," BEG does *not* appear. If the TI BAII PLUS is in "begin mode," the symbol BGN appears in the display; if it is in "end mode," BGN does *not* appear. Here is how we can change the mode:

HP 10BII+	TI BAII PLUS
▼ Beg/End	2ND BGN 2ND SET 2ND QUIT

Example 5

Rework Example 4, assuming the deposits were made at the beginning of each year.

N	i	PV	PMT	FV
4	6		-100 Begin	463.71

Because this problem is unique, calculator keystrokes are shown:

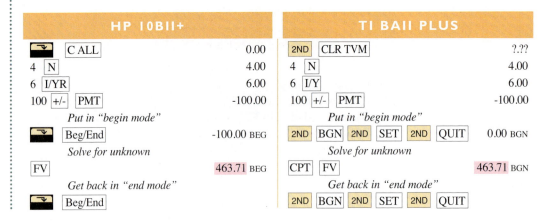

Notice that the answer to Example 5 ($463.71) matches the answer we got without our TVM registers.

TIP — don't be a "beginner"

Most TVM problems are *end-mode* problems, so here is a helpful suggestion: Immediately after getting the answer to a *begin-mode* problem, put your calculator back in "end" mode (as we did in the keystrokes of Example 5). If you forget, your answers to *end-mode* problems will be wrong, and you won't know it; that's what we call going through life as a "beginner"!

Some books use special terminology for a series of payments: if payments are made at the end of each period, the series of payments is referred to as an **ordinary annuity**; if payments are made at the beginning of each period, the series of payments is referred to as an **annuity due**. We will not use that terminology; instead, we will simply state for each problem whether payments are made at the end, or beginning, of each period.

To help visualize Examples 4 and 5, here is a cash flow diagram for each:

The next example shows the importance of starting to save as soon as possible.

Example 6

Kristen and Erica are twins. On her 20th birthday, Kristen starts a savings plan by depositing $50 at the beginning of each month. Erica starts a savings plan 25 years later by depositing $100 at the beginning of each month. Both savings plans earn 6% compounded monthly. Find their account balances when they turn 70.

N	i	PV	PMT	FV
50 × 12 = 600	6 ÷ 12 = 0.50		-50 Begin	190,306.35
25 × 12 = 300	↑		-100 Begin*	69,645.89

*Note: Don't forget to put back in "end" mode.

In Example 6, Kristen ends up with much more than Erica. Notice they both deposited a total of $30,000. Kristen earned interest of $160,306.35 ($190,306.35 - $30,000 deposited) and Erica earned interest of only $39,645.89 ($69,645.89 - $30,000 deposited).

To help visualize the difference between the two savings plans, here are cash flow diagrams:

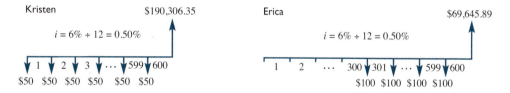

TIP   **sooner or later?**

Many people delay starting a savings plan because they think a small amount set aside each month will not amount to much later. Perhaps the best investment advice is to "Just Get Started." And the sooner, the better, as pointed out in Example 6.

Let's try a few fun problems in the U-Try-It set. I'll bet you are saying "fun" problems is a contradiction of terms! The two "fun" problems provide a different twist, so be sure to give them a try. In the first "fun" problem, an initial deposit is made into a savings plan and then is followed by a series of deposits. In the second "fun" problem, a series of deposits is made and then the money is left alone, without more deposits, for some additional time.

U-Try-It (Unit 12.3)

1. You start a savings plan by making an initial deposit of $1,250. You then deposit $100 at the end of each quarter for 10 years. What will your balance be in 10 years, assuming you earn 4% compounded quarterly?

2. Sarah Sharp, a 30-year-old insurance broker, decides to start a retirement plan. She figures that her income for the next 25 years will be sufficient to deposit $1,000 at the end of each quarter into her retirement plan. She will let the money sit for another 10 years until she is 65 years old. If Sarah's retirement plan earns 6% compounded quarterly, what amount will she have when she turns 65?

Answers: (If you have a different answer, check the solution in Appendix A.)
1. $6,749.72   2. $415,052.93

Unit 12.4 Present value

In this unit, we will find the value, in today's dollars, of future cash flows. That value is referred to as **present value**. We can find the present value of a single sum to be received in the future, the present value of a series of payments to be received in the future, or the present value of a single sum plus a series of payments. Let's start by finding the present value of a single sum.

For many prizes, such as prizes from gameshows, lotteries, or casino jackpots, the winners do not get the money all at once—it is paid over time. The real value (present value) of the prize is much less than the stated prize money because we have to wait for the money.

ⓐ Finding the present value of a single sum to be received in the future

In Example 1 of Unit 12.3, you deposit $400 in a savings plan and let the money sit for 3 years earning 5% compounded annually. The balance grew to $463.05 in 3 years. Let's look at this problem from a different angle. Suppose your aunt says she will give you $463.05 in 3 years. Assuming that you can earn 5% compounded annually on your money, the real value of her promise, in today's dollars (the present value), is $400 because you could invest the $400 and end up with $463.05. Illustration 12-1 shows this graphically. Notice the two-way arrow: with a rate of 5% compounded annually, $400 will grow to $463.05 in 3 years and the *present value* of $463.05 to be received in 3 years is $400.

Let's use our TVM registers to find the present value of your aunt's promise.

Example 1 Your aunt says she will give you $463.05 in 3 years. Assuming that you can earn 5% compounded annually, what is the real value of her promise, in today's dollars?

N	i	PV	PMT	FV
3	5	-400.00		463.05

The present value is $400.

Notice that the answer to Example 1 is a negative value (-400.00), indicating that someone should be willing to *pay* $400 now to get $463.05 in 3 years. Sign convention is not critical for this problem because we enter only one dollar value (463.05); if we had entered the 463.05 as a negative, the answer would still be 400, but positive.

260   Chapter 12   Future Value and Present Value: Using Financial Calculators

Illustration 12-1 Relationship between Present Value and Future Value

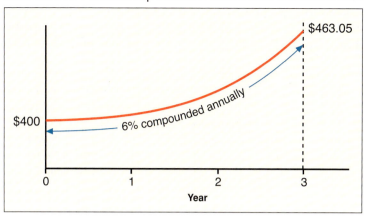

Conclusions
1. $400 invested at 5% compounded annually will grow to $463.05 in 3 years.
2. Assuming that money can earn 5% compounded annually, the present value of $463.05 to be received in 3 years is $400.

ⓑ Finding the present value for a series of payments

In Example 1, we found the present value of a *single sum* to be received in the future. We can also find the present value of a *series of payments*. For instance, we might want to know the present value of $2,000 to be received at the end of each year for 3 years.

Example 2

You are selling a valuable coin. You have two offers. The first offer is for $5,500 cash. With the second offer, the buyer will pay you $2,000 at the end of each year for 3 years. Assuming that you can earn 8% compounded annually on your money, which offer is better?

Your first reaction may be to accept the second offer because you will receive a total of $6,000. But you would be ignoring the time value of money. Let's calculate the present value of the second offer.

N	i	PV	PMT	FV
3	8	-5,154.19	2,000	

The present value of the second offer is $5,154.19, considerably less than the $5,500 cash offer. You should accept the first offer.

In Example 2, you may have been tempted to treat the $6,000 total as the FV variable. But no one pays or receives $6,000 at the end of the last period, so it is not a future value. If the offer had instead been for the buyer to pay you $6,000 at the end of 3 years, we could find the present value ($4,762.99).

There are lots of practical applications for finding the present value of a series of payments. We explore three common applications in this chapter: (1) finding the amount to pay for a promissory note, (2) determining the value of bonds, and (3) finding the value of a long-term project.

Finding the amount to pay for a promissory note. Someone who borrows money is generally required to sign a **promissory note**, which spells out terms of repayment. An owner of a note (a lender) who needs cash may sell the note to a third party. The price is based on the rate of return (referred to as **yield**) the investor demands. As an example, suppose Randy loaned Jinny $15,000 at 6% interest, with quarterly payments of $500. Jinny has been making payments for awhile and the balance is now $11,363.36; she still owes 28 quarterly payments of $500. Randy needs some money for a business venture and asks you to buy the note, in which case you would receive the remaining 28 payments from Jinny. If you are satisfied with the **note rate** of 6%, you would pay the **note balance** of $11,363.36; the note is said to be sold at **par**. If you are satisfied with a rate less than the note rate, you could pay a **premium**. If you require a yield greater than the note rate you would buy the note at a **discount**. In Example 2 of Unit 12.2, we found the amount you should pay if you want to earn 8% compounded quarterly: $10,640.64.

Determining the value of bonds. Corporations, the U.S. government, and local governmental agencies often need large sums of money. They often raise the money by selling bonds to the public. A **bond** is a written promise to repay the owner of the bond (**bondholder**) a specified amount (**maturity value**) at a future date (**maturity date**). Bondholders also earn interest, generally paid semiannually or annually.

Corporate bonds are generally issued in $1,000 denominations. Many beginning investors think that a $1,000 bond is always worth $1,000. While a $1,000 bond is worth $1,000 at maturity, the same bond may be worth more or less than the $1,000 *prior* to maturity, depending on the prevailing rate for similar bonds. For example, if you own a bond paying 6% and new bonds are paying 8%, investors will buy the 8% bond instead of yours; to attract a buyer you will have to sell it for less than $1,000 (at a *discount*) so that the buyer can earn 8%. On the other hand, if your bond pays 10%, an investor would be willing to pay you more than $1,000 (at a *premium*). In the next example, we will determine the value of a bond.

Example 3

Eight years ago you bought a 20-year 6% $1,000 bond. The bond pays interest each 6 months. You want to sell the bond. You just received the 16th semiannual interest payment, in the amount of $30 ($1,000 × 3% periodic rate = $30). Similar bonds are being issued that pay 8% semiannually. What is your bond worth today?

Let's look at this *from the standpoint of an investor* who might buy your bond. The investor would receive $30 interest checks at the end of each 6 months for the next 12 years plus the $1,000 maturity value in 12 years.

N	i	PV	PMT	FV
12 × 2 = 24	8 ÷ 2 = 4	-847.53	30	1,000

Your $1,000 bond is worth only $847.53.

Finding the value of a long-term project. Finding the present value of future cash flows is also valuable in deciding whether a business should spend money on a long-term project, like buying machinery or expanding a plant. The evaluation of a long-term project is known as **capital budgeting**.

Example 4

You own a manufacturing business and are considering the purchase of a labor-saving device for $100,000. You project that the device will last 15 years and save you $900 per month in labor costs (assume that the savings are realized at the end of each month). At the end of the 15 years, you project you can sell the device for a salvage value of $7,000. Assuming that you can earn 10.25% compounded monthly on your money, find the value of the device. Then decide whether you should buy the device.

You will save a total of $162,000 (180 months × $900). You will also get the $7,000 salvage value, for a total dollar return of $169,000. Because the total return is more than the $100,000 cost, you may conclude that you should buy the device. But, we need to find the present value of those amounts.

N	i	PV	PMT	FV
15 × 12 = 180	10.25 ÷ 12 = 0.85416*	-84,086.80	900	7,000

*Note: The underlined 6 means the 6 is a repeating digit (the 6s continue forever). By dividing 10.25 by 12 and transferring the result in the interest rate register, we enter the *internal, more accurate value* (approximately 0.854166667).

The device has a value of $84,086.80. Because the value ($84,086.80) is less than the cost of the device ($100,000), you should not buy the device.

> **TIP** — don't round the rate before entering
>
> Don't make the common mistake of entering a periodic rate as a rounded value. In Example 4, the annual rate was 10.25%. By dividing 10.25 by 12 and transferring the result directly into the interest rate register, we enter the *internal, more accurate* value. Don't make the mistake of entering a *rounded* periodic rate (such as 0.85); the answer of Example 4 would be off ($84,331.90)!

Congratulations on finishing this chapter. Financial calculators provide a great way to solve a variety of time-value-of-money problems. Let's do the U-Try-It exercises to get a little more practice finding the present value of money to be received in the future.

U-Try-It (Unit 12.4)

1. Marcus's rich aunt promises to give him $100,000 on his 25th birthday, 21 years from now. If money is worth 6% compounded annually, what is today's value of her promise?
2. You win a $10,000,000 lottery. When you go to collect your money, you find out the $10,000,000 will be paid with 40 annual payments of $250,000 (totaling $10,000,000). The payments will be made at the end of each year. What is the real value of your prize, in today's dollars, assuming that you can earn 6% compounded annually?
3. You own a manufacturing business and are considering the purchase of a labor-saving device for $100,000. You project that the device will last 15 years and save you $1,500 per month in labor costs (assume that the savings are realized at the end of each month). At the end of the 15 years, you project you can sell the device for a salvage value of $5,500. Assuming that you can earn 12% compounded monthly, find the value of the device.
4. Refer to Problem 3. Should you buy the device?

Answers: (If you have a different answer, check the solution in Appendix A.)
1. $29,415.54 **2.** $3,761,574.22 **3.** $125,899.80 **4.** Yes, because the device is worth more than it costs.

Chapter in a Nutshell

Objectives	Examples

Unit 12.1 Time-value-of-money terminology

(a) Understanding time-value-of-money terminology

You deposit $500 today and an additional $175 at the end of each 6 months for 5 years. You earn 6% compounded semiannually. TVM variables?

$n = 5 \times 2 = 10$ $i = 6\% \div 2 = 3\%$ PV = $500   PMT = $175   FV = Not given

Unit 12.2 Financial calculators

(a) Understanding the basics of using a financial calculator

Step 1 Clear the TVM registers.
Step 2 Enter the given data (money received is positive; money paid is negative).
Step 3 Solve for the unknown.

Unit 12.3 Future value

(a) Finding what a single deposit will grow to

You deposit $125 in a savings plan earning 5% compounded annually. Balance in 30 years?

N	i	PV	PMT	FV
30	5	-125		540.24

(b) Finding what a series of deposits will grow to

You deposit $25 at the end of each quarter into a savings plan earning 6% compounded quarterly. Balance in 10 years?

N	i	PV	PMT	FV
10 × 4 = 40	6 ÷ 4 = 1.5		-25	1,356.70

Chapter in a Nutshell (concluded)

Objectives	Examples

Unit 12.4 Present value

a Finding the present value of a single sum to be received in the future

You win a contest that pays $5,000 in one lump-sum 5 years from now. What is the value of the prize if money is worth 6% compounded annually?

N	i	PV	PMT	FV
5	6	-3,736.29		5,000

b Finding the present value for a series of payments

You invent a product and sell it to a corporation. You will receive $30,000 at the end of each year for 10 years. If money is worth 8% compounded annually, what is the value of your invention?

N	i	PV	PMT	FV
10	8	-201,302.44	30,000	

Enrichment Topics

The following Enrichment Topic, which goes a bit beyond what is in the text, is available for this chapter:

If Compounding Period and Deposit Period Differ

If your instructor doesn't cover this topic in class and you would like to dig in deeper on your own, please send a request to *studentsupport@olympuspub.com*. You can also request a set of keystrokes for your particular calculator.

Think

1. Rosa Ramos bought some IBM stock 15 years ago for $2,000. She sold the stock today for $8,000. Which value—$2,000 or $8,000—is the present value, and why?
2. Suppose you invent a product and sell the patent to a large corporation. The corporation agrees to pay you $5,000 each quarter for 10 years. For each question, select the best choice (choose from $150,000, $200,000, and $270,000). Explain your reasoning. *Note:* For questions (b) and (c), don't do any calculations.
    a. What is the total amount of money you will receive?
    b. If you deposit the $5,000 payments into a savings plan, what will the balance be in 10 years?
    c. What is the value of your invention?
3. Suppose Ted deposits $10,000 in a savings plan earning 5% compounded annually and Tess deposits $10,000 in a savings plan earning 10% compounded annually. Both leave their money on deposit for 40 years. Because Tess's rate is twice as great as Ted's rate, is it true that Tess will earn twice as much interest? Explain why or why not. Then show calculations to support your point of view.
4. Refer to the cash flow diagrams of Unit 12.3. Create a cash flow diagram for each of the U-Try-It exercises of Unit 12.3.

Explore

1. Refer to Appendix E. Review the explanations for using Excel to solve time-value-of-money problems. Then use Excel to solve each of the U-Try-It problems from Units 12.3 and 12.4.
2. Go to **www.webbertext.com** and click Online Calculator. Using the online calculator and the guidelines shown on that page, solve each of the U-Try-It problems from Units 12.3 and 12.4.
3. Compare the answers using each method (financial calculators, Excel, and the online calculator). Which answers are different, if any, and why?

Apply

1. **Costs in the Future.** Pick 5 items that you have bought in the last year (like a car, home, gallon of milk, dozen eggs, tuition, gallon of gasoline, etc.) or one that you would like to buy (like a car or home). Based on annual inflation rates of 3%, 5%, and 8%, use your financial calculator to project the cost of each item in 10 years, 20 years, 30 years, and 40 years. *Hint:* Treat the current cost as PV, and the cost later as FV.

Chapter Review Problems

Unit 12.1 Time-value-of-money terminology

For Problems 1-5, assume you deposit $1,000 today in a savings account. You earn 6% compounded quarterly. You deposit an additional $50 each quarter, starting in 3 months. At the end of 3 years, you withdraw the balance of $1,847.68. Identify each value.

1. n?
2. i?
3. PV?
4. PMT?
5. FV?

For Problems 6-8, assume you purchased some corporate stock 8 years ago for $4,000. You received dividends of $50 each quarter; your dividends total $1,600 (32 dividend checks × $50 = $1,600). You sold the stock today for $6,000.

6. The PV is $6,000 because that is the amount you received today (in the present). (T or F)

7. Which variable (PV, PMT, or FV) does $1,600 represent?

8. What is the FV amount?

Unit 12.2 Financial calculators

9. When should we clear the TVM registers, and when should we not clear the TVM registers?

10. What is the advantage of setting our "periods per year" register at 1?

11. Unfortunately, we cannot review the values in the TVM registers. (T or F)

12. Values must be entered in the TVM registers in a certain order: from left to right. (T or F)

13. For any TVM problem, what is the minimum number of variables that must be given?

14. When entering dollar amounts we should enter amounts *received* as positive numbers, and amounts *paid* as negative numbers. (T or F)

15. If you make a total of six $100 payments, you should enter $600 in the PMT register. (T or F)

Unit 12.3 Future value

16. Your great-great-great-great-grandfather lost $42 playing poker at a fur-trading post in Wyoming 170 years ago. If he had not been tempted to get into the poker game and instead had deposited the $42 in a savings account earning 4% compounded annually, how much money would be in the account today?

17. Tammy Brown is 35 years old and deposits $2,000 at the end of each year into an individual retirement account (IRA). If the account earns 8% compounded annually, how much will Tammy have when she retires 30 years later?

18. Jed Redmond just turned 22. He decides to empty the change out of his pocket each day—averaging a dollar a day—and set it aside. Then, at the end of each year, Jed will deposit the $365 in a savings plan earning 2% compounded annually. How much will Jed have when he turns 62, after his final deposit?

19. Jack Green spends $135 a month on cigarettes and is considering kicking the habit. If Jack just turned 19 and deposits the $135 at the end of each month into a savings plan earning 7.5% compounded monthly, how much will he have in his savings plan at age 70?

20. Refer to Problem 19. What if Jack makes deposits at the *beginning* of each month?

21. Refer to Problem 20. How much interest will Jack's savings plan earn?

22. Refer to a business magazine article, shown to the right. Assuming that interest is compounded monthly and deposits are made at the end of each month, calculate the *precise* savings plan balance you will have at ages 35, 45, 55, and 65.

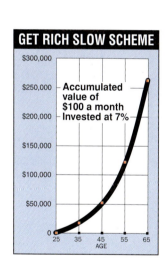

23. The average growth rate for a certain corporate stock over the last 100 years is 12%. If your great-great-grandmother had invested $500 in the stock 100 years ago and received the 12% return, what would her investment be worth today?

24. Tuition at a local college is currently $2,550 per year. You want your newborn daughter to attend when she turns 18. If tuition rates are expected to increase at an annual rate of 5%, what will the annual tuition be at the college 18 years from now?

25. Suppose there are an estimated 4,400 elephants in a certain region. If the elephant population is decreasing 5% per year, what will the elephant population be 40 years from now?

Unit 12.4 Present value

26. Bob's grandfather gives each of his grandchildren $5,000 on their 30th birthday. Bob just turned 20. What is the value of the $5,000 gift, in today's dollars, assuming that Bob can earn 3% compounded annually?

27. Cicily Montague, an author from Paris, sells the movie rights to her book and will receive 600,000 euros at the end of each quarter for the next 4 years. Assuming that money is worth 6% compounded quarterly, what is the value of the movie rights?

For Problems 28-31, assume you own a manufacturing business and are thinking about purchasing a labor-saving device at a cost of $150,000. The device will last 15 years and save you $1,300 per month in labor costs (assume that the savings are realized at the end of each month). You project there will be no salvage value.

28. If you buy the device, what is the total amount of labor costs you will save?

29. Does having the answer to Problem 28 make it possible for you to decide if you should buy the device?

30. Assuming that you need to earn 9% compounded monthly on your money, what is the value of the device?

31. Should you buy the device?

32. You have the chance to buy a promissory note in which you will receive 100 monthly payments of $700, starting a month from now. If you buy the note, what is the total amount you will receive?

33. Refer to Problem 32. If you want to earn 6% compounded monthly, what price should you pay for the note?

34. Seven years ago you bought a 20-year 6% $1,000 bond. The bond pays interest each 6 months. You want to sell the bond. You just received the 14th semiannual interest payment of $30 ($1,000 × 3% periodic rate = $30). Similar bonds are being issued that pay 8% semiannually. What is your bond worth today?

35. Refer to Problem 34. Why is your bond worth less than the $1,000 face value?

36. Some bonds, referred to as *zero-coupon bonds*, pay no periodic interest; instead the bondholder buys the bond at a discount and receives the maturity value on the maturity date. In effect, interest is received in one lump-sum when the bond matures. Suppose a corporation issues 20-year $1,000 zero-coupon bonds. Calculate the price you must pay for one of these bonds based on a prevailing 8% annual rate.

37. You rent an apartment for $700 a month and offer to prepay 6 months' rent. If the landlord can earn 9% compounded monthly, what amount should the landlord accept? *Hint*: Remember, rent is always paid in advance, at the *beginning* of each month (unless the landlord is *exceptionally nice*).

Challenge problems

38. You invest $5,800 today in a savings plan earning 8% compounded semiannually. You then invest $100 each 6 months (starting in 6 months). What will your balance be at the end of 5 years?

For Problems 39-42, consider Social Security and Medicare payroll deductions. As of December, 2015, the federal government requires employees to pay tax of 7.65% on the first $118,500 earned each year plus 1.45% of the remainder. Employers must contribute a matching amount. Assume that an employee earns $45,000 each year during a 40-year working career.

39. Based on these rates, what is the amount withheld from the employee's pay each year?

40. What is the total amount contributed by the employee and employer each year?

41. The money is remitted to the government quarterly. What is the quarterly deposit?

42. Assuming that the deposits were made to a savings plan at the end of each quarter (instead of with the IRS), earning 7% compounded quarterly, how much would the employee have in the savings plan at the end of a 40-year working career?

43. An accomplished pianist lost his right hand in an accident. He successfully sued the party responsible. You, as a member of the jury, are trying to decide what amount the pianist should receive as a settlement. You have determined that the pianist was able to earn $25,000 net income from concerts each month and would have been able to continue earning that amount for another 28 years. Assuming that money is worth 9% compounded monthly and that the $25,000 was received at the end of each month, what is a fair settlement?

44. You leased retail space 5 years ago for $22,000 per month, payable at the beginning of each month. Your lease is for 25 years and allows you to sublease the space. You have outgrown the space and sublease to Smith Furniture Company for the remaining 20 years. Smith will pay you $27,500 at the beginning of each month. What is the value of your position in the lease (referred to as a *leasehold interest*), assuming that money is worth 9% compounded monthly?

45. You win a $5,000,000 lottery. When you go to collect your money, you find out the $5,000,000 will be paid with 10 annual payments of $500,000, starting in 1 year. What is the real value of your prize, in today's dollars, assuming that you can earn 8% compounded annually?

46. Refer to Problem 45. If you invest the lottery payments in a savings plan earning 8% compounded annually, how much will you end up with in 10 years, after your final deposit?

47. Melvin Maxwell, a 30-year-old real estate broker, decides to start a retirement plan. He figures that his income for the next 25 years will be sufficient to deposit $750 at the end of each quarter into his retirement plan earning 6% compounded quarterly. After 25 years he will let the money sit for another 10 years, without making additional deposits, until he is 65 years old. What amount will Melvin have when he turns 65?

Practice Test

1. You deposit $500 today in a savings account that earns 6% compounded quarterly and leave the money there for 5 years. What is the *n*-value?

2. You deposited $420 in a savings account 13 years ago, earning 5% compounded quarterly. Today, you withdraw the entire balance of $801.29. What is the present value?

3. The average growth rate for a certain stock over the last 50 years is reported to be 12% compounded annually. If your grandmother had invested $500 in the stock 50 years ago, what would her investment be worth today?

4. Maria Martinez is a soda pop "addict" and wonders how much money she could accumulate if she stopped drinking soda pop and deposited the $100 per month she spends on the stuff into a savings plan. If Maria is 20 years old, what amount would she have at retirement, 50 years from now, if she deposited $100 at the end of each month and her savings plan earned 6.75% compounded monthly?

5. Tuition at a local college is currently $3,800 per year. If tuition rates are expected to increase at an annual rate of 4%, what will the annual tuition be 18 years from now?

6. A corporation issues 20-year $1,000 zero-coupon bonds. If you buy one of these bonds you will receive no interest checks during the 20 years, but will receive the $1,000 maturity value in 20 years. Based on a prevailing 8% annual rate, what price must you pay for one of the bonds?

7. You own a manufacturing business and are considering the purchase of a labor-saving device. You project that the device will last 12 years and save you $800 per month in labor costs (assume that the savings are realized at the end of each month). At the end of 12 years, you project you can sell the device for a salvage value of $8,000. Assuming that you can earn 9.75% compounded monthly on your money, what is the value of the device?

FUN CORNER

Quotable Quip
There's no reason to be the richest man in the cemetery.
– Colonel Sanders, Kentucky Fried Chicken

Roth IRA vs Regular IRA
Educated investors rushed to open Roth IRAs when the plan was introduced in 1998. If you don't understand the difference between a regular IRA (Individual Retirement Account) and a Roth IRA, here is a brief explanation. With a regular IRA, contributions are tax-deductible in the year they are made, and earnings are tax-deferred. When you withdraw the money it is taxed at regular rates. With a Roth IRA, contributions are not tax-deductible. But, if you've owned the account for at least 5 years and you're over $59\frac{1}{2}$ years old, all money you withdraw is tax-free. The Roth IRA can be left to your heirs income-tax-free if you have held it for at least 5 years.

If you have children who earn money babysitting or mowing lawns, convince them to open a Roth IRA; it can grow into a small tax-free fortune.

As with any government-approved plan, there are special restrictions on contributions and withdrawals. Be sure to check with a tax advisor.

The Millionaire Next Door
In the top-selling book, *The Millionaire Next Door*, the authors found some common traits of wealthy people.
- Most millionaires have incomes of less than $100,000.
- They own a modest home (the average value is $278,000).
- They are self-employed.
- They are frugal. They clip coupons, buy on sale, and they buy based on needs, not wants.
- They are not material people. Their typical car is American-made, 3 years old, with the most common being a Ford F-150 pickup truck.

Consumer Price Index
The consumer price index (CPI) measures inflation by tracking the cost of a "basket of goods" (food, housing, medical care, fuel, etc.). The base year of the current index is 1983, when the basket of goods cost $100. The CPI was introduced in 1913, when the index was 9.9 (meaning that same basket of goods cost about $9.90).

Year	CPI	Year	CPI
1913	9.9	1970	38.8
1920	20.0	1980	82.4
1930	16.7	1990	130.7
1940	14.0	2000	172.2
1950	24.1	2010	218.1
1960	29.6	2015	238.7

Source: U.S. Dept of Labor, Bureau of Labor Statistics

"I think it's about time I started putting some money aside for my retirement."

Sinking Funds, Annuities, and More: Using Financial Calculators

13

In Chapter 12, we solved for future value and present value using financial calculators. Now you're in for more fun!

In this chapter, we will figure out how much money we must set aside to reach a goal (this type of problem is known as a *sinking fund* problem). Then we will explore options we have for withdrawing the money that we have saved up (this type of problem is known as an *annuity* problem). And we will calculate a monthly payment on a car loan and a home loan. Sounds fun, don't you think?

Unit Objectives

Unit 13.1 Sinking funds
- **a** Finding the required deposit(s) to reach a goal
- **b** Finding the required time to reach a goal
- **c** Understanding the effect of rate

Unit 13.2 Annuities
- **a** Making annuity calculations

Unit 13.3 Loan payments
- **a** Calculating a payment on an installment loan
- **b** Calculating a payment on a mortgage loan
- **c** Finding the remaining term (*n*)

Unit 13.1 Sinking funds

People often save money for a specific purpose, like a down payment on a home, a college fund, or retirement. The money set aside is known as a sinking fund.

We introduced calculator time-value-of-money (TVM) registers in Chapter 12. You may want to review the concepts of Unit 12.2 before proceeding with this chapter.

Money set aside for a specific purpose is referred to as a **sinking fund**. For example, you might want to establish a college fund for a child, needing $30,000 in 18 years. Or you might need $20,000 in 10 years to replace an apartment building roof. Corporations use sinking funds to replace worn-out equipment, to repay bondholders the principal portion of the debt, etc. A *sinking fund* is not a fund that is slowly sinking; it is a fund in which we *sink* money.

a Finding the required deposit(s) to reach a goal

We can determine the dollar amount of deposits if we know how much money we want to accumulate, when we will need the money, and what interest rate our deposits will earn. Deposits may consist of one lump-sum (Example 1), periodic deposits (Example 2), or a combination of both (Example 3). We can also determine how long it will take to accumulate the desired sum (Example 4).

Example 1 You want to accumulate $200,000 for retirement in 40 years. You can earn 6.75% compounded monthly. What amount must you deposit today in one lump-sum to have $200,000 in 40 years?

N	i	PV	PMT	FV
40 × 12 = 480	6.75 ÷ 12 = 0.5625*	−13,543.18		200,000

Note: With 2 decimal places, the periodic rate is 0.56. Internally, the value is the more accurate 0.5625. By dividing 6.75 by 12 and entering the result in the *i-register*, the internal, more accurate value is entered.

By depositing $13,543.18 today, you will have $200,000 in 40 years.

> **TIP** don't round the rate before entering
>
> A fairly common mistake is to enter a periodic rate as a rounded value. In Example 1, the annual rate was 6.75%. By dividing 6.75 by 12 and transferring the result directly into the interest rate register, we enter the *internal, more accurate* value (0.5625). Don't make the mistake of entering a *rounded* periodic rate (0.56); the answer of Example 1 would be wrong ($13,705.75).

274   Chapter 13   Sinking Funds, Annuities, and More: Using Financial Calculators

Example 2 Refer to Example 1. Suppose you don't have $13,543.18 to deposit today and instead consider making monthly deposits. What amount must you deposit at the end of each month in order to accumulate $200,000 in 40 years?

_____

N	i	PV	PMT	FV
↑*	↑*	0	-81.71	↑*

Note: When a problem is a variation of a preceding problem, it is not necessary to re-enter values. We can simply enter the values that are different. Values that are the same are shown with an upward arrow (↑).

Instead, you can deposit $81.71 at the end of each month.

Example 3 Refer to Examples 1 and 2. You have $3,000 to deposit into the savings plan today. What additional amount must you deposit at the end of each month in order to accumulate the $200,000?

_____

N	i	PV	PMT	FV
↑	↑	-3,000	-63.61	↑

If you deposit $3,000 today and $63.61 at the end of each month for 40 years, you will have $200,000 in 40 years. You deposit a total of $33,532.80 ($3,000 + 480 deposits of $63.61), meaning you earn interest of $166,467.20 ($200,000 you end up with - $33,532.80 deposited)!

b Finding the required time to reach a goal

If we know the dollar amount of deposits we can afford for a sinking fund, we can determine how long it will take to reach our goal.

Example 4 You want to start a restaurant business and estimate it will take $28,000 to get started. You currently have $3,000 and can deposit an additional $425 at the end of each month. If your sinking fund will earn 9% compounded monthly, in how many months can you start your business?

_____

N	i	PV	PMT	FV
46.83	9 ÷ 12 = 0.75	-3,000	-425	28,000

You can start your business in 47 months. The more precise *n*-value of 46.83 indicates that you must make 46 deposits of $425; the final deposit will be about 83% (or .83) of the regular $425 deposit.

> **TIP** **begin mode?**
>
> In Example 4, you may have been tempted to set your calculator to "begin" mode, since you deposited $3,000 at the beginning of the first period. But remember that PV *always* occurs at the beginning of the first period and does not affect the mode; it is the PMT that dictates the mode. For problems in which the periodic payments start immediately (at the beginning of the first period), we must set our calculator to "being" mode; if the periodic payments start after one period has lapsed, we must set our calculator to "end" mode.

c Understanding the effect of rate

The interest rate is a significant factor in savings plan problems, as shown in the next example.

Example 5 You want to give your newborn son $1,000,000 for his retirement at age 65. If you establish a savings plan, how much do you need to deposit at the end of each month, provided that the fund earns (a) 3% compounded monthly, (b) 9% compounded monthly, and (c) 15% compounded monthly.

N	i	PV	PMT	FV
65 × 12 = 780	3 ÷ 12 = 0.25		-415.86	1,000,000
↑	9 ÷ 12 = 0.75		-22.14	↑
↑	15 ÷ 12 = 1.25		-0.77	↑

To have $1,000,000 in 65 years, you must make monthly deposits of $415.86, $22.14, or $0.77 (that's right, 77¢), depending on the rate you earn.

As you can see, the rate makes a dramatic difference. You may ask, Is a 9% or 15% rate reasonable? When most people think of savings rates, they limit their thinking to passbook savings accounts, which currently pay very low rates. Rates on passbook savings will likely never rebound to the 14% rates of the 1980s but other investments such as stocks, bonds, real estate, and mutual funds can, over the long haul, provide substantial returns.

Let's try the U-Try-It exercises to find out how much about *sinking* funds *sunk* in.

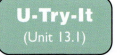

1. While your dentist is filling a cavity in one of your teeth, he is talking with his dental assistant about the new dental equipment he wants to buy in $3\frac{1}{2}$ years for $30,000. He wonders how much money he must deposit today in order to accumulate the $30,000. You get his attention and tell him that if he will quit drilling for a minute you will help him calculate the amount. What amount is required if he can earn 6% compounded quarterly?
2. Refer to Problem 1. If your dentist wants to instead make quarterly deposits, what amount must he deposit at the end of each quarter?

Answers: (If you have a different answer, check the solution in Appendix A.)
1. $24,355.48 2. $1,941.70

Unit 13.2 Annuities

Accumulating savings is the hard part. Spending is the fun part. The money received back from a savings plan is known as an **annuity**. We will refer to an annuity more specifically—as a repetitive, uniform withdrawal of funds. A savings fund could be created slowly by making deposits over a long period of time. Or we could inherit a large sum of money all at once or win the lottery. Once the annuity plan is funded, we can start making withdrawals.

a Making annuity calculations

A savings plan continues to earn interest during the withdrawal (annuity) stage. If the withdrawals are *identical* to the amount of interest earned, the savings plan balance will remain the same.

Example 1 Suppose you have accumulated $500,000, perhaps from many years of savings or from an inheritance. You put the money in a savings plan earning 6% compounded monthly. If you want to live off the interest without disturbing the $500,000 balance, what amount can you withdraw each month?

Let's use the *simple interest formula* to calculate the monthly interest:

$$I = PRT = \$500,000 \times 6\% \times \tfrac{1}{12} = \$2,500$$

You can withdraw $2,500 each month forever.

By withdrawing exactly $2,500 at the end of each month, your savings plan balance will remain at $500,000. By withdrawing more than $2,500 each month the balance will decrease, because withdrawals are more than the interest you earn. By withdrawing less than $2,500 each month, your savings plan balance will increase, because withdrawals are less than the interest you earn.

Example 2 Refer to Example 1. You want the plan to last 40 years. How much can you withdraw at the end of each month?

N	i	PV	PMT	FV
40 × 12 = 480	6 ÷ 12 = 0.50	-500,000	2,751.07	0

You can withdraw $2,751.07 at the end of each month for 40 years. Then it's time to go back to work because the savings plan will have no money left in it.

In Example 2, you are able to withdraw a total of $1,320,513.60 (480 × $2,751.07), meaning your savings plan earns $820,513.60 interest ($1,320,513.60 - $500,000 deposited). Your money is at work for you, even though you are gradually depleting the fund.

Example 3 Refer to Example 2. If you instead withdraw $4,000 at the end of each month, how long before the savings plan is exhausted?

N	i	PV	PMT	FV
196.66 months	↑	↑	4,000	0

You can withdraw $4,000 a month for about 197 months (16 years and 5 months); then it's off to work because the savings plan balance is zero!

Example 4 Refer to Example 2. If you instead withdraw $2,000 at the end of each month, what will the balance be after 20 years?

N	i	PV	PMT	FV
20 × 12 = 240	↑	↑	2,000	731,020.45

After withdrawing $2,000 a month for 20 years, your savings plan balance will have grown from $500,000 to $731,020.45. That's because your plan earned more interest than you withdrew.

Well, that's it for this unit. Let's try some U-Try-It questions.

U-Try-It (Unit 13.2)

Your Aunt Irene has been making deposits to a savings plan for the last 35 years. Her account balance is now $420,000 and her plan earns 8% compounded monthly. Aunt Irene just turned 60 and asks for your advice.
1. What amount can Aunt Irene withdraw at the end of each month so that the plan balance will stay the same?
2. If Aunt Irene wants the plan to last exactly 25 years, what amount can she withdraw at the end of each month?
3. If she withdraws $3,500 at the end of each month, how long will the savings plan last?
4. If she withdraws $2,500 at the end of each month, what will the balance be in 25 years?

Answers: (If you have a different answer, check the solution in Appendix A.)
1. $2,800   2. $3,241.63   3. 242.22 months   4. $705,307.92

Unit 13.3 Loan payments

When money is borrowed, it must be repaid. Unless we borrow from a rich, very nice relative, we must pay interest in addition to the amount borrowed. In this unit we will calculate a monthly payment on an installment loan (Example 1) and on a mortgage loan (Example 2). We will also calculate the remaining term of a loan (Example 4).

People often get loans to buy costly items, without considering alternatives. Instead of buying an expensive recreational vehicle (with hefty loan payments), consider buying a nice, loan-free tent!

a Calculating a payment on an installment loan

An **installment loan** is a loan that is paid off with payments of an equal amount. People get installment loans to buy cars, boats, furniture, and other costly items.

Let's see how an installment loan might work. Assume Casey wants to buy a car and finds one he likes, priced at $13,000. With tax and license fees the total amount comes to $14,200. Suppose Casey has $700 saved up for the car purchase. Where will the remaining $13,500 come from? If he's like most of us, he will borrow the $13,500 from a bank or credit union. Depending on the make and model of the car, as well as his credit history, the lender will decide what interest rate to charge and the length of the loan. The lender will calculate a monthly payment that will be sufficient to pay back the principal (the $13,500 Casey borrows) plus interest. We can calculate a monthly payment using our TVM registers.

Example 1

Casey gets a 5-year $13,500 car loan at 7.5% interest. Calculate his monthly payment.

If Casey paid no interest, his monthly payment would be $225 ($13,500 ÷ 60 months). Because he must pay interest, his monthly payment will be more.

N	i	PV	PMT	FV
5 × 12 = 60	7.5 ÷ 12 = 0.625	13,500	-270.51	

Casey's monthly payment is $270.51. He will pay the lender a total of $16,230.60 (60 payments × $270.51), which means he pays $2,730.60 interest ($16,230.60 repaid - $13,500 principal).

We will explore installment loans more in Chapter 14.

b Calculating a payment on a mortgage loan

Real estate, unlike *personal property*, is immovable. Real estate includes land and buildings. Personal property includes things like cars and furniture. A loan secured by real estate is known as a **mortgage loan**.

Tara has been collecting rent receipts for awhile and has decided to buy a home. After looking at quite a few homes, Tara finds her "dream home," priced at $180,000. She makes an offer of $165,000. The seller is not happy with that price and makes a *counteroffer* of $168,000. Tara accepts the seller's counteroffer.

Tara has saved up some cash but needs to borrow $160,000. Before making an offer on the home, Tara visited a lender to get pre-approved for a mortgage loan. The lender has offered two choices: (1) a 30-year loan at 7.75% or (2) a 15-year loan at 7.25%.

Example 2 Tara needs to borrow $160,000 to buy her dream home. She can get a 30-year loan at 7.75% or a 15-year loan at 7.25%. Calculate the monthly payment for each.

___

If Tara paid no interest, her monthly payment would be $444.44 on the 30-year loan ($160,000 ÷ 360 months) and $888.89 on the 15-year loan ($160,000 ÷ 180 months). Because she pays interest, her monthly payment will be considerably more.

N	i	PV	PMT	FV
30 × 12 = 360	7.75 ÷ 12 ≈ 0.64583*	160,000	-1,146.26	
15 × 12 = 180	7.25 ÷ 12 ≈ 0.60416*	↑	-1,460.58	

Note: The underlined 3 is a repeating digit (the 3s continue forever). By dividing 7.75 by 12 and transferring the result in the interest rate register, we enter the *internal, more accurate value* (approximately 0.645833333). Follow the same procedure for the 15-year loan.

Tara's mortgage payment would be $1,146.26 for the 30-year loan, compared to $1,460.58 for the 15-year loan. Her first reaction may be to get the 30-year loan because she could save $314.32 each month. But let's figure the total interest on each loan. *Warning*: The result may take your breath away!

Example 3 Refer to Example 2. What is the total interest for each loan?

___

30-year loan (total number of payments = 30 years × 12 payments per year = 360)

Total paid: 360 × $1,146.26 =	$412,653.60
Less principal portion (loan amount)	-160,000.00
Interest portion	$252,653.60

15-year loan (total number of payments = 15 years × 12 payments per year = 180)

Total paid: 180 × $1,460.58 =	$262,904.40
Less principal portion (loan amount)	-160,000.00
Interest portion	$102,904.40

The interest is bad enough with the 15-year loan ($102,904.40) but with the 30-year loan, interest is about two and one-half times as much ($252,653.60). Also, notice that the interest on the 30-year loan is more than the $160,000 borrowed!

Some books refer to a series of payments in which payments are made at the end of each period as an **ordinary annuity** and to a series of payments in which payments are made at the beginning of each period as an **annuity due**. Instead of using that terminology we will, for each problem, simply state whether payments are made at the end, or beginning, of each period.

> **TIP** — begin or end?
>
> A car payment or mortgage loan payment may be due on the first day of each month, but the due date is not the deciding factor in determining *begin* or *end* mode. The key is whether payments start immediately upon getting the loan or start after 1 period has lapsed. With car loans and mortgage loans, the first monthly payment is due after 1 period has lapsed, meaning payments are made at the *end* of each period.

C Finding the remaining term (*n*)

We can find the remaining term of a loan as shown in the next example.

Example 4 Refer to Example 3. Tara likes the idea of the 7.25% 15-year loan but does not feel comfortable *promising* to pay $1,460.58 per month. She is thinking about getting the 7.75% 30-year loan but making payments of $1,460.58. How long would it take to pay off the loan?

The advantage of signing a 30-year mortgage loan is that Tara is obligated to pay only $1,146.26 per month. The disadvantage of signing a 30-year loan is that she is stuck with a higher interest rate (7.75% vs. 7.25%). Let's solve for *n*:

N	i	PV	PMT	FV
190.95	7.75 ÷ 12 ≈ 0.64583*	160,000	-1,460.58	

It will take 190.95 months.

If Tara signs the 15-year mortgage loan it will take 180 months to pay off the loan. By signing the 30-year loan but making monthly payments of a 15-year loan, Tara must make 10.95 extra monthly payments (190.95 - 180 = 10.95). That's because of the higher interest rate (7.75% vs. 7.25%). She would pay approximately $16,000 more interest than if she were to sign the 15-year loan ($1,460.26 × 10.95 months = $15,989.85). Tara is now in a better position to make an informed decision.

Mortgage rates are often quoted in "eighths," such as $3\frac{5}{8}$%. Before we key an interest rate into the interest rate register of a calculator, we must be able to convert the rate to a decimal number. As a reminder, here are decimal equivalents for eighths:

$$\frac{1}{8} = .125 \qquad \frac{3}{8} = .375 \qquad \frac{5}{8} = .625 \qquad \frac{7}{8} = .875$$

($\frac{5}{8}$ *means* "5 ÷ 8," *resulting in* .625, *so* $3\frac{5}{8}$ *is* 3.625 *in decimal form*)

We will explore home ownership and mortgage loans more in Chapter 15. And we will solve for *i* (APRs on loans and yields on contemplated investments) in Chapter 17.

If you get or suspect a bad answer using your TVM registers, here are a few troubleshooting ideas:

> **TIP** — troubleshooting
>
> If you get or suspect a bad answer:
>
> 1. Recall (RCL) the value in each register. Have you entered a wrong amount, used the wrong sign (+ or -), or left a previous amount in an unused register?
> 2. Is your calculator in the correct mode (begin or end)?
> 3. Is your calculator set at 1 period per year?
>
>   For the HP 10BII, when clearing the TVM registers, the P/YR setting will briefly appear. To check the P/YR setting during keystrokes, press RCL ▼ P/YR.
>
>   For the TI BAII PLUS, press 2ND P/Y to observe the current setting, and then press 2ND QUIT.

Congratulations on finishing this chapter. Hopefully, you see how valuable financial calculators can be in solving real-world problems. Now, let's try the last set of U-Try-It exercises.

U-Try-It
(Unit 13.3)

1. You are thinking about buying a piano. You can get a 6-year $7,000 loan at 9.5% interest from your bank. Calculate your monthly payment.
2. You buy a home for $200,000. If you have $20,000 for a down payment and borrow $180,000 for 30 years at $5\frac{7}{8}$% interest, what is your monthly mortgage payment?
3. Refer to Problem 2. How much interest will you pay over the 30 years?
4. Several years ago you got a mortgage loan at 8.5% interest. You just received a mortgage loan statement, showing you owe $105,286.67. Your monthly payment is $922.69. How long until the loan is paid off?

Answers: (If you have a different answer, check the solution in Appendix A.)
1. $127.92 **2.** $1,064.77 **3.** $203,317.20 **4.** 234 months

Chapter in a Nutshell

Objectives	Examples

Unit 13.1 Sinking funds

a Finding the required deposit(s) to reach a goal	You want to accumulate $200,000 for retirement 25 years from now. You can earn 8% compounded semiannually. What amount must you deposit at the end of each 6 months to have $200,000 in 25 years?	

N	i	PV	PMT	FV
25 × 2 = 50	8 ÷ 2 = 4		-1,310.04	200,000

b Finding the required time to reach a goal	See above. How long will it take to accumulate $200,000 if you deposit $1,500 at the end of each 6 months?

N	i	PV	PMT	FV
47.06 ÷ 2 = 23.53 yrs	↑		-1,500	↑

c Understanding the effect of rate	See above. If you want to accumulate $200,000 in 25 years, what amount must you deposit at the end of each 6 months if you can earn 16% compounded semiannually?

N	i	PV	PMT	FV
25 × 2 = 50	16 ÷ 2 = 8		-348.57	↑

Unit 13.2 Annuities

a Making annuity calculations	You deposit $42,000, earning 3% compounded monthly. If you want the savings plan to last 40 years, how much can you withdraw at the end of each month?

N	i	PV	PMT	FV
40 × 12 = 480	3 ÷ 12 = 0.25	-42,000	150.35	

Chapter in a Nutshell (concluded)

Objectives	Examples

Unit 13.3 Loan payments

a Calculating a payment on an installment loan

Calculate your monthly payment on a 6-year $15,000 car loan at 3.5% interest.

N	i	PV	PMT	FV
6 × 12 = 72	3.5 ÷ 12 = 0.291<u>6</u>	15,000	-231.28	

b Calculating a payment on a mortgage loan

What is the monthly payment on a 30-year 4.75% $250,000 mortgage loan?

N	i	PV	PMT	FV
30 × 12 = 360	4.75 ÷ 12 = 0.3958<u>3</u>	250,000	-1,304.12	

c Finding the remaining term (*n*)

Mortgage balance = $125,162.20; 4.5% rate; monthly payment = $1,126.47. How many months left on the loan?

N	i	PV	PMT	FV
144 months	4.5 ÷ 12 = 0.375	125,162.20	-1,126.47	

Enrichment Topics

The following Enrichment Topics, which go a bit beyond what is in the text, are available for this chapter:

Funding an Annuity to Produce Specified Withdrawals
Semimonthly and Biweekly Mortgages
Installment Loan Incentive Programs
Disguised Prices
Affordable Price

If your instructor doesn't cover these topics in class and you would like to dig in deeper on your own, please send a request to *studentsupport@olympuspub.com*. You can also request a set of keystrokes for your particular calculator.

Think

1. Explain the difference between a future value problem, a sinking fund problem, and an annuity problem. Then give an example of each type of problem.
2. Suppose you want to accumulate $20,000 in 20 years and can earn 10% compounded annually. Determine the amount you must deposit today in one lump-sum to accumulate the $20,000. Now assume that you can earn only 5% compounded annually. Does it follow that because the interest rate is half as great you must deposit exactly twice as much today to reach your goal? Explain your reasoning. Then show calculations to support your point of view.
3. You may have heard of the Rule of 72. The Rule of 72 is a guideline for *approximating* how long it will take to double money left on deposit. To find the number of years, we divide 72 by the annual rate (without the percent sign). Figure how many years it would take to double money for rates of 4%, 6%, 8%, 9%, and 12%. Then, use your TVM registers to find the precise time for each rate.

Explore

1. Refer to Appendix E. Review the explanations for using Excel to solve time-value-of-money problems. Then use Excel to solve the U-Try-It problems of Unit 13.3.
2. Go to **www.webbertext.com** and click Online Calculator. Using the online calculator and the guidelines shown on that page, solve the U-Try-It problems of Unit 13.3.
3. Compare the answers using each method (financial calculators, Excel, and the online calculator). Which answers are different, if any, and why?

Apply

1. **The Car Loan.** Visit a bank or credit union. Ask for help with this school project. Make a list of available car loans for new vehicles and used vehicles. Show interest rates and resulting monthly payments. What front-end loan fees are there, if any?. Do they offer adjustable rate loans and, if so, how do these loans work? How is interest calculated? Are you penalized if you pay off the loan early? How are late fees calculated? Prepare a report on your findings.
2. **The Inflation Factor.** Research the cost of at least 4 products or services that were advertised in newspapers or magazines more than 25 years ago. Then find the current cost. Using your financial calculator, calculate the annual rate of increase (or decrease) in prices between the two points in time. Include copies of the articles as well as your solutions. *Note:* To find the old advertisements or articles you can go online or visit a local library.
3. **Retirement.** Figure out a retirement plan for yourself (and spouse, if applicable). Make some assumptions: (1) an interest rate the plan will earn; (2) how much money you need each month to live on today; (3) how much you will need each month during retirement (based on a certain rate of inflation between now and retirement); (4) how much Social Security you will receive each month during retirement; (5) how many years until retirement; and (6) how long you will live. For simplicity, ignore inflation *during* retirement. Assume that for the 10 years before retirement, your earnings will decline and you will not make deposits to the plan. Calculate how much you must deposit at the end of each month into your retirement plan.

Chapter Review Problems

Unit 13.1 Sinking funds

1. Uncle Ted promises to give his niece Beth $50,000 on her 30th birthday, $6\frac{1}{2}$ years from now. Uncle Ted can earn 8% compounded quarterly. What amount could Uncle Ted deposit today in a savings plan so that the plan would have the required $50,000 in $6\frac{1}{2}$ years?

2. Refer to Problem 1. If, instead, Uncle Ted elects to make quarterly deposits into the plan (starting in 3 months), what is the required quarterly deposit?

3. Refer to Problems 1 and 2. If Uncle Ted deposits $4,700 today, what additional amount must he deposit at the end of each quarter?

4. While your dentist is filling a cavity in one of your teeth, he is talking with his dental assistant about the new dental equipment he wants to buy in $4\frac{1}{2}$ years for $40,000. He wonders how much money he must deposit at the end of each quarter to accumulate $40,000. You get his attention and tell him if he will quit drilling for a minute you will help him calculate the amount. What amount is required if he can earn 3% compounded quarterly?

For Problems 5–7, help a British auto manufacturer make calculations on some bonds. The company issues £86,500,000 of 6% 20-year bonds to upgrade its assembly line. Terms of the bond require annual interest payments to bondholders plus annual deposits to a sinking fund for retirement of the bonds when they mature.

5. How much interest must the corporation pay to the bondholders each year?

6. Assuming the corporation can earn 8% compounded annually on its sinking fund, how much must it deposit into the fund at the end of each year?

7. What is the total amount the corporation needs each year to meet its obligations on the bonds?

8. Kristi just turned 28 and can save $180 per month, starting in 1 month. If Kristi can earn 8% compounded monthly, what age will she be when she accumulates $1,000,000?

Unit 13.2 Annuities

For Problems 9-14, pretend you receive an inheritance of $500,000 and deposit it in a savings plan that earns 6.75% compounded monthly.

9. If you want to live off the interest without withdrawing any of the $500,000 principal, what amount can you withdraw at the end of each month?

10. How much can you withdraw at the end of each month if you want the plan to last 40 years?

11. How much can you withdraw at the end of each month if you want the plan to last 30 years?

12. If you withdraw $3,500 at the end of each month, how long will the plan last?

13. If you withdraw less than the amount you calculated in Problem 9, what will happen to the plan balance?

14. If you withdraw $2,700 at the end of each month, what will the balance be in 25 years?

15. A wealthy citizen sets up a trust for scholarships at a local community college. The gift is for $4,000,000 and the money is to be distributed at the beginning of each year over the next 150 years. If the trust earns 5.5% compounded annually, how much is available for scholarships each year?

Unit 13.3 Loan payments

16. You are thinking about buying a sports car priced at $28,500. Your bank will loan you $27,500 at 6.5% for 6 years. Determine your monthly payment.

17. Refer to Problem 16. What is the total amount of interest you will pay over the 6 years?

18. If you purchase a big screen TV for $900 and the store finances the entire amount over 24 months at a monthly rate of 1.75%, what is your monthly payment?

For Problems 19-22, assume you need a $150,000 mortgage loan but are unsure whether to get a 7.25% 15-year loan or a 7.5% 30-year loan.

19. Calculate the monthly payment for each.

20. How much more per month will you pay with the 15-year loan?

21. Find the total amount of interest for each loan.

22. How much more interest will you pay with the 30-year loan?

23. Calculate the monthly payment on a 20-year $365,000 mortgage loan at $4\frac{7}{8}$% interest.

24. Several years ago you got a mortgage loan at 8.75% interest. You currently owe $138,743.03 with a monthly payment of $1,180.05. How long until the loan will be paid off?

25. Refer to Problem 24. How many months will it take until the loan will be paid off if you pay an extra **(a)** $10 each month or **(b)** $100 each month?

Challenge problems

26. You serve as a member of the board of directors for a tennis facility. Courts must be resurfaced in 5 years. The cost of resurfacing today is $400,000, and the cost is estimated to increase at an annual rate of 4%. What will the cost be in 5 years?

27. Refer to Problem 26. What amount must be deposited into a sinking fund at the beginning of each quarter to accumulate the amount needed if the fund earns 6% compounded quarterly?

28. Calculate the term for an 8% $500 loan with monthly payments of $5.

29. Refer to Problem 28. Calculate the term with monthly payments of $10.

30. Refer to Problems 28 and 29. By doubling the monthly payment, do you exactly halve the term? Explain why or why not.

31. You have just made your $326.14 monthly payment on your 11% car loan. Your balance, after the payment, is $13,841.90. How many months will it take to pay off the loan?

32. Refer to Problem 31. You just received an income tax refund of $834. If you apply the refund as an extra principal payment immediately after making the above monthly payment, how many monthly payments will you save?

33. You see a car advertisement, showing the dealer will give the buyer either **(a)** a $3,500 cash rebate or **(b)** 2.9% financing for 5 years. The dealer's price (before rebate) is $25,500, and the current interest rate on 5-year car loans is 8.5%. Calculate a monthly payment for each choice, assuming that you use the cash rebate to reduce the loan amount.

34. You can afford a monthly mortgage payment of $900 and can get a 30-year 4.75% loan. What is the maximum loan you can get so your payment does not exceed $900?

35. Jacob Mullin is 25 years old. Some of Jacob's older relatives have retired, having no income other than Social Security. Jacob does not want to be caught in that situation, so he is thinking about setting up a retirement plan. Jacob wants to retire at age 60, 35 years from now, and wants his retirement plan to provide $2,000 a month for 30 years (until he is 90). His plan can earn 6% compounded monthly. What amount must Jacob deposit at the end of each month for the next 35 years so that he can then start receiving $2,000 at the end of each month for the following 30 years?

36. Refer to Problem 35. How much interest will Jacob's retirement plan earn over the 65 years?

37. In 8 years, Yu Chen's daughter will be entering college and Yu would like to help financially. Tuition is currently $6,000 a year, but is expected to increase at a rate of 4% compounded annually. Yu decides to create a college fund and make 8 annual deposits, starting in 1 year. In 8 years, he would like his daughter to be able to make 4 annual withdrawals from the fund (at the beginning of each year) that will cover her annual tuition. If the college fund earns 6% compounded annually, how much must Yu deposit at the end of each year? *Note*: Assume that tuition will remain the same for the 4 years of college.

Practice Test

1. You want to accumulate $35,000 in 18 years for your child's education, and you can earn 6% compounded monthly. What amount must you deposit each month if the first of your deposits is made today?

2. You want to start an accounting business and estimate it will take $22,000 to get started. You currently have $5,500 and can deposit an additional $400 at the end of each month. If your savings plan will earn 6% compounded monthly, in how many months can you start your business?

3. Your uncle dies and your 62-year-old aunt receives $250,000 life insurance proceeds. She needs monthly income and expects to live for approximately 30 years. If she invests the insurance money, earning 6.5% compounded monthly, how much can she withdraw at the end of each month?

4. Determine your monthly payment on a 4-year $13,500 car loan at 6.5% interest.

5. Determine your monthly payment on a 20-year $140,000 mortgage loan at $7\frac{5}{8}$% interest.

6. You are thinking about getting a 40-year $180,000 mortgage loan at 7.25% interest. How much interest would you pay over the 40 years?

FUN CORNER

Highest Car Mileage
The highest documented mileage for a car is 3,039,122 miles, as of May 2014. The car (a 1966 Volvo P-1800S) and owner (Irvin Gordon of Long Island, New York) are pictured above on a road trip in Alaska. The car, still running, has been to 9 countries and has been in 11 accidents in 48 years.

Source: Guinness World Record

Credit Card Tips
- Pay more than the minimum payment; if you don't, it can take forever to pay off the balance. If you have more than one card, pay the extra amount on the one with the highest interest rate.
- Put charge receipts in a folder and then use them to reconcile your monthly statement. When you pay the bill, staple the receipts to your section of the statement and file it.
- When you call the company about a bill, write down the date, time, who you spoke to, and promises made.

Most Credit Cards
Walter Cavanagh (pictured above) of Santa Clara, California, has 1,497 individual credit cards, which together have a credit limit of over $1,700,000.

Source: Guinness World Records

Quotable Quip
If you think nobody cares if you're alive, try missing a couple of car payments

– Earl Wilson, columnist

Opt Out
If you receive too many credit card solicitations, you can request they stop by calling 1-888-567-8688.

"Thanks for the college money, Uncle Ned. How can I ever repay you?" "With monthly payments over three years, including interest at eight percent." ????

Installment Loans and Open-End Credit

One way to acquire costly items (such as furniture, boats, and cars) is to save enough money to pay cash for them. In today's world of credit, however, the more common method is to borrow part or all of the purchase price. Credit is a "double-edged sword" that has advantages and disadvantages. By using credit instead of paying cash for everything, we can purchase more items and start using them sooner. However, we must pay interest and may end up buying nonessential things because they are so easy to get with credit. Lots of financial difficulties arise from using credit unwisely.

With a simple interest loan, the borrower makes one payment, including interest, on the maturity date. This chapter deals with another type of loan—one that is repaid with multiple payments such as a car loan or a credit card loan. For these loans, the agony is prolonged—the payments may seem to go on forever! Hopefully, as a result of studying this chapter, we will be able to make well-informed decisions regarding installment purchases.

Unit Objectives

Unit 14.1 Cost of installment buying
  a Determining the loan amount
  b Figuring finance charge
  c Figuring total cost

Unit 14.2 Paying off an installment loan
  a Finding interest, principal, and remaining balance
  b Calculating a payoff amount

Unit 14.3 Open-end credit
  a Evaluating annual and periodic rates
  b Calculating an average daily balance
  c Calculating interest for open-end credit

Unit 14.1 Cost of installment buying

When money is borrowed, it must be repaid. Unless we borrow from a rich, very nice relative, we must pay interest in addition to the amount borrowed. One way to repay the money is with an **installment loan**. An installment loan is paid off with payments of an equal amount. In this unit, we will examine the effect of interest on a purchase. We will follow the adventures of Casey, who is buying his first vehicle.

Most people, when buying a vehicle, borrow all or part of the purchase price. Getting a loan adds to the overall cost because, in addition to the cost of the vehicle, the owner must pay interest.

a Determining the loan amount

Casey has been looking for a vehicle and has finally found the object of his affection—a shiny, yellow two-seat convertible. The car is 4 years old.

> **TIP**   car-buying tips
>
> **Tip 1** Read consumer magazines and test drive several models before deciding on a car. Take your time.
> **Tip 2** Decide whether a new or used car is right for you. A new car loses quite a bit of value as soon as you drive it off the lot but comes with a warranty, has lower repair costs, and smells better! In Think Activity 8, we compare the cost of owning a new car, owning a used car, and leasing a car.
> **Tip 3** Don't base your decision on monthly payment (which depends on the number of years you pay).
> **Tip 4** Don't talk trade-in until you have negotiated a cash price; otherwise you won't know the *real* price of the vehicle you're buying.
> **Tip 5** Compare financing from several sources before signing a contract.
> **Tip 6** Think twice about adding extras you may not need (like credit insurance and service contracts).
> *Additional things to do for used cars:*
> **Tip 7** Check values on Internet sites like **www.edmunds.com**.
> **Tip 8** Check the history of a vehicle (odometer readings and damage through car crashes) by paying a fee to a company like *Carfax* (1-800-274-2277).
> **Tip 9** Get the vehicle checked by a certified mechanic before buying it.

Casey and the car dealer have agreed upon a price of $14,500. Casey must also pay $900 for tax and license fees. He has saved $2,000 for a down payment and hopes to get a loan for the remainder of the money. For a vehicle loan, the loan amount, interest rate, and length of the loan depend on the make and model of the vehicle, as well as the borrower's credit history. Casey calls a few lenders and decides that his credit union has the best deal; they will loan him the additional money he needs with a 5-year loan at 7.5% interest. Let's help Casey figure out how much money he needs to borrow.

Example 1 Casey wants to buy a used car priced at $14,500. He must also pay tax and license fees of $900. He has $2,000. His credit union will make him an installment loan for 5 years at 7.5% interest; they charge a $100 fee for making the loan. Help Casey calculate the amount he needs to borrow.

Price of car	$14,500
Tax and license fees	+ 900
Loan fee	+ 100
Total amount needed	$15,500
Less down payment	− 2,000
Required loan	**$13,500**

Chapter 14 Installment Loans and Open-End Credit

Casey needs to borrow $13,500. If there were no interest charged, Casey would pay $225 each month ($13,500 ÷ 60 months = $225). But Casey is not that lucky; with interest, his monthly payment will be more than $225.

We calculated Casey's monthly payment—for a 5-year $13,500 loan at 7.5% interest—in previous chapters: Example 1 of Unit 11.3 (using formulas), and Example 1 of Unit 13.3 (using financial calculators). We got the same answer with each method: $270.51.

> ### payments
>
> Installment loan payments typically start after one period has lapsed. For example, if Casey gets his truck loan on August 5, his first payment will be due September 5. Interest for each payment is figured through the date the payment is received by the lender (interest is paid in *arrears*). When a lender calculates an actual payment, the amount may be slightly different if the due date of the first payment is *not* exactly 1 month after getting the loan.

b Figuring finance charge

In the next example, we will help Casey figure the **finance charge** on the loan. Finance charges are total costs that must be paid as a condition of getting the loan; finance charges include interest and prepaid loan costs (such as Casey's $100 fee).

> ### finance charge
>
> **Step 1** Find the total of all payments.
>
> **Step 2** Subtract the loan amount (principal portion of payments). The result is the interest portion of payments.
>
> **Step 3** Add prepaid loan costs.

Example 2 Refer to Example 1. Help Casey figure out the total *finance charge* assuming a 5-year loan with monthly payments of $270.51.

Step 1	(total of all payments): 60 × $270.51	$16,230.60
Step 2	(subtract loan amount)	- 13,500.00
	Interest portion of payments	$ 2,730.60
Step 3	(add prepaid loan costs)	+ 100.00
	Total finance charges	$ 2,830.60

Casey will repay the credit union $16,230.60, of which $13,500 is principal (the amount he borrowed). The remainder ($2,730.60) is interest. In addition, Casey must pay a $100 fee to get the loan, resulting in total finance charges of $2,830.60.

> ### TIP   did we count the $100 fee twice?
>
> We took into account the $100 loan fee in Example 1 and again in Example 2, so you may wonder if we counted the fee twice in coming up with total finance charges of $2,830.60. We did not. Here's why. Once Casey gets the $13,500 loan, he pays $2,730.60 in interest, but Casey had to pay $100 to get the loan, resulting in total finance charges of $2,830.60. Is that as clear as mud?

Most lenders use the **U.S. Rule** to calculate interest. With the U.S. Rule, interest is calculated on the unpaid balance to the date payment is *received* and on the basis of a 365-day year. If a lender using the U.S. Rule charges no front-end loan costs, the *real* interest rate (called the **annual percentage rate**, or **APR**) is the same as the stated annual rate. However, if a lender does not use the U.S. Rule or if the lender charges front-end loan costs, the APR will be different (usually *higher*) than the stated annual rate.

Illustration 14-1: Truth in Lending Disclosure Statement

Annual Percentage Rate The cost of your credit as a yearly rate **7.81%**	Finance Charge The dollar amount the credit will cost you **$2,830.60**	Amount Financed The amount of credit provided to you or on your behalf **$13,400.00**	Total of Payments The amount you will have paid after you have made all payments as scheduled **$16,230.60**

You agree to repay $ 13,500.00 at a rate of 7.5% over 60 months, resulting in the following monthly payments:

Number of payments	Amount of payments	When payments are due
60	$270.51	Monthly beginning September 5, 20xx

Security: You are giving a security interest in:
- ☑ The goods or property being purchased
- ☐ Other: _____

Late Charge: If a payment is over ten (10) days late, you will be assessed a late charge of $25 or 5% of your monthly payment, whichever is greater. The finance charge shown is the actual finance charge if you make all payments exactly as scheduled. If you make payments early, the actual finance charge will be less. If you pay late, the actual finance charge will be more.

Prepayment: If you pay the loan off early, you
- ☐ may   ☑ will not   have to pay a penalty.
- ☐ may   ☑ will not   be entitled to a refund of finance charges (finance charges are calculated each day and not in advance, so no refund is due).

Calculations:
Block 3 (Amount Financed): $13,500 loan amount - $100 origination fee = $13,400 net proceeds
Block 4 (Total of Payments): 60 × $270.51 = $16,230.60
Block 2 (Finance Charge): $16,230.60 (from block 4) - $13,400 (from block 3) = $2,830.60

Casey will be required to sign a **promissory note**, which spells out terms of repayment. His car will be used as **collateral** (also called **security**) for the loan; collateral is an asset owned by the borrower that the lender can claim if the borrower quits making payments.

Before having Casey sign the promissory note, the lender is required by the **Truth in Lending Act** (also known as **Regulation Z**) to inform Casey how much extra money he is paying as a result of borrowing the money (this is the *finance charge* we calculated in Example 2) and the APR he is paying. The lender informs the borrower on a form called a **disclosure statement**. The disclosure statement provided to Casey is shown as Illustration 14-1. Notice that the Finance Charge and Total of Payments match the amounts we calculated in Example 2. Also notice that the Annual Percentage Rate is greater than the 7.5% stated annual rate. That's because the lender is charging Casey a $100 front-end fee, which is like prepaid interest, having the effect of increasing the interest rate. *Note:* We calculate Casey's 7.81% APR in Chapter 17.

Here are a few things to remember about the Truth in Lending Act.

Truth in Lending Act (also known as Regulation Z)

- The Truth in Lending Act does *not* establish maximum interest rates, nor does it dictate the method for calculating interest; many states provide these regulations.
- The Truth in Lending Act applies only to those who are customarily engaged in loaning money or extending credit for personal, family, or household purposes; such loans are known as **consumer loans**. The law does *not* apply to loans for business purposes, loans over $25,000 not secured by real estate, most public utility fees, stock brokerage accounts, and student loan programs.
- APRs reported to the borrower must be accurate to $\frac{1}{8}$ of 1 percent.

c Figuring total cost

As you can see, buying things on credit has a price. For Casey, the price is $2,830.60. In Example 3, we will help Casey figure out the total cost of his car, including finance charges.

> **total cost, including finance charges**
>
> **Step 1** Figure the total cost of the purchase, excluding finance charges.
> **Step 2** Add the finance charges.

Example 3 Help Casey figure the total cost of his car, including finance charges.

Step 1	(cost of the purchase): $14,500 + $900 tax and license fees	$15,400.00
Step 2	(add finance charges): from Example 2	+ 2,830.60
	Total cost, including finance charges	$18,230.60

Casey must pay the dealer a total of $15,400. This would be Casey's total cost if he didn't need financing. His total cost including finance charges is $18,230.60.

> **TIP** **wants vs needs**
>
> People who get in financial trouble often do so because they buy things based on "wants" rather than "needs." Surveys of millionaires have found a common trait: the vast majority of millionaires are *not* extravagant spenders—on the contrary, they are very frugal, buying things based on needs, not wants. Take a tip from these millionaires: Avoid buying things you may want but don't really need!

Casey now has signed the loan documents and is driving around town in his yellow convertible. In 1 month, Casey must make his first monthly payment; we'll join Casey in Unit 14.2 for that event.

Let's test our understanding of this unit by doing the U-Try-It exercises.

U-Try-It (Unit 14.1)

You are thinking about buying a piano at a price of $8,500 plus $510 sales tax. You have $1,200 cash.
1. You can get a 10-year loan from your bank for the remainder of the money. Determine the loan amount.
2. Your monthly payment is $94.76. Calculate the finance charge.
3. Figure the total cost of the piano, including finance charge.

Answers: (If you have a different answer, check the solution in Appendix A.)
1. $7,810   2. $3,561.20   3. $12,571.20

Unit 14.2 Paying off an installment loan

Getting a loan, for most people, is the easy part. Paying it off is more of a headache. In this unit we will explore how to calculate the interest and principal portion of each payment, as well as the remaining balance after a payment is made. We will also explore ways of paying off a loan sooner.

a Finding interest, principal, and remaining balance

A promissory note specifies how interest is calculated. As mentioned, most lenders rely on the U.S. Rule, in which interest is calculated on the unpaid balance to the date payment is received by the lender. In figuring how much of each payment is interest and how much is principal, we first calculate the interest. The remainder of the payment is principal and reduces the loan balance.

> **calculating interest, principal, and remaining balance**
>
> **Step 1** Determine the number of days for which interest is charged.
> **Step 2** Calculate interest: $I = PRT$.
> **Step 3** The remainder of the payment is principal: Principal = Total paid − Interest portion (Step 2).
> **Step 4** New balance = Previous balance − Principal portion of payment (Step 3).

In figuring interest for each monthly payment we must know how many days there are in each payment period. One way to determine the number of days is to count days on a calendar; the day after the date of the loan (or last payment) is day 1, and so on. Two other methods are illustrated below, assuming that Casey got his car loan on August 5 and made his first payment on September 3.

Day-of-the-year calendar. Refer to Appendix D, page D-1, in which each day is numbered; August 5 is day 217 (it is the 217th day of the year), and September 3 is day 246 (it is the 246th day of the year).

Sep. 3 → Day   246
Aug. 5 → Day −217
                29 days

Days-in-a-month. With this method, shown in Appendix D, page D-2, we remember how many days there are in each month. Notice the memory aids on that page.

Days in August: 31 − 5 =   26   *August has 31 days; not charged interest for first 5 days*
Days in September   +3
                    29 days

For installment loans with monthly payments, it is probably easier to count days using the days-in-a-month method; that is the method we will use in this chapter.

If a borrower makes a larger payment than is required, the extra money is applied to the principal and reduces the loan balance. As a result, the borrower will be charged less interest for future payments and the length of the loan will be shortened.

We left Casey, in Unit 14.1, driving his convertible around town. It's now time for Casey to make his first monthly payment.

Example 1 On August 5, Casey got a $13,500 loan at 7.5% interest. Payments of $270.51 are due on the 5th of each month, starting September 5. To save interest and pay off the loan sooner, Casey pays a bit extra: $400 on September 3 and $375 on October 6. Help Casey calculate the interest and principal portion for the first two payments, as well as the remaining balance after each payment.

Payment number	Date received	Total payment	Interest	Principal	Balance
New loan	Aug. 5	—	—	—	$13,500.00
1	Sep. 3	$400.00	$80.45	$319.55	$13,180.45
2	Oct. 6	$375.00	$89.37	$285.63	$12,894.82

Procedure for September 3 payment
Step 1 Number of days: 26 days in Aug. (31 − 5 = 26) + 3 days in Sep. = 29
Step 2 $I = PRT = \$13{,}500 \times 7.5\% \times \frac{29}{365} = \$80.45$
Step 3 Principal = $400.00 − $80.45 = $319.55
Step 4 Balance = $13,500.00 − $319.55 = $13,180.45

Procedure for October 6 payment
Step 1 Number of days: 27 days in Sep. (30 − 3 = 27) + 6 days in Oct. = 33
Step 2 $I = \$13{,}180.45 \times 7.5\% \times \frac{33}{365} = \$89.37$
Step 3 Principal = $375.00 − $89.37 = $285.63
Step 4 Balance = $13,180.45 − $285.63 = $12,894.82

b Calculating a payoff amount

Often, borrowers pay loans off early. For example, you may sell your vehicle before the loan is scheduled to be paid off (in which case, you must pay the loan balance). Or you may have extra money and use it to pay off the loan, thereby saving interest. Or you may decide to **refinance** the loan; refinancing a loan means you get a new loan and use part or all of the proceeds to pay off your old loan. People refinance to get additional cash, to decrease a payment, or simply to get a lower interest rate.

Doing calculations for the final payment is a bit different. We calculate interest the same way. To end up with a zero balance, the principal portion of the payment must be the previous balance. The total payment (referred to as the **payoff amount**) is the sum of the interest and principal.

Example 2 Casey has been making larger payments when he can. Casey made payment 31 on March 5 (about $2\frac{1}{2}$ years after getting the loan). His balance after that payment was $3,181.85. He just received a large income tax refund and decides to use part of the money to pay off the loan on April 2. Calculate the payoff amount.

Payment number	Date received	Total payment	Interest	Principal	Balance
31	Mar. 5	—	—	—	$3,181.85
32	Apr. 2	$3,200.16	$18.31	$3,181.85	$0.00

Number of days: 26 days in Mar. (31 − 5 = 26) + 2 days in Apr. = 28
$I = PRT = \$3{,}181.85 \times 7.5\% \times \frac{28}{365} = \$18.31$
Principal: $3,181.85 (the previous balance)
Total payment = $18.31 + $3,181.85 = $3,200.16

By making a payment of $3,200.16 on April 2, the loan will be paid in full. No more payments!

Casey now has paid off his car loan, so he can really drive around town in style. Later, if Casey needs some money for something, he can get another loan on his car.

If a borrower quits making payments on a secured loan (like an auto loan), the lender can reclaim the security and sell it. The proceeds from the sale are applied to the amount owed (including interest, legal fees, and other costs); any surplus is given to the borrower. If the proceeds from the sale do not cover the amount owed, many states allow the lender to collect the difference from the borrower after the sale (by getting a **deficiency judgement** against the borrower).

> **TIP** one of the most valuable things you will ever own
>
> Don't underestimate the value of having good credit. By paying bills on time and maintaining good credit, we will have a much easier time getting a loan when needed and at a decent interest rate. Good credit is an extremely valuable possession. Don't let it get tarnished.
>
> Interest rates on car loans can be 21%, or even higher, with bad credit. A monthly payment on a 4-year $10,000 car loan at 21% is $309.66; for the same loan at 3.5% the monthly payment is $223.56. That's a penalty of $86.10 a month—$4,132.80 over 4 years—for having bad credit!

Rule of 78

Most lenders use the U.S. Rule to calculate interest on installment loans. Another method, the **Rule of 78,** is losing popularity and is currently not allowed in most states (probably because it works to the disadvantage of a borrower in the event the loan is paid off early). As a result, we will not cover the Rule of 78 in the text. If the text is being used for a course in a state that uses the Rule of 78, your instructor may cover this method in detail as an Enrichment Topic.

U-Try-It (Unit 14.2)

Well, that finishes up this unit. Do you have *interest* in doing the U-Try-It questions?

You buy a motorcycle and get an installment loan of $8,000 at 11.25% interest to be repaid over 3 years at $262.86 per month.

1. You got the loan on July 15 and make a $400 payment on August 12. Calculate interest, principal, and the new balance.
2. After making payment 21 on April 14 (almost 3 years later), you still owe $495.50. If you pay off the loan on May 3, what is the payoff amount?

Answers: (If you have a different answer, check the solution in Appendix A.)
1. Interest: $69.04; Principal: $330.96; Balance: $7,669.04   **2.** $498.40

Unit 14.3 Open-end credit

With **open-end credit** (also referred to as **revolving credit**), a person can borrow up to an approved credit limit. The most common types of open-end credit are **credit cards** (such as VISA, MasterCard, and department store cards) and **home equity credit lines**. With open-end credit, it is not necessary to apply for credit each time money is needed; the borrower is already approved, up to a certain limit (called the **line of credit**).

Using a credit card wisely is a good way to establish a good credit rating. But many people use credit cards unwisely and get into financial trouble.

a Evaluating annual and periodic rates

A **periodic rate** is an interest rate per period (such as 1.5% per month) and is frequently used for open-end credit. To find the periodic rate, we divide the annual rate (also called the **nominal rate**) by the number of periods per year.

periodic rate formula

$$\text{Periodic rate} = \frac{\text{Annual rate}}{\text{Periods per year}}$$

Example 1 For an annual rate of 18%, find **(a)** the monthly periodic rate and **(b)** the daily periodic rate.

a. Monthly periodic rate $= \frac{\text{Annual rate}}{\text{Periods per year}} = \frac{18}{12} = 1.5(\%)$

b. Daily periodic rate $= \frac{\text{Annual rate}}{\text{Periods per year}} = \frac{18}{365} \approx .04931507(\%)$

An 18% annual rate is identical to a monthly periodic rate of 1.5% (a borrower is charged 1.5% each month) and is equivalent to a daily periodic rate of approximately .04931507% (a borrower is charged .04931507% each day).

To change a periodic rate to an annual rate, we multiply the periodic rate by the number of periods per year.

annual rate formula

Annual rate = Periodic rate × Periods per year

Example 2 You are thinking about getting a credit card. One credit card company charges interest at 1.25% per month. Another charges interest at 13.9% per year. Which rate is lower?

Let's convert the 1.25% periodic rate to an annual rate: 1.25 × 12 = 15(%)

The 1.25% monthly rate is identical to a 15% annual rate. The 13.9% rate is lower.

b Calculating an average daily balance

For most loans with an open-end line of credit, interest is calculated on the basis of the **average daily balance**. Interest is *not* charged on the unused part of a credit line.

calculating an average daily balance

Step 1 Multiply the balance by the number of days it remained the same; this gives a subtotal for those days.

Step 2 Add the subtotals.

Step 3 Divide by the number of days in the billing period. When counting days, remember to count *both the first and last days* of the billing period but *not* the last day of the previous billing period.

Example 3 You have a charge card. You receive a bill, dated October 15. Your previous bill was dated September 15. Calculate your average daily balance.

Charge card statement: October 15			
Date	Item	Amount	New balance
9/16	Previous balance brought forward		$520
9/22	Charge	$40	$560
9/23	Payment	$200 Credit	$360
9/27	Charge	$100	$460
10/8	Charge	$50	$510

```
Number of days                              Balance       Subtotal
  6  (Sep. 16, 17, 18, 19, 20, 21)    ×      $520    =    $ 3,120 ⎫
  1  (Sep. 22)                        ×       560    =        560 ⎪
  4  (Sep. 23, 24, 25, 26)            ×       360    =      1,440 ⎬ Step 1
 11  (Sep. 27, 28, 29, 30; Oct. 1–7)  ×       460    =      5,060 ⎪
 +8  (Oct. 8, 9, 10, 11, 12, 13, 14, 15) ×    510    =     +4,080 ⎭
 30                                                       $14,260  ← Step 2
```

Average daily balance = $\frac{\$14{,}260}{30}$ = $475.33 ← Step 3

c Calculating interest for open-end credit

For credit cards, guidelines (including interest rate) are determined by the company that issues the credit card. Guidelines are different from card to card and from institution to institution.

> **TIP**   not all credit cards are the same
>
> Not all credit cards are the same. Here are some things to consider when selecting a credit card:
> - Credit limit
> - Annual or monthly fee (such as $40 per year)
> - Points earned, which can be redeemed for cash, airline tickets, or gift cards
> - Cash advance fee (such as 2% of any cash advances)
> - Minimum payment (such as $20 per month)
> - Late fees (such as $25 if over 20 days late)
> - Interest rate
> - The amount upon which interest is calculated. Most charge on the average daily balance. Many charge no interest if the balance is paid in full each month; as a result, many cardholders pay their account in full each month.

Interest is referred to as "finance charge" on most credit cards and home equity loan statements. Interest is generally calculated using one of two methods.

> **calculating interest for open-end credit**
>
> **Method 1**   Multiply a certain balance (like the average daily balance) by a *monthly* periodic rate.
>
> **Method 2**   Multiply a certain balance by a *daily* periodic rate and then multiply the result by the number of days in the billing cycle.

Example 4   Calculate the monthly finance charge for a credit card with an average daily balance of $475.33 and a monthly periodic rate of 1.5%.

$475.33 × 1.5% = $7.13

> **TIP**   a sure-fire way to earn 18% interest
>
> Most of us would jump at the chance to earn 18% interest. Well, here is the easiest way in the world to do it: Pay off those credit cards that are charging 18%! By avoiding paying 18% interest we are, in effect, earning 18% interest on the money we use to pay off the debt.

Example 5   Calculate the finance charge on a home equity loan based on an average daily balance of $62,300 during a 31-day billing period. The lender charges 9.25% interest and calculates interest based on the resulting daily periodic rate.

Daily periodic rate = $\frac{9.25}{365}$ ≈ .02534247(%)

Interest = $62,300 × .02534247% × 31 = $489.44

In Example 5, we would get the same answer if we used the simple interest formula: $I = PRT$ = $62,300 × 9.25% × $\frac{31}{365}$ = $489.44. But that's too easy; most lenders calculate interest on home equity loans using a daily periodic rate.

Congratulations on finishing this chapter. Now, let's *charge* ahead to the U-Try-It problems.

U-Try-It (Unit 14.3)

1. You are thinking about getting a credit card. One company charges interest at 1.5% per month and a second charges 18% per year. Which rate is lower?
2. Calculate the average daily balance for the following charge card statement, dated June 5. The previous statement was dated May 5.

Charge card statement: June 5			
Date	Item	Amount	New balance
5/6	Previous balance brought forward		$460
5/17	Charge	$60	$520
5/18	Payment	$250 Credit	$270
5/27	Charge	$120	$390
6/1	Charge	$30	$420

3. Calculate the finance charge on a home equity loan based on an average daily balance of $34,100 during a 31-day billing period. The lender charges 9.75% interest and calculates interest on the resulting daily periodic rate (rounded to 8 decimal places).

Answers: (If you have a different answer, check the solution in Appendix A.)
1. The rates are identical   2. $389.03   3. $282.38

Chapter in a Nutshell

Objectives	Examples

Unit 14.1 Cost of installment buying

a Determining the loan amount

You are buying a car for $8,300. You must also pay tax and license fees of $700. You have $1,100. Amount you need to borrow?

$8,300 + $700 - $1,100 = **$7,900**

b Figuring finance charge

Refer back. You get a 4-year $7,900 loan at 6.5% interest. Monthly payment = $187.35. Total finance charge?

Total finance charge = ($187.35 × 48) - $7,900 = $8,992.80 - $7,900 = **$1,092.80**

c Figuring total cost

Refer back. Total cost of the car, including finance charges?

$8,300 + $700 + $1,092.80 = **$10,092.80**

Unit 14.2 Paying off an installment loan

a Finding interest, principal, and remaining balance

Refer back. You got the loan on July 10 and make a $250 payment on August 7. Calculate interest, principal, and remaining balance.

Step 1 Number of days: 21 days in Jul. (31 - 10 = 21) + 7 days in Aug. = 28
Step 2 $I = PRT = \$7{,}900 \times 6.5\% \times \frac{28}{365} =$ **$39.39**
Step 3 Principal = $250.00 - $39.39 = **$210.61**
Step 3 Balance = $7,900 - $210.61 = **$7,689.39**

b Calculating a payoff amount

Refer back. After making payment 38 on July 10 (3 years later), you still owe $1,448.80. You have extra money and decide to pay off the loan on July 26. What is the payoff amount?

Number of days: 26 - 10 = 16
$I = PRT = \$1{,}448.80 \times 6.5\% \times \frac{16}{365} = \$4.13$
Principal = $1,448.80 (previous balance)
Payoff amount = $4.13 + $1,448.80 = **$1,452.93**

Chapter in a Nutshell (concluded)

Objectives | **Examples**

Unit 14.3 Open-end credit

a Evaluating annual and periodic rates

13.5% annual rate. Daily periodic rate? $\frac{13.5}{365} \approx .03698630(\%)$

1.75% monthly periodic rate. Annual rate? $1.75 \times 12 = 21(\%)$

b Calculating an average daily balance

Charge card bill, dated August 8. Previous bill dated July 8. Average daily balance?

Date	Item	Amount	New balance
July 9	Previous balance brought forward		$700
July 14	Payment	$400 Credit	$300
July 27	Charge	$140	$440

```
 5 days × $700  = $ 3,500
13 days × $300  =   3,900
13 days × $440  = + 5,720
31                $13,120 ÷ 31 days = $423.23 average daily balance
```

c Calculating interest for open-end credit

Calculate finance charge on a 5.5% home equity loan based on an average daily balance of $85,700 during a 30-day billing period using a daily periodic rate.

Daily periodic rate = $\frac{5.5}{365} \approx .01506849(\%)$ $85,700 \times .01506849\% \times 30 = \$387.41$

Enrichment Topics

The following Enrichment Topic, which goes a bit beyond what is in the text, is available for this chapter:

Rule of 78

If your instructor doesn't cover this topic in class and you would like to dig in deeper on your own, please send a request to *studentsupport@olympuspub.com*.

Think

1. Explain the concept of "wants vs needs" and how ignoring this concept can lead to financial troubles. Give some examples of things you may want but don't really need.
2. Under what conditions is an APR greater than the stated annual rate; give a logical explanation for this.
3. Do you think the Truth in Lending Act is a good thing? Why?
4. Which types of loans are exempt from the Truth in Lending Act? Give a logical explanation of why they may be exempt.
5. Suppose, as part of a special promotion, you got a 0.9% car loan. Assume you have an extra $2,000 and are trying to decide whether you should use the money to pay down your car loan or put the $2,000 in a savings account earning 3.5%. Which is the wiser move and why?
6. What are some advantages and disadvantages of using credit cards?
7. Do you know someone who has gotten into financial trouble? If so, without giving names, expalin what lead to his or her financial troubles.
8. Do you think it is smarter to (a) buy a new car, (b) lease a new car, or (c) buy a used car? Compare the cost of each over, say, a 5-year period; consider gasoline, repairs, insurance, licensing/registration, taxes, car payments, and depreciation.

Explore

1. Calculate a car payment on a 4-year $7,000 car loan at 6.5% interest, using either compound interest formulas (Unit 11.3), or financial calculators (Unit 13.3). Your instructor may ask you to use more than one method.
2. See Activity 1. Calculate the same payment using Excel (see instructions in Appendix E).
3. See Activity 1. Use the online calculator on our Web site (**www.webbertext.com**) to calculate the same payment. Follow the accompanying guidelines.
4. See Activity 1. Search on the Internet for a site that calculates car payments. Use that site to calculate the same payment.
5. Refer to Activities 1-4. Are any of the payments different? If so, which do you suppose are incorrect, and why?
6. Go to **www.myfico.com/crediteducation/calculators/loanrates.aspx**. Find current interest rates for car loans in your area, based on different credit scores. Then figure out how much more total interest a person with a poor credit score would have to pay over the life of a 4-year $15,000 loan than a person with an excellent credit score.

Apply

1. **What's It Worth?** Visit a website (like **edmunds.com**) that shows values of used vehicles. Determine the value of your current vehicle (edmunds.com shows 3 values: (1) retail price charged by a car dealer, (2) sale between individuals, and (3) trade-in value). Print and submit.
2. **Comparing Plastic.** Get the following information on three different credit cards: (1) interest rate, (2) credit limit, (3) annual or monthly fees, (4) cash advance fees, (5) minimum payment, (6) late fees, (7) the amount upon which interest is charged, (8) whether you are charged interest if you pay the entire balance with each statement, and (9) other features. Conclude by stating which card best suits your needs and why.

Chapter Review Problems

Unless noted otherwise, use 2 decimal places for answers.

Unit 14.1 Cost of installment buying

1. Maria Sanchez is thinking about buying a car and getting a 4-year car loan from her credit union in the amount of $8,500. Her monthly payment will be **(a)** $177.08, **(b)** less than $177.08, or **(c)** greater than $177.08.

2. Suppose you get a 6.5% installment loan and are charged a $50 front-end application fee. Your APR will be **(a)** 6.5% **(b)** greater than 6.5%, or **(c)** less than 6.5%.

For Problems 3–5, assume that you are thinking about buying a sports car.

3. The sports car you have in mind is priced at $28,500. You must pay tax and license fees of $1,700. You have $3,000. Your bank will make you a loan at 7.5% for 4 years. They charge a $300 origination fee for making the loan. If you use your $3,000 toward the purchase, how much will you need to borrow?

4. You get the loan. Your monthly payment is $664.92. What is your total finance charge?

5. What is the total cost of the car, including finance charges?

6. You are thinking about buying a tent trailer, priced at $6,200. You must pay tax and license fees of $500. You have $1,500 and your credit union will loan you the remaining $5,200 with 24 monthly payments of $235.18; there are no front-end loan fees. What is the total cost of the tent trailer, including finance charges?

Unit 14.2 Paying off an installment loan

7. Interest is always more during the latter part of an installment loan. (T or F)

8. With the U.S. Rule, interest is calculated on the basis of a 360-day year. (T or F)

9. With the U.S. Rule, the lender calculates interest through which date: (a) the due date, (b) the date shown on the borrower's check, (c) the postmark date on the borrower's envelope, (d) the date received by the lender?

10. You get a car loan on June 12. Your first monthly payment is due July 12. The lender receives your payment on July 16. For how many days is interest calculated?

11. You buy a motorcycle on July 1 for $1,500 with $500 down. You agree to pay the seller the remaining $1,000 at 9% interest with four monthly payments of $254.71. Your first payment is due August 1. Calculate interest, principal, and remaining balance for each payment using the U.S. Rule. Payment dates are shown in the table. Remember, the final payment may be slightly different because of rounding and actual payment date.

Due date	Date received	Total payment	Interest	Principal	Balance
July 1	(Start)	—	—	—	$1,000.00
Aug. 1	July 28	$254.71			
Sep. 1	Aug. 29	$254.71			
Oct. 1	Sep. 27	$254.71			
Nov. 1	Nov. 1				$0.00

12. Amir Rafati has been making payments on his 13.5% boat loan for what seems like forever! Amir made a payment October 1. His balance after that payment was $2,182.64. He just sold some stock and decides to use part of the money to pay off the boat loan on October 27. Calculate the payoff amount.

Unit 14.3 Open-end credit

13. For an annual rate of 13%, find (a) the monthly periodic rate and (b) the daily periodic rate (using a 365-day year). Express each rate with 6 decimal places.

14. You are thinking about getting a credit card. One credit card company charges interest at 1.75% per month. Another charges interest at 15.9% per year. Which rate is lower?

15. You have a charge card. You receive a bill dated July 10. Your previous bill was dated June 10. Calculate your average daily balance.

Charge card statement: July 10			
Date	Item	Amount	New balance
6/11	Previous balance brought forward		$420
6/18	Charge	$50	$470
6/24	Payment	$150 Credit	$320
6/30	Charge	$80	$400
7/5	Charge	$40	$440

16. Refer to Problem 15. Calculate the monthly finance charge, assuming you are charged a monthly periodic rate of 1.25%.

17. Calculate the finance charge on a home equity loan based on an average daily balance of $48,700 during a 31-day billing period. The lender charges 8.75% interest and calculates interest based on the resulting daily periodic rate. Assume a 365-day year and round the daily periodic rate to 8 decimal places.

Challenge problems

For Problems 18-22, assume that you buy a car for $8,300. You must also pay tax and license fees of $550. You have $700. Your bank will make you a 3-year car loan at 5.5% interest, but will charge you a $50 processing fee.

18. What amount do you need to borrow?

19. You get the loan on September 8, with monthly payments of $247.61. What is your total finance charge?

20. What is the total cost of the car, including finance charges?

21. Your monthly payments are due on the 8th of each month, starting October 8. The lender receives your first monthly payment ($247.61) on October 6. For your second monthly payment, you pay $300; the lender receives the payment on November 10. Calculate interest, principal, and remaining balance for each payment using the U.S. Rule.

Due Date	Date Received	Total Payment	Interest	Principal	Balance
Sep. 8	(Start)	—	—	—	$8,200.00
Oct. 8	Oct. 6	$247.61			
Nov. 8	Nov. 10	$300.00			

22. Two and one-half years later, after making payment 30 on April 8, your balance is $418.22. You get your income tax refund and decide to use part of the money to pay off the loan on May 3. Calculate the payoff amount.

Practice Test

1. You buy a truck for $22,200. You must also pay tax and license fees of $1,500. You borrow $20,000 at 6% interest for 5 years with monthly payments of $386.66. What is the total cost of the truck, including tax and license fees and finance charges?

2. On July 5, you get a car loan. Your first payment is due August 5. You write out your check on August 3, drop it in a mailbox on August 4, it gets postmarked on August 5, and the lender receives the payment on August 7. For how many days is interest calculated?

3. On November 18, you get a 10% $2,400 furniture loan with monthly payments of $100. Your first payment is due December 18. What is the balance after your first payment, assuming the lender receives your payment on December 16?

4. On May 24, Whitney Nickle made a payment on her 7.9% car loan. After making the payment, the balance was $1,489.23. Whitney got her income tax refund, and on June 2 she pays off the loan. What is the payoff amount?

5. Calculate the finance charge on a home equity loan based on an average daily balance of $92,817 during a 30-day billing period. The lender charges 8.5% interest and calculates interest based on a daily periodic rate. Assume a 365-day year and round the daily periodic rate to 8 decimal places.

Classroom Notes

FUN CORNER

Location, Location

Home values vary a lot, depending on location. Here are the 5 most expensive areas in the United States. Average (median) prices are shown.

1. San Jose, CA	$980,000
2. San Francisco, CA	$841,600
3. Anaheim, CA	$713,200
4. Honolulu, HI	$698,600
5. San Diego, CA	$547,800

Note: The average home price in the U.S. is $229,400.

Source: National Association of Realtors, June, 2015

Quotable Quip

I'm a marvelous housekeeper. Every time I leave a man, I keep his house.

– Zsa Zsa Gabor, actress

Home Ownership

From *Homes and Other Black Holes*
by Dave Barry

The Ritual Closing Ceremony. The Ritual Closing Ceremony is an important and highly traditional part of the home-buying process, the last major hurdle you must clear before you become an Official Homeowner. Essentially, what you must do, in the Ritual Closing Ceremony, is go into a small room and write large checks to total strangers. According to tradition, anybody may ask you for a check, for any amount, and you may not refuse. Once you get started handing out money, the good news will travel quickly through the real estate community via joyful shouts: "A Closing Ceremony is taking place!" Soon there will be a huge horde of people—lawyers, bankers, brokers, insurance people, termite inspectors, caterers, photographers, people you used to know in high school—crowding into the closing room and spilling out into the street. You may be forced to hurl batches of signed blank checks out the window, just to make sure that everyone is accommodated in the traditional way.

Traditional Activities of Homeowners. Once you become a homeowner you can immerse yourself in the many rewarding and traditional activities that new homeowners engage in, such as trying to figure out how to make the mortgage payment and, simultaneously, not starve to death. Here's a suggestion. If you go to any major hotel or country club on a weekend, chances are you'll find a large formal wedding reception going on, featuring serving people walking around and actually giving away teeny little sandwiches with the crust cut off. This is an excellent source of food for you, the new homeowner. You just walk in there, looking like you are a close personal friend of either the bride or the groom, and help yourself to as many trays as you feel you will need during this particular mortgage payment period.

Eye of the Beholder

Here's how your home looks to:

THE OWNER

THE BUYER

THE LENDER

THE TAX ASSESSOR

"I thought we qualified for more than this!"

Home Ownership and Mortgage Loans

15

For most people, a home is their largest single lifetime investment. Most people don't have lots of cash sitting around, so they borrow part of the purchase price; the loan is called a mortgage loan. Generally, a mortgage loan is repaid with a series of equal monthly payments (*lots* of them, unfortunately). In this chapter we will explore home ownership and mortgage loans.

UNIT OBJECTIVES

Unit 15.1 Home ownership and mortgage payments

- a Understanding home ownership
- b Getting prequalified for a mortgage loan
- c Figuring total interest
- d Calculating a payment for an escrow account

Unit 15.2 Paying off a mortgage loan and increasing equity

- a Preparing an amortization schedule—breaking down the payment
- b Determining equity

Unit 15.3 Amortization with a financial calculator

- a Using amortization registers of a financial calculator

Unit 15.4 Repayment variations and loan charges

- a Understanding repayment variations
- b Understanding loan charges on a mortgage loan

Unit 15.1 Home ownership and mortgage payments

In this chapter we will follow the adventures of Tara. She has been renting an apartment for several years and is considering buying a home.

a Understanding home ownership

Owning a home is a big part of the American Dream. Lots of people figure a home is their castle and it isn't right for the king or queen to be *renting* the castle.

Tara has been collecting rent receipts and is thinking about the American Dream. After talking with relatives and friends, she has come up with some advantages and disadvantages of home ownership.

Homes come in all shapes, sizes, and locations. When choosing a home, make sure it's right for you.

---

 a few pros and cons of home ownership

A few benefits of home ownership:
- You can make and benefit from improvements to the property.
- You have monthly payments that, for most loans, do not escalate like rent.
- You can deduct interest and property taxes on an income tax return.
- You can benefit from increases in property values.

A few disadvantages of home ownership:
- You must generally use a large amount of cash as a down payment.
- You, rather than a landlord, are responsible for repairs.
- You take the risk of home values decreasing.
- You have the responsibility of selling the home when moving.

Note: Chapter 17 includes an Enrichment Topic that does a financial comparison of renting vs. buying.

Real estate, unlike *personal property*, is immovable. Real estate includes land and buildings. Personal property includes things like cars, furniture, money, stock certificates, and promissory notes.

A loan that is secured by real estate is known as a **mortgage loan**. Owners may have more than one mortgage loan on a property at the same time. The first loan obtained is called a **first mortgage**; the second loan is called a **second mortgage**; and so forth. If a borrower stops making payments to one or more of the lenders, the borrower is said to be in **default** and the property may be sold at a *foreclosure sale*. Proceeds from the sale are used to pay lenders in order (the first lender gets paid in full first, then the second lender, and so on); any surplus is paid to the borrower. In some cases, proceeds from the sale are not enough to cover the amounts owed to lenders; many states allow lenders to collect the difference (called a **deficiency**) from the borrower following a foreclosure sale. Because second lenders are not as well protected as first lenders, second lenders charge higher rates and make shorter-term loans.

Example 1 Alma Noble lost his job and got in financial trouble. He quit making his mortgage payments and the property was sold at a foreclosure sale. He owes $110,300 on his first mortgage (including past-due interest, attorney fees, and court costs) and $22,300 on his second mortgage (including past-due interest, attorney fees, and court costs). What will happen to the money at the foreclosure sale, assuming the foreclosure price is **(a)** $100,000, **(b)** $120,000, and **(c)** $140,000?

$100,000. The first lender will receive all of the money. The second lender gets nothing. In states that allow deficiency judgments, the first lender can get a deficiency judgment against Alma for $10,300 and the second lender can get a deficiency judgment for $22,300.

$120,000. The first lender gets $110,300. The second lender gets the remaining $9,700; if that state allows deficiency judgments, they can get a deficiency judgment for $12,600 ($22,300 - $9,700).

$140,000. The first lender gets $110,300. The second lender gets $22,300. Alma gets the remaining $7,400.

> **TIP — expect the unexpected**
>
> Owning a home can be a drain on the pocketbook. People find out, after buying a home, there are lots of things to spend money on: landscaping, painting, new carpet or cabinets, repairs, furniture and decorating, large utility bills, and the list goes on. For those who can't afford the additional expenses, the American Dream (of owning a home) can become an American Nightmare! Don't make the mistake of using every last penny to buy a home; have some extra money set aside for the unexpected!

It is a good idea for those venturing into real estate to get help from professionals. A **real estate appraiser** can assist in estimating the value of a property; lenders hire appraisers to estimate the value before making a loan. A **real estate broker** can assist in locating a property; generally, real estate brokers charge a commission only to the seller of the property, often about 5% to 7% of the selling price.

b Getting prequalified for a mortgage loan

There are three basic types of mortgage loans:

- A **conventional loan**.
- An **FHA loan**, which must be approved by the Federal Housing Administration (FHA). Payments are made to the lending institution *not* to the FHA.
- A **VA loan**, which must be approved by the Veterans Administration (VA). The borrower must be a qualified veteran. Payments are made to the lending institution *not* to the VA.

Mortgage rates change depending on supply and demand. As of the writing of the text (October 2015), mortgage rates are near an all-time low; borrowers can get 30-year loans at an interest rate as low as 3.75% and 15-year loans as low as 3%. Mortgage rates hit an all-time high of 18.16% in September 1981. Illustration 15-1 shows mortgage rates from 1972 to 2015. In the examples that follow, we use a variety of interest rates so you can see the impact of different rates.

Mortgage lenders decide whether to make loans, and at what interest rate, based on (1) the property (or **collateral**) securing the loan, and (2) the borrower's ability to make the payments.

Illustration 15-1 Average Mortgage Rates, 1972 to 2015 (30-year fixed, July of each year). Source: Freddie Mac

1972.......7.40%	1981.......16.83%	1990.......10.04%	1999.......7.73%	2008.......6.43%
1973.......8.05%	1982.......16.82%	1991.......9.85%	2000.......8.15%	2009.......5.22%
1974.......9.28%	1983.......13.43%	1992.......8.13%	2001.......7.13%	2010.......4.56%
1975.......8.89%	1984.......14.67%	1993.......7.21%	2002.......6.49%	2011.......4.55%
1976.......8.93%	1985.......12.03%	1994.......8.61%	2003.......5.63%	2012.......3.55%
1977.......8.94%	1986.......10.51%	1995.......7.61%	2004.......6.05%	2013.......4.37%
1978.......9.74%	1987.......10.28%	1996.......8.24%	2005.......5.70%	2014.......4.13%
1979.......11.09%	1988.......10.43%	1997.......7.49%	2006.......6.76%	2015.......4.05%
1980.......12.19%	1989.......9.88%	1998.......6.95%	2007.......6.70%	

When evaluating the collateral, lenders get an appraisal (generally paid for by the borrower) to make sure that the loan amount does not exceed the value. The percent of value loaned is referred to as the **loan-to-value ratio (LTV ratio)**. A loan with an 80% LTV ratio (the loan amount is 80% of the home's value) is more attractive to a lender than a loan with a 98% LTV ratio, because there is less risk to the lender.

When evaluating the borrower, lenders consider the borrower's credit history, income and expenses, job stability, and cash reserves. To determine the maximum mortgage payment, lenders use two qualifying ratios:

> The **housing ratio** or **front-end ratio** is the percentage of monthly gross income needed to pay housing costs: monthly mortgage payment, property taxes, and home insurance.

> The **debt-to-income ratio** or **back-end ratio** is the percentage of monthly gross income needed to pay housing costs *and* consumer debt: car payments, credit card payments (minimum amount required), and other installment loan payments but it does not include utilities, phone bills, and auto insurance.

Monthly gross income includes wages (before tax), self-employment income, alimony, child support, Social Security, retirement or VA benefits, interest income, and other regular income.

FHA guidelines, as of the writing of the text, state that a 29% front-end ratio and 41% back-end ratio are acceptable, often written as 29/41. The VA does not have a front-end ratio guideline, but the back-end ratio is 41%. For conventional loans, the ratios vary from lender to lender, and depend on the amount of down payment, borrower's credit, and other criteria.

TIP — don't put the cart before the horse

Home buyers often spend months finding their "dream home," only to discover they cannot qualify for the loan they need. Then they have to start looking all over again. Smart buyers contact a mortgage lender to find out in advance what size loan they can get; this is known as getting *prequalified*.

After weighing the pros and cons of owning a home, Tara decides to take the plunge. She decides that it would be a good idea to get prequalified to determine what price home she can afford *before* she starts looking at homes. In Example 2, we use front-end and back-end ratios to determine her maximum monthly payment; in Example 3, we determine the loan amount that results in that monthly payment; in Example 4, we factor in down payment to determine the maximum price home she can afford.

determining a maximum monthly payment using front-end and back-end ratios

Step 1 Determine monthly gross income.

Step 2 Use the front-end ratio:

 a. Multiply monthly gross income by the front-end ratio (like 29%); this is the amount available for housing costs (monthly payment, property taxes, insurance).
 b. Subtract monthly amount needed for property taxes and insurance.
 c. The result is the amount available for the monthly payment.

Step 3 Use the back-end ratio:

 a. Multiply monthly gross income by the back-end ratio (like 41%); this is the amount available for housing costs and consumer debt.
 b. Subtract monthly property tax and insurance.
 c. Subtract consumer debt.
 d. The result is the amount available for the monthly payment.

Step 4 Compare the results of Steps 2 and 3; the maximum monthly payment is the lesser of the two.

Example 2 Before shopping for homes, Tara decides to get prequalified for a loan. The lender she goes to has qualifying ratios of 29/41. Tara earns $5,000 a month in wages, $1,000 a month from a rental property, and has interest income of $650 a year. Based on the price of the home Tara hopes to buy, the lender figures property taxes to be $1,600 a year and insurance to be $520 a year. Tara's car payment is $347, and her minimum required payment on her credit card is $25. What is the maximum monthly payment she qualifies for?

Step 1 Monthly gross income: $5,000 (wages) + $1,000 (rental income) + $54.17 (monthly interest) = $6,054.17

Step 2 Use the front-end ratio (29%):

a. Amount available for housing costs: $6,054.17 × 29%	$1,755.71
b. Subtract monthly property taxes and insurance: ($1,600 + $520) ÷ 12	- 176.67
c. Amount available for monthly payment	$1,579.04

Step 3 Use the back-end ratio (41%):

a. Amount available for housing costs and consumer debt: $6,054.17 × 41%	$2,482.21
b. Subtract monthly property taxes and insurance (see above)	- 176.67
c. Subtract consumer debt: $347 (car payment) + $25 (credit card)	- 372.00
d. Amount available for monthly payment	$1,933.54

Step 4 Using the front-end ratio, Tara's maximum monthly payment is $1,579.04. Using the back-end ratio, the maximum monthly payment is $1,933.54. Tara's maximum monthly payment is the lesser of the two: $1,579.04.

Tara qualifies for a maximum monthly payment of $1,579.04. Based on that payment, the lender tells her she can get a 7.75% 30-year mortgage loan of $220,400. With the cash she has for a down payment, she could buy a home priced at $240,000. She has seen some of her friends mortgage their homes to the max and later get in financial trouble. So, she decides to look at homes in a slightly lower price range. After looking at quite a few homes, Tara finds her "dream home," priced at $180,000.

> **TIP** what's included, and what's not included?
>
> One of the main arguments buyers and sellers have in a transaction is what is included in the sale and what is not. For example, the buyer may be expecting to get the refrigerator, but the seller does not think the refrigerator is included and takes it when moving out.
>
> As mentioned earlier, real estate is immovable. Unless specifically included in an offer, personal property is not included as part of the property. So, refrigerators and slide-in ranges would not be included. Drapery rods would be included because they are attached to the walls but drapes hung from the rods would not be included. Levelor blind brackets would be included but blinds that can be snapped out of the brackets would not be included. And free-standing fireplace equipment, spring-loaded shower rods, removable parts of certain toilet paper holders, and even lightbulbs would not be included.
>
> To avoid arguments, buyers and sellers should specify which items are included in the sale. Many states have preprinted forms that address certain items, such as light bulbs. If the seller wants to exclude certain attached items, such as a dining room chandelier the seller brought from Italy, the seller should exclude it in the written offer; better yet, the seller should remove the chandelier and replace it with a standard light fixture before showing the property to prospective buyers.

> **TIP** — **don't buy a pig in a poke**
>
> Back in the old days, con men used to put a cat in a poke (bag) and sell it to an unsuspecting buyer as a pig, telling the buyer not to open the bag or the pig would get out and run away. When a buyer insisted on seeing what he was getting and the seller opened the bag, he "let the cat out of the bag." When buying a home, don't buy a pig in a poke. Here are two suggestions.
> - Hire a competent inspector to evaluate the condition of the home and its components.
> - Don't buy without having a title insurance policy. The seller may not even own the home. Or the seller may have mortgage balances, liens, or judgments that you will inherit when you buy the home. A title search will determine the status.

Tara decides to make an offer. Her real estate agent suggests the offer specify what is included in the sale and requires the seller to provide Tara with a policy of title insurance. Her agent also suggests that the offer be subject to (1) Tara obtaining a mortgage loan that is satisfactory to Tara and (2) Tara's approval of a physical inspection of the property. These "subject-to" provisions, known as **contingencies**, allow Tara to nullify the offer if the conditions are not met. Tara makes an offer of $165,000 (rather than the $180,000 asking price). The seller is not happy with that price and makes a *counteroffer* of $168,000. Tara accepts the counteroffer.

Buying a home can be an exciting experience. But take your time. Buy in the right area. Don't buy more than you need. And be careful when making an offer.

C Figuring total interest

Tara decides to get a $160,000 loan. The lender gives her two choices: (1) a 30-year loan at 7.75% or (2) a 15-year loan at 7.25% interest. *Note:* Lenders do, in fact, offer lower rates for shorter-term loans because they have less risk on shorter-term loans. We calculated Tara's monthly payment on each choice in previous chapters: Example 2 of Unit 11.3 (using formulas), and Example 2 of Unit 13.3 (using financial calculators). We got the same monthly payment using each method: $1,146.26 for the 30-year loan and $1,460.58 for the 15-year loan. Tara's first reaction may be to get the 30-year loan because she could save $314.32 each month. But she may want to figure how much interest she would pay over the life of the loan.

> **figuring total interest on a mortgage loan**
>
> **Step 1** Multiply the monthly payment by the number of payments to be made. This is the total amount that will be paid to the lender.
>
> **Step 2** Subtract the loan amount (the principal portion of payments). The result is the interest portion of payments.

316 Chapter 15 Home Ownership and Mortgage Loans

Example 3 Tara can get a 30-year $160,000 loan with monthly payments of $1,146.26 or a 15-year $160,000 loan with monthly payments of $1,460.58. Calculate the total interest she would pay for each loan.

30-year loan

Total amount to be repaid: 360 × $1,146.26 =	$412,653.60	← Step 1
Subtract principal portion (loan amount)	-160,000.00	← Step 2
Interest portion of payments	$252,653.60	

15-year loan

Total amount to be repaid: 180 × $1,460.58 =	$262,904.40	← Step 1
Subtract principal portion (loan amount)	-160,000.00	← Step 2
Interest portion of payments	$102,904.40	

In Example 3, the interest for the 30-year loan is about two and one-half times as much as for the 15-year loan! In fact the interest on the 30-year loan is more than the $160,000 borrowed! That's pretty astounding, isn't it? Tara decides to get the 15-year loan.

d Calculating a payment for an escrow account

Mortgage lenders require borrowers to pay *property tax* and to have adequate *hazard insurance* to cover losses from fire, accidents, and other risks. In many cases lenders require borrowers to maintain a separate account with the lender, from which the lender pays property taxes and insurance on behalf of the borrower. The account is referred to by various titles, including **escrow account, reserve account**, and **impound account**. The money in the account *belongs to the borrower* but is held by the lender. Some lenders pay interest on escrow accounts (some states require that interest be paid).

Tara's monthly payment ($1,460.58) covers principal and interest. If an escrow account is required, the borrower must pay an additional amount each month ($\frac{1}{12}$ of the annual property tax and insurance) for deposit into the escrow account.

Example 4 Tara can get a $160,000 mortgage loan with a monthly payment (PI) of $1,460.58. The lender requires an escrow account for payment of annual property taxes and insurance. Property taxes are currently $1,600 per year and insurance is $520. Calculate Tara's total monthly payment (PITI).

Principal and interest (PI)		$1,460.58
Taxes and insurance (TI):		
Property taxes	$1,600	
Insurance	+ 520	
Total tax and insurance	$2,120 ÷ 12 =	+ 176.67
Total monthly payment (PITI)		$1,637.25

Tara's total monthly payment will start out at $1,637.25. While the principal and interest (PI) portion of the payment does not change, the tax and insurance (TI) portion changes to reflect an increase or decrease in property tax and insurance. The total payment (PITI) is therefore subject to change.

TIP   should I or should I not?

For many loans, escrow accounts are required; for some they are not. If you have a choice, here are some pros and cons of having an escrow account:

Pros An escrow account forces you to set money aside so that you don't have to come up with a large amount of money all at once to pay property taxes and insurance.

Cons Most escrow accounts pay no interest. By putting the money aside yourself, you can earn interest on the money. And, if you have an escrow account, you must check to make sure that deposits into the account and payments from the account are correct.

Let's try some U-Try-It questions to see how we're doing.

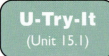
U-Try-It
(Unit 15.1)

1. You are getting prequalified for a mortgage loan. You earn $4,200 a month. Based on the price home you hope to buy, the lender figures property taxes will be $1,300 per year and insurance will be $480. Based on a front-end qualifying ratio of 29%, what is the maximum monthly payment you qualify for?
2. Suppose you get a 30-year $185,000 mortgage loan with a monthly payment of $1,293.55. Based on making 360 payments of $1,293.55, how much interest will you pay over the 30 years?
3. Lucy gets a 30-year $175,000 mortgage loan at 5.625% interest, resulting in a monthly payment (PI) of $1,007.40. The lender requires an escrow account. Property taxes are $1,450 per year and insurance is $600. Calculate the total monthly payment (PITI).

Answers: (If you have a different answer, check the solution in Appendix A.)
1. $1,069.67   **2.** $280,678.00   **3.** $1,178.23

Unit 15.2 Paying off a mortgage loan and increasing equity

A loan paid off with a series of equal periodic payments is called an **amortized loan**. As you may recall, with installment loans (like a car loan), we calculate interest using the U.S. Rule. With the U.S. Rule, we calculate interest to the day payment is received by the lender. For most mortgage loans, we calculate interest *per period*, regardless of the day payment is received; so, for monthly payments, the borrower is charged $\frac{1}{12}$ of a year's interest for each payment.

Preparing an amortization schedule—breaking down the payment

In figuring how much of each payment is interest and how much is principal, we first calculate interest. The remainder of the principal and interest (PI) portion of the payment is principal and reduces the loan balance.

> **breaking down a mortgage payment:**
> **interest, principal, and new balance**
>
> **Step 1** $I = PRT$ = Previous loan balance × Annual rate × $\frac{1}{12}$ of a year.
>
> (*Note*: As you may recall, multiplying by $\frac{1}{12}$ is the same as dividing by 12.)
>
> **Step 2**   Principal portion of payment = Total PI payment − Interest (from Step 1)
>
> **Step 3**   New balance = Previous balance − Principal (from Step 2)

We left Tara enjoying her home. A month has gone by and it's time for her to make her first payment. Let's help Tara figure the interest, principal, and remaining balance for her first two payments.

Example 1 Tara got a $160,000 15-year mortgage loan at 7.25% on April 1. Her monthly payment is $1,460.58 (PI) + $176.67 (TI). For the first two payments, calculate interest, principal, and remaining balance.

The TI portion of the payment does not apply to the debt.

Payment number	Due date	Total payment	Interest	Principal	Balance
New loan	Apr. 1	—	—	—	$160,000.00
1	May 1	$1,460.58	$966.67	$493.91	$159,506.09
2	June 1	$1,460.58	$963.68	$496.90	$159,009.19

Procedure for May 1 payment
Step 1 $I = PRT = \$160{,}000 \times 7.25\% \times \frac{1}{12} = \$966.67$
Step 2 Principal = $1,460.58 - $966.67 = $493.91
Step 3 Balance = $160,000.00 - $493.91 = $159,506.09

Procedure for June 1 payment
Step 1 $I = PRT = \$159{,}506.09 \times 7.25\% \times \frac{1}{12} = \$963.68$
Step 2 Principal = $1,460.58 - $963.68 = $496.90
Step 3 Balance = $159,506.09 - $496.90 = $159,009.19

In Example 1, we didn't have to count days like we do for car loans. That's because interest is calculated for 1 month ($\frac{1}{12}$ of a year) regardless of payment date. That is true for most mortgage loans. The exception is for home equity loans and mortgage loans on business properties; for many of these, interest is calculated using the U.S. Rule to the date payment is received.

Also, notice in Example 1 that interest *decreases* with each payment. That's because interest is charged on the unpaid balance, and the balance is gradually decreasing. On the flip side, principal *increases* with each payment (because the interest portion of each payment is decreasing).

Because interest is greater during the first part of a mortgage loan than at the end, the balance decreases slowly at first and then takes a nosedive near the end of the loan; this is shown in Illustration 15-2.

A payment schedule that shows the interest and principal portion of payments as well as the unpaid balance is known as an **amortization schedule**. An amortization schedule cannot be prepared *in advance* for loans that use the U.S. Rule because interest depends on the actual payment date. But we can prepare an amortization schedule in advance for a mortgage loan that calculates interest per period (like monthly) regardless of payment date. Many computer programs are available for creating amortization schedules. Portions of a computer-generated amortization schedule for Tara's 15-year mortgage loan appear as Illustration 15-3, several pages later. Notice that the interest, principal, and remaining balance for payments 1 and 2 match those of Example 1.

Illustration 15-2 Loan Balance for an Amortized Loan

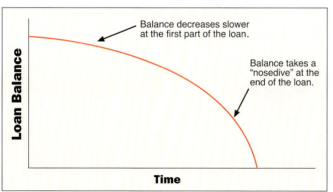

> **TIP** — don't leave it to chance!
>
> If you pay more than your scheduled payment and your mortgage loan has an escrow account, be sure to include a note telling the lender that you want the extra money applied to *principal*. Otherwise, the lender may put the extra money in your escrow account.

b Determining equity

As Tara makes payments on her mortgage loan, she builds equity in her home. **Equity** is the difference between the value of the home and the mortgage balance(s) owed on the home. So, as the mortgage balance goes down, the equity goes up. Another way Tara's equity can go up is if her home increases in value—either by Tara making improvements to her home or by home values increasing in her area.

Example 2

Tara has owned her home for 5 years. She has made some improvements to her home and values have increased a bit in her neighborhood. Her home is currently worth about $270,000. The balance on her first mortgage is $124,410. She got a second mortgage to make some home improvements and owes $17,340 on that loan. What is Tara's equity?

Value	$ 270,000
Amounts owed: $124,410 + $17,340	- 141,750
Equity	$128,250

Tara's equity is $128,250. If she were to sell her home for $270,000, she would receive $128,250 from the sale, less any selling expenses (like real estate commissions and title insurance).

> **TIP** — another income tax benefit of owning a home
>
> One advantage of home ownership is that we can deduct interest and property taxes on our federal income tax return. Here is another tax benefit, as of the writing of this text. If a person has lived in his or her home for at least 2 out of the last 5 years, the first $250,000 of gain from the sale of the home is not taxed on the federal income tax return; for a married couple filing jointly, the first $500,000 of gain is not taxable. This is a HUGE tax benefit.
>
> Keep in mind the $250,000 applies to gain, not sales price. To illustrate, suppose you buy a home for $200,000 and spend $40,000 for improvements (like a new kitchen, bathroom, deck, and fence). Your total cost would be $240,000. Suppose you sell the home several years later for $550,000, and incur selling expenses of $20,000. Your gain would be $550,000 - $20,000 - $240,000 = $290,000. If you qualify for the deduction, you would have to report only a $40,000 gain; if you were married filing jointly, you would not have to report any gain.
>
> *Caution:* Before planning a sale, be sure to check with the IRS or a tax consultant to make sure the rules are still in place and that you qualify for the deduction.

Let's try the U-Try-It exercise to determine how much we remember.

U-Try-It (Unit 15.2)

1. You get a $200,000 mortgage loan for 30 years at 8.75% interest. Your monthly payment (PI) is $1,573.40. Calculate interest, principal, and remaining balance for each of the first two monthly payments.
2. Your home has a current value of $320,000 and you owe $197,400. What is your equity in the home?

Answers: (If you have a different answer, check the solution in Appendix A.)
1. *Payment 1:* Interest = $1,458.33; Principal = $115.07; Balance = $199,884.93
   Payment 2: Interest = $1,457.49; Principal = $115.91; Balance = $199,769.02
2. $122,600

Unit 15.3 Amortization with a financial calculator

As mentioned, a loan paid off with a series of equal periodic payments is called an **amortized loan**. The word *amortize* comes from the Latin word *amort*, which means to "kill off." With mortgage loans that are structured to pay some of the balance each month, we are slowly "killing off" the loan.

a Using amortization registers of a financial calculator

In Example 1 of Unit 15.2 we calculated interest, principal, and remaining balance on Tara's $160,000 15-year mortgage loan at 7.25% interest.

Financial calculators have special registers to figure interest, principal, and remaining balance. In the next example we will rework Example 1 of Unit 15.2 using these special registers.

amortization registers

Here are a few things to remember about amortizing:
- When interest is calculated on loans, it is figured to the nearest penny (2 decimal places). So, to amortize correctly, we must have our decimal set at 2 places. If we incorrectly set the decimal at, say, 4 places, the calculator rounds the interest portion of each payment to 4 places, in which case our results differ from those obtained in the business world.
- **HP 10BII+**. We can slice out any series of payments by keying in the beginning payment number, pressing INPUT, and keying in the ending payment number followed by AMORT. Then, pressing = gives principal, next = gives interest, next = gives balance. Press = to go through the cycle again. If the next series is for the same number of payments, press AMORT.
- **TI BAII PLUS**. We use the amortization (AMORT) worksheet. We provide beginning (P1) and ending (P2) payment numbers. Then, we scroll down (↓) to get the balance, principal, and interest. If the next series is for the same number of payments, press CPT at the P1 prompt.
- When amortizing with a calculator, be sure to give the calculator time to complete a calculation before pressing the next key; look at your display after pressing each key.

Example 1 Tara got a $160,000 15-year mortgage loan at 7.25% on April 1, 2010. Calculate her monthly payment. Then using the amortization registers of your calculator, find interest, principal, and remaining balance for the first two payments.

Continued on next page…

HP 10BII+			TI BAII PLUS		
▼ C ALL		0.00	2ND CLR TVM		?.??
calculate payment			*calculate payment*		
15 × 12 = N		180.00	15 × 12 = N		N=180.00
7.25 ÷ 12 = I/YR		0.60	7.25 ÷ 12 = I/Y		I/Y=0.60
160,000 PV		160,000.00	160,000 PV		PV=160,000.00
PMT		-1,460.58	CPT PMT		PMT= -1,460.58
amortize (must have decimal at 2)			*amortize (must have decimal at 2)*		
▼ AMORT		1 - 1	2ND AMORT 2ND CLR WORK		P1=1.00
=		-493.91 PRIN	↓		P2=1.00
=		-966.67 INT	↓		BAL=159,506.09
=		159,506.09 BAL	↓		PRN= -493.91
▼ AMORT		2 - 2	↓		INT= -966.67
=		-496.90 PRIN	↓ CPT		P1=2.00
=		-963.68 INT	↓		P2=2.00
=		159,009.19 BAL	↓		BAL=159,009.19
			↓		PRN= -496.90
			↓		INT= -963.68
			2ND QUIT		

Note: Don't clear your calculator; the next example is a continuation.

The results match the answers we got in Example 1 of Unit 15.2.

For federal income tax purposes, interest on many mortgage loans can be claimed as a deduction. Most taxpayers are on a calendar-year basis for income taxes, so they include all deductions *paid* during the calendar year (January through December). As a result, calendar-year interest is important. In the next example, we will calculate Tara's interest for each of the first 3 calendar-years.

Example 2 Refer to Example 1. Calculate interest, principal, and remaining balance for each of the first *3 calendar-years*.

Tara's first payment is due May 1, so she will make 8 payments during the first calendar-year. During the second calendar-year, she will make 12 payments (payments 9 through 20). Calculator keystrokes can be continued from Example 1.

HP 10BII+			TI BAII PLUS		
1 INPUT 8 ▼ AMORT		1 - 8	2ND AMORT 2ND CLR WORK		P1=1.00
=		-4,035.88 PRIN	↓ 8 ENTER		P2=8.00
=		-7,648.76 INT	↓		BAL=155,964.12
=		155,964.12 BAL	↓		PRN= -4,035.88
9 INPUT 20 ▼ AMORT		9 - 20	↓		INT= -7,648.76
=		-6,430.46 PRIN	↓ 9 ENTER		P1=9.00
=		-11,096.50 INT	↓ 20 ENTER		P2=20.00
=		149,533.66 BAL	↓		BAL=149,533.66
▼ AMORT *		21 - 32	↓		PRN= -6,430.46
=		-6,912.45 PRIN	↓		INT= -11,096.50
=		-10,614.51 INT	↓ CPT *		P1=21.00
=		142,621.21 BAL	↓		P2=32.00
			↓		BAL=142,621.21
			↓		PRN= -6,912.45
			↓		INT= -10,614.51
			2ND QUIT		0.00

Note: For the second calendar-year, there were 12 payments. Because the next series of payments (the third calendar-year) also includes 12 payments, we don't have to tell the calculator the beginning and ending payment numbers.

Note: Don't clear your calculator; the next example is a continuation.

Illustration 15-3 Amortization Schedule (selected portions)

		OrigBal $160,000	IntRate 7.25%	Term 15.00	1st PMT May-06			
Pmt #	Date	Yr Rate	P&I Payment	Principal	Interest	Extra Prin	New Balance	Cum. Interest	Yearly Total Int
	Apr-10						$160,000.00		
1	May-10	7.25%	$1,460.58	$493.91	$966.67	$0.00	$159,506.09	$966.67	$966.67
2	Jun-10	7.25%	$1,460.58	$496.90	$963.68	$0.00	$159,009.19	$1,930.35	$1,930.35
3	Jul-10	7.25%	$1,460.58	$499.90	$960.68	$0.00	$158,509.29	$2,891.03	$2,891.03
4	Aug-10	7.25%	$1,460.58	$502.92	$957.66	$0.00	$158,006.37	$3,848.69	$3,848.69
5	Sep-10	7.25%	$1,460.58	$505.96	$954.62	$0.00	$157,500.41	$4,803.31	$4,803.31
6	Oct-10	7.25%	$1,460.58	$509.02	$951.56	$0.00	$156,991.39	$5,754.87	$5,754.87
7	Nov-10	7.25%	$1,460.58	$512.09	$948.49	$0.00	$156,479.30	$6,703.36	$6,703.36
8	Dec-10	7.25%	$1,460.58	$515.18	$945.40	$0.00	$155,964.12	$7,648.76	$7,648.76
9	Jan-11	7.25%	$1,460.58	$518.30	$942.28	$0.00	$155,445.82	$8,591.04	$942.28
10	Feb-11	7.25%	$1,460.58	$521.43	$939.15	$0.00	$154,924.39	$9,530.19	$1,881.43
11	Mar-11	7.25%	$1,460.58	$524.58	$936.00	$0.00	$154,399.81	$10,466.19	$2,817.43
12	Apr-11	7.25%	$1,460.58	$527.75	$932.83	$0.00	$153,872.06	$11,399.02	$3,750.26
13	May-11	7.25%	$1,460.58	$530.94	$929.64	$0.00	$153,341.12	$12,328.66	$4,679.90
14	Jun-11	7.25%	$1,460.58	$534.14	$926.44	$0.00	$152,806.98	$13,255.10	$5,606.34
15	Jul-11	7.25%	$1,460.58	$537.37	$923.21	$0.00	$152,269.61	$14,178.31	$6,529.55
16	Aug-11	7.25%	$1,460.58	$540.62	$919.96	$0.00	$151,728.99	$15,098.27	$7,449.51
17	Sep-11	7.25%	$1,460.58	$543.88	$916.70	$0.00	$151,185.11	$16,014.97	$8,366.21
18	Oct-11	7.25%	$1,460.58	$547.17	$913.41	$0.00	$150,637.94	$16,928.38	$9,279.62
19	Nov-11	7.25%	$1,460.58	$550.48	$910.10	$0.00	$150,087.46	$17,838.48	$10,189.72
20	Dec-11	7.25%	$1,460.58	$553.80	$906.78	$0.00	$149,533.66	$18,745.26	$11,096.50
21	Jan-12	7.25%	$1,460.58	$557.15	$903.43	$0.00	$148,976.51	$19,648.69	$903.43
22	Feb-12	7.25%	$1,460.58	$560.51	$900.07	$0.00	$148,416.00	$20,548.76	$1,803.50
23	Mar-12	7.25%	$1,460.58	$563.90	$896.68	$0.00	$147,852.10	$21,445.44	$2,700.18
24	Apr-12	7.25%	$1,460.58	$567.31	$893.27	$0.00	$147,284.79	$22,338.71	$3,593.45
25	May-12	7.25%	$1,460.58	$570.73	$889.85	$0.00	$146,714.06	$23,228.56	$4,483.30
26	Jun-12	7.25%	$1,460.58	$574.18	$886.40	$0.00	$146,139.88	$24,114.96	$5,369.70
27	Jul-12	7.25%	$1,460.58	$577.65	$882.93	$0.00	$145,562.23	$24,997.89	$6,252.63
28	Aug-12	7.25%	$1,460.58	$581.14	$879.44	$0.00	$144,981.09	$25,877.33	$7,132.07
29	Sep-12	7.25%	$1,460.58	$584.65	$875.93	$0.00	$144,396.44	$26,753.26	$8,008.00
30	Oct-12	7.25%	$1,460.58	$588.18	$872.40	$0.00	$143,808.26	$27,625.66	$8,880.40
31	Nov-12	7.25%	$1,460.58	$591.74	$868.84	$0.00	$143,216.52	$28,494.50	$9,749.24
32	Dec-12	7.25%	$1,460.58	$595.31	$865.27	$0.00	$142,621.21	$29,359.77	$10,614.51
177	Jan-25	7.25%	$1,460.58	$1,425.81	$34.77	$0.00	$4,329.65	$102,852.31	$34.77
178	Feb-25	7.25%	$1,460.58	$1,434.42	$26.16	$0.00	$2,895.23	$102,878.47	$60.93
179	Mar-25	7.25%	$1,460.58	$1,443.09	$17.49	$0.00	$1,452.14	$102,895.96	$78.42
180	Apr-25	7.25%	$1,460.91	$1,452.14	$8.77	$0.00	$0.00	$102,904.73	$87.19

Notice in Example 2 that the interest for year 3 is less than for year 2. This is based on the fact that interest is charged on the unpaid balance and as the balance decreases so does interest. You may wonder why the interest is more for year 2 than for year 1. The answer: there are only 8 payments in year 1.

Portions of a computer-generated amortization schedule for Tara's 15-year mortgage loan appear as Illustration 15-3. Notice that the answers of Examples 1 and 2 match the numbers of the amortization schedule.

> **TIP — are all amortization programs accurate?**
>
> There are lots of amortization programs, including many on the Internet. Most are not accurate; they neglect to round the interest portion of each payment to the nearest penny. Before relying on a certain program, make sure it is accurate; a program is accurate if the results match what you get with your HP 10BII+ or TI BAII PLUS calculator (with the decimal set at 2 places).

In the next example, we will calculate Tara's interest for the entire 15 years.

Example 3 Calculate the total interest Tara will pay on her 15-year loan.

Keystrokes are continued from Example 2. Be sure to give your calculator time to complete a calculation before pressing the next key; look at your display after pressing each key.

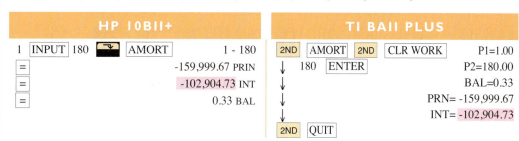

Unit 15.3 Amortization with a financial calculator

The final payment on a mortgage loan is rarely the same as the other payments. That's because when a payment is calculated it is rounded to the nearest penny. Notice in Example 3 the balance, after the 180th payment, is $0.33. Tara's final payment needs to be 33¢ more so that the balance will be exactly zero. The amortization schedule for Tara's loan, shown in Illustration 15-3, shows the final payment is $1,460.91 instead of the regular $1,460.58.

We calculated total interest on Tara's loan in Example 3 of Unit 15.1—in the amount of $102,904.40. In Example 3 that we just did we found a different amount: $102,904.73. Which one is right, you ask? The one we got with our amortization registers, of course; the amount from earlier is based on all 180 payments being $1,460.58. As we now know, the final payment is 33¢ more, so we can modify our earlier estimate:

Total paid: 179 payments of $1,460.58 + 1 payment of $1,460.91 =	$262,904.73
Less principal portion (loan amount)	- 160,000.00
Total interest	$102,904.73

Let's try the U-Try-It exercises to see how much we remember.

U-Try-It (Unit 15.3)

On July 1 you get a $200,000 mortgage loan for 30 years at 8.25% interest.
1. Your first monthly payment is due August 1. Calculate interest, principal, and remaining balance for the first *calendar-year*.
2. Calculate interest for the entire 30 years.

Answers: (If you have a different answer, check the solution in Appendix A.)
1. Interest: $6,866.17; Principal: $646.48; Balance: $199,353.52   2. $340,915.75

Unit 15.4 Repayment variations and loan charges

People get mortgage loans when purchasing a home or other real estate. People also get mortgage loans to **refinance** their current mortgage loan, meaning they get a new loan and use part or all of the proceeds to pay off the old loan. People refinance to get additional cash, to reduce a payment, or to get a lower interest rate.

In this unit, we will explore a few creative ways mortgages can be repaid. We will also explore various loan charges a borrower must pay when getting a mortgage loan.

a Understanding repayment variations

Tara's interest rate (7.25%) and monthly PI payment ($1,460.58) remain fixed for the entire 15 years; her loan is referred to as a **fixed-rate loan**. Let's examine a few other types of mortgage loans.

- With an **adjustable-rate mortgage (ARM)**, the interest rate changes at set intervals (like each year). ARMs often start out with a rate lower than that of fixed-rate loans. The interest rate is tied to an index (such as the 1-year T-bill rate). Payments change to reflect the new rate. Most ARMs provide for a maximum interest rate change each year (*annual cap*) and during the life of the loan (*lifetime cap*). ARMs work well for borrowers when rates drop, but can be costly when rates rise.
- A **balloon payment** pays off a loan with one large payment. A monthly payment is calculated using, say, a 30-year term but the borrower is required to pay the lender whatever balance is still unpaid at the end of, say, 5 years; the required final payment is called a balloon payment.
- With an **interest-only mortgage**, the borrower pays interest only (no principal) for the first few years. If Tara had selected an interest-only mortgage, her payment would be $966.67 ($160,000 × 7.25% × $\frac{1}{12}$). A borrower has an easier time qualifying because qualification is based on a lower payment. But the loan balance stays the same and when the loan stops being *interest-only*, the monthly payment jumps considerably.
- With a **negative amortization loan**, the monthly payment starts out less than what is required to cover interest. This makes qualifying for the loan easier. The disadvantage is that the payment is not enough to cover the interest so the loan balance *increases*. And when the

negative amortization period ends, the monthly payment jumps considerably.
- With a **graduated equity mortgage (GEM)**, monthly payments increase at set intervals. With a 15-year GEM, Tara's monthly payment (PI) may be $1,300 for the first 3 years, $1,400 for the second 3 years, then $1,592.25 for the remaining 9 years.
- With **seller financing**, the seller provides financing to the buyer. For instance, a buyer paying $160,000 for a home could pay $30,000 down and pay the seller the remaining $130,000 at 7% interest with monthly payments. The buyer saves the expense of loan costs. The seller earns the interest that a bank would earn; it may be a greater rate than the seller could earn from a savings plan. The seller should get an adequate down payment and verify the creditworthiness of the buyer.
- With a **biweekly mortgage**, the borrower makes payments every 2 weeks; each payment is half of a monthly PI payment. By paying every 2 weeks the term of the loan is shortened. But the borrower pays more money each year because there are about 26, *not* 24, payments per year: 365.25 days in an average year ÷ 14 days = 26.09 payments per year.
- A **home-equity loan** provides a line of credit; the line of credit is based on a certain loan-to-value (LTV) ratio, such as 80% of the home's value, less the first mortgage. Borrowers are given a checkbook; to borrow money, borrowers simply write a check. Most home-equity loans are ARMs. Some require an interest-only payment, while others require some principal. To attract borrowers, many lenders pay for the appraisal, recording, and title fees.
- A **reverse mortgage** is ideal for older homeowners who need cash for living expenses. With a reverse mortgage, the homeowner borrows against the equity in the home, often getting fixed monthly checks. The loan balance goes up with each check, to a designated maximum amount. The debt is repaid when the homeowner or the homeowner's estate sells the home.

Example 1

You get a 30-year ARM at a rate of 4.75%. The rate is adjusted each year to the 1-year T-bill rate plus 0.5%. The loan has a 1% annual cap and a 5% lifetime cap. One year later the T-bill rate is 5.5%. In 2 years, the T-bill rate is 5.85%. What rate will you pay for the second and third years?

Year 2 5.5% T-bill rate + 0.5% = 6%. However, because of the annual cap, your rate cannot increase more than 1%, so your rate will be: 4.75% + 1% = 5.75%

Year 3 5.85% + 0.5% = 6.35%

You will be charged 4.75% for the first year, 5.75% for the second year, and 6.35% for the third year.

> **TIP** — can rates increase dramatically?
>
> You may wonder if rates really change much. To answer that question, refer back to Illustration 15-1; during the early 1980s, mortgage rates were over 16%. People with ARMs or people who had to get a new loan were forced to pay the increased rate! Be careful, especially with ARMs and balloon payments.

Example 2

In Unit 15.1, Tara got a $160,000 loan at 7.25% with monthly payments of $1,460.58. Assume, instead, Tara got a negative amortization loan, with monthly payments of $900. Calculate interest, principal, and remaining balance for the first payment.

$$I = PRT = \$160{,}000 \times 7.25\% \times \tfrac{1}{12} = \$966.67$$

Principal = $900 paid - $966.67 interest = negative $66.67

(Notice, the $900 monthly payment is not enough to cover interest, so the balance will *increase*.)

Balance = $160,000 + $66.67 = $160,066.67

Tara's balance goes up because the $900 payment is not enough to cover the interest. Tara's interest the next month will be even more because interest is based on the new balance ($160,066.67).

> **TIP** — **just because you can doesn't mean you should**
>
> Home buyers often try to get the largest loan possible. Interest-only loans and negative amortization loans, in particular, make qualifying much easier. As a result, many people get homes they cannot really afford and get in financial trouble later. Don't fall into the trap of buying the most expensive home you "qualify" for; make sure you can really afford it!

Example 3   You apply for a home-equity loan. The lender gets an appraisal on your home, showing a value of $255,000. You have a first mortgage with a current balance of $121,900. Based on a 75% LTV ratio, what is the maximum line of credit you can get?

Maximum total balances allowed: $255,000 × 75% =	$ 191,250
Less current loan balance	− 121,900
Available line of credit	$ 69,350

b Understanding loan charges on a mortgage loan

People getting a mortgage loan may be overwhelmed by the volume of paperwork and loan charges. A description of some of these charges is shown in Illustration 15-4.

> **TIP** — **good faith estimate**
>
> Not all mortgage lenders charge the same fees. When getting a mortgage loan, check around with a few lenders to determine what fees they charge. Be sure to get a **good faith estimate**, which shows the interest rate, as well as the dollar amount of each loan charge.

Illustration 15-4   A Few Common Loan Charges

Basic fees
a. An **origination fee** is usually charged, often $\frac{1}{2}$% to 1% of the loan amount.
b. **Points** are used to buy down the interest rate. For example, a lender may offer a 5.75% rate with no points or a 5.25% rate with $1\frac{1}{2}$ points. Each point represents 1% of the loan amount.
c. Some loans require the borrower to provide **mortgage insurance**, which insures the lender for an agreed-upon sum in the event the loan is not repaid. Mortgage insurance is generally not required if the LTV ratio is 80% or less. Depending on the type of loan, the mortgage insurance may be paid up-front, monthly, or both.
d. Miscellaneous fees paid to the lender, such as a *processing fee, mortgage broker fee,* or *application fee.*

Fees paid to third parties (called pass-through fees)
e. Fees for preparing documents.
f. Credit report fee.
g. Appraisal fee.
h. Fee for title insurance, which insures against losses arising from certain defects in the title to the property. Typically, a seller provides a buyer with a policy of title insurance and the buyer (borrower) provides the lender with a separate policy, called a *lender's policy.*
i. Fee to record documents with the county recorder's office.

Insurance, deposits to an escrow account, and interest adjustment
j. Annual premium for hazard insurance, which provides reimbursement for losses arising from damage to the property such as from fire.
k. If an escrow account is required, the borrower must make an initial deposit into the account so that when the first property tax or insurance payment is due, sufficient funds will be in the account.
l. An interest adjustment may be necessary. If there is less than an exact month before the first monthly payment is due, the borrower will receive an interest *credit;* if there is more than an exact month before the first payment is due, the borrower will be *charged* additional interest.

Example 4

You get a $140,000 mortgage loan. You incur the following loan costs: $\frac{1}{2}$% origination fee, $\frac{3}{4}$ of a point, mortgage insurance of $2,030 (paid up-front), $40 credit report fee, $425 appraisal fee, $640 title insurance fee, $350 document preparation fee, and $70 for recording. What are your total loan costs?

Origination fee: $140,000 × 0.5% =	$ 700
Points: $140,000 × 0.75% =	1,050
Mortgage insurance	2,030
Credit report	40
Appraisal fee	425
Title insurance	640
Document preparation	350
Recording	70
Total loan costs	$5,305

Your loan costs total $5,305. Your net proceeds, after deducting loan costs, are $134,695.

As part of getting her $160,000 15-year loan at a **note rate** of 7.25%, Tara will sign a **promissory note,** which spells out terms of repayment. In many areas, the promissory note is called a **Trust Deed Note,** and the borrower signs an accompanying **Trust Deed**, which spells out what the lender can do (like foreclose) in the event the borrower defaults on the loan.

When we get a mortgage loan, we must pay interest (referred to as *finance charge*) to the lender. Loan costs add to the *finance charges* of the loan, thereby increasing the *real* interest rate. The *real* interest rate is called the **annual percentage rate (APR).**

Tara's lender is required by the **Truth-in-Lending Act** (also known as **Regulation Z**) to inform Tara (1) how much extra money she is paying as a result of borrowing the money (this is the *finance charge*) and (2) the resulting APR. This is done on a form called a **disclosure statement**, similar to the disclosure statement of Illustration 14-1 in Chapter 14. Tara's APR is considerably higher than the 7.25% note rate. That's because of front-end loan costs, which are, in effect, prepaid interest. We calculate Tara's APR (7.93%) in Chapter 17.

Some lenders offer a *no-cost* or *low-cost loan*, which means the lender waives part or all of the loan charges. This may sound like a great deal, but the lender needs to earn a certain yield. They do so by charging a higher interest rate; in Tara's case, the interest rate would likely be in the range of the 7.93% APR. For a borrower who projects paying off a loan in a few years, a no-cost or low-cost loan may be a good choice because even though the borrower pays a higher rate for a few years, he or she saves the up-front loan charges. To protect themselves when this happens, some lenders require the borrower to pay a **prepayment penalty** if the loan is paid off within a specified number of years.

Congratulations on finishing this chapter. Are you ready to do one last set of U-Try-It exercises?

U-Try-It (Unit 15.4)

1. You get a 30-year ARM at an introductory rate of 4.5%. The rate will adjust each year to the 1-year T-bill rate plus 0.75%. The loan has a 1% annual cap. In 1 year, the T-bill rate is 5.28%. In 2 years the T-bill rate is 5.43%. What will your rate be for the second and third years?
2. You get an 8.5% $130,000 interest-only mortgage, in which you will make interest-only payments during the first 5 years. Calculate your interest-only payment.
3. You get a 6.5% $150,000 mortgage loan, with a monthly payment (PI) of $700. Calculate your remaining balance after the first payment.
4. You apply for a home-equity loan. You have a first mortgage, with a balance of $92,200. Based on an appraisal of $175,000 and an 80% LTV ratio, what is your maximum line of credit?
5. You get a $120,000 mortgage loan. You incur the following loan costs: a 1% origination fee, $1\frac{1}{4}$ points; mortgage insurance of $1,980, $60 credit report fee, $450 appraisal fee, $490 title insurance fee, $300 document preparation fee, and $85 for recording. What are your total loan costs?

Answers: (If you have a different answer, check the solution in Appendix A.)
1. Yr 2: 5.5%; Yr 3: 6.18%   **2.** $920.83   **3.** $150,112.50   **4.** $47,800   **5.** $6,065

Chapter in a Nutshell

Objectives	Examples

Unit 15.1 Home ownership and mortgage payments

(a) Understanding home ownership

Marcia quit making her mortgage payments. Property sold at foreclosure sale for $140,000. She owes $122,000 on first mortgage and $28,000 on second mortgage. How much does each lender get?

First lender gets $122,000. Second lender gets the $18,000 remainder; if Marcia's state allows deficiency judgments, the second lender can get a deficiency judgment against Marcia for the unpaid $10,000.

(b) Getting prequalified for a mortgage loan

Travis earns $3,500 a month. Property taxes = $750; insurance = $450. Front-end ratio = 29%. Maximum monthly payment?

Amount available for housing costs: $3,500 × 29%	$1,015
Subtract monthly property taxes and insurance: ($750 + $450) ÷ 12	− 100
Amount available for mortgage payment	$ 915

(c) Figuring total interest

Travis gets a 30-year $150,000 mortgage loan at 5.5% interest, with a monthly payment (PI) of $851.68. Based on making 360 payments of $851.68, how much interest will Travis pay over the 30 years?

360 × $851.68	$306,604.80
Less principal portion (loan amount)	− 150,000.00
Interest portion	$156,604.80

(d) Calculating a payment for an escrow account

Refer back. Annual property taxes are $750 and insurance is $450. PITI?

Principal and interest (PI)	$851.68
TI portion of payment: ($750 + $450) ÷ 12	+100.00
Total monthly payment (PITI)	$951.68

Unit 15.2 Paying off a mortgage loan and increasing equity

(a) Preparing an amortization schedule—breaking down the payment

Refer back. Calculate interest, principal, and remaining balance for first payment.

Interest: $I = PRT = \$150,000 \times 5.5\% \times \frac{1}{12} = \$687.50$
Principal: $851.68 − $687.50 = $164.18
Balance: $150,000 − $164.18 = $149,835.82

(b) Determining equity

Home value = $375,000. First mortgage balance = $124,200. Second mortgage balance = $21,400. Equity?

$375,000 − $124,200 − $21,400 = $229,400

Chapter in a Nutshell (concluded)

Objectives	Examples

Unit 15.3 Amortization with a financial calculator

a Using amortization registers of a financial calculator

Calculate the monthly payment on a 30-year 8.5% $250,000 mortgage loan. Then, use amortization registers to find (a) interest, principal, and remaining balance for first payment, (b) interest for first 8 payments, and (c) interest for all 360 payments.

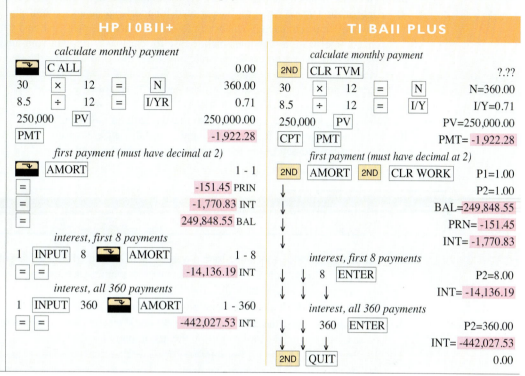

Unit 15.4 Repayment variations and loan charges

a Understanding repayment variations

ARM. Interest rate changes at set intervals (like each year).
Balloon. Pays off with one large payment (in, say, 5 years).
Interest-only mortgage. During early years, payment = interest. Balance stays same.
Negative amortization. Payment starts out less than what interest is; balance increases.
GEM. Payments increase at set intervals.
Seller financing. Seller provides financing to buyer.
Biweekly mortgage. Payments are made every 2 weeks.
Home-equity loan. Can borrow up to approved line of credit.
Reverse mortgage. Ideal for older homeowners who need cash for living expenses.

b Understanding loan charges on a mortgage loan

You get a $160,000 mortgage loan, with $\frac{1}{2}$% origination fee, $\frac{3}{4}$ of a point, $1,250 mortgage insurance, $500 appraisal fee, $440 title insurance fee, and $70 recording. Total loan costs?

($160,000 × 0.5%) + ($160,000 × 0.75%) + $1,250 + $500 + $440 + $70 =
   $800   + $1,200   + $1,250 + $500 + $440 + $70 = **$4,260**

Enrichment Topics

The following Enrichment Topic, which goes a bit beyond what is in the text, is available for this chapter:

ARMS, GEMS, Negative Amortization, and Balloon Payments

If your instructor doesn't cover this topic in class and you would like to dig in deeper on your own, please send a request to *studentsupport@olympuspub.com*. You can also request a set of keystrokes for your particular calculator.

Think

1. Discuss the benefits and disadvantages of owning a home. Does home ownership make sense for you personally and why?
2. What are the advantages and disadvantages of having an escrow account? Would you personally prefer to have an escrow account or not? Give your reasons.
3. Is it easier to calculate interest for a car loan or a mortgage loan? Give reasons for your answer.
4. Amortization schedules are often printed for mortgage loans, so both the lender and borrower know how much of each payment is interest, how much is principal, and what the balance is. Do printed amortization schedules make sense for car loans? Explain your answer.
5. Lenders may offer an introductory rate on ARMs that is lower than the interest rate on fixed-rate loans. Suppose a person needs a mortgage loan and will be transferred to another area in, say, 3 years. Is an APR a good choice for this person? Explain why or why not.
6. What are some disadvantages of ARMs?
7. What can go wrong if a person has to make a balloon payment?
8. For a mortgage loan, the final payment is usually different from the other payments. Explain why and how to determine the amount of the final payment.

Explore

1. Calculate a monthly mortgage loan payment on a 30-year $180,000 loan at 6% using either (1) compound interest formulas (Unit 11.3), or (3) financial calculators (Unit 13.3). Your instructor may ask you to use more than one method.
2. See Problem 1. Calculate the same payment using Excel (see instructions in Appendix E).
3. See Problem 1. Use the online calculator on our Web site (**www.webbertext.com**) to calculate the same payment. Be sure to follow the accompanying guidelines.
4. See Problem 1. Search on the Internet for a site that calculates mortgage loan payments. Use that site to calculate the same payment.
5. Refer to Activities 1-4. Are any of the payments different? If so, which do you suppose are incorrect, and why?
6. Search the Internet for *home buying tips*. Explore several sites and write a report on things to consider before buying a home.
7. Search the Internet for *average home prices, by city* (metropolitan area, or region) on sites such as the National Association of Realtors. Determine which cities or metropolitan areas have the highest-priced homes and which have the lowest-priced homes. Find the average price of a home in your area. Write a report on your findings.
8. Go to **www.myfico.com/crediteducation/calculators/loanrates.aspx**. Find current interest rates for mortgage loans in your area, based on different credit scores. Then, figure out how much more total interest a person with a poor credit score would have to pay over the life of a 30-year $250,000 loan than a person with an excellent credit score.
9. Refer to Examples 1 and 3 of Unit 15.3. Notice that total interest for the 180 months is $102,904.73. Search on the Internet for *amortization schedules*. Find a site that will calculate interest, principal, and remaining balance on a mortgage loan. Using the data of Example 1, compare the amortization program of that site with the results of Example 3. If the results do not match, explain why.
10. See Problem 1. Use an Excel amortization program to compute the interest, principal, and remaining balance on the mortgage loan. Compare the Excel results with the result in Example 3. If the values do not match, determine for which payments the values differ, and why. Be specific.

Apply

1. **Mortgage Loan.** Contact a mortgage loan company and ask for help with this project. Compare features of FHA, conventional, and other types of loans that are available. Answer the following questions about each type of loan:

   A. Based on your income and debt, determine the maximum loan amount you qualify for.
   B. What is the maximum percent of the purchase price that can be borrowed?
   C. What length of loan is available?
   D. Assuming that you have the required cash for a down payment, what interest rates are available? What points are charged for each interest rate?
   E. What loan costs will be incurred? Include a dollar amount for each.
   F. Can the loan be assumed by the buyer (can the buyer take over the payments)? If so, what must a buyer do to assume the loan? If assumed, are you still responsible for the loan in the event the buyer quits making payments?
   G. Is mortgage insurance required? If so, what is the front-end premium, and what are the monthly premiums? Can mortgage insurance be discontinued after the loan is paid down to a certain amount? Will a partial refund be made if the loan is paid off early?
   H. Is an escrow account required? If so, does it earn interest?
   I. What extra fees, if any, must be paid if the loan is paid off early?
   J. When are late fees imposed? How are late fees calculated?

   Submit your findings. Include a *good faith estimate*, the name of the mortgage loan company, and the name of the loan officer.

2. **Amortization Schedule.** Using an Excel spreadsheet, create an amortization schedule that matches Illustration 15-2; include payments 33 through 176 (which are omitted in Illustration 15-2). *Tip:* When calculating interest for each payment, be sure to use the "Round" function so that interest will be calculated (not just displayed) to the nearest penny. Here is an example of the "Round" function, assuming that the mortgage balance is in col G and the interest rate is in col C: =ROUND((G1*C2/12),2)

Chapter Review Problems

Use 2 decimal places for all answers.

Unit 15.1 Home ownership and mortgage payments

1. Your personal residence is considered personal property rather than real estate because you hold it for personal use. (T or F)

2. In the event a foreclosure sale does not provide a lender with all the money due, the lender can, in some states, collect the deficiency from the borrower. (T or F)

3. Nash Quinn stops making his mortgage payments and his home sells at a foreclosure sale for $140,000. Nash owes $123,200 on his first mortgage (including past-due interest, attorney fees, and court costs) and owes $24,400 on a second mortgage. How will the $140,000 be distributed?

4. Refer to Problem 3. How will the money be distributed if the home sells for $155,000 at the foreclosure sale?

5. Mortgage interest rates have been the same for the last 40 years (T or F)

6. Before shopping for a home, Todd and Jenn decide to get prequalified for a loan. The lender has qualifying ratios of 29/41. Todd earns $3,600 a month and Jenn earns $1,300 a month. Based on the price of the home they hope to find, the lender estimates property taxes at $1,700 a year and insurance at $575. Todd's car payment is $295; Jenn's car is paid off. They each have a minimum credit card payment of $20. What is the maximum monthly payment they qualify for?

For Problems 7-10, assume you get a 30-year $150,000 mortgage loan at 7.75% interest, with monthly payments (PI) of $1,074.62.

7. Based on making 360 payments of $1,074.62, how much interest will you pay over the 30 years?

8. The lender requires an escrow account. Property taxes are currently $1,725 per year and insurance is $575. What additional amount is required each month for taxes and insurance (TI)?

9. What is your total monthly payment (PITI)?

10. Is your payment subject to change? If so, why?

Unit 15.2 Paying off a mortgage loan and increasing equity

11. Refer to Problems 7-10. Calculate interest, principal, and remaining balance for the first two monthly payments.

12. The final payment of a mortgage loan is usually different from the other payments. (T or F)

13. Amortization schedules are often printed for mortgage loans, so both the lender and borrower know the interest portion of each payment, the principal portion, and the unpaid balance. It is also a good idea to get a printed amortization schedule for a car loan. (T or F)

14. You bought a home 6 years ago for $180,000 and got a $160,000 mortgage loan. You spent $22,000 on improvements. Your mortgage balance is currently $147,300. Your home is now worth $315,000. Calculate your equity.

Unit 15.3 Amortization with a financial calculator

15. Assume you get a 30-year $120,000 mortgage loan at 6% interest. Use your financial calculator to determine (a) your monthly payment; (b) interest, principal, and remaining balance for the first monthly payment; (c) interest for the first 8 payments; (d) balance after payment 102; (e) interest for the entire 30-year term; and (f) exact amount of the final payment.

16. Assume you buy a 6-unit apartment building for $550,000 and give the seller $200,000 down. The seller finances the remaining $350,000 over 25 years at 10.25% interest. Use your financial calculator to determine your monthly payment. Then, assuming your first payment is due August 1 of this year, find interest, principal, and remaining balance for each of the first 3 calendar-years.

For Problems 17-24, assume you get a 30-year $100,000 mortgage loan at 9% interest.

17. Calculate the monthly payment (PI).

18. Based on making 360 payments of $804.62, what is the total interest over the 30 years?

19. Use your amortization registers to calculate (a) interest for the entire 30 years and (b) balance after 360 payments of $804.62.

20. Compare the total interest of Problem 18 with the total interest of Problem 19. If there is a difference, explain which answer is correct, and why.

21. After making payments for 15 years, what is your balance?

22. After 15 years, you have made half of the payments. Why isn't the loan half repaid?

23. How many months will be left on the loan when the balance is half repaid?

24. How many years will it take for the loan to be half repaid?

Unit 15.4 Repayment variations and loan charges

25. You get a 30-year ARM at a rate of 5.5%. The rate is adjusted each year to the 1-year T-bill rate plus 0.50%. The loan has a 1% annual cap. One year later the T-bill rate is 6.10%. What rate will you pay the second year?

26. Refer to Problem 25. What happens to your monthly payment in year 2?

27. You get an interest-only mortgage loan of $340,000 at 9.75%. For the first 3 years, your monthly payments are interest-only. What is your monthly payment for those 3 years?

28. Refer to Problem 27. What is the mortgage balance after making 22 monthly payments?

29. You get a $225,000 mortgage loan at 7% interest. Your monthly payment (PI) is $1,100. Calculate the balance after the first monthly payment.

30. You apply for a home-equity loan. You have a first mortgage, with a current balance of $172,200. Based on an appraisal of $265,000 and a 75% LTV, what is the maximum line of credit you can get?

31. Points are used to buy down the interest rate. (T or F)

32. You get a $700,000 mortgage loan with $1\frac{1}{4}$ points. What dollar amount do you pay for points?

33. Calculate total loan costs on a $320,000 loan with a $\frac{1}{2}$% origination fee, $\frac{3}{4}$ of a point, $750 processing fee, $70 credit report fee, $700 appraisal fee, $970 title insurance fee, $400 document preparation fee, $200 closing fee, and $95 for recording.

34. The APR is greater than the note rate if the borrower pays front-end loan costs. (T or F)

Challenge problems

For Problems 35-43, assume Mort and Carla Palmer are interested in buying a home. Determine the maximum monthly mortgage payment they qualify for. Mort earns $1,250 a month and Carla earns $1,100 a month. Carla receives child support of $760 a month from an ex-husband. Mort gets $120 annual interest from some bonds he owns. Based on the price range they are thinking about, annual property taxes are estimated at $975 and insurance at $490.

35. Based on a front-end ratio of 30%, what is the maximum mortgage payment they qualify for?

36. Mort has a car payment of $110 and a credit card payment of $30. Carla's car is paid off, but she has a credit card payment of $10. They have a furniture loan with a monthly payment of $45. Based on a back-end ratio of 41%, what is the maximum mortgage payment they qualify for?

37. What is their maximum monthly mortgage payment?

38. They buy a home for $135,000 and get a 40-year $115,000 mortgage loan at 7% interest, with a monthly payment (PI) of $714.65. The lender requires an escrow account. Property taxes on the home they ended up buying are $948 per year and insurance is $520 a year. Calculate their total (PITI) payment.

39. Mort and Carla sign the loan documents on April 27 and are required to deposit $270 into the escrow account at that time. Their first payment is due June 1. The lender pays property taxes of $948 from their escrow account on November 15. Calculate the escrow balance at the end of the calendar year.

40. Calculate their mortgage balance after the first monthly payment.

41. Two years after buying the home, Mort and Carla borrow $22,000 on a home-equity loan to upgrade the kitchen and bathrooms. Four years after buying the home, their first mortgage is paid down to $112,581 (rounded), and their home-equity loan has a balance of $18,300. They get an appraisal, showing the home is worth $142,000. What is their equity in the home?

42. Assume that a year later, Mort loses his job and they get behind on their mortgage payments. The balance on the first mortgage (including court costs and attorney fees) is $116,100 and the balance on the second mortgage (home-equity loan) is $20,000. The home is sold at a foreclosure sale for $134,500. Who gets the money from the sale?

43. Assume, instead, that Mort and Carla weather the storm and bring their payments current. During the next several years, home values increase dramatically, and they sell their home for $180,000. They owe $108,434 on the first mortgage and $4,500 on the second. They pay a 6% real estate commission and other selling expenses of $2,200. What amount will they receive from the sale?

Practice Test

1. Enrique and Rosie are getting prequalified for a VA mortgage loan. Enrique earns $4,550 a month and Rosie earns $5,200. Based on the price home they hope to buy, the lender estimates property taxes at $2,780 a year and insurance at $750. Enrique has a car payment of $391; Rosie's is $275. They have a furniture loan with a monthly payment of $318, and Enrique pays child support to his ex-wife of $1,350 a month. They each have a minimum credit card payment of $25. Based on a back-end ratio of 41%, what is the maximum monthly payment they qualify for?

2. You get a $105,000 mortgage loan at 6.5% with a monthly payment (PI) of $663.67. What is your balance after your first payment?

3. You get a mortgage loan with a monthly payment (PI) of $872.55. The lender requires an escrow account. Property taxes are $1,325 per year and insurance is $710 per year. Calculate your total monthly payment (PITI).

4. You get a 20-year mortgage loan of $270,000 at 4.75% interest. You make your first payment on April 1. Use your financial calculator to calculate the *calendar-year* interest for Year 2.

5. You get a 30-year ARM at a rate of 5.5%. The rate is adjusted each year to the 1-year T-bill rate plus $\frac{1}{2}$%. The loan has a 1% annual cap. One year later the T-bill rate is 5%. In 2 years the T-bill rate is 6.25%. What is your interest rate for the third year?

6. You apply for a home-equity loan. Your first mortgage has a current balance of $103,200. Based on an appraisal of $174,500 and an 80% LTV ratio, what is the maximum line of credit you can get?

7. You get a $170,000 mortgage loan and incur the following loan costs: $\frac{1}{2}$% origination fee, $\frac{7}{8}$ of a point, $70 credit report fee, $475 appraisal fee, $630 title insurance fee, $400 processing fee, $125 closing fee, and $70 for recording. What are your total loan costs?

FUN CORNER

15-Year-Old Stock Advisor
In March 1986, 15-year-old Jennifer Sanchez, a self-proclaimed "computer geek" invested her $750 life savings into a new stock—Microsoft. Back then, Microsoft was a small firm with an uncertain future. Jennifer even talked her parents into investing. Are they glad they did! By early 2000, Jennifer's $750 turned into $450,000 plus a new Porsche 911 convertible. Her parent's $10,000 investment had grown to $7.1 million.

Quotable Quip
An investment in knowledge always pays the highest dividends.
— Author unknown

Observation
Why is the person who invests all your money called a *broker*?

Bear? Bull?
You may wonder why the terms "bear" and "bull" are used. Here's why. A bear market refers to a downward market and comes from the fact that bears swipe downward when they attack. A bull market refers to rising prices and comes from the fact that bulls fling their horns upward when they attack.

Oldest Stock Exchange
The Stock Exchange in Amsterdam, Netherlands, was founded in the Oude Zijds Kapel in 1602, for dealings in printed shares of the United East Indian Company of the Netherlands.

The King Of Rock 'n' Roll
When he graduated from high school, his goal was to become a truck driver like his father, but all that changed. It didn't take long for Elvis Presley to become a rock'n'roll star. He made millions of dollars. But, in his early forties, he faced financial ruin. Here's why. Elvis used his father who had served a prison sentence for passing bad checks, as his business advisor. He didn't take advantage of tax shelters, and he gave away cash and expensive gifts on impulse.

Elvis made lots of money, but he spent even more. So, what's the point? It's always easier to spend than to save. Life will be easier if we put some planning in our investment goals.

"Investment opportunities are everywhere, Jenkins. Let's buy the tide when it's low and sell when it's high."

Stocks, Bonds, and Mutual Funds

Most people earn more during the middle part of their life. Later in life, their earnings decrease. Investing means limiting consumption in the present (when earning power is high) to provide for the future (when earning power decreases). In this chapter we will examine a few traditional investments: stocks, bonds, and mutual funds. Maybe the stuff in this chapter will help us get rich for later in life.

Unit Objectives

Unit 16.1 Stocks
- a. Calculating dividends
- b. Understanding how to buy and sell stock
- c. Calculating a price–earnings ratio

Unit 16.2 Bonds
- a. Understanding how bonds work
- b. Understanding bond quotations

Unit 16.3 Mutual funds
- a. Calculating net asset value
- b. Understanding mutual fund quotations

Unit 16.1 Stocks

The three main forms of business ownership are sole proprietorship, partnership, and corporation. When a corporation is organized, it raises money by selling **corporate stock** to the public. The buyers of the stock (called **stockholders**) become owners of the corporation.

a Calculating dividends

Corporations distribute their profits in the form of **dividends**. Corporations generally distribute between 25% and 75% of their earnings, keeping the remainder for future development and contingencies. To protect creditors, corporations cannot distribute more than their earnings; the undistributed portion of accumulated earnings is called **retained earnings** on the corporation's balance sheet.

In most cases corporations issue only **common stock**. In some cases, corporations also issue **preferred stock**. While owners of common stock and owners of preferred stock both own part of the company, their rights and claims toward earnings differ.

- Owners of common stock generally can vote at the annual stockholder's meeting; preferred stockholders generally have no vote.
- Dividends are not guaranteed. However, preferred stockholders receive dividends (often for fixed amounts) before any dividends are paid to common stockholders. Some preferred stock is *cumulative*, which means that dividends not paid in the past are paid from future profits before dividends are paid to common stockholders.
- If a corporation goes out of business, creditors are paid first, preferred stockholders next, and finally common stockholders.

Some investors consider preferred stock a safer investment than common stock because preferred stockholders have prior claim on dividends and assets. Other investors favor common stock because of the potential to share a larger portion of the company's profits.

Example 1 XYZ Corporation has 1,250,000 shares of common stock and 300,000 shares of cumulative preferred stock. The annual dividend on the preferred stock is $2 per share. No dividends were paid last year. This year the board of directors decided to distribute $4,000,000 in dividends. You own 100 shares of XYZ common stock. Determine the amount of your annual dividend.

Total dividends			$4,000,000
Dividends for preferred stock:			
for last year: 300,000 shares × $2	$600,000	}	– 1,200,000
for this year: 300,000 shares × $2	+600,000		
Dividends available to common stockholders			$2,800,000

Dividends per share of common stock: $2,800,000 ÷ 1,250,000 shares = $2.24
Your dividend: 100 shares × $2.24 per share = **$224.00**

b Understanding how to buy and sell stock

A **stock exchange** is a place where **stockbrokerage firms** meet to buy and sell stocks and other securities for their investors. The largest stock exchange in the world is the **New York Stock Exchange** (NYSE), located on Wall Street in New York City. Because individual investors do not belong to a stock exchange, they cannot buy and sell stock directly at the stock exchange. Instead, investors buy or sell stock through a stockbroker who has a membership (called a *seat*) on the stock exchange. Often stockbrokerage firms buy large quantities of stock for their own investment portfolio and resell to investors. In other cases, stockbrokerage firms act only as an agent, handling a transaction on behalf of a buyer and seller.

This is one of the trading "floors" of the New York Stock Exchange—the AMEX floor—located a few blocks from Wall Street in New York City.

You may wonder how the price of a stock is determined. The price is simply a function of demand—it is based on how much buyers are willing to pay for it. If the demand for a particular stock increases, the price of the stock will increase; if the demand decreases, the price of the stock will decrease.

Often, many stock prices rise or fall together, depending on how investors feel about the overall economy and stock market. When investors are optimistic, stock prices rise; this is referred to as a **bull market**. When investors are pessimistic, stock prices fall; this is referred to as a **bear market**. Several stock indexes monitor general fluctuations in the stock market. The most well-known index is the **Dow Jones Industrial Average** (DJIA), which monitors the price changes of 30 stocks.

---

the 30 stocks in the Dow Jones Industrial Average (as of October 20, 2015)

American Express	General Electric	Minnesota Mining & Mfg (3M)
Apple	Goldman Sachs	Nike
Boeing	Home Depot	Pfizer
Caterpillar	IBM	Procter & Gamble
Chevron	Intel	Travelers
Cisco Systems	Johnson & Johnson	United Health Group
Coca-Cola	JP Morgan Chase & Co.	United Technologies
Disney	McDonald's	Verizon
Dupont	Merck & Co.	Visa
ExxonMobil	Microsoft	Walmart

The "Dow" was originated by Charles Henry Dow in 1884. Eleven stocks were included in the first index. In 1928, the DJIA expanded to 30 stocks. The stocks that are included periodically change to reflect mergers and companies going out of business. Because of mergers and stock splits, the index is adjusted to maintain historical continuity (it is *not* found by adding the price per share of the 30 stocks). On September 16, 2015, for example, the Dow closed at 16,743.52, up 142.24 from the previous day.

Stock prices are quoted in the financial section of many newspapers and on the Internet. Prices are quoted in dollars and cents. The format of stock quotes varies, depending on the source. A stock quote for McDonald's is shown in Illustration 16-1. Pay special attention to the explanation of column headings, found under the stock quote.

Illustration 16-1   Stock quote from the NYSE—McDonald's

| 52 weeks | | Stock | Sym | Div | Yld% | PE Ratio | Vol 100s | Close | Net Chg |
Hi	Lo								
98.53	72.14	McDon	MCD	2.80	2.84	19	58000	98.48	0.45

52-week Hi: The highest price during the last 52 weeks (excluding the current day).
52-week Lo: The lowest price during the last 52 weeks.
Stock: The name of the stock (abbreviated, if necessary).
Sym: This is the symbol (used to identify the stock on the Internet, price boards, etc.).
Div: Dividends per share during the last 12 months.
Yld %: This is the dividend rate (not a rate of return), found by dividing the amount in the "Div" column by the amount in the "Close" column.
PE Ratio: This is the price–earnings ratio (to be studied in detail later). If no number is shown, it is generally because the company lost money.
Vol 100s: This is the number of shares traded this day (in hundreds; so multiply by 100).
Close: This is the last price of the day.
Net Chg: This is the change in price from the previous day (the closing price today minus the closing price of the preceding day).

Example 2 Refer to Illustration 16-1. Answer the following questions about McDonald's stock.
a. What is the highest price during the last 52 weeks?
b. What is the lowest price during the last 52 weeks?
c. How many shares traded this day?
d. What is the closing price?
e. How did the price change from the preceding day?
f. If you have owned 200 shares, what are the total dividends you have received over the last 12 months?
g. Verify the Yld%.

---

a. $98.53   b. $72.14   c. 5,800,000 shares (58,000 × 100 = 5,800,000)
d. $98.48   e. The price increased $0.45 (45¢)
f. 200 shares × $2.80 = $560
g. 2.80 (amount in "Div" column) ÷ 98.48 (amount from "Close" column) = 0.0284 (with decimal set at 4 places) ≈ 2.84%

You may wonder from Example 2(g), why an investor would settle for yearly dividends that are only 2.84% of the price; after all, an investor could probably earn a higher rate on other investments. Here is the reason. Investors are hoping the price of the stock will go up, thereby providing a much better *total* return.

Stockbrokers charge a fee to a buyer and seller for handling a transaction; the fee, or commission, varies depending on the services the stockbroker provides. Incidental fees may be charged, such as transfer taxes and Securities and Exchange Commission (SEC) fees.

> **TIP**   **on-line trading and day-trading**
>
> Some investors prefer going through a broker. Others, because of lower fees, do transactions *on-line*. Many on-line trades are done as a long-term investment, but some are done by *day-traders*. A day-trader is a person who rides the momentum of a stock and gets out quickly (maybe the same day) before it loses value. Day-trading is extremely risky, especially for a beginning investor!

>   **brokerage fees**
>
> **When buying:** Brokerage fees *increase* the cost of the stock.
> **When selling:** Brokerage fees *decrease* the proceeds from the sale.

Example 3 You purchase 300 shares of stock at a price of 22.75 and incur brokerage fees totaling $75. What is your total cost?

Price of stock: 300 shares × $22.75	$6,825
Brokerage fees	+ 75
Total cost	$6,900

Example 4 Refer to Example 3. Five years later you sell the stock at a price of 34.63 and incur brokerage fees totaling $85. Calculate your net proceeds.

Price of stock: 300 shares × $34.63	$10,389
Brokerage fees	− 85
Net proceeds	$10,304

C Calculating a price–earnings ratio

Stock advisory reports—such as Standard & Poor's and Moody's—provide information about specific corporations that can help an investor evaluate a potential stock investment. These reports are available at stockbrokerage firms, most public libraries, and on the Internet.

Investors often rely on numerical indicators when considering stock investments. One popular indicator, the **price–earnings ratio** (abbreviated **PE ratio**) is the price per share divided by annual **earnings per share**. *Earnings per share* is not included in some stock quotes but is reported by the company (it is found by dividing the company's profit for the last four quarters by the number of shares owned by stockholders).

= price–earnings ratio

$$\text{PE ratio} = \frac{\text{Price per share}}{\text{Annual earnings per share}}$$

Example 5

McDonald's annual earnings per share is reported at $5.11 (not given in stock quotes). Confirm the PE ratio of 19 found in Illustration 16-1.

$$\text{PE} = \frac{P}{E} = \frac{\$98.48}{\$5.11} \approx 19.27 \approx 19$$

Let's make sure we understand what *earnings per share* and *PE ratio* mean. If we owned stock in McDonald's, our share of earnings would be $5.11 for each share of stock we owned. Someone willing to pay $98.48 for a share of stock would be paying about $19 for each $1 of annual earnings (assuming that annual earnings remain constant); *for each $19 spent, they would get $1 back in earnings*. Naturally, investors would rather spend less (a low PE ratio) to get $1 back. The PE ratio varies greatly between stocks, often ranging from about 7 to 20. A low PE ratio may indicate a good buy other investors are not aware of (referred to as a "sleeper"), or it may indicate that investors think the company's future earnings will decline. A high PE ratio may indicate that the price of the stock is too high, or it may indicate that investors think the company's future earnings will increase.

The bottom line is, of course, what an investor's *actual* return turns out to be. Investors try to select stocks that have a better future than is indicated by the price. They hope that dividends will be large and that the stock can be sold for much more than its cost.

TIP — **don't be a hog**

If a stock price goes up dramatically, don't be afraid to sell and take your profit. Lots of people make the mistake of being a "hog," waiting for the value to go up even more. Often, after a dramatic increase, stock prices go down.

Are you up to doing the U-Try-It exercises?

1. A company has issued 500,000 shares of common stock and 100,000 shares of cumulative preferred stock. The annual dividend of the preferred stock is 75¢ per share. No dividends were distributed last year. $1,000,000 is available for dividends this year. You own 50 shares of common stock. What is your dividend?

2. Observe the following stock quote. What are **(a)** the highest price during the last 52 weeks, **(b)** the lowest price during the last 52 weeks, **(c)** the last price this day, and **(d)** the change in price this day. Confirm **(e)** the Yld% and **(f)** the PE Ratio, assuming annual earnings per share of $3.60.

52 weeks		Div	Yld%	PE Ratio	Vol 100s	Close	Net Chg
Hi	Lo						
63.94	39.25	.80	1.47	15	19781	54.56	-1.50

3. You buy 100 shares of the stock in Problem 2 at the "closing" price and incur brokerage fees of $150. What is your total cost?

Answers: (If you have a different answer, check the solution in Appendix A.)
1. $85   **2a.** $63.94   **2b.** $39.25   **2c.** $54.56   **2d.** -$1.50   **2e.** 1.47%   **2f.** 15   **3.** $5,606

Unit 16.2 Bonds

A person investing in corporate stock becomes an *owner* of the corporation. That is not the case with bonds. A person investing in corporate bonds is *lending* money to the corporation. Some people hesitate to invest in stock because of the volatility of the stock market. Many of these people invest in bonds.

Bonds are issued by corporations, the U.S. government, and local governments. Local governments issue bonds to pay for things like airports, schools, parks, and libraries.

A **bond** is a written promise to repay the owner of the bond (**bondholder**) a specified amount (called the **face value, par value,** or **maturity value**) at a future date (**maturity date**). Bondholders also earn interest, generally paid semiannually or annually. The interest rate is referred to as the **coupon rate** (named for *coupons* of some bonds that are exchanged for an interest check.) Some bonds, referred to as **zero-coupon bonds**, pay no periodic interest; instead, the bondholder buys the bond at a discount and receives the face value at maturity. In effect, interest is received in one lump-sum when the bond matures.

a Understanding how bonds work

Corporations, the U.S. government, and local governmental agencies often need large sums of money. They often raise the money by selling bonds to the public. Here is a brief description of each.

- **Corporate bonds** are often in denominations of $1,000 and generally pay interest semiannually or annually. Interest received from corporate bonds is taxable, just like interest from a savings account. For zero-coupon bonds, the interest is received in one lump-sum when the bond matures, but the owner must report a prorated portion of the interest each year rather than report all of the interest when the bond matures.
- U.S. government bonds, called **U.S. securities**, have different names depending on the maturity date. *Treasury bills* (*T-bills*) mature in 1 year or less and pay no interest until maturity (they are zero-coupon bonds). *Treasury notes* mature between 2 and 10 years and pay interest semiannually. *Treasury bonds* mature in 30 years and pay interest semiannually. *Savings bonds* are purchased at half of the face value. Interest from U.S. securities is exempt on many state income tax returns.
- States, counties, cities, and other municipal agencies sell bonds (called **municipal bonds**) to the public. Most municipal bonds have at least a 20-year maturity, pay periodic interest, and are often sold in denominations of $5,000. Interest from many municipal bonds is tax-exempt for federal income tax purposes and is tax-exempt on some state income tax returns.

> **TIP**   **aren't all municipal bonds tax-exempt?**
>
> Don't be misled into believing that interest from all municipal bonds is tax-exempt. Before buying a municipal bond, determine whether the bond is tax-exempt from federal and state income tax.

Example 1   You buy a 6% $1,000 corporate bond that matures in 20 years. Interest is paid semiannually. How much money will you receive and when?

The bond pays an annual rate of 6%. But interest is paid every 6 months, so you will receive an *interest rate per period* of 3% (6% ÷ 2 periods per year = 3%). This means you will get a check each 6 months for $30 ($1,000 face value × 3% = $30). In 20 years, you will receive $1,030 (your 40th interest check of $30 plus the $1,000 face value).

346   Chapter 16   Stocks, Bonds, and Mutual Funds

Some bonds are safer than others. Some corporations or governmental agencies go broke, leaving bondholders with worthless bonds. Bonds that have minimal safety are referred to as **junk bonds**. To help investors evaluate the quality of a bond, companies such as Moody's and Standard & Poor's provide **bond reports**. Ratings generally range from AAA (pronounced "triple A"), the safest, to D, the least safe. U.S. securities are not rated, because for all practical purposes they are considered risk-free.

The interest rate for bonds is a function of supply and demand. When bonds are originally issued and when they are resold, the rate of return must be high enough to attract investors. If an investor is able to get some income tax advantages from a bond, the investor is willing to accept a lesser rate (as with tax-exempt municipal bonds). Another factor is risk; bonds with a higher degree of risk must provide a higher rate to attract investors.

> **TIP**   100% × 6% > 0% × 18%
>
> Some bond investors sacrifice safety in favor of a high rate. Others sacrifice a high rate in favor of safety. *Remember, 100% of a small return is more than 0% of a large return.*

Bond prices plummet in weeklong selling frenzy

NEW YORK (UPI)—Bond prices plummeted and yields surged in a weeklong selling frenzy ignited by signs that a real economic rebound is finally beginning to emerge.

The market's bellwether security, the 30-year Treasury, which climbed two full points last week, fell 1-16/32 points. The issue's yield, which moves in the opposite direction of its price, climbed to 6.21 percent—its highest level since November.

Bond investors do not like news of economic strength because they worry that a strong economy will lead to higher inflation and interest rates, trends that reduce the value of bonds.

Many beginning investors think that a $1,000 bond is always worth $1,000. While a $1,000 bond is worth $1,000 at maturity, the same bond may be worth more or less than $1,000 *prior* to maturity, depending on the prevailing rate for similar bonds. For example, if you own a bond paying 6% and new bonds are paying 8%, investors will buy the 8% bond instead of yours; to attract a buyer you will have to sell it for less than $1,000 (at a **discount**) so that the buyer can earn 8%. On the other hand, if your bond pays 10%, an investor would be willing to pay you more (a **premium**) for your bond. If your bond pays 8%, you could sell your bond at face value (called **par**). *Bond values decline when prevailing interest rates increase; bond values increase when prevailing interest rates decline,* as pointed out in the newspaper article on the left.

We calculate bond values in Unit 10.3 (using formulas) and Unit 12.4 (using financial calculators).

b Understanding bond quotations

A bond quote for an IBM bond is shown in Illustration 16-2. Pay special attention to the footnotes, which explain the headings.

In the bond quote, the closing price of 105.348 indicates this bond is selling for 105.348% of its face value.

Illustration 16-2   Bond Quote—an IBM bond

Bond	Cur Yld	Vol	Close	Net Chg
IBM 6½ 28	6.17	10	105.348	+ 0.314

Bond: This is the abbreviated name, the coupon rate, and the year of maturity.
Cur Yld: "Cur Yld" stands for current yield, found by dividing the coupon rate by the value in the "Close" column.
Vol: This is the number of bonds that were sold for the day. Unlike stocks, this is *not* stated in 100s.
Close: This is the percent of face value for the last bond sold that day.
Net Chg: This is the difference (as a percent of face value) between the last price paid today and the previous day.

Example 2 Refer to Illustration 16-2. Answer the following questions about the IBM bond.
  a. What is the coupon rate?
  b. In what year does the bond mature?
  c. How many of these bonds were sold on this day?
  d. Assuming a $1,000 face value, what was the price for the last bond traded?
  e. How did the price change from the preceding day?
  f. Confirm the "Cur Yld."

---

  a. The "6½" in the bond column is the coupon rate: 6½% or **6.5%**
  b. The "28" in the bond column signifies the year: the bond matures in the year **2028**
  c. **10 bonds**
  d. $1,000 × 105.348% = **$1,053.48**
  e. The price increased 0.314%: $1,000 × 0.314% = **$3.14 increase**
  f. Cur Yld = $\dfrac{\text{Coupon rate}}{\text{Close column value}}$ = $\dfrac{6.5}{105.348}$ ≈ .0617 ≈ **6.17%**

In Example 2, the IBM bond is selling for a *premium* (105.348% of face value). Apparently, this bond is in demand because similar newly-issued bonds have a *lower* interest rate than this bond.

Quotes for municipal bonds are like those of corporate bonds, but U.S. securities are different. Prices for U.S. Treasury notes and bonds are quoted in 32nds. For example, a quote of 106:14 means that the price is 106¹⁴/₃₂% of face value. Before we proceed, let's make sure we remember how to convert a fraction to a decimal number. As you may recall, a fraction like 14/32 means 14 ÷ 32, which is .4375 (try it with your calculator, if you'd like). So, the bond price is 106.4375% of face value. Let's try another fraction: 5/32 means 5 ÷ 32, or .15625.

Example 3 You buy four $5,000 U.S. Treasury notes at a price of 106:14. What is the total price?

The decimal equivalent of 14/32 is .4375 (14 ÷ 32 = .4375), so:

Cost per bond: $5,000 × 106¹⁴/₃₂% = $5,000 × 106.4375% =	$5,321.875
Number of bonds	× 4
Total price	**$21,287.50**

Investors generally buy and sell corporate and municipal bonds through stockbrokers. U.S. securities can be purchased through stockbrokers and banks and directly from the Federal Reserve. As with buying or selling stock, brokerage fees may be incurred.

---

brokerage fees

When buying: Brokerage fees *increase* the cost of the bond. Generally, stockbroker's commissions are built into the purchase price of bonds rather than being shown separately.
When selling: Brokerage fees *decrease* the proceeds from the sale.

That's it for bonds. Before we do the U-Try-It questions, let's review some differences between stocks and bonds.

Stocks	Bonds
Stockholders own part of a corporation.	Bondholders lend money to the corporation or governmental agency.
Some stockholders receive dividends; dividends depend on profits.	Most bondholders receive interest checks (not dependent on profits, just solvency).
Selling price is unknown at the time of the investment; stock values can increase or decrease dramatically.	Bondholders know the maturity value at the time of the investment.

U-Try-It (Unit 16.2)

For questions 1-5, assume that you buy one of the $1,000 bonds from the following bond quote.

Bond	Cur Yld	Vol	Close	Net Chg
IBM $6^{1}/_{2}$ 28	5.91	60	110	+ $1^{3}/_{4}$

1. What is the price you will pay for one of these bonds if you pay the closing price?
2. In what year does the bond mature?
3. How many of these bonds were sold on this day?
4. Assuming interest is paid annually, how much interest will you receive each year?
5. Based on the price you paid for the bond, is the prevailing rate (a) less than 6.5%, (b) exactly 6.5%, or (c) greater than 6.5%?
6. You buy two $5,000 U.S. Treasury notes at a price of 97:18. What is the total price?

Answers: (If you have a different answer, check the solution in Appendix A.)
1. $1,100   2. 2028   3. 60 bonds   4. $65   5. (a) less than 6.5%   6. $9,756.25

Unit 16.3 Mutual funds

A **mutual fund** is a company that pools money from investors (shareholders) and invests in a diversified portfolio of securities (stocks, bonds, etc.). According to a recent report, there are an estimated 95 million Americans who own mutual fund shares; there are over 8,200 different funds, controlling over $6 trillion of assets. Some mutual funds specialize in a particular type of investment. For example, one mutual fund may invest only in U.S. government bonds, another only in well-proven stocks, and another only in tax-exempt municipal bonds. Other mutual funds invest in a variety of investments.

One reason people invest in mutual funds is to spread their risk; when we invest in a mutual fund, we own a small portion of several different things, rather than a larger portion of one thing. Spreading risk is referred to as **diversification**. Another reason people choose mutual funds is that they don't have to worry about specific investment decisions; the mutual fund company makes the decisions.

a Calculating net asset value

When we invest in a mutual fund, we receive shares. The price of a share, called the **net asset value (NAV)**, is found by dividing the fund's *net assets* (assets minus liabilities) by the number of shares. The asset values are calculated at the end of each business day by adding the "closing" value of all the individual securities in the fund.

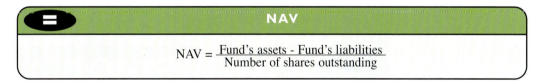

$$\text{NAV} = \frac{\text{Fund's assets - Fund's liabilities}}{\text{Number of shares outstanding}}$$

Example 1 A mutual fund has investments with closing prices totaling $8,350,000, liabilities of $620,000, and 700,000 shares outstanding. What is the NAV?

$$\text{NAV} = \frac{\$8,350,000 - \$620,000}{700,000} = \frac{\$7,730,000}{700,000} = \$11.04$$

Each share is valued at $11.04.

Illustration 16-3 Mutual Fund Quotations, Putnam Funds

Name	Sym	NAV	Net Chg	YTD % ret
Muni	PMO	12.56	+ 0.02	+ 1.10
IncGr	PCONX	20.53	+ 0.07	+ 2.96
Hlth	PHSTX	49.20	- 0.13	- 4.80

Name: Name of fund, abbreviated.
Sym: This is the symbol (on the Internet, etc.).
NAV: Net asset value (price per share).
Net Chg: The price change (in dollars and cents) from the previous closing price.
YTD% ret: The increase in NAV so far this calendar year.

b Understanding mutual fund quotations

Quotations for mutual funds are shown in many newspapers. Illustration 16-3 shows recent mutual fund quotes from *The Wall Street Journal* for a few funds from the Putnam "family of funds" (Putnam, like most mutual fund companies, has many individual funds to choose from).

Example 2 For the Putnam Income and Growth Fund (PCONX), what are the **(a)** NAV, **(b)** change in price this day, and **(c)** year-to-date percentage increase in value.

a. $20.53 per share
b. Increased $0.07 (7¢) per share
c. Increased 2.96% so far this year

A **no-load mutual fund** does not charge a transaction fee (the buyer pays only the NAV). With a no-load mutual fund, shares are purchased directly from the mutual fund company; advertising and selling expenses are built into the fund's management fee. Some mutual funds are sold through stockbrokers or investment advisors, who provide information and advice to the investor. With these, a fee is charged, either when shares are purchased (called a **front-end load**) or when shares are sold (called a **back-end load**). The fee is used to compensate salespeople selling the fund. For back-end loads, the fee decreases for each year of ownership, until after 5 years of ownership there is no fee at all. Mutual fund companies charge an annual management fee for managing the fund. Fees vary from fund to fund.

Some funds are **closed-end funds**; after the initial offering, no additional shares are sold. If an investor wants to sell these shares, he or she must do so through a brokerage company. Most funds are **open-end funds**; additional shares can be purchased at any time, and shares can be *redeemed* through the mutual fund company (the company pays the NAV). By the way, the price used is the NAV at the "close" of business. So if we place an order to buy or sell shares, the price is not established until later, at the end of the day, when the NAV is calculated.

Funds make money from the individual securities in the fund, either from interest, dividends, or selling the securities at a profit (these profits are called **capital gains**). The fund periodically distributes each investor's portion. Investors generally have the choice of receiving money or *reinvesting* (in which case their distribution is used to buy additional shares or fractions of shares).

> **TIP** do your homework
>
> Before investing in a mutual fund, here are a few ideas.
> - Read the **prospectus** (a document that explains the fund and it's objectives).
> - Check out the recent performance of the fund. You can find reports on the Internet or at most public libraries.
> - Each fund has a fund manager and team of associates. Check out the performance of other funds they have managed.
> - Determine what fees there are for buying and selling and what the management fees are.
> - Find out if you can switch from one fund to another (within the same family of funds) without penalty.

Let's try some U-Try-It questions to see how we're doing.

U-Try-It
(Unit 16.3)

1. A mutual fund has investments with closing prices totaling $43,580,000, liabilities of $1,300,000, and 2,100,000 shares outstanding. What is the NAV?
2. Refer to Illustration 16-3. What was the NAV of the Putnam Health (PHSTX) fund at the *beginning* of the calendar year? *Hint:* Write an equation to help with the arithmetic (you may want to use equation-solving skills found in Chapter 3).

Answers: (If you have a different answer, check the solution in Appendix A.)
1. $20.13 **2.** $51.68

Chapter in a Nutshell

Objectives	Examples
Unit 16.1 Stocks	
a Calculating dividends	200,000 shares of common stock and 50,000 shares of cumulative preferred stock (with an annual dividend of $1 per share). No dividends last year. $500,000 available this year. Your dividend for 100 shares of common stock? $500,000 - $50,000 (preferred last year) - $50,000 (preferred this year) = $400,000 for common $400,000 ÷ 200,000 common shares = $2 per share; $2 × 100 shares = $200
b Understanding how to buy and sell stock	Buy 400 shares of stock at price of 11.88; $150 brokerage fees. Sell for 14.75; $200 brokerage fees. Total cost: (400 × $11.88) + $150 = $4,902 Net proceeds: (400 × $14.75) - $200 = $5,700
c Calculating a price–earnings ratio	Closing price of $38.25; earnings per share of $1.22. PE ratio? $PE = \frac{P}{E} = \frac{\$38.25}{\$1.22} \approx 31.35 \approx 31$
Unit 16.2 Bonds	
a Understanding how bonds work	Buy 7% $1,000 corporate bond that pays interest each 6 months. Dollar amount of interest checks? Interest rate per period = 7 ÷ 2 = 3.5 $1,000 × 3.5% = $35
b Understanding bond quotations	$1,000 "ATT 8⅝ 31" bond at a price of 107.424: **a.** matures? **b.** interest check each year? **c.** price? **a.** 2031 **b.** $1,000 × 8.625% = $86.25 **c.** $1,000 × 107.424% = $1,074.24
Unit 16.3 Mutual funds	
a Calculating net asset value	Fund has asset closing prices totaling $18,400,000, liabilities of $400,000, and 942,000 shares. NAV? $NAV = \frac{\$18,400,000 - \$400,000}{942,000} = \frac{\$18,000,000}{942,000} = \$19.11$
b Understanding mutual fund quotations	Refer to Illustration 16-3. For Putnam Muni (PMO): **a.** NAV? **b.** Daily change? **c.** % calendar-year change? **a.** $12.56 **b.** + $0.02 **c.** + 1.10%

Enrichment Topics

The following Enrichment Topic, which goes a bit beyond what is in the text, is available for this chapter:

Selecting an Investment: The 8 Investment Criteria

If your instructor doesn't cover this topic in class and you would like to dig in deeper on your own, please send a request to *studentsupport@olympuspub.com*.

Think

1. Suppose a corporate bond pays 8% interest and a tax-free municipal bond pays 6%. For which investors is the municipal bond a better deal? Prove your point of view with calculations.
2. Under what conditions do bonds sell at a premium? Under what conditions do they sell at a discount?
3. Many young investors prefer investing in stocks, while older people often prefer investing in bonds. Why do you suppose that is?
4. What are some advantages and disadvantages of investing in mutual funds?
5. Look at the stock quotations in a newspaper. Did most of the stock prices go up or go down for this day? How is it possible for some prices to go up and others to go down?

Explore

1. Search the Internet for *Dow Jones Industrial Average*. Write a report on its history. What are the stocks that are currently used in computing the DJIA? Which 3 companies have been on the list the longest, and which 3 companies are newest to the list?
2. Select 5 companies that make products that you use on a regular basis (the companies can be those referred to in Activity 1). For each company, list the ticker symbol, a recent closing price, the price-earnings ratio, and any relevant trends that might affect your interest in buying or not buying the stock. Conclude by rating the 5 stocks, best to worst buys, from your personal standpoint. *Note:* You can refer to analyst opinions found on the Internet to justify your opinions; be sure to cite sources you use.
3. Search the Internet for the *Richest People in the World*. Summarize your findings on the 5 richest people (who they are, their net worth, how they have earned their fortune, where they are from, etc.).

Apply

1. **Interview Investors.** Interview three different investors: one whose main investments are stocks, one whose main investments are bonds, and one whose main investments are in real estate. Write a report for each investor, indicating why the investor selected his or her particular type of investment and how each got started investing. Determine their investment strategies—how they decide whether to invest in a particular investment and how long to keep the investment. Ask each investor to tell you about other investors who have lost money investing and what caused the loss. Summarize your findings by telling which of the three types of investments appeals most to you and why.
2. **Stockbroker's Opinions.** Contact a stockbroker and ask for his or her help with this project. Determine the following:
   A. What is a *blue-chip* stock? List three specific stocks that could be classified as blue-chip stocks.
   B. What is an *income* stock? List three specific stocks.
   C. What is a *growth* stock? List three specific stocks.
   D. What is a *cyclical* stock? List three specific stocks.
   E. What is a *defensive* stock? List three specific stocks.
   F. An industry whose future looks good for the upcoming 5 years and why.
   G. An industry whose future looks bad for the upcoming 5 years and why.
   H. A type of stock that does well during times of inflation and why.
   I. A type of stock that does well during recession and why.
   J. A prediction for the Dow Jones Industrial Average during the upcoming 12 months and the basis for the prediction.
   K. A prediction about the possibility of a 20% drop in the Dow during the next 2 years and a basis for the prediction.

   Submit your findings. Then, name a few stocks in which you would consider investing and why.

Chapter Review Problems

State all stock and bond prices in dollars and cents.

Unit 16.1 Stocks

1. When a corporation earns a profit, the board of directors is obligated by law to immediately distribute 100% of the profits to stockholders. (T or F)

2. If a corporation goes out of business, preferred stockholders are paid before creditors. (T or F)

3. ABC Corporation has 1,150,000 shares of common stock and 200,000 shares of cumulative preferred stock. The annual dividend on the preferred stock is $3 per share. The only dividends paid last year were to preferred stockholders in the amount of $1 per share. This year the board of directors decided to distribute $1,575,000 in dividends. If you own 75 shares of common stock, what is the amount of your annual dividend?

4. All stockbrokerage companies charge the same commission. (T or F)

5. The largest stock exchange in the United States is the Dow Jones Stock Exchange. (T or F)

6. A "bear market" occurs when investors are pessimistic about the overall economy and the stock market. (T or F)

7. Observe the following stock quote. What are (a) the highest price during the last 52 weeks, (b) the lowest price during the last 52 weeks, (c) the last price this day, (d) the change in price this day, and (e) the number of shares traded this day? Confirm (f) the Yld% and (g) the PE Ratio, assuming annual earnings per share of $3.21.

| 52 weeks | | Div | Yld% | PE Ratio | Vol 100s | Close | Net Chg |
Hi	Lo						
92.13	78.25	1.40	1.62	27	352	86.56	-0.63

For Problems 8 and 9, evaluate an investment in 100 shares of stock.

8. You buy the 100 shares at a price of 38.50 and incur brokerage fees totaling $80. What is your total cost?

9. Four years later, you sell the stock at a price of 46.00 and incur brokerage fees totaling $120. What are your net proceeds?

10. Data for three companies is shown. Calculate the PE ratio for each. Use 2 decimal places in the ratio.

Company	Price per share	Earnings per share	PE ratio
A	$65.00	$8.13	
B	$65.00	$5.91	
C	$65.00	$2.22	

11. Refer to Problem 10. For Company A, what does the PE ratio of 8.0 mean?

12. Refer to Problem 10. Based on the PE ratios (i.e., assume that future earnings will remain the same as recent earnings), which of the three stocks is the best buy?

13. Refer to Problem 10. What accounts for the high PE ratio for Company C? (short answer)

Unit 16.2 Bonds

14. Corporate bonds are generally in denominations of $1,000. (T or F)

15. Treasury bills are a form of zero-coupon bond. (T or F)

16. All municipal bonds are tax-exempt. (T or F)

17. Bonds that have a high degree of risk must provide a high interest rate to attract investors. (T or F)

For Problems 18 and 19, assume you own a 30-year 7% bond that pays interest annually and matures in 24 years. You are thinking about selling the bond.

18. If the prevailing rate for similar bonds is 6%, your bond will be priced at (a) par, (b) a discount, or (c) a premium.

19. If the prevailing rate for similar bonds is 8%, your bond will be priced at (a) par, (b) a discount, or (c) a premium.

For Problems 20–26, refer to the following bond quote.

Bond	Cur Yld	Vol	Close	Net Chg
ATT $8^5/_8$ 26	6.80	30	126.765	- 0.583

20. What is the coupon rate?
21. In what year does the bond mature?
22. How many bonds were sold this day?
23. Based on a $1,000 face value, what was the price for the last bond traded?

24. Why do you suppose the bond is priced at a premium?

25. What happened to the price this day?
26. Confirm the "Cur Yld" quote.

27. You buy three $5,000 Treasury bonds at a price of 133:13. What is the total price?

Unit 16.3 Mutual funds

28. One reason people invest in mutual funds is that mutual funds provide *diversification*. (T or F)

29. For each fund, find the NAV.

Fund assets	Fund liabilities	Shares outstanding	NAV
$23,478,000	$4,122,000	800,000	
$8,155,000	$1,050,000	450,000	
$745,000,000	$192,000,000	5,820,000	

30. With a closed-end mutual fund, no additional shares are sold by the company after the initial offering. (T or F)

31. With a front-end load mutual fund, an investor pays a fee when the shares are purchased. (T or F)

Challenge problems

For Problems 32–36, tell whether the statement refers to stock, a bond, or both.

32. With this investment, you become an owner of a corporation.

33. For this investment, you may receive dividends.

34. A quote in the financial section of a newspaper looks like this: StdOil $8^{3}/_{8}$ 22.

35. The value of this investment can change during ownership.

36. With this investment, you are a lender.

37. Assuming a 28% tax rate, which bond, purchased at par, has the greater after-tax rate of return: **(a)** a corporate bond paying 6.75% or **(b)** a tax-free municipal bond paying 5.25%?

38. Which bond purchased at par provides the greater return: a 7.6% corporate bond paying interest *annually* or a 7.5% corporate bond paying interest *semiannually*?

Practice Test

1. Aztec Corporation has 562,500 shares of common stock and 200,000 shares of cumulative preferred stock. The annual dividend of the preferred stock is $2 per share. The only dividends paid last year were to preferred stockholders in the amount of $1 per share. This year the board of directors decided to distribute $1,275,000 in dividends. If you own 150 shares of common stock, what is the amount of your annual dividend?

2. Refer to the following stock quote. Determine (a) the highest price during the last 52 weeks, (b) the number of shares traded this day, and (c) dividends during the last 12 months.

52 weeks		Div	Yld%	PE Ratio	Vol 100s	Close	Net Chg
Hi	Lo						
51.38	38.25	.60	1.34	25	1613	44.94	-0.88

3. Refer to the stock quote of Problem 2. Assume you buy 125 shares of stock at the closing price and incur brokerage fees of $120. What is your total cost?

4. A company reported annual earnings per share of $2.28. If the price is currently $86.75 per share, what is the PE ratio?

5. Refer to the following bond quote. Suppose you sold one of these $1,000 bonds at the closing price and incurred brokerage fees of $75. Calculate your net proceeds.

Bond	Cur Yld	Vol	Close	Net Chg
IBM $8^{3}/_{8}$ 18	6.31	30	132.758	+ 1.27

6. Refer to the bond quote of Problem 5. Assuming the bonds pay interest annually, what is the dollar amount of interest the buyer will receive each year?

7. Refer to the bond quote of Problem 5. Is the prevailing rate (a) less than the coupon rate, (b) greater than the coupon rate, or (c) equal to the coupon rate?

8. You buy four $5,000 Treasury bonds at a price of 112:17. What is the total price?

9. A mutual fund has investments with assets totaling $12,742,000, liabilities of $3,450,000, and 900,000 shares outstanding. What is the NAV?

Classroom Notes

FUN CORNER

Prices in the Good Old Days

People often talk about how cheap things were in the good old days. For example, in 1964 a loaf of bread would set you back 21 cents, a pound of butter 75 cents, a gallon of milk $1.06, a gallon of gasoline 30 cents, a new Ford auto $3,495, and an average home $13,050.

But, ignoring inflation makes these comparisons meaningless. Inflation from 1964 to 2015 has averaged 4.1% per year. Based on this rate, compounded annually here is what these same products would cost today:

Loaf of bread	$1.63
Pound of butter	$5.82
Gallon of milk	$8.23
Gallon of gasoline	$2.33
Average car	$27,129
Average home	$101,297

Earn 50% Interest

If you work for a company that makes matching contributions to a retirement plan, take advantage of it. Say your company makes a matching contribution of 50 cents for each dollar you put in, it's like 50% interest the first year. Where else can you get that kind of return?

Quotable Quip

A billion dollars is not what it used to be.
– Nelson Bunker Hunt

The Midas Touch

Perhaps you have heard the expression, He (or she) has the Midas touch. It refers to the ability to make money in anything the person does. Here's where the saying came from. In Greek mythology, Midas was a legendary king of Phrygia; in return for kindness, Dionysus gave him the power to turn anything he touched into gold. When Midas found that even his food was turning into gold, he begged to have the favor withdrawn, and Dionysus let him wash it away.

"Don't worry sir, Walters is crunching the numbers on his calculator as we speak."

Additional Applications Using Financial Calculators

17

In Chapters 12 and 13, we explored some basic time-value-of-money applications using financial calculators. In Chapter 15, we used our amortization registers. In this chapter we will explore a few additional—and extremely valuable—applications. We will (1) calculate APRs for a variety of loans, (2) determine growth rates, (3) calculate yields on a variety of investments, and (4) calculate what is called *net present value* for situations in which the payments change.

UNIT OBJECTIVES

Unit 17.1 Solving for interest rate paid

- **a** Calculating an APR using the add-on method
- **b** Calculating an APR for an installment plan
- **c** Calculating an APR for an installment loan with front-end loan charges
- **d** Calculating an APR for a mortgage loan with front-end loan charges

Unit 17.2 Growth rates

- **a** Finding growth rates

Unit 17.3 Solving for interest rate earned

- **a** Calculating a yield on a non-income-producing asset
- **b** Calculating a yield on stock
- **c** Calculating a yield on bonds
- **d** Calculating a yield on mutual funds
- **e** Calculating a yield on a promissory note

Unit 17.4 Cash flow problems

- **a** Calculating an internal rate of return (IRR)
- **b** Calculating net present value (NPV)

Unit 17.1 Solving for interest rate paid

The **Truth in Lending Act**, also known as **Regulation Z**, requires lenders to notify the borrower of (1) how much extra money the borrower is paying (known as **finance charge**) as a result of borrowing the money, and (2) the **annual percentage rate (APR)** the borrower is paying. The Truth in Lending Act does *not* set maximum interest rates; however, many states set limits. The law does not apply to business loans, loans over $25,000 (unless they are secured by real estate), most public utility fees, and student loan programs.

In Chapter 9 we calculated APRs for simple interest loans. In this unit, we will calculate APRs for a variety of other loans. As you will see, calculating APRs allows us to make better-informed decisions.

a Calculating an APR using the add-on method

Some lenders have tricky ways of calculating interest. One fairly common method is the **add-on method**, in which interest is figured in advance using the formula $I = PRT$. Here is how we calculate the payment.

calculating a payment using the add-on method

Step 1 Determine the dollar amount of interest as though this were a simple interest loan: $I = PRT$.
Step 2 Add the result of Step 1 to the loan amount.
Step 3 Divide by the total number of payments. This is the periodic payment.

I = Dollar amount of interest P = Principal R = Annual rate of interest T = Time (in years)

Example 1 John Paul gets a $6,000 three-year 8% loan from Jim Roberts. They agree to use the add-on method. First calculate the monthly payment. Then calculate John's APR.

Step 1 (dollar amount of interest): $I = PRT = \$6{,}000 \times 8\% \times 3 = \$1{,}440$
Step 2 (add to loan amount): $\$6{,}000 + \$1{,}440 = \$7{,}440$
Step 3 (divide by total number of payments): $\$7{,}440 \div 36 = \$206.67$

N	i	PV	PMT	FV
3 × 12 = 36	1.21 × 12 ≈ 14.55	6,000	-206.67	

John is really paying 14.55% interest (and Jim is *earning* 14.55%).

In Example 1, the APR (14.55%) is considerably higher than the stated rate (8%). Here is the reason. Using the add-on method, John is charged interest on $6,000 for the entire time even though he is gradually repaying the loan and should be charged only on the unpaid balance. If Jim does not lend money *on a regular basis*, he would not be required by the Truth in Lending Act to inform John of the APR; it would be up to John to figure the APR. John should probably check around to see if he can get a loan with a lower APR, because Jim's 8% loan is not really an 8% loan!

TIP troubleshooting

If you get or suspect a bad answer with your financial registers:
1. Recall (RCL) the value in each register. Have you entered a wrong amount, used the wrong sign (+ or -), or left a previous amount in an unused register?
2. Is your calculator in the correct mode (begin or end)?
3. Is your calculator set at 1 period per year?

   For the HP 10BII+, when clearing the TVM registers, the P/YR setting will briefly appear. To check the P/YR setting during keystrokes, press RCL ▽ P/YR.

   For the TI BAII PLUS, press 2ND P/Y to observe the current setting, then press 2ND QUIT.

Refer to Chapter 12 if you need more details.

b Calculating an APR for an installment plan

Some bills, like insurance bills, allow us to pay with installments. If we elect the installment plan, we may have to pay a bit extra as a service fee. The interest rate can be surprising.

Example 2 You get your car insurance bill. The company gives you the option of paying the entire 6-month premium of $480 now or paying with 6 monthly installments of $87 (starting today). What interest rate (APR) will you be paying if you elect to pay with the installment method?

N	i	PV	PMT	FV
6	3.48 × 12 = 41.79	480	- 87 Begin*	

*Note: You should be in "begin" mode because your payments start immediately; don't forget to put back in "end" mode when finished.

You will be paying 41.79% interest! If you don't have the money to pay the entire $480 now, consider borrowing the money elsewhere (like from a credit card that charges 18% interest).

> **TIP** *i-register* represents interest rate per period
>
> Remember, the *i-register* represents the interest rate *per period*, not the annual rate. In Example 2, when we solved for *i* we got 3.48, which is the interest rate per period—in this case the interest rate per month. You may have been tempted to multiply the periodic rate by 6, since you will make payments for only 6 months. But to get the annual rate, we must multiply by the number of periods in a year (12). Even though you would be paying a rate of 41.79% for only 6 months, the annual rate is 41.79%!

c Calculating an APR for an installment loan with front-end loan charges

An APR *relates the amount and timing of value received by the borrower to the amount and timing of payments made*. So, if front-end loan costs are charged, we figure the APR based on **net proceeds** (after deducting front-end loan costs). In Chapter 14, Casey got a 5-year $13,500 car loan at 7.5% interest. The lender charged Casey a front-end fee. Front-end fees are a form of interest—just paid in advance—so Casey's APR will be higher than his 7.5% **note rate** (the stated annual rate). In the next example we will calculate Casey's APR.

> **calculating an APR on an installment loan with front-end loan charges**
>
> **Step 1** Determine the monthly payment, ignoring the loan charges.
>
> **Step 2** Substitute the *net proceeds* for the present value (loan amount), then solve for *i*. Remember *i* represents the interest rate period, so multiply by 12 to get the annual rate.

Example 3 Casey gets a 5-year $13,500 car loan at 7.5% interest. The lender charges a $100 front-end fee. Calculate Casey's APR. *Tip:* Your calculator should be back in "end" mode.

N	i	PV	PMT	FV
5 × 12 = 60	7.5 ÷ 12 ≈ 0.63*	13,500	**-270.51**	
↑	0.65 × 12 = 7.81	13,400**	↑	

*Note: In Step 1, the 7.5% rate divided by 12 = 0.625, but with 2 decimal places appears as 0.63. By dividing 7.5 by 12 and transferring the result in the interest rate register, we enter the *internal, more accurate value* (0.625). Don't make the common mistake of entering a rounded rate (0.63) in the interest rate register.

**Note: In Step 2, $13,500 - $100 front-end fee = net proceeds of $13,400.

Casey's APR is 7.81%. Looking at this another way, if Casey were to get a $13,400 loan with no loan costs at an interest rate of 7.81% (7.814%, to be more exact), the payment would be $270.51.

Please take a moment to refer to Illustration 14-1 of Chapter 14, which is the disclosure statement Casey's lender was required to provide to Casey. Notice that the APR on the disclosure statement is 7.81%, the answer we got in Example 3.

d Calculating an APR for a mortgage loan with front-end loan charges

In Chapter 15, Tara got a $160,000 15-year mortgage loan at 7.25%. Tara must pay front-end loan charges. Illustration 17-1 is a brief summary of common mortgage loan charges. (For a detailed explanation of the charges, refer to Illustration 15-4.)

Because Tara paid front-end loan charges, her APR will be greater than the 7.25% note rate. Notice the footnote to Illustration 17-1, which shows what charges are used in APR calculations; the footnote suggests there is more than one type of APR for mortgage loans. We will, in fact, calculate three different APRs: a *reportable* APR (Example 4), a *real* APR (Example 5), and a *real APR reflecting an early payoff* (Example 6).

Reportable APR

A **reportable APR** is the APR that must be reported by the lender, and considers only a *few* of the loan charges (items *a-d* of Illustration 17-1). Document preparation fees, even if paid to the lender, are not used in calculating a *reportable APR*. The steps in calculating a *reportable APR* for a mortgage loan are similar to the steps used in calculating an APR for an installment loan.

> **calculating a reportable APR on a mortgage loan**
>
> **Step 1** Determine the monthly payment, ignoring loan charges.
>
> **Step 2** Subtract items *a-d* of Illustration 17-1 from the loan amount. Substitute the result for the present value (loan amount), and then solve for *i*. Remember, *i* represents the interest rate per period, so multiply by 12 to get the annual rate.

Illustration 17-1 Brief Summary of Common Loan Charges (see Illustration 15-4 for more detail)

Basic fees
a. Origination fee
b. Points
c. Mortgage insurance
d. Miscellaneous fees to lender

Fees paid to third parties
e. Document preparation
f. Credit report
g. Appraisal
h. Lender's title policy
i. Recording

Insurance, escrow, interest adjustment
j. Insurance premium
k. Initial escrow deposit
l. Interest adjustment

Note: Items *a-d* are used by a lender in calculating a *reportable APR*.
Items *a-i* (items in the left column and middle column, combined) are used by a borrower in calculating a *real* APR.
Items *j-l* are *not* used in APR calculations.

Example 4

Tara got a $160,000 15-year mortgage loan at 7.25%. She was charged a 1% origination fee, $1\frac{1}{2}$ points, and a one-time $2,560 mortgage insurance premium. Calculate the *reportable APR*.

The loan costs used in calculating a *reportable APR* are:

Origination fee: $160,000 × 1% =	$1,600
Points: $160,000 × 1.5% =	2,400
Mortgage insurance	2,560
Total	$6,560

N	i	PV	PMT	FV
15 × 12 = 180	7.25 ÷ 12 ≈ 0.6041<u>6</u>	160,000	**-1,460.58**	
↑	0.66 × 12 = 7.93	153,440*	↑	

Note: $160,000 - $6,560 qualified loan charges = $153,440.

The *reportable APR* is 7.93%.

Real APR

In Example 4, we found the *reportable APR* is 7.93%. This is the rate the lender must disclose on a **disclosure statement**. The 7.93% *reportable APR* disregards additional loan costs that Tara pays, namely items *e-i* of Illustration 17-1. The borrower's **real APR** is based on net proceeds after items *a-i* are deducted and, as a result, is even higher than the *reportable APR*. Notice in Illustration 17-1, items *j-l* are not used in calculating an APR. Here's why. Hazard insurance (item *j*) is something the buyer needs even if there is no mortgage, so it is not a cost of getting the loan. Money put into an escrow account (item *k*) still belongs to the borrower (like savings account money). And an interest adjustment (item *l*) is part of the basic interest on the loan.

Example 5

Refer to Example 4. Tara incurred some additional loan costs, including $50 for a credit report, $450 for an appraisal, $700 for lender's title insurance, $250 for document preparation, and $50 for recording. Calculate Tara's *real APR*.

$6,560 (costs from Example 4) + $50 + $450 + $700 + $250 + $50 = $8,060

N	i	PV	PMT	FV
15 × 12 = 180	7.25 ÷ 12 = 0.6041<u>6</u>	160,000	**-1,460.58**	
↑	0.67 × 12 ≈ 8.10	151,940	↑	

Tara's real APR is 8.10%.

Notice that the APR of Example 5 (8.10%) is higher than the APR of Example 4 (7.93%) because in Example 5 we considered *all* of the loan costs.

Real APR reflecting an early payoff

Most borrowers pay off mortgage loans early. Some do so because they sell the property before the loan is scheduled to be paid off (in which case they must pay the loan balance). Some get a bunch of money (like from an inheritance, retirement plan, or sale of other investments) and use the money to pay off their mortgage loan. Some people **refinance** their mortgage loan, meaning they get a new loan and use part or all of the proceeds to pay off the old loan. People refinance to get additional cash, to reduce a payment, or to get a lower interest rate.

When a mortgage loan is paid off early, loan costs, for APR purposes, are spread over a shorter period of time than anticipated, *increasing the real APR*. The next example shows how to modify the real APR to reflect an early payoff. We will use three steps.

> **calculating real APR to reflect an early payoff**
>
> **Step 1** Calculate the monthly payment using the loan amount and note rate.
>
> **Step 2** Calculate the remaining balance (using amortization registers) after the designated time.
>
> **Step 3** Calculate the real APR by (1) putting the remaining balance (the result of Step 2) in the FV register (as a negative value), (2) changing the N-value, and (3) changing PV to the net proceeds (after loan costs are deducted).

Example 6 Refer to Example 5. Assume Tara will pay off the loan at the end of 7 years. Calculate Tara's real APR, reflecting the early payoff.

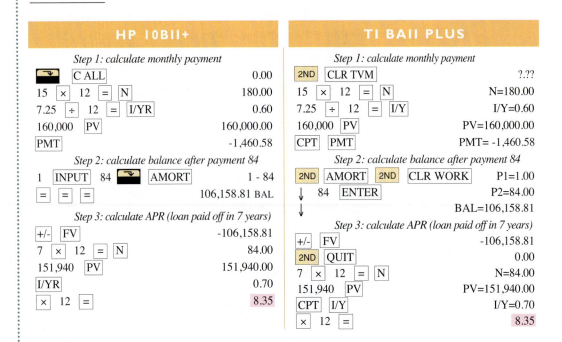

Tara signs a promissory note for $160,000 at 7.25% interest, requiring a monthly payment of $1,460.58. However, because of the loan costs and paying off the loan at the end of 7 years, Tara receives and pays different amounts (and that is the basis for the APR). She receives net proceeds of $151,940, makes 84 monthly payments of $1,460.58, and pays the lender an additional $106,158.81 at the end of the 84th month. *As a result, Tara pays an actual rate of 8.35% on the $151,940 she has use of.* Here is how it looks using our time-value-of-money format:

N	i	PV	PMT	FV
15 × 12 = 180	7.25 ÷ 12 = 0.60416	160,000	-1,460.58	
7 × 12 = 84	0.70 × 12 ≈ 8.35	151,940	↑	-106,158.81

Here is a summary of Tara's interest rates:

Note rate	7.25%
Reportable APR	7.93%
Real APR, assuming the loan is not paid off early	8.10%
Real APR, assuming the loan is paid off in 7 years	8.35%

Notice that the APR increased with each modification. You may wonder which rate is the most meaningful. The *note rate* (7.25%) ignores all loan costs. The *reportable APR* (7.93%) ignores many of the loan costs. The third rate (8.10%) disregards the likelihood of paying off the loan early. The real APR assuming an early payoff, 8.35%, is the most meaningful one.

Selecting a mortgage loan is a big decision, and using APRs to compare loans is extremely valuable. Loan costs vary from lender to lender. Even with the same lender we may have several choices. To compare the choices, we can calculate an APR for each loan using the method of Example 6. The loan with the lowest APR is the best choice. We will do this in the upcoming U-Try-It (I'll bet you can't wait).

Calculating an APR is also valuable in deciding whether to refinance. Suppose Tara, rather than getting the 7.25% loan to *buy a home*, is thinking about getting the loan to *pay off an existing 8.25% loan*. Your first reaction may be that she should, since the note rate of the new loan (7.25%) is less than the note rate of her existing loan (8.25%). But we would be ignoring all of the loan costs she would incur in getting the new loan, and the resulting APR she will pay.

> **refinance or not—that is the question**
>
> To decide whether to refinance, compare the APR on the contemplated loan with the note rate of the old loan. If the APR on the contemplated loan is less, it is probably a good idea to refinance.

Example 7

Tara has an existing mortgage loan at 8.25%. She is thinking about refinancing with a 15-year $160,000 mortgage loan at 7.25% interest. She will incur loan costs totaling $8,060, and she figures she will pay off the loan at the end of 7 years. If her main goal is getting a lower interest rate, should she refinance?

We calculated Tara's real APR, reflecting the early payoff, in Example 6: 8.35%. Because the APR on the contemplated loan is greater than the note rate of the existing loan (8.25%), Tara should not refinance.

> **TIP   resist temptation**
>
> In Example 7, we compared the APR on the new loan with the note rate on the old loan. You may wonder, Why don't we compare the APR on the new loan with the APR on the old loan? The answer: The loan costs on the old loan are already "down the drain." From this point on, Tara is paying only the note rate (8.25%) on the old loan.

Hope you're doing okay. While the stuff in this unit is a bit tricky, it is extremely valuable. Let's try calculating a few more APRs in the U-Try-It set.

U-Try-It (Unit 17.1)

1. You buy a big-screen TV for $4,800. The retailer agrees to finance the entire amount for 2 years at 10% interest using the add-on method. You must make monthly payments, starting in 1 month. Calculate your APR.
2. You get your car insurance bill. The company gives you the option of paying the entire 6-month premium of $450 now or paying with 6 monthly installments of $80 (starting today). If you elect to pay on the installment method, what interest rate (APR) will you pay?
3. You buy a boat and need a loan. You can get a 3-year $10,000 loan at 9.25% with no front-end loan costs or a 3-year loan at 7.75% with a $250 set-up fee (in which case you will borrow $10,250 and receive net proceeds of $10,000). You will make monthly payments. Which loan results in a lower APR?
4. You need a 30-year $140,000 mortgage loan. You have two choices: (**1**) an 8.25% loan with loan costs totaling $4,000 or (**2**) a 7.875% loan with loan costs totaling $8,000. You project paying off the loan at the end of 10 years. If you base your decision on the real APR, reflecting the early payoff, which loan should you get?
5. You currently owe $110,474.65 on your mortgage loan, with monthly payments of $807.18 (PI) at 8.25% interest. You are considering refinancing with a 15-year $115,000 loan at 7% interest, in which case you will incur loan costs of $4,500. You project paying off the new loan at the end of 6 years. Should you refinance now?

Answers: (If you have a different answer, check the solution in Appendix A.)
1. 18.16%   **2.** 31.88%   **3.** 9.25% loan has 9.25% APR (other loan has 9.43% APR)   **4.** The first choice provides the lower APR (8.70% vs. 8.78%), so you should get the 8.25% loan.   **5.** The APR on the contemplated loan (7.93%) is lower than the note rate on the existing loan (8.25%). Unless you foresee interest rates dropping in the future—and in the absence of any other material factors—you should refinance now.

Unit 17.2 Growth rates

a Finding growth rates

Most time-value-of-money problems involve *receipts* and *expenditures of money*. Some problems, such as changes in the population of a town, do not.

We can use financial calculators to find growth rates, such as changes in the consumer price index (CPI), stock indexes, tuition, and population of a town.

> **🔑 changes over time not involving receipts and expenditures of money**
>
> - The first value to occur (it occurs at the beginning of the first period) is considered the present value; the last to occur (it occurs at the end of the last period) is the future value.
> - One of the values—present value or future value—will be positive and the other will be negative; our solutions will show present value as the negative value.

Example 1 Four years ago the population of a town in Alberta, Canada, was 8,570. If the population is now 11,677, what is the annual growth rate of the town?

N	i	PV	PMT	FV
4	8.04	-8,570*		11,677

*Note: One of the population values must be entered as a negative; otherwise a solution is not possible.

The population has increased at an annual rate of 8.04%.

Longhand calculator proof: 8,570 + 8.04% + 8.04% + 8.04% + 8.04% ≈ 11,677

Example 2 The Dow Jones Industrial Average (DJIA) is an index that monitors changes in the stock market. On December 31, 1903, the DJIA was 49.11; on December 31, 2014, the DJIA was 17,832.99. Calculate the average annual increase in the index.

N	i	PV	PMT	FV
111	5.45	-49.11		17,832.99

Let's check the growth rate of our knowledge by trying a U-Try-It question.

U-Try-It (Unit 17.2)

1. Tuition at a local college has increased over the last 15 years from $650 per year to $3,600 per year. What is the average annual rate of increase?

Answers: (If you have a different answer, check the solution in Appendix A.)
1. 12.09%

Unit 17.3 Solving for interest rate earned

When we make an investment, we hope to get back more than we invest. We can easily calculate the dollar amount of profit by subtracting the amount invested from the amount we get back. But a more valuable indicator is our annual **rate of return**, often referred to as our **yield** from the investment.

In this unit, we will calculate yields from several popular investments: non-income-producing assets, stock, bonds, mutual funds, and promissory notes.

a Calculating a yield on a non-income-producing asset

Some people invest in assets that do not produce any income during the investment period, such as gold, rare coins, baseball cards, etc. These investments provide no return on the investment other than the sales proceeds. We can calculate the yield as shown in Example 1.

Example 1 Dale bought a rare baseball card 3 years ago for $1,500. He just sold the card for $2,000 to get some money for his college tuition. What interest rate, compounded annually, did Dale earn on his investment? Use 4 decimal places in the rate.

_____

You may be tempted to treat the $2,000 as a present value because Dale received it today (in the present). But Dale paid the $1,500 at the beginning of the first period, making it the present value. He got the $2,000 at the end of the last period, making it the future value.

N	i	PV	PMT	FV
3	10.0642	-1,500		2,000

Dale earned 10.0642%, compounded annually.

You may wonder if an answer, like the one to Example 1, can be relied upon. After all, you are not doing the arithmetic, a machine is. One way to feel comfortable about an answer is to determine whether it sounds reasonable. In Example 1, Dale's profit was $500, which is about 33% of the $1,500 cost. That's about 11% per year. The 11% is a *simple interest* rate, however. If compounded annually, the rate could be less and still end up with a value of $2,000. As found in Example 1 that rate, compounded annually, is 10.0642%. Let's do a calculator proof to see if that rate works: $1,500 + 10.0642% + 10.0642% + 10.0642% = $2,000.00. Our calculators must know what they're doing!

b Calculating a yield on stock

When a corporation is organized, it raises money by selling **corporate stock** to the public. The buyers of the stock (called **stockholders**) become owners of the corporation. Many corporations distribute a portion of their profits in the form of **dividends**. An investor who receives no dividends during the investment period can calculate his or her rate of return as shown in Example 1. An investor who receives regular dividends can calculate a rate of return as shown in the next example.

Example 2 You purchased some corporate stock 5 years ago for $1,650 plus brokerage fees of $50. You received dividends of $25 at the end of each quarter. Immediately after receiving the 20th quarterly dividend, you sold the stock for $2,200 less brokerage fees of $100. Calculate your rate of return.

_____

N	i	PV	PMT	FV
5 × 4 = 20	2.40 × 4 = 9.60	-1,700	25	2,100

You earned 9.60% compounded quarterly.

> **TIP** what does the *i-register* represent?
>
> Don't forget that the *i-register* represents the *interest rate per period*. In Example 2, we solved for *i* and got 2.40%. As an annual rate, that is lousy; we could get a better annual rate of return elsewhere. Fortunately, the 2.40% is the periodic rate (in this case the interest rate per quarter). To find the annual rate we multiply by the periods per year (4), getting 9.60%.
>
> In Example 2, you earned 2.40% each quarter, so you may conclude that you earned "2.40% compounded quarterly." While the *periodic rate* is 2.40%, the rate you earned is stated as "9.60% compounded quarterly."

C Calculating a yield on bonds

Corporations, the U.S. government, and local governmental agencies often need large sums of money. They often raise money by selling bonds to the public. A person buying a bond is loaning money to the corporation or governmental agency. A **bond** is a written promise to repay the owner of the bond (**bondholder**) a specified amount (called the **maturity value**) at a future date (**maturity date**). Bondholders earn interest at a specified rate (known as the **coupon rate**). Interest is generally paid semiannually or annually. To illustrate, a 6% $1,000 bond that pays interest semiannually would pay $30 interest each 6 months: $1,000 × 3% periodic rate = $30.

Many beginning investors think that a $1,000 bond is always worth $1,000. While a $1,000 bond is worth $1,000 at maturity, the same bond may be worth more or less than $1,000 *prior* to maturity, depending on the prevailing rate for similar bonds. For example, if you own a bond paying 6% and new bonds are paying 8%, investors will buy the 8% bond instead of yours; to attract a buyer you must sell it for less than $1,000 (at a **discount**) so that the buyer can earn 8%. On the other hand, if your bond pays 10%, an investor would be willing to pay you more (a **premium**) for your bond. We calculated bond values in Unit 12.4.

Some bonds are safer than others. Bonds with a higher degree of risk must provide a higher rate to attract investors.

We can calculate a yield on a bond as shown in the next two examples. If a bond is held to maturity, the yield is called **yield to maturity (YTM).**

Example 3 You buy a 7% corporate bond for $1,050. You will receive the $1,000 maturity value in 18 years. You will receive interest checks at the end of each 6 months. Calculate your YTM.

N	i	PV	PMT	FV
18 × 2 = 36	3.26 × 2 = 6.52	-1,050	35*	1,000

Note: Semiannual interest check = $1,000 × 3.5% periodic rate = $35.

Your YTM is 6.52% compounded semiannually.

In Example 3, the 7% coupon rate was apparently greater than the prevailing rate on similar bonds because you paid a *premium* for the bond ($1,050 for this $1,000 bond). As a result of paying a premium, your YTM (6.52%) is less than the coupon rate (7%).

If bonds are sold before the maturity date, we can calculate our rate of return (called a **yield during ownership**) based on the net proceeds from the sale.

Example 4 Refer to Example 3. Twelve years after buying the bond you sell it for $980, less brokerage fees of $50. Calculate your yield during ownership.

N	i	PV	PMT	FV
12 × 2 = 24	3.00 × 2 = 6.00	-1,050	35	930

You earned 6.00% compounded semiannually. Because you sold the bond at a discount, your yield (6%) is less than the projected YTM (6.52%).

Bonds sold by local governmental agencies are known as **municipal bonds**. Municipal bonds are often sold in denominations of $5,000. Interest from many municipal bonds is tax-exempt for federal and state income tax purposes. Not all municipal bonds are tax-exempt, so before buying one determine whether it is tax-exempt.

d Calculating a yield on mutual funds

A **mutual fund** is a company that pools money from investors (**shareholders**) and invests in a diversified portfolio of assets (stocks, bonds, etc.). When we invest in a mutual fund, we receive shares. Many mutual fund companies allow investors to invest a fixed amount at set intervals, like $50 a month. Distributions are made based on profits, but shareholders can elect to reinvest the distributions to buy additional shares (or fractional parts). In the next example, we will calculate a rate of return on a mutual fund investment.

Example 5 You invest $50 each month (starting today) into a mutual fund. You reinvest distributions. At the end of 3 years, you sell all of your shares and receive $1,650. Calculate your rate of return.

N	i	PV	PMT	FV
3 × 12 = 36	-0.48 × 12 = -5.71		-50 Begin*	1,650

Note: Don't forget to put your calculator back in "end" mode.

You lost money (you put in $1,800 and only got back $1,650). Your rate of return was a *negative* 5.71% compounded monthly.

As illustrated in Example 5, it is possible to lose money on investments. I could tell you a few stories, but you've probably heard plenty from friends and relatives.

e Calculating a yield on a promissory note

Someone who borrows money is generally required to sign a **promissory note**, which spells out terms of repayment. Notes are often sold by individuals and businesses that need cash. Notes are often sold at a discount (referred to as **discounting notes**), so that the buyer of the note can get a yield greater than the note rate. In the next example we will calculate the yield from buying a promissory note.

Example 6 Six years ago, Samantha sold her home to Ali for $250,000. Ali paid $50,000 down and agreed to pay Samantha the remaining $200,000 over 20 years at 7% interest, resulting in a monthly payment of $1,550.60. Ali has just made payment 72, and the balance is $165,768.15 (you can confirm the balance with your amortization registers). Samantha needs some cash and asks you to buy the note for $150,000. Find your yield if you pay $150,000.

You will be buying the note at a discount ($150,000, compared to the $165,768.15 balance), so your yield will be greater than the 7% note rate. Let's find your exact yield. *Note:* Your calculator should be back in "end" mode.

N	i	PV	PMT	FV
168*	0.73 × 12 = 8.74	-150,000	1,550.60	

Note: 240 total scheduled payments - 72 payments made = 168 payments remaining.

If you pay $150,000, you will earn 8.74% compounded monthly.

In Example 6, if you buy the note for $150,000 you will collect the remaining 168 monthly payments from Ali. You will receive a total of $260,500.80 (168 × $1,550.60). You will earn 8.74%, compounded monthly, on your money.

> **TIP** when stating a yield, mention the compounding period
>
> In Example 6, you will earn 8.74% compounded monthly. That's a better rate than 8.74% compounded annually. In fact, using the concepts of Unit 9.3, the APY for 8.74% compounded monthly is 9.10%! So, if the yield is not based on annual compounding, always refer to the compounding period along with the rate.
>
> You may wonder if we should state the compounding period for APRs (Annual Percentage Rates) on loans. APRs are almost always based on monthly interest calculations, and as a common practice APRs are stated without referring to the compounding period.

That finishes up this unit. Let's try calculating a few rates of return in the U-Try-It exercises. The first problem is a true story.

U-Try-It (Unit 17.3)

1. (True story) Anne Scheiber, shown in this passport photo, retired in 1944 after a 23-year career with the Internal Revenue Service. She invested her $5,000 savings in the stock market. When she died in 1995 at the age of 101, her nest egg had grown to $22 million, which she left to Yeshiva University. What average annual rate of return did her investment fund earn over the 51 years?

2. Four years ago, Matilda Merkel bought 5 corporate bonds for $918.50 each. The bonds pay interest of $30 per bond at the end of each 6 months. Matilda just sold the bonds for $1,180 each, less brokerage fees totaling $350. What is Matilda's yield during ownership?

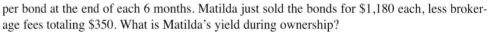

Answers: (If you have a different answer, check the solution in Appendix A.)
1. 17.88%   **2.** 10.83% compounded semiannually

Unit 17.4 Cash flow problems

Many investments, such as this rental property, provide cash flows that change from year to year. With some calculators, we can calculate a rate of return, even though the cash flows are uneven.

We have solved a variety of time-value-of-money (TVM) problems with our financial calculators. In this unit, we will solve a different type of problem, known as a *cash flow problem*. To illustrate the difference between a TVM problem and a cash flow problem, assume that you purchased some stock for $2,000, received dividends of different amounts each year, and then sold the stock for $2,700. We cannot calculate your rate of return with the TVM registers because the periodic payment changes.

A problem in which the periodic payment changes is known as a **cash flow problem**. For cash flow problems, we refer to the interest rate as an **internal rate of return** (or **IRR**), and we refer to the present value as **net present value** (or **NPV**). To solve a cash flow problem we use a different set of registers, referred to as *cash flow registers*.

370   Chapter 17   Additional Applications Using Financial Calculators

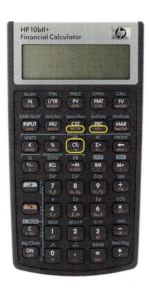

> **cash flow registers**
>
> **HP 10BII+.** Cash flows are entered in CFj (stands for cash flow); if a certain cash flow repeats, the number of times it happens is entered in the Nj register. After cash flows are entered, we can solve for IRR (internal rate of return) or NPV (net present value).
>
> **TI BAII PLUS.** Cash flow worksheet (CF) allows us to enter cash flows: CFo (initial cash flow), C01 (first periodic cash flow), F01 (frequency of first periodic cash flow), C02 (second periodic cash flow), etc. After cash flows are entered, we can solve for IRR (internal rate of return) or NPV (net present value).

a Calculating an internal rate of return (IRR)

An internal rate of return (IRR) is defined technically as the rate that equates the cash outflows (cost) of an investment with the cash inflows. Put simply, an IRR is *an interest rate earned*; it considers the dollar amounts of cash flows (positive and negative) and when each cash flow occurs.

In the upcoming example, we will calculate your rate of return on the stock investment referred to earlier, using the cash flow registers. As you will see, the cash flow registers are a piece of cake to use.

Example 1

Four years ago, you purchased some corporate stock for $2,000. You received dividends as follows: $100 at the end of year 1, $150 at the end of year 2, nothing at the end of year 3, and $125 at the end of year 4. Immediately after receiving the final dividend check, you sold the stock for $2,700. What is your annual rate of return?

HP 10BII+						TI BAII PLUS					
	C ALL				0.00	CF	2ND	CLR WORK			CFo=0.00
2,000	+/-	CFj			-2,000.00	2,000	+/-	ENTER			CFo= -2,000.00
100	CFj				100.00	↓	100	ENTER			C01=100.00
150	CFj				150.00	↓	↓	150	ENTER		C02=150.00
0	CFj				0.00	↓	↓	0	ENTER		C03=0.00
125	+	2,700	=	CFj*	2,825.00	↓	↓	125	+	2,700	= * 2,825.00
	IRR/YR				12.06	ENTER					C04=2,825.00
	DISP	4			12.0628	IRR	CPT				IRR=12.06
	DISP	2			12.06	2ND	FORMAT	4	ENTER	2ND	QUIT
						IRR					IRR=12.0628
						2ND	FORMAT	2	ENTER	2ND	QUIT 0.00

Note: Because the final dividend and the sales proceeds both occur at the end of year 4, we combine before entering.

In Example 1, we found that you earned 12.0628% (with 4 decimal places) on your money. You may wonder if the answer can be relied upon. Let's find out by doing a longhand proof. To make the process more understandable let's think of your money being in a savings account. At the end of each year, we will add interest at the 12.0628% rate and then subtract withdrawals (the dividend checks received); your ending balance should be $2,825 (the total amount you get from the stock at the end of year 4).

Unit 17.4 Cash flow problems 371

Balance at the end of year 1: $2,000 + 12.0628% - $100 withdrawal =	$2,141.26
Balance at the end of year 2: + 12.0628% - $150 withdrawal =	$2,249.55
Balance at the end of year 3: + 12.0628% =	$2,520.91
Balance at the end of year 4: + 12.0628% =	**$2,825.00**

There is no other interest rate—except 12.0628%—that will result in an exact ending balance of $2,825. Our longhand proof assures us that our cash flow registers can be trusted.

> **TIP** combine, and don't skip nothing
>
> Here are a few common errors in solving cash flow problems:
> - In Example 1, two cash flows occurred in year 4; the two amounts were combined before entering: $125 + $2,700 = $2,825. Entering the amounts separately would put $125 in year 4 and $2,700 in year 5; we would get a wrong answer (remember, "garbage in, garbage out").
> - By not entering zero for a cash flow of zero, the calculator will incorrectly assume that the next cash flow occurs sooner. Don't skip nothing!

b Calculating net present value (NPV)

In Example 1, we found the rate of return (IRR) when the payment amount changes. Now we will find the present value of a series of payments when the payment amount changes.

Example 2   Florence Curtis decides to sell her office supply business. Ishiro Suma offers to buy the business for $240,000 cash. Michael Gabriel offers to buy the business by paying $2,000 at the end of each month for 10 years, followed by $3,000 at the end of each month for 5 years. Assuming that money is worth 8.5% compounded monthly (that is the rate that Florence can earn on her money), which offer is better?

Michael will pay a total of $420,000: (120 × $2,000) + (60 × $3,000). But because the money is to be received in the future, the value is less than $420,000. Let's find the present value of Michael's offer.

Step 1   PV of the first stream of payments (120 payments of $2,000):

N	i	PV	PMT	FV
120	8.5 ÷ 12 = 0.708<u>3</u>	**-161,308.94**	2,000	

Step 2   PV of the second stream of payments (60 payments of $3,000):

N	i	PV	PMT	FV
60	8.5 ÷ 12 = 0.708<u>3</u>	**-146,223.55**	3,000	

Step 3   The value in Step 2 ($146,223.55) is the value at the *beginning* of that stream of payments (120 months from now), so the present value *today* is:

N	i	PV	PMT	FV
120	8.5 ÷ 12 = 0.708<u>3</u>	**-62,685.67**	0	146,223.55

Step 4   Find total PV

PV of first stream of payments (from Step 1)	$161,308.94
PV of second stream of payments (from Step 3)	+ 62,685.67
Total PV	**$223,994.61**

The real value of Michael's offer is $223,994.61. Ishiro's $240,000 cash offer is better.

We can solve Example 2 an easier way—with our cash flow registers! Remember, for cash flow problems the present value is referred to as net present value (NPV).

Example 3 Rework Example 2 using cash flow registers.

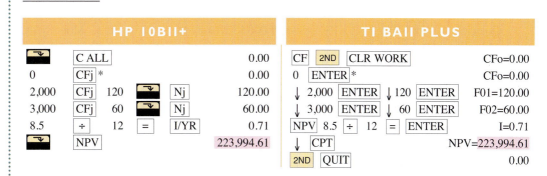

Note: For Michael's offer, the cash flow at the beginning of the first period is zero, so you may have been tempted to skip this cash flow. But, by doing so, you would not be able to solve the problem correctly.

We got identical answers in Examples 2 and 3 but the method of Example 3 (with cash flow registers) is considerably easier.

Let's try a few more cash flow problems in the U-Try-It exercises. The first is an investment in a rental property.

U-Try-It (Unit 17.4)

1. Hunter purchased a 2-unit rental property (a duplex) for $250,000. He paid $50,000 down and got a mortgage loan for the remaining $200,000. He collected rents and paid expenses (including his mortgage payments). The cash flows are summarized below. Notice that Hunter had negative cash flow the first 2 years because his expenses and mortgage payments exceeded the rent he collected. At the end of year 5, Hunter sold the property for $275,000. He had to pay selling expenses of $18,000 and his mortgage balance of $173,000, so he ended up receiving $84,000 ($275,000 - $18,000 - $173,000). Calculate Hunter's rate of return (IRR). *Note:* Assume that the cash flows are received at the end of each year (this is standard practice for real estate investors), and figure the IRR on cash flows, *not* on prices.

   Year 1: -$3,000   Year 2: -$1,000   Year 3: $4,000
   Year 4: $9,500   Year 5: $14,000   From sale (year 5): $84,000

2. You win the lottery and will collect $15,000 at the end of each month for 5 years, and then $20,000 at the end of each month for the following 5 years. If money is worth 8.25% compounded monthly, what is the value of your prize, in today's dollars?

Answers: (If you have a different answer, check the solution in Appendix A.)
1. 16.52%   **2.** $1,385,478.36

Chapter in a Nutshell

Objectives | **Examples**

Unit 17.1 Solving for interest rate paid

a Calculating an APR using the add-on method

You get a 7% 2-year $5,000 loan using the add-on method. Monthly payment? APR?

I = PRT = $5,000 × 7% × 2 = $700; $5,000 + $700 = $5,700; $5,700 ÷ 24 = $237.50

N	i	PV	PMT	FV
24	1.08 × 12 = 12.91	5,000	-237.50	

b Calculating an APR for an installment plan

Your insurance bill allows you to pay the $300 premium now or with 6 monthly payments of $55, starting today. APR if you elect to pay on the installment plan?

N	i	PV	PMT	FV
6	3.98 × 12 = 47.74*	300	-55 Begin**	

*Note: You may be tempted to multiply periodic rate by 6 (because n is 6) but there are 12 periods per year.
**Note: Don't forget to put back in "end" mode.

c Calculating an APR for an installment loan with front-end loan charges

You get a 3-year 7% $8,000 car loan. You must pay a $200 front-end fee. APR?

N	i	PV	PMT	FV
3 × 12 = 36	7 ÷ 12 = 0.58$\underline{3}$	8,000	**-247.02**	
↑	0.73 × 12 = 8.72	7,800	↑	

d Calculating an APR for a mortgage loan with front-end loan charges

You are thinking about getting a 15-year 6% $175,000 mortgage loan. You will incur loan costs totaling $7,000. Assume you will pay off the loan in 7 years. Real APR, reflecting the early payoff?

N	i	PV	PMT	FV
15 × 12 = 180	6 ÷ 12 = 0.50	175,000	**-1,476.75**	
84	0.57 × 12 = 6.85	168,000	↑	-112,373.47*

*Note: This is the balance after payment 84 (found by amortizing 84 payments); must *pay* this at the end of 7 years.

Unit 17.2 Growth rates

a Finding growth rates

Your annual salary 5 years ago was $18,000; it is now $24,000. Average annual increase?

N	i	PV	PMT	FV
5	5.92	-18,000		24,000

Unit 17.3 Solving for interest rate earned

a Calculating a yield on a non-income-producing asset

You bought a rare coin 10 years ago for $2,000. Sold it today for $3,000. Yield?

N	i	PV	PMT	FV
10	4.14	-2,000		3,000

b Calculating a yield on stock

You bought stock 4 years ago for $1,500. Received $50 dividends at the end of each quarter. Sold today for $4,300, less $150 brokerage fees, immediately after receiving the 16th dividend. Yield?

N	i	PV	PMT	FV
4 × 4 = 16	8.79 × 4 = 35.14	-1,500	50	4,150

Chapter in a Nutshell (continued)

Objectives	Examples
c Calculating a yield on bonds	You buy a 7% $1,000 corporate bond for $955. The bond pays interest at the end of each 6 months and matures in 13 years. YTM?

N	i	PV	PMT	FV
13 × 2 = 26	3.77 × 2 = 7.55	-955	35	1,000

Objectives	Examples
d Calculating a yield on mutual funds	You buy 25 mutual fund shares at $21.71 per share. You reinvest distributions and, as a result, own 34.127 shares in 5 years. You sell the shares at $24.52 per share. Yield?

N	i	PV	PMT	FV
5	9.04	-542.75		836.79

Objectives	Examples
e Calculating a yield on a promissory note	You are thinking about buying a promissory note for $73,000, in which case you will receive 207 monthly payments of $700, starting in 1 month. Yield compounded monthly if you buy it?

N	i	PV	PMT	FV
207	0.76 × 12 = 9.10	-73,000	700	

Unit 17.4 Cash flow problems

Objectives	Examples
a Calculating an internal rate of return (IRR)	Three years ago, you bought some corporate stock for $2,800. You received annual dividends as follows: $200 at the end of year 1, nothing for year 2, and $350 at the end of year 3. Immediately after getting the $350 check, you sold the stock for $4,300. What is your annual rate of return (IRR)?

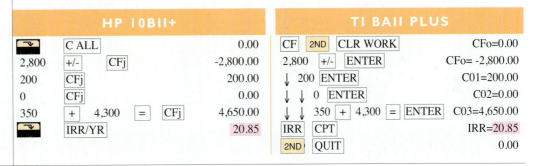

Objectives	Examples
b Calculating net present value (NPV)	A real estate broker is to receive a lease commission payable over the next 10 years: $5,000 at the end of each 6 months for 5 years, followed by $7,000 each 6 months for another 5 years. Assuming money is worth 9% compounded semiannually, what is the value of the future commissions?

HP 10BII+							TI BAII PLUS				
▼	C ALL					0.00	CF 2ND CLR WORK				CFo=0.00
0	CFj					0.00	0 ENTER				CFo=0.00
5,000	CFj	10	▼	Nj		10.00	↓ 5,000 ENTER ↓ 10 ENTER				F01=10.00
7,000	CFj	10	▼	Nj		10.00	↓ 7,000 ENTER ↓ 10 ENTER				F02=10.00
9	÷	2	=	I/YR		4.50	NPV 9 ÷ 2 = ENTER				I=4.50
▼	NPV					75,230.12	↓ CPT				NPV=75,230.12
							2ND QUIT				0.00

Chapter in a Nutshell 375

Chapter in a Nutshell (concluded)

Objectives | **Examples**

Enrichment Topics

The following Enrichment Topics, which go a bit beyond what is in the text, are available for this chapter:

Buy or Rent a Home? Buy or Lease a Car?
Rent-to-Own Option
Finding FV for a Series of Unequal Deposits
Capital Budgeting
Bonds with a Call Feature
Valuation of Common Stock

If your instructor doesn't cover these topics in class and you would like to dig in deeper on your own, please send a request to *studentsupport@olympuspub.com*. You can also request a set of keystrokes for your particular calculator.

Think

1. A lender must disclose an APR on a Disclosure Statement. Why, then, would a borrower want to calculate his or her own APR? As part of your answer, explain the difference between calculating the APR the lender discloses and the APR a borrower should calculate on his or her own? Which APR will be greater and why?
2. If you have a choice between two mortgage loans, why not just select the one with the lower stated interest rate?
3. If you are thinking about refinancing your mortgage loan, explain why you shouldn't decide by comparing the APR on the new loan with the APR on the old loan.
4. For what types of problems can we use the time-value-of-money registers of financial calculators, and for what types of problems must we use the cash flow registers?
5. Suppose you bought some stock 10 years ago for $10,000, received a $500 dividend check at the end of each year, and just sold the stock for $15,000. Can we calculate the rate of return using time-value-of-money registers? Can we, instead, use the cash flow registers? Try solving the problem both ways. What conclusions can you draw?

Explore

1. Go to www.webbertext.com and click Online Calculator. Using the online calculator and the guidelines shown on that page, solve each of the U-Try-It problems from Unit 17.3.
2. Refer to Appendix E. Review the explanations for using Excel to solve for IRR and NPV. Then use Excel to solve each of the U-Try-It problems from Unit 17.4.
3. Research the cost of at least 4 products or services that were advertised in newspapers or magazines more than 25 years ago. Then find the current cost. Calculate the annual rate of increase (or decrease) in prices between the two points in time. Include copies of the articles as well as your solutions. *Note:* To find the old advertisements or articles you can search the Internet or visit a local library.

Apply

1. **Comparing APRs.** Contact a mortgage loan company and ask for help with this project. Get information about two different types of mortgage loans for a specified amount, including interest rate, term, loan costs, points, and other fees. Submit a *good faith estimate* for each loan. Project how long you will keep the loan before paying it off. Calculate your APR for each loan, based on the early payoff. Submit all calculations; include the names of the mortgage loan company and the loan officer.

Chapter Review Problems

Unit 17.1 Solving for interest rate paid

1. You are thinking about getting a $27,500 loan at 7.2% interest with monthly payments over 4 years. Your bank will withhold $300 for an origination fee. What is the APR?

2. You buy some furniture for $2,500. You pay $350 down and the retailer finances the remainder with 36 monthly payments of $77.64. Calculate your APR.

3. You buy a used pick-up truck from a friend for $4,000. Your friend agrees to finance the entire amount with payments of $135 per month for 36 months, starting in 1 month. If you can borrow the $4,000 from your credit union at 11.75%, should you do so? Explain your answer by determining the rate that your friend is charging.

4. You buy some furniture for $800. The retailer finances the entire amount for 1 year and says you will be charged 10% interest. However, the retailer uses the add-on method. First calculate your monthly payment. Then calculate the real rate you are paying.

5. You just received your car insurance bill. The company gives you a choice of paying the entire 6-month premium of $470 now or paying with 6 monthly installments of $83.50 (starting today). What interest rate (APR) will you be paying if you elect to pay with the installment method?

For Problems 6–11, assume you buy a home and borrow $90,000 at 6.5% for 25 years. You pay a total of $4,525 for origination fee, points, and mortgage insurance. In addition, you pay other loan costs of $1,128. You pay the first year's hazard insurance premium of $400 and are required to deposit $425 into an escrow account.

6. What is the reportable APR?

7. What is your real APR, assuming the loan is not paid off early?

8. Without calculating a precise APR, decide if, by prepaying the loan, your APR will be more or less than the APR found in Problem 14.

9. Assume you will pay off the loan at the end of 6 years. What is your real APR, reflecting the early payoff?

10. Assume, before you get this loan, you are offered another loan: $90,000 over 25 years at 6.875% interest. You must pay loan costs totaling $3,853 (you save $1,800 in points for getting the higher interest rate loan). Assuming you will pay off the loan at the end of 6 years, what is your real APR on this loan, reflecting the early payoff?

11. Refer to Problems 9 and 10. Which loan has the lower APR?

12. You currently owe $77,848.89 on your mortgage loan, with an interest rate of 11.5%. Interest rates are currently 9.5%, and you are thinking about refinancing, in which case you will borrow $80,000 for 30 years. You will incur loan costs of $2,300 on the new loan (payable in cash when you get the loan), and you must pay a prepayment penalty of $3,000 on the old loan for paying it off early. Calculate your APR on the new loan assuming you pay off the new loan in 8 years (there is no prepayment penalty on the new loan).

13. Refer to Problem 12. Should you refinance?

Unit 17.2 Growth rates

14. (True Story) Clara Patterson and Bill Mayne got married in 1940. A year later, they bought a home in Salt Lake City, Utah, for $2,450. They lived in the home, in romantic bliss, until 2003; the home was worth $165,000. At what average annual rate did the home increase in value?

15. One way of measuring inflation is through the use of the consumer price index (CPI), which tracks the cost of a "basket of goods" (food, housing, medical care, fuel, etc.). The base year of the current index is 1983, when the basket of goods cost $100. The CPI was 9.9 in 1913 (meaning the same basket of goods cost $9.90), 30.6 in 1963, and 238.7 in 2015. Calculate the average annual rate of inflation for the following periods: **(a)** 1913 to 1963, **(b)** 1963 to 1983, **(c)** 1983 to 2015, and **(d)** 1913 to 2015.

16. Your annual salary 12 years ago was $15,600; it is now $23,000. If the inflation rate over the last 12 years has averaged 3.5% per year, has your salary kept up with inflation?

17. In 1943 a gallon of milk cost $0.62. In 2015, a gallon of milk cost $4.05. What is the average annual rate of increase?

18. If gasoline prices increased over a 35-year period from 35.9 cents per gallon to $4.399 per gallon, what is the average annual rate of increase?

Unit 17.3 Solving for interest rate earned

19. Joe Salazar purchased some vacant land 4 years ago for $28,500. He just sold the land for $40,000. What interest rate, compounded annually, did Joe earn on the investment?

For Problems 20–24, assume you just bought a 7% $1,000 bond for $940, immediately after the annual interest payment was paid to the previous owner. The bond matures in 8 years.

20. What is the YTM?

21. Why were you able to buy this bond for less than the $1,000 face value?

22. Why was your YTM greater than the 7% coupon rate?

23. You sell the bond in 5 years for $1,170, less brokerage fees of $40. What is your yield during ownership?

24. Why is your yield during ownership greater than the YTM of Problem 20?

25. Bonds that have a high degree of risk must provide a high interest rate to attract investors. (T or F)

26. All municipal bonds are tax-exempt. (T or F)

27. You buy 25 mutual fund shares at a price of $12.23 per share. You elect to reinvest distributions and, as a result, own 38.214 shares in 5 years. You sell the shares at a price of $24.44, less fees of $55. Calculate your annual rate of return.

28. You invest $40 each month (starting today) into a mutual fund. You reinvest distributions. At the end of 6 years, you sell all your shares and receive $2,522. Calculate your rate of return.

29. (True Story) In March, 1986, 15-year-old Jennifer Sanchez, a self-proclaimed "computer geek," invested her $750 life savings into a new stock—Microsoft. 14 years later, her investment turned into $450,000 plus a new Porsche 911 convertible, worth $82,500. Calculate Jennifer's average annual rate of return.

Unit 17.4 Cash flow problems

30. You have the chance to buy a promissory note in which you will receive 66 monthly payments of $500 (starting a month from now), followed by 120 monthly payments of $750. If you buy the note, what is the total amount you will receive?

31. Refer to Problem 30. What is your yield if you buy the note for $60,000?

32. You and three friends are thinking about buying a 6-unit rental property for $425,000, by paying $50,000 down and paying the seller the remaining $375,000 with monthly payments. Your projected cash flows for each year are shown below. You project you will be able to sell the property at the end of year 5 for $455,000; your selling expenses will be $30,000 and you will still owe the seller $341,000. Calculate the IRR, based on your projections. *Note:* Assume that the cash flows are received at the end of each year.

| Year 1: -$5,200 | Year 2: -$1,400 | Year 3: $3,500 |
| Year 4: $7,700 | Year 5: $10,000 | From sale (year 5): $84,000 |

33. You have the chance to buy a promissory note in which you will receive 42 monthly payments of $700 (starting a month from now), followed by 180 monthly payments of $800. What is the total amount you will receive?

34. Refer to Problem 33. If you want to earn 8.75% compounded monthly, what price should you pay for the note?

Challenge problems

35. For which investment(s) can we determine a yield *before* buying: (a) stock, (b) bond, (c) mutual fund, (d) promissory note?

36. You bought 100 shares of stock at a price of $38.50 per share and incurred brokerage fees totaling $80. Four years later, you sold the stock at a price of $46 per share and incurred brokerage fees totaling $120. Calculate your rate of return.

37. Refer to Problem 36. Assume you received dividends of 75¢ per share at the end of each year and you received your fourth annual dividend immediately before selling the stock. Calculate your rate of return.

38. Refer to Problem 37. Assume you received dividends of $75 at the end of year 1, $100 at the end of year 2, nothing at the end of year 3, and $150 at the end of year 4 (just before you sold the stock). Calculate your rate of return.

39. Refer to the newspaper article. What is the average annual rate of return?

Ben Franklin is still saving pennies

Birthday gift. Bequest has grown from $4,000 to $520,000 and will be used to help students of trades, crafts and the applied sciences.

PHILADELPHIA (UPI) — The proceeds of Benjamin Franklin's estate will be used to help educate young Philadelphians in the trades and applied sciences, city officials and members of a blue-ribbon panel said Tuesday.

The planned use of the bequest was announced on the 200th anniversary of Franklin's death, the date when Franklin instructed his trust was to be terminated.

The bequest has grown from about $4,000 to $520,000, and the prospect of using his legacy drew more than 300 proposals from various groups...

40. Assuming a 28% tax rate, which bond, purchased at par, has the greater after-tax rate of return: **(a)** a corporate bond paying 6.75% or **(b)** a tax-free municipal bond paying 5.25%?

For Problems 41–44, assume you have a chance to buy a promissory note in which you will receive 157 monthly payments of $550, starting a month from now.

41. What is the total amount you will receive?

42. The seller of the note asks you to pay $55,000 for the note. If you do, what will your yield be?

43. If you want to earn 8.5% compounded monthly, can you pay more, or must you pay less than $55,000?

44. What price should you pay for the note if you want to earn 8.5% compounded monthly?

45. Which bond purchased at par ($1,000 face value) provides the greater return: A 7.6% bond paying interest *annually* or a 7.5% bond paying interest *semiannually*?

Practice Test

1. Your insurance bill allows you to pay the $345 six-month premium now or with 6 monthly payments of $62.50, starting today. What APR would you pay with the installment plan?

2. You are thinking about getting a 20-year $220,000 mortgage loan at 6.75%. You will incur a total of $7,200 for origination fee, points, mortgage insurance, and other loan costs. In addition, you will have to pay the first year's hazard insurance premium of $400 and put $350 into an escrow account. You project paying off the loan at the end of 6 years. What is your real APR, reflecting the early payoff?

3. If the average value of homes in your area has increased over the last 10 years from $155,000 to $238,000, what is the average annual rate of increase?

4. You buy a 7.5% $1,000 corporate bond for $965. The bond pays interest at the end of each 6 months and matures in 17 years. What is your YTM?

5. Junko Fujimoto purchased some corporate stock 8 years ago for $12,000. Junko received quarterly dividends of $200 at the end of each quarter for the first 5 years, nothing for the sixth year, and $250 at the end of each quarter for the last 2 years. Immediately after receiving the last quarterly dividend, Junko sold the stock for $17,300. What interest rate, compounded quarterly, did Junko earn?

6. You have the chance to buy a promissory note in which you receive 34 monthly payments of $650 (starting a month from now), followed by 180 monthly payments of $850. If you want to earn 9% compounded monthly, what price should you pay for the note?

Quotable Quip
Success in business is 1% inspiration and 99% perspiration.
— Thomas Edison

Quotable Quip
I should like to live like a poor man, with a great deal of money.
— Pablo Picasso

Quotable Quip
The only place where success comes before work is in a dictionary.
— Vidal Sassoon

Quotable Quip
By working faithfully eight hours a day, you may eventually get to be a boss and work twelve hours a day.
— Robert Frost

Individual Net Worth
The U.S. Federal Reserve System gathers data on individual net worth. Here are recent averages (median), by age and education level:

By Age
Under 25	$1,475
25–34	$8,525
35–44	$51,575
45–54	$98,350
55–64	$180,125
65+	$232,000

By Education
No high school diploma	$20,600
High school diploma	$68,700
Some college	$69,300
College degree	$226,100

Public Debt of the U.S.
As of Oct. 10, 2015, the national debt was approximately $18,150,500,000,000 (over $18 trillion). Based on a U.S. population of about 322,000,000, each person's share (including children) is about $56,368. Here are the historic numbers.

Year	Debt ($billions)	Debt per person
1870	$2.4	$61.06
1880	$2.0	$41.60
1890	$1.1	$17.80
1900	$1.2	$16.60
1910	$1.1	$12.41
1920	$24.2	$228
1930	$16.1	$131
1940	$43.0	$325
1950	$256.1	$1,688
1960	$284.1	$1,572
1970	$370.1	$1,814
1980	$907.7	$3,985
1990	$3,233.3	$13,000
2000	$5,674.2	$20,591
2010	$13,561.6	$44,031
2015	$18,150.5	$56,368

Top 5 U.S. Companies (Sales, 2014)
1. Wal-Mart $485,651,000,000
2. Exxon Mobil $382,597,000,000
3. Chevron $203,784,000,000
4. Berkshire Hathaway $194,673,000,000
5. Apple $182,795,000,000

Source: Fortune Magazine, 2014

"My accountant says I've got all the money I'll ever need — if I die by Tuesday."

Financial Statements: How to Read and Interpret

18

Approximately 75,000 businesses go broke each year in the United States. Many do so because their owners become lost in the day-to-day operations of the business and do not take the time to see the big picture in the financial reports of the business.

Bookkeepers record transactions of a business and accountants summarize the data into financial reports. The purpose of this chapter is not to show how to record the transactions or assemble the data into financial reports. Instead, *this chapter focuses on reading and interpreting the reports*. Being able to read and interpret financial reports is crucial not only for a business owner or manager but also for others such as bankers and investors who are evaluating a company.

We will begin the chapter by exploring the two main types of financial statements: income statements and balance sheets. We will finish by studying trends and ratios that are important to businesses.

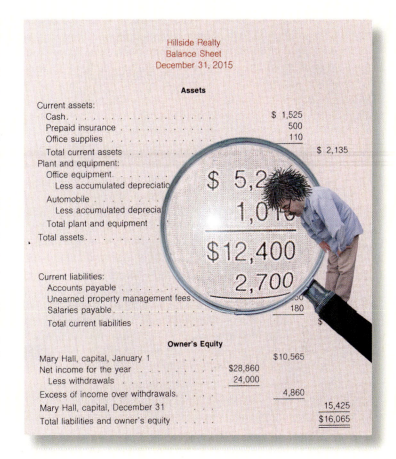

Unit Objectives

Unit 18.1 Income statements

a. Interpreting an income statement for a service company
b. Interpreting an income statement for a merchandising company

Unit 18.2 Balance sheets

a. Identifying assets and liabilities
b. Determining owner's equity

Unit 18.3 Trend and ratio analysis

a. Evaluating trends through vertical and horizontal analysis
b. Evaluating business ratios

Unit 18.1 Income statements

Robin has been working at a gift shop and is thinking about starting her own gift shop. While Robin has not had many business classes, she is excited to learn about businesses. She has learned a bit about the basic forms of business ownership, all of which are created under state law.

A **sole proprietorship** has 1 owner.

A **partnership** has 2 or more owners. A **partnership agreement** spells out each partner's duties and rights; partners do not necessarily share profits equally.

A **corporation** is a separate entity, like a person: able to buy assets, borrow money, and perform other business activities. The corporation issues shares of **stock** to investors (called **stockholders**), who become owners of the corporation. The stockholders elect a board of directors, whose members in turn select officers to oversee the day-to-day operations. Corporations can have as few as 1 stockholder or can have millions of stockholders.

A **limited liability company (LLC)** is a special type of ownership that limits the personal liability of its owners (resulting in the title *limited liability* company). An LLC has 1 or more owners.

Later (at the end of Unit 18.2), we will explore some pros and cons of each form of ownership.

Robin has also been learning about financial statements. An **income statement**, sometimes referred to as a **profit and loss statement** or an **operating statement**, shows the profitability of a business *over a period of time*. When revenues exceed expenses, the business has a **profit**; when expenses exceed revenues, the business has a **loss**.

Robin has figured out there are two types of business operations: those that provide *services*, such as accountants, lawyers, real estate brokers, engineers, doctors, and architects; and those that sell *products* (known as merchandising companies), such as grocery stores, department stores, gasoline stations, wholesalers, and manufacturers. Robin's gift shop would be a merchandising company. Income statements for service companies are slightly different from those of merchandising companies. Let's start with the easier of the two: service companies.

Many people, like Robin, dream of owning their own business. Before doing so, it is wise to understand the basics of business ownership and financial statements.

a Interpreting an income statement for a service company

For service companies, profit (or **net income**) is figured by deducting expenses from revenues.

service company income statement formula

Net income = Revenues - Expenses

An income statement for an appraisal business is shown in Illustration 18-1.

388   Chapter 18   Financial Statements: How to Read and Interpret

Illustration 18-1 Income Statement for a Service Company

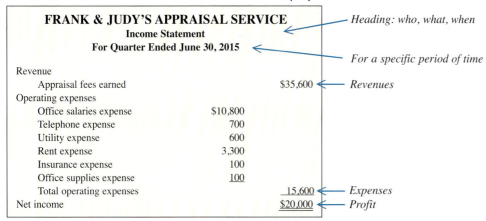

FRANK & JUDY'S APPRAISAL SERVICE
Income Statement
For Quarter Ended June 30, 2015

Revenue		
Appraisal fees earned		$35,600
Operating expenses		
Office salaries expense	$10,800	
Telephone expense	700	
Utility expense	600	
Rent expense	3,300	
Insurance expense	100	
Office supplies expense	100	
Total operating expenses		15,600
Net income		$20,000

Heading: who, what, when
For a specific period of time
Revenues
Expenses
Profit

Example 1 Evaluate the income statement of Illustration 18-1 by answering the following questions.
 a. How much money was earned from customers?
 b. What are total operating expenses?
 c. What is the net income (profit)?
 d. Income and expenses are for what period of time?

 _____

 a. $35,600   b. $15,600   c. $20,000   d. April 1 through June 30 (3 months)

b Interpreting an income statement for a merchandising company

Merchandising companies must pay for the goods they sell. Think of the **cost of goods sold** as an expense of the company to be deducted from sales revenue before other expenses are subtracted. Robin's Uncle Jerry is a stockholder in Bonneville Electric Supply (a wholesaler of electrical supplies). Because Robin is thinking about starting a merchandising business (a gift shop), she asks Uncle Jerry to explain income statements. An abbreviated income statement for Bonneville is shown as Illustration 18-2; it is referred to as an *abbreviated* income statement because it merely shows the major items. The same income statement is expanded (with more detail) in Illustration 18-3. *Pay special attention to the footnotes.*

Illustration 18-2 Abbreviated Income Statement for a Merchandising Company

BONNEVILLE ELECTRIC SUPPLY, INC.
Income Statement, Abbreviated
For Year Ended December 31, 2015

Net sales	$973,400
Less cost of goods sold	702,700
Gross profit	$270,700
Less expenses	187,300
Net income (before income taxes)	$83,400

Illustration 18-3 Expanded Income Statement for a Merchandising Company

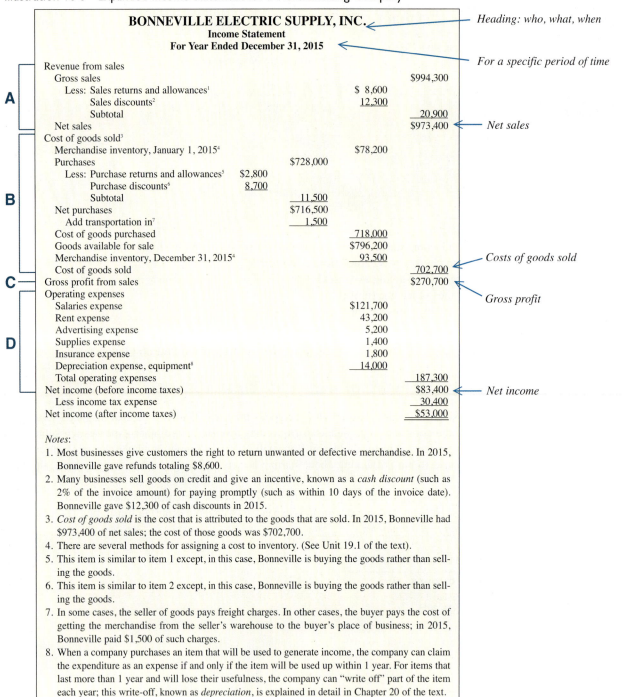

Notice, Illustration 18-3 is divided into four sections. Let's take a closer look at how each section is built.

formulas for a merchandising company income statement

Section A: **Net sales** = Gross sales - Sales returns - Sales discounts

Section B: **Cost of goods sold** = Beginning inventory + Cost of goods purchased (Purchases - Returns - Discounts + Transportation in) - Ending inventory

Section C: **Gross profit** = Net sales - Cost of goods sold

Section D: **Net income** = Gross profit - Operating expenses

Example 2   Refer to Illustration 18-3. Verify net sales ($973,400), cost of goods sold ($702,700), gross profit ($270,700), and net income ($83,400).

Net sales = Gross sales - Sales returns - Sales discounts
= $994,300 - $ 8,600 - $12,300 = $973,400

Cost of goods sold = Beginning inventory + Cost of goods purchased - Ending inventory
= $ 78,200 + $718,000 - $93,500 = $702,700

Gross profit = Net sales - Cost of goods sold
= $973,400 - $702,700 = $270,700

Net income = Gross profit - Operating expenses
= $270,700 - $187,300 = $83,400

how are income taxes handled?

In Illustration 18-3, the next to last line provides for income taxes. Business profits are subject to federal income tax (most states and some cities also charge income tax). Here is how federal income tax is handled:

- **Corporations.** For corporations (like Bonneville), the income and expenses of the corporation are shown on a *corporate income tax return* and income taxes are paid by the corporation.
- **Sole proprietorships.** The income and expenses of the business are reported on the owner's personal income tax return (on *Schedule C*); the net income is added to the owner's other income before calculating the tax.
- **Parnerships.** The income and expenses are reported on a *partnership income tax return*, submitted by the partnership. The tax return is for informational purposes only; taxes are not paid by the partnership. Instead, each owner reports his or her share of the net income on his or her personal income tax return (on *Schedule E*).
- **LLC.** Before doing business, the LLC, as part of getting an Employer Identification Number (EIN), must select how it wishes to be taxed. If the LLC has only one owner, it must be taxed like a sole proprietorship. If the LLC has more than one owner, it can elect to be taxed as either a corporation or partnership.

TIP   pay yourself a salary or not?

The greater a company's net income, the greater the income taxes. Salaries are treated as an expense of the business, so you may wonder if, as a sole proprietor, you should pay yourself a salary, thereby reducing the business net income. By doing so, the net income of the business is, in fact, less. But the money paid to yourself is added to your personal income; your total taxable income will be the same whether you pay yourself a salary or not.

U-Try-It (Unit 18.1)

1. A business had $13,600 monthly revenues and $8,400 expenses. What is the net income?
2. A convenience store had monthly gross sales of $52,000; sales returns of $800; beginning inventory of $6,500; cost of goods purchased of $31,700; ending inventory of $7,100; and operating expenses of $9,400. Calculate **(a)** net sales **(b)** costs of goods sold, **(c)** gross profit, and **(d)** net income.

Answers: (If you have a different answer, check the solution in Appendix A.)
1. $5,200   **2a.** $51,200   **2b.** $31,100   **2c.** $20,100   **2d.** $10,700

Unit 18.2 Balance sheets

As mentioned, income statements show the profitability of a business for a certain period of time. A **balance sheet** shows a company's financial position on a certain date (the close of business on that date), after taking into account preceding profits; it lists all of the **assets** and **liabilities** together with the resulting **equity** (value) of the business. Robin would like to know more about assets, liabilities, and equity.

Identifying assets and liabilities

An asset is something of value that is *owned*. Assets are often divided into four categories.
- **Current assets** consist of cash (including checking and savings account balances) and other assets that can be converted into cash within 1 year (or a normal operating cycle for some businesses).
- **Plant and equipment** are assets that will last longer than 1 year and that are used in the operation of the business, such as equipment, business vehicles, buildings, and land used for the business.
- **Investment assets** include things like land for future expansion, stocks, and bonds.
- **Intangible assets** include things like patents and trademarks.

> **at what value should assets be listed on a balance sheet: cost or current value?**
>
> Suppose 10 years ago a company paid $50,000 for a future business site; the site (still vacant) is now believed to be worth $400,000. Accounting principles require that *assets be shown at cost rather than current value*. So, the land should be shown at $50,000 not $400,000. You may wonder why this is done. Suppose the business owner is trying to get a bank loan and shows the value at $2,000,000 on the balance sheet. The bank would be misled into thinking the business is worth more than it really is. To avoid this problem, assets are listed at cost rather than at an arbitrary value.

A liability is an obligation that is *owed* to someone else. Liabilities are divided into two categories.
- **Current liabilities** are debts that must be paid within 1 year (or one operating cycle for some businesses), like accounts payable.
- **Long-term liabilities** are debts that are not "current."

Part of a debt may be classified as a current liability while the remainder is classified as a long-term liability. Assume, for example, that a business owes $120,000 on a mortgage loan. The portion of the loan amount that is to be repaid within 1 year (only the *principal* portion, not the *interest* portion) is considered a current liability, whereas the remainder of the loan balance is considered a long-term liability.

Example 1 Classify the following seven items as either a current asset, plant and equipment, investment asset, intangible asset, current liability, or long-term liability:
- a. accounts receivable
- b. accounts payable
- c. trademark
- d. office equipment
- e. building and land for present location
- f. land for future expansion
- g. mortgage payable (10 years remaining)

---

a. current asset   **b.** current liability   **c.** intangible asset   **d.** plant and equipment
e. plant and equipment   **f.** investment asset   **g.** part current liability; part long-term liability

ⓑ Determining owner's equity

Owner's equity is found by subtracting liabilities from assets; it represents the net value of the business to the owner. To illustrate, suppose a company quits doing business. The company must pay creditors any amounts owed; the balance goes to the owner. This leads to the following formula.

=	owner's equity formula
	Owner's equity = Assets - Liabilities

Example 2 Paula O'Malley, MD, owns a medical practice. On December 31, her business had total assets of $438,600 and total liabilities of $62,100. Calculate Paula's equity in the business.

Owner's equity = Assets - Liabilities = $438,600 - $62,100 = $376,500

A modification of the owner's equity formula is known as the **accounting equation.**

=	accounting equation
	Assets = Liabilities + Owner's equity

Example 3 For Example 2, show that the accounting equation is in balance.

Assets = Liabilities + Owner's Equity
$438,600 = $62,100 + $376,500
$438,600 = $438,600   *(Assets do, in fact, equal liabilities plus owner's equity.)*

🔑	official title of equity section
	Here are the most common titles used in the equity section of a balance sheet:
	For a sole proprietorship: Owner's equity
	For a partnership: Partners' capital
	For a corporation: Stockholders' equity
	For an LLC: Members' capital

Robin is now ready to study the balance sheet of Bonneville, shown as Illustration 18-4. Pay special attention to the footnotes.

Notice in Illustration 18-4 that total assets ($361,800) equal total liabilities plus stockholders' equity ($361,800); because the accounting equation is in balance, both figures are double-underlined.

Illustration 18-4 Balance Sheet for a Merchandising company

BONNEVILLE ELECTRIC SUPPLY, INC.
Balance Sheet
December 31, 2015

Heading: who, what, when
Specific date

Assets

Current assets
  Cash $85,000
  Accounts receivable[1] 60,000
  Merchandise inventory[2] 93,500
  Prepaid expenses[3] 1,500
  Total current assets $240,000
Plant and equipment
  Store and office equipment $85,000
  Less accumulated depreciation[4] 43,200
     41,800
Investment assets
  Land for future location 80,000
Total assets $361,800

Liabilities

Current liabilities
  Accounts payable[5] $61,700
  Notes payable[6] 5,000
Total liabilities $66,700

Totals balance, so double underlined

Stockholders' Equity

Common stock: 20,000 shares authorized and outstanding at $10 a share[7] $200,000
Retained earnings[8] 95,100
Total stockholders' equity 295,100
Total liabilities and stockholders' equity $361,800

Notes:
1. Some of Bonneville's customers buy merchandise with an agreement to pay later; customers owe Bonneville a total of $60,000 on December 31, 2015.
2. This is inventory on December 31, 2015 (at Bonneville's cost). Notice that this is the same as the ending inventory of Illustration 18-3.
3. Bonneville has prepaid some of its expenses (such as rent, insurance, and unused office supplies).
4. This is the total depreciation taken so far.
5. Bonneville purchases goods on account. The balance owed on December 31, 2015, is $61,700; most is probably for inventory.
6. In addition to accounts payable, Bonneville owes creditors $5,000 for which Bonneville has signed promissory notes.
7. Bonneville has issued (sold) 20,000 shares of stock to the public at a price of $10 per share; Bonneville collected a total of $200,000 from these stock sales.
8. Retained earnings are Bonneville's earnings (since inception of the corporation) that have not been distributed as dividends.

> **TIP** distinction between an income statement and a balance sheet
>
> We have studied income statements and balance sheets. An income statement reflects the *profitability* of a business *over a given period of time*. A balance sheet reflects a company's *financial position* at a certain point in time after taking into account preceding profits. A heading for an income statement should *always* show the period of time for which revenues and expenses occurred. For example, if an income statement shows a profit of $20,000 but no time period, owners (as well as new creditors) would like to know how long it took to earn the $20,000 profit. A heading for a balance sheet should *always* state a specific date (not a period of time).

A **personal financial statement** is the name given to a balance sheet for *individuals* (as opposed to businesses). While the primary focus of the text is on balance sheets for businesses, here is some helpful information for preparing a personal financial statement.

  personal financial statement

> A personal financial statement lists assets and liabilities of an individual or married couple; when liabilities are subtracted from assets, the result is called **net worth** (not equity). Unlike the case of a balance sheet for a business, assets for a personal financial statement are often shown at current value rather than at cost; a footnote should indicate when this is done.

Robin is feeling pretty comfortable with business financial statements. She is, however, wondering which form of ownership (sole proprietorship, partnership, corporation, or LLC) might be best for her. Uncle Jerry provided the following food for thought.

which form of ownership is best?

Personal liability

For some forms of ownership, owners are *personally liable* to creditors; for others their liability is limited to their investment. For a sole proprietorship, the owner is personally liable. For a **general partnership** (the typical partnership), each partner is personally liable, and remember that a creditor can collect 100% of the debt from any or all partners. For a **limited partnership** (requiring special legal documentation), there are two types of partners: one or more general partners, who run the business, and one or more **limited partners,** who contribute money but are not actively involved in the business. General partners are personally liable; limited partners are not. For corporations, stockholders are not personally liable beyond their contribution, or in the case of fraud. For an LLC, owners (referred to as *members*) are not personally liable beyond their contribution or in the case of fraud. Because of the limited liability, a corporation or LLC may have difficulty getting a loan unless someone personally guarantees the loan.

Distributions of cash

Businesses often have extra cash. For sole proprietorships and partnerships, distributions of excess cash are tax-free (owners have already paid taxes on profits). For corporations, the distributions are referred to as **dividends**. As of writing this text, dividends are taxable to stockholders. The corporation pays tax on the corporation's profit, then the owner must pay income tax on the remainder if distributed as dividends. This *double taxation* is a drawback of corporations. For some corporations (those with no more than 35 stockholders), the corporation can apply with the IRS to be treated as an **S Corporation**; if approved, the corporation files a tax return for informational purposes, and stockholders report their share of corporate profits on their personal income tax return. Dividends for an S Corporation are, under most conditions, tax-free. For an LLC, distributions of excess cash are treated according to how the LLC elected to be taxed (as a corporation, partnership, or sole proprietorship) when it applied for an Employer Identification Number.

Let's try a U-Try-It problem to check our understanding of balance sheets.

U-Try-It (Unit 18.2)

1. A gift shop has $15,000 cash; $11,000 accounts payable; $95,000 store and office equipment; $38,700 accumulated depreciation on store and office equipment; $18,000 accounts receivable; $2,000 notes payable; and $24,000 inventory. What is the owner's equity?

Answers: (If you have a different answer, check the solution in Appendix A.)
1. $100,300

Unit 18.3 Trend and ratio analysis

In this unit, we will examine ways business owners can determine how their business is doing. One way to analyze a business is to compare financial statements from two or more successive accounting periods. This is known as **trend analysis**.

a Evaluating trends through vertical and horizontal analysis

Business owners and managers should take the time to analyze financial statements to determine how the business is doing.

To determine whether a business is improving, financial statements from two or more successive accounting periods can be placed side by side and compared. When the data from these financial statements are placed on one report, the report is called a **comparative statement**. Comparative statements generally include two types of analysis: **vertical analysis**, in which we go up and down columns to determine what part of a whole each dollar amount is, and **horizontal analysis**, in which we move across the columns to determine the increase or decrease between successive accounting periods (the increase or decrease is often stated as both a dollar amount and a percent). A comparative income statement and balance sheet for Bonneville are shown as Illustrations 18-5 and 18-6. For identification purposes, lines are numbered 1 through 27 and columns are lettered A through F. The data in column A come from Illustrations 18-3 and 18-4. Data for the preceding year (2014) are shown in column B. *Vertical analysis* is performed in columns C and D, and *horizontal analysis* is performed in columns E and F.

You may wonder how the amounts were found for columns C and D (vertical analysis) and E and F (horizontal analysis). Here is a summary:

---

vertical and horizontal analysis

vertical analysis

Column C for Income Statement. Divide each amount in column A by "net sales" of column A to determine what part of net sales each amount is.

Column C for Balance Sheet. Divide each amount in column A by "total assets" (or the equivalent "total liabilities and SH equity") to determine what part of the total each asset, liability, or equity item is.

Column D. Same procedure as for column C, except use amounts in column B instead of column A.

horizontal analysis

Column E. Column A (most recent year) - Column B (prior year); this gives the *dollar amount* of increase or decrease.

Column F. Column E (the dollar amount of increase) ÷ Column B (prior year); this gives the *percent* increase or decrease.

Remember: A negative value divided by a positive value results in a negative value.

Example 1 Refer to Illustrations 18-5 and 18-6. Verify the amounts for lines 7 and 16, columns C through F.

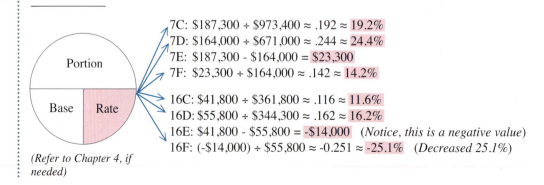

7C: $187,300 ÷ $973,400 ≈ .192 ≈ **19.2%**
7D: $164,000 ÷ $671,000 ≈ .244 ≈ **24.4%**
7E: $187,300 - $164,000 = **$23,300**
7F: $23,300 ÷ $164,000 ≈ .142 ≈ **14.2%**
16C: $41,800 ÷ $361,800 ≈ .116 ≈ **11.6%**
16D: $55,800 ÷ $344,300 ≈ .162 ≈ **16.2%**
16E: $41,800 - $55,800 = **-$14,000**   (Notice, this is a negative value)
16F: (-$14,000) ÷ $55,800 ≈ -0.251 ≈ **-25.1%**   (Decreased 25.1%)

(Refer to Chapter 4, if needed)

Illustration 18-5 Comparative Income Statement for Bonneville (2015 vs 2014)

	Annual Amounts		Percent of Net Sales		Increase (or Decrease)	
	A	B	C	D	E	F
	2015	2014	2015	2014	Amount	Percent
① Gross sales	$994,300	$685,600	102.1%	102.2%	$308,700	45.0%
② Sales returns and allowances	8,600	6,200	0.9%	0.9%	2,400	38.7%
③ Sales discounts	12,300	8,400	1.3%	1.3%	3,900	46.4%
④ Net sales	$973,400	$671,000	100.0%	100.0%	$302,400	45.1%
⑤ Cost of goods sold	702,700	452,300	72.2%	67.4%	250,400	55.4%
⑥ Gross profit	$270,700	$218,700	27.8%	32.6%	$52,000	23.8%
⑦ Total operating expenses	187,300	164,000	19.2%	24.4%	23,300	14.2%
⑧ Net income (before income taxes)	$83,400	$54,700	8.6%	8.2%	$28,700	52.5%
⑨ Less income taxes	30,400	20,000	3.1%	3.0%	10,400	52.0%
⑩ Net income (after income taxes)	$53,000	$34,700	5.4%	5.2%	$18,300	52.7%

Illustration 18-6 Comparative Balance Sheet for Bonneville (Dec. 31, 2015 vs Dec. 31, 2014)

	Year-end Amounts		Percent of Total		Increase (or Decrease)	
	A	B	C	D	E	F
	2015	2014	2015	2014	Amount	Percent
Assets						
Current assets						
⑪ Cash	$85,000	$82,700	23.5%	24.0%	$2,300	2.8%
⑫ Accounts receivable	60,000	47,000	16.6%	13.7%	13,000	27.7%
⑬ Merchandise inventory	93,500	78,200	25.8%	22.7%	15,300	19.6%
⑭ Prepaid expenses	1,500	600	0.4%	0.2%	900	150.0%
⑮ Total current assets	$240,000	$208,500	66.3%	60.6%	$31,500	15.1%
⑯ Plant and equipment, net	41,800	55,800	11.6%	16.2%	(14,000)	(25.1)%
⑰ Investment assets	80,000	80,000	22.1%	23.2%	0	0%
⑱ Total assets	$361,800	$344,300	100.0%	100.0%	$17,500	5.1%
Liabilities						
Current liabilities						
⑲ Accounts payable	$61,700	$56,100	17.1%	16.3%	$5,600	10.0%
⑳ Notes payable	5,000	4,000	1.4%	1.2%	1,000	25.0%
㉑ Total current liabilities	$66,700	$60,100	18.4%	17.5%	$6,600	11.0%
㉒ Long-term liabilities	0	0	0%	0%	0	0%
㉓ Total liabilities	$66,700	$60,100	18.4%	17.5%	$6,600	11.0%
Stockholders' equity						
㉔ Common stock	$200,000	$200,000	55.3%	58.1%	$0	0%
㉕ Retained earnings	95,100	84,200	26.3%	24.5%	10,900	12.9%
㉖ Total stockholders' equity	$295,100	$284,200	81.6%	82.5%	$10,900	3.8%
㉗ Total liabilities and SH equity	$361,800	$344,300	100.0%	100.0%	$17,500	5.1%

> **TIP** — percentage increase or decrease
>
> As you may recall, to figure a percentage increase (or decrease), we divide the amount of increase or (decrease) by the *original amount*. Don't make the common mistake of dividing by the new amount. In Example 1, to calculate item 7F:
>
> | Correct | Incorrect |
> |---|---|
> | $23,300 (increase) ÷ $164,000 (original amount) ≈ .142 | $23,300 (increase) ÷ $187,300 (new amount) ≈ .124 |

Robin decides to review Bonneville's comparative statements to see if she can notice any trends.

Example 2 — Refer to Illustrations 18-5 and 18-6. Help Robin list a few noteworthy items that might make stockholders happy or concerned.

Listing noteworthy items is somewhat subjective. However, here are a few things that might make stockholders happy or concerned.

- Gross sales have increased 45% (item 1F). This should make stockholders extremely happy.
- Sales returns have increased 38.7% (2F); while this is a dramatic increase, sales returns have not increased as much as sales. Once again, this should make stockholders happy.
- Costs of goods sold was 72.2% of net sales in 2015, but only 67.4% of net sales in 2014 (5C and 5D). This is a potential concern. Maybe goods are being sold too cheaply; maybe Bonneville is paying too much for its goods; possibly Bonneville planned a strategy for reducing prices, thereby increasing sales. Management should determine the reason for the increased percentage.
- Operating expenses increased 14.2% (7F); however, expenses might be expected to increase more dramatically in light of a 45% increase in sales. Management should be happy.
- Net income (after taxes) increased 52.7% (10F). This is mainly due to increased sales.
- Accounts receivable increased 27.7% (12F); this is expected, in light of the 45% increase in sales.
- Merchandise inventory increased 19.6% (13F); this is also expected because of the 45% increase in sales. Maybe the increase in inventory is a result of increased sales; maybe the increased sales is a direct result of increasing inventory.
- Prepaid expenses increased 150% (14F). While this sounds dramatic, the dollar amount ($900) makes the percent insignificant.
- Plant and equipment decreased $14,000 (16E). This is a result of depreciation, not the sale of assets, and is nothing to be concerned about.

ⓑ Evaluating business ratios

The previous few pages were devoted to *comparing a company with itself over a period of time*. Robin has figured out how to use comparative statements, but she is now interested in evaluating a company *compared with its competitors*. This is what we will focus on now.

Most public libraries have reference books that contain industry averages. These books contain ratios for hundreds of types of businesses. A **ratio** is a comparison of numbers. Businesses can compare their ratios with those of preceding years and with ratios of competitors. Illustration 18-7 is a summary of a few key ratios; ratios 1 through 3 measure *liquidity* of a business (liquidity means the ability to pay debts), ratios 4 and 5 measure *efficiency*, and ratios 6 and 7 measure *profitability*. Also included are calculations for Bonneville (for the year 2015), recent industry averages (for electrical parts wholesalers), and ideas if the ratio is bad.

In comparing ratios for other electrical parts wholesalers (shown in the second column of Illustration 18-7), Robin concludes that Bonneville is doing pretty well. With respect to *liquidity* (ratios 1 through 3), Bonneville is in a much better position to pay its debts than other electrical parts wholesalers. With respect to *efficiency* (ratios 4 and 5), Bonneville is right on target with the industry average. With respect to *profitability* (ratios 6 and 7), Bonneville comes through with flying colors.

Illustration 18-7 Summary of Key Ratios

Ratio and formula	Bonneville calculations, 2015	What it says	Ideas if the ratio is bad
1. Current ratio = $\dfrac{\text{Current assets}}{\text{Current liabilities}}$	$\dfrac{\$240{,}000}{\$66{,}700} \approx 3.6$ (Industry average = 2.1)	Measures a company's ability to pay its bills. Bonneville has about \$3.60 in current assets for each \$1 of current liabilities.	Increase profits. Increase long-term financing. If sole proprietorship or partnership, contribute cash. If corporation, reduce dividends; sell additional stock.
2. Acid-test ratio = $\dfrac{\text{Cash + Accounts receivable}}{\text{Current liabilities}}$	$\dfrac{\$85{,}000 + \$60{,}000}{\$66{,}700} \approx 2.2$ (Industry average = 1.1)	Like current ratio, except more stringent; assumes inventory may be hard to sell during a recession. Bonneville had about \$2.20 for each \$1 of current liabilities.	Same as for current ratio. Also, reduce inventory.
3. Debt ratio = $\dfrac{\text{Total liabilities}}{\text{Total assets}}$	$\dfrac{\$66{,}700}{\$361{,}800} \approx .184 \approx 18.4\%$ (Industry average = 50.8%)	Measures the long-run solvency of the business. For each dollor of assets, Bonneville owes 18.4¢.	Increase profits. If sole proprietorship or partnership, contribute cash. If corporation, reduce dividends; sell additional stock.
4. Inventory turnover = $\dfrac{\text{Cost of goods sold}}{\text{Average inventory}}$ Note: Average inventory is found by adding beginning inventory to ending inventory and dividing the result by 2. Beginning inventory is the ending inventory from the previous year.	$\dfrac{\$702{,}700}{(\$78{,}200 + \$93{,}500) \div 2}$ $= \dfrac{\$702{,}700}{\$85{,}850} \approx 8.2$ (Industry average = 7.8)	Measures how many times per year the inventory is sold (turned over). During 2015, Bonneville sold its inventory 8.2 times (about once each 6 weeks: 52 weeks ÷ 8.2 ≈ 6).	Do more advertising. Increase or improve sales staff. Reducing inventory may help, but in the process, sales (and thus profits) may decrease.
5. Cost of goods sold as % of net sales = $\dfrac{\text{Cost of goods sold}}{\text{Net sales}}$	$\dfrac{\$702{,}700}{\$973{,}400} \approx .722 \approx 72.2\%$ (Industry average = 73.6%)	Measures cost of goods as a percent of net sales. During 2015, Bonneville's goods cost 72.2% of what they sold for.	If percent is too high, compare prices from other vendors. Increase prices to customers. Decrease inventory, spoilage, and theft.
6. Profit margin, before tax = $\dfrac{\text{Net income, before tax}}{\text{Net sales}}$	$\dfrac{\$83{,}400}{\$973{,}400} \approx .086 \approx 8.6\%$ (Industry average = 3.8%)	Measures the efficiency of the business. Bonneville's profit is 8.6% of net sales.	Review pricing structure, cost of goods, and operating expenses.
7. Return on equity = $\dfrac{\text{Net income, after tax}}{\text{Equity}}$	$\dfrac{\$53{,}000}{\$295{,}100} \approx .180 \approx 18.0\%$ (Industry average = 12.9%)	Measures profitability to owners, based on invested capital. Bonneville's profit is 18% of stockholders' equity.	Increase profits by increasing sales and/or decreasing expenses.

Well, Robin is feeling pretty comfortable reading and interpreting financial statements. Learning this stuff has helped her make a final decision to open her own gift shop business. Let's find out if we've learned as much as Robin, by doing the U-Try-It exercises.

U-Try-It
(Unit 18.3)

1. Refer to Illustration 18-5. For line 6, verify the amounts in columns C through F.
2. Refer to Illustrations 18-5 and 18-6. Calculate the following ratios for the year 2014:
   a. Current ratio
   b. Inventory turnover (beginning inventory = \$71,300)
   c. Profit margin, before tax
3. Refer to Problem 2. Explain the meaning of the results.

Answers: (If you have a different answer, check the solution in Appendix A.)
1. 6C: 27.8%; 6D: 32.6%; 6E: \$52,000; 6F: 23.8%   **2a.** 3.5   **2b.** 6.1   **2c.** 8.2%   **3a.** Bonneville had about \$3.50 in current assets for each \$1 in current liabilities.   **3b.** During the year, Bonneville sold its inventory 6.1 times.   **3c.** Bonneville's profit during the year was 8.2% of net sales.

Chapter in a Nutshell

Objectives	Examples

Unit 18.1 Income statements

a Interpreting an income statement for a service company

$240,000 revenues; $112,000 expenses. Net income?

Net income = Revenues - Expenses = $240,000 - $112,000 = **$128,000**

b Interpreting an income statement for a merchandising company

Given: $96,000 gross sales; $1,500 sales returns; $19,000 beginning inventory; $44,000 cost of goods purchased; $20,000 ending inventory; $14,000 operating expenses.

Find: Net sales, cost of goods sold, gross profit, and net income

Net sales = Gross sales - Sales returns = $96,000 - $1,500 = **$94,500**
Cost of goods sold = Beginning inventory + Cost of goods purchased - Ending inventory
 = $19,000 + $44,000 - $20,000 = **$43,000**
Gross profit = Net sales - Cost of goods sold = $94,500 - $43,000 = **$51,500**
Net income = Gross profit - Operating expenses = $51,500 - $14,000 = **$37,500**

Unit 18.2 Balance sheets

a Identifying assets and liabilities

Given: $32,000 cash; $45,000 accounts receivable; $31,000 accounts payable; $5,000 patent; $40,000 land for future expansion; $52,000 inventory; $5,000 note payable.

Find: Total assets and total liabilities

Assets = $32,000 (cash) + $45,000 (accounts receivable) + $5,000 (patent) + $40,000
 (land) + $52,000 (inventory) = **$174,000**
Liabilities = $31,000 (accounts payable) + $5,000 (note payable) = **$36,000**

b Determining owner's equity

Refer back.

Owner's equity = Assets - Liabilities = $174,000 - $36,000 = **$138,000**

Accounting equation:
Assets	=	Liabilities + Owner's equity
$174,000	=	$36,000 + $138,000
$174,000	=	**$174,000**

Unit 18.3 Trend and ratio analysis

a Evaluating trends through vertical and horizontal analysis

	Annual amounts		Percent of net sales		Increase (or Decrease)	
	A 2015	**B** 2014	**C** 2015	**D** 2014	**E** Amount	**F** Percent
Net sales	$154,200	$158,800	100.0%	100.0%	($4,600)	(2.9)
Operating expenses	$34,000	$32,500	22.0%	20.5%	$1,500	4.6

Net sales: Col. E = $154,200 - $158,800 = **-$4,600**
 Col. F = (-$4,600) ÷ $158,800 ≈ -.029 ≈ **-2.9%**
Expenses: Col. C = $34,000 ÷ $154,200 ≈ .220 ≈ **22.0%**
 Col. D = $32,500 ÷ $158,800 ≈ .205 ≈ **20.5%**
 Col. E = $34,000 - $32,500 = **$1,500**
 Col. F = $1,500 ÷ $32,500 ≈ .046 ≈ **4.6%**

Chapter in a Nutshell (concluded)

Objectives	Examples
b Evaluating business ratios	Given: $37,000 cash; $33,000 accounts receivable; $142,000 total current assets; $268,000 total assets; $59,000 total current liabilities; $132,000 total liabilities; $335,000 cost of goods sold; $44,000 beginning inventory; $48,000 ending inventory; $495,000 net sales; $24,000 net income, before tax; $19,000 net income, after tax; and $136,000 stockholders' equity.

$$\text{Current ratio} = \frac{\text{Current assets}}{\text{Current liabilities}} = \frac{\$142,000}{\$59,000} \approx 2.4$$

$$\text{Acid-test ratio} = \frac{\text{Cash + Accounts receivable}}{\text{Current liabilities}} = \frac{\$37,000 + \$33,000}{\$59,000} \approx 1.2$$

$$\text{Debt ratio} = \frac{\text{Total liabilities}}{\text{Total assets}} = \frac{\$132,000}{\$268,000} \approx .493 \approx 49.3\%$$

$$\text{Inventory turnover} = \frac{\text{Cost of goods sold}}{\text{Average inventory}} = \frac{\$335,000}{(\$44,000 + \$48,000) \div 2} = \frac{\$335,000}{\$46,000} \approx 7.3$$

$$\text{Cost of goods sold as \% of net sales} = \frac{\text{Cost of goods sold}}{\text{Net sales}} = \frac{\$335,000}{\$495,000} \approx .677 \approx 67.7\%$$

$$\text{Profit margin, before tax} = \frac{\text{Net income, before tax}}{\text{Net sales}} = \frac{\$24,000}{\$495,000} \approx 0.048 \approx 4.8\%$$

$$\text{Return on equity} = \frac{\text{Net income, after tax}}{\text{Equity}} = \frac{\$19,000}{\$136,000} \approx .140 \approx 14.0\%$$

Think

1. What is the difference between an income statement and a balance sheet?
2. Name a few businesses that could be classified as a service company. Name a few that could be classified as a merchandising company. What differences are there on an income statement? On a balance sheet?
3. Brandi Lewis is trying to get a business loan from her bank. She provides a balance sheet for her business showing some vacant land listed at $200,000. Brandi paid $10,000 for the land 10 years ago. Is Brandi being ethical? Why or why not? Who will her actions hurt, if anyone?
4. What are the differences between a balance sheet and a personal financial statement?
5. What is the purpose of (1) vertical analysis and (2) horizontal analysis?
6. What are the benefits of computing business ratios and comparing the ratios with those of competitors?

Explore

1. Refer to Illustrations 18-5 (Comparative Income Statement) and 18-6 (Comparative Balance Sheet). Create an Excel spreadsheet that includes the data of both illustrations. Don't worry about displaying dollar signs ($). Write formulas in the last 4 columns so your spreadsheet results will match those of the illustrations. *Tip:* When referencing a *specific* cell in several other cells, use a dollar sign symbol ($). For example, if Annual Amounts is in row 1, years are in row 2, and $973,400 (net sales) is in cell B6, we can find percents for column D, rows 3-12 as follows: In cell D3, type =B3/B$6. Then copy the formula into cells D4 through D12 and E3 to E12; the value in cell B6 is applied to the formula in each of these cells.
2. Refer to Chapter Review Problem 30 (for BBB Office Supply). Using an Excel spreadsheet, write formulas in the last 4 columns to find the missing numbers.

Apply

1. **The Personal Financial Statement.** Prepare a personal financial statement, showing assets (cash, stocks, real estate, autos, furniture, etc.), liabilities (loans on cars, furniture, appliances, real estate, credit cards, etc.), and resulting net worth. If you are married, the financial statement should be for you and your spouse. Do not include social security numbers and birthdates.

2. **Company Study.** Submit a recent income statement and balance sheet for a specific company. Try to base your study on a company in which you have a personal interest or of which you know an owner. If you cannot find such a company, use stock report information; stock reports can be obtained from a stockbroker, through most public libraries, or on the Internet. Submit a copy of industry averages for the type of company you are studying. Compare industry averages with those of the company you are studying. Draw conclusions about how the company you are studying is doing.

Chapter Review Problems

Unit 18.1 Income statements

1. When revenues exceed expenses, is the result (a) net income or (b) net loss?
2. Do income statements reflect profits of a business (a) on a certain date or (b) over a given period of time?
3. Cost of goods sold is an important part of an income statement for service companies. (T or F)

For Problems 4–6, fill in the missing amounts. Each problem represents a different situation. Negative values are in parentheses.

	4.	5.	6.
Revenues	$108,000	$120,000	
Total expenses	$ 28,000		$42,000
Net income (or loss)		($10,000)	$27,000

7. Calculate net sales based on gross sales of $805,000; sales returns of $5,400; and sales discounts of $15,700.

8. Calculate cost of goods sold based on $82,400 beginning inventory; $264,000 cost of goods purchased; and $94,800 ending inventory.

9. Refer to Problems 7 and 8. Calculate gross profit.

10. Refer to Problem 9. Calculate net income based on operating expenses of $371,300.

Unit 18.2 Balance sheets

For Problems 11–20, identify the item by placing the appropriate letter in the space.

	Item	Choose from
11. ___	Accounts receivable	A. Current asset
12. ___	Accounts payable	B. Plant and equipment
13. ___	Office equipment	C. Investment asset
14. ___	Owner's equity	D. Intangible asset
15. ___	Cash	E. Current liability
16. ___	Land held for future expansion	F. Long-term liability
17. ___	Trademark	G. Equity item
18. ___	Mortgage payable (monthly payments)	
19. ___	Building and land for present location	
20. ___	Retained earnings	

21. Bihn Pham owns an engineering consulting business. Total assets are $135,700. Total liabilities are $24,800. What is Bihn's equity in the business?

22. Assets should be shown on balance sheets at current value, not original cost. (T or F)

For Problems 23–25, fill in the missing amounts. Each problem represents a different situation.

	23.	24.	25.
Total assets	$128,000	$820,000	
Total liabilities	$ 65,000		$192,000
Equity		$672,000	$27,000

26. For corporations, the equity section of a balance sheet is called corporate equity. (T or F)

27. For a personal financial statement, assets are often shown at current value, not at cost. (T or F)

28. For a personal financial statement, the difference between assets and liabilities is referred to as personal equity. (T or F)

Unit 18.3 Trend and ratio analysis

29. Vertical and horizontal analysis are used to evaluate the progress of a company over two or more accounting periods. (T or F)

30. Comparative data for BBB Office Supply is given in the first two columns of the following pair of tables. Complete the remaining columns using vertical and horizontal analysis. Show percents with 1 decimal place. You can, if you want, use an Excel spreadsheet to find the missing values (by writing formulas in the last 4 columns of the spreadsheet; see tips in Explore Activity 1).

BBB OFFICE SUPPLY, INC.
Comparative Income Statement (2015 vs 2014)

	Annual Amounts		Percent of Net Sales		Increase (or Decrease)	
	2015	2014	2015	2014	Amount	Percent
Gross sales	$346,200	$364,900				
Sales returns	3,800	1,700				
Net sales	$342,400	$363,200				
Cost of goods sold	153,100	148,700				
Gross profit	$189,300	$214,500				
Total operating expenses	177,700	153,400				
Net income (before income taxes)	$11,600	$61,100				
Less income taxes	4,000	22,000				
Net income (after income taxes)	$7,600	$39,100				

BBB OFFICE SUPPLY, INC.
Comparative Balance Sheet (Dec. 31, 2015 vs Dec. 31, 2014)

	Year-end Amounts		Percent of Total		Increase (or Decrease)	
	2015	2014	2015	2014	Amount	Percent
Assets						
Current assets						
Cash	$23,100	$36,100				
Accounts receivable	42,000	45,100				
Merchandise inventory	58,100	73,800				
Prepaid expenses	300	300				
Total current assets	$123,500	$155,300				
Plant and equipment, net	7,100	7,900				
Total assets	$130,600	$163,200				
Liabilities						
Accounts payable	$18,000	$19,000				
Total liabilities	$18,000	$19,000				
Stockholders' Equity						
Common stock	$100,000	$100,000				
Retained earnings	12,600	44,200				
Total stockholders' equity	$112,600	$144,200				
Total liabilities and SH equity	$130,600	$163,200				

31. Refer to Problem 30. List a few noteworthy items that might make stockholders happy or concerned.

For Problems 32–38, use the data of Problem 30 to calculate the requested ratio or percent for 2015. Use one decimal place in all ratios or percents. Then, state what the ratio means.

32. Current ratio.

33. Acid-test ratio.

34. Debt ratio.

35. Inventory turnover.

36. Cost of goods sold as % of net sales.

37. Profit margin, before tax.

38. Return on equity.

39. LMN, Inc., has a current ratio of 1.3. The industry average for its type of business is 1.8. Is LMN's current ratio (a) better or (b) worse than the industry average?

40. Refer to Problem 39. What can LMN do to improve its current ratio?

41. Would a business prefer having a (a) high or (b) low inventory turnover?

42. What can be done to improve inventory turnover?

Challenge problems

For Problems 43–47, answer from the following choices: sole proprietorship, general partnership, and corporation.

43. For which entity or entities are the owner(s) personally responsible for the company's debts?

44. Which entity or entities file a federal income tax return?

45. Which entity or entities pay federal income tax directly to the IRS?

46. For which entity or entities are distributions of extra cash taxable to the owners?

47. Which entity or entities can be owned by only one person?

48. A three-person general partnership quits doing business and has only $60,000 with which to pay $90,000 of debt. Which statement is true? (a) The partners are not personally liable for the $30,000 difference; (b) each partner is liable for exactly $10,000; (c) any of the partners may be sued for the entire $30,000 difference.

49. ABC Corporation had annual profit of $1,200,000. Assume that the corporation pays 34% of profit as federal and state income taxes; the remainder is paid to stockholders as dividends. Assuming that stockholders pay 35% of dividends as federal and state income taxes, determine the total percent of income taxes paid as a result of the $1,200,000 profit.

50. Prepare an income statement for Fisher's Clothing Store, Inc. Income statement items for the first 3 months of 2016 were as follows: gross sales, $1,653,800; sales returns, $143,700; beginning inventory, $436,000; purchases, $922,800; purchase returns, $5,300; purchase discounts, $13,800; transportation in, $3,400; ending inventory, $461,900; total operating expenses, $296,600; income taxes, $110,000. Use the format of Illustration 18-3.

51. Wayne's Corner Market, Inc., had assets and liabilities on June 30, 2016, as follows: cash, $22,800; accounts payable, $38,100; store equipment, $42,000 less accumulated depreciation of $10,500; merchandise inventory, $42,200; notes payable, $5,000 (the entire amount is due in 18 months); prepaid expenses, $800. So far, 1,000 shares of stock have been issued (at $20 per share). Prepare a classified balance sheet like that of Illustration 18-4. In the process, determine the amount of retained earnings.

Practice Test

1. What, if anything, is wrong with this income statement heading?

   > ALPINE ENGINEERING
   > Income Statement
   > June 30, 2016

2. Given: gross sales, $220,000; sales returns, $1,500; sales discounts, $2,000; beginning inventory, $92,000; cost of goods purchased, $145,000; ending inventory, $95,000; operating expenses, $30,000. Calculate: **(a)** net sales, **(b)** cost of goods sold, **(c)** gross profit, and **(d)** net income.

3. Given: cash, $28,000; accounts receivable, $52,000; merchandise inventory, $60,000; prepaid expenses, $2,000; land for future expansion, $50,000; accounts payable, $24,000. Calculate the equity of the business.

4. Given: net sales, $152,800; total operating expenses, $42,100. What percent of net sales are operating expenses? Round to the nearest tenth of a percent.

5. For each item, calculate (a) the dollar amount of increase and (b) the percent change (rounded to the nearest tenth of a percent).

Item	2016	2015	Increase (or Decrease)	
			Amount	Percent
Cash	$27,000	$23,000		
Accounts receivable	$52,000	$58,000		

6. Given: total current assets, $120,000; total assets, $280,000; total current liabilities, $72,000; total liabilities, $150,000; beginning inventory, $60,000; ending inventory, $68,000; cost of goods sold, $140,000. Calculate (a) current ratio, (b) debt ratio, and (c) inventory turnover. Use 1 decimal place in each ratio. For each ratio, tell what it means.

Classroom Notes

FUN CORNER

Which Inventory Method Is the Most Popular?

According to a recent survey of the 600 largest U.S. companies, conducted by the American Institute of Certified Public Accountants, here is a summary of preferred inventory valuation methods:

FIFO	42%
LIFO	35%
Weighted average	19%
Other	.4%

10 Fastest Growing U.S. Franchises

Here is a list of the fastest growing U.S. franchises, together with minimum start-up cost.

1. Subway .... $117,000–$263,000
2. Dunkin' Donuts .... $217,000–$2,000,000
3. Cruise Planners (Travel Agency) ..... $2,000–$23,000
4. Jimmy John's .... $323,000–$544,000
5. Vanguard Cleaning Systems .... $11,000–$36,000
6. Great Clips .... $122,000–$233,000
7. Taco Bell .... $1,000,000–$3,000,000
8. Bricks 4 Kidz .... $34,000–$51,000
9. McDonald's .... $989,000–$2,000,000
10. Sports Clips .... $168,000–$327,000

Source: Entrepreneur Magazine, 2015

Inventory Shrinkage

Shoplifting and employee theft are the two major causes of "inventory shrinkage" for the retail industry.
Recent figures indicate that about $37.1 billion of inventory is lost each year, of which approximately $16.2 billion is due to employee theft, $12.1 billion is from shoplifting, $4.8 billion is due to administrative error, and $2 billion is due to fraud from suppliers.

Source: National Retail Security Survey, 2011

Controlling Overhead

The American Institute of Certified Public Accountants routinely examines cost control policies of companies throughout the country. In a recent study, it surveyed over 650 companies, including about half in the Fortune 100. Here is what it found.

- The average company spends $3.55 to process a single invoice. The most efficient firms need just 35 cents.
- The average company spends $6.05 to handle an employee expense report. The most efficient firms do it for 27 cents.
- It takes the average firm $1.91 to process each paycheck. The most efficient firms spend just 36 cents.

You may think these cost savings are insignificant. But suppose you work at a company that has 12,000 employees who receive 52 paychecks a year, and you figure out how to lower the cost of processing a paycheck from $1.91 down to 36 cents. You'd save your company $967,200 a year! Now assume your company rewards creative employees by paying 10% of savings. You would get an extra $96,720 each year!

"I'm sorry ma'am, I can't sell it to you. Our computer says we don't have any in stock."

Inventory and Overhead

19

In this chapter, we will examine a few topics that play a key role in the preparation and understanding of financial statements: inventory and overhead.

You may be asking why a company needs to know the dollar amount of inventory. Here's why. A merchandising company cannot prepare an income statement and balance sheet without knowing the cost of its ending inventory. As a result, we must be able to attach a specific value to the inventory.

With respect to overhead, many businesses like to allocate expenses (like rent and advertising) by department so that they can determine the profitability of each department. We will examine different methods used to make this allocation.

Sound like fun? Probably not, huh? While these may not be the most fun topics of the text, they are vital to a merchandising business. We'll try to have a little fun along the way!

Unit Objectives

Unit 19.1 Inventory methods: Assigning a cost to ending inventory

- **a** Using the specific identification method
- **b** Using the weighted average method
- **c** Using the first-in, first-out method (FIFO)
- **d** Using the last-in, first-out method (LIFO)
- **e** Determining the effect of ending inventory on profit and equity

Unit 19.2 Overhead: Spreading expenses to departments

- **a** Allocating overhead

Unit 19.1 Inventory methods: Assigning a cost to ending inventory

Scanners help stores to monitor their inventory. Even when scanners are used, stores generally rely on a physical count to verify inventory.

Many businesses sell products; examples are grocery stores, gasoline stations, car dealerships, wholesalers, and manufacturers. Their goods, called **inventory,** are often a large percent of the company's assets.

Most businesses use computers to keep track of their inventory, using what is called a **perpetual inventory** system. A *bar code, RFID chip,* or other product code is attached to each item. When the store receives an item from a supplier, the product code is scanned and the item is added to the store's inventory. Then, when the cashier scans the product code at the check-out register, the item is subtracted from the store's inventory. With the perpetual inventory system a business can tell, at any time, which items are in stock, and in what quantity. But, because some merchandise may be lost to spoilage or theft, the perpetual inventory system is not always 100% accurate. So they rely on a physical count of merchandise to verify computer counts.

Relying on a physical count of merchandise is called a **periodic inventory** system; it is utilized by businesses that do not use a perpetual inventory system as well as many businesses that like to verify their perpetual inventory records. In a periodic inventory system, a physical count of each product is taken at regular intervals (like monthly, quarterly, or annually). The count for each product is multiplied by its cost; subtotals for the various products are then added.

Assigning a cost to each inventory item creates no problem if merchandise costs remain fixed. However, *when identical items are purchased at different costs, a problem arises regarding which cost applies to the ending inventory.* This is the dilemma we will address in this unit. We will examine four methods used to value the ending inventory: specific identification; weighted average; first-in, first-out (FIFO); and last-in, first-out (LIFO).

a Using the specific identification method

Action Sports Company carries a W-2 model tennis racket. They had 10 of these rackets on hand at the beginning of the year (at a cost of $58 each), and they purchased an additional 60 rackets during the year at various prices. So they had a total of 70 rackets available for sale during the year. In the next example, we will determine the total cost of W-2 rackets available for sale during the year.

Example 1 Action Sports Company had 10 W-2 rackets at the beginning of the year at a cost of $58 each. They purchased 20 rackets in March for $60 each, 30 in May for $65 each, and 10 in July for $70 each. Calculate the total cost of rackets available for sale.

Beginning inventory:	10 × $58	$ 580
March:	20 × $60	1,200
May:	30 × $65	1,950
July:	10 × $70	+ 700
Totals	70	$4,430

Assume Action conducted a physical inventory at the end of the year; they had 12 of these rackets. The question we will now address is, What cost do we assign to these 12 rackets?

When it is possible to identify each inventory item with a specific purchase (such as from tagging or marking each item), the **specific identification** method may be used.

> **ending inventory: specific identification method**
>
> **Step 1** For each cost per unit, multiply the number of units by the cost per unit.
>
> **Step 2** Add the subtotals.

Example 2 Refer to Example 1. Action had 12 of these rackets in ending inventory and they were identified: 1 was from the beginning inventory, 4 were from the March purchase, and 7 were from the July purchase. Calculate the total cost of the 12 rackets.

```
 1 × $58      $ 58
 4 × $60        240
 7 × $70       +490
12            $788
```

Ending inventory, using the specific identification method is $788.

b Using the weighted average method

With the **weighted average** method, ending inventory is based on an average unit cost.

> **ending inventory: weighted average method**
>
> **Step 1** Find the average unit cost by dividing the total cost available for sale by the number of units available for sale. Round to the nearest penny.
>
> **Step 2** Multiply the result by the number of units in ending inventory.

Example 3 Refer to Example 1. Use the weighted average method to determine the cost of the 12 rackets in ending inventory.

From Example 1

$$\text{Average unit cost} = \frac{\text{Total cost available for sale}}{\text{Number of units available for sale}} = \frac{\$4{,}430}{70} = \$63.29$$

Ending inventory = 12 × $63.29 = **$759.48**

Ending inventory using the weighted average method is $759.48.

> **TIP — round the average**
>
> When using the weighted average method, remember to round the average unit cost to the nearest penny. In Example 3, if we had used chain calculations instead of rounding the average unit cost, we would get an *incorrect* answer:
>
> $$\frac{\$4{,}430}{70} \times 12 = \$759.43 \quad \leftarrow \text{Wrong}$$

c Using the first-in, first-out method (FIFO)

The **first-in, first out** method, referred to as **FIFO,** assumes that the first goods purchased are the first to be sold. This method conforms to actual selling practices of most companies and is a commonly used method for valuing ending inventory.

> **ending inventory: FIFO method**
>
> **Step 1** List the units to be included in the ending inventory, assuming they are the last ones purchased. For each cost per unit, multiply the number of units by the cost per unit.
>
> **Step 2** Add the subtotals.

Example 4   Refer to Example 1. Use the FIFO method to determine the cost of the 12 rackets in ending inventory.

Because the FIFO method assumes that the oldest goods were sold first, if follows that the 12 rackets in ending inventory are the most recently purchased. So

10 rackets purchased in July:	10 × $70	$700
2 rackets purchased in May:	2 × $65	+130
12		$830

Ending inventory using the FIFO method is $830.

d Using the last-in, first-out method (LIFO)

The **last-in, first-out** method, referred to as **LIFO,** is the opposite of FIFO and assumes that ending inventory consists of the oldest goods. Although the LIFO method generally does not conform to actual selling practices, it is an acceptable method that is still used by some businesses. As you will see later, the LIFO method results in tax savings for businesses during periods of rising prices.

ending inventory: LIFO method

Step 1   List the units to be included in the ending inventory, assuming they are the oldest goods. For each cost per unit, multiply the number of units by the cost per unit.

Step 2   Add the subtotals.

Example 5   Refer to Example 1. Use the LIFO method to determine the cost of the 12 rackets in ending inventory.

Because the LIFO method assumes that the ending inventory consists of the oldest goods,

10 rackets from beginning inventory:	10 × $58	$580
2 rackets from March purchase:	2 × $60	+120
12		$700

Ending inventory using the LIFO method is $700.

TIP   is that a catchy title, or what?

The title of each inventory method can be helpful in determining ending inventory:

Method	Clue
Specific identification	*Specific* cost is used for each item.
Weighted average	Different costs are *averaged*.
FIFO	*First in* are gone, so most recent goods are used.
LIFO	*Last in* are gone, so oldest goods are used.

e Determining the effect of ending inventory on profit and equity

Now we will summarize the results of Examples 1 through 5. The cost of goods available for sale ($4,430 from Example 1) can be divided into two components: cost of goods *not* sold (ending inventory) and **cost of goods sold.** In Examples 2 through 5, we determined the first component (cost of goods *not* sold); the second component (cost of goods sold) is found by subtracting ending inventory from the cost of goods available for sale.

cost of goods sold (COGS) formula

COGS = Cost of goods available for sale - Ending inventory

In Example 1, we found cost of goods available for sale was $4,430. In Examples 2 through 5, we found ending inventory:

Using the specific identification method: $788.00
Using the weighted average method: $759.48
Using the FIFO method: $830.00
Using the LIFO method: $700.00

Determine COGS using each inventory method.

COGS = Cost of goods available for sale - Ending inventory, so:

Specific identification: $4,430 - $788 = $3,642.00
Weighted Average: $4,430 - $759.48 = $3,670.52
FIFO: $4,430 - $830 = $3,600.00
LIFO: $4,430 - $700 = $3,730.00

You may wonder why establishing the cost of ending inventory is so important. The cost of ending inventory has a significant effect on a company's profit (found on an income statement) and equity (found on a balance sheet).

The effect on profit. As shown in Example 6, a larger ending inventory results in a lower cost of goods sold. By thinking of the cost of goods sold as an expense of a business, it is easy to see that the smaller the cost of goods sold, the larger the profit. So, *the greater the ending inventory, the greater the profit* (Is that as clear as mud?). You may think businesses want to have larger profits; however, remember that the higher the profit, the more income taxes the company must pay. So, many businesses select an inventory method that will result in the least profit. In Example 6, the LIFO method has the smallest ending inventory and thus the smallest profit, while the FIFO method has the greatest ending inventory and thus the greatest profit.

The effect on equity. For balance sheet purposes, ending inventory is an asset of a company. And the greater the assets, the greater the resulting equity of a business (remember that Assets - Liabilities = Equity.) So, *the greater the ending inventory, the greater the equity (or value) of a business*. In Example 6, the FIFO method, with the greatest ending inventory, results in the greatest equity; the LIFO method, with the smallest ending inventory, results in the smallest equity.

Because an inventory valuation method affects company profits and equity, the valuation method should be shown on the company's financial statements by means of a footnote. Remember, the ending inventory becomes the beginning inventory of the next accounting cycle. So the beginning inventory of the 12 W-2 tennis rackets for the next accounting cycle would be $788, $759.48, $830, or $700, depending on which inventory method is used.

Now let's take *inventory* of what we've learned by doing the U-Try-It exercises.

A computer store carries a TX600 model computer. The company had 4 of these computers at the beginning of the year at a cost of $1,200 each, purchased 15 in January at $1,150 each, and purchased 12 in March at $1,065 each (the cost is decreasing).
1. Calculate the total cost of TX600s available for sale.
2. Inventory is taken March 31, with 5 computers on hand. Calculate ending inventory using the specific identification method, assuming 2 of the computers are from beginning inventory and 3 are from the March purchase.
3. Calculate ending inventory for the 5 computers using the weighted average method.
4. Calculate ending inventory for the 5 computers using the FIFO method.
5. Calculate ending inventory for the 5 computers using the LIFO method.
6. For each method, calculate COGS.

Answers: (If you have a different answer, check the solution in Appendix A.)
1. $34,830 2. $5,595 3. $5,617.75 4. $5,325 5. $5,950 6. spec. ident. $29,235; wtd. ave. $29,212.25; FIFO $29,505; LIFO $28,880

Unit 19.2 Overhead: Spreading expenses to departments

In this unit, we will focus our attention on Food4U, a grocery store with four departments: bakery, grocery, meat, and produce. Many businesses that have divisions or departments, like Food4U, want to know how profitable each department is. As an example, some of Food4U's expenses, such as the cost of meat and wages of meat department employees, can be used in calculating the profit of the meat department. Other expenses of the store—such as utilities, advertising, rent, and office wages—do not apply to any single department and must be shared (allocated) by departments. These expenses are referred to as **common expenses,** or **overhead.** Let's say the monthly utility bill is $10,000 and $\frac{1}{10}$ of the store's space is used for the meat department; $1,000 ($\frac{1}{10}$ of the $10,000 total) could be allocated to the meat department.

a Allocating overhead

No hard-and-fast rules apply to allocating common expenses to each department. Instead, judgment should dictate how the allocation is made. Here are a few ideas.

- **Utility expense.** Utilities are used fairly uniformly throughout the store, so allocation is often based on *floor space* of each department.
- **Advertising expense.** One way to allocate advertising is by square inches of advertising for each department. However, one purpose of advertising is to get customers into the store; once customers are in the store, they buy goods in all departments. So advertising is often allocated based on *departmental sales*.
- **Rent expense.** One way to allocate rent is on the basis of floor space. However, backroom storage space is cheaper to build than display space. So a more valid approach might be to allocate based on the *building value* per department.
- **Wages for supervisors and office personnel.** If the time spent by supervisors and office personnel is directly proportional to departmental sales, it might be fair to allocate based on departmental sales. On the other hand, if these employees spend their time supervising departmental employees, it might make more sense to allocate based on the *number of employees* per department.

In upcoming examples, we will allocate expenses by using ratios. Remember, a ratio is a comparison of two numbers, often written as a fraction, with one number as the numerator and the other as the denominator.

---

allocating overhead

For each department

Step 1 Establish a ratio, written as a fraction. The numerator is the *department amount* (such as floor space, sales, number of employees, or building value). The denominator is the *total amount* (such as total floor space, total sales, total number of employees, or total building value).

Step 2 Multiply the ratio by the total dollar amount to be allocated. Because allocated amounts are only estimates, they are often rounded.

Then

Step 3 Add each department's share to verify the sum is the same as the total amount being allocated.

In Example 1, we will allocate $7,600 utility expense between the four departments of Food4U, based on floor space. As you will see, the ratio for the meat department is not $\frac{1}{10}$ used in the unit introduction; it is $\frac{5,000}{62,000}$.

Example 1 Food4U had utility expense of $7,600 for the last month. Calculate each department's share (rounded to the nearest dollar), based on floor space.

Department	Square footage
Bakery	5,000
Grocery	45,000
Meat	5,000
Produce	+7,000
Total	62,000

Bakery: $\frac{5,000}{62,000}$ × $7,600 = $612.90 ≈ $\boxed{\$\ 613}$ ← *Square footage of Bakery Department / Total utility expense / Bakery department's share of utility expense*

Grocery: $\frac{45,000}{62,000}$ × $7,600 = $5,516.13 ≈ $\boxed{\$5,516}$ *Total square footage in store*

Meat: $\frac{5,000}{62,000}$ × $7,600 = $612.90 ≈ $\boxed{\$\ 613}$

Produce: $\frac{7,000}{62,000}$ × $7,600 = $858.06 ≈ $\boxed{\$\ 858}$

Total allocation $7,600

We can do the arithmetic of Example 1 using a calculator. Keystrokes for the Bakery Department are shown below.

Keystrokes (for most calculators)

5,000 ÷ 62,000 × 7,600 =   **612.90**

what if it doesn't add up?

Because of rounding (to the nearest penny, dollar, or $100), allocated amounts may not add up to the total amount being allocated. When this happens, one of the allocated amounts must be adjusted; *the one to be adjusted is the one that will result in the lowest difference between the unrounded amount and the adjusted amount.*

Example 2 Food4U paid $40,000 monthly rent. Calculate each department's share (rounded to the nearest $100), based on building value.

Department	Building value
Bakery	$ 300,000
Grocery	2,400,000
Meat	250,000
Produce	+ 320,000
Total	$ 3,270,000

Bakery: $\frac{300,000}{3,270,000}$ × $40,000 = $3,669.72 ≈ $ 3,700 $\boxed{\$\ 3,700}$

Grocery: $\frac{2,400,000}{3,270,000}$ × $40,000 = $29,357.80 ≈ 29,400 $\boxed{\$29,300}$ ←

Meat: $\frac{250,000}{3,270,000}$ × $40,000 = $3,058.10 ≈ 3,100 $\boxed{\$\ 3,100}$

Produce: $\frac{320,000}{3,270,000}$ × $40,000 = $3,914.37 ≈ + 3,900 $\boxed{\$\ 3,900}$

Total allocation $40,100 $40,000

Note: Incorrect total! One department's share must be decreased $100.

Grocery department's share decreased $100. Now the total is correct.

Unit 19.2 Overhead: Spreading expenses to departments

In Example 2, we had to decrease one department amount by $100 so that the total allocation would be $40,000. Decreasing the bakery total to $3,600 would result in rounding down *$69.72* ($3,669.72 - $3,600); decreasing grocery to $29,300 results in rounding down *$57.80* ($29,357.80 - $29,300); decreasing meat to $3,000 would result in rounding down *$58.10* ($3,058.10 - $3,000); decreasing produce to $3,800 would result in rounding down *$114.37* ($3,914.37 - $3,800). Because reducing grocery results in the lowest adjustment ($57.80), that is the department that is reduced.

Well, that finishes up this chapter. Let's do a U-Try-It problem to find out if the stuff about overhead went "over our heads" (that's pretty sick humor, isn't it?).

U-Try-It (Unit 19.2)

1. A business with 2 departments spent $48,300 for advertising last month. Calculate each department's share (to the nearest dollar), based on monthly sales.

Department	Monthly sales
A	$ 913,000
B	+ 422,000
Total	$1,335,000

Answers: (If you have a different answer, check the solution in Appendix A.)
1. Dept. A $33,032; Dept. B $15,268

Chapter in a Nutshell

Objectives | **Examples**

Unit 19.1 Inventory methods: Assigning a cost to ending inventory

a Using the specific identification method

A furniture store carries a certain leather sofa. The company had 3 of these sofas at the beginning of the year at a cost of $910 each, purchased 8 during January at $930 each, and 10 during March at $935 each.

Total cost of these sofas available for sale:
Beginning inventory:	3 × $910	$ 2,730
January purchase:	8 × $930	7,440
March purchase:	10 × $935	+ 9,350
Totals	21	$19,520

Inventory is taken March 31, with 6 sofas on hand. Find cost of ending inventory, using the **specific identification** method. Assume 1 sofa is from beginning inventory and 5 are from the March purchase.

(1 × $910) + (5 × $935) = **$5,585**

b Using the weighted average method

See above. Use **weighted average** method.

$19,520 (cost available for sale) ÷ 21 (number of sofas available for sale) = $929.52
6 × $929.52 = **$5,577.12**

c Using the first-in, first-out method (FIFO)

See above. Use **FIFO** method.

First-in are gone, so 6 in ending inventory are from most recent purchase (March):

6 × $935 = **$5,610**

d Using the last-in, first-out method (LIFO)

See above. Use **LIFO** method.

Last-in are gone, so 6 in ending inventory are the oldest: (3 × $910) + (3 × $930) = **$5,520**

Chapter in a Nutshell (concluded)

Objectives	Examples
(e) Determining the effect of ending inventory on profit and equity	See above. The greater the ending inventory, the greater the equity of the business, so the FIFO method (with ending inventory of $5,610) results in the greatest equity. COGS for each method: COGS = Cost of goods available for sale - Ending inventory **Specific identification:** $19,520 - $5,585 = $13,935 **Weighted average:** $19,520 - $5,577.12 = $13,942.88 **FIFO:** $19,520 - $5,610 = $13,910 **LIFO:** $19,520 - $5,520 = $14,000 The method with the lowest COGS (FIFO with $13,910) results in the greatest profit.
Unit 19.2 Overhead: Spreading expenses to departments	
(a) Allocatiing overhead	A business has 2 departments. Department A has 14 employees, Department B has 18. The company also has supervisors who oversee the 32 employees. Wages for the supervisors are $8,000 per month. Find each department's share based on *number of employees:* A: $\frac{14}{32}$ × $8,000 = $3,500 B: $\frac{18}{32}$ × $8,000 = $4,500 Total $8,000

Think

1. If you had a retail business, which inventory method (specific identification, weighted average, FIFO, or LIFO) would you use and why?
2. Suppose you own a fish market. Which inventory method do you think would best reflect what your inventory actually consists of? Please explain. Suppose you own a gas station with underground storage tanks. Which inventory method would best reflect what your inventory actually consists of? Please explain.
3. During a period of rising prices, which inventory method results in the least income tax? Explain.
4. Why would a store expand floor space of one department by reducing the floor space of another? Do you know of any stores that have done that? Did the strategy produce greater profits?

Explore

1. Refer to Example 1 of Unit 19.2. Create an Excel spreadsheet that allocates each department's share of utility expense. Show departments in column A, square footage in column B, allocated amounts (to the nearest penny) in column C, and allocated amounts (to the nearest dollar) in column D. *Tip:* When rounding amounts to the nearest dollar, be sure to use the "Round" function so that the amount will be rounded (not just displayed) to the nearest dollar. For example, to round an amount in cell C4 and put the result in cell D4, type:=ROUND(C4, 0); the "0" inside the parentheses means to round to zero decimal places (or the nearest whole number).

Apply

1. **How Do They Count?** Meet with the owner, manager, or accountant of a local retailer and ask for his or her help with this project. Write a report that covers these points:
    A. About how many different items are carried in inventory?
    B. What is the beginning and ending inventory for the last accounting period?
    C. Which inventory system does the company use (perpetual inventory or periodic inventory)?
    D. How often does the company take a physical count of inventory? Who does it? How long does it take?
    E. What method is used for assigning a cost to ending inventory (specific identification, weighted average, FIFO, LIFO, or some other method)?

    Write a concluding paragraph describing how efficient the company's inventory system is. Include any suggestions you have for improving their system.

2. **Is It over Your Head?** Find a local retailer that allocates expenses to departments and ask for help with this project. Write a report explaining which expenses are allocated as well as the method of allocation. Provide a copy of its most recent income statement, showing the allocated expenses. Include your calculations showing how the allocation was made.

Chapter Review Problems

Unit 19.1 Inventory methods: Assigning a cost to ending inventory

1. Car dealers often use a perpetual inventory. (T or F)

For Problems 2–9, we will keep inventory for a bunch of hammers. A hardware store carries a True-Balance model hammer. Assume that the company had 8 of these hammers at the beginning of the year at a cost of $11.35 each and purchased additional True-Balance hammers as follows: 12 at $11.62 each on March 23, 17 at $11.55 each on May 5, 25 at $12.25 each on July 23, and 15 at $12.47 each on September 18.

2. Calculate the total number of hammers available for sale and the total cost of hammers available for sale.

3. Use the specific identification method to determine ending inventory on December 31. Assume that 1 hammer was from beginning inventory, 1 was from the March 23 purchase, 2 were from the July 23 purchase, and 3 were from the September 18 purchase.

4. Use the weighted average method to determine the cost of the 7 hammers in ending inventory. *Note:* Round the cost per hammer to the nearest penny before multiplying by the quantity on hand.

5. Use the FIFO method to determine the cost of the 7 hammers in ending inventory.

6. Use the LIFO method to determine the cost of the 7 hammers in ending inventory.

7. For each method (specific identification, weighted average, FIFO, and LIFO), determine COGS.

8. Which method will contribute to the greatest profit?

9. Which method will contribute to the greatest equity on December 31?

Unit 19.2 Overhead: Spreading expenses to departments

10. Common expenses (overhead) should always be allocated based on floor space. (T or F)

For Problems 11–14, we will allocate some common expenses for a store that has three departments. Information for each department is given in the table.

Department	Floor space (sq ft)	Number of employees	Building value	Monthly sales
A	12,000	16	$365,000	$422,000
B	18,500	15	$420,000	$377,000
C	53,900	33	$1,065,000	$813,000
Totals	84,400	64	$1,850,000	$1,612,000

11. Allocate $65,000 monthly rent to each department based on building value. Round to the nearest $100.

12. Allocate $40,000 monthly advertising to each department based on sales. Round to the nearest dollar.

13. Allocate $7,100 monthly utility expense to each department based on floor space. Round to the nearest $10.

Challenge problems

14. See above. Allocate $18,210 monthly administrative wages to each department based on the number of employees. Round to the nearest dollar.

15. A-1 Office Supply has a beginning inventory of 4 copy machines at a cost of $480 each. During the year, the company purchased 10 copy machines at $490, 12 at $495, and 20 at $520. At the end of the year, the company had 3 copy machines left. Calculate the cost of ending inventory using these methods: weighted average, FIFO, and LIFO.

Practice Test

1. Rocky Mountain Outdoor Products has a beginning inventory of 12 backpacks at a cost of $180 each. During the year, the company purchased 10 backpacks at $190, 12 at $195, and 25 at $200. At the end of the year, the company had 8 backpacks left. Calculate the cost of ending inventory using these methods: weighted average, FIFO, and LIFO.

2. Extreme Sports has a beginning inventory of 35 snowboards at a cost of $340 each. During the year, the company purchased 40 snowboards at $350 and 150 at $335. First, figure the ending inventory using the specific identification method. The ending inventory of 34 snowboards consisted of 12 from beginning inventory, 4 from the first purchase, and 18 from the last purchase. Then, figure the COGS.

3. Which criteria would be more meaningful in allocating advertising expense to departments?
   a. Building value per department
   b. Number of employees per department
   c. Monthly sales per department
   d. Floor space per department

4. A store had monthly utility expense of $15,788. Determine the share for Department 1, based on floor space for each department as follows:

   Dept. 1: 22,000 sq ft   Dept. 2: 37,000 sq ft   Dept. 3: 25,000 sq ft   Dept. 4: 18,000 sq ft

FUN CORNER

Depreciation: Real Estate Appraisals

If you ever see a real estate appraisal, say of a home or office building, you will see that "depreciation" is a key element in estimating the value of the property. You may think that the amount of depreciation represents the amount of depreciation taken on the asset. That is not the case.

Depreciation for real estate appraisals is an entirely different application, representing an estimate of *actual loss in value* for an asset. To illustrate, suppose you are thinking about buying a 12-unit apartment building. To verify its value, you hire a real estate appraiser. The appraisal report may show the building would cost $700,000 to build, new. But, because of the age of the building the appraiser has deducted say 20%, or $140,000 for depreciation. The $140,000 does *not* represent how much depreciation the previous owner has taken on the building. Instead, it represents how much less this building is worth than a new one.

Depreciation on Intangible Assets

Depreciation reflects a loss of usefulness for a tangible asset. A *tangible* asset is one that we can *touch*, like a computer or apartment building. For *intangible* assets, such as patents, copyrights, or goodwill, the loss of usefulness is referred to as *amortization*, not depreciation. Under Generally Accepted Accounting Principles, a company must generally use the straight-line method to amortize its intangible assets.

Straight-Line Wins Out

According to a recent survey of the 600 largest U.S. companies by the American Institute of Certified Public Accountants, it was found that a whopping 80% of depreciation is done using straight-line depreciation. The second most popular method is units-of-production, with 7%.

Avoid Being Upside-Down

Many people who get loans find they are "upside-down," meaning the loan balance is greater than the value of the asset they financed.

Here's how that happens. The asset is depreciating faster than the loan balance is going down. As an example, when you drive off the dealer's lot in your new car, it loses quite a bit of value because it is now a used car instead of a new car. Each month you own the car it loses more value. If you want to pay off the loan, chances are the loan balance will be greater than the value of the car. That means you will have to pay money to get rid of it!

To avoid being caught upside-down, try to purchase models that hold their value. Also, finance for a shorter period of time (so the loan pays off quicker).

"I claimed depreciation on my sports car because it WILL generate income. I'm using it to attract a younger woman who can support me later in life."

Depreciation

20

Depreciation reflects the *loss of usefulness* for an asset. Assets such as equipment lose their usefulness because of (1) wear and tear, (2) inadequacy as a result of the company's growth, or (3) advances in technology, which make the asset obsolete. The amount of depreciation depends on the cost of the asset, the projected useful life, the projected value at the end of the useful life, and the depreciation method used.

For federal income tax, depreciation (referred to as MACRS) provides a tax deduction; depreciation methods and useful life are prescribed by the IRS. Many businesses do not consider the amount of depreciation under federal income tax rules to be realistic; in some cases it may be considered too high and in others too low. So, many businesses prepare two sets of financial statements: one for financial accounting purposes (reflecting a "realistic" amount of depreciation) and another for federal income tax purposes (reflecting the "theoretical" amount of depreciation required by the IRS).

We will study three depreciation methods used for financial accounting (straight-line, units-of-production, and declining-balance) as well as MACRS—a bit boring perhaps, but valuable.

Unit Objectives

Unit 20.1 Depreciation for financial accounting

- **a** Understanding depreciation terminology
- **b** Calculating straight-line depreciation
- **c** Calculating units-of-production depreciation
- **d** Calculating declining-balance depreciation
- **e** Calculating depreciation for partial years

Unit 20.2 Depreciation for federal income taxes (MACRS)

- **a** Calculating depreciation using MACRS
- **b** Calculating Section 179 expense deduction

Unit 20.1 Depreciation for financial accounting

Many people get confused with depreciation terminology. Many of the terms sound alike. So we'll start off slowly, reviewing the "language of depreciation."

a Understanding depreciation terminology

The cost of an asset is referred to as its **basis.** The number of years the asset will be useful is referred to as **useful life.** **Salvage value** (sometimes called *residual value, scrap value,* or *trade-in value*) is the projected value of the asset at the end of its useful life. An asset's **depreciable basis** is its basis (cost) minus salvage value; this is the amount that can be depreciated. **Depreciation expense,** which represents the asset's loss of usefulness during an accounting period, is shown on an income statement and, like other expenses, reduces the company's profit. Depreciation expense is only a "paper entry" and is *not a cash outlay* like most expenses. **Accumulated depreciation** represents the total amount of depreciation expense for the asset to date. The basis (original cost) minus accumulated depreciation is the asset's **adjusted basis** or **book value**; the book value may not go below the salvage value.

Example 1 Your business buys a copy machine for $3,000. You anticipate that the copy machine will be useful for 5 years; you project that you can sell the copy machine at the end of 5 years for $500.

a. What is the asset's basis?
b. What is its useful life?
c. What is its salvage value?
d. What is its depreciable basis?
e. If you take depreciation expense of $500 per year for 2 years, what is the accumulated depreciation at the end of year 2?
f. What is the book value at the end of year 2?

---

a. $3,000 (the cost)
b. 5 years
c. $500
d. $2,500 ($3,000 basis - $500 salvage value)
e. $1,000 ($500 × 2 years)
f. $2,000 ($3,000 basis - $1,000 accumulated depreciation)

The purchase price of a business building must be broken into two parts: (1) land, which cannot be depreciated, and (2) building, which can be depreciated.

Businesses take depreciation expense on some assets but not on others. Here are a few guidelines for taking depreciation:

- **The business must own the asset.** So, for instance, a business would take depreciation for a delivery truck that the business owns but would not take depreciation for a leased vehicle (they would instead treat the lease payments as a business expense).
- **The property must have a life longer than 1 year.** So, desks, copy machines, and computers would be depreciated because they have a life longer than 1 year. But money spent for office supplies (with a life less than 1 year) is treated as an expense. Businesses generally prefer to expense all of a purchase in 1 year instead of depreciating a portion each year.
- **It must be something that wears out or becomes obsolete.** Land can't be depreciated

because land doesn't wear out or become obsolete. So if a business buys an office building, the price must be broken into two parts: land, which cannot be depreciated, and the building, which can be depreciated.

b Calculating straight-line depreciation

Straight-line depreciation, the simplest method of depreciation, assumes that the asset loses an equal amount of usefulness each year.

straight-line depreciation

$$\text{Annual depreciation} = \frac{\text{Depreciable basis}}{\text{Useful life}}$$

Example 2 Your business buys a copy machine for $3,000 on January 1. You anticipate that the copy machine will be useful for 5 years; you project that you can sell the copy machine at the end of 5 years for $500. Calculate the annual depreciation using straight-line depreciation.

$$\text{Annual depreciation} = \frac{\text{Depreciable basis}}{\text{Useful life}} = \frac{\$2,500}{5} = \$500$$

You can claim $500 depreciation each year for 5 years.

Illustration 20-1, known as a *depreciation schedule,* gives a summary of the copy machine depreciation over the 5-year period.

In Example 2, the copy machine was purchased on January 1, so the first year you were able to take a full year's depreciation. You're probably wondering what would happen if you purchased the copy machine later. After all, not many purchases are made on January 1—(we're still partying!). We will address the question of depreciation for partial years later, in Example 5 (I'll bet you can hardly wait).

c Calculating units-of-production depreciation

The purpose of depreciation is to charge each year with its fair share of an asset's cost. The straight-line method charges an equal amount to each year. However, some assets are used more in one year than in another. For these instances, the **units-of-production depreciation** is ideal. Using this method, depreciation is calculated on a per-unit basis, such as hours of operation, miles driven, or units produced.

units-of-production depreciation

Step 1 $\text{Depreciation per unit} = \dfrac{\text{Depreciable basis}}{\text{Total estimated units of production}}$

9400

Step 2 Annual depreciation = Annual units × Depreciation per unit (from Step 1)

Note: Book value cannot go below salvage value.

Illustration 20-1 Depreciation Schedule (Straight-line Method)

Year	Depreciation expense	Accumulated depreciation	Book value
Begin	—	—	$3,000
1	$500	$500	$2,500
2	$500	$1,000	$2,000
3	$500	$1,500	$1,500
4	$500	$2,000	$1,000
5	$500	$2,500	$500

Depreciation is same for each full year.   Accumulated depreciation increases by $500 each year.   Book value decreases $500 each year until salvage value of $500 is reached.

Example 3 Refer to Example 2. You estimate that the copy machine will produce 500,000 copies during its useful life; its salvage value after producing 500,000 copies is projected to be $500. The copy machine produced 88,800 copies in year 1; 105,400 in year 2; 132,600 in year 3; 128,200 in year 4; and 120,500 in year 5. Calculate depreciation for each year using the units-of-production method.

Step 1 Depreciation per unit = $\frac{\text{Depreciable basis}}{\text{Total estimated units of production}} = \frac{\$2,500}{500,000} = \$0.005$

Depreciation is based on $\frac{1}{2}$ of a cent per copy (.005 dollars = .5 cent).

Step 2 Annual depreciation (rounded to the nearest dollar) is found by multiplying annual units by $0.005; notice that book value is found by subtracting annual depreciation from prior book value.

Year	Annual depreciation	Book value
Begin	—	$3,000
1	88,800 copies × $0.005 = $444	$2,556
2	105,400 copies × $0.005 = $527	$2,029
3	132,600 copies × $0.005 = $663	$1,366
4	128,200 copies × $0.005 = $641	$725
5	120,500 copies × $0.005 ≈ $603; limited to $225 *	$500
Total	$2,500	NA

Note: Because book value cannot go below the $500 salvage value, year 5 depreciation is limited to $225.

d Calculating declining-balance depreciation

Declining-balance depreciation is a type of **accelerated depreciation** (a form of depreciation that allows more depreciation expense during the early years of an asset's life and less in later years). With this method, depreciation is found by multiplying a fixed rate by the declining book value of the asset, without considering salvage value. The fixed rate depends on which declining-balance method is used; the three common declining-balance methods are 200% declining-balance (also referred to as **double-declining-balance depreciation**), 150% declining-balance, and 125% declining-balance. Of the three, the 200% declining-balance method provides the greatest depreciation during the early years, followed by 150% and 125%.

declining-balance depreciation

Step 1 Find the fixed rate by dividing the appropriate percent (200%, 150%, or 125%) by the useful life of the asset.

Step 2 For each year, multiply the previous year-end book value by the fixed rate. Remember, *salvage value is not deducted from the basis* before the rate is applied, but book value cannot go below the designated salvage value.

Example 4 Refer to Example 2. Calculate depreciation for each year (rounded to the nearest dollar) using the 200% declining-balance method.

Step 1 Rate = $\frac{200\%}{5}$ = 40%

Step 2 For each year, multiply the previous year-end book value by 40%.

(Continued on next page)

Year	Annual depreciation	Book value
Begin	—	$3,000
1	$3,000 × 40% = $1,200	$1,800
2	$1,800 × 40% = $720	$1,080
3	$1,080 × 40% = $432	$648
4	$648 × 40% ≈ 259; limited to $148 *	$500
5	$0	$500
Total	$2,500	NA

Note: Because the book value cannot go below the designated salvage value of $500, depreciation for year 4 is limited to $148, and no depreciation is taken in year 5.

> **TIP** declining-balance method: the "weird" one
>
> With the declining-balance method, unlike the other methods, we do *not* deduct salvage value before figuring depreciation. Using Example 4:
>
> | | Correct | Incorrect |
> |---|---|---|
> | Year 1 depreciation: | $3,000 × 40% = $1,200 | $2,500 × 40% = $1,000 |

We have calculated annual depreciation for a $3,000 copy machine using three different methods. The results are summarized in Illustration 20-2. Notice that the straight-line method results in the same amount of depreciation each year, while the declining-balance method results in more depreciation in the early years and less in later years. *A method should be selected that best predicts the asset's loss of usefulness.*

e Calculating depreciation for partial years

Depreciation begins when the asset is placed in service. When an asset is placed in service at some time other than the beginning of an accounting period or taken out of service at some time other than the end of an accounting period, depreciation must be prorated. Depreciation to the nearest full month is considered sufficiently accurate. As a general rule, depreciation is calculated for a full month on assets placed in service during the first 15 days of the month and depreciation is not taken on assets placed in service after the 15th of the month. Preceding examples were based on buying a copy machine on January 1. In the next two examples, we will assume the copy machine is purchased later.

Illustration 20-2 Comparison of Depreciation Methods

Year	Straight-line (Example 2)		Units-of-production (Example 3)		200% Declining-balance (Example 4)	
	Depreciation	Book value	Depreciation	Book value	Depreciation	Book value
Begin	—	$3,000	—	$3,000	—	$3,000
1	$500	$2,500	$444	$2,556	$1,200	$1,800
2	$500	$2,000	$527	$2,029	$720	$1,080
3	$500	$1,500	$663	$1,366	$432	$648
4	$500	$1,000	$641	$725	$148	$500
5	$500	$500	$225	$500	$0	$500
Total	$2,500	NA	$2,500	NA	$2,500	NA

Example 5 You purchased a copy machine for $3,000 on April 13 and paid for the copier on April 28. The machine was delivered on April 25; but because you were remodeling your office, you did not begin using the copier until May 12. Using 5-year straight-line depreciation, with a salvage value of $500, figure depreciation (rounded to the nearest dollar) for each of the first 2 calendar-years.

The determining factor is when the asset is *placed in service* (May 12). You are entitled to depreciation for the month of May, since the machine was placed in service during the first 15 days of the month. You are also entitled to depreciation for the months of June through December. So you will get 8 months or $\frac{8}{12}$ of a year's depreciation for Year 1.

Depreciable basis: $3,000 (basis) - $500 (salvage value) = $2,500

Depreciation expense, by year:

Year 1: $\frac{\$2,500}{5} \times \frac{8}{12} \approx$ $333   **Year 2:** $\frac{\$2,500}{5} =$ $500

For the units-of-production method, there is no need to prorate for partial years since the method is based on use and not on time; for only part of a year, the asset would not get as much use, thereby resulting in less depreciation.

With the declining-balance method, depreciation must be divided into accounting periods. For example, depreciation for the copy machine using the 200% declining-balance method is $1,200 for the first 12 months and $720 for the second 12 months (see Example 4). If the copier is placed in service on May 12, the machine will be in use for $\frac{8}{12}$ of the first calendar-year. So, this period should be charged with $\frac{8}{12}$ of the $1,200 amount. The second calendar-year should be charged with the remaining $\frac{4}{12}$ of the $1,200 amount plus $\frac{8}{12}$ of the $720 amount. Similar calculations should be used for the remaining periods.

Example 6 Refer to Example 4. Calculate depreciation for the first 2 calendar-years, using the 200% declining-balance method.

In Example 4, we calculated depreciation: $1,200 for the first 12 months and $720 for the second 12 months. Now we will divide these amounts into accounting periods (calendar-years).

Year 1: $1,200 $\times \frac{8}{12} =$ $800   **Year 2:** ($1,200 $\times \frac{4}{12}$) + ($720 $\times \frac{8}{12}$)

= $400 + $480 = $880

Now let's try the U-Try-It questions to see how we're doing.

U-Try-It (Unit 20.1)

Your business buys a delivery truck for $32,000 on January 1. You anticipate that the truck will be useful for 5 years; you project that you can sell the truck at the end of 5 years for $7,000. Calculate depreciation (rounded to the nearest dollar) for each year using:
1. Straight-line method.
2. Units-of-production method. You estimate that the truck can be driven a total of 125,000 miles during its useful life; its salvage value after that will be $7,000. The truck was driven 35,000 miles in year 1; 32,000 miles in year 2; 28,000 miles in year 3; 25,000 miles in year 4; and 18,000 miles in year 5.
3. 150% declining-balance method.

For Problems 4 and 5 assume that the delivery truck was placed in service on October 22.
4. Calculate straight-line depreciation for the first 2 calendar-years.
5. Calculate depreciation for the first 2 calendar-years using the 150% declining-balance method.

Answers: (If you have a different answer, check the solution in Appendix A.)
1. $5,000 each year   2. $7,000; $6,400; $5,600; $5,000; $1,000   3. $9,600; $6,720; $4,704; $3,293; $683   4. $833; $5,000
5. $1,600; $9,120

Unit 20.2 Depreciation for federal income taxes (MACRS)

For income tax purposes, assets have a useful life dictated by MACRS. For example, a desk has a useful life of 7 years.

For federal income taxes, the depreciation system is the **Modified Accelerated Cost Recovery System (MACRS,** pronounced "makers"). MACRS is used for all property placed in service after 1986. As mentioned, many businesses prepare two sets of financial statements: one for financial accounting purposes (to reflect a "realistic" amount of depreciation) and another for federal income taxes (based on MACRS that is required by the IRS).

For income tax purposes, assets are classified by useful life, referred to as **recovery period.** The recovery period dictated by the IRS is often different from the useful life used for financial accounting. Illustration 20-3 shows a few assets for the eight recovery periods.

> **TIP** save taxes by taking a depreciation deduction
>
> Taking depreciation on an income tax return provides a tax deduction, thereby decreasing income tax. Don't be misled into thinking taxpayers can claim depreciation expense on any asset; the asset *must be used for the production of income.* We cannot, for example, take depreciation on an auto or computer used for *personal* use. Another point to remember: the business must *own* the asset. Depreciation is not allowed, for example, on a *leased* car (the business would instead treat the lease payments as a business expense).

a Calculating depreciation using MACRS

The IRS publishes tables showing the annual depreciation percentages that are used with MACRS. Illustration 20-4 is a table for 3-, 5-, 7-, 10-, 15-, and 20-year property; Illustration 20-5 is a table for 27.5-year property; and Illustration 20-6 is a table for 39-year property.

Taxpayers who have certain types of income or deductions may owe an additional federal income tax, called Alternative Minimum Tax. One of the items that can trigger this tax is using a recovery period of less than 40 years when calculating depreciation for rental property. As a result, *many taxpayers elect to use an optional 40-year method for rental property,* reflected in Illustration 20-7.

Illustration 20-3 MACRS Class Recovery Periods

Recovery period (useful life)	Examples of assets
3 years	Tractor units for use over the road; racehorse over 2 years old
5 years	Automobiles, taxis, buses, trucks, computers, office machinery (such as typewriters and copiers); breeding cattle and dairy cattle
7 years	Office furniture, fixtures (such as desks and files), and restaurant equipment
10 years	Water transportation equipment (such as vessels, barges, and tugs); any single-purpose agricultural structure; any tree or vine bearing fruits or nuts
15 years	Land improvements (such as sidewalks, roads, fences, and shrubbery)
20 years	Farm buildings (other than those included as 10-year property)
27.5 years	Residential rental property (such as rental houses and apartments)
39 years	Nonresidential rental property (such as office buildings, retail stores, warehouses, and hotels)

Illustration 20-4 MACRS Rates for 3-, 5-, 7-, 10-, 15-, and 20-Year Property

Year	Recovery Period					
	3 Years	5 Years	7 Years	10 Years	15 Years	20 Years
1	33.33%	20.00%	14.29%	10.00%	5.00%	3.750%
2	44.45	32.00	24.49	18.00	9.50	7.219
3	14.81	19.20	17.49	14.40	8.55	6.677
4	7.41	11.52	12.49	11.52	7.70	6.177
5		11.52	8.93	9.22	6.93	5.713
6		5.76	8.92	7.37	6.23	5.285
7			8.93	6.55	5.90	4.888
8			4.46	6.55	5.90	4.522
9				6.56	5.91	4.462
10				6.55	5.90	4.461
11				3.28	5.91	4.462
12					5.90	4.461
13					5.91	4.462
14					5.90	4.461
15					5.91	4.462
16					2.95	4.461
17						4.462
18						4.461
19						4.462
20						4.461
21						2.231

Illustration 20-5 MACRS Rates for Residential Rental Property (27.5 Years)

Year	Month Property Initially Placed in Service											
	Jan.	Feb.	Mar.	Apr.	May	June	July	Aug.	Sep.	Oct.	Nov.	Dec.
1	3.485%	3.182%	2.879%	2.576%	2.273%	1.970%	1.667%	1.364%	1.061%	.758%	.455%	.152%
2–9	3.636	3.636	3.636	3.636	3.636	3.636	3.636	3.636	3.636	3.636	3.636	3.636
Even years: 10–26	3.637	3.637	3.637	3.637	3.637	3.637	3.636	3.636	3.636	3.636	3.636	3.636
Odd years: 11–27	3.636	3.636	3.636	3.636	3.636	3.636	3.637	3.637	3.637	3.637	3.637	3.637
28	1.970	2.273	2.576	2.879	3.182	3.485	3.636	3.636	3.636	3.636	3.636	3.636
29							.152	.455	.758	1.061	1.364	1.667

Illustration 20-6 MACRS Rates for Nonresidential Rental Property (39 Years)

Year	Month Property Initially Placed in Service											
	Jan.	Feb.	Mar.	Apr.	May	June	July	Aug.	Sep.	Oct.	Nov.	Dec.
1	2.461%	2.247%	2.033%	1.819%	1.605%	1.391%	1.177%	0.963%	0.749%	0.535%	0.321%	0.107%
2–39	2.564	2.564	2.564	2.564	2.564	2.564	2.564	2.564	2.564	2.564	2.564	2.564
40	0.107	0.321	0.535	0.749	0.963	1.177	1.391	1.605	1.819	2.033	2.247	2.461

Illustration 20-7 MACRS Alternative Rates for Residential and Nonresidential Rental Property (40 Years)

Year	Month Property Initially Placed in Service											
	Jan.	Feb.	Mar.	Apr.	May	June	July	Aug.	Sep.	Oct.	Nov.	Dec.
1	2.396%	2.188%	1.979%	1.771%	1.563%	1.146%	1.354%	0.938%	0.729%	0.521%	0.313%	0.104%
2–40	2.500	2.500	2.500	2.500	2.500	2.500	2.500	2.500	2.500	2.500	2.500	2.500
41	0.104	0.312	0.521	0.729	0.937	1.146	1.354	1.562	1.771	1.979	2.187	2.396

> ## key points of MACRS
>
> - MACRS ignores salvage value.
> - Assets with a 3-, 5-, 7-, 10-, 15-, and 20-year life (Illustration 20-4) are presumed to have been purchased in the middle of the year (this is the *half-year convention*). For example, if you purchase a computer (whether you buy it on January 4 or September 30), you will get a half-year's depreciation for the first year. An exception: If more than 40% of these assets are placed in service during the last 3 months of the year, the taxpayer must use a *mid-quarter convention* (different charts are used).
> - Rental property with a 27.5-, 39-, or the alternative 40-year life are presumed to have been purchased in the middle of the month (this is the *mid-month convention*). For example, if you purchase an apartment building on May 29, you will get $7\frac{1}{2}$ months' depreciation (half of May, plus June through December).
> - Assets with a 3-, 5-, 7-, and 10-year life use a 200% declining-balance method and switch to straight-line when straight-line depreciation provides a larger deduction.
> - Assets with a 15- and 20-year life use a 150% declining-balance method before switching to straight-line depreciation.
> - Rental properties use straight-line depreciation.
>
> *Note:* MACRS charts (Illustrations 20-4, 20-5, 20-6, and 20-7) incorporate the above guidelines. As a result, *all we have to do is multiply the basis of the property by the rate shown in the table*. As a general rule, depreciation expense is rounded to the nearest dollar.

In Examples 2 through 4 of Unit 20.1, we calculated depreciation on a copy machine purchased on January 1 for $3,000, with a useful life of 5 years and a salvage value of $500. Three methods were used: straight-line, units-of-production, and declining-balance. In the next example, we will calculate depreciation for *federal income tax purposes,* so we must use MACRS.

Example 1

Your business buys a copy machine for $3,000 on January 1. Calculate depreciation (rounded to the nearest dollar) under MACRS.

We do not choose useful life; it is dictated by the IRS. Copy machines are listed as a 5-year property. Also, notice, we ignore salvage value. We simply multiply the basis ($3,000) by the rates found in the "5 Years" column of Illustration 20-4.

Year	Depreciation expense	Adjusted basis (book value)
Begin	—	$3,000
1	$3,000 × 20% = $600	$2,400
2	$3,000 × 32% = $960	$1,440
3	$3,000 × 19.20% = $576	$864
4	$3,000 × 11.52% ≈ $346	$518
5	$3,000 × 11.52% ≈ $346	$172
6	$3,000 × 5.76% ≈ $173; limited to $172*	$0
Total	$3,000	NA

*Note: Year 6 depreciation is limited to $172, so the copy machine will not be *overdepreciated.*

Depreciated to $0.00; no salvage value.

You may wonder why, if a computer is a 5-year property, depreciation is taken for 6 years. Remember, taxpayers receive only half a year's depreciation for the first year; this carries some depreciation into the sixth year.

> **TIP** with declining balance, don't we multiply rate by a declining amount?
>
> The "5-year" rates of Illustration 20-4 are based on 200% *declining-balance depreciation*. So many people make the mistake of multiplying the rates by the *adjusted basis* rather than the original basis. Using the data of Example 1:
>
> | | **Correct** | **Incorrect** |
> |---|---|---|
> | year 2 depreciation | $3,000 × 32% = $960 | $2,400 × 32% = $768 |

The column headings of Illustrations 20-5, 20-6, and 20-7 represent the month that the rental property is placed in service. If a property is placed in service in May, for example, the rates in the May column apply to that property throughout its entire recovery period. Remember that land cannot be depreciated. The purchase price must be broken into two parts: (1) building and (2) land. The allocation should be made based on the percent of total value in a county assessor's valuation or an appraisal.

Example 2

You purchased a six-unit apartment building on May 29 for $500,000. Just prior to buying the property, you obtained an appraisal, indicating that land value was 15% of the total value and buildings were 85% of total value. Calculate MACRS depreciation for each of the first 3 years using a 27.5-year life.

Building value: $500,000 × 85% = $425,000

Depreciation (using May column of Illustration 20-5)

Year 1: $425,000 × 2.273% ≈ $9,660
Year 2: $425,000 × 3.636% = $15,453
Year 3: $425,000 × 3.636% = $15,453

Although most taxpayers use the regular MACRS method (for which Illustrations 20-4, 20-5, and 20-6 apply), a few alternative methods are available for most assets. These alternative methods result in less depreciation in the early years of an asset. One alternative method is using a 40-year recovery period for rental property, reflected in Illustration 20-7. Rate charts for other alternative methods appear in IRS Publication 946.

ⓑ Calculating Section 179 expense deduction

Under current federal income tax rules, a taxpayer may elect to treat part or all of the cost of certain depreciable property as an expense rather than depreciate it over a number of years. This deduction is known as a **Section 179 expense deduction.** Buildings (with a few exceptions) are *not* eligible for the deduction.

The maximum deduction changes from year to year, depending on how much the U.S. Congress wants to stimulate economic growth. The rules are aimed at helping small and mid-sized companies; to prevent large companies from receiving the tax benefit, there is a phase-out amount. Taxpayers who place more Section 179 property into service during the taxable year than allowed must reduce their Section 179 deduction dollar for dollar by the amount exceeding the phase-out amount. Here are the limits for Years 2007 through 2015:

Year	Maximum deduction	Phase-out amount
2007	$150,000	$500,000
2008	$250,000	$800,000
2009	$250,000	$800,000
2010 thru 2015	$500,000	$2,000,000

When a taxpayer elects to take a Section 179 expense deduction, the amount of the deduction reduces the depreciable basis.

Example 3

In June of 2015, you purchased and placed in service 5-year business property at a cost of $2,130,000. Assuming that the property qualifies for a Section 179 expense deduction, and you placed no additional Section 179 property in service during 2015, determine **(a)** the maximum Section 179 expense deduction and **(b)** MACRS depreciation for the year.

    a. Section 179 expense deduction

Limit for 2015	$500,000
Excess over phase-out limit: $2,130,000 - $2,000,000 limit	- 130,000
Section 179 expense deduction	$370,000

    b. MACRS depreciation

        Depreciable basis: $2,130,000 - $370,000 = $1,760,000
        MACRS Depreciation: $1,760,000 × 20% = $352,000

You could write off a total of $722,000 in 2015. In 2016, you can claim MACRS depreciation of $563,200 ($1,760,000 × 32%).

> **TIP** — details, details
>
> Depreciation is one of the most complicated subjects in tax accounting. We have covered the basic concepts of MACRS and Section 179. Remember, tax laws change frequently. For up-to-date details and limitations on MACRS and Section 179 expense deduction, see IRS Publication 946 or contact the IRS or a tax expert.

Now, let's *tax* our brains by doing the U-Try-It exercises on income tax depreciation.

U-Try-It (Unit 20.2)

Using the rates of Illustrations 20-4, 20-5, 20-6, and 20-7 calculate first-year depreciation for the following assets.

1. A $2,000 computer purchased on April 13; you use the computer for personal use.
2. A $1,200 desk purchased on February 26. The desk is used for business. You figure it has a useful life of 5 years with a $200 salvage value.
3. An office building purchased on August 22 for $850,000. The county assessor shows 20% of the value is for land and 80% for buildings. You elect to use the alternative 40-year recovery period.
4. 5-year business property of $512,000 placed in service on May 5, 2015. Assuming that the property qualifies for a Section 179 expense deduction and you take the maximum deduction, what is the amount of MACRS for the year?

Answers: (If you have a different answer, check the solution in Appendix A.)
1. None can be taken   **2.** $171   **3.** $6,378   **4.** $2,400 (total deduction = $502,400)

Chapter in a Nutshell

Objectives	Examples
Unit 20.1 Depreciation for financial accounting	

(a) Understanding depreciation terminology	Your business buys a copy machine on January 1 for $2,000. You project a 5-year life and $500 salvage value, and take depreciation of $300 per year. What is the **(a)** basis, **(b)** depreciable basis, **(c)** accumulated depreciation at end of year 3, and **(d)** book value at end of year 3?
	    a. Basis = $2,000
	    b. Depreciable basis = $2,000 (basis) - $500 (salvage value) = $1,500
	    c. Accumulated depreciation at end of year 3 = $900 ($300 per year × 3 years)
	    d. Book value at end of year 3 = $2,000 (basis) - $900 (accumulated depreciation) = $1,100

Chapter in a Nutshell (concluded)

Objectives	Examples

b Calculating straight-line depreciation

Refer back. Straight-line depreciation?

Year 1: $\frac{\$1,500}{5} = \$300$ **Year 2:** $\frac{\$1,500}{5} = \$300$

c Calculating units-of-production depreciation

Refer back. You estimate that the copy machine will produce 200,000 copies during its useful life. If the machine produced 45,000 copies in year 1 and 50,000 copies in year 2:

Depreciation per unit = $\frac{\text{Depreciable basis}}{\text{Total estimated units of production}} = \frac{\$1,500}{200,000} = \$0.0075$

Year 1: 45,000 copies × $0.0075 ≈ **$338**   **Year 2:** 50,000 copies × $0.0075 = **$375**

d Calculating declining-balance depreciation

Refer back. 200% declining-balance depreciation?

Rate = $\frac{200\%}{5}$ = 40%. Remember, do not deduct salvage value.

Year	Annual depreciation	Book value
Begin	—	$2,000
1	$2,000 × 40% = **$800**	$1,200
2	$1,200 × 40% = **$480**	$720

e Calculating depreciation for partial years

Refer back. Instead assume that you placed the copy machine in service on August 18.

Get no depreciation for August (placed in service *after* the 15th of the month), so get depreciation for 4 months out of 12 ($\frac{4}{12}$ of a year).

Straight-line depreciation

Year 1: $\frac{\$1,500}{5} \times \frac{4}{12} = \$100$ **Year 2:** $\frac{\$1,500}{5} = \$300$

200% declining-balance depreciation (see Objective d, above)

Year 1: $800 × $\frac{4}{12}$ ≈ **$267**   **Year 2:** ($800 × $\frac{8}{12}$) + ($480 × $\frac{4}{12}$)

= $533.33 + $160 ≈ **$693**

Unit 20.2 Depreciation for federal income taxes (MACRS)

a Calculating depreciation using MACRS

Refer back. Assume copy machine is placed in service on August 18. MACRS?

Refer to Illustration 20-3 to determine useful life: 5 years

Year 1: (Illustration 20-4, Year 1, 5-year column): $2,000 × 20% = **$400**
Year 2: $2,000 × 32% = **$640**

Buy four-unit residential rental property May 22 for $480,000. 75% allocated to buildings. MACRS, using a 27.5-year life:

Building value = $480,000 × 75% = $360,000

Year 1: $360,000 (building value) × 2.273% (Illustration 20-5, Year 1, May column) ≈ **$8,183**
Year 2: $360,000 × 3.636% ≈ **$13,090**

b Calculating Section 179 expense deduction

5-year business property of $547,400 placed in service June 25, 2015; no more Section 179 property placed in service that year. Determine maximum you can claim in the year 2015 for Section 179 expense deduction and MACRS depreciation.

Section 179 expense deduction (maximum in year 2015)   **$500,000**
MACRS depreciation
  Depreciable basis: $547,400 - $500,000 = $47,400
  MACRS Depreciation: $47,400 × 20%   **$9,480**

Chapter in a Nutshell (concluded)

Objectives	Examples

Enrichment Topics

The following Enrichment Topics, which go a bit beyond what is in the text, are available for this chapter:

Gain on Sale of Depreciable Property
Depletion of Natural Resources

If your instructor doesn't cover these topics in class and you would like to dig in deeper on your own, please send a request to *studentsupport@olympuspub.com*.

Think

1. What type of property can be depreciated? What cannot be depreciated?
2. Why do you suppose some businesses use a depreciation method other than straight-line?
3. If, for income tax purposes, a business must use MACRS, why would the business use a different method for financial accounting purposes?
4. Why, with the units-of-production method, is there no need to prorate for partial years?
5. With MACRS, salvage value is ignored, so the asset should be fully depreciated over its recovery period. Use the numbers in the 7-year column of Illustration 20-4 to prove that the asset will, in fact, be fully depreciated. Explain why there are eight sets of numbers in the 7-year column.

Explore

1. Refer to Example 4 of Unit 20.1. Create an Excel spreadsheet that will compute depreciation each year, as well as the resulting book value. *Tip:* The book value can be no lower than the salvage value ($500). To prevent this from happening, we can use an Excel "If" statement, such as: =IF(C2 500>C2*0.4,C2*0.4,C2 500). An "If" statement is divided into 3 parts, separated by commas. The first part is the argument. The second part gives a depreciation value if the argument is true. The third part gives a depreciation value if the argument is false.

Apply

1. **How do they do it?** Meet with the owner, manager, or accountant of a local company and ask for his or her help with this project. List at least 10 depreciable assets owned by the company. For each asset, list (1) useful life, (2) depreciable basis, (3) the depreciation method used for financial accounting, (4) accumulated depreciation, and (5) current adjusted basis. Include your calculations to confirm the company's numbers. Then, for each asset, determine these items for federal income tax: (1) depreciable basis, (2) recovery period, (3) current year's depreciation, (4) accumulated depreciation, and (5) adjusted basis. Include your calculations to confirm the company's numbers.

Chapter Review Problems

Unit 20.1 Depreciation for financial accounting

1. Depreciation for financial accounting is identical to depreciation for federal income tax purposes. (T or F)

For Problems 2–7, assume that your business buys a computer for $1,300 on January 12. You project that the computer will be worth $150 at the end of its 5-year useful life.

2. What is the asset's basis?

3. What is the useful life?

4. What is the salvage value?

5. What is the depreciable basis?

6. If you take depreciation expense of $230 per year, what is the accumulated depreciation at the end of year 3?

7. What is the book value at the end of year 3?

8. A business can take depreciation on a delivery truck that it leases from someone. (T or F)

9. Suppose an office supply business buys a building for $800,000. If the building is used as a retail location, the business can depreciate the entire $800,000. (T or F)

For Problems 10–13, assume that your business buys a copy machine for $2,400 on January 1. You project that you can sell the copy machine at the end of its 5-year useful life for $400.

10. Calculate the annual depreciation using straight-line depreciation.

11. Prepare a depreciation schedule for the 5-year useful life (show depreciation expense, accumulated depreciation, and book value).

12. Calculate depreciation for each year (to the nearest dollar) using the units-of-production method. Assume that the copy machine will produce 160,000 copies during its useful life; its salvage value after producing the 160,000 copies is projected to be $400. The machine produced copies as follows:

    Year 1: 34,200   Year 2: 35,800   Year 3: 30,100   Year 4: 38,400   Year 5: 35,200

13. Calculate depreciation for each year (to the nearest dollar) using the 200% declining-balance method.

For Problems 14 and 15, assume you buy a business desk.

14. You purchased the desk on May 27 and paid for the desk on June 10. The desk was delivered on June 4; but because you were remodeling your office, you did not begin using the desk until June 17. For how many months can you take depreciation in the first calendar-year?

15. The desk cost $1,800. Using 7-year straight-line depreciation, with a $400 salvage value, figure depreciation for each of the first 2 calendar-years.

Unit 20.2 Depreciation for federal income taxes (MACRS)

16. For MACRS, salvage value is ignored. (T or F)

17. For MACRS purposes, assets with a 27.5-year recovery period are presumed to have been purchased in the middle of the year, regardless of the actual purchase date. (T or F)

For Problems 18–21, determine the recovery period.

18. Computer.

19. Car.

20. Warehouse building.

21. Desk.

For Problems 22–27, find MACRS depreciation (to the nearest dollar).

22. Year 1 for a 5-year $2,500 property.

23. Year 4 for a 3-year $8,000 property.

24. Year 2 for a 5-year $800 property.

25. Year 1 for 27.5-year property purchased August 2 (building value = $220,000).

26. Year 12 for 39-year property purchased May 27 (building value = $970,000).

27. Refer to problem 26. You elect to use the alternative 40-year method. What is year 12 MACRS?

28. Your business buys a copy machine for $1,500 on January 12. You project a 3-year useful life, with a salvage value of $500. Determine MACRS depreciation, rounded to the nearest dollar, for each year.

29. Refer to Problem 28. Why, if the copy machine has a 5-year recovery period, is depreciation taken for 6 years?

30. You purchased a duplex on September 29 for $250,000. The county assessor's valuation of the property indicates that 20% of the total value is for land and 80% for buildings. Calculate MACRS depreciation for each of the first 3 years, using a 27.5-year life.

31. Refer to Illustration 20-5. Explain why the January rate for year 1 is less than the rate for year 2.

32. In May 2015, Prince & Rulon, Attorneys at Law, purchased office furniture at a cost of $572,000. The furniture qualifies for a Section 179 expense deduction. Determine (a) the maximum Section 179 expense deduction and (b) MACRS depreciation for the year.

Challenge problems

For Problems 33–36, assume your business buys a delivery truck for $35,000 on May 22.

33. You project the truck will have a salvage value of $8,000 at the end of it's 5-year useful life. Calculate straight-line depreciation for each of the first 3 calendar-years.

34. Calculate depreciation for the first 3 calendar-years using the 200% declining-balance method.

35. Calculate MACRS depreciation for the first 3 calendar-years.

36. Which of the three methods provides the greatest depreciation expense for the first 3 calendar-years?

Practice Test

For all problems, round annual depreciation amounts to the nearest dollar.

1. Your business buys a delivery van for $30,000. You figure the van will be useful for 5 years and have a value of $5,000 at the end of the 5-year period. What are the **(a)** basis, **(b)** useful life, **(c)** salvage value, **(d)** depreciable basis, **(e)** accumulated depreciation at the end of year 2 if you take $5,000 depreciation each year, and **(f)** the book value at the end of year 2?

2. Your business buys a copy machine for $6,000 on January 1. You estimate that the copy machine will produce 250,000 copies during its useful life; its salvage value after producing the 250,000 copies is projected to be $1,000. The copy machine produced 78,200 copies in year 1 and 65,300 copies in year 2. Calculate depreciation for each of the first two years using the units-of-production method.

3. Your business buys a desk on January 10 for $2,000 with an 8-year useful life and a $500 salvage value. Calculate depreciation for each of the first 2 years using the 125% declining-balance method.

4. See Problem 3. Assume, instead, the desk is purchased September 18. Calculate depreciation for each of the first 2 calendar-years using the 125% declining-balance method.

5. See Problem 3. Calculate MACRS depreciation for each of the first 2 calendar-years.

6. Suppose you buy an apartment building for $850,000 on July 28. Land value represents 20% of the purchase price. Calculate MACRS depreciation for each of the first 2 calendar-years, using a 27.5-year life.

7. Your business buys office furniture on February 26, 2015, for $508,000. The furniture qualifies for a Section 179 expense deduction. Determine **(a)** the maximum Section 179 expense deduction and **(b)** MACRS depreciation for the year.

Classroom Notes

Quotable Quip
The Income Tax has made more liars out of the American people than golf balls.
– Will Rogers

Tax Freedom Day
Tax Freedom Day is the day on which the average American has earned enough to pay all federal, state, and local taxes for the year. Here are a few Tax Freedom Days; asterisks indicate a leap year.

1965	Apr. 6	1970	Apr. 17
1975	Apr. 15	1980*	Apr. 20
1985	Apr. 17	1990	Apr. 21
1995	Apr. 24	2000*	May 2
2005	Apr. 21	2010	Apr. 11
2015	Apr. 24		

Source: Tax Foundation

Another way to look at tax freedom is to figure how much of an 8-hour day is to pay taxes. If you start work at 8 AM, for 2015 you would work until 10:30 AM to pay your taxes! Earnings for the rest of the day are yours (to pay other bills).

Quotable Quip
The hardest thing in the world is to understand the income tax.
– Albert Einstein

Income Tax
From *Dave Barry's Greatest Hits*
by Dave Barry

There are a number (23,968,847) of significant differences between this year's tax form and last year's, but it shouldn't be too much trouble as long as you avoid Common Taxpayer Errors. "For example," reminds IRS Helpful Hint Division Chief Rexford Pooch, Jr., "taxpayers who make everything up should use numbers that sound sort of accurate, such as $3,847.62, rather than the obvious fictions like $4,000.

Also, we generally give much closer scrutiny to a return where the taxpayer gives a name such as "Nick 'The Weasel' Testosterone."

Today, the tax system is a mess. And it is unfair. I personally called for reform nearly two years ago, when I proposed a simple and fair three-pronged tax system called the You Pay Only $8.95 Tax Plan, which worked as follows:

PRONG ONE: You would pay $8.95 in taxes.

PRONG TWO: Cheating would be permitted.

PRONG THREE: Anybody who has parked his or her car diagonally across two parking spaces would be shot without trial. (This prong is not directly related to tax reform, but everybody I discussed it with feels it should be included anyway.)

5 Highest Taxed States
Taxes vary from state to state. Here are the five U.S. states with the highest combined 2015 state taxes (property, sales, state income tax, state corporate income tax, and other taxes). (Tax Freedom Day, after allowing for state taxes, is shown in parentheses)
1. Connecticut & New Jersey, tie (May 13)
3. New York (May 8)
4. Maryland (May 5)
5. California (May 3)

Note: The states with the lowest combined taxes are Louisiana (Apr 2), Mississippi (Apr 4), South Dakota (Apr 8), Tennessee & Alabama (Apr 9).

Source: Tax Foundation

A History Lesson
In 1864, the federal government decided to create an income tax to fund the Civil War. The tax was 3 percent on all incomes over $800. In 1872 the tax was discontinued.

In 1913, the income tax as we know it now became law. From 1913 to 1915 the rate was 1 percent.

In 1945, the instructions for the basic 1040 income tax form ran all of four pages. The instruction booklet is now over 150 pages long. Since 1954, Congress has changed the tax code every 15 months, on average. The actual tax code consists of over 12,000 pages.

"You've got two hours to deliver, dear, or we lose an exemption for this year!"

Taxes: Income, Sales, and Property

21

Governments provide services such as national defense, highways and streets, education, police and fire protection, libraries, parks and recreation facilities, health services, and public assistance to the needy. In order to pay for these services, a variety of taxes is collected.

If you are like the rest of us, you ask, But why do I have to pay the entire tax burden all by myself? It has been said the two things people cannot avoid are death and taxes. In this chapter, we won't talk about death, but we will examine a few taxes: federal income tax for individuals and corporations, sales tax, and property tax.

UNIT OBJECTIVES

Unit 21.1 Federal income tax
  a Calculating federal income tax for individuals
  b Calculating federal income tax for corporations

Unit 21.2 Sales tax
  a Calculating sales tax

Unit 21.3 Property tax
  a Finding assessed value
  b Establishing the tax rate
  c Calculating property tax

Unit 21.1 Federal income tax

Individuals and corporations must pay federal income tax on their income. Most states and a few cities also have income taxes; but since rules and rates are different for each, we will limit our study to *federal* income tax. The rules for federal income tax are complex and change from year to year. As a result, we will not attempt to cover the volumes of tax laws used in determining what income must be reported and what expenses can be deducted on a tax return. Instead, we will cover the highlights and then calculate the tax, based on certain amounts of taxable income. Let's start out by examining federal income tax for *individuals*.

a Calculating federal income tax for individuals

Income tax is withheld from an employee's paychecks. The amounts are applied against the *actual* tax liability on the taxpayer's income tax return. If too much was withheld, the taxpayer gets a refund; if not enough was withheld, the taxpayer owes the balance at the time the income tax return is submitted.

Federal income tax returns must be mailed before midnight on April 15.

TIP — **preparing an income tax return**

About 4:00 P.M. on April 15, many of us remember that we have forgotten something—to file our federal income tax return (due by midnight, April 15). Have you wondered whether you should fill out your own income tax return or have someone prepare it for you? Here are a few ideas.

- The IRS provides forms (many can be found on the IRS website: **www.irs.gov**), and instruction booklets. The IRS also provides tax advice (800-829-1040). Remember, however, that if the IRS gives faulty advice, the taxpayer is still responsible for the accuracy of the return.
- Computer software packages are available to help guide us through the process and print the results on tax forms.
- Because tax laws are so complex and change so frequently, many taxpayers hire a professional tax preparer. The taxpayer must still supply all information; a good tax preparer asks the right questions, inserts the client's data in the correct places, and does the calculations.

In calculating federal income tax, taxpayers must determine the amount that is subject to tax; this amount is called **taxable income.** As stated, we will not study the detailed rules or calculate taxable income. But for information, here are the highlights of finding *taxable income*:

---

 finding taxable income

Step 1 *Find total income.* Include: interest earned; dividends; alimony (not child support); net income from self-employment, rental properties, and farming (net income is income minus expenses, including depreciation); gain from the sale of property (such as stocks and real estate); pensions and taxable portions of IRA distributions; taxpayer's share of net income from partnerships, estates, and trusts; unemployment compensation; taxable portions of Social Security benefits; prizes and gambling winnings.

(continues)

finding taxable income (conclusion)

Step 2 *Make adjustments to income.* Can subtract: qualified deductions to an IRA, SEP, or Keogh plan; one-half of self-employment FICA tax; certain health insurance premiums paid by self-employed taxpayers; alimony paid; qualified moving expenses; student loan interest.

Step 3 *Subtract the larger of standard deduction or itemized deductions.*

Step 4 *Subtract a specified amount for each exemption.* You get one exemption for yourself, one for your spouse, and one for each other dependent (such as children), provided you, spouse, and children are not claimed as a dependent on another tax return.

The result is the *taxable income;* this is the amount on which the tax is figured.

Once we have determined taxable income, we can calculate federal income tax.

calculating federal income tax

- If taxable income is *less than $100,000,* we use the **tax table.** The tax table consists of several pages; selected portions of the 2014 tax table are shown as Illustration 21-1.
- If taxable income is *$100,000 or more,* we use the **tax rate schedules,** shown as Illustration 21-2.

Jack and Betty Green, a married couple, have 2014 taxable income of $42,452. Calculate their federal income tax.

Because taxable income is less than $100,000 we use the tax table (Illustration 21-1). We look for the range that includes $42,452; the range reads "at least $42,450 but less than $42,500." By following across this line to the "married filing jointly" column, we see that their tax is $5,464.

Calculating federal income tax using the tax rate schedules is a bit more complicated.

using the tax rate schedules (for taxable incomes of $100,000 or more)

Step 1 Locate the schedule that corresponds to the filing status.
Step 2 Find the range that includes the taxable income.
Step 3 Find the difference between taxable income and the base amount (in right-hand column).
Step 4 Multiply the result of Step 3 by the rate listed for that range.
Step 5 Find the tax by adding the result of Step 4 to the base tax for that range.

Tom Brown, whose filing status is single, has 2014 taxable income of $112,014. Calculate his federal income tax.

Because Tom's taxable income is at least $100,000, we must use the tax rate schedules (Ill. 21-2).

Step 1 (locate the schedule): Because Tom is single, we use Schedule X.
Step 2 (find the range): "over $89,350 but not over $186,350"
Step 3 (difference between taxable income and base amount): $112,014 - $89,350 = $22,664
Step 4 (multiply by rate): $22,664 × 28% = $6,345.92
Step 5 (tax): $6,345.92 + $18,193.75 = $24,540 (rounded to the nearest dollar)

The arithmetic of Example 2 can be done on a calculator, as shown below:

Keystrokes (for most calculators)	
112,014 − 89,350 =	22,664.00
× 28 % =	6,345.92
+ 18,193.75 =	**24,539.67**

Illustration 21-1 Selected Portions of the 2014 Tax Table (for taxable income under $100,000)

If line 43 (taxable income) is—		And you are—				If line 43 (taxable income) is—		And you are—				If line 43 (taxable income) is—		And you are—			
At least	But less than	Single	Married filing jointly*	Married filing separately	Head of a household	At least	But less than	Single	Married filing jointly*	Married filing separately	Head of a household	At least	But less than	Single	Married filing jointly*	Married filing separately	Head of a household
		Your tax is—						Your tax is—						Your tax is—			
15,000						**42,000**						**69,000**					
15,000	15,050	1,800	1,503	1,800	1,606	42,000	42,050	6,363	5,396	6,363	5,656	69,000	69,050	13,113	9,446	13,113	11,669
15,050	15,100	1,808	1,508	1,808	1,614	42,050	42,100	6,375	5,404	6,375	5,664	69,050	69,100	13,125	9,454	13,125	11,681
15,100	15,150	1,815	1,513	1,815	1,621	42,100	42,150	6,388	5,411	6,388	5,671	69,100	69,150	13,138	9,461	13,138	11,694
15,150	15,200	1,823	1,518	1,823	1,629	42,150	42,200	6,400	5,419	6,400	5,679	69,150	69,200	13,150	9,469	13,150	11,706
15,200	15,250	1,830	1,523	1,830	1,636	42,200	42,250	6,413	5,426	6,413	5,686	69,200	69,250	13,163	9,476	13,163	11,719
15,250	15,300	1,838	1,528	1,838	1,644	42,250	42,300	6,425	5,434	6,425	5,694	69,250	69,300	13,175	9,484	13,175	11,731
15,300	15,350	1,845	1,533	1,845	1,651	42,300	42,350	6,438	5,441	6,438	5,701	69,300	69,350	13,188	9,491	13,188	11,744
15,350	15,400	1,853	1,538	1,853	1,659	42,350	42,400	6,450	5,449	6,450	5,709	69,350	69,400	13,200	9,499	13,200	11,756
15,400	15,450	1,860	1,543	1,860	1,666	42,400	42,450	6,463	5,456	6,463	5,716	69,400	69,450	13,213	9,506	13,213	11,769
15,450	15,500	1,868	1,548	1,868	1,674	42,450	42,500	6,475	5,464	6,475	5,724	69,450	69,500	13,225	9,514	13,225	11,781
15,500	15,550	1,875	1,553	1,875	1,681	42,500	42,550	6,488	5,471	6,488	5,731	69,500	69,550	13,238	9,521	13,238	11,794
15,550	15,600	1,883	1,558	1,883	1,689	42,550	42,600	6,500	5,479	6,500	5,739	69,550	69,600	13,250	9,529	13,250	11,806
15,600	15,650	1,890	1,563	1,890	1,696	42,600	42,650	6,513	5,486	6,513	5,746	69,600	69,650	13,263	9,536	13,263	11,819
15,650	15,700	1,898	1,568	1,898	1,704	42,650	42,700	6,525	5,494	6,525	5,754	69,650	69,700	13,275	9,544	13,275	11,831
15,700	15,750	1,905	1,573	1,905	1,711	42,700	42,750	6,538	5,501	6,538	5,761	69,700	69,750	13,288	9,551	13,288	11,844
15,750	15,800	1,913	1,578	1,913	1,719	42,750	42,800	6,550	5,509	6,550	5,769	69,750	69,800	13,300	9,559	13,300	11,856
15,800	15,850	1,920	1,583	1,920	1,726	42,800	42,850	6,563	5,516	6,563	5,776	69,800	69,850	13,313	9,566	13,313	11,869
15,850	15,900	1,928	1,588	1,928	1,734	42,850	42,900	6,575	5,524	6,575	5,784	69,850	69,900	13,325	9,574	13,325	11,881
15,900	15,950	1,935	1,593	1,935	1,741	42,900	42,950	6,588	5,531	6,588	5,791	69,900	69,950	13,338	9,581	13,338	11,894
15,950	16,000	1,943	1,598	1,943	1,749	42,950	43,000	6,600	5,539	6,600	5,799	69,950	70,000	13,350	9,589	13,350	11,906
16,000						**43,000**						**70,000**					
16,000	16,050	1,950	1,603	1,950	1,756	43,000	43,050	6,613	5,546	6,613	5,806	70,000	70,050	13,363	9,596	13,363	11,919
16,050	16,100	1,958	1,608	1,958	1,764	43,050	43,100	6,625	5,554	6,625	5,814	70,050	70,100	13,375	9,604	13,375	11,931
16,100	16,150	1,965	1,613	1,965	1,771	43,100	43,150	6,638	5,561	6,638	5,821	70,100	70,150	13,388	9,611	13,388	11,944
16,150	16,200	1,973	1,618	1,973	1,779	43,150	43,200	6,650	5,569	6,650	5,829	70,150	70,200	13,400	9,619	13,400	11,956
16,200	16,250	1,980	1,623	1,980	1,786	43,200	43,250	6,663	5,576	6,663	5,836	70,200	70,250	13,413	9,626	13,413	11,969
16,250	16,300	1,988	1,628	1,988	1,794	43,250	43,300	6,675	5,584	6,675	5,844	70,250	70,300	13,425	9,634	13,425	11,981
16,300	16,350	1,995	1,633	1,995	1,801	43,300	43,350	6,688	5,591	6,688	5,851	70,300	70,350	13,438	9,641	13,438	11,994
16,350	16,400	2,003	1,638	2,003	1,809	43,350	43,400	6,700	5,599	6,700	5,859	70,350	70,400	13,450	9,649	13,450	12,006
16,400	16,450	2,010	1,643	2,010	1,816	43,400	43,450	6,713	5,606	6,713	5,866	70,400	70,450	13,463	9,656	13,463	12,019
16,450	16,500	2,018	1,648	2,018	1,824	43,450	43,500	6,725	5,614	6,725	5,874	70,450	70,500	13,475	9,664	13,475	12,031
16,500	16,550	2,025	1,653	2,025	1,831	43,500	43,550	6,738	5,621	6,738	5,881	70,500	70,550	13,488	9,671	13,488	12,044
16,550	16,600	2,033	1,658	2,033	1,839	43,550	43,600	6,750	5,629	6,750	5,889	70,550	70,600	13,500	9,679	13,500	12,056
16,600	16,650	2,040	1,663	2,040	1,846	43,600	43,650	6,763	5,636	6,763	5,896	70,600	70,650	13,513	9,686	13,513	12,069
16,650	16,700	2,048	1,668	2,048	1,854	43,650	43,700	6,775	5,644	6,775	5,904	70,650	70,700	13,525	9,694	13,525	12,081
16,700	16,750	2,055	1,673	2,055	1,861	43,700	43,750	6,788	5,651	6,788	5,911	70,700	70,750	13,538	9,701	13,538	12,094
16,750	16,800	2,063	1,678	2,063	1,869	43,750	43,800	6,800	5,659	6,800	5,919	70,750	70,800	13,550	9,709	13,550	12,106
16,800	16,850	2,070	1,683	2,070	1,876	43,800	43,850	6,813	5,666	6,813	5,926	70,800	70,850	13,563	9,716	13,563	12,119
16,850	16,900	2,078	1,688	2,078	1,884	43,850	43,900	6,825	5,674	6,825	5,934	70,850	70,900	13,575	9,724	13,575	12,131
16,900	16,950	2,085	1,693	2,085	1,891	43,900	43,950	6,838	5,681	6,838	5,941	70,900	70,950	13,588	9,731	13,588	12,144
16,950	17,000	2,093	1,698	2,093	1,899	43,950	44,000	6,850	5,689	6,850	5,949	70,950	71,000	13,600	9,739	13,600	12,156
17,000						**44,000**						**71,000**					
17,000	17,050	2,100	1,703	2,100	1,906	44,000	44,050	6,863	5,696	6,863	5,956	71,000	71,050	13,613	9,746	13,613	12,169
17,050	17,100	2,108	1,708	2,108	1,914	44,050	44,100	6,875	5,704	6,875	5,964	71,050	71,100	13,625	9,754	13,625	12,181
17,100	17,150	2,115	1,713	2,115	1,921	44,100	44,150	6,888	5,711	6,888	5,971	71,100	71,150	13,638	9,761	13,638	12,194
17,150	17,200	2,123	1,718	2,123	1,929	44,150	44,200	6,900	5,719	6,900	5,979	71,150	71,200	13,650	9,769	13,650	12,206
17,200	17,250	2,130	1,723	2,130	1,936	44,200	44,250	6,913	5,726	6,913	5,986	71,200	71,250	13,663	9,776	13,663	12,219
17,250	17,300	2,138	1,728	2,138	1,944	44,250	44,300	6,925	5,734	6,925	5,994	71,250	71,300	13,675	9,784	13,675	12,231
17,300	17,350	2,145	1,733	2,145	1,951	44,300	44,350	6,938	5,741	6,938	6,001	71,300	71,350	13,688	9,791	13,688	12,244
17,350	17,400	2,153	1,738	2,153	1,959	44,350	44,400	6,950	5,749	6,950	6,009	71,350	71,400	13,700	9,799	13,700	12,256
17,400	17,450	2,160	1,743	2,160	1,966	44,400	44,450	6,963	5,756	6,963	6,016	71,400	71,450	13,713	9,806	13,713	12,269
17,450	17,500	2,168	1,748	2,168	1,974	44,450	44,500	6,975	5,764	6,975	6,024	71,450	71,500	13,725	9,814	13,725	12,281
17,500	17,550	2,175	1,753	2,175	1,981	44,500	44,550	6,988	5,771	6,988	6,031	71,500	71,550	13,738	9,821	13,738	12,294
17,550	17,600	2,183	1,758	2,183	1,989	44,550	44,600	7,000	5,779	7,000	6,039	71,550	71,600	13,750	9,829	13,750	12,306
17,600	17,650	2,190	1,763	2,190	1,996	44,600	44,650	7,013	5,786	7,013	6,046	71,600	71,650	13,763	9,836	13,763	12,319
17,650	17,700	2,198	1,768	2,198	2,004	44,650	44,700	7,025	5,794	7,025	6,054	71,650	71,700	13,775	9,844	13,775	12,331
17,700	17,750	2,205	1,773	2,205	2,011	44,700	44,750	7,038	5,801	7,038	6,061	71,700	71,750	13,788	9,851	13,788	12,344
17,750	17,800	2,213	1,778	2,213	2,019	44,750	44,800	7,050	5,809	7,050	6,069	71,750	71,800	13,800	9,859	13,800	12,356
17,800	17,850	2,220	1,783	2,220	2,026	44,800	44,850	7,063	5,816	7,063	6,076	71,800	71,850	13,813	9,866	13,813	12,369
17,850	17,900	2,228	1,788	2,228	2,034	44,850	44,900	7,075	5,824	7,075	6,084	71,850	71,900	13,825	9,874	13,825	12,381
17,900	17,950	2,235	1,793	2,235	2,041	44,900	44,950	7,088	5,831	7,088	6,091	71,900	71,950	13,838	9,881	13,838	12,394
17,950	18,000	2,243	1,798	2,243	2,049	44,950	45,000	7,100	5,839	7,100	6,099	71,950	72,000	13,850	9,889	13,850	12,406

Note: The Married filing jointly column must also be used by a qualifying widow(er).

Illustration 21-2 Tax Rate Schedules, 2014 (for taxable income of $100,000 or more)

2014 Tax Rate Schedules

 Use **only** if your taxable income is $100,000 or more. If less, use the **Tax Table**. Even though you cannot use the Tax Rate Schedules below, if your taxable income is less than $100,000, all levels of taxable income are shown so taxpayers can see the tax rate that applies to each level.

Schedule X—If your filing status is **Single**

If your taxable income is: Over—	But not over—	The tax is:	of the amount over—
$0	$9,075	10%	$0
9,075	36,900	$907.50 + 15%	9,075
36,900	89,350	5,081.25 + 25%	36,900
89,350	186,350	18,193.75 + 28%	89,350
186,350	405,100	45,353.75 + 33%	186,350
405,100	406,750	117,541.25 + 35%	405,100
406,750	-----------	118,118.75 + 39.6%	406,750

Schedule Y-1—If your filing status is **Married filing jointly** or **Qualifying widow(er)**

If your taxable income is: Over—	But not over—	The tax is:	of the amount over—
$0	$18,150	10%	$0
18,150	73,800	$1,815 + 15%	18,150
73,800	148,850	10,162.50 + 25%	73,800
148,850	226,850	28,925 + 28%	148,850
226,850	405,100	50,765 + 33%	226,850
405,100	457,600	109,587.50 + 35%	405,100
457,600	-----------	127,962.50 + 39.6%	457,600

Schedule Y-2—If your filing status is **Married filing separately**

If your taxable income is: Over—	But not over—	The tax is:	of the amount over—
$0	$9,075	10%	$0
9,075	36,900	$907.50 + 15%	9,075
36,900	74,425	5,081.25 + 25%	36,900
74,425	113,425	14,462.50 + 28%	74,425
113,425	202,550	25,382.50 + 33%	113,425
202,550	228,800	54,793.75 + 35%	202,550
228,000	-----------	63,981.25 + 39.6%	228,800

Schedule Z—If your filing status is **Head of household**

If your taxable income is: Over—	But not over—	The tax is:	of the amount over—
$0	$12,950	10%	$0
12,950	49,400	$1,295 + 15%	12,950
49,400	127,550	6,762.50 + 25%	49,400
127,550	206,600	26,300 + 28%	127,550
206,600	405,100	48,434 + 33%	206,600
405,100	432,200	113,939 + 35%	405,100
432,200	-----------	123,424 + 39.6%	432,200

> **TIP** — what tax bracket are we in?
>
> The tax rate schedules can be used to determine our tax bracket. In Example 2, Tom's taxable income over $89,350 is taxed at a 28% *tax rate;* so we say Tom is in a 28% **tax bracket.** This does *not* mean that Tom pays 28% of his taxable income as federal income tax; it means that for each *additional* dollar of taxable income, Tom must pay 28% to the IRS. To find the rate of tax for the *average dollar* of taxable income, we can divide actual tax by taxable income. For Tom:
>
> $$\frac{\$24{,}540 \text{ tax}}{\$112{,}014 \text{ taxable income}} \approx .2191 \approx 21.91\%$$
>
> So, even though Tom is in a 28% tax bracket, he pays a tax of only 21.91% of his taxable income.
>
> Knowing our tax bracket lets us know how much more tax we must pay for any additional income (the bad news) but also lets us know how much we will save from additional deductions (the good news).

b Calculating federal income tax for corporations

Business profits are also subject to federal income tax (nobody escapes the tax man). Profit is determined by subtracting business expenses from business revenues. For a *sole proprietorship*, the income and expenses are reported on the owner's individual income tax return (on Schedule C). So the taxpayer's federal income tax liability reflects his or her business income. For a *partnership*, the income and expenses are reported on a partnership return (Form 1065). Taxes are *not* paid by the partnership. Instead, each owner reports his or her share of the profit on his or her individual income tax return (on Schedule E). For a *corporation*, the income and expenses are reported on a corporate return (Form 1120), and income taxes are paid by the corporation. Corporate tax rates for 2014 are shown in Illustration 21-3.

A *limited liability company* (LLC) is another type of ownership. Before doing business, the LLC, as part of getting an Employer Identification number (EIN), must select how it wishes to be taxed. If the LLC has only one owner, it must be taxed like a sole prorietorship. If the LLC has more than one owner, it can elect to be taxed as either a corporation or partnership.

> **using the corporate tax rate schedule**
>
> **Step 1** Find the range that includes the taxable income.
> **Step 2** Find the difference between the taxable income and the base amount (in right-hand column).
> **Step 3** Multiply the result of Step 2 by the rate listed for that range.
> **Step 4** Find the tax by adding the result of Step 3 to the base tax for that range.

Illustration 21-3 Federal Tax Rate Schedule for Corporations, 2014

Tax Rate Schedule

If taxable income is:

Over—	But not over—	Tax is:	Of the amount over—
$0	$50,000	15%	$0
50,000	75,000	$7,500 + 25%	50,000
75,000	100,000	13,750 + 34%	75,000
100,000	335,000	22,250 + 39%	100,000
335,000	10,000,000	113,900 + 34%	335,000
10,000,000	15,000,000	3,400,000 + 35%	10,000,000
15,000,000	18,333,333	5,150,000 + 38%	15,000,000
18,333,333	-----	35%	0

Example 3 ABC Corporation has 2014 taxable income of $352,400. Calculate ABC's federal income tax.

Step 1 (find the range): "over $335,000 but not over $10,000,000"
Step 2 (find difference between taxable income and base amount): $352,400 - $335,000 = $17,400
Step 3 (multiply by rate): $17,400 × 34% = $5,916
Step 4 (find the tax): $5,916 + $113,900 = $119,816

> **TIP** — simplified tax return
>
> You may have heard about the development of a new simplified tax return.
>
> NEW SIMPLIFIED TAX RETURN
> 1. How much money did you make? _____
> 2. Send it in.
>
> Well, things aren't quite that bad yet! But understanding federal income tax rules is not *simple,* and the rules and rates change frequently. For up-to-date rules and rates, contact the IRS or a tax expert.

That does it for this unit. Are you ready for some U-Try-It questions?

U-Try-It (Unit 21.1)

Calculate 2014 federal income tax for each of the following situations:
1. A single taxpayer with taxable income of $16,750.
2. A married couple filing jointly, with taxable income of $145,666.
3. A corporation with taxable income of $145,666.

Answers: (If you have a different answer, check the solution in Appendix A.)
1. $2,063   2. $28,129   3. $40,060

Unit 21.2 Sales tax

In this unit, we will study a tax charged on the sale of products: sales tax.

a Calculating sales tax

All but a few states and local governments charge a tax to *consumers* called a **sales tax.** Here are a few things to remember about sales tax:

- Sales tax is charged *only to consumers* (not to someone who will resell the merchandise) and is a percent of selling price, *after any discounts.* Generally, the **sales tax rate** is applied to the total amount of the sale unless the sale consists of different kinds of merchandise that are taxed at different rates.
- There is no federal sales tax (you're relieved to hear that, I'll bet).
- Sales tax rates vary from state to state (from about 4% to 8.25%). In addition, counties and cities often impose sales tax, making the rates go even higher. Retailers collect the sales tax from consumers and forward it to the appropriate government agency.
- Certain items are excluded from sales tax. For example, some states do not charge sales tax on food, prescriptions, services (such as legal and accounting), and repair labor (such as car repairs).
- In some states, sales tax for vehicles is referred to as a state excise tax rather than a sales tax.

Some state and local governments provide retailers with a **sales tax table,** showing the amount of sales tax that should be collected. Illustration 21-4 is a selected portion of a typical sales tax table.

Illustration 21-4 Part of a Typical Sales Tax Table, 6%

Price	Sales Tax
$19.92–20.08	$1.20
20.09–20.24	1.21
20.25–20.41	1.22
20.42–20.58	1.23
20.59–20.74	1.24
20.75–20.91	1.25
20.92–21.08	1.26

When a consumer buys merchandise, sales tax is added to the price of the merchandise to determine the total amount due.

total amount due

Total amount due = Price of merchandise + Sales tax

Example 1 Cindy McGrath bought $20.28 of school supplies from Valley Office Supply. Using the 6% sales tax table of Illustration 21-4, calculate the total amount Cindy must pay.

Cost of merchandise	$20.28
Sales tax (from table)	+ 1.22
Total amount due	$21.50

For many areas, sales tax tables are optional. Retailers can instead calculate sales tax by multiplying the selling price by the sales tax rate and rounding the result to the nearest penny. Most cash registers automatically calculate and add the sales tax.

Example 2 Refer to Example 1. Calculate the sales tax without a sales tax table; then determine the total amount Cindy must pay.

Cost of merchandise	$20.28	
Sales tax: $20.28 × 6%	+ 1.22	
Total amount due	$21.50	Same amount as in Example 1

We can use a calculator to simplify the arithmetic of Example 2.

Keystrokes (for most calculators)

20.28 [+] 6 [%] [=]   **21.50**

Often, when people buy a vehicle from a dealer, they give the dealer a *trade-in vehicle* as part of the purchase price. Some states allow the value of the trade-in vehicle to be deducted from the selling price before sales tax is calculated.

Example 3 You are thinking about buying a car for $19,300. If you trade in your old vehicle (with a value of $5,000), calculate the 6% sales tax assuming that sales tax is figured on the net price.

Price of new car	$19,300
Less trade-in	- 5,000
Net price	$14,300 × 6% = $858

Chapter 21 Taxes: Income, Sales, and Property

Now, let's try a short U-Try-It set on sales tax.

U-Try-It
(Unit 21.2)

1. You are shopping for a car. You can buy the car from a dealer in your city for $19,300. The sales tax rate in your city is 6.75%. You can buy the car for the same price from a dealer in a different part of the state with a 6% sales tax rate. How much sales tax will you save if you buy the car from the second dealer?
2. You buy a new shiny red convertible for $41,000. The dealer gives you $2,000 credit for your old beat-up wreck. You must pay sales tax of 5.5% based on the "net price." Calculate the sales tax.

Answers: (If you have a different answer, check the solution in Appendix A.)
1. $144.75   2. $2,145

Unit 21.3 Property tax

Property may be classified as either **real property** or **personal property.** Real property, also called **real estate,** includes land and things permanently attached to it, such as buildings, fences, trees, and sidewalks. All property other than real property is personal property and includes things like cars, business inventory, and equipment. Local governments and independent taxing districts (such as schools and parks) get much of their revenue from property taxes.

Public schools are funded primarily from property taxes.

a Finding assessed value

The process of determining property tax begins by establishing a **fair market value** of each property being taxed. The fair market value is an estimated amount for which the property could be sold, generally estimated by a government **tax assessor.** Because higher valuations result in higher property tax, the property owner has the right to appeal the tax assessor's value.

Many local governments base their property tax not on the fair market value of the property, but on another value called **assessed value.** Assessed value is generally a certain percent (such as 25%) of the fair market value.

Example 1 Milt Hendrickson owns a home. The county assessor estimated the fair market value to be $275,000. If this type of property is assessed at 40% of fair market value, what is the assessed value of Milt's home?

$275,000 fair market value × 40% = $110,000

Milt's home has an assessed value of $110,000.

b Establishing the tax rate

In Example 1, we found assessed value, *not* the property tax ($110,000 would be a pretty hefty tax, wouldn't it?). In order to find the property tax, we must know the **property tax rate** that is applied to the assessed value. The tax rate varies from year to year depending on the financial budget of each taxing entity in which the property is located. The tax rate for each taxing entity is found by dividing the entity's total budget by the total assessed value of property within its jurisdiction.

> **tax rate formula**
>
> $$\text{Tax rate} = \frac{\text{Total budget of the taxing entity}}{\text{Total assessed value within the taxing entity}}$$
>
> *Note:* To ensure adequate revenues, taxing districts customarily round *up* the last digit, even if the following digit is less than 5.

Example 2 Refer to Example 1. Milt's home is within the boundaries of Riverside School District. The school district has an annual budget of $18,723,000 and total assessed property value within its jurisdiction of $2,236,289,100. Determine the tax rate for the school district. *Note:* Express the rate as a decimal number with 6 decimal places; round the last digit up.

$$\text{Tax rate} = \frac{\text{Total budget of the taxing entity}}{\text{Total assessed value within the taxing entity}} = \frac{\$18,723,000}{\$2,236,289,100} \approx .0083724 \approx .008373$$

We need to know the result with 7 decimal places, so that we can round up and express the answer with 6 decimal places

The tax rate of Example 2 is .008373. On the basis of this tax rate, the school district's revenues should be: $2,236,289,100 (total assessed values) × .008373 (tax rate) = $18,724,448.63, which is slightly more than the budget requires. Illustration 21-5 is a tax notice for Milt's home. Notice that the assessed value is $110,000 (the same amount we found in Example 1); the first taxing district, Riverside School District, has a tax rate of .008373 (the rate we found in Example 2). There are eight other taxing entities that service Milt's home. Each needs money and determines a tax rate as shown in Example 2; the sum of all the tax rates (called the **total tax rate**) is .019033.

C Calculating property tax

To find the **property tax,** we multiply the assessed value by the total tax rate.

Illustration 21-5   Property Tax Notice

PROPERTY TAX NOTICE Parcel Number: 16-05-105-012	Assessed To: Milt Hendrickson 555 E Any Street Anytown, CA		
Taxing District	**Tax Rate**	**Valuation**	
Riverside School District	.008373	Fair Market Value	
County General Fund	.005912	Land	$105,000
Flood Control	.001477	Buildings	$170,000
County Health Department	.001332	Total FMV	$275,000
Planetarium	.000811		× 40%
Water District	.000716	**Assessed Value**	**$110,000**
Mosquito Abatement District	.000184		
Parks Department	.000145		
Library Fund	.000083		
Total Tax Rate	.019033	**Property Tax:**	**$2,093.63**

property tax formula

Property tax = Assessed value × Total tax rate

Example 3 On the basis of the total tax rate of Illustration 21-5, calculate Milt's property tax.

Property tax = Assessed value × Total tax rate = $110,000 × .019033 = **$2,093.63**

Milt's property tax is $2,093.63. *Note:* This amount is shown at the lower right corner of the tax notice of Illustration 21-5.

In Example 3, the tax rate was expressed as a decimal number (.019033). Some places express the tax rate in a different form: as a percent; per $100 of assessed value; per $1,000 of assessed value; or in mills (a **mill** is $\frac{1}{10}$ of a cent or $\frac{1}{1,000}$ of a dollar). Here are some formulas used to find property tax, based on tax rates in various forms.

calculating property tax with tax rates in various forms

If tax rate is expressed	Formula
as a decimal number	Property tax = Assessed value × Tax rate
as a percent	Property tax = Assessed value × Tax rate
per $100 of assessed value	Property tax = $\frac{\text{Assessed value}}{\$100}$ × Tax rate
per $1,000 of assessed value	Property tax = $\frac{\text{Assessed value}}{\$1,000}$ × Tax rate
in mills	Property tax = $\frac{\text{Assessed value}}{1,000}$ × Mill levy

Example 4 Milt's property has an assessed value of $110,000. Find his property tax based on each of the following tax rates: **(a)** .019033, **(b)** 1.9033%, **(c)** $1.9033 per $100 of assessed value, **(d)** $19.033 per $1,000 of assessed value, and **(e)** 19.033 mills.

a. Property tax = $110,000 × .019033 = **$2,093.63**
b. Property tax = $110,000 × 1.9033% = **$2,093.63**
c. Property tax = $\frac{\$110,000}{\$100}$ × $1.9033 = **$2,093.63**
d. Property tax = $\frac{\$110,000}{\$1,000}$ × $19.033 = **$2,093.63**
e. Property tax = $\frac{\$110,000}{1,000}$ × 19.033 = **$2,093.63**

Using a calculator makes the arithmetic easier for Example 4. For parts a–c, for example:

Keystrokes (for most calculators)

110,000 × .019033 =	2,093.63
110,000 × 1.9033 % =	2,093.63
110,000 ÷ 100 × 1.9033 =	2,093.63

Notice that Example 4(a) is the same problem as Example 3 (with the same answer, of course). The answers for parts a–e are identical, making it apparent that the five tax rates are equivalent.

Well, that's it for this chapter. Let's try the U-Try-It exercises on property taxes.

U-Try-It (Unit 21.3)

Roy and Beth Nielson own a home. The county assessor estimates the fair market value to be $228,000.

1. If their property is assessed at 35% of fair market value, what is the assessed value?
2. Their home is within the boundaries of the Jubilee Planetarium. The planetarium has an annual budget of $14,372,000 and total assessed property within its jurisdiction of $4,259,445,120. Determine the tax rate for the planetarium. *Note:* Express the rate as a decimal number with 6 decimal places; round the last digit up.
3. If the total tax rate for Roy and Beth's property is .031764, calculate their property tax.

Find property tax for each property.

4. Assessed value = $150,000; tax rate = $2.925 per $100
5. Assessed value = $115,000; mill levy = 14.654

Answers: (If you have a different answer, check the solution in Appendix A.)
1. $79,800 2. .003375 3. $2,534.77 4. $4,387.50 5. $1,685.21

Chapter in a Nutshell

Objectives	Examples
Unit 21.1 Federal income tax	

a Calculating federal income tax for individuals	Single taxpayer with 2014 taxable income of $70,422.
	  Use tax table (because taxable income is less than $100,000).
	  Find range "at least $70,400 but less than $70,450"; single column; Tax = **$13,463**
	Married couple filing jointly with 2014 taxable income of $245,100.
	  Use tax rate schedules (because taxable income is $100,000 or more).
	  Step 1 (locate correct schedule): Schedule Y-1 (married filing jointly)
	  Step 2 (find range): "over $226,850 but not over $405,100"
	  Step 3 (find difference): $245,100 - $226,850 = $18,250
	  Step 4 (multiply by rate): $18,250 × 33% = $6,022.50
	  Step 5 (find the tax): $6,022.50 + $50,765 = $56,787.50 = **$56,788 (rounded)**

b Calculating federal income tax for corporations	Corporation has taxable income of $104,200.
	  Step 1 (find range): "over $100,000 but not over $335,000"
	  Step 2 (find difference): $104,200 - $100,000 = $4,200
	  Step 3 (multiply by rate): $4,200 × 39% = $1,638
	  Step 4 (find the tax): $1,638 + $22,250 = **$23,888**

Unit 21.2 Sales tax	

a Calculating sales tax	Big-screen TV costs $3,495. Total amount due, including 6.375% sales tax?
	  Cost of merchandise $3,495.00
	  Sales tax: $3,495 × 6.375% + 222.81
	  Total amount due **$3,717.81**

Unit 21.3 Property tax	
a Finding assessed value	Fair market value of home = $180,000. If assessed at 30%, what is assessed value? $180,000 × 30% = **$54,000**
b Establishing the tax rate	Total budget of County Health Department is $31,085,000. Total assessed value within its jurisdiction is $3,578,215,000. Tax rate? Write as a decimal number with 6 decimal places; round last digit up. Tax rate = $\dfrac{\text{Total budget of the taxing entity}}{\text{Total assessed value within the taxing entity}} = \dfrac{\$31,085,000}{\$3,578,215,000} \approx .0086873 \approx$ **.008688**

456   Chapter 21   Taxes: Income, Sales, and Property

Chapter in a Nutshell (concluded)

Objectives	Examples
C Calculating property tax	Assessed value = $54,000. Find property tax based on five different tax rates.

Tax rate	Property tax
a. .026633	$54,000 × .026633 = **$1,438.18**
b. 1.9542%	$54,000 × 1.9542% = **$1,055.27**
c. $3.1455 per $100	$\frac{\$54,000}{\$100}$ × $3.1455 = **$1,698.57**
d. $25.328 per $1,000	$\frac{\$54,000}{\$1,000}$ × $25.328 = **$1,367.71**
e. 30.655 mills	$\frac{\$54,000}{1,000}$ × 30.655 = **$1,655.37**

Think

1. Some people propose that we have a "flat tax" for federal income tax. What do you think? What problems do you see? Would a flat tax be fair or unfair?
2. In Illustration 21-1, tax for taxable income of $42,000 is greater for a single taxpayer than for a married couple filing jointly. Is this fair?
3. Some states have no sales tax. Some have sales tax but exempt things like food. Rates vary from state to state. Should all states have the same sales tax? Explain.
4. Many sales on the Internet are not currently subject to sales tax. Do you favor or oppose having sales over the Internet being subject to sales tax? Explain why or why not.
5. Some states set a maximum for property tax, such as 1% of the value of the property. Do you favor or oppose a limit? Explain.
6. If there were only one tax each person had to pay to fund the federal, state, and local governments, which tax do you think is the most fair (income tax, sales tax, property tax, or some other type of tax)?

Explore

1. Go to **www.irs.gov**. Search for the most recent Tax Rate Schedules. Compare the Tax Rate Schedules with the ones in Illustration 21-2 by figuring the tax on taxable income of $105,000 for (a) a single taxpayer and (b) a married couple filing jointly. Write a report on your findings; show your calculations.
2. Use the Internet to learn about *Tax Freedom Day*. Write a report explaining what Tax Freedom Day represents and the trend over the last 20 years.

Apply

1. **Where Does It All Go?** Submit a copy of a property tax notice for real estate. Submit another property tax notice for personal property. For each, identify the fair market value, assessed (or taxable) value, and tax rates. Find out what each taxing entity uses the money for. Determine the procedure the taxing authority uses to establish fair market value and assessed (or taxable) value. Find out whether certain types of real property and certain types of personal property are assessed differently from others. Submit the names of all people you talk to, along with your findings.

2. **Price, PLUS.** Write a report on sales tax in your area. Determine the percent charged by the state and the percent charged by local governments. Find out what the sales tax is applied to and what is excluded. Get copies of three different types of invoices (or register tapes) showing the dollar amount of sales tax. For each, calculate the sales tax rate; submit your calculations. Submit all of your findings, including the name and position of each person you talk to.

3. **April 15!** Go to www.irs.gov. Once on the site, search for the most recent Form 1040 (2 page form); print the two pages. Print a copy of Schedule A (Itemized Deductions). Complete a federal income tax return based on the following instructions:
    A. Do not do the return for real people. Use any fictitious name(s), address, and social security number(s) you would like. Use any filing status and number of exemptions you would like.
    B. Assume that the taxpayer (and spouse) had wages. You determine the amount(s). Assume that the taxpayer(s) had interest income of $355 and dividends of $250.
    C. Assume that the taxpayer(s) made maximum IRA contributions; research the rules, if necessary, to determine the amount(s). Enter the amount on the appropriate line near the bottom of page 1, Form 1040.
    D. Assume that the taxpayer is not sure whether to itemize deductions or take a standard deduction. Using Schedule A, you determine the amounts for each itemized deduction; if the total itemized deductions does not exceed the standard deduction, take the standard deduction.

Chapter Review Problems

Unit 21.1 Federal income tax

1. Taxpayers are not responsible for errors on a federal income tax return if the error is based on faulty advice given by the IRS. (T or F)

2. If taxable income is less than $100,000, which do we use to calculate federal income tax: **(a)** tax tables or **(b)** tax rate schedules?

For Problems 3 and 4, figure 2015 federal income tax, based on the given taxable income and filing status.

3. Taxable income = $16,458; single.

4. Taxable income = $133,400; married filing jointly.

For Problems 5–8, consider the tax situation of Tom and Shauna Pfaff, a married couple.

5. Tom and Shauna have 2015 taxable income of $162,400. Assuming they file jointly, what is their federal income tax?

6. Assume, instead, Tom and Shauna's marriage is on the rocks and they file separately. Tom's taxable income is $42,000 and Shauna's is $120,400. Calculate the amount of tax for each.

7. Assume, instead, Tom and Shauna got divorced and file with a single status. Calculate the amount of tax for each.

8. Refer to Problems 5 through 7. For each problem, their combined taxable income is $162,400. Which filing status results in the least amount of tax, and which results in the greatest amount of tax?

9. Landmark, Inc., has 2014 taxable income of $12,525,000. Calculate federal income tax.

Unit 21.2 Sales tax

10. When retailers buy goods for resale, they must pay sales tax on the net price of goods, after discounts. (T or F)

11. Sidney Marshall bought some golf balls for $20.49. Using the 6% sales tax table of Illustration 21-4, calculate the total amount Sidney must pay.

12. Refer to Problem 11. Calculate the total amount due without a sales tax table.

13. You are thinking about buying a car for $22,400. If you trade in your old vehicle for $6,500, calculate the 6.5% sales tax assuming that sales tax is figured on the net price.

14. You are shopping for a car. You can buy the car from a dealer in your city for $18,700, with sales tax of 6.5%. You can buy the car for $18,300 from a dealer in a different part of the state, with sales tax of 7.25%. Figure the total amount due from each dealer.

Unit 21.3 Property tax

15. In the U.S., property tax is charged by (a) the federal government, (b) state and local governments, or (c) federal, state, and local governments.

For Problems 16–19, we will help Rex and Barbara Frazier figure their property tax.

16. Rex and Barbara own a home. The county assessor estimated the fair market value to be $350,000. If this type of property is assessed at 50% of fair market value, what is the assessed value of their home?

17. The home is within the boundaries of Granite School District. The school district has an annual budget of $25,194,500 and total assessed values within its jurisdiction of $3,825,876,200. Determine the tax rate for the school district. Express the rate as a decimal number with 6 decimal places; round the last digit up.

18. Refer to Problem 17. Why, if the tax rate is expressed with 6 decimal places, isn't the rate rounded to .006585 rather than .006586?

19. Rex and Barbara's tax notice shows a total tax rate of .024593. What is their property tax?

For Problems 20–22, determine property tax based on the given assessed value and tax rate.

20. Assessed value = $175,000; tax rate = $2.452 per $100

21. Assessed value = $248,000; tax rate = 1.8565%

22. Assessed value = $720,000; tax rate = 21.344 mills

Challenge problems

For Problems 23–29, we will help Cary and Judy Self with their income tax.

23. Cary and Judy have 2014 taxable income of $70,824. If they file as married filing jointly, what is their federal income tax?

24. The tax rate schedules of Illustration 21-2 are not used for taxable incomes under $100,000. Just for the heck of it, figure Cary and Judy's tax using the tax rate schedules.

25. Compare the result of Problem 23 with that of Problem 24.

26. If the tax rate schedules result in the same tax as tax tables, why doesn't the IRS use only tax rate schedules?

27. What tax bracket are Cary and Judy in?

28. What does the tax bracket from Problem 27 mean?

29. Find the rate of tax for Cary and Judy's average dollar of taxable income. Express the rate with 2 decimal places.

30. Suppose your home has a fair market value of $200,000 and homes are assessed at 25% of value. Based on a tax rate of 51.044 mills, what is your property tax?

Practice Test

1. Jose Montero has 2014 taxable income of $43,824. Jose is single. What is his federal income tax?

2. Dan and Margaret Engler have 2014 taxable income of $182,488. What is their federal income tax, assuming their status is married filing jointly?

3. Pacific Health Care, Inc., has 2014 taxable income of $35,911,080. What is their federal income tax?

4. You buy a big-screen TV for $6,800. Based on sales tax of 6.75%, what is the total amount due?

5. You buy a new 4-wheel drive vehicle for $47,500. The dealer gives you $8,000 credit for your old vehicle. You must pay sales tax of 7% based on the net price. Calculate the sales tax.

6. Your home is within the boundaries of a certain school district. The school district has an annual budget of $8,255,500 and total assessed property value within its jurisdiction of $952,844,200. Determine the tax rate as a decimal number with 6 decimal places; round the last digit up.

7. Find property tax for a property with an assessed value of $450,000 and a tax rate of $2.628 per $100.

Classroom Notes

FUN CORNER

U.S. Life Expectancy

At age	Men	Women
0	75.5	80.5
10	66.2	71.1
20	56.5	61.5
30	47.2	51.5
40	37.9	41.9
50	29.0	32.7
60	20.9	24.0
70	13.7	16.0
80	7.9	9.4
90	4.1	4.8

Source: U.S. Census Bureau, 2012

Quotable Quip

Insurance companies stay in business because deductibles are usually greater than the claim.
– Author unknown

Close But No Cigar
(True Story, We Think)

CHARLOTTE, NC—A Charlotte, NC lawyer purchased a box of very expensive cigars, then insured them against fire. During the next month he smoked them, then filed an insurance claim stating the cigars were lost "in a series of small fires." When the insurance company said they would not pay, the lawyer sued and won, collecting $15,000.

After the lawyer cashed the check, the insurance company had him arrested for 24 counts of arson, claiming the lawyer had intentionally burned the insured property. The lawyer was sentenced to 24 months in jail and fined $24,000.

Source: Criminal Lawyers Award Contest

How to Lower Your Auto Insurance Premium

The average auto insurance premium in the United States is about $650 per year. Premiums are higher in some states than others. The states with the highest average (over $800) are California, Connecticut, Hawaii, and Rhode Island. The lowest (about $400) are Idaho, Iowa, North Dakota, South Dakota, and Wyoming. Other than moving to a cheaper state, here are a few ideas to reduce your auto insurance premiums.

- Compare premiums of different insurance companies. Make sure coverage is the same for each quote (so that you are comparing apples with apples).
- When shopping for a car, consider the insurance premium. Rates vary a lot from car to car, depending on things like repair rates and the probability of that model being stolen.
- Increase your deductibles. A higher deductible results in a lower premium. The insurance company saves money by not having so many claims and you save on the premium.
- Consider dropping collision coverage on older cars, because the insurance company won't pay much to repair an old car.
- Inquire about special discounts, such as a good student discount (there really is one), low mileage discount, multiple car discount, accident-free discount, anti-theft device discount, and anti-lock brake discount.

22

Insurance

Insurance is based on "shared risk." An insurance company (called the **insurer**) collects fees (**premiums**) from people (the **insured**) who want to be reimbursed if certain events take place. The premiums are then used to reimburse the unlucky people who have losses. The insurance company determines the mathematical probability that the events insured against will take place and sets premiums accordingly; the premiums must be large enough to cover the actual losses, overhead, and profit for the insurance company.

Most adults have insurance, such as car insurance or life insurance. But many don't understand the options that are available and what is insured against. For example, do you understand what *comprehensive coverage* on an auto policy covers? Do you understand the difference between *whole-life insurance* and *term insurance*? As a result of studying this chapter, we should end up with a good basic understanding of different insurance choices.

Unit Objectives

Unit 22.1 Property insurance

- **a** Understanding how property insurance works
- **b** Determining a premium for homeowner's insurance
- **c** Determining a premium for a business building
- **d** Understanding auto coverage

Unit 22.2 Life insurance

- **a** Calculating premiums on various types of life insurance
- **b** Understanding nonforfeiture options and death benefit options

Unit 22.1 Property insurance

In this unit, we will examine insurance on homes, business buildings, and autos. First though, let's review how property insurance works.

a Understanding how property insurance works

Most businesses and individuals have insurance to protect against losses to their property, such as from fire.

Most people purchase insurance *only for those events that would cause a financial hardship;* buying more insurance than a person needs is called "overinsuring." To illustrate, Jack may need glass coverage for his business because he cannot afford to replace the front window if broken. Sally, who can afford to replace her front window, could exclude glass coverage, pay a lower premium, and take her chances.

An insurance policy is for a stated period of time. Many policies are for a 1-year period. Auto insurance is often for a 6-month period. Premiums are generally due at the start of the policy, although some companies give the insured a choice of paying the premium in installments (in which case a service charge may be added).

Some people have the false impression that insurance provides reimbursement for losses, no matter what caused the loss. For example, suppose you have an insurance policy on your home and suffer a $30,000 loss as a result of a large tree falling on your home. You may or may not be reimbursed for this loss, depending on your specific coverage. Each insurance policy explains for what **hazards** you will be reimbursed. When purchasing insurance, find out which hazards are covered and which are not.

Many policies provide reimbursement based on **replacement cost** (the cost to replace the damaged or lost property). Some provide reimbursement based on **value** (the loss in value).

Example 1 Your carport collapses from too much snow. You built the carport 10 years ago at a cost of $2,500. The carport, because of its age, is worth only $2,000. To build an identical carport today would cost $3,500. Assuming you have adequate insurance, determine the amount you will receive from the insurance company if reimbursement is based on **(a)** replacement cost or **(b)** value.

If reimbursement is based on replacement cost, you will receive $3,500. If reimbursement is based on value, you will receive $2,000; you must come up with the additional $1,500 to rebuild the carport.

Many insurance policies require that the insured pay a certain dollar amount of each loss. This amount is called the **deductible.** For example, a policy may require the insured to pay the first $500 of a loss; the insurance company will pay the remainder. Often, insurance companies offer several deductible choices; the higher the deductible, the lower the cost of insurance. The deductible applies to each occurrence.

Example 2 On Tuesday, your TV is stolen. That same day, your carport collapses. Assuming your policy insures those events for $550 and $3,500, respectively, what amount will you be reimbursed if you have a $500 deductible policy?

Because these losses occurred as a result of two separate events, the deductible will be applied to each loss. You will receive $50 for the TV ($550 - $500 deductible) and $3,000 for the carport ($3,500 - $500 deductible).

Some policies require that the property be insured for a certain percent of value (or replacement cost). For example, a policy may require that a home be insured for at least 80% of its replacement cost. If a loss is sustained and it is discovered that the property was *underinsured,* the insured may receive payment for only part of the loss. If you have too much coverage (*overinsured*), the insurance company will pay based on the amount of the loss, rather than the amount of coverage.

An insurance policy may be canceled by the insurance company or by the insured. When this happens, the insured is entitled to a refund. In most cases, companies prorate based on a 365-day year.

Example 3   XYZ Insurance Company does a property inspection of Gail Eggman's home. They notify Gail that she must install railing on her patio to reduce the chance that someone will fall off the patio. Gail does not comply with the request, so the insurance company cancels the policy. Based on an annual premium of $414, and assuming that Gail's policy provided protection for 108 days before cancellation, calculate the amount of Gail's refund (assume the company uses a 365-day year to prorate).

Total annual premium	$414.00
Earned portion: $414 × $\frac{108}{365}$	- 122.50
Refund	$291.50

Gail will get a refund of $291.50. The company will keep $122.50 of the original $414 premium.

We can find the earned portion from Example 3 with calculators:

Keystrokes (for most calculators)

414 × 108 ÷ 365 =   **122.50**

b Determining a premium for homeowner's insurance

For single-family homes occupied by the owner, most people purchase **homeowner's insurance.** There are several basic "packages" available, identified as HO-1, HO-2, HO-3, and so on. The majority of homeowners get either an HO-3 or HO-5 policy. Many homeowner's packages insure the homeowner against losses from fire, lightning, windstorm, hail, riot, civil commotion, and aircraft crashing into the property. In addition, most provide liability coverage in case a visitor is injured or a visitor's property is damaged while on the property. Most do not insure against losses from floods, landslides, and earthquakes. Before buying a homeowner's policy, make sure you understand what hazards you are protected against; here are some specific hazards you might ask about: (a) explosions, including bursting hot water appliances and heating systems; (b) damage by vehicles to buildings, fences, driveways, walks, trees, shrubs, and lawn; (c) smoke damage from a fireplace, heating unit, or cooking unit; (d) vandalism or malicious mischief; (e) water damage from backed up sewers and drains; (f) leaks from plumbing, heating, or air-conditioning systems; (g) rain through bad roof, windows, or doors; (h) freezing of plumbing and heating systems; (i) sonic boom; (j) falling objects, including trees; (k) weight of ice, snow, and sleet; (l) collapse of building; (m) glass breakage; and (n) theft.

> **TIP**   dirt doesn't burn
>
> Suppose you buy a home for $200,000. You may be under the false impression that your homeowner's policy should be for $200,000 of coverage. But part of the purchase price is for land, and land doesn't need to be insured. So, depending on whether you get coverage for *value* of improvements or *replacement cost* of improvements, your coverage may be able to be less than the $200,000 purchase price. And less coverage means a lower premium.

Illustration 22-1 shows typical rates for an HO-3 policy. Premiums are based on the dollar amount of coverage and the "premium group." The premium group reflects the likelihood of a loss. For instance, a home located near a fire hydrant, not far from a fire station, and built with fire-resistant materials will have a lower premium than a frame home next to a paint store, located miles from a fire station. The rates are *basic* rates, from which discounts may be given. For example, a company may offer a 12% discount for homes less than 10 years old, a 5% discount if the home has a burglar alarm, and a 2% discount if the home has deadbolts and smoke alarms. When discounts are given, they are figured *one after the other* and rounded to the nearest dollar at the end of the calculation.

Illustration 22-1 Typical Basic Rates for an HO-3 Policy

Coverage for dwelling	Premium groups							
	1	2	3	4	5	6	7	8
$95,000	$230	$271	$317	$396	$419	$524	$237	$278
100,000	244	286	336	419	444	554	251	294
110,000	271	319	374	467	494	618	279	328
120,000	299	351	412	514	545	681	307	361
130,000	327	384	450	562	595	744	336	395
140,000	354	416	488	610	646	807	364	428
150,000	382	449	526	657	696	870	393	462
160,000	409	481	564	705	747	933	421	495
170,000	437	514	603	753	797	996	449	528
180,000	465	546	641	800	848	1060	478	562

Example 4 You buy an HO-3 basic policy in the amount of $120,000. Calculate your annual premium using the basic rates of Illustration 22-1. Assume that (a) your home is classified in premium group 2, (b) you get a 5% discount for having a burglar alarm, (c) you get a "new home discount" of 12%, (d) you get a 2% discount for having a smoke alarm, and (e) you pay an extra $45 for additional liability coverage.

Basic premium (look across $120,000 row to column 2)	$351.00
Burglar alarm discount: $351.00 × 5%	- 17.55
Subtotal	$333.45
New home discount: $333.45 × 12%	- 40.01
Subtotal	$293.44
Smoke alarm discount: $293.44 × 2%	- 5.87
Subtotal	$287.57
Premium for additional liability coverage	+ 45.00
Total annual premium	$332.57 ($333 rounded)

Your total annual premium is $333. Remember, the answer is the same if you apply the discounts in a different order; you may want to check this yourself.

Homeowner's policies insure the home for a stated amount, called the **face value** of the policy, and generally extend coverage for other things as a percent of face value. For example, suppose you get a homeowner's policy with a face value of $120,000 and the policy insures your personal property up to 70% of face value, other structures up to 10% of face value, and loss of use up to 20% of face value. Your home is insured for $120,000; your furniture, appliances, and other personal belongings are insured up to $84,000 ($120,000 × 70%); other buildings (such as a detached garage, carport, shed) are insured for a total of $12,000 ($120,000 × 10%); if you are forced to live elsewhere while your home is being repaired, you will be reimbursed for up to $24,000 ($120,000 × 20%) of living expenses.

Many people do not own their own home but instead rent from someone else. Tenants can obtain **renter's insurance** to protect their belongings and to provide liability protection (in the event a visitor is injured as a result of something that is the tenant's fault). Insurance rates are much less than homeowner's insurance because there is no building to insure; the annual premiums are often about $100 to $200 depending on the type and amount of coverage. Just as with homeowner's insurance, find out what hazards are covered in the policy. Ask if your belongings are covered from losses due to fire, water damage, theft, and other occurrences. And ask about the amount and type of liability coverage.

Condominium associations typically purchase insurance for buildings and common areas. Each owner pays his or her fair share through condo fees. The insurance purchased through the condo association does not cover any personal belongings of the individual owners and may not insure some of the interior features, such as wall coverings, baseboard, and cabinets. Individual owners can purchase **condominium unit owner's insurance** to protect their personal belongings and interior features and to provide liability protection. Protection and rates are similar to those for renter's insurance.

Illustration 22-2 Typical Rate Table for Apartment Buildings (per $1,000 of replacement cost)

# units	Premium groups 1–4			Premium groups 5–6			Premium groups 7–8		
	Frame	Masonry	FireResist	Frame	Masonry	FireResist	Frame	Masonry	FireResist
5–10	$3.30	$1.80	$1.80	$4.20	$2.20	$2.10	$5.50	$2.90	$2.60
11–30	3.90	2.20	1.80	5.00	2.80	2.10	6.80	3.70	2.60
>30	4.30	2.70	1.80	5.60	3.60	2.10	7.50	4.90	2.60

Rates are for $500 deductible:
- For $1,000 deductible, subtract 4%   • For $2,500 deductible, subtract 6%.

To increase liability coverage to $1,000,000 pay an extra $0.20 per $1,000 of replacement cost.

c Determining a premium for a business building

Business buildings (such as offices, warehouses, stores, and apartment buildings) should be insured. Rates vary greatly depending on the use. For example, a paint store, which stores highly flammable materials, will have a very high premium. The standard insurance policy protects against losses arising from fire and lightning. An additional package, known as **extended coverage,** can be purchased to protect against additional losses. When purchasing a policy, find out what types of losses are covered. Get an extended coverage package that matches your needs. And make sure there is ample liability coverage. Businesses should also insure their inventory, fixtures, equipment, and other business property.

Illustration 22-2 is a typical rate table for an apartment building. Rates are per $1,000 of replacement cost and include an extended coverage package for losses due to hail, riot, explosion, smoke, sonic boom, falling objects, weight of ice and snow; $500,000 of liability coverage; and reimbursement for lost rents (up to 12 months) as a result of any of the covered hazards. Properties are classified in a premium group according to risk. The "Frame" column is used for frame construction (wood and stucco); the "Masonry" column is used if at least 60% of the exterior is masonry (brick, for example); and the "FireResist" column is used if the walls and roof are made of precast fire-resistant materials (like concrete).

To find the basic premium, we divide the replacement cost by $1,000 and multiply the result by the rate.

= finding premium for business buildings using rate table per $1,000

$$\text{Basic premium} = \frac{\text{Replacement cost}}{\$1{,}000} \times \text{Rate}$$

Example 5 Jeremy and Simone Silverman own a 24-unit apartment complex. Using the rates of Illustration 22-2, calculate their annual premium based on (a) premium group 4; (b) masonry construction; (c) replacement cost of $820,000; (d) a $1,000 deductible; and (e) $1,000,000 liability coverage.

Basic premium: $\frac{\$820{,}000}{\$1{,}000} \times \$2.20$	$1,804.00
Discount for having $1,000 deductible: $1,804 × 4%	− 72.16
Subtotal	$1,731.84
Additional liability coverage: $\frac{\$820{,}000}{\$1{,}000} \times \$0.20$	+ 164.00
Total annual premium	$1,895.84 ($1,896 rounded)

The annual premium is $1,896. Notice, the 4% discount was not applied to the additional liability coverage.

d Understanding auto coverage

Just as with other types of insurance, the amount and type of automobile coverage varies from policy to policy. A few typical types of coverage for auto insurance include:

- **Liability.** For damage to others, including bodily injury, and damage to their property.
- **Medical.** When you, family members, and your passengers are injured in an auto accident.

- **Collision.** When the insured's car is damaged by collision.
- **Comprehensive.** When the insured's car is damaged except by collision.
- **Uninsured motor vehicle.** When the other car or driver is uninsured.
- **Underinsured motor vehicle.** When the other car or driver is underinsured.
- **Emergency road service.** When the insured's car breaks down and needs to be towed.
- **Car rental.** When the insured needs to rent a car because of damage to the insured's car.

Auto insurance policies often state the amount of coverage as a sort of code. For example, liability coverage of "25/50/20" may mean the policy will pay up to $25,000 for bodily injury per person, up to a total of $50,000 for bodily injury to all people, and $20,000 for property damage.

Many states require owners of vehicles to carry minimum amounts of liability insurance. In most states, the person at fault must pay for any damage caused by an automobile accident. In some states, the person at fault is the *owner* of the vehicle at fault; in other states, the person at fault is the *driver* of the vehicle at fault (a car could be driven by someone other than the owner). Typically, the insurance company of the person at fault pays for damage to other people or other people's property. For example, if Ted is at fault in an accident and Becky's car is damaged, Ted's insurance company pays to repair Becky's car, provides Becky with a rental car, and pays other expenses incurred by Becky. Some states require **no-fault insurance.** With no-fault insurance, reimbursement for bodily injury (up to a certain dollar limit) is made *without regard* to who was at fault. A person sustaining injuries exceeding the dollar limit who is not at fault can collect the excess from the insurance company of the person at fault; if the insurance policy does not provide adequate coverage, the injured person must collect the remainder directly from the party at fault.

Example 6 While driving, Emerson ran a red light and hit Whitney's car. Whitney sustained injuries of $38,000 and her new $42,000 car was totaled. Their state requires no-fault insurance of $3,000. Emerson carried liability coverage of "25/50/20" but had no medical or collision coverage. His medical expenses came to $7,000 and his $15,000 car was totaled. How will the expenses be covered?

Because of the no-fault law, Emerson's company will pay the first $3,000 of Emerson's medical expenses, even though he was at fault. Because Emerson has no medical coverage, he must pay the remaining $4,000 out of his own pocket. Because he had no collision coverage, he is out of luck for the damage to his car. Whitney's company will pay the first $3,000 of her medical expenses through her no-fault coverage; Emerson's company will pay the next $25,000 through Emerson's 25/50/20 liability coverage. Emerson's company will also pay the first $20,000 of damage to Whitney's car through Emerson's 25/50/20 liability coverage. Whitney must collect the remaining $10,000 ($38,000 - $3,000 - $25,000) of medical expenses and the remaining $22,000 ($42,000 - $20,000) damage to her car directly from Emerson (through the courts, if Emerson refuses to pay).

Here is a summary of Example 6:

	Total	Whitney's Ins. Co.	Emerson's Ins. Co.	Emerson
Whitney's injuries	38,000	3,000	25,000	10,000
Whitney's car	42,000		20,000	22,000
Emerson's injuries	7,000		3,000	4,000
Emerson's car	15,000			15,000
Totals	102,000	3,000	48,000	51,000

Auto insurance rates are figured as a bunch of individual amounts. For example, the amount for collision coverage is figured separately, depending on several factors including the age and make of the car, driver's age and driving record, how many miles the car is driven per week, and the area. Discounts may be offered for some of the components. For example, a 10% "accident-free discount" may apply to the collision and liability portions of the premium. Discounts on medical coverage or no-fault coverage are often given for having air bags. Once each component rate is determined, the amounts are totaled to find the total premium. Companies often give "multiple car" discounts for insuring more than one vehicle. Because there are so many rate tables involved, and because the rate tables vary from company to company, we will not attempt to calculate an auto insurance premium. When buying auto insurance, ask for a breakdown of the premium by components. Make sure you have adequate coverage.

Most car owners have a loan on their vehicle. If the borrower defaults on the loan, the lender gets the vehicle. To protect the lender, borrowers are generally required to carry certain types of coverage (such as collision insurance).

Let's try some U-Try-It questions to see what we remember.

U-Try-It
(Unit 22.1)

1. Your fence is damaged due to high winds. You installed the fence 6 years ago at a cost of $4,000. Because of its age, it is worth only $3,300. To install an identical fence today would cost $6,000. Assuming that you have a $500 deductible insurance policy that covers the loss, based on value, how much will you receive from the insurance company?
2. You buy a $150,000 HO-3 homeowner's policy. Calculate your annual premium using the basic rates of Illustration 22-1. Assume (a) your home is classified in premium group 4, (b) you get a new home discount of 12%, (c) you get a 2% discount for having a smoke alarm, and (d) you pay an extra $85 for additional liability coverage.
3. The MacArthurs own a 24-unit apartment building. Using the rates of Illustration 22-2, calculate their annual premium, based on (a) being in premium group 3, (b) masonry construction, (c) replacement cost of $975,000, (d) $1,000 deductible, and (e) $1,000,000 of liability coverage.
4. While driving, Brandi rear-ended Bronson's car. Brandi was determined responsible for the accident. Bronson sustained medical expenses of $46,000, and his $16,000 car was totaled. Their state requires no-fault insurance of $10,000. Brandi carried liability coverage of "25/50/25." How will Bronson's expenses be covered?

Answers: (If you have a different answer, check the solution in Appendix A.)
1. $2,800 **2.** $652 **3.** $2,254 **4.** The first $10,000 of Bronson's medical expenses are paid by Bronson's insurance company. Brandi's company will pay the next $25,000. Brandi must pay the remaining $11,000. Brandi's company will pay $16,000 for damage to Bronson's car.

Unit 22.2 Life insurance

In most cases, **life insurance** is used to provide compensation to families following the death of someone they depend on for income. To become insured, a person's health must be good enough to meet the insurance company's guidelines. If the insured person dies while insured, the life insurance company pays an agreed-upon sum (most policies, however, do not pay for suicide during the first part of the policy, such as the first 2 years). Obviously the money cannot be paid to the insured, so it is paid to a designated person known as the **beneficiary.** In this unit, we will examine different types of life insurance. We will do so through the eyes of Jed Watkins. Jed is 35 years old and wants to get some life insurance that will pay his wife $150,000 in the event he dies. To start off, Jed wants to know what types of life insurance are available and what the cost is.

This is a grave marker in historic Boot Hill, Kansas. For most people, life insurance is not a pleasant thing to buy because we don't like to think about dying. But, dying without insurance can be financially devastating to those we leave behind.

a Calculating premiums on various types of life insurance

One of the most difficult tasks associated with buying life insurance is deciding what type of policy to get. Jed has lots of choices. Here are a few.

- **Term insurance** provides protection for a given period of time (or term), such as 1, 5, 10, 15, 20, or 30 years. The face value is paid if the insured dies within the given term. Some policies can be renewed without showing evidence of good health.
- **Decreasing term** is a form of term insurance, in which coverage decreases over the life of the policy, until at the end of the term, the coverage is zero. The premium is level for the life of the policy. This is used where more insurance is needed now than in the future. It is often used in

conjunction with a loan (in which case it is referred to as *credit life insurance*). The death benefit is used to pay off the loan; the amount of coverage decreases as the loan balance decreases.

- **Whole-life insurance** (also referred to as **straight life** or **ordinary life insurance**) has a level premium for life. During the early years of the policy, the premiums are higher than those of term insurance; the excess goes to a cash reserve (referred to as the **cash value** of the policy). This cash reserve is necessary to keep the premiums level in later years when the cost of insurance is higher. Whole-life insurance is often thought of as insurance plus savings; the cash reserve, or savings portion, earns interest. The premium is determined by the insured's age when the policy begins. The beneficiary is paid the face value of the policy upon the death of the insured.
- **Universal life.** Unlike most whole-life insurance, the policyholder can increase, decrease, or suspend premiums, provided some cash reserve is maintained. Any extra money paid by the policyholder increases the cash reserve. If the policyholder does not make a full payment, the cash reserve is used to pay the balance of the premium. The company invests the cash reserves at whatever rates can be earned. The company guarantees a certain rate, but that minimum rate is generally lower than the guaranteed rate of ordinary whole-life policies.
- **Variable life** is similar to universal life except that the policyholder can instruct the insurance company how to invest the cash reserves (with limitations). For example, a policyholder may be able to choose from a mortgage loan fund, a stock fund, a bond fund, and mixed funds. The policyholder is allowed to switch from one fund to another a certain number of times each year.
- **First-to-die insurance** insures more than one person, and the death benefit is paid when the first dies. This type of insurance is commonly used for partnerships. The partnership pays the premiums and the death benefit is used to buy the deceased partner's interest in the business from the estate of the deceased.
- **Second-to-die insurance** insures two people, but the death benefit is paid only after both have died. This policy is often used in connection with estate planning in which there are no federal and state estate taxes until the second of a married couple dies.

To have life insurance, Jed (or his wife) must pay a fee (premium) to the insurance company. The premium is based on several factors, including the insured's age and health. Smokers often pay higher rates than nonsmokers (because smokers do not live as long). Rates for women are slightly less than for men (because women live longer). Insurance companies have tables showing premiums for various types of insurance. Because providing a premium table for each type of insurance would be cumbersome, premium tables will be shown for only two types: 15-year term and whole-life. Illustration 22-3 shows typical premiums (per $1,000 of insurance). Rates, of course, vary from company to company. The older a person is, the sooner the person will likely die, so premiums increase with age.

Illustration 22-3 Typical Annual Premium per $1,000 of Life Insurance

Age	15-year term	Whole-life	Age	15-year term	Whole-life
20	2.54	6.24	31	2.74	10.10
21	2.54	6.49	32	2.82	10.58
22	2.54	6.76	33	2.92	11.11
23	2.54	7.06	34	3.06	11.68
24	2.54	7.39	35	3.22	12.29
25	2.54	7.75	40	4.48	15.73
26	2.54	8.07	45	6.58	20.25
27	2.54	8.42	50	10.36	26.97
28	2.54	8.79	55	16.52	32.97
29	2.60	9.20	60	26.32	41.81
30	2.66	9.63			

Rates shown are typical rates for a male in good health. Rates may be higher for smokers. Rates for females are approximately those of a male 4 years younger.

To find the annual premium using the rates of Illustration 22-3, we divide the amount of coverage by $1,000 and multiply by the appropriate rate (based on age and type of insurance):

> **= finding annual insurance premium using rates of Illustration 22-3**
>
> $$\text{Annual Premium} = \frac{\text{Amount of coverage}}{\$1,000} \times \text{Rate}$$

Example 1 Jed Watkins, age 35, is thinking about purchasing $150,000 of 15-year term insurance. Calculate his annual premium for each of the first 30 years.

Jed's premium for the first 15 years is based on age 35:

$$\text{Annual Premium} = \frac{\$150,000}{\$1,000} \times \$3.22 = \$483$$

Jed's premium for the second 15 years is based on age 50:

$$\text{Annual Premium} = \frac{\$150,000}{\$1,000} \times \$10.36 = \$1,554$$

Jed must pay $483 per year for the first 15 years and $1,554 per year for the second 15 years.

For most term insurance policies, if the insured does not show evidence of good health at the beginning of each renewal period, the premiums are higher. For example, if Jed is in poor health at the start of the second 15-year period, Jed's premiums will be greater than the $1,554 of Example 1.

Example 2 Using the rates of Illustration 22-3, calculate Jed's annual premium with whole-life insurance.

$$\text{Annual Premium} = \frac{\$150,000}{\$1,000} \times \$12.29 = \$1,843.50$$

Jed must pay $1,843.50 each year for the rest of his life. When he dies, his beneficiary will receive $150,000.

Annual premiums are due at the beginning of each year. Policyholders are often given the option of paying premiums semiannually, quarterly, or monthly (in which case a service charge is added).

> **TIP — compare apples with apples**
>
> For many life insurance policies, the company pays policyholders part of the company profits; this is like a premium rebate and is called a dividend. A policy that pays policyholders part of the company profits is known as a **participating policy.** When comparing policies, estimate the "net premium." For example, suppose you have a choice of paying a $500 annual premium for a participating policy or $400 for a nonparticipating policy. And suppose dividends for the participating policy have historically been $150 per year. While future dividends are not guaranteed, if future dividends continue at $150 per year, your net annual premium will be only $350 ($500 - $150 dividend), which is less than the policy with the $400 premium.

An insurance policy can provide additional benefits by attaching a **rider** to the policy. A rider, of course, results in additional premium. Here are a few common riders:

- **Accidental death rider** (often called a *double indemnity rider*). The insurance company will pay extra (often double) if the insured dies from accidental causes rather than illness.
- **Premium waiver rider.** In the event the insured is disabled and unable to work, the premium for the policy will be waived so long as that condition continues.
- **Family insurance rider.** Provides insurance for present and future family members.
- **Guaranteed insurability rider.** Provides the option to purchase additional amounts of insurance in the future without having to provide evidence of good health.

Illustration 22-4 Cash Value for a Typical Whole-Life Policy ($150,000 of Coverage)

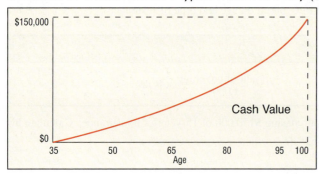

b Understanding nonforfeiture options and death benefit options

Term insurance has no cash reserve (cash value). Whole-life insurance has a cash value that increases over the life of the policy. Illustration 22-4 shows the approximate cash value of a $150,000 whole-life policy.

Policies with a cash value provide three options (called **nonforfeiture options**) if the insured wants to cancel the policy or stop paying premiums.

Option 1 (Cash value). Receive cash equal to the cash value of the policy. The policy is then terminated.

Option 2 (Reduced paid-up insurance). Reduce the amount of coverage. The cash value buys a certain amount of coverage without paying any more premiums. The policy continues for life (with reduced coverage). The greater the cash value, the greater the coverage.

Option 3 (Extended term). Keep the coverage the same, but for a limited amount of time. The length of time depends on the cash value and the insured's age. This option is used automatically if the policyholder fails to pay premiums and does not elect another option.

Typical nonforfeiture values for a whole-life policy issued at age 35 are shown in Illustration 22-5. Nonforfeiture values vary from policy to policy and from company to company.

Example 3 Assume Jed got the $150,000 whole-life policy of Example 2. Then assume he quits paying premiums after 15 years. Based on the nonforfeiture values of Illustration 22-5, determine Jed's options.

Option 1. Get cash value: $\frac{\$150,000}{\$1,000} \times \$147 = \$22,050$

Option 2. Reduce the coverage: $\frac{\$150,000}{\$1,000} \times \$370 = \$55,500$

Option 3. Keep $150,000 coverage, but for a shorter term: 20 years, 162 days

Jed could get $22,050 in cash, reduce the coverage for life to $55,500 (paying no more premiums), or keep $150,000 of coverage for 20 years and 162 days (paying no more premiums).

Illustration 22-5 Typical Nonforfeiture Options of Whole-Life Coverage (issued at age 35)

Years policy in force	Option 1 Cash value (per $1,000)	Option 2 Paid-up insurance (per $1,000)	Option 3 Extended term (face value)
5	$ 29	$ 86	9 years, 89 days
10	$ 96	$258	18 years, 74 days
15	$147	$370	20 years, 162 days
20	$264	$548	21 years, 296 days

In Example 3 Jed's cash value, after paying premiums for 15 years, would be $22,050. Jed would have paid a total of $27,652.50 (15 years × $1,843.50 from Example 2). Part of his premiums went to buy insurance. The remainder went to the the cash value portion; with interest, the amount has grown to $22,050.

As mentioned, the beneficiary (in Jed's case, his wife) is entitled to receive the face value of the policy upon the death of the insured (Jed). A lump-sum death benefit received by the beneficiary is, in most cases, not taxable for federal income tax purposes; this is an appealing feature of life insurance.

In many cases, the beneficiary would prefer to receive the money in installments rather than in one lump-sum. Several options, defined in each policy, are available. Here are a few:

- **Fixed Amount Annuity.** The beneficiary selects a fixed amount to receive each period (such as $1,500 per month). The beneficiary will receive this amount until the money from the death benefit, together with interest, is used up.
- **Fixed Period Annuity.** The beneficiary selects a period of time (such as 25 years). Based on the period of time, the insurance company determines what dollar amount can be paid each period. The payment continues for exactly that period of time. If the beneficiary dies before the period of time is up, the payments are made to other designated heirs.
- **Annuity for life.** The insurance company determines an amount to be paid each period for as long as the beneficiary lives, based on the age and sex of the beneficiary. When the beneficiary dies, payments stop.
- **Annuity for life, guaranteed.** With an annuity for life (the previous option), if the beneficiary dies shortly after payments start, not much is received and family members who depend on the income are out of luck. So many prefer an annuity for life, *guaranteed*. Here, if the beneficiary dies during a certain time period (like 15 years), the payments continue to designated heirs until the guaranteed time period is up. If the beneficiary lives past the guaranteed time period, payments continue until the death of the beneficiary. The dollar amount of the payment is less with this option than with an annuity for life because of the guaranteed time period.

Well, that does it for this unit. Are you ready to test your knowledge with some U-Try-It questions?

U-Try-It (Unit 22.2)

1. Chelsea Clark is 32 years old and has two children. She wants to get some life insurance that will pay her kids $200,000 if she dies. She likes the idea of a 15-year term policy. Using the rates of Illustration 22-3, help Chelsea determine her annual premium. (*Hint:* Pay special attention to the footnote of Illustration 22-3 regarding rates for females.)
2. Yi Chung purchased a $125,000 whole-life insurance policy when he was 35 years old. He quit paying his premiums 20 years later. Based on the values of Illustration 22-5, what are his three options?

Answers: (If you have a different answer, check the solution in Appendix A.)
1. $508 2. $33,000; $68,500; 21 years, 296 days

Chapter in a Nutshell

Objectives	Examples
	Unit 22.1 Property insurance
a Understanding how property insurance works	Your carport is damaged. You built the carport 15 years ago at a cost of $3,200. The carport, because of its age, is worth only $2,500. To build an identical carport today would cost $5,400. You have a $500 deductible policy. What will you receive if reimbursement is based on (a) replacement cost and (b) value? a. Replacement cost: $5,400 - $500 = $4,900 b. Value: $2,500 - $500 = $2,000

Chapter in a Nutshell (concluded)

Objectives	Examples
(b) Determining a premium for homeowner's insurance	You get a $180,000 HO-3 homeowner's policy. Use Illustration 22-1 to figure your annual premium. Assume (a) premium group 3, (b) 12% new home discount, and (c) $70 extra for additional liability coverage. Basic premium $641.00 New home discount: $641 × 12% − 76.92 Subtotal $564.08 Premium for additional liability coverage + 70.00 Total annual premium $634.08 (**$634** rounded)
(c) Determining a premium for a business building	$650,000 insurance on an 8-unit apartment building. Use Illustration 22-2 to figure annual premium. Assume (a) premium group 6, (b) frame construction, (c) $2,500 deductible, and (d) $1,000,000 liability coverage. Basic premium: $\frac{\$650,000}{\$1,000} \times \$4.20$ $2,730.00 Discount for $2,500 deductible: $2,730 × 6% − 163.80 Subtotal $2,566.20 Additional liability coverage: $\frac{\$650,000}{\$1,000} \times \$0.20$ + 130.00 Total annual premium $2,696.20 (**$2,696** rounded)
(d) Understanding auto coverage	**Liability:** For damage to others, including bodily injury, and damage to their property. **Medical:** When you, family members, and your passengers are injured in an auto accident. **Collision:** When the insured's car is damaged by collision. **Comprehensive:** When the insured's car is damaged except by collision. **Uninsured motor vehicle:** When the other car or driver is uninsured. **Underinsured motor vehicle:** When the other car or driver is underinsured. **Emergency road service:** When the insured's car breaks down and needs to be towed. **Car rental:** When the insured needs to rent a car because of damage to the insured's car. **No-fault coverage:** Reimbursement for bodily injury is made *without regard to who was at fault*.

Unit 22.2 Life insurance

(a) Calculating premiums on various types of life insurance	Ian McGregor is 25 years old. Use Illustration 22-3 to find annual premium for 15-year, $100,000 term insurance for each of the first 45 years. First 15 years (age 25): $\frac{\$100,000}{\$1,000} \times \$2.54 =$ **$254 per year** Second 15 years (age 40): $\frac{\$100,000}{\$1,000} \times \$4.48 =$ **$448 per year** Third 15 years (age 55): $\frac{\$100,000}{\$1,000} \times \$16.52 =$ **$1,652 per year**
(b) Understanding nonforfeiture options and death benefit options	Santiago Gomez got a $200,000 whole-life policy at age 35. If Santiago quits paying premiums after 20 years, what are his nonforfeiture options, based on the values of Illustration 22-5? **Option 1.** Get cash value: $\frac{\$200,000}{\$1,000} \times \$264 =$ **$52,800** **Option 2.** Reduce the coverage: $\frac{\$200,000}{\$1,000} \times \$548 =$ **$109,600** **Option 3.** Keep $200,000 coverage, but for a shorter term: **21 years, 296 days**

Enrichment Topics

The following Enrichment Topic, which goes a bit beyond what is in the text, is available for this chapter:

  Term or Whole Life Insurance?

If your instructor doesn't cover this topic in class and you would like to dig in deeper on your own, please send a request to *studentsupport@olympuspub.com*.

Think

1. What type of insurance do you currently have? What other insurance do you think you need? What is a good strategy for deciding what, and how much, insurance to have?
2. What types of coverage for an auto policy do you personally think you need, and why?
3. Why is the premium for whole-life insurance greater than the premium for a term policy?
4. When comparing life insurance premiums, why is it important to know if the policy is a participating policy?
5. Life insurance premiums are higher for males than for females. Is that fair, and why?

Explore

1. Search the Internet to determine what minimum auto insurance is required in your state. Write a report about your findings.

Apply

1. **Apartment and Car** Base your work for this project on the apartment or home you rent and the vehicle you currently own. If you are not a tenant or do not own a vehicle, use a place you would like to rent and/or a vehicle you would like to own. Meet with an insurance agent and ask for his or her help on this project. Determine the premium for a renter's policy that meets your personal needs. Write a report that describes what type of coverage the policy has as well as how the premium is determined. Then determine a premium for your vehicle based on coverage that matches your needs. Explain the specific coverage included and how the premium is figured. Include the name and phone number of the insurance agent.

Chapter Review Problems

Unit 22.1 Property insurance

1. If an insured property is damaged, the insured will be reimbursed for the loss, no matter what caused the loss. (T or F)

For Problems 2–4, evaluate insurance coverage on a video camera you bought 2 years ago for $800. Because of its age, the camera is now worth only $600. A similar video camera costs $750 new. Assume that your camera is stolen and you have insurance that covers theft.

2. What amount will you receive from the insurance company if the reimbursement is based on replacement cost?

3. What amount will you receive if reimbursement is based on value?

4. What amount will you receive if reimbursement is based on replacement cost and you have a $500 deductible policy?

5. ABC Insurance Company cancels Michelle Schreiber's policy. Based on an annual premium of $280, 218 days of protection before cancellation, and a 365-day year for prorating, what amount will be refunded?

6. All homeowner's policies cover the same hazards. (T or F)

7. You buy an HO-3 basic policy in the amount of $170,000. Calculate your annual premium (to the nearest dollar) using the basic rates of Illustration 22-1. Assume that (a) your home is classified in premium group 4, (b) you get a 5% discount for having a security system, and (c) you pay an extra $60 for additional liability coverage.

8. With most homeowner's policies, personal belongings are not insured. (T or F)

9. Use the rates of Illustration 22-2 to calculate the annual premium (to the nearest dollar) for a 36-unit apartment building with a replacement cost of $1,550,000. Assume (a) the building is masonry and is in premium group 3, (b) $1,000 deductible, and (c) $1,000,000 of liability coverage.

10. For auto insurance, collision coverage pays for damage to the other driver's car. (T or F)

11. No-fault insurance takes effect when the police cannot determine who is at fault. (T or F)

Unit 22.2 Life insurance

12. All people, regardless of age, sex, and medical condition, pay the same rates for life insurance. (T or F)

For Problems 13–16, name the type of insurance that matches the special features.

13. With this type of insurance, coverage decreases over the life of the policy.

14. Has a level premium for life.

15. The policyholder can increase, decrease, or suspend premiums, provided some cash reserve is maintained.

16. Provides a certain amount of protection for a given period of time.

For Problems 17–21, calculate annual premiums for Justin Lee using the rates of Illustration 22-3. Justin is 30 years old and wants $200,000 of insurance.

17. 15-year term insurance for Year 1.

18. 15-year term insurance for Year 2.

19. 15-year term insurance for Years 16–30.

20. Whole-life insurance for Year 1.

21. Whole-life insurance for Year 30.

22. Mandy Phillips just turned 27. Using the rates and footnotes of Illustration 22-3, calculate her annual premium for a $120,000 whole-life policy.

23. A guaranteed insurability rider provides the option to purchase additional coverage in the future without having to provide evidence of good health. (T or F)

For Problems 24–26, assume that Tim Morley, age 45, decides to quit paying premiums on a $100,000 whole-life policy that he got when he was 35.

24. If Tim elects to receive the cash value, what amount will he receive?

25. If Tim elects to have insurance for the remainder of his life without paying any more premiums, what amount of coverage will he have?

26. If Tim elects to maintain $100,000 of coverage, for what period of time will he be covered if he pays no more premiums?

27. When the insured dies, the beneficiary must receive the death benefit in one lump sum. (T or F)

Challenge problems

*Note: Problems 28–30 are time-value-of-money problems; refer to Chapter 17, if neccessary or to the online calculator on our website (**www.webbertext.com**).*

28. You get a bill for your auto insurance premium. You can pay the 6-month premium of $450 today, or you can pay with monthly installments (starting today). With monthly installments, a $10 carrying charge will be added to each payment. If you elect to pay on the installment method, what annual interest rate are you, in effect, paying?

29. Igor Tosic is trying to decide whether to get whole-life insurance (with an annual premium of $892) or 15-year term insurance (with an annual premium of $177). His insurance agent tells him that the cash value for the whole-life policy will be $17,870 in 15 years. Calculate the rate Igor earns on the savings plan portion of the whole-life policy.

30. Jay Sullivan dies. Cindy, his wife, is the beneficiary of his $150,000 life insurance policy. She is thinking about taking the money as a "fixed period annuity" instead of taking the $150,000 in one lump sum. With the fixed period annuity, she will receive $975 at the end of each month for 20 years. If Cindy elects to take the money monthly, what interest rate will she earn on the money?

Practice Test

1. Your TV is stolen. You bought the TV 3 years ago for $570 but because of its age, it is worth only $425. Similar new TVs are selling for $650. Assuming that you have coverage for theft, with a $500 deductible, what amount will you receive from the insurance company if reimbursement is based on replacement cost?

2. Security Insurance Company cancels Jay Paul's homeowner's policy. Based on an annual premium of $620, 145 days of protection before cancellation, and a 365-day year for prorating, what amount will be refunded?

3. Use Illustration 22-1 to figure the annual premium (to the nearest dollar) for a $180,000 homeowner's HO-3 policy. Assume your home is classified in premium group 3. You get these discounts: 5% for having a burglar alarm, 3% for having a smoke alarm, and 10% "new home discount."

4. Use Illustration 22-2 to figure the annual premium (to the nearest dollar) on a 12-unit apartment complex. Assume (a) the property is in premium group 4, frame construction, (b) $700,000 replacement cost, (c) $2,500 deductible, and (d) $1,000,000 of liability coverage.

5. Which, if any, is true about auto insurance?

   a. Collision coverage pays for damage to the other driver's car.
   b. No-fault insurance applies only if you are not responsible for the accident.
   c. If another driver damages your car and has no insurance, your insurance company automatically pays for your loss.

6. With a variable life policy, the policyholder can instruct the insurance company how to invest the cash reserves (with limitations). (T or F)

7. Why is a premium for term insurance less than a premium for whole-life coverage? (short answer)

8. Tammy Jorgensen, age 28, gets $70,000 of whole-life insurance. Using the rates and footnotes of Illustration 22-3, determine her premium for Year 7.

9. Chih Ho got a $200,000 whole-life insurance policy when he was 35 years old. He is now 55 years old and decides to quit paying premiums. How much insurance can Chih have for the rest of his life if he pays no more premiums?

FUN CORNER

Guinness World Records

Here are a few world records according to *Guinness World Records*.

- **Biggest pizza.** A pizza with a diameter of 122 ft 8 in. was baked at Norwood Hypermarket, Norwood, South Africa, on Dec. 8, 1990.
- **Longest paper-clip chain.** A paper clip chain 22.14 miles long was completed by 9th grade students from Eisenhower Junior High School, Taylorsville, Utah, on March 26-27, 2004.
- **Longest walk on hands.** Johann Hurlinger (Austria) walked 870 miles on his hands in 1900. He walked from Vienna, Austria, to Paris, France, in 55 daily 10-hour stints, averaging a speed of 1.58 m.p.h.

Have You Heard This One?

What do you get if you divide the circumference of an apple by its diameter?

Answer: Apple π.

Figure Your Gas Mileage

Have you figured the gas mileage for your vehicle? Many people haven't because they don't know how.

To figure out how many miles per gallon our vehicle gets, we must figure out how much gas is used and how many miles we travel (like on a trip, or for a week around town).

1. Gallons of gas

Fill your tank. The initial number of gallons is *not* used in calculations; you must begin with a full tank. Each time you add gas to your tank, record the number of gallons; it is not necessary to fill the tank each time. At the end, fill your gas tank; the number of gallons is used in calculations because you must end with a full tank.

2. Number of miles

Record your odometer reading at the start when you initially fill your gas tank. Subtract that amount from your odometer reading at the end. This is the number of miles traveled.

3. Time to divide

Miles *per* gallon means miles *divided* by gallons. So, we divide the number of miles traveled by the gallons of gas needed to travel those miles. This is your gas mileage (mpg).

Can You Guess?

If all the inhabitable land on earth were divided equally among all the people now living, how much land would each person have?

A. 5 sq ft
B. 50 sq ft
C. 5 acres
D. 50 acres

Answer: C. 5 acres. There are about 58 million sq mi of inhabitable land and about 7 billion people, so 58,000,000 sq mi = (58,000,000 × 640) acres = 37,120,000,000 acres = 37,120,000,000 ÷ 7,400,000,000 people ≈ 5.02 acres per person.

Brainteasers

1. There is a 10 foot steel ladder attached to the side of a boat. The rungs on the ladder are exactly one foot apart with the bottom rung resting exactly on the top of the water. If the tide rises 1 foot every half hour, how long will it take to cover the first three rungs on the ladder?
2. A man builds a house with four sides. The house is rectangular in shape. Each side faces south. A big bear comes wandering by. What color is the bear?

Answers: 1. The water will never cover the rungs (the boat rises with the tide). 2. White (polar bear; house is at north pole).

"It's got the 4,000 square feet, just like you wanted!"

Measurements: Real-World Applications

23

In this chapter, we will solve problems involving length, area, and volume. As you will see, there are lots of real-world applications. For example, builders, lenders, real estate brokers, appraisers, and insurance agents must frequently calculate the square footage (area) of homes. A homeowner must frequently calculate area; for example, the amount of roofing material needed is based on roof area. Topsoil and concrete are sold by volume. And the list goes on and on.

In addition to solving problems involving length, area, and volume, we will find unit costs, such as the cost per square foot to build a home. Finally, we will review how to convert measurements; in this chapter, we will limit our study to the U.S. system of measurements (the metric system is explored in Unit 24.2).

Working with measurements scares some people. We will start slowly and build to a "mild roar." Hopefully, you will find this stuff not only valuable but also fun.

UNIT OBJECTIVES

Unit 23.1 Length, area, and volume: Applications

- **a** Calculating length
- **b** Calculating area
- **c** Calculating volume

Unit 23.2 Unit costs and converting measurements (U.S. to U.S.)

- **a** Calculating unit costs
- **b** Converting measurements (U.S. to U.S.)

Unit 23.1 Length, area, and volume: Applications

Before we start solving problems involving length, area, and volume, let's take a moment to review angles. An **angle** exists when two straight lines join at a point. Angles are measured in degrees; this type of degree is different from the degrees used to measure temperature. The more rapidly two lines separate as you get away from their common point, the greater the angle. By definition, there are 360° (degrees) in a circle. Here are various angles.

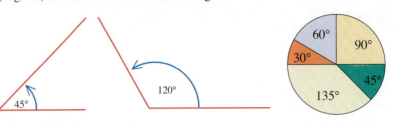

Notice the upper and lower halves of the circle each contain 180°. The entire circle contains 360°.

Two lines that meet at a 90° angle (like a floor and wall) are said to be **perpendicular**; the 90° angle is referred to as a **right angle**. Two lines side by side that travel in the same direction and will never cross (like railroad tracks) are said to be **parallel**.

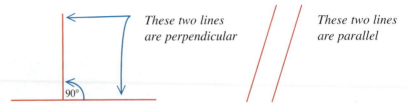

There are lots of two-dimensional shapes; here are some common ones:

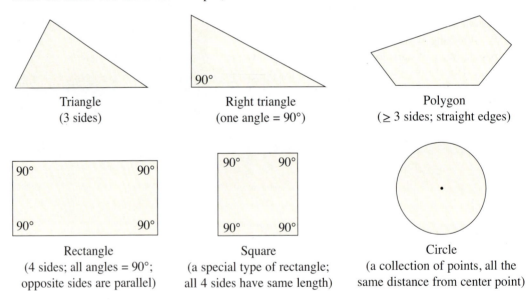

a Calculating length

Length represents the distance from one point to another and is often referred to as a *linear measurement*. U.S. units of length include inches, feet, yards, and miles; one increment is generally more appropriate in a given context than another. For example, the width of copy paper is stated in inches; football fields use yards; distance between cities is stated in miles.

One common linear measurement is called a **perimeter**. A perimeter is the distance *around* an object and is found by adding the lengths of the sides.

perimeter

Perimeter is found by adding the lengths of the sides.

Example 1 You are building a swimming pool with a tile border along the edge. Dimensions shown in the figure are in feet. How many linear feet (ft) of tile are needed?

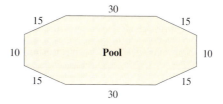

We are asked to find the perimeter of the pool. Starting from the top and working clockwise:

30 ft + 15 ft + 10 ft + 15 ft + 30 ft + 15 ft + 10 ft + 15 ft = 140 ft

A **square** has four sides of equal length. As a *shortcut* in finding the perimeter, we can multiply the length of one side by 4. A **rectangle** has two pairs of sides with equal length, so as a *shortcut* in finding the perimeter we can add twice the length to twice the width; an alternative method is to add the length and width together and then double the result.

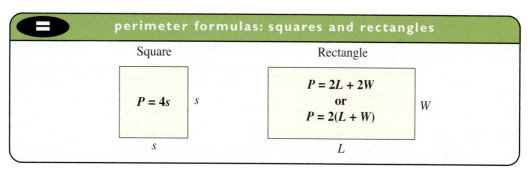

Example 2 Farmer Brown has two separate pastures for his cows, as shown. Determine how many linear feet of fencing are needed to enclose each pasture.

Pasture A: $P = 4s = 4(1{,}200 \text{ ft}) = 4{,}800 \text{ ft}$
Pasture B: $P = 2(L + W) = 2(2{,}000 \text{ ft} + 400 \text{ ft}) = 2(2{,}400 \text{ ft}) = 4{,}800 \text{ ft}$

Farmer Brown will need 4,800 linear feet of fencing for each pasture.

The perimeter of a circle has a special name: **circumference**. The distance from the center of a circle to the outside is called the **radius**, and the distance across a circle (twice the radius) is called the **diameter**. There is a relationship between the circumference and the diameter that can be found by measuring the diameter and circumference of numerous circles. The circumference is *always* 3.1415926536 (rounded to 10 decimal places) times the diameter. This value is known as π, pronounced "pie." For our purposes, we will consider π to be 3.14.

linear formulas for a circle

If we want to know	And we know	Use this formula
diameter (d)	radius (r)	$d = 2r$
radius (r)	diameter (d)	$r = \frac{d}{2}$
circumference (C)	radius (r)	$C = 2\pi r$
circumference (C)	diameter (d)	$C = \pi d$
diameter (d)	circumference (C)	$d = \frac{C}{\pi}$

Example 3 Each wheel of a bicycle has a diameter of 28 inches. How far does the bicycle travel for each revolution of the wheels?

Notice that we use the "approximately equal to" symbol because 3.14 is the approximate value of π

We want to know C and we know d, so: $C = \pi d \approx 3.14(28 \text{ in.}) \approx 87.92 \text{ in.}$

The bike travels approximately 88 inches (a little over 7 feet) for each revolution of the wheels.

Example 4 You discover a large redwood tree. You run a tape measure around the tree and get a measurement of 47 feet. How can you determine the thickness (diameter) of the tree?

You cannot measure the diameter because you cannot place a tape measure *through* the tree. Instead, let's use the circumference (47 feet) to find the diameter. We want to know d and we know C, so:

$d = \frac{C}{\pi} \approx \frac{47 \text{ ft}}{3.14} \approx 14.97 \text{ ft}$

The tree is about 15 feet thick.

b Calculating area

Calculating area, like figuring the square footage of a home, is a common mathematical problem. In some cases the calculations can be a bit tricky.

Calculating area is one of the most common mathematical problems. Area is expressed in *square units*, such as square inches (sq in.) square feet (sq ft), square yards (sq yd), or square miles (sq mi). Remember, *area is found by multiplying two dimensions*; just as 4 × 4 can be written as 4^2, a dimension such as ft × ft can be written as ft^2 or sq ft.

If we know how to find the area of a few basic shapes (rectangles, triangles, and circles), we can determine the area of most two-dimensional figures. The following table shows how to calculate the area of these basic shapes and includes a logical explanation for why the formula works (the explanation might help us remember the formulas).

calculating area of basic shapes

Shape	Formula and example	Justification for formula
Rectangle $W = 3$ ft, $L = 4$ ft	Area = (Length)(Width) $$A = LW$$ $A = (4\text{ ft})(3\text{ ft})$ $\quad = 12\text{ ft}^2$ ($A =$ 12 sq ft)	Notice in the picture that there are 12 squares, each measuring 1 ft by 1 ft (1 square foot), confirming that there are 12 square feet. The formula "$A = LW$" also applies to squares, since a square is a form of a rectangle.
Right triangle / **Any triangle** $h = 4$ in., $b = 5$ in.	Area = $(\frac{1}{2})$(Base)(Height) $$A = \tfrac{1}{2}bh$$ $A = \tfrac{1}{2}(5\text{ in.})(4\text{ in.})$ $\quad = \tfrac{1}{2}(20\text{ in.}^2)$ $\quad = 10\text{ in.}^2$ ($A =$ 10 sq in.)	In the first picture (right triangle), by adding another triangle of equal size we have a rectangle. In the second picture, we have two right triangles; by adding a triangle on the left and one on the right we have a rectangle. Since the overall area of the rectangle is "bh", $\tfrac{1}{2}$ of the area (that of the triangle) is $\tfrac{1}{2}bh$.
Circle $r = 6$ in.	Area = π(radius)(radius) $$A = \pi r^2$$ $A \approx 3.14(6\text{ in.})(6\text{ in.})$ $\quad \approx 3.14(36\text{ in.}^2)$ $\quad \approx 113.04\text{ in.}^2$ ($A \approx$ 113.04 sq in.) *Remember, r^2 means r multiplied by itself, or in this case (6 in.)(6 in.).*	(diagram: large square of side d divided into four small squares of side r; $A = r^2$. Circle with radius r and diameter d; $A = \pi r^2 \approx 3.14 r^2$.) Notice the large square has length and width of d; Each of the four small squares has length and width of r, so $A = LW = (r)(r) = r^2$. The area of the circle is "πr^2" or 3.14 times as great as each small square. You can prove this by duplicating the two diagrams (only larger). Then, cut the square portion into the four squares; use three squares plus .14 of the fourth square (discard the .86 of fourth square). The pieces will fit into the circle (by trimming off edges and shaping into smaller pieces).

Unit 23.1   Length, area, and volume: Applications   487

Example 5 The outside dimensions of an odd-shaped home are shown below. Dimensions are in feet. The curved area is half of a circle. Calculate the area.

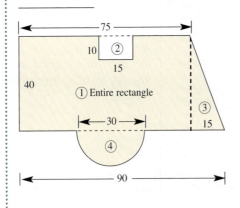

Let's divide into separate areas and combine the square footage of each:

① Entire rectangle

$A = LW = (75)(40) =$ 3,000.00

② Deduct small rectangle

$A = LW = (15)(10) =$ − 150.00

③ Triangle

$A = \frac{1}{2} bh = \frac{1}{2}(15)(40) =$ + 300.00

④ Half circle (r = 15)

$A = \frac{1}{2}(\pi r^2) \approx \frac{1}{2}(3.14)(15)(15) \approx$ + 353.25

Total square footage ≈   **3,503.25**

The home contains 3,503.25 square feet.

> **TIP**   **visualize the answer**
>
> To help understand how large an area is, try "visualizing." For Example 5, imagine a square piece of paper measuring 1 ft (12 in.) on each edge; the floor space of the home is equivalent to 3,503 of these squares.

C Calculating volume

Volume is used for *three-dimensional objects* and is expressed in *cubic units*, such as cubic inches (cu in.), cubic feet (cu ft), and cubic yards (cu yd). *Volume is found by multiplying three dimensions;* just as $4 \times 4 \times 4$ can be written as 4^3, a dimension such as ft × ft × ft can be written as ft^3. While there are lots of three-dimensional objects, we will study the two most common ones: rectangular solids and cylinders.

The volume of a **rectangular solid** is the number of unit cubes it takes to fill it.

Unit cube

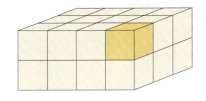
Volume = 24

In this drawing, there are 12 cubes in each level (4 wide × 3 long = 12) and there are two levels; so there are 24 cubes (12 cubes per level × 2 levels = 24 cubes). The volume of rectangular solids is found by multiplying the area of its base by its height. Since the area (A) of the base = LW, the volume (V) = LWH.

volume of a rectangular solid

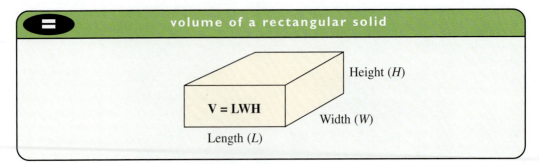

Example 6 To determine what size furnace to install, a heating contractor needs to know how many cubic feet a home contains. The home measures 32 feet by 45 feet. Based on a ceiling height of 9 feet, how many cubic feet are there?

$V = LWH = (32\text{ ft})(45\text{ ft})(9\text{ ft}) = 12{,}960\text{ ft}^3$

The home contains 12,960 cubic feet (cu ft) of airspace.

> **TIP** — visualize the answer
>
> To help understand the answer to Example 6, picture a cubic box measuring 1 ft by 1 ft by 1 ft. The home is large enough to hold 12,960 of these cubes.

A **cylinder**, often referred to as a *right circular cylinder*, has the same diameter from top to bottom, and its sides are perpendicular to the base. The process of determining the volume of a cylinder is similar to that of determining the volume of a rectangular solid: we find the area of the base and multiply the result by the height. Since the base is a circle and the area (A) of a circle $= \pi r^2$, it follows that $V = \pi r^2 h$.

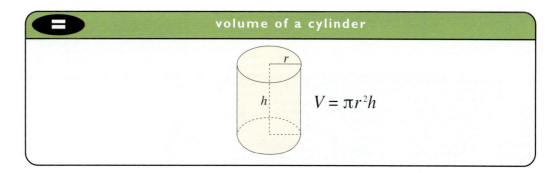

volume of a cylinder

$V = \pi r^2 h$

Example 7 Find the volume of a grain silo that has a diameter of 28 feet and a height of 36.5 feet.

Because a grain silo is a cylinder, we use the formula $V = \pi r^2 h$. We know that $h = 36.5$ ft. And $r = \frac{d}{2} = \frac{28\text{ ft}}{2} = 14$ ft.

$V = \pi r^2 h \approx 3.14(14\text{ ft})(14\text{ ft})(36.5\text{ ft}) \approx 22{,}463.56\text{ ft}^3$

The silo contains about 22,463.56 cu ft. For comparison, that is almost double the volume of the home in Example 6.

> **TIP** — answer in (1) feet, (2) square feet, or (3) cubic feet?
>
> Some people aren't sure whether to write an answer in units, square units, or cubic units. Here is a guide that might help:
> - For **length** problems (these involve only *one dimension*), the answer is in plain old *units* (such as 140 ft).
> - For **area** problems (these involve *two dimensions*), the answer is in *square units* (such as 3,503 sq ft).
> - For **volume** problems (these involve *three dimensions*), the answer is in *cubic units* (such as 12,960 cu ft).

That does it for this unit. Let's *measure* our understanding of this unit by doing the U-Try-It exercises.

Unit 23.1   Length, area, and volume: Applications   489

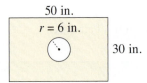

U-Try-It (Unit 23.1)

1. A farmer wants to fence a field measuring 1,650 feet × 660 feet. How many feet of fencing are required?
2. The earth has a circumference of approximately 25,000 miles. What is the distance to the center of the earth?
3. Determine the area of the shaded region.

   50 in.
   $r = 6$ in.
   30 in.

4. An underground gasoline storage tank has a diameter of 26 feet and is 12 feet tall. What is its volume?

Answers: (If you have a different answer, check the solution in Appendix A.)
1. 4,620 ft 2. 3,980.89 mi 3. 1,386.96 sq in. 4. 6,367.92 cu ft

Unit 23.2 Unit costs and converting measurements (U.S. to U.S.)

ⓐ Calculating unit costs

Can you figure out the cost per square inch of pizza? See Example 3.

Measurements are frequently used to compare or evaluate costs. When determining a **unit cost**, such as cost per ounce or cost per square foot, the word "per" means "divided by." So, to find the *cost per unit*, we divide the cost (in dollars) by the number of units (for example, ounces or square feet).

= cost per unit

$$\text{Cost per unit} = \frac{\text{Cost}}{\text{Number of units}}$$

Example 1 An 18-ounce container of ketchup sells for $1.39. A 32-ounce container is advertised on sale for $2.59. Which container costs the least per ounce?

✓ *To change from dollars to cents, move the decimal point 2 places to the right.*

18 oz: Cost per ounce = $\frac{\text{Cost}}{\text{Number of ounces}} = \frac{\$1.39}{18 \text{ oz}} \approx \$0.0772$ per oz ≈ **7.72¢ per oz**

32 oz: Cost per ounce = $\frac{\text{Cost}}{\text{Number of ounces}} = \frac{\$2.59}{32 \text{ oz}} \approx \$0.0809$ per oz ≈ **8.09¢ per oz**

The 18-ounce container is cheaper per ounce than the container that is "on sale."

Example 2   You are thinking about building a home containing 3,100 sq ft of floor space. The builder has given you a bid of $294,000 for the construction of the home. What is the cost per square foot?

$$\text{Cost per sq ft} = \frac{\text{Cost}}{\text{Number of sq ft}} = \frac{\$294{,}000}{3{,}100 \text{ sq ft}} \approx \$94.84 \text{ per sq ft}$$

On average, each square foot of space will cost $94.84.

Example 3   You are about to order a pepperoni pizza but are unsure whether to order a 12-inch pizza at a cost of $9.95 or a 14-inch pizza at a cost of $12.75. Which pizza has the lower cost per square inch? *Hint*: The stated size of a round pizza is the *diameter*.

Your first impulse may be to divide $9.95 by 12 to get $0.83 and $12.75 by 14 to get $0.91, but by doing this you would have determined the cost per *linear* inch of diameter, not the cost per *square* inch. First, let's calculate the area (square inches) for each pizza.

12-inch: $A = \pi r^2 \approx 3.14(6 \text{ in.})(6 \text{ in.}) \approx 113.04 \text{ in.}^2$
14-inch: $A = \pi r^2 \approx 3.14(7 \text{ in.})(7 \text{ in.}) \approx 153.86 \text{ in.}^2$

Picture a piece of pizza measuring 1 inch by 1 inch.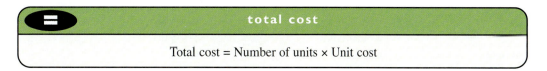

The 12-inch pizza contains the equivalent of 113.04 of these bite-size pieces; the 14-inch pizza contains the equivalent of 153.86 pieces. Now, let's calculate the cost per square inch.

12-inch: $\text{Cost per square inch} = \dfrac{\text{Cost}}{\text{Number of sq in.}} = \dfrac{\$9.95}{113.04 \text{ sq in.}} \approx \$0.0880 \approx 8.80\text{¢ per sq in.}$

14-inch: $\text{Cost per square inch} = \dfrac{\text{Cost}}{\text{Number of sq in.}} = \dfrac{\$12.75}{153.86 \text{ sq in.}} \approx \$0.0829 \approx 8.29\text{¢ per sq in.}$

The 12-inch pizza costs 8.80 cents per square inch. Each time you eat a piece measuring 1 inch by 1 inch, it costs 8.80 cents. The 14-inch pizza costs less (8.29 cents for each square inch). *Note*: Next time you order pizza with your friends, impress everybody by pulling out your calculator to determine which pizza has the lowest cost per square inch. It's a real crowd-pleaser!

In the previous examples we determined *unit cost*. On the flip side, we can determine total cost by multiplying the number of units by the unit cost.

> **total cost**
>
> Total cost = Number of units × Unit cost

Example 4   You want to install floor tile in your kitchen. If the cost per square foot is $9.75 and your kitchen contains 208 square feet, what is the total cost?

Total cost = Number of units × Unit cost = 208 × $9.75 = $2,028

ⓑ Converting measurements (U.S. to U.S.)

A measurement must sometimes be converted to another denomination. Illustration 23-1 is a table that can be used to convert a U.S. measurement to another U.S. measurement. Pay special attention to the footnote of Illustration 23-1. *Note*: Metrics are covered in Unit 24.2.

Illustration 23-1   Conversion Table (U.S. to U.S.)

	To convert from	To	Multiply by*
Units	dozen (doz)	units	12
	gross (gr)	dozen (doz)	12
	gross (gr)	units	144
Time	minutes (min)	seconds (sec)	60
	hours (hr)	minutes (min)	60
	days	hours (hr)	24
	weeks (wk)	days	7
	nonleap years (yr)	days	365
	leap years (yr)	days	366
	centuries (C)	years (yr)	100
Linear (distance)	feet (ft)	inches (in.)	12
	yards (yd)	feet (ft)	3
	yards (yd)	inches (in.)	36
	miles (mi)	yards (yd)	1,760
	miles (mi)	feet (ft)	5,280
	rods (rd)	feet (ft)	16.5
	chains (ch)	feet (ft)	66
Area	square feet (sq ft)	square inches (sq in.)	144
	square yards (sq yd)	square feet (sq ft)	9
	square yards (sq yd)	square inches (sq in.)	1,296
	acres (A)	square feet (sq ft)	43,560
	square miles (sq mi) or sections	acres (A)	640
	townships	sections	36
Volume—liquid	tablespoons (tbsp)	teaspoons (tsp)	3
	ounces (oz)	tablespoons (tbsp)	2
	cups (c)	tablespoons (tbsp)	16
	cups (c)	ounces (oz)	8
	pints (pt)	cups (c)	2
	pints (pt)	ounces (oz)	16
	quarts (qt)	pints (pt)	2
	quarts (qt)	ounces (oz)	32
	gallons (gal)	quarts (qt)	4
	gallons (gal)	ounces (oz)	128
	gallons (gal)	cubic inches (cu in.)	231
Volume—dry	cubic feet (cu ft)	cubic inches (cu in.)	1,728
	cubic yards (cu yd)	cubic feet (cu ft)	27
	cubic yards (cu yd)	cubic inches (cu in.)	46,656
	pecks (pk)	quarts (qt)	8
	bushels (bu)	pecks (pk)	4
Weight	pounds (lb)	ounces (oz)	16
	tons (T)	pounds (lb)	2,000
Angles	degrees (°)	minutes (')	60
	minutes (')	seconds (")	60

Note: If converting in the opposite direction, divide rather than multiply.

Example 5   1.5 lb = __?__ oz.

The abbreviation lb stands for pounds and oz stands for ounces; both are units of weight. Find "Weight" in the left-hand column of Illustration 23-1. Then find the line that has both pounds and ounces. To convert from pounds to ounces, we multiply the number of pounds by 16.

1.5 lb = (1.5 × 16) oz = 24 oz

Example 6 You are thinking about buying some vacant land for your dream home. The land is rectangular in shape and measures 228 ft by 350 ft. Calculate the number of acres (to the nearest hundredth).

First, let's find the area (in square feet): $A = LW = (228 \text{ ft})(350 \text{ ft}) = 79{,}800$ sq ft

Now, let's convert from square feet to acres. Find "Area" in the left-hand column of Illustration 23-1. Then find the line that has both square feet and acres. To convert from square feet to acres (rather than acres to square feet), we *divide* the number of square feet by 43,560.

$$79{,}800 \text{ sq ft} = \left(\frac{79{,}800}{43{,}560}\right) \text{acres} \approx 1.83 \text{ acres}$$

When measurements are given in more than one unit (such as one measurement in feet and another in inches), we must convert to the same type of unit before doing calculations.

TIP — choices, choices

There are often several different ways a problem can be solved. However, there is often an easy way and a hard way. For example, assume we are asked to find how many cubic yards of concrete are in a driveway that measures 24 ft long, 18 ft wide, and 4 in. thick. We have three choices.

Choice 1 Convert all measurements to *inches* before multiplying (24 ft = 288 in.; 18 ft = 216 in.). Then, find cubic inches. Finally, convert from cubic inches to cubic yards.

Choice 2 Convert all measurements to *feet* before multiplying (4 in. = $\frac{4}{12}$ ft). Then, find cubic feet. Finally, convert from cubic feet to cubic yards.

Choice 3 Convert all measurements to *yards* before multiplying (24 ft = 8 yd; 18 ft = 6 yd; 4 in. = $\frac{4}{36}$ yd).

Notice that choice 3 results in the fewest number of steps. This is because the final answer is to be in cubic *yards*, and by converting all measurements to yards *first*, we save some effort.

Example 7 Concrete is sold by the cubic yard. You want to install a concrete driveway, measuring 24 ft by 18 ft. If the concrete is to be 4 inches thick, how many cubic yards of concrete do you need? Express your answer as a decimal number with 2 decimal places.

To convert from ft to yd, we divide the number of feet by 3

$$V = LWH = (24 \text{ ft})(18 \text{ ft})(4 \text{ in.}) = \left(\frac{24}{3} \text{ yd}\right)\left(\frac{18}{3} \text{ yd}\right)\left(\frac{4}{36} \text{ yd}\right) = (8 \text{ yd})(6 \text{ yd})\left(\frac{1}{9} \text{ yd}\right) = \frac{48}{9} \text{ yd} \approx 5.33 \text{ cu yd}$$

To convert from in. to yd, we divide the number of inches by 36

You will need 5.33 cubic yards of concrete. To picture how much this is, imagine a cubic box measuring 3 ft by 3 ft by 3 ft; you will need enough concrete to fill 5.33 of these boxes.

That finishes up this chapter. Let's find out how much sunk in by doing another U-Try-It set.

U-Try-It (23.2)

1. You just got your accounting degree and are considering opening an office at one of two locations. The first measures 18 ft × 30 ft and rents for $525 a month. The second measures 22 ft × 24 ft and rents for $480 a month. Which office has the lower rent per square foot?
2. You are thinking about replacing the carpet in your family room. The room measures 15 ft × 22.5 ft. If the new carpet costs $28 per square yard, what will it cost to replace the carpet in your family room?

Answers: (If you have a different answer, check the solution in Appendix A.)
1. Office 2 ($0.91 per sq ft) **2.** $1,050

Chapter in a Nutshell

Objectives	Examples

Unit 23.1 Length, area, and volume: Applications

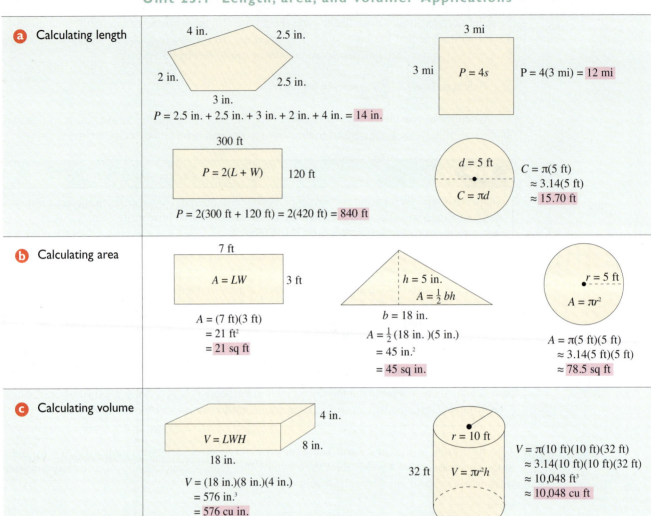

Unit 23.2 Units costs and converting measurements (U.S. to U.S.)

(a) Calculating unit costs

$1,275 monthly rent on 850 sq ft office. Rent per square foot?

$$\text{Rent per sq ft} = \frac{\text{Rent}}{\text{Number of sq ft}} = \frac{\$1{,}275}{850 \text{ sq ft}} = \$1.50 \text{ per sq ft}$$

A contractor gives a bid of $2.75 per sq ft for installing concrete drive. Drive measures 18 ft × 32 ft. Total cost?

$A = LW = (18 \text{ ft})(32 \text{ ft}) = 576 \text{ sq ft}$
Total cost = Number of units × Unit cost = 576 × $2.75 = **$1,584**

(b) Converting measurements (U.S. to U.S.)

100 yd = __?__ in.   100 yd = (100 × 36) in. = **3,600 in.**

405 sq ft = __?__ sq yd   405 sq ft = $\left(\frac{405}{9}\right)$ sq yd = **45 sq yd**

405 cu ft = __?__ cu yd   405 cu ft = $\left(\frac{405}{27}\right)$ cu yd = **15 cu yd**

Chapter in a Nutshell (concluded)

Objectives | **Examples**

Enrichment Topics

The following Enrichment Topics, which go a bit beyond what is in the text, are available for this chapter:

Pythagorean Formula
Measurement Calculations in Graphic Design

If your instructor doesn't cover these topics in class and you would like to dig in deeper on your own, please send a request to *studentsupport@olympuspub.com*.

Think

1. For each problem, which choice (50 ft, 50 sq ft, or 50 cu ft) would be a possible answer, and how do you know?
    a. Area problem   b. Volume problem   c. Perimeter problem
2. How big is 1 square foot? How big is 1 cubic foot? How big is 12 square feet? How big is 8 cubic feet?
3. Which has a greater area: A square measuring 8 ft on each side or a circle 8 ft across?
4. Name some situations for which you might want to know a cost per unit. For each case, how would you find the cost per unit?
5. A square measures 6 feet × 6 feet. A second square measures 3 feet × 3 feet. The dimensions of the first square are twice the dimensions of second square. Is the area of the first square twice the area of the second square?
6. A cube measures 4 feet × 4 feet × 4 feet. A second cube measures 2 feet × 2 feet × 2 feet. The dimensions of the first cube are twice the dimensions of the second cube. Is the volume of the first cube twice the volume of the second cube?

Explore

1. Search the Internet for *geometry formulas*. Find a site that has some additional area and volume formulas. Submit a report on your findings; include drawings and your calculations.

Apply

1. **How Big Is The Home.** Determine the measurements below for a home. You can use your own home or the home of a friend or relative.
   A. The square footage of the improvements: (1) living space, (2) garage or carport, (3) decks, (4) driveway, (5) other improvements (shed, playhouse, gazebo, etc.)
   B. Assuming that the driveway is 4 inches thick, calculate the cubic yards of concrete that were used.

   Submit drawings of each of the improvements, indicating dimensions. Dimensions should be determined using a measuring tape and should indicate feet and inches for each measurement. Drawings can be rough and do not have to be to scale.

2. **Pizza, Pizza.** Examine a menu for a local pizza restaurant that has at least three sizes of pizza. Calculate the cost per square inch for each size; assume identical toppings for each (if pizza slices are identified with words, such as "large," you will have to determine the diameter of each). Submit all of your data. Include the name of the pizza establishment.

3. **How Far on a Gallon.** Determine the gas mileage for your vehicle for a 2-week period. Include your beginning odometer reading, gallons of gas used, and ending odometer reading. For each gas purchase, state the date, dollar amount, number of gallons, and place of purchase. Indicate whether each purchase is a fill-up; for fill-ups, include your odometer reading. After calculating the miles per gallon, determine the total cost (gasoline only) per mile traveled.

4. **Distance, Area, Volume.** Using a ruler or tape measure, make calculations for each of the following:
   A. Textbook: width, height, thickness, area of cover, volume
   B. Wood door: width, height, thickness, area of one side, volume
   C. U.S. quarter: diameter, thickness, area, volume. Hint: To measure small objects (like a quarter), stack several (say, 20 quarters), measure the stack, and then divide that measurement by the number of objects (in this case 20) to get the measurement per object.

Chapter Review Problems

Unless instructed otherwise, use up to 2 decimal places for final answers. Assume π = 3.14.

Unit 23.1 Length, area, and volume: Applications

1. If the ground is level, at what angle should the wall of a building be in relation to the ground?

2. A square is a type of rectangle. (T or F)

For Problems 3–5 find the perimeter. Some dimensions are intentionally not shown.

3.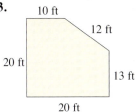

4.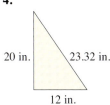

5.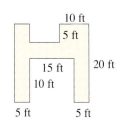

6. A farmer wants to fence a field measuring 660 ft × 330 ft. How many feet of fencing are required?

7. Write in order from smallest to largest: diameter (*d*), radius (*r*), circumference (*c*).

8. Marla is making a round table cloth that is 48 inches wide. She wants to attach a piece of trim on the edge. Help Marla figure out how many inches of trim material she needs to buy.

9. You see a large redwood tree. You run a tape measure around the tree and get a measurement of 44 ft. How thick is the tree?

For Problems 10 and 11, determine the area of the shaded region.

10.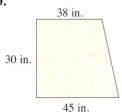

11.

12. A home has measurements as shown. Dimensions are in feet. What is the square footage of the home?

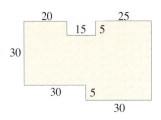

13. From a fire observation tower, a forest ranger can see a distance of 50 miles in all directions. How many square miles can be observed from the tower?

For Problems 14–16, find the volume of the object.

14.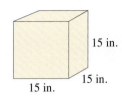

15.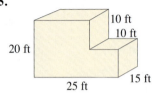

16.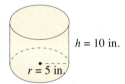

17. A theater is 40 ft wide, 90 ft deep, and 18 ft high. Allowing 250 cubic feet of airspace per patron, what is the maximum number of tickets that should be sold for each movie?

18. An underground gasoline storage tank has a diameter of 28 ft and is 15 ft tall. Find the volume.

19. If all the gold in the world were gathered together, it would reportedly form a cube 18 yards on a side. Find the volume of the world's gold (in cubic yards).

Unit 23.2 Unit costs and converting measurements (U.S. to U.S.)

20. You have a choice of buying a 68-oz bottle of soda pop for $1.19 or a six-pack of 12-oz cans for $1.49. Which is cheaper per ounce? Hint: Figure the cost per ounce in *cents* not dollars.

21. A fence is to be built around an outdoor basketball court measuring 40 ft × 30 ft. If fencing costs $4.75 per linear foot, what will the fencing cost?

22. A rollerskating rink is shown with dimensions in feet. How much will the hardwood flooring cost, based on a cost of $6.50 per square foot?

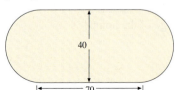

23. You want to lay sod in an area measuring 74 ft × 62 ft. If sod costs 22¢ per square foot plus $35 for delivery, what is the total cost?

24. Refer to Problem 12. What is the cost to build the home, based on a cost per square foot of $120?

25. Determine the total shipping weight of a carton containing two dozen cans of beans. Each can contains 12 oz of beans. Each can (empty) weights 1 oz, and the cardboard carton (empty) weighs 10 oz. Express the total shipping weight in pounds.

26. You are adding a new family room to your home. The room measures 24 ft × 15 ft. Calculate the cost of carpeting based on a cost of $21.50 per square yard. Assume there is no waste.

27. A utility company is buying a right-of-way through a farm. If the strip of land is 2,640 ft long and 100 ft wide and the utility company is paying $22,000 per acre, how much will the farmer receive? *Remember*: Don't round intermediate results.

28. During a basketball game, you figure you ran an average of 65 ft each time you ran to the other end of the court. If you changed ends a total of 150 times, how many miles (to the nearest hundredth of a mile) did you run during the game?

29. How many days will 100 yards of dental floss last if you use 15 inches each time you floss your teeth and you floss each morning and evening?

Challenge problems

30. The distance from Miami to Seattle is 3,403 miles. A car is driven this distance using tires with a radius of 15 inches. How many revolutions does each tire make?

31. The earth has a circumference of about 25,000 miles. If a satellite is in orbit 200 miles above the surface of the earth, how many miles does it travel each time it circles the earth?

32. You are planning on painting a room that measures 14 ft × 18 ft, with a ceiling height of 9 ft; you will paint the walls with one color and the ceiling with another. There are 3 windows in the room, each measuring 3 ft × 4 ft. The door measures 3 ft × 7 ft. Assume that a gallon of paint will cover 200 square feet; you cannot buy part of a gallon. Find the cost of the paint, if the paint costs $32.95 per gallon.

33. You have purchased some land for your dream home. The land is below street grade and requires fill dirt to bring it to proper grade. Your land measures 115 ft × 280 ft and is an average of 27 in. below grade. How many cubic yards of fill dirt are required?

34. A farmer has land measuring 2,640 feet × 2,640 feet. The farmer is thinking about installing a circular sprinkling system to water crops, with the sprinkling system revolving around the center of the land. How many square feet of land will *not* be farmed if a circular sprinkling system is installed?

35. Refer to Problem 34. What *percent* of the land will not be farmed?

36. An 18-hole golf course has a total of 7,122 yards. If there are 125 yards from the clubhouse to the first tee, an average of 50 yards between each green and the next tee, and 125 yards from the 18th green to the clubhouse, how many miles would you walk for an 18-hole round (from clubhouse to clubhouse)? *Hint to nongolfers*: Each hole has a tee (where the golfer begins the hole) and a green (where the hole is completed).

37. You want to install a concrete driveway with dimensions of 27 ft 6 in. × 18 ft. The concrete is to be 4 in. thick. If concrete costs $85 per cubic yard, what is the total cost?

38. A container made of wood measures 6 ft long, 4 ft deep, and 3 ft high. How many square feet of wood are required to build the container? Remember, the container is closed on all sides.

39. Jilly Bean's time for a 100-yard dash is 10.5 seconds. Calculate Jilly's speed in miles per hour (mph) to the nearest tenth.

40. Refer to the newspaper article to the right. Assuming that the plot of land is a rectangle, figure the length of the plot to the nearest hundredth of an inch.

Park is world's smallest at only 2 feet wide

PORTLAND, Ore. (AP) — If you're searching for a wide open space to bring your picnic basket, there's no point heading to Mill Ends Park. It's only 2 feet wide.

At 452 square inches, Mill Ends is the smallest park in the world. It was created to offer a base for a light pole on busy Front Avenue. The pole never came, but the weeds did.

Journalist Dick Fagan got tired of gazing down from the old Oregon Journal Building to the weedy plot. He planted some flowers and Mill Ends Park became an official city park shortly after.

Practice Test

For all problems, express the final answer with up to 2 decimal places. Assume $\pi = 3.14$.

1. A farmer wants to fence a field measuring 1,200 ft × 600 ft. How many feet of fencing are required?

2. A ball has a circumference of 31.5 inches. What is the diameter?

3. Find the area. Dimensions are in feet.

   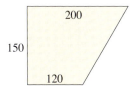

4. A circular fountain is surrounded by a circular walkway 4 feet wide. The fountain has a diameter of 20 feet. What is the area of the walkway?

5. The city is excavating for a landfill. If the area measures 1,000 ft × 270 ft and must be dug to a depth of 12 ft, how many cubic yards of earth must be removed?

6. Find the volume of a grain silo that has a diameter of 24 feet and a height of 45 feet.

7. You are thinking about building a home containing 2,320 sq ft. You have been told that homes cost about $95 to $120 per sq ft, depending on the quality, etc. Your builder gives you a cost of $242,000 for your home. Is that cost within the $95 to $120 per sq ft range?

8. You are thinking about buying some recreational land for a cabin, measuring 1,320 ft × 660 ft. How many acres is it?

FUN CORNER

World's 5 Biggest Employers
employees
1. Wal-Mart (U.S.) 2,100,000
2. McDonald's (U.S.) 1,900,000
3. National Health Service (U.K.) 1,700,000
4. China National Petroleum (China) . . . 1,600,000
5. Grid Corporation of China (China) . 1,500,000

Source: Wikipedia, 2015

Extreme Temperatures
The highest recorded temperature is in El Azizia, Libya on Sep. 13, 1922: 136°F (58°C). The highest temperature in the U.S. is in Death Valley, CA on Jul. 10, 1913: 134°F (57°C). The lowest temperature is in Vostok, Antarctica on Jul. 21, 1983: -129°F (-89°C). The lowest temperature in the U.S. is in Prospect Creek, Alaska on Jan. 23, 1971: -80°F (-62°C)

World's 10 Most Populous Countries, 2014
1. China 1,355,692,576
2. India 1,236,344,631
3. United States 318,892,103
4. Indonesia 253,609,643
5. Brazil 202,656,788
6. Pakistan 196,174,830
7. Nigeria 177,155,754
8. Bangladesh 166,280,712
9. Russia 142,470,272
10. Japan 127,103,388

Source: Infoplease.com

Blunders
U.S. companies have made a few blunders in foreign markets because they did not fully understand foreign differences. Here are a few examples.

- An outdoor products company, about to introduce coolers in Europe, realized in the nick of time that soda pop is often sold in 2-liter bottles, requiring a taller cooler than the ones sold in the U.S.
- Many a U.S. businessman, after completion of a deal, has flashed the OK signal by connecting his or her thumb and forefinger to form a letter O. In Japan, the signal means that a bribe has been asked for; in southern France, the gesture means the deal is worthless; and in Brazil, the signal is grossly insulting.
- The Dutch exchange Christmas gifts on December 6. In its first year in the Netherlands a U.S. electronic's retailer planned a major advertising campaign for the middle of December, only to find that Dutch consumers had already completed their Christmas shopping.

Brainteaser
How many cubic meters of dirt in a circular hole that is 10 feet deep and 8 feet across?

Answer: There is no dirt in a hole.

"Congratulations, Giovanni. You just won a million lira — or if you'd prefer, fifty-two dollars."

International Business: Exchange Rates and Metrics

24

Lots of products and services are in demand worldwide. As a result, many companies, both large and small, are doing business internationally. Some companies **import** raw materials, parts, finished products, or services from other countries. Some **export** to other countries. Some companies establish branches in more than one country.

Doing business internationally requires an understanding of differences in laws, import and export regulations and fees, languages, cultures, seasons, time zones, competition, monetary systems, and measurements. Companies have made lots of costly blunders in foreign markets because they did not understand these differences (a few blunders are included in the Fun Corner, to the left). It is critical for a company venturing abroad to have contacts who are highly familiar with the country in which business is to be conducted. While it might be more fun to study *marketing* aspects of international business, we'll limit our study to a few math-related topics. We'll try to have some fun along the way. So let's enter the international market!

Unit Objectives

Unit 24.1 Monetary exchange rates: Significance in international business

- ⓐ Determining how exchange rates affect international sales
- ⓑ Determining how exchange rates affect international investments

Unit 24.2 Metric system: Significance in international business

- ⓐ Writing metric terms
- ⓑ Converting metric to metric
- ⓒ Converting metric to U.S. and U.S. to metric
- ⓓ Making temperature conversions

Unit 24.1 Monetary exchange rates: Significance in international business

If you are involved in an international transaction, agree in advance which currency will be used.

A *worldwide* currency does not exist. Instead, countries have different currencies. Without a universal currency, a system is required that will allow for the transfer of money between a company in one country and a company in another country. For example, if a U.S. company sells a computer to a company in Japan, the Japanese company probably does not have U.S. dollars on hand to make payment and the U.S. company cannot use Japanese yen to run its business. An international banking system allows the Japanese company to pay in Japanese yen and the U.S. company to receive U.S. dollars.

A few recent monetary exchange rates are shown in Illustration 24-1. Current rates appear in most daily newspapers and on the Internet (on sites like **www.xe.com**); the exchange rates fluctuate throughout the day. Pay special attention to the conversion guidelines at the bottom of Illustration 24-1.

a Determining how exchange rates affect international sales

Buyers and sellers that do not use the same currency must agree in advance which currency will be used to make payment.

Example 1 A U.S. company negotiates the sale of a $20,000 computer to a Japanese firm. Calculate the price, in *Japanese yen*, based on the exchange rate of 1 U.S. dollar = 115.700 yen.

To convert U.S. dollars to Japanese yen, we *multiply* the number of U.S. dollars by the exchange rate:

$20,000 = (20,000 × 115.700) Japanese yen = **2,314,000 Japanese yen**

Example 2 Refer to Example 1. In 45 days, the U.S. company receives a check for 2,314,000 Japanese yen. The U.S. company goes to its bank to exchange the check for U.S. funds only to discover that the exchange rate has changed dramatically. How much will it receive on the basis of a current exchange rate of 127.400?

To convert Japanese yen to U.S. dollars, we *divide* the number of Japanese yen by the exchange rate:

2,314,000 Japanese yen = $\left(\frac{2,314,000}{127.400}\right)$ U.S. dollars = **$18,163.27**

> **TIP** — multiply or divide?
>
> If you are not sure whether to *multiply* or *divide* by the exchange rate, try both and see which answer seems *reasonable*. In Example 2, if we had *multiplied* 2,314,000 by the exchange rate of 127.400 we would get $294,803,600! That answer is unreasonable, so we would know we should have *divided*.

Illustration 24-1 A Few Monetary Exchange Rates (September 22, 2015)

Currency	1 U.S. dollar can be exchanged for
British pound	0.65159
Canadian dollar	1.32818
Euro	0.90006
Japanese yen	120.270
Mexican peso	16.9023
Swiss franc	0.97604

To convert from U.S. dollars to the foreign currency, *multiply* the number of U.S. dollars by the exchange rate.
To convert from foreign currency to U.S. dollars, *divide* the units of foreign currency by the exchange rate.

In Example 2, the U.S. company received only $18,163.27 ($1,836.73 less than anticipated). If the exchange rate had gone down (say to 105.200), the U.S. company would have received more than anticipated ($21,996.20).

> **TIP** — how to make money and lose it at the same time
>
> Suppose in Example 2, the U.S. firm had a $1,000 profit built into the $20,000 selling price. They would have made $1,000 but lost $1,836.73 because of the exchange rate, thereby losing money on the deal. Example 2 points out the risk when a price is agreed upon but payment is made in a foreign currency. One way to avoid this risk is to have prices quoted and require payment in your own currency, whether you are a buyer or seller. If the other party insists that payment be made in its currency, the risk can be offset by buying their currency, currency options, or futures at the time the sale is made; contact the international services department of a bank or a stock brokerage firm for more information.

In Example 2, the Japanese company made payment with a company check. A more common method of payment is by electronic transmission, called a **wire transfer.** The Japanese company could write a check to its bank for 2,314,000 Japanese yen (or simply authorize its bank to withdraw funds from the company's account). The Japanese bank would then electronically transfer the funds (through a system of international banks) to the U.S. firm's bank. The U.S. firm's bank would then credit the amount (in U.S. dollars) to the account of the U.S. firm.

When products are sold internationally between two parties who know little about each other, the buyer does not want to make payment until the goods are received, and the seller is reluctant to ship goods until payment is made. They are both saying, no way! One way to resolve this dilemma is with a **letter of credit.** Here is how a typical letter of credit works.

1. The buyer asks his or her bank to guarantee payment once certain conditions are met. Typically, these conditions consist of proof that the goods have been shipped and insured. The letter of credit is sent to the seller, who now has assurance of payment. The bank normally charges a fee for issuing the credit, paid by its customer, the buyer.
2. The shipping company notifies the bank when the goods are shipped.
3. The bank requests payment from its customer (the buyer) and remits the money to the seller (or the seller's bank). Payment is made after goods are shipped, quite often before goods are received. If the buyer fails to pay the bank, the bank is still obligated to pay the seller.

A letter of credit is based on *documents, not on the condition of goods.* With a letter of credit, the seller has a promise from the buyer's bank that payment will be made. The seller, however, does not know much about the creditworthiness of the buyer's bank. As a result, the seller might ask its own bank to guarantee payment; this is known as a **confirmed letter of credit.** With a confirmed letter of credit, the promise of the seller's bank is added to the promise of the buyer's bank. If payment is not made by the buyer's bank, the seller's bank must pay. Of course, the seller's bank will charge the seller a fee for issuing a confirmed letter of credit.

b Determining how exchange rates affect international investments

As illustrated in the next few examples, foreign investments are affected by exchange rates.

Example 3 A U.S. hotel chain buys a hotel in Geneva for 7,500,000 Swiss francs. Calculate the price in U.S. dollars, rounded to the nearest dollar, based on the exchange rate of 1 U.S. dollar = 1.28503 Swiss francs.

To convert Swiss francs to U.S. dollars, we *divide* the number of Swiss francs by the exchange rate:

$$7{,}500{,}000 \text{ Swiss francs} = \left(\frac{7{,}500{,}000}{1.28503}\right) \text{ U.S. dollars} = \$5{,}836{,}440 \text{ (rounded)}$$

Example 4 Refer to Example 3. The hotel is not as profitable as anticipated, and the U.S. firm sells the hotel for 7,500,000 Swiss francs (the same price they paid). Calculate the price in U.S. dollars, based on an exchange rate of 1.01500.

$$7{,}500{,}000 \text{ Swiss francs} = \left(\frac{7{,}500{,}000}{1.01500}\right) \text{ U.S. dollars} = \$7{,}389{,}163 \text{ (rounded)}$$

In Example 4, the U.S. firm sold the hotel for quite a profit ($1,552,723) because of a beneficial change in exchange rates. Of course, they could have lost a substantial amount if the exchange rates had moved in the opposite direction.

Let's try the U-Try-It problems.

U-Try-It (Unit 24.1)

1. A U.S. company negotiates a $45,000 sale of vegetables to a British firm. Based on an exchange rate of 1 U.S. dollar = 0.50822 British pounds, calculate the price in British pounds.
2. Sixty days later, the U.S. company gets a check for the amount determined in Problem 1. On the basis of a current exchange rate of .58420, what amount, in U.S. dollars, will the U.S. firm receive from its bank?
3. A U.S. investor buys an office building in Canada at a price of 850,000 Canadian dollars, based on an exchange rate of 1 U.S. dollar = 1.1510 Canadian dollars. The investor just sold the building at a price of 775,000 Canadian dollars based on an exchange rate of 1 U.S. dollar = 1.0183 Canadian dollars. How much money, in U.S. dollars, did the investor make or lose on the deal?

Answers: (If you have a different answer, check the solution in Appendix A.)
1. 22,869.90 pounds   2. $39,147.38   3. Made $22,584.11

Unit 24.2 Metric system: Significance in international business

The **metric system** was established over 200 years ago. The United States is the only industrial nation that has not switched to the metric system. Many industries in the United States now use the metric system and many people predict that the metric system will replace the U.S. system of measurements, meaning that measurements like inches, gallons, and pounds will be discontinued. Illustration 24-2 is a comparison between the metric system and the U.S. system of measurements.

a Writing metric terms

To specify multiple units or fractions of a unit, the basic unit (meter, liter, or gram) is preceded by a prefix:

kilo (k) means 1,000   **hecto (h)** means 100   **deka (da)** means 10

deci (d) means $\frac{1}{10}$ **centi (c)** means $\frac{1}{100}$ **milli (m)** means $\frac{1}{1{,}000}$

For example, a kilogram is 1,000 grams; a centimeter is $\frac{1}{100}$ of a meter. Metric measurements are written by following the number of units by the symbol of the prefix (k, h, da, d, c, or m) and the symbol of the base unit (m, ℓ, or g).

Illustration 24-2 Comparison Between Metric System and U.S. System

Type of measurement	Instead of	The metric system uses	Which is
length	inches, yards, miles	meter (m)	a little more than a yard
volume	quarts, gallons	liter (ℓ)	a little more than a quart
weight	ounces, pounds	gram (g)	about the weight of a raisin

Example 1   Write "7 centimeters" using the standard metric abbreviations.

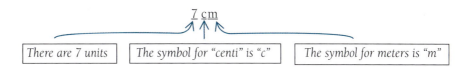

Example 2   Explain what these metric terms mean: **a.** 210 mm   **b.** 67 g

a. The first m is the symbol for the prefix milli. The second m is the symbol for the base unit meter. So 210 mm is read "210 millimeters" and means $\frac{210}{1,000}$ of a meter.

b. The g is the symbol for the base unit gram. There is no prefix. So 67g is read "67 grams" and means simply 67 grams.

---

derivation of meter, liter, and gram

Here is some interesting information. You don't need to read this, but you'll be missing out on some fun stuff if you don't.

The basic measurement of the metric system is the meter. A meter is a precise distance that was originally thought to be $\frac{1}{10,000,000}$ of the distance from the north pole to the equator. However, errors were made in the original calculations. The meter is now officially defined in relation to a certain wavelength in the atmosphere: 1,650,763.73 wavelengths of the orange light emitted from the isotope krypton 86 (that's probably more than you wanted to know). This provides a way to recalculate the exact length of a meter (most of us, however, would have a rough time even finding the wavelength, let alone measuring it).

The precise definitions of the liter and gram are derived from the meter. One liter is defined as the capacity of a cube that measures 1 decimeter on each edge. One gram is defined as the weight of 1 cubic centimeter of pure water at 4° Celsius.

---

special rules for writing metric terms

Rule	Correct	Incorrect
1. Unit names are not capitalized except for "Celsius"	I ran 100 meters.	I ran 100 Meters.
2. Leave a single space between a numeral and a symbol (°C is the exception).	My car weighs 1,455 kg.	My cars weighs 1,455kg.
3. Unit symbols are not followed by a period except at the end of a sentence.	The rope is 100 m long.	The rope is 100 m. long.
4. Write all symbols in the singular form.	The car weighs 1,400 kg.	The car weighs 1,400 kgs.
5. Use a zero before the decimal point for quantities smaller than 1; always use decimals, not fractions.	The pencil lead has a diameter of 0.2 cm.	The diameter is .2 cm. The diameter is $\frac{2}{10}$ cm.
6. Use exponents to indicate square and cubic symbols.	I need 30 m² of carpeting.	I need 30 sq m of carpeting.
7. A single space is used instead of a comma to separate numerals into groups of three digits.	Last year, I drove my car 22 345 km.	Last year, I drove my car 22,345 km.

Note: To avoid confusion, we *will disregard Rule 7*; we will use commas.

Illustration 24-3 Metric Line Indicator

The "base units" of the metric system are meter (m), liter (ℓ), and gram (g).

Prefix:	kilo (k)	hecto (h)	deka (da)	Base unit	deci (d)	centi (c)	milli (m)
Means:	1,000	100	10		$\frac{1}{10}$	$\frac{1}{100}$	$\frac{1}{1,000}$

Example 3 A U.S. auto manufacturer exports cars to Canada, providing an advertising brochure that contains the following statements. Correct any errors.

> Model R-2 has a wheelbase of 4.1 Meters, giving great stability. The car weighs only 1,210 kgs. This contributes to a fantastic 480km on a tank of gas. The spacious trunk contains 3.1 cu m of space.

> Model R-2 has a wheelbase of 4.1 meters, giving great stability. The car weighs only 1,210 kg. This contributes to a fantastic 480 km on a tank of gas. The spacious trunk contains 3.1 m³ of space.

ⓑ Converting metric to metric

Illustration 24-3 is a **metric line indicator**; it simplifies conversions from one metric measurement to another. To convert from one metric measurement to another, we move the decimal point in the direction and number of decimal places on the line indicator; add zeros if needed.

Example 4 Make these conversions: **a.** 22 km to cm **b.** 1,156 mg to g

a. Start at kilo on the line indicator of Illustration 24-3. Move to centi (5 places to the right). Move the decimal point 5 places to the right, getting

   22 km = 2200000 km = 2,200,000 cm

b. Start at milli on the line indicator. Move to the base unit (3 places to the left). Move the decimal point 3 places to the left, getting

   1,156 mg = 1156 mg = 1.156 g

ⓒ Converting metric to U.S. and U.S. to metric

Companies that do business internationally must often convert a metric measurement to a U.S. measurement or a U.S. measurement to a metric measurement. Illustration 24-4 is a conversion table for a few common measurements. Notice that the conversions require the use of *approximate* equivalents.

For products that are sold both in the U.S. and elsewhere, the label should include the U.S. measurement and the metric equivalent.

Illustration 24-4 Converting Metric to U.S. and U.S. to Metric

To convert from metric	To U.S.	Multiply by	To convert from U.S.	To metric	Multiply by
Distance					
cm	in.	.3937	in.	cm	2.54
m	in.	39.37	in.	m	.0254
m	ft	3.2808	ft	m	.3048
m	yd	1.09361	yd	m	.9144
km	mi	.62137	mi	km	1.60935
Volume					
ml	in.³	.0610247	in.³	ml	16.3868
l	qt (dry)	.9081	qt (dry)	l	1.1012
l	qt (liquid)	1.05668	qt (liquid)	l	.94636
l	gal (liquid)	.26417762	gal (liquid)	l	3.785332
l	bushel (dry)	.02837757	bushel (dry)	l	35.2391
m³	yd³	1.30794	yd³	m³	.76456
Weight					
g	oz	.035274	oz	g	28.3495
kg	lb	2.2046	lb	kg	.4536
t (metric ton)	T (ton)	1.1023	T	t	.9072

Example 5 Your company decides to market mustard worldwide. Each container holds 8 ounces. What metric weight (to the nearest gram) should appear on the label?

We will convert from ounces to grams using the right half of the weight section of Illustration 24-4.

8 oz ≈ (8 × 28.3495) g ≈ 227 g

If your primary market is in the United States, the label might state "8 oz (227 g)"; if your primary market is outside the United States, the label might state "227 g (8 oz)."

Example 6 Your company decides to market apple cider worldwide. You elect to package the cider in a 2-liter container. For labeling purposes, what is the equivalent U.S. measurement, in quarts? Round to the nearest hundredth of a quart.

We will convert from liters to quarts (liquid), using the left half of the volume section of Illustration 24-4:

2 l ≈ 2(1.05668) liquid quarts ≈ 2.11 quarts

Your label should state "2 l (2.11 quarts)."

d Making temperature conversions

In the metric system, temperature is measured in degrees **Celsius** (called **centigrade** until 1948). Anders Celsius is the name of a Swedish astronomer (1701–1744) who devised the Celsius scale; water freezes at 0°C and boils at 100°C. In the U.S. system, temperature is measured in degrees **Fahrenheit.** Gabriel Fahrenheit (1686–1736) is the name of a German physicist who devised the Fahrenheit scale; water freezes at 32°F and boils at 212°F. The Fahrenheit numbers (32° and 212°) are odd numbers, aren't they? Well, the scale was originally based on a mixture of salt and water freezing at 0°F; 100°F represents the temperature inside Gabriel Fahrenheit's mouth (I know, you didn't need to hear that!).

We convert temperatures as shown below.

> **= temperature conversions**
>
> To find Fahrenheit temperature if we know Celsius temperature, use the formula $F = \frac{9}{5}C + 32$.
>
> *First, multiply Celsius temperature by 9, divide by 5, add 32.*
>
> To find Celsius temperature if we know Fahrenheit temperature, use the formula $C = \frac{5}{9}(F - 32)$.
>
> *First, subtract 32 from Fahrenheit temperature, multiply by 5, divide by 9.*

Example 7 A U.S. company markets camera film internationally. In the United States, directions state that subjecting film to temperatures over 75°F can affect the color of the prints. What temperature (to the nearest degree) should be stated for international marketing?

$$C = \frac{5}{9}(F - 32) = \frac{5}{9}(75 - 32) = \frac{5}{9}(43) \approx 23.89 \approx 24°C$$

Subjecting film to temperatures over 24°C can affect the color of the prints.

Well, that's it for this unit. Are you ready for the U-Try-It exercises?

U-Try-It (Unit 24.2)

1. Write 15 kilograms using standard metric abbreviations.
2. Explain what 22 cm means.
3. 24.8 mm = _____ cm
4. A U.S. automaker determines that one of its cars can travel 328 miles on a tank of gas. The company is preparing an advertising brochure to be used in Europe. Find the distance in kilometers (to the nearest whole kilometer).
5. A Chamber of Commerce is preparing a brochure inviting people in Europe to vacation in Florida. If the average daily temperature during January is 72°F, what is the equivalent Celsius temperature (to the nearest whole degree)?

Answers: (If you have a different answer, check the solution in Appendix A.)
1. 15 kg   2. $\frac{22}{100}$ of a meter   3. 2.48 cm   4. 528 km   5. 22°C

Chapter in a Nutshell

Objectives	Examples

Unit 24.1 Monetary exchange rates: Significance in international business

a Determining how exchange rates affect international sales	$85,000 = _____ pesos (using Ill. 24-1): $85,000 = (85,000 × 16.9023) pesos = 1,436,695.50 pesos	
	2,230,000 Japanese yen = $_____ (using Ill. 24-1): ($\frac{2,230,000}{120.270}$) dollars = $18,541.61	
b Determining how exchange rates affect international investments	Bought storage facility in Germany for 8,500,000 euros. Sold for 8,500,000 euros. Purchased in U.S. dollars at exchange rate of 1.1230; sold at exchange rate of 0.8100. Profit or loss in U.S. dollars?	
	Sold for 8,500,000 euros = $\left(\frac{8,500,000}{0.8100}\right)$ U.S. dollars	$10,493,827.16
	Purchased for 8,500,000 euros = $\left(\frac{8,500,000}{1.1230}\right)$ U.S. dollars	- 7,569,011.58
	Profit	$ 2,924,815.58

Chapter in a Nutshell (concluded)

Objectives	Examples

Unit 24.2 Metric system: Significance in international business

a	Writing metric terms	28 centimeters, using symbols: 28 cm 150 kg means: k stands for kilo and g stands for gram, so 150 kg means 150 kilograms
b	Converting metric to metric	1.2 km = _____ cm Start at kilo on line indicator of Illustration 24-3. Move to centi (5 places to the right). Move decimal point 5 places to the right: 1.2 km = 120,000 cm
c	Converting metric to U.S. and U.S. to metric	75 kg = _____ lbs. Using Illustration 24-4: 75 kg ≈ (75 × 2.2046) lb ≈ 165.35 lb
d	Making temperature conversions	45°C = _____ °F $F = \frac{9}{5}C + 32 = \frac{9}{5}(45) + 32 = 81 + 32 = $ 113°F

Enrichment Topics

The following Enrichment Topic, which goes a bit beyond what is in the text, is available for this chapter:

Medical Dosages

If your instructor doesn't cover this topic in class and you would like to dig in deeper on your own, please send a request to *studentsupport@olympuspub.com*.

Think

1. Name some specific problems a business might encounter by doing business in a foreign country.
2. Is it possible to make a profit on an international investment and still lose money? Give an example.
3. The United States is the only industrial nation that does not use the metric system. Why do you think the United States has been slow to switch? Do you think the United States should make the switch, and why?
4. There is a temperature that is the same in both Celsius and Fahrenheit. Figure out that temperature.

Explore

1. Search on the Internet for *currency conversions* to locate 3 or 4 sites that will convert currency from one denomination to another. Decide which site you like the best. Write a report, indicating which currencies can be converted, and some of your findings.
2. Search on the Internet for currency conversions. Find the conversion rate between U.S. currency (or the country you reside in) and two countries you would like to visit.
3. Search on the Internet for *metric conversion* to locate 3 or 4 sites that have a metric conversion calculator. Experiment with each conversion calculator and decide which you like best. Write a report, indicating which conversions the metric conversion calculator performs, and some of the values you converted from U.S. to metric, and metric to U.S.

Apply

1. **Living in a Metric World**
   Record the following things in both U.S. measurements and metric measurements:
   A. Your own measurements
      Height:_____ in.; _____ cm   Waist:_____ in.; _____ cm   Weight:_____ lb; _____ kg
   B. Measurements for your home or apartment:
      Floor space:_____ sq ft; _____ m^2
      Perimeter of your kitchen:_____ ft; _____ m
      Total carpeting in your home or apartment:_____ sq yd; _____ m^2
      Total wall and ceiling area of your largest bedroom:_____ sq ft; _____ m^2
      Volume (airspace) of your home or apartment:_____ cu ft; _____ m^3
      Land size:_____ sq ft; _____ acres; _____ m^2
   C. Measurements for your auto:
      Length (bumper to bumper):_____ ft; _____ m   Wheelbase:_____ ft; _____ m
      Fuel tank volume:_____ gal; _____ ℓ   Mileage (per odometer):_____ mi; _____ km
      Top speed reading on your speedometer:_____ miles per hour; _____ km per hour
      Your gas mileage for last week:_____ miles per gallon; _____ km per liter
   D. Products in your home:
      Weight of a nonliquid product (such as pakcake mix):____ oz; ____ g (Describe product)
      Capacity of a liquid product (such as oil):_____ oz; _____ ℓ (Describe product)
   E. Temperature. Yesterday's high:_____ °F; _____ °C   Yesterday's low:_____ °F; _____ °C

2. **Investing in Money.** Suppose you purchased each foreign currency listed in Illustration 24-1. Using the exchange rates of Illustration 24-1, determine the amount of each currency you would get with an investment of 1,000 U.S. dollars. Then determine how much each currency is worth now in U.S. dollars based on *current* exchange rates. Determine which investments made money and which lost money. Which was the best investment? Submit a copy of the published current exchange rates. Show all of your calculations.

Chapter Review Problems

Unit 24.1 Monetary exchange rates: Significance in international business

1. A worldwide currency has existed since October 18, 1878. (T or F)

For Problems 2–4, use the exchange rates of Illustration 24-1 to find the equivalent amount, in the foreign currency, of 2,300 U.S. dollars. Use 2 decimal places in your answer.

2. Euros
3. British pounds
4. Japanese yen

For Problems 5–7, use the exchange rates of Illustration 24-1 to calculate the equivalent amount, in U.S. dollars.

5. 21,300 Canadian dollars
6. 975,000 British pounds
7. 65 Swiss francs
8. A U.S. company negotiates the sale of a $128,000 tractor to a Swiss firm. Using an exchange rate of 1 U.S. dollar = 1.5247 Swiss francs, calculate the price in Swiss francs.

9. Sixty days later, the U.S. company receives a check for the amount determined in Problem 8. On the basis of a current exchange rate of 1.3822, what amount, in U.S. dollars, will the U.S. firm receive from its bank?

10. Refer to Problem 9. What if the current exchange rate is 1.6744?

11. The simplest way to avoid the risk associated with fluctuating exchange rates is to insist that payment be made in your country's currency. (T or F)

12. International payments are always made by either personal or company check. (T or F)

13. A U.S. real estate investment company buys an office building in Montreal for 5,300,000 Canadian dollars. Using an exchange rate of 1 U.S. dollar = 1.0510 Canadian dollars, calculate how much money, in U.S. dollars, is needed to buy the building.

14. Refer to Problem 13. Three years later, the U.S. firm sells the building for 5,500,000 Canadian dollars. The exchange rate has changed to 1.1587. How much money, in U.S. dollars, will the U.S. firm receive?

15. Refer to Problems 13 and 14. How much money, in U.S. dollars, did the U.S. firm make or lose on the investment?

Unit 24.2 Metric system: Significance in international business

16. Very few countries use the metric system (T or F)

For Problems 17–20, pick the best choice. Try to estimate using Illustration 24-2.

17. A grapefruit weighs about (a) 2 cg or (b) 200 g.
18. A professional basketball player is how tall? (a) 2 m or (b) 2 km.
19. The distance between Los Angeles and San Francisco is (a) 650 cm or (b) 650 km.
20. An auto gas tank holds about how much gas? (a) 65 ℓ or (b) 65 mℓ.

For Problems 21–23, write the value using standard metric abbreviations.

21. 112 kilometers

22. 25 milligrams

23. 82 liters

For Problems 24–26, indicate which measurement is larger.

24. mm or cm

25. km or m

26. cg or kg

For Problems 27–29, make the conversion.

27. 850 mm = _____ cm

28. 12 hg = _____ cg

29. 1,300 mℓ = _____ ℓ

For Problems 30–35, use the approximate equivalents of Illustration 24-4 to convert the measurement. Use 2 decimal places in your answer.

30. 24 kg = _____ lb

31. 100 m = _____ yd

32. 62 ℓ = _____ gal (liquid)

33. 17.5 in. = _____ cm

34. 38 yd³ = _____ m³

35. 14.2 oz = _____ g

36. Standard-sized copy paper is 8.5 in. × 11 in. What are the metric dimensions? Use 2 decimal places for each dimension.

37. A company sells pancake mix in 60-oz packages. What is the metric equivalent (to the nearest gram)?

38. The high temperature in Chicago was 95°F. The high temperature in Rome on the same day was 38°C. Which city was warmer?

39. A normal body temperature is 98.6°F. What is the equivalent Celsius temperature?

40. On a certain winter day in Alaska, the temperature was minus 60°F (-60°F). What is the equivalent Celsius temperature (to the nearest tenth of a degree)?

Challenge problems

For Problems 41–43, consider an international transaction.

41. A U.S. firm needs 15 U.S. tons (T) of a certain mineral. How many metric tons (t) does it need? Express your answer with 3 decimal places.

42. The seller quotes a price of 975 British pounds per metric ton. Using an exchange rate of 1 U.S. dollar = .62570 British pounds, determine the equivalent U.S. price per metric ton.

43. What is the total price of the order, in U.S. dollars?

44. A plumber used the following lengths of pipe: 1.6 m, 2.5 m, 83 cm, and 4.7 m. How many total meters of pipe were used?

45. While driving to Montreal, Canada, you see a sign that reads "Montreal 483 km." If you generally drive an average of 50 miles per hour, how many hours will it take to get to Montreal?

46. After arriving in Canada on a vacation, you pull into a gas station. You notice that the price of gas is 1.40 Canadian dollars per liter. Based on an exchange rate of 1 U.S. dollar = 1.05 Canadian dollars, calculate your cost, in U.S. dollars, per U.S. gallon. *Note:* Use chain calculations, without rounding until the final answer is obtained.

47. The Washington High School track record for the 100-meter dash is 10.94 seconds. The Lincoln High School record for the 100-yard dash is 10.03 seconds. Which recordholder ran the fastest?

Practice Test

1. A U.S. company sells a $38,000 product to a Mexican firm. Calculate the price, in Mexican pesos, based on an exchange rate of 1 U.S. dollar = 10.2350 pesos.

2. Eight years ago, a U.S. company purchased an office building in London for 6,800,000 British pounds, based on an exchange rate of 1 U.S. dollar = .65320 pounds. They just sold the building for 7,500,000 British pounds, based on an exchange rate of 1 U.S. dollar = .71450 pounds. How much money, in U.S. dollars, did they make or lose on the deal?

3. Write 25 kilometers using standard metric abbreviations.

4. Convert 1.05 mg to g.

5. Your company markets almonds worldwide. Each container holds 12.5 ounces. Use the approximate equivalents of Illustration 24-4 to determine what metric weight (to the nearest gram) should appear on the label.

6. While vacationing in New Zealand, you hear that the temperature is 30°. You realize, since it is a nice warm day, the temperature is stated in degrees Celsius. What is the equivalent Fahrenheit temperature?

Classroom Notes

FUN CORNER

The 50-50-90 Rule
Anytime you have a 50-50 chance of getting something right, there is a 90% probability you'll get it wrong.

Quotable Quip
It is proven that the celebration of birthdays is healthy. Statistics show that those people who celebrate the most birthdays become the oldest.
– S. den Hartog, PhD,
Univ. of Groningen

Worth Repeating
A statistician had his head in a hot oven and his feet in a bucket of ice. When asked how he felt, he replied "On average, I feel fine."

Lawn-Care Statistics
**From *Homes and Other Black Holes*
by Dave Barry**

We Americans can make the proud boast that no other nation cares for its lawns as much as we do. Lawn care has made America what it is today, as can be shown by this chart:

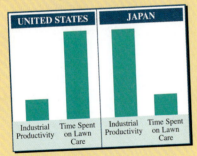

I have, over the years, learned a few basic facts about lawn care, the two major ones being:

- If you fail to feed, fertilize, and water your lawn, it will die.
- If you feed, fertilize, and water your lawn, it will die.

Quotable Quip
Statistics show that marriage is the leading cause of divorce.
– Groucho Marx

Quotable Quip
Statistics show that if you drop a piece of bread, it always lands buttered-side down.
– Author unknown

"We've done an in-depth study, and found that 42% of all statistics are wrong."

Statistics: An Introduction

25

Statistics is the process of collecting, organizing, interpreting, and presenting numerical data. There are entire volumes written on the subject of statistics; this chapter is intended only as an introduction.

Business decisions are often based on raw numerical data. For example, before building a theater complex, a prospective owner would be interested in several kinds of data, including: (a) population within a certain radius, (b) age-group breakdown for the population, (c) spendable income of the population, (d) attendance and ticket prices at nearby theaters, and (e) growth trends and economic forecast. While we will not focus on gathering the raw data, we will study several methods used to interpret and present the data.

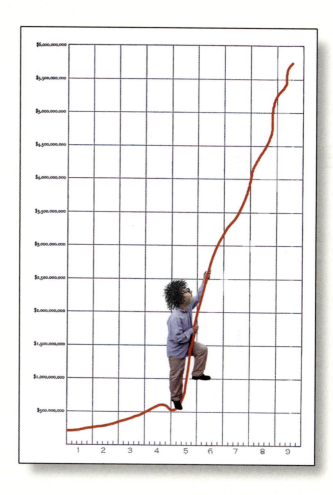

Unit Objectives

Unit 25.1 The three Ms: Mean, median, and mode
- **a** Finding the mean
- **b** Finding the median
- **c** Finding the mode

Unit 25.2 Graphs: Presenting data so it is easy to understand
- **a** Preparing a line graph
- **b** Preparing a bar graph
- **c** Preparing a circle graph
- **d** Graphing grouped data

Unit 25.3 Measures of dispersion
- **a** Finding the range
- **b** Finding the standard deviation

Unit 25.1 The three Ms: Mean, median, and mode

In this unit, we will examine ways of finding a single number that is designed to represent an entire group of numbers; this single number is said to be the average for the entire group of numbers. The most common averages are the three Ms: mean, median, and mode.

a Finding the mean

The **mean** is the *arithmetic average* and is found by dividing the sum of values by the number of values.

> **mean**
>
> $$\text{Mean} = \frac{\text{Sum of values}}{\text{Number of values}}$$

Example 1 A movie theater recorded its weekly ticket sales as shown. Determine the average (mean) ticket sales per week for the 5-week period.

Week 1: 8,515   Week 2: 7,722   Week 3: 7,185   Week 4: 7,904   Week 5: 9,439

$$\text{Mean} = \frac{\text{Sum of values}}{\text{Number of values}} = \frac{8{,}515 + 7{,}722 + 7{,}185 + 7{,}904 + 9{,}439}{5} = \frac{40{,}765}{5} = 8{,}153$$

The average number of tickets sold per week was 8,153.

When values appear more than once, we can use a shortcut to find the mean. Rather than add all individual values, we multiply the frequency by each value to get a product; then we add the products and divide by the total number of frequencies. The result is referred to as a **weighted mean** (or **weighted average**).

> **weighted mean**
>
> $$\text{Weighted mean} = \frac{\text{Sum of products}}{\text{Sum of frequencies}}$$

Example 2 You own a company that manufactures tennis rackets. You make four models. Price and monthly sales for each model are shown in the table. Determine the average price per racket sold during the month.

Model	Price per racket	Number sold
beginner model	$45	28
basic	$57	42
midsize	$68	65
widebody	$97	38

Value		Frequency		Product
$45	×	28	=	$ 1,260
$57	×	42	=	2,394
$68	×	65	=	4,420
$97	×	38	=	3,686
		173		$11,760

$$\text{Weighted mean} = \frac{\text{Sum of products}}{\text{Sum of frequencies}} = \frac{\$11{,}760}{173} = \$67.98$$

The average price per racket sold for the month is $67.98.

In Example 2, the relative importance of each price is different depending on the number of rackets sold, so each price is "weighted" according to its frequency. A **grade point average (GPA)** is based on a weighted average; a GPA is the *average grade per hour of credit*. Getting an A in a 5-hour class has the same effect on a GPA as five 1-hour As. For those who get all As, figuring a GPA is not difficult. But some of us get an occasional B (or worse), don't we? The next example shows how to calculate a GPA.

Statistics are useful in evaluating performance. A grade point average (GPA) is a statistical measure that reflects the average grade per credit hour.

Example 3   Tom Bryant's school uses the following grade points:

A	4.0	B+	3.3	C+	2.3	D+	1.3	F	0.0
A-	3.7	B	3.0	C	2.0	D	1.0		
		B-	2.7	C-	1.7	D-	0.7		

For this last semester, Tom got a B- in Accounting (5 hours), a B+ in Computer Science (3 hours), an A in Tennis (1 hour), and an A in Business Math (5 hours). Help Tom calculate his GPA (Tom probably doesn't need help if he got an A in Business Math, does he?).

_____

Course	Grade	Hours	Grade-point units
Accounting	B-	5	2.7 × 5 = 13.50
Computer Science	B+	3	3.3 × 3 = 9.90
Tennis	A	1	4.0 × 1 = 4.00
Business Math	A	5	4.0 × 5 = 20.00
		14	47.40 ÷ 14 ≈ **3.39**

Tom's GPA for the last semester is 3.39 (slightly higher than a B+).

b   Finding the median

If a group of numbers has one or more *extremely* low or high numbers, the mean is distorted and may not properly represent the average of the values.

Example 4   A real estate office sold five homes during the week: $185,000, $165,000, $135,000, $190,000, and $1,875,000. Find the mean (average) price.

_____

$$\text{Mean} = \frac{\text{Sum of values}}{\text{Number of values}} = \frac{\$185{,}000 + \$165{,}000 + \$135{,}000 + \$190{,}000 + \$1{,}875{,}000}{5} = \frac{\$2{,}550{,}000}{5} = \mathbf{\$510{,}000}$$

In Example 4, notice how the $1,875,000 sale distorted the average. The mean ($510,000) is much larger than the second highest price and doesn't seem to represent the average selling price. When a group of numbers has an extreme value, the **median** may be a better indicator of the average. The median is the *value at the midpoint* when the numbers from a set are arranged from high to low.

> **median**
>
> **Step 1**   Arrange the values from high to low.
>
> **Step 2**   Find the midpoint: Midpoint = $\dfrac{\text{Number of values} + 1}{2}$
>
>   **a.** *Odd number of values.* Median is the midpoint.
>   **b.** *Even number of values.* There will be two values that share the midpoint, so the median is the average of the two middle numbers.

Unit 25.1   The three Ms: Mean, median, and mode

Example 5   Refer to Example 4. Find the median value.

Step 1 (arrange values)   **Step 2 (find midpoint)**

$1,875,000   Midpoint = $\frac{\text{Number of values} + 1}{2} = \frac{5+1}{2} = \frac{6}{2} = 3$

$190,000

$185,000 ← *The median is the third highest value*

$165,000

$135,000

The median price is $185,000.

Example 5 had an *odd* number of values (5). The next example has an *even* number of values.

Example 6   Silvana Gonzalez owns an appliance store. Weekly sales for the month of February are shown. Calculate the median weekly sales.

Week 1: $42,000   Week 2: $34,000   Week 3: $64,500   Week 4: $45,800

Step 1 (arrange values)   **Step 2 (find midpoint)**

$64,500   Midpoint = $\frac{\text{Nubmer of values} + 1}{2} = \frac{4+1}{2} = \frac{5}{2} = 2.5$

$45,800

$42,000   *The midpoint is between the second and third values*: ($45,800 + $42,000) ÷ 2 = $43,900

$34,000

C Finding the mode

The **mode** is the value that occurs the *most often*. We do not have to arrange the numbers from high to low, although doing so may make it easier to identify the mode.

Example 7   Scores on a business math exam were: 95, 100, 80, 75, 85, 100, 95, 65, 75, 70, 85, 90, and 100. What is the mode?

Because 100 is listed most often (3 times), the mode is 100.

As in Example 7, the mode often does not represent the *average* value; it merely shows which value occurs most often.

If each value in a set of numbers occurs the same number of times, there is no mode (such as with scores of 100, 98, 95, 92, and 71). If two or more values occur most often, we have more than one mode; for scores of 100, 95, 95, 90, 85, 85, and 70, there are two modes (95 and 85).

Well, that does it for this unit. Let's see if our understanding is above or below *average* by doing the U-Try-It exercises.

U-Try-It (Unit 25.1)

Taufa Pua owns a computer store. Six computers were sold at the following prices. $1,350, $850, $1,475, $850, $3,900, and $1,100.
1. What is the mean price?
2. What is the median price?
3. What is the mode?
4. Which indicator (mean, median, or mode) best represents the average selling price?

Answers: (If you have a different answer, check the solution in Appendix A.)
1. $1,587.50   2. $1,225   3. $850   4. Median

Unit 25.2 Graphs: Presenting data so it is easy to understand

Data is often presented in table form. Illustration 25-1 shows departmental sales for ABC Grocery over the last 5 years.

Illustration 25-1   Sales, ABC Grocery, Last 5 Years

Department	Year 1	Year 2	Year 3	Year 4	Year 5
Bakery	$174,000	$228,000	$234,000	$250,000	$289,000
Frozen Food	279,000	312,000	344,000	301,000	323,000
Grocery	441,000	442,000	474,000	488,000	527,000
Meat	235,000	245,000	305,000	354,000	391,000
Produce	102,000	112,000	148,000	195,000	170,000
Totals	$1,231,000	$1,339,000	$1,505,000	$1,588,000	$1,700,000

Data is easier to understand if it can be visualized. A **graph** allows us to visualize complex data in an understandable way. The most common graphs are line graphs, bar graphs, circle graphs, and graphs for grouped data.

a Preparing a line graph

The table of Illustration 25-1 contains lots of data but is not great for seeing the big picture at a glance. A **line graph** is ideal for showing trends over a period of time. Some line graphs show the trend for several items, each represented by a different line. Illustration 25-2 shows ABC's departmental sales for the last 5 years.

> **preparing a line graph**
>
> In preparing a line graph, here are a few guidelines:
> - Time intervals are on the horizontal (bottom) axis.
> - Amounts (with even increments) are on the vertical (left) axis.
> - Points are plotted that correspond to the year and dollar amount.
> - The points are connected with straight lines.

Illustration 25-2   Line Graph Showing Departmental Sales, ABC Grocery, Last 5 Years

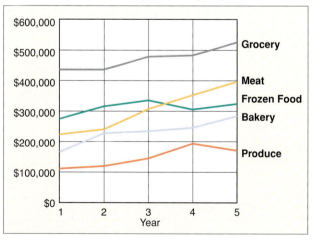

> **TIP** — don't be a victim of graph abuse
>
> Graphs can make good trends look better. These two graphs show identical data for ABC's Grocery Department for the last 5 years. The graph on the left has a vertical scale starting at zero; this graph is prepared properly. The graph on the right does not start at zero and squeezes the years closer together, giving the false impression that sales have skyrocketed. Graphs can also make bad trends look not so bad. By elongating the horizontal time line and squeezing the vertical dollar line closer together, downward trends appear flatter, giving the false impression that sales are not dropping as rapidly as they are. *Don't be misled by improperly prepared graphs.*
>
>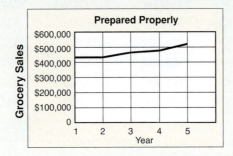

b Preparing a bar graph

A **bar graph** shows quantities by the length of vertical or horizontal bars and allows us to see the relationship between values quickly. We will study two types of bar graphs: standard and stacked. Let's first look at a *standard bar graph*, shown in Illustration 25-3; this shows ABC's frozen food sales over the last 5 years. Notice that sales volume is indicated on the vertical (left) axis and bars extend *vertically* (up); this type of bar graph is called a *vertical bar graph*. A bar graph in which bars run *horizontally* (from left to right) is called a *horizontal bar graph*.

> **preparing a bar graph**
>
> In preparing a bar graph, here are a few guidelines:
> - Bars should be the same width.
> - The length of the bar is, of course, determined by the data.
> - Customarily, a space is left between the axis and the first bar and a space is left between bars; the space is about one-half the width of the bar itself.
> - Even increments should be used for the vertical or horizontal scales.

Illustration 25-3   Standard Bar Graph, ABC's Frozen Food Sales, Last 5 Years

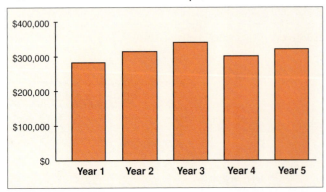

Illustration 25-4 Stacked Bar Graph Showing Sales, ABC Grocery, Last 5 Years

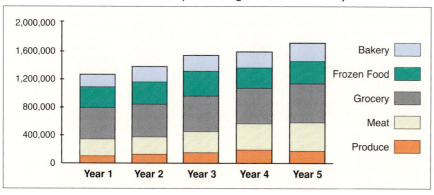

With a **stacked bar graph**, two or more bars are stacked together to show parts of a whole. Illustration 25-4 is a stacked bar graph showing ABC sales for the last 5 years.

C Preparing a circle graph

A **circle graph**, also known as a **pie chart**, is an ideal way to present parts of a whole. Illustration 25-5 is a circle graph that shows the Year 5 sales data for ABC. Preparing a circle graph is trickier than preparing a line graph or bar graph; here are some steps to follow.

---

preparing a circle graph

Step 1 Determine the percent for each segment; do this by dividing each portion by the whole amount.

Step 2 Multiply the percent for each segment by 360 degrees (360°); remember, there are 360° in a complete circle. The result is the number of degrees that should be allocated to that segment.

Step 3 Draw a circle. Use a protractor to divide the circle; start at the top (12:00 position) and move clockwise.

In reviewing Illustration 25-5, pay special attention to the calculations. As you may recall, to convert a decimal number to a percent, we move the decimal point two places to the right and add a percent sign.

You may wonder which type of graph is best. It depends on the situation. Line graphs and bar graphs are ideal for showing a trend. To show trends for several departments, a line graph with a line for each department is probably better than a bar graph. To show parts of a whole for one period, a circle graph is ideal; for successive periods, a stacked bar graph works well.

Illustration 25-5 Circle Graph Showing Departmental Sales, ABC Grocery, Most Recent Year

Department	Step 1 (find percents)	Step 2 (find degrees)	Step 3 (divide circle)
Bakery	$289,000 ÷ $1,700,000 = .17 = 17%	.17 × 360° = 61.20°	
Frozen food	$323,000 ÷ $1,700,000 = .19 = 19%	.19 × 360° = 68.40°	
Grocery	$527,000 ÷ $1,700,000 = .31 = 31%	.31 × 360° = 111.60°	
Meat	$391,000 ÷ $1,700,000 = .23 = 23%	.23 × 360° = 82.80°	
Produce	$170,000 ÷ $1,700,000 = .10 = 10%	.10 × 360° = 36.00°	
	$1,700,000 100%	360.00°	

Unit 25.2 Graphs: Presenting data so it is easy to understand

Illustration 25-6 Bar Graph (Grouped Data), Joe's Used Cars

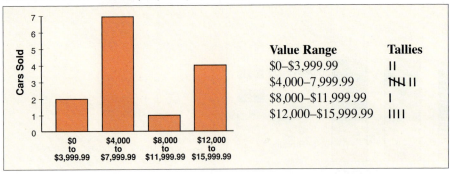

Value Range	Tallies
$0–$3,999.99	II
$4,000–7,999.99	ℍ II
$8,000–$11,999.99	I
$12,000–$15,999.99	IIII

d Graphing grouped data

Often, it makes sense to graph data in groups. For example, assume that Joe's Used Cars sold 14 cars during the week, at prices of $3,700; $5,800; $7,900; $14,700; $9,500; $2,100; $12,600; $12,400; $15,800; $6,200; $5,100; $7,400; $4,100; and $7,600. Joe likes to know the number of sales within each $4,000 price increment. Illustration 25-6 is a bar graph showing the number of sales for increments of $4,000. Included is the tally count for each price range.

> **preparing a bar graph for grouped data**
>
> In addition to the guidelines for preparing a basic bar graph, here are a few additional guidelines.
> - Use groups of equal increments (like the $4,000 increment of Illustration 25-6).
> - Prepare a tally sheet showing the number within each interval.
> - The length of the each bar corresponds to the number within that interval.

> **TIP   computer aids**
>
> Many computer software programs will prepare graphs. For example, with data in table form, we can choose to have the data printed as a line graph, bar graph, or circle graph. We can make lots of choices, such as having the graph in three dimensions and color. Explore Activity 2 gives the opportunity to do this.

Let's try a few U-try-It questions about graphs.

U-Try-It (Unit 25.2)

1. Prepare a line graph showing annual revenues for an accounting business for the last 5 years.
   Year 1: $64,000   Year 2: $78,000   Year 3: $112,000   Year 4: $115,000   Year 5: $184,000
2. Prepare a standard bar graph showing convenience store sales for the most recent month.
   Food: $155,000   Beverages: $230,000   Gas: $370,000
3. Prepare a circle graph for a car dealership based on a percent of sales revenue.
   New cars: 58%   Used cars: 12%   Service department: 22%   Parts department: 8%

Answers: Because the answers are graphs, they are shown only in Appendix A.

Unit 25.3 Measures of dispersion

In Unit 25.1, we calculated the mean, median, and mode. The mean, median, and mode are often referred to as *measures of central tendency* because they represent the average, center, or most often occurring value for a group of numbers. But to get the big picture we also need to know how "scattered" (or dispersed) the numbers are. We will examine two measure of dispersion: range and standard deviation.

a Finding the range

The simplest measure of dispersion, the **range**, is the difference between the highest value and the lowest value in a set of data.

Example 1 A tent manufacturing company observes 6 sewing specialists and records the time it takes each to sew a tent: 83 minutes, 77 minutes, 91 minutes, 73 minutes, 80 minutes, and 82 minutes. What is the range?

Range = 91 (highest value) - 73 (lowest value) = 18

The range is 18 minutes.

b Finding the standard deviation

The range tells us the difference between the highest and lowest value, but does not tell us how scattered the other values are. The most widely used measure of dispersion is the **standard deviation**. The standard deviation indicates how much each value in a data set deviates from the mean.

Data are often gathered for an entire group. A study that gathers data from every member of a group it wishes to draw conclusions about is known as a **population study**. To calculate the standard deviation for a population study, we first find the mean. We then subtract the mean from each value to determine how much it differs (deviates) from the mean. For statistical reasons, we square each deviation, add all the squared deviations, and divide by the number of values in the set. Finally, we calculate the square root to obtain the standard deviation.

You are probably saying, Are you kidding me? But as you will see, the process is not as tricky as it may first appear. As you may recall, to square a number we multiply the number by itself. And, the square root is a number that when multiplied by itself equals the value we are finding the square root of; for example, the square root of 16 is 4, since 4 × 4 = 16. We can find the square root of a number by trial and error, or we can use a calculator with a square root key ($\sqrt{\ }$).

standard deviation for a population study

Step 1 Find the mean.
Step 2 Subtract the mean from each value to find each deviation.
Step 3 Square each deviation (multiply each deviation by itself).
Step 4 Add all squared deviations
Step 5 Divide the sum of the squared deviations by n, where n equals the number of values in the set.
Step 6 Find the square root of the result of Step 5.

Example 2 A tent manufacturing company has 6 sewing specialists. Each specialist is observed to determine the time it takes to sew a tent: 83 minutes, 77 minutes, 91 minutes, 73 minutes, 80 minutes, and 82 minutes. Find the standard deviation.

Step 1 Mean = $\frac{\text{Sum of values}}{n}$ = $\frac{83 + 77 + 91 + 73 + 80 + 82}{6}$ = $\frac{486}{6}$ = 81

Step 2 (Subtract Mean)	Step 3 (Square the result)
83 - 81 = 2	(2)(2) = 4
77 - 81 = -4	(-4)(-4) = 16
91 - 81 = 10	(10)(10) = 100
73 - 81 = -8	(-8)(-8) = 64
80 - 81 = -1	(-1)(-1) = 1
82 - 81 = 1	(1)(1) = 1

Step 4 (add squared deviations): 4 + 16 + 100 + 64 + 1 + 1 = 186

Step 5 (divide by *n*): 186 ÷ 6 = 31

Step 6 (square root): Find the square root of 31.

One way to find the square root is by trial and error. 5 × 5 = 25; we want the result to be 31, so 5 is too low. 6 × 6 = 36, so 6 is too high. The square root of 31 is somewhere between 5 and 6, but closer to 6. Let's try 5.55: 5.55 × 5.55 = 30.80 (too low). Let's try 5.57: 5.57 × 5.57 = 31.02 (very close). The square root of 31 is approximately 5.57.

An easier way to find the square root is to use a calculator that has a square root key. For most calculators, enter 31, and then press the square root key ($\sqrt{}$). The result appears: 5.57 (with 2 decimal places).

The standard deviation is about 5.57; this means that, on average, these sewing specialists took 5.57 minutes more, or 5.57 minutes less, than the 81-minute average.

In some cases, gathering data on an *entire group* is not practical. For example, if a light bulb manufacturer wants to determine the life span of all light bulbs, each light bulb could be tested to see how long it lasts. It is hard, however, to find buyers for burned out light bulbs! In this case a population study (one in which we gather data from every member of the group we want to draw conclusions about), is not practical. Instead, for a batch of 20,000 bulbs, the company could randomly select and test 100 bulbs. The 100 bulbs tested are known as a *sample*, and the study is known as a **sample study**. Test results from the sample of 100 bulbs is deemed to be representative of the entire population of 20,000 bulbs.

In Example 2, we assumed that the company has only 6 sewing specialists. If the company has a total of 50 sewing specialists, the observation of 6 of the specialists could be considered a sample study to draw conclusions about all 50; the data from the 6 sewing specialists are an *approximate* representation of the entire population. To allow some room for error in the standard deviation of the sample so it is likely more representative of the whole population set, we divide the sum of the squared deviations (in Step 5) by (*n* - 1) rather than by *n*; this has the effect of increasing the standard deviation.

standard deviation for a sample study

Step 1 Find the mean.
Step 2 Subtract the mean from each value to find each deviation.
Step 3 Square each deviation (multiply each deviation by itself).
Step 4 Add all squared deviations
Step 5 Divide the sum of the squared deviations by (*n* - 1), where *n* equals the number of values in the set.
Step 6 Find the square root of the result of Step 5.

Example 3   A tent manufacturing company has 50 sewing specialists. A sample study is conducted in which 6 of the specialist are observed to draw conslusions about all 50 sewing specialists. Here are the times it took each of the 6 specialists to sew a tent: 83 minutes, 77 minutes, 91 minutes, 73 minutes, 80 minutes, and 82 minutes. Find the standard deviation for the entire group of sewing specialists.

Refer to Example 2. For Example 3, the only difference is in Step 5 (we divide the result of Step 4 by (n - 1) instead of by n. So, rather than re-do Steps 1 through 4, let's start with the result of Step 4 from Example 2:

Step 4 (add squared deviations): 4 + 16 + 100 + 64 + 1 + 1 = 186

Step 5 (divide by (n - 1): 186 ÷ 5 = 37.20

Step 6 (square root): Find the square root of 37.20.

Using a calculator that has a square root key, enter 37.20, an then press the square root key ($\sqrt{}$). The result appear: 6.10 (with 2 decimal places).

The standard deviation is about 6.10. In drawing conclusions *about all 50 sewing specialists*, we can conclude that, on average, the specialists take 6.10 minutes more, or 6.10 minutes less, than the 81-minute average.

The standard deviation for a sample study (6.10 in Example 3) is always greater than the standard deviation for a population study (5.57 in Example 2). That's because statisticians want to allow a little room for error on a sample study because the data are from only part of the entire group they want to draw conclusions about.

Finding the mean, median, mode, and standard deviation can be time-consuming. To save time, we can calculate mean, median, mode, range, and standard deviation by using Excel®; see the instructions for Explore Activity 1. We can also use calculators that have statistical keys. Let's use the HP 10BII+ and TI BAII PLUS to confirm the results of Examples 2 and 3.

HP 10BII+			TI BAII PLUS			
clear statistics registers			*clear statistics registers*			
▼ C STAT		0.00	2ND DATA 2ND CLR WORK			X01 0.00
enter data			*enter data*			
83	Σ+	1.00	83	ENTER		X01= 83.00
77	Σ+	2.00	↓ ↓ 77	ENTER		X02= 77.00
91	Σ+	3.00	↓ ↓ 91	ENTER		X03= 91.00
73	Σ+	4.00	↓ ↓ 73	ENTER		X04= 73.00
80	Σ+	5.00	↓ ↓ 80	ENTER		X05= 80.00
82	Σ+	6.00	↓ ↓ 82	ENTER		X06= 82.00
find mean			*find mean*			
▼ $\bar{x},\bar{y}$		81.00	2ND STAT 2ND SET…, if necessary*			1-V
find std dev of population study			↓ ↓			$\bar{x}$= 81.00
▼ σx,σy		5.57	*find std dev of sample study*			
find std dev of sample study			↓			Sx= 6.10
▼ Sx,Sy		6.10	*find std dev of population study*			
			↓			σx= 5.57
			2ND QUIT			0.00

*Note: Press 2ND SET until "1-V" appears

You may say, Why did we waste our time doing these calculations the long way when they are so easy to do on a calculator? The reason, of course, was to insure that concepts are understood.

Well, that's if for this unit, this chapter, and *the entire text!* Congratulations! Hopefully as a result of completing the text you feel more confident about business and investing. Good luck in your ventures.

U-Try-It (Unit 25.3)

Jill Davies teaches Business Math. Her 10:00 class has 6 students. Test scores on a certain test are 100, 87, 92, 71, 78, and 100.
1. What is the range?
2. What is the standard deviation for this class?
3. Jill teaches two other business math classes. What is the standard deviation of all 3 classes, using the class of 6 students as a simple study?

Answers: (If you have a different answer, check the solution in Appendix A.)
1. 29   2. 10.75   3. 11.78

Chapter in a Nutshell

Objectives	Examples

Unit 25.1 The three Ms: Mean, median, and mode

a Finding the mean

Jared's business math test scores: 72, 90, 78, 84, 95, 100, and 90. Average (mean) score?

$$\text{Mean} = \frac{\text{Sum of values}}{\text{Number of values}} = \frac{72 + 90 + 78 + 84 + 95 + 100 + 90}{7} = \frac{609}{7} = 87$$

Tina owns a 24-unit apartment building. Ten rents are $600, eight are $625, and six are $700. Average rent?

Value	Frequency	Product
$600	× 10 =	$ 6,000
$625	× 8 =	5,000
$700	× 6 =	4,200
	24	$15,200

$$\text{Weighted Mean} = \frac{\text{Sum of products}}{\text{Sum of frequencies}} = \frac{\$15,200}{24} = \$633.33$$

b Finding the median

A-1 Realty home sales for week: $245,000, $128,000, $475,000, $185,000, $240,000. Median price?

Step 1 (arrange values)
$475,000
$245,000
$240,000 ← The median is the third highest value
$185,000
$128,000

Step 2 (find midpoint)

$$\text{Midpoint} = \frac{\text{Number of values} + 1}{2} = \frac{5+1}{2} = \frac{6}{2} = 3$$

c Finding the mode

Ages of students in an accounting class: 18, 21, 38, 19, 20, 18, 19, 20, 19, 57, 19, 32, and 18. Mode?

19 occurs the most often (4 times), so the mode is 19 (more students are 19 than any other age).

Unit 25.2 Graphs: Presenting data so it is easy to understand

a Preparing a line graph

Number of accounting clients:
Year 1: 18
Year 2: 23
Year 3: 60

b Preparing a bar graph

See above.

530   Chapter 25   Statistics: An Introduction

Chapter in a Nutshell (concluded)

Objectives	Examples
c Preparing a circle graph	Of 120 employees, 18 are administrators, 30 are in sales, and 72 are in manufacturing.

Department	Percent of Total	Degrees
Administration	$18 \div 120 = .15 = $ 15%	$.15 \times 360° = 54°$
Sales	$30 \div 120 = .25 = $ 25%	$.25 \times 360° = 90°$
Manufacturing	$\underline{72} \div 120 = .60 = \underline{60\%}$	$.60 \times 360° = \underline{216°}$
	120 100%	360°

d Graphing grouped data

Friendly Computer Company sold 18 computers this week: $795; $1,900; $1,300; $690; $2,400; $1,200; $759; $895; $995; $1,100; $1,100; $1,900; $690; $1,750; $1,200; $2,400; $895; and $1,300. Owner wants to see a bar graph, grouping in increments of $1,000.

Value range	Tallies
$0–$999.99	∭ II
$1,000–$1,999.99	∭ IIII
$2,000–$2,999.99	II

Unit 25.3 Measures of dispersion

a Finding the range

Ages of students in a college class: 19, 21, 47, 33, 18, and 24. Range? $47 - 18 = 29$

b Finding the standard deviation

See above. Standard deviation for this class?

Step 1   Mean = $\dfrac{\text{Sum of values}}{n} = \dfrac{19 + 21 + 47 + 33 + 18 + 24}{6} = \dfrac{162}{6} = 27$

Step 2 (Subtract Mean)	**Step 3** (Square the result)
19 - 27 = -8	(-8)(-8) = 64
21 - 27 = -6	(-6)(-6) = 36
47 - 27 = 20	(20)(20) = 400
33 - 27 = 6	(6)(6) = 36
18 - 27 = -9	(-9)(-9) = 81
24 - 27 = -3	(-3)(-3) = 9

Step 4 (add squared deviations): 64 + 36 + 400 + 36 + 81 + 9 = 626

Step 5 (divide by *n*): 626 ÷ 6 = 104.33

Step 6 (square root): The square root of 104.33 is 10.21

See above. Draw conclusions about all 250 business students at the college, using this class as a sample study. Standard deviation?

Step 4 (above): 626

Step 5 (divide by *n* - 1): 626 ÷ 5 = 125.20

Step 6 (square root): The square root of 125.20 is 11.19

Enrichment Topics

The following Enrichment Topics, which go a bit beyond what is in the text, are available for this chapter:

Normal Curve
Linear Regression
Calculating the Probability of Something Happening

If your instructor doesn't cover these topics in class and you would like to dig in deeper on your own, please send a request to *studentsupport@olympuspub.com*.

Think

1. Explain the difference between mean, median, and mode.
2. Give an example of when a mean might not be the best indicator of an average for a group of numbers.
3. Explain why we might want to show data in graph form, rather than in table form.

Explore

1. We can use Excel to determine the mean, median, and mode of a set of numbers. For example, if you enter data in Cells B2 through B26, we can calculate the mean in Cell B27 by typing =AVERAGE(B2:B26). To find the median, we type =MEDIAN(B2:B26). To find the mode, we type =MODE(B2:B26). To find the range, we type =RANGE(B2:B26). To find the standard deviation for a population study, we type =STDEVP(B2:B26). To find the standard deviation for a sample study, we type =STDEV(B2:B26). Use the data of Chapter Review Problems 4-7, in which home sales during the week were $125,000, $115,000, $195,000, $88,000, $150,000, $135,000, $245,000, $110,000, $165,000, $88,000, $665,000, and $145,000. Enter the prices in Column A, Rows 1 through 12. In Cell A14, type a formula for mean. In Cell A15, type a formula for median. In Cell A16, type a formula for mode. Compare your results with the answers to Chapter Review Problems 4-6. Then, in Cell A17, type a formula for range. In Cell A18, type a formula to find the standard deviation for a population study. In Cell A19, type a formula to find the standard deviation for a sample study.
2. Refer to Illustration 27-1 (Sales, ABC Grocery, Last 5 Years). Enter the same data on an Excel spreadsheet (rows 1-6) and write formulas for the Totals row (Row 7). Then use Excel to show the data as a line graph, standard bar graph, stacked bar graph, and circle graph. For all graphs except the circle graph, highlight data on all rows except Row 7 (totals), click the Insert tab, then select the type of graph so it resembles Ill. 25-2, 25-3, and 25-4. Move each graph to a sheet at the bottom of the worksheet (you may have to create extra sheets). For the circle graph, highlight the data in Year 5 (except the total), click the Insert tab, pie chart, and then select the type of chart that shows %.

Apply

1. **Conduct a Survey.** Select something you think is normally distributed at your college (such as age, grade point average, height of men, height of women, neck size, years a person has owned the same car, and hours working each week). Gather the data on at least 100 people (include the names of all people; get their permission). Calculate the mean, median, mode, range, and standard deviation for those 100 people. Decide which measure best represents the average. Submit all of your data and calculations.

Chapter Review Problems

Unit 25.1 The three Ms: Mean, median, and mode

For Problems 1-3, consider test scores: 79, 87, 94, 67, 92, 94, 82.

1. What is the mean?

2. What is the median?

3. What is the mode?

For Problems 4–7, consider the 12 home sales of Action Real Estate during the week: $125,000; $115,000; $195,000; $88,000; $150,000; $135,000; $245,000; $110,000; $165,000; $88,000; $665,000; and $145,000.

4. What is the mean?

5. What is the median?

6. What is the mode?

7. Which indicator (mean, median, or mode) best represents the average selling price?

For Problems 8 and 9, consider July sales for Bob's Hot Tubs. Bob sells four models.

Model	Price	Number sold
Economy	$4,700	8
Midsize	$5,900	13
Large	$6,800	11
Luxury	$8,700	5

8. What is the average (mean) price of the product line?

9. What is the average (mean) price of hot tubs sold during July?

10. Assume that your school uses grade points shown below. Calculate your GPA (with two decimal places) based on the following grades: a B+ in Accounting (5 hrs), a B- in Computer Science (3 hrs), an A in Golf (1 hr), and an A- in Management (3 hrs).

A 4.0	B+ 3.3	C+ 2.3	D+ 1.3	F 0.0
A- 3.7	B 3.0	C 2.0	D 1.0	
	B- 2.7	C- 1.7	D- 0.7	

Unit 25.2 Graphs: Presenting data so it is easy to understand

For Problems 11 and 12, consider revenues of Rocky Mountain River Expeditions.

Year 1: $452,000   Year 2: $585,000   Year 3: $813,000   Year 4: $638,000   Year 5: $955,000

11. Prepare a line graph; use increments of $200,000.   **12.** Prepare a vertical bar graph; use increments of $200,000.

For Problems 13–15, consider the following horizontal bar graph, showing the length of the five longest rivers in the world.

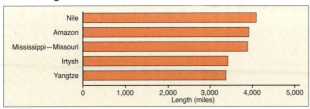

13. Which river is the longest?

14. Approximately how long is the Amazon?

15. Approximately how much longer is the Nile than the Mississippi–Missouri?

For Problems 16 and 17, suppose a survey shows how many hours per week the average American adult spends for various activities: 54 hours for sleep, 27 hours for work, 14 hours for family care, 23 hours for personal care, and 50 hours for leisure.

16. In constructing a circle graph, how many degrees (to the nearest tenth) are allocated to each activity? Remember, use chain calculations.

17. Use a protractor to construct a circle graph. Show percents (to the nearest tenth of a percent) for each segment.

18. A used car dealer sold 15 cars during the week at prices of $4,200; $13,300; $7,900; $1,800; $12,000; $12,800; $8,300; $4,900; $10,800; $7,700; $5,100; $6,600; $7,500; $3,300; and $10,900. Prepare a bar graph for grouped data using increments of $3,000 (the first increment is $0 to $2,999.99).

19. A department manager is preparing a line graph reflecting department sales. Which graph (a, b, or c) makes the bad trend look not so bad?

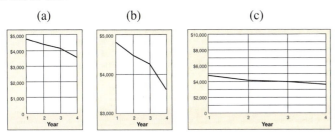

For Problems 20–22, refer to the stacked bar graph, showing the number of cars sold by price range.

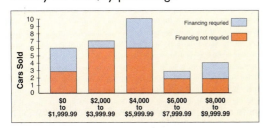

20. Which increment has the most cars sold?

21. How many cars were sold in the $2,000 to $3,999.99 range?

22. How many cars required financing in the $0 to $1,999.99 range?

Unit 25.3 Measures of dispersion

23. You survey 5 members of a college class about how many hours of exercise they get per week: 5 hours, 7 hours, 1 hour, 14 hours, and 8 hours. What is the range?

24. Refer to Problem 23. What is the standard deviation for these 5 students?

25. Refer to Problems 23 and 24. The class has a total of 24 students. Based on the findings from the 5 students your interviewed, what is the standard deviation for the entire class?

Challenge problems

26. Your savings account balance at the end of May was $400. You made a $225 deposit on June 5 and withdrew $150 on June 28. Calculate your average (mean) daily balance for June.

27. Your test scores so far are 84, 93, 87, 94, and 88. What score do you need on your last test to end up with an average (mean) score of 90?

28. Refer to Problem 10. Your cumulative GPA, prior to that semester, was 2.92 for 42 credit hours. What is your new cumulative GPA for the total 54 hours?

Practice Test

1. We-Sell-Em Real Estate had 6 home sales during the week: $120,000; $140,000; $210,000; $178,000; $2,400,000; and $120,000. What is the mean?

2. Refer to Problem 1. What is the median?

3. Refer to Problem 1. What is the mode?

4. Refer to Problems 1–3. Which indicator (mean, median, or mode) best represents the average selling price?

5. Venetta Beckstrom sells copy machines. She carries three models. Price and monthly sales for each model are shown. Determine the average price per copy machine sold during the month.

Model	Price	Number sold
Workmaster	$550	52
Auto-Feed	$850	18
Deluxe	$2,300	6

6. Enrollment at a community college for the last 4 years is shown. Show the data on (a) a line graph and (b) a bar graph.

   Year 1: 2,400   Year 2: 3,000   Year 3: 2,800   Year 4: 3,500

7. Clinton Dunn owns a tent manufacturing business. He makes four different models. Sales for May are shown. In constructing a circle graph, how many degrees (to the nearest tenth of a degree) should be used for the 10 × 12 model?

Model	Number sold
4 × 7	252
5 × 8	144
10 × 12	211
12 × 15	128

8. You throw a football as far as you can 4 times, recording the distance for each throw: 45 yards, 38 yards, 42 yards, and 51 yards. If you want to draw conclusions about the standard deviation of, say 50 throws, what would the standard deviation be?

Classroom Notes

Classroom Notes

Classroom Notes

Classroom Notes

A Step-by-Step Solutions
U-Try-It Exercises

Unit 1.1

1a. Seventy-two thousand, one hundred sixty-eight   1b. Thirty-two and eighty-four thousandths

2a. 328,608   2b. 500.014   2c. 48.2 million → 48,2 → **48,200,000**

3a. 12,448 → 1<u>2</u>,448 → **12,000**   3b. 12.86513 → 12.8<u>6</u>513 → 12.87000 → **12.87**

3c. 72,971 → 72,<u>9</u>71 → **73,000**

Unit 1.2

1.   3172
     283
 +1765
  5220

2.   1283   1283
 -718   +718 ↑
  565   565

3a.   4721 ⎫ Put smaller number
 ×   48 ⎭ on bottom.
 37 768
 188 84
 226,608

3b. 34000 ⎫ →   34
 ×   140 ⎭   ×14
             136
              34
             476 $\xrightarrow[\text{4 zeros}]{\text{attach}}$ **4,760,000**

4.   **29** R1
28)813
  56↓
  253
  252
    1

Unit 1.3

1. *word problem guide*

1. Solving for	Total monthly rents
2. Known facts	2 units at $750 each 4 units at $770 each
3. Procedure	2 × $750 = $1500 4 × $770 = +3080 **$4580**

2. *word problem guide*

1. Solving for	Average miles per gallon
2. Known facts	Traveled 756 miles Used 42 gallons of gasoline

3. Procedure	Miles *per* gallon means miles *divided by* gallons
	    18 You got 18 miles per gallon. (For each gallon of gas, you traveled 18 miles.)
	42)756
	  42↓
	  336
	  336

3a. $1329 ⎫ $1300
   598 ⎬ →   600
 + 379 ⎭ + 400
             $2300

3b. $1329 ⎫ $1000
   598 ⎬ →   600
 + 379 ⎭ + 400
             $2000

3c. $1329
   598
 + 379
  $2306

3d. Rounding to the nearest hundred dollars ($2,300) is closer to the actual price ($2,306).

Unit 1.4

1. $45.$
    4.76
    $+12.8652$

    $\longrightarrow$

    45.0000
    4.7600
    $+12.8652$
    62.6252

2. $\$385.21$
    -48.17
    $\$337.04$

3a. 12.64 2 decimals
    $\times 32.1$ 1 decimal
    1264
    2528
    3792
    405.744

3b. $12.63 \times 1{,}000 \rightarrow 12.630 \rightarrow \mathbf{12{,}630}$

4a. $42.3 \overline{)791.01} \rightarrow 423 \overline{)7910.1}$ = 18.7
    423
    3680
    3384
    2961
    2961

4b. $1.67 \div 100 \rightarrow 01.67 \rightarrow .0167$

Unit 2.1

1. $4\frac{3}{8} = \frac{(4 \times 8) + 3}{8} = \frac{35}{8}$

2. $3 \overline{)11} = 3\frac{2}{3}$
   9
   2

3a. $\frac{3}{4} = \frac{?}{16} \rightarrow \frac{3}{4} = \frac{12}{16}$ (×4)

3b. $\frac{8}{3} = \frac{?}{24} \rightarrow \frac{8}{3} = \frac{64}{24}$ (×8)

4a. $\frac{14}{21} = \frac{14 \div 7}{21 \div 7} = \frac{2}{3}$

4b. $52 \overline{)195} \rightarrow 39\overline{)52} \rightarrow 13\overline{)39}$ = 3, 1, 3
    $156 39 39$
    $39 13 0$

    GCD is last divisor (13), so: $\frac{52}{195} = \frac{52 \div 13}{195 \div 13} = \frac{4}{15}$

Unit 2.2

1a. $\frac{5}{12} + \frac{11}{12} - \frac{7}{12} = \frac{5 + 11 - 7}{12} = \frac{9}{12} = \frac{3}{4}$

1b. $\frac{3}{4} + \frac{1}{2} - \frac{1}{6} = \frac{?}{12} + \frac{?}{12} - \frac{?}{12} = \frac{9}{12} + \frac{6}{12} - \frac{2}{12} = \frac{9 + 6 - 2}{12} = \frac{13}{12}$

1c. $\frac{7}{8} \times \frac{1}{4} = \frac{7 \times 1}{8 \times 4} = \frac{7}{32}$

1d. $\frac{4}{3} \div \frac{1}{2} = \frac{4}{3} \times \frac{2}{1} = \frac{8}{3}$

2. $2\frac{2}{3} \rightarrow 2\frac{8}{12}$
   $\frac{3}{4} \rightarrow \frac{9}{12}$
   $+1\frac{1}{2} \rightarrow +1\frac{6}{12}$
   Need LCD $\rightarrow 3\frac{23}{12} = 3 + \frac{23}{12} = 3 + 1\frac{11}{12} = 4\frac{11}{12}$

3a. $4\frac{1}{2} \rightarrow 4\frac{2}{4}$
    $-1\frac{1}{4} \rightarrow -1\frac{1}{4}$
    Need LCD $\rightarrow 3\frac{1}{4}$

3b. $3\frac{1}{6} \rightarrow 3\frac{1}{6} \rightarrow 2\frac{7}{6}$ $\left(\frac{6}{6} + \frac{1}{6}\right)$
    $-1\frac{2}{3} \rightarrow -1\frac{4}{6} \rightarrow -1\frac{4}{6}$
    Need LCD   Need to borrow $1\frac{3}{6} = 1\frac{1}{2}$

4. Flour: $1\frac{1}{2} \times 2\frac{1}{2} = \frac{3}{2} \times \frac{5}{2} = \frac{15}{4} = 3\frac{3}{4}$ cups

   Chocolate chips: $\frac{1}{3} \times 2\frac{1}{2} = \frac{1}{3} \times \frac{5}{2} = \frac{5}{6}$ cup

   Butter: $\frac{1}{4} \times 2\frac{1}{2} = \frac{1}{4} \times \frac{5}{2} = \frac{5}{8}$ cup

   Eggs: $4 \times 2\frac{1}{2} = \frac{2\cancel{4}}{1} \times \frac{5}{\cancel{2}_1} = \frac{10}{1} = 10$ eggs

5. $5\frac{1}{3} \div 1\frac{1}{2} = \frac{16}{3} \div \frac{3}{2} = \frac{16}{3} \times \frac{2}{3} = \frac{32}{9} = 3\frac{5}{9}$ *(Final answer is written as a mixed number because we started with one)*

Unit 2.3

1a. $15.76 = 15\frac{76}{100} = 15\frac{19}{25}$ 1b. $.6 = \frac{6}{10} = \frac{3}{5}$

2.
```
     .4166  → Repeating decimal .416̄
12)5.0000
   4 8↓
     20
     12↓
      80
      72↓
       80
       72
        8 (repeating)
```

3a. $\frac{7}{12} = .58\overline{3}$ (repeating)   3b. $\frac{3}{16} = .1875$ (terminating)   3c. $\frac{5}{9} = .\overline{55}$ (repeating)

4.
```
    .875 + 61 = 61.875
8)7.000
  6 4↓
    60
    56↓
     40
     40
```

Unit 3.1

1. $3y$, $3 \cdot y$, $3(y)$, $(3)(y)$ 2. 3^4 3. $18^3 = (18)(18)(18) = 5{,}832$

4a. $3 + 2(5 + 3)^2 = 3 + 2(8)^2 = 3 + 2(64) = 3 + 128 = \mathbf{131}$ 4b. $2[4 + 3(5 - 2)] = 2[4 + 3(3)] = 2[4 + 9] = 2[13] = \mathbf{26}$

5. $3 + (5 - 3) + (2 - 3) - (4 - 2) - (1 - 6)$
   $= 3 + (+2) + (-1) - (+2) - (-5)$
   $= 3 + 2 - 1 - 2 + 5 = \mathbf{7}$

6a. $(-2)(-4) = \mathbf{8}$ (Multiplying 2 negatives results in a positive.)   6b. $\frac{-8}{2} = \mathbf{-4}$ (A negative divided by a positive is a negative.)

7. $2(3a + 2) - 1 + 2a = 2(3a) + 2(2) - 1 + 2a = 6a + 4 - 1 + 2a = \mathbf{8a + 3}$

Unit 3.2

1a. $m - 3 = 5$ 1b. $a + 6 = -2$ 1c. $4b = 5$ 1d. $\frac{x}{4} = 3$ 1e. $\frac{2}{3}y = 10$

   $\underline{+3 \quad +3}$ $\underline{-6 \quad -6}$ $\frac{\cancel{4}b}{\cancel{4}} = \frac{5}{4}$ $\frac{\cancel{4}}{1}\left(\frac{x}{\cancel{4}}\right) = 4(3)$ $\frac{\cancel{3}}{\cancel{2}}\left(\frac{\cancel{2}}{\cancel{3}}\right)y = \frac{3}{2}\left(\frac{10}{1}\right)$

   $m \quad\ \ = 8$ $a \quad\ = -8$ $b = \frac{5}{4}$ $x = 12$ $y = 15$

1f. $2(p + 6) - 4 = 3(2p - 2) + 3p$
    $2(p) + 2(6) - 4 = 3(2p) + 3(-2) + 3p$
    $2p + 12 - 4 = 6p - 6 + 3p$
    $2p + 8 \quad = 9p - 6$
    $\underline{-2p \qquad\quad\ -2p}$
    $8 \quad = 7p - 6$
    $\underline{+6 \qquad\quad +6}$
    $14 \quad = 7p$
    $\frac{14}{7} \quad = \frac{\cancel{7}p}{\cancel{7}}$
    $2 = p$

2. $V = \pi r^2 h$ Formula for volume

   $\frac{V}{\pi r^2} = h$ Divide both sides by πr^2

   $h = \frac{V}{\pi r^2}$ Rearrange so "h" is on the left

Unit 3.3

1a. $4m$ 1b. $a + 3$ (or $3 + a$) 1c. $b - 8$ 1d. $p + q + r$

2. $b = a + 5$ (or $b = 5 + a$)

3.
word problem guide

1. Solving for	Stocks (S), bonds (B), and mutual funds (M)		
2. Write equation	? = $4,500,000		Something = $4,500,000
	S + B + M = $4,500,000		S + B + M = $4,500,000
3. Substitute known facts	2M + $1,200,000 + M = $4,500,000		Substitute: B = $1,200,000; S = 2M
4. Solve for unknown	3M + $1,200,000 = $4,500,000		Combine terms on left
	3M = $3,300,000		Subtract $1,200,000 from both sides
	M = $1,100,000		Divide both sides by 3
	× 2		
	S = $2,220,000		Amount to invest in stocks
5. Check answer	Stocks $2,200,000		
	Bonds 1,200,000		
	Mutual funds 1,100,000		
	$4,500,000		Total ($4,500,000) is correct

Unit 4.1

1. $.6\underline{2} = 62\%$ 2. $.00\underline{3} = .3\%$ 3. $3.4 = 3.4\underline{0} = 340\%$ 4. $3\underline{7}.2\% = .372$ 5. $2.8\% = 0\underline{2}.8\% = .028$

6. $132\frac{1}{4}\% = 13\underline{2}.25\% = 1.3225$ 7. $\frac{1}{8}\% = 0\underline{0}.125\% = .00125$ 8. $\frac{1}{4} = .2\underline{5} = 25\%$ 9. $\frac{7}{8} = .8\underline{7}5 = 87.5\%$

10. $36\% = 36 \times \frac{1}{100} = \frac{36}{100} = \frac{9}{25}$ 11. $62\frac{1}{2}\% = \frac{125}{2}\% = \frac{125}{2} \times \frac{1}{100} = \frac{125}{200} = \frac{5}{8}$

12. $18.75\% = 18\frac{3}{4}\% = \frac{75}{4}\% = \frac{75}{4} \times \frac{1}{100} = \frac{75}{400} = \frac{3}{16}$

Unit 4.2

1. Portion = Base × Rate = $370 × 27% = $370 × .27 = **$99.90**

2. Portion = Base × Rate = 1,200 × 74% = 1,200 × .74 = **888**

3. Base = $\frac{Portion}{Rate}$ = $\frac{33}{20\%}$ = $\frac{33}{.20}$ = **165**   Check answer: 165 × 20% = 33

4. Base = $\frac{Portion}{Rate}$ = $\frac{\$1,470}{70\%}$ = $\frac{\$1,470}{.70}$ = **$2,100**   Check answer: $2,100 × 70% = $1,470

5. Rate = $\frac{Portion}{Base}$ ≈ $\frac{210}{870}$ ≈ .241$\underline{3}$8 ≈ 24.1$\underline{3}$8% ≈ **24.1%**

6. Rate = $\frac{Portion}{Base}$ = $\frac{\$45}{\$600}$ = .07$\underline{5}$ = **7.5%**

7. **Katherine:** Portion = Base × Rate = $82,300 × 40% = **$32,920**
   Rachel: Portion = Base × Rate = $82,300 × 35% = **$28,805**
   Meghan: Portion = Base × Rate = $82,300 × 25% = **$20,575**
                                              100% $82,300

8. *word problem guide*

1. Solving for	Rate (percent correct)
2. Formula	Rate = $\frac{Portion}{Base}$
3. Known facts	= $\frac{31}{35}$
4. Procedure	≈ .88571
	≈ 88.5$\underline{7}$1%
	≈ **88.6%**

Questions correct (35 − 4)
Portion (31)
Base (35)   Rate (?)
Total questions   Percent correct

9. *word problem guide*

1. Solving for	Base (retail price)
2. Formula	Base = $\frac{\text{Portion}}{\text{Rate}}$
3. Known facts	= $\frac{\$7.70}{40\%}$
4. Procedure	= $\frac{\$7.70}{.40}$
	= **$19.25**

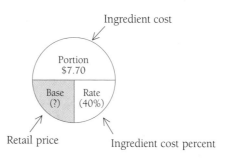

Unit 4.3

1. *word problem guide*

1. Solving for	Portion (new salary)
2. Formula	Portion = Base × Rate
3. Known facts	= $40,000 × 115%
4. Procedure	= $40,000 × 1.15
	= **$46,000**

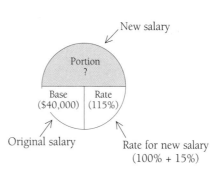

2. *word problem guide*

1. Solving for	Base (price)
2. Formula	Base = $\frac{\text{Portion}}{\text{Rate}}$
3. Known facts	= $\frac{\$1,381.79}{106.375\%}$
4. Procedure	= $\frac{\$1,381.79}{1.06375}$
	= **$1,298.98**

Check answer
Price $1,298.98
Sales tax: $1,298.98 × 6.375%   +   82.81
Total amount $1,381.79

3. *word problem guide*

1. Solving for	Base (original price)
2. Formula	Base = $\frac{\text{Portion}}{\text{Rate}}$
3. Known facts	= $\frac{\$312}{60\%}$
4. Procedure	= $\frac{\$312}{.60}$
	= **$520**

Check answer
Original price $520
Discount: $520 × 40%   -208
Reduced price $312

4. Percent increase = $\frac{\text{Amount of increase}}{\text{Original amount}}$ = $\frac{\$2,417 - \$2,135}{\$2,135}$ = $\frac{\$282}{\$2,135}$ ≈ .132084 ≈ 13.2084% ≈ **13.2%**

5. Percent decrease = $\frac{\text{Amount of decrease}}{\text{Original amount}}$ = $\frac{518 - 497}{518}$ = $\frac{21}{518}$ ≈ .040541 ≈ 4.0541% ≈ **4.05%**

Unit 5.1

1. Trade discount amount = List price × Trade discount rate
   = $1,300 × 30%
   = $1,300 × .30
   = **$390**

   Net price = List price - Trade discount amount
   = $1,300 - $390
   = **$910**

2. **Step 1** Complement = 100% - 20% = 80%
   Step 2 Net price = List price × Complement
   = $800 × 80%
   = $800 × .80
   = **$640**

3. List price $995.00
   Less first discount: $995 × 25%   - 248.75
   Price after first discount $746.25
   Less second discount: $746.25 × 15%   - 111.94
   Net price **$634.31**

4. **Step 1 (complements)**   **Step 2 (multiply)**   **Step 3 (complement of Step 2)**
   25% 10%   75% × 90%   100.0%
   ↓   ↓   = .75 × .90   - 67.5%
   75% 90%   = .675   **32.5%**
                                  = 67.5%

Unit 5.2

1. List price $850.00
   Less returned goods   - 45.00
   Price after returns $805.00
   Less trade discount: $805 × 30%   - 241.50
   Net price $563.50
   Less cash discount: $563.50 × 6%   - 33.81
   Net price, less cash discount $529.69
   Add freight charges   + 73.00
   Net amount due **$602.69**

2. Apr. 4 + 15 → **Apr. 19**

3. July 28 → Day 209
              + 45
   Sep. 11 ←   254

4. Nov. 12 → Day 316
              + 90
                 406
              -365
   Feb. 10 ←   41

Last day discount period	Last day of credit period
5. July 18 + 10 = **July 28**	July 18 → Day 199 +60 Sep. 16 ← 259
6. Mar. 17 → Day 76 +15 **Apr. 1** ← 91	Mar. 17 → Day 76 +45 **May 1** ← 121
7. June 30 + 15 days → **July 15**	July 15 → Day 196 Additional 20 days +20 **Aug. 4** ← 216
8. Oct. 19 → Day 292 +90 382 -365 **Jan. 17** ← 17	

9. Amount credited = $\frac{\text{Amount paid}}{\text{Complement of cash discount rate}}$ = $\frac{\$5,000}{100\% - 5\%}$ = $\frac{\$5,000}{95\%}$ = $\frac{\$5,000}{.95}$ = **$5,263.16**

10. Rate = $\frac{\text{Cash discount rate}}{\text{Complement of cash discount rate}}$ × $\frac{365}{\text{Days in credit period - days in discount period}}$

    = $\frac{5}{95}$ × $\frac{365}{60-10}$ = $\frac{5}{95}$ × $\frac{365}{50}$ = $\frac{5 \times 365}{95 \times 50}$ = $\frac{1,825}{4,750}$ ≈ .3842 ≈ **38.42%**

Unit 6.1

1. S = C + M = $38,500 + $2,150 = **$40,650**

2. *word problem guide*

1. Solving for	Selling price	
2. Formula	S = C + M	*Markup formula*
3. Known facts	S = C + 80%(C)	M = 80% of cost
	S = $25 + 80%($25)	C = $25
4. Procedure	S = $25 + $20	80%($25) = $20
	S = **$45**	$25 + $20 = $45

3. *word problem guide*

1. Solving for	Selling price	
2. Formula	S = C + M	*Markup formula*
3. Known facts	100%S = $550 + 60%S	"S" means "100%S; M = 60% of selling price
4. Procedure	40%S = $550	Subtract "60%S" from both sides of the equation
	.40S = $550	Convert "40%" to a decimal number
	$\frac{.40S}{.40} = \frac{\$550}{.40}$	Divide both sides of the equation by .40
	S = **$1,375**	Simplify

Unit 6.2

1a. M = S − C = $2,070 − $1,800 = **$270**

1b. Percent markup on cost = $\frac{\$270}{\$1,800}$ = .1500 = **15%**

1c. Percent markup on selling price = $\frac{\$270}{\$2,070}$ ≈ .1304 ≈ **13.04%**

The symbol "≈" means "approximately equal to"

2. Let's find Yoko's equivalent percent markup on selling price (we could instead find her competitor's equivalent percent markup on cost):

$$\text{Equivalent percent markup on selling price} = \frac{\text{Percent markup on cost}}{100\% + \text{Percent markup on cost}}$$

$$= \frac{30\%}{100\% + 30\%} = \frac{30\%}{130\%} = \frac{30}{1.30} \approx .2308 \approx \mathbf{23.08\%}$$

Yoko's 20% markup on cost is equivalent to a 23.08% markup on selling price, which is less than her competitor's 25% markup on selling price.

Unit 6.3

1. | | |
    |---|---:|
    | Original marked price | $1,500.00 |
    | Markdown 1: $1,500 × 25% | - 375.00 |
    | Reduced price, after markdown 1 | $1,125.00 |
    | Markdown 2: $1,125 × 10% | - 112.50 |
    | Reduced price, after markdown 2 | $1,012.50 |
    | Markdown 3: $1,012.50 × 20% | - 202.50 |
    | Reduced price, after markdown 3 | **$ 810.00** |

2. Total dollar markdown = Original marked price - Final reduced price = $1,500 - $810 = $690

    $$\text{Percent markdown} = \frac{\text{Dollar markdown}}{\text{Original marked price}} = \frac{\$690}{\$1,500} = .4600 = \mathbf{46\%}$$

3. **Step 1** Determine desired sales proceeds from all 30 computers

    word problem guide

1. Solving for	Sales proceeds from entire stock	
2. Formula	S = C + M	*Markup formula*
3. Known facts	S = $36,000 + 25%($36,000)	C = 30 × $1,200 = $36,000; M = 25% of cost
4. Procedure	S = $36,000 + $9,000	25%($36,000) = $9,000
	S = $45,000	$36,000 + $9,000 = $45,000

    Step 2 Deduct proceeds from products sold at a discount

    6 computers (30 computers × 20%) will be sold at $840 each ($1,200 cost × 70%), so

Desired sales proceeds (from Step 1)	$45,000
Less proceeds from computers sold at a discount: 6 computers × $840	- 5,040
Proceeds required from computers sold at original marked price	$39,960

    Step 3 Find original marked price

    24 computers will sell at original marked price, so: $39,960 ÷ 24 = **$1,665 each**

4. Price/Cost ratio = $\frac{\text{Selling price}}{\text{Cost}} = \frac{\$1,665}{\$1,200} = 1.3875$

    Next shipment: $1,175 × 1.3875 = **$1,630.32 each** (Always round *up*)

Unit 6.4

1. | | | | |
    |---|---:|---|---:|
    | List price | $ 92.80 | | |
    | Trade discount: $92.80 × 20% | - 18.56 | | |
    | Cost | $ 74.24 | Cost (from left) | $74.24 |
    | Markup: $74.24 × 35% | + 25.98 | Amount to cover operating expenses: $74.24 × 20% | +14.85 |
    | Original marked price | **$100.22** | Break-even price | **$89.09** |

2. Batch 1 ($100.22). Greater than break-even price ($89.09): $100.22 - $89.09 break-even price = **$11.13 profit**

   Batch 2 ($85). Greater than cost ($74.24) but less than break-even price ($89.09):

   $89.09 break-even price - $85 = **$4.09 operating loss**

   Batch 3 ($70). Less than cost. $74.24 cost - $70 = **$4.24 absolute loss**

3. Fixed costs allocated to tents: $17,920 × 60% = $10,752

   $$\text{Number of units needed} = \frac{\text{Fixed costs}}{\text{Selling price per unit - Variable cost per unit}} = \frac{\$10{,}752}{\$180 - \$52} = \frac{\$10{,}752}{\$128} = \mathbf{84 \text{ tents}}$$

Unit 7.1

1.

Check Number	Date	Description of Transaction	(-) Payment/Debit	(+) Deposit/Credit	Balance
	9-5	Open account		1,700.00	**1,700.00**
101	9-7	ABC Grocery	275.00		**1,425.00**
102	9-12	Car Specialists; car repair	283.00		**1,142.00**
	9-15	Paycheck		2,800.00	**3,942.00**
103	9-15	Homestead Mortgage; mortgage payment	958.00		**2,984.00**
104	9-23	ABC Grocery	173.25		**2,810.75**
105	9-30	Electricity bill	98.32		**2,712.43**

2. $0.00 (previous balance) + $4,507.85 (total deposits) - $1,516.00 (total checks) - $23.25 (other debits) = **$2,968.60**

3. Refer to Problems 1 and 2. Complete a bank reconciliation.

   Reconciliation Period Ending _September 25, 20xx_

CHECKBOOK BALANCE	
1. Ending balance in your check register	$2,810.75
2. Add: September interest	7.85
3. Subtotal	$2,818.60
4. Subtract: Ck printing charges	23.25
5. TOTAL	**$2,795.35**

BANK STATEMENT	
1. Ending balance on bank statement	$2,968.60
2. Add: Outstanding deposits	
3. Subtotal	$2,968.60
4. Subtract: Ck 104	173.25
5. TOTAL	**$2,795.35**

These two totals are the same

The ending checkbook balance ($2,810.75) is through September 25 (the bank statement date)

4. **Step 1 (review outstanding deposits).** There are no outstanding deposits.
   Step 2 (review outstanding checks). Check 104 has not been outstanding for very long.
   Step 3 (enter adjustments). There are two adjustments on the left side of the reconciliation. These must be entered in the check register: September interest ($7.85) must be added to the balance, and check printing charges ($23.25) must be subtracted from the balance.

Unit 8.1

1. Overtime hours: 46.5 total hours - 40 regular hours = 6.5 hours
   Overtime rate: $9.25 regular rate × 1.5 = $13.875

Pay for regular hours: 40 × $9.25	$370.00
Pay for overtime hours: 6.5 × $13.875	+ 90.19
	$460.19

2. Monthly: $3,000 × 12 — $36,000.00
   Semimonthly: $1,450 × 24 — $34,800.00
   Biweekly: $1,375 × 26.07 — $35,846.25
   Weekly: $700 × 52.14 — **$36,498.00**
   Hourly: $17 × 40 hrs × 52.14 — $35,455.20

3. Base salary: 38 hours × $6 — $228
   Piecework:
   400 × $0.30 — $120
   200 × $0.40 — 80
   +344 × $0.50 — +172
   944
   — 372
   Total gross pay — **$600**

4. Salary 2 × $600 — $1,200
   -Commission:
   Net sales: $97,300 - $5,800 — $91,500
   Base amount — -60,000
   Overage — $31,500 × 3% — 945
   Gross pay — **$2,145**

Unit 8.2

1. Social Security:
   Limit — $118,500
   Prior earnings — -115,500
   Amount subject to Social Security tax — $ 3,000 × 6.2% = **$186.00**

   Medicare: $10,500 × 1.45% — **$152.25**

2. **Step 1** Illustration 8-2, monthly: $333.30 × 3 allowances = $999.90

   Step 2 Subtract the result of Step 1 from gross pay: $10,500 - $999.90 = $9,500.10

   Step 3 Illustration 8-3, monthly, married, over $6,958, but not over $13,317:
   Amount = $859.30 + 25%($9,500.10 - $6,958)
   = $859.30 + 25%($2,542.10)
   = $859.30 + $635.53
   = **$1,494.83**

3. State income tax withholding: $10,500 × 5.5% = $577.50
   Net pay: $10,500 - $186 - $152.25 - $1,494.83 - $577.50 = **$8,089.42**

Unit 8.3

1. Match employees' contribution: $136.40 (Social Security) + $31.90 (Medicare) = **$168.30**

2. | Employee | FUT | SUT |
   |---|---|---|
   | Tina | $600 | $ 800 |
   | Andy | + 0 | + 800 |
   | Total | $600 × 0.6% = **$3.60** | $1,600 × 2.5% = **$40** |

3. **Step 1** $97,400 × 92.35% = $89,949 (rounded)
   Step 2 FICA tax: $89,949 × 15.3% = **$13,762** (rounded)

4.
Amounts owed to IRS		Amounts already paid to IRS	
Income tax liability	$23,382	Federal income tax w/h from Marilyn	$ 6,122
Ed's self-employment FICA tax	+13,762	Estimated payments: 4 × $7,000	+28,000
	$37,144		$34,122

Ed and Marilyn underpaid. **They owe an additional $3,022** ($37,144 − $34,122) to the IRS; they may also owe an underpayment penalty.

Unit 9.1

1a. $I = PRT = \$8,000 \times 11\% \times \frac{18}{12} = \$1,320$ 1b. $M = P + I = \$8,000 + \$1,320 = \$9,320$

2. Aug. 5 → Day 217
    +180
    397 (*Greater than 365, so subtract 365*)
    −365
   Feb. 1 ← 32

3. Oct. 14 → Day 287
   May 22 → Day −142
    **145 days**

4a. 365-day year: $I = PRT = \$15,000 \times 9.25\% \times \frac{90}{365} = \$342.12$

4b. 360-day year: $I = PRT = \$15,000 \times 9.25\% \times \frac{90}{360} = \$346.88$

5.
Day number	Total payment	Interest	Principal	Balance
0	—	—	—	$20,000.00
40	$8,000.00	$230.14	$7,769.86	$12,230.14
115	$12,494.01	$263.87	$12,230.14	$ 0.00
Totals	$20,494.01	$494.01	$20,000.00	—

Procedure for payment on day 40
$I = PRT = \$20,000.00 \times 10.5\% \times \frac{40}{365} = \$230.14$
Principal = $8,000.00 − $230.14 = **$7,769.86**
Balance = $20,000.00 − $7,769.86 = **$12,230.14**

Procedure for payment on day 115
$I = PRT = \$12,230.14 \times 10.5\% \times \frac{75}{365} = \$263.87$ (115 days − 40 days = 75 days)
Principal = **$12,230.14** (previous balance)
Total payment = $263.87 + $12,230.14 = **$12,494.01**

Unit 9.2

1. $P = \frac{I}{RT} = \frac{\$157.50}{9\% \times \frac{6}{12}} = \frac{\$157.50}{.09 \times \frac{6}{12}} = \frac{\$157.50}{0.045} = \$3,500$

   Check answer: $I = PRT = \$3,500 \times 9\% \times \frac{6}{12} = \$157.50$

2. $T = \frac{I}{PR} = \frac{\$78.90}{\$4,000 \times 8\%} = \frac{\$78.90}{\$320} = .2465625 \longrightarrow 365 \text{ days} \times .2465625 = \textbf{90 days}$

   Check answer: $I = PRT = \$4,000 \times 8\% \times \frac{90}{365} = \$78.90$

3. Principal for APR purposes: $5,000 − $150 = $4,850
   Interest for APR purposes:

   $I = PRT = \$5,000 \times 10.5\% \times \frac{180}{360} = \$262.50$
   Document preparation fee +150.00
   Total finance charges $412.50

   $R = \frac{I}{PT} = \frac{\$412.50}{\$4,850 \times \frac{180}{365}} \approx .1725 \approx \textbf{17.25\%}$

Unit 9.3

1. Yr. 1: $I = PRT = \$500.00 \times 5\% \times 1 = \$25.00$ $M = P + I = \$500.00 + \$25.00 = \$525.00$
   Yr. 2: $I = PRT = \$525.00 \times 5\% \times 1 = \$26.25$ $M = P + I = \$525.00 + \$26.25 = \$551.25$
   Yr. 3: $I = PRT = \$551.25 \times 5\% \times 1 = \$27.56$ $M = P + I = \$551.25 + \$27.56 = \$578.81$
   Yr. 4: $I + PRT = \$578.81 \times 5\% \times 1 = \$28.94$ $M = P + I = \$578.81 + \$28.94 = \mathbf{\$607.75}$

   Use a calculator to increase the balance 5% each year.

   Keystrokes (for most calculators)

500 [+] 5 [%] [=]	525.00
[+] 5 [%] [=]	551.25
[+] 5 [%] [=]	578.81
[+] 5 [%] [=]	**607.75**

2. Periodic rate: $\frac{4.5}{4} = 1.125$

	Interest	Balance
Beginning	—	$1,200.00
3 months	$1,200.00 × 1.125% = $13.50	$1,213.50
6 months	$1,213.50 × 1.125% = $13.65	$1,227.15
9 months	$1,227.15 × 1.125% = $13.81	$1,240.96
12 months	$1,240.96 × 1.125% = $13.96	**$1,254.92**

3. Periodic rate: $\frac{6.75}{4} = 1.6875(\%)$

   $100 + 1.6875\% =$ $101.69
   $+ 1.6875\% =$ $103.40*
   $+ 1.6875\% =$ $105.15*
   $+ 1.6875\% =$ $106.92 ⟶ APY = **6.92%**

   Note: Use chain calculations (don't round intermediate results)

Unit 10.1

1. n = 10 years × 4 periods per year = **40**
   i = 6% ÷ 4 periods per year = **1.5%**
   PV = **$300** (this is the one-time amount that happens at the beginning of the first period)
   PMT = **$100** (this happens every period)
   FV = **Unknown** (this is what we want to know)

Unit 10.2

1. What $1,250 will grow to. Formula 1A ($n = 10 \times 4 = 40$; $i = 4\% \div 4 = 1\% = .01$):

   $FV = PV(1 + i)^n = \$1{,}250(1.01)^{40} =$ $1,861.08

   What $100 quarterly payments will grow to. Formula 1B:

   $FV = PMT\left[\dfrac{(1+i)^n - 1}{i}\right] = \$100\left[\dfrac{(1.01)^{40} - 1}{.01}\right] =$ +4,888.64

   Total FV   **$6,749.72**

2. First, let's find the balance 25 years from now. Formula 1B ($n = 25 \times 4 = 100$; $i = 6\% \div 4 = 1.5\% = .015$):

   $FV = PMT\left[\dfrac{(1+i)^n - 1}{i}\right] = \$1000\left[\dfrac{(1.015)^{100} - 1}{.015}\right] = \$228{,}803.04$

   Now, let's find what $228,803.04 will grow to over the final 10 years. Formula 1A ($n = 10 \times 4 = 40$; $i = 6\% \div 4 = 1.5\% = .015$):

   $FV = PV(1 + i)^n = \$228{,}803.04(1.015)^{40} = \mathbf{\$415{,}052.93}$

Unit 10.3

1. Formula 2A ($n = 21$; $i = 6\% = .06$): $PV = \dfrac{FV}{(1+i)^n} = \dfrac{\$100{,}000}{(1.06)^{21}} = \$29{,}415.54$

2. Formula 2B ($n = 40$; $i = 6\% = .06$): $PV = PMT\left[\dfrac{1 - \dfrac{1}{(1+i)^n}}{i}\right] = \$250{,}000\left[\dfrac{1 - \dfrac{1}{(1.06)^{40}}}{.06}\right] = \$3{,}761{,}574.22$

3. $n = 15 \times 12 = 180$; $i = 12\% \div 12 = 1\% = .01$:

    PV, annual savings: $PV = PMT\left[\dfrac{1 - \dfrac{1}{(1+i)^n}}{i}\right] = \$1{,}500\left[\dfrac{1 - \dfrac{1}{(1.01)^{180}}}{.01}\right] = \$124{,}982.50$

    PV, salvage value: $PV = \dfrac{FV}{(1+i)^n} = \dfrac{\$5{,}500}{(1.01)^{180}} =$ + 917.31

    Total PV   **$125,899.81**

4. **Yes**, because the value of the device ($125,899.81) is greater than the its cost ($100,000).

Unit 11.1

1. Formula 2A ($n = 3.5 \times 4 = 14$; $i = 6\% \div 4 = 1.5\% = .015$): $PV = \dfrac{FV}{(1+i)^n} = \dfrac{\$30{,}000}{(1.015)^{14}} = \$24{,}355.48$

2. Formula 4A ($n = 3.5 \times 4 = 14$; $i = 6\% \div 4 = 1.5\% = .015$):

    $PMT = \dfrac{FV(i)}{(1+i)^n - 1} = \dfrac{\$30{,}000(.015)}{(1.015)^{14} - 1} = \$1{,}941.70$

Unit 11.2

1. $I = PRT = \$420{,}000 \times 8\% \times \dfrac{1}{12} = \$2{,}800$

2. Formula 4B ($n = 25 \times 12 = 300$; $i = 8\% \div 12 \approx .6666667\% \approx .006666667$):

    $PMT = \dfrac{PV(i)}{1 - \dfrac{1}{(1+i)^n}} = \dfrac{\$420{,}000(.006666667)}{1 - \dfrac{1}{(1.006666667)^{300}}} = \$3{,}241.63$

Unit 11.3

1. Formula 4B ($n = 6 \times 12 = 72$; $i = 9.5\% \div 12 \approx .7916667\% \approx .007916667$):

    $PMT = \dfrac{PV(i)}{1 - \dfrac{1}{(1+i)^n}} = \dfrac{\$7{,}000(.007916667)}{1 - \dfrac{1}{(1.007916667)^{72}}} = \$127.92$

2. Formula 4B ($n = 30 \times 12 = 360$; $i = 5.875\% \div 12 \approx .4895833\% \approx .004895833$):

    $PMT = \dfrac{PV(i)}{1 - \dfrac{1}{(1+i)^n}} = \dfrac{\$180{,}000(.004895833)}{1 - \dfrac{1}{(1.004895833)^{360}}} = \$1{,}064.77$

3. $(360 \times \$1{,}064.77) - \$180{,}000 = \$383{,}317.20 - \$180{,}000 = \mathbf{\$203{,}317.20}$

4. Formula 5 ($i = 8.5\% \div 12 \approx .7083333\% \approx .007083333$):

    $n = \dfrac{-\ln\left[\dfrac{PV + \left(\dfrac{PMT}{i}\right)}{\dfrac{PMT}{i} - FV}\right]}{\ln(1+i)} = \dfrac{-\ln\left[\dfrac{\$105{,}286.67 + \left(\dfrac{-\$922.69}{.007083333}\right)}{\dfrac{-922.69}{.007083333} - \$0}\right]}{\ln(1.007083333)} = \mathbf{234\text{ months}}$

Unit 11.4

1. $i = \left(\dfrac{FV}{PV}\right)^{\frac{1}{n}} - 1 = \left(\dfrac{\$22{,}000{,}000}{\$5{,}000}\right)^{\frac{1}{51}} - 1 = .1788 = \mathbf{17.88\%}$

2. Formulas are not designed to solve for *i* when periodic payments are involved. Let's use the Guess and Check Method.

   Step 1 Calculate the monthly payment: $PMT = \dfrac{PV(i)}{1 - \dfrac{1}{(1+i)^n}} = \dfrac{\$12{,}000(.00625)}{1 - \dfrac{1}{(1.00625)^{60}}} = \$240.46$

   Step 2 Calculate the APR (*i*) based on net proceeds of $11,800. Let's use Formula 4B and guess rates until we get close to our target figure of $240.46 (the monthly payment). The note rate is 7.5% but because there is a front-end fee, the APR will be a bit higher. Let's try a periodic rate of 8% ($i = 8\% \div 12 \approx .6666667\% \approx .006666667$):

   $PMT = \dfrac{PV(i)}{1 - \dfrac{1}{(1+i)^n}} = \dfrac{\$11{,}800(.006666667)}{1 - \dfrac{1}{(1.006666667)^{60}}} = \$239.26$

   A rate of 8% results in a monthly payment of $239.26, less than our $240.46 target figure, so we need to use a higher rate. Let's try 8.25% ($i = 8.25\% \div 12 = .6875\% = .006875$):

   $PMT = \dfrac{PV(i)}{1 - \dfrac{1}{(1+i)^n}} = \dfrac{\$11{,}800(.006875)}{1 - \dfrac{1}{(1.006875)^{60}}} = \$240.68$

   A rate of 8.25% results in a monthly payment of $240.68, just a bit greater than our $240.46 target figure. Let's try 8.21% ($i = 8.21\% \div 12 \approx .6841667\% \approx .006841667$):

   $PMT = \dfrac{PV(i)}{1 - \dfrac{1}{(1+i)^n}} = \dfrac{\$11{,}800(.006841667)}{1 - \dfrac{1}{(1.006841667)^{60}}} = \$240.45$

   The rate of 8.21% results in a monthly payment that is very close to our $240.46 target figure. The APR is about **8.21%**.

Unit 12.1

1. $n = 10$ years × 4 periods per year = **40**
   $i = 6\% \div 4$ periods per year = **1.5%**
   PV = **$300** (this is the one-time amount that happens at the beginning of the first period)
   PMT = **$100** (this happens every period)
   FV = **Unknown** (this is what we want to know)

Unit 12.2

1. -$30,000 (negative because you *paid* the money)

2. **False.** Known values can be entered in any order.

3. **True.**

Unit 12.3

1.

N	i	PV	PMT	FV
10 × 4 = 40	4 ÷ 4 = 1	-1,250	-100	6,749.72

   Note: If you forgot to set your calculator back to "end" mode after doing Example 6, you will get a wrong answer ($1,154,526.44).

2.

N	i	PV	PMT	FV
25 × 4 = 100	6 ÷ 4 = 1.50		-1,000	228,803.04
10 × 4 = 40	↑	-228,803.04	0	415,052.93

Unit 12.4

1.

N	i	PV	PMT	FV
21	6	-29,415.54		100,000

2.

N	i	PV	PMT	FV
40	6	-3,761,574.22	250,000	

3.

N	i	PV	PMT	FV
15 × 12 = 180	12 ÷ 12 = 1	-125,899.80	1,500	5,500

4. **Yes**; the value of the device ($125,899.80) is greater than its cost ($100,000).

Unit 13.1

1.

N	i	PV	PMT	FV
3.5 × 4 = 14	6 ÷ 4 = 1.50	-24,355.48		30,000

2.

N	i	PV	PMT	FV
↑	↑	0	-1,941.70	30,000

Unit 13.2

1. $I = PRT = \$420{,}000 \times 8\% \times \frac{1}{12} = \$2{,}800$

2.

N	i	PV	PMT	FV
25 × 12 = 300	8 ÷ 12 = 0.6̲6̲	-420,000	**3,241.63**	0

3.

N	i	PV	PMT	FV
242.22 months	↑	↑	3,500	0

4.

N	i	PV	PMT	FV
25 × 12 = 300	↑	↑	2,500	**705,307.92**

Unit 13.3

1.

N	i	PV	PMT	FV
6 × 12 = 72	9.5 ÷ 12 = 0.791̲6̲	7,000	**-127.92**	

2.

N	i	PV	PMT	FV
30 × 12 = 360	5.875 ÷ 12 = 0.48958̲3̲	180,000	**-1,064.77**	

3. (360 × $1,064.77) - $180,000 = $383,317.20 - $180,000 = **$203,317.20**

4.

N	i	PV	PMT	FV
234.00 months	8.5 ÷ 12 = 0.708̲3̲	105,286.67	-922.69	

Unit 14.1

1. $8,500 (price) + $510 (sales tax) - $1,200 (cash) = **$7,810**

2. (120 × $94.76) - $7,810 (principal portion) = $11,371.20 - $7,810 = **$3,561.20**

3. $8,500 (price) + $510 (sales tax) + $3,561.20 (finance charge) = **$12,571.20**

Unit 14.2

1.

Payment number	Date received	Total payment	Interest	Principal	Balance
New loan	July 15	—	—	—	$8,000.00
1	Aug. 12	$400.00	**$69.04**	**$330.96**	**$7,669.04**

Step 1 Number of days: 16 days in Jul. (31 - 15 = 16) + 12 days in Aug. = 28
Step 2 $I = PRT = \$8{,}000 \times 11.25\% \times \frac{28}{365} = \$69.04$
Step 3 Principal = $400.00 - $69.04 = $330.96
Step 4 Balance = $8,000.00 - $330.96 = $7,669.04

2.

Payment number	Date received	Total payment	Interest	Principal	Balance
21	Apr. 14	—	—	—	$495.50
22	May 3	**$498.40**	$2.90	$495.50	$0.00

Step 1 Number of days: 16 days in Apr. (30 - 14 = 16) + 3 days in May = 19
Step 2 $I = PRT = \$495.50 \times 11.25\% \times \frac{19}{365} = \$2.90$
Step 3 Principal: $495.50 (previous balance)
Step 4 Total payment = $2.90 + $495.50 = $498.40

Unit 14.3

1. 1.5 × 12 months = 18(%). **The two companies charge identical rates.**

2.
Number of days		Balance		Subtotal
11 (May 6, 7, 8, 9, 10, 11, 12, 13, 14, 15, 16)	×	$460	=	$ 5,060
1 (May 17)	×	520	=	520
9 (May 18, 19, 20, 21, 22, 23, 24, 25, 26)	×	270	=	2,430
5 (May 27, 28, 29, 30, 31)	×	390	=	1,950
+ 5 (June 1–5)	×	420	=	+ 2,100
31				$12,060

Average daily balance = $\frac{\$12{,}060}{31}$ = **$389.03**

3. Daily periodic rate = $\frac{9.75}{365} \approx .02671233(\%)$

Interest = $34,100 × .02671233% × 31 = **$282.38**

Unit 15.1

1. Amount available for housing costs: $4,200 × 29% $1,218.00
Subtract monthly property taxes and insurance: ($1,300 + $480) ÷ 12   - 148.33
Amount available for mortgage payment   **$1,069.67**

2. (360 × $1,293.55) - $185,000 (principal portion) = $465,678.00 - $185,000 = **$280,678.00**

3. PI: $1,007.40
TI: ($1,450 + $600) ÷ 12 =   + 170.83
PITI   **$1,178.23**

Unit 15.2

1.

Payment number	Total payment	Interest	Principal	Balance
New loan	—	—	—	$200,000.00
1	1,573.40	**1,458.33**	**115.07**	199,884.93
2	1,573.40	1,457.49	115.91	199,769.02

Payment 1. $I = PRT = \$200{,}000 \times 8.75\% \times \frac{1}{12} = \$1{,}458.33$; Principal = $1,573.40 - $1,458.33 = $115.07; Balance = $200,000 - $115.07 = $199,884.93.

Payment 2. $I = PRT = \$199{,}884.93 \times 8.75\% \times \frac{1}{12} = \$1{,}457.49$; Principal = $1,573.40 - $1,457.49 = $115.91; Balance = $199,884.93 - $115.91 = $199,769.02.

2. $320,000 - $197,400 = **$122,600**

Unit 15.3

1.

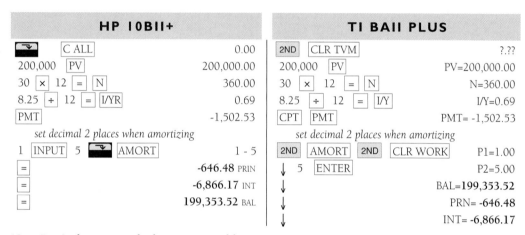

Note: Don't clear your calculator; next problem is a continuation.

2.

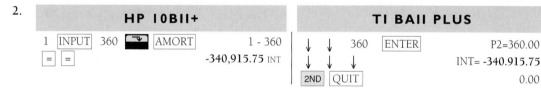

Unit 15.4

1. **Year 2** 5.28% T-bill rate + .75% = 6.03%. Because of 1% anual cap: 4.5% + 1% annual cap = **5.5%**
   Year 3 5.43% T-bill rate + .75% = **6.18%**

2. $I = PRT = \$130{,}000 \times 8.5\% \times \frac{1}{12} = $ **$920.83**

3. $I = PRT = \$150{,}000 \times 6.5\% \times \frac{1}{12} = \$812.50$
   Principal = $700 - $812.30 = -$112.50 (interest is more than total payment, so balance will increase)
   Balance = $150,000 + $112.50 = **$150,112.50**

4. 80%($175,000) - $92,200 = $140,000 - $92,200 = **$47,800**

5. ($120,000 × 1%) + ($120,000 × 1.25%) + $1,980 + $60 + $450 + $490 + $300 + $85 = **$6,065**

Unit 16.1

1. $1,000,000 - $75,000 (preferred last year) - $75,000 (preferred this year) = $850,000 for common stock
   $850,000 ÷ 500,000 common shares = $1.70 per share; $1.70 × 50 shares = **$85**

2a. **$63.94** per share 2b. **$39.25** per share 2c. **$54.56** per share 2d. **Decreased $1.50** per share
2e. .80 (amount in "Div" column) ÷ 54.56 (amount in "Close" column) ≈ .0147 ≈ **1.47%**
2f. $PE = \frac{P}{E} = \frac{\$54.56}{\$3.60} \approx 15.16 \approx \mathbf{15}$

3. (100 × $54.56) + $150 = $5,456 + $150 = **$5,606**

Unit 16.2

1. $1,000 × 110% = **$1,100**

2. **2028** (from "Bond" column)

3. **60 bonds** (from "Vol" column)

4. $1,000 × 6.5% = **$65**

5. **(a) less than 6.5%.** Your bond has a better rate than the prevailing rate, evidenced by the "110" premium price.

6. Cost per bond: $5,000 × 97 18/32% = $5,000 × 97.5625% = $4,878.125
   Number of bonds   ×   2
   Total price   **$9,756.25**

Unit 16.3

1. $NAV = \frac{\$43,580,000 - \$1,300,000}{2,100,000} = \frac{\$42,280,000}{2,100,000} = \mathbf{\$20.13}$

2.
?	= $49.20	something = $49.20
L - D	= $49.20	last year's NAV - decrease = $49.20
100%L - 4.80%L	= $49.20	substitute: D = 4.80% of last year's value
95.20%L	= $49.20	100%L - 4.80%L = 95.20%L
L	= **$51.68**	divide both sides by 95.20%

   <u>check answer</u>
   Last year's price $51.68
   Decrease in value: $51.68 × 4.80% =   - 2.48
   Current price $49.20

Unit 17.1

1. **Step 1** I = PRT = $4,800 × 10% × 2 = $960
   Step 2 $4,800 + $960 = $5,760
   Step 3 $5,760 ÷ 24 = $240 (this is your monthly payment)

N	i	PV	PMT	FV
24	1.51 × 12 ≈ 18.16	4,800	- 240	

2.
N	i	PV	PMT	FV
6	2.66 × 12* ≈ 31.88	450	- 80 Begin**	

   *Note: Even if the term is less than a full year, there are still 12 months in a year.
   **Note: Don't forget to put back in "end" mode.

3. The 9.25% loan has no front-end fees, so the APR is 9.25%. The APR on the 7.75% loan can be calculated as follows:

N	i	PV	PMT	FV
3 × 12 = 36	7.75 ÷ 12 = 0.64583	10,250	- 320.02	
↑	0.79 × 12 ≈ 9.43	10,000	↑	

   The 9.25% loan has the lower APR.

4. Let's calculate the APR on both loans using the three-step approach. First, we will calculate the monthly payment. Next, we will calculate the remaining balance at the designated time (10 years). Finally, we will calculate the APR by (1) putting the remaining balance (after payment 120) in the FV register (as a negative value), (2) changing N to 120, and (3) changing PV to the net proceeds (after loan costs are deducted). Here are the results.

Choice 1

N	i	PV	PMT	FV
30 × 12 = 360	8.25 ÷ 12 = 0.6875	140,000	**-1,051.77**	
10 × 12 = 120	0.72 × 12 ≈ **8.70**	136,000	↑	-123,438.61*

*Note: The FV amount ($123,438.61) is the unpaid balance, found by amortizing 120 payments.

Choice 2

N	i	PV	PMT	FV
30 × 12 = 360	7.875 ÷ 12 = 0.65625	140,000	**-1,015.10**	
10 × 12 = 120	0.73 × 12 ≈ **8.78**	132,000	↑	-122,495.55*

*Note: The FV amount ($122,495.55) is the unpaid balance, found by amortizing 120 payments.

The first choice provides the lower APR (8.70% vs 8.78%), so you should get the 8.25% loan.

5. Let's calculate the APR on the contemplated loan.

N	i	PV	PMT	FV
15 × 12 = 180	7 ÷ 12 = 0.58$\underline{3}$	115,000	-1,033.65	
6 × 12 = 72	0.66 × 12 ≈ **7.93**	110,500	↑	-82,650.92*

*Note: The FV amount ($82,650.92) is the unpaid balance, found by amortizing 72 payments.

The APR on the contemplated loan (7.93%) is lower than the note rate on the existing loan (8.25%). Unless you foresee interest rates dropping in the future—and in the absence of any other material factors—you should refinance now.

Unit 17.2

1.

N	i	PV	PMT	FV
15	12.09	-650		3,600

Unit 17.3

1.

N	i	PV	PMT	FV
51	17.88	-5,000		22,000,000

2.

N	i	PV	PMT	FV
4 × 2 = 8	5.42 × 2 = 10.83	-4,592.50	150	5,550*

*Note: (5 × $1,180) - $350 = $5,550

Unit 17.4

1.

HP 10BII+			TI BAII PLUS	
▼ C ALL	0.00		CF 2ND CLR WORK	CFo=0.00
50,000 +/− CFj	−50,000.00		50,000 +/− ENTER	CFo= −50,000.00
3,000 +/− CFj	−3,000.00		↓ 3,000 +/− ENTER	C01= −3,000.00
1,000 +/− CFj	−1,000.00		↓ ↓ 1,000 +/− ENTER	C02= −1,000.00
4,000 CFj	4,000.00		↓ ↓ 4,000 ENTER	C03=4,000.00
9,500 CFj	9,500.00		↓ ↓ 9,500 ENTER	C04=9,500.00
14,000 + 84,000 = CFj	98,000.00		↓ ↓ 14,000 + 84,000 =	98,000.00
▼ IRR/YR	16.52		ENTER	C05=98,000.00
			IRR CPT	IRR=16.52
			2ND QUIT	

2. You will collect a total of $2,100,000 (60 months × $15,000 + 60 months × $20,000). But because the money is to be received over time, the value, in today's dollars, is less. Because the payments change, we will use the cash flow registers:

HP 10BII+			TI BAII PLUS	
▼ C ALL	0.00		CF 2ND CLR WORK	CFo=0.00
0 CFj	0.00		0 ENTER	CFo=0.00
15,000 CFj 60 ▼ Nj	60.00		↓ 15,000 ENTER ↓ 60 ENTER	F01=60.00
20,000 CFj 60 ▼ Nj	60.00		↓ 20,000 ENTER ↓ 60 ENTER	F02=60.00
8.25 ÷ 12 = I/YR	0.69		NPV 8.25 ÷ 12 = ENTER	I=0.69
▼ NPV	1,385,478.36		↓ CPT	NPV=1,385,478.36
			2ND QUIT	

Unit 18.1

1. Net income = Revenues − Expenses = $13,600 − $8,400 = **$5,200**

2a. Net sales = Gross sales − Sales returns = $52,000 − $800 = **$51,200**

2b. Cost of goods sold = Beginning inventory + Cost of goods purchased − Ending inventory
    = $6,500 + 31,700 − $7,100 = **$31,100**

2c. Gross profit = Net sales − Cost of goods sold = $51,200 − $31,100 = **$20,100**

2d. Net income = Gross profit − Operating expenses = $20,100 − $9,400 = **$10,700**

Unit 18.2

1. Total assets = $15,000 (cash) + $18,000 (accounts receivable) + $24,000 (inventory) + $56,300 (store and office equipment, depreciated) = $113,300

   Total liabilities = $11,000 (accounts payable) + $2,000 (notes payable) = $13,000

   Owner's equity = $113,300 (total assets) − $13,000 (total liabilities) = **$100,300**

Unit 18.3

1. 6C: $270,700 ÷ $973,400 ≈ .278 ≈ **27.8%**
   6D: $218,700 ÷ $671,000 ≈ .326 ≈ **32.6%**
   6E: $270,700 − $218,700 = **$52,000**
   6F: $52,000 ÷ $218,700 ≈ .238 ≈ **23.8%**

2a. Current ratio = $\frac{\text{Current assets}}{\text{Current liabilities}} = \frac{\$208,500}{\$60,100} ≈ \mathbf{3.5}$

2b. Inventory turnover = $\frac{\text{Cost of goods sold}}{\text{Average inventory}} = \frac{\$452,300}{(\$71,300 + \$78,200) \div 2} = \frac{\$452,300}{\$74,750} ≈ \mathbf{6.1}$

2c. Profit margin, before tax = $\frac{\text{Net income, before tax}}{\text{Net sales}} = \frac{\$54,700}{\$671,000} \approx .082 \approx 8.2\%$

3a. Bonneville had about $3.50 in current assets for each $1 in current liabilities.

3b. During the year, Bonneville sold its inventory 6.1 times.

3c. Bonneville's profit during the year was 8.2% of net sales.

Unit 19.1

1. Beginning inventory: 4 × $1,200 $ 4,800
   January: 15 × $1,150   17,250
   March: 12 × $1,065   12,780
   Totals: 31 $34,830

2. 2 × $1,200 $2,400
   3 × $1,065   +3,195
   5            $5,595

3. Average unit cost = $\frac{\text{Total cost available for sale}}{\text{Number of units available for sale}} = \frac{\$34,830}{31} = \$1,123.55$

   Ending inventory = 5 × $1,123.55 = **$5,617.75**

4. 5 computers purchased in March: 5 × $1,065 = **$5,325**

5. 4 computers from beginning inventory: 4 × $1,200 $4,800
   1 computer purchased in January: 1 × $1,150   +1,150
   Totals   5 $5,950

6. Specific identification: $34,830 - $5,595   = **$29,235.00**
   Weighted average: $34,830 - $5,617.75 = **$29,212.25**
   FIFO: $34,830 - $5,325   = **$29,505.00**
   LIFO: $34,830 - $5,950   = **$28,880.00**

Unit 19.2

1. Department A: $\frac{913,000}{1,335,000}$ × $48,300 = $33,032.13 ≈ **$33,032**

   Department B: $\frac{422,000}{1,335,000}$ × $48,300 = $15,267.87 ≈ **$15,268**

   Total $48,300

Unit 20.1

1. **Straight-line method**

   Depreciable basis = $32,000 - $7,000 = $25,000

Year	Annual depreciation	Book value
Begin	—	$32,000
1	$\frac{\$25,000}{5}$ = **$5,000**	$27,000
2	**$5,000**	$22,000
3	**$5,000**	$17,000
4	**$5,000**	$12,000
5	**$5,000**	$ 7,000
Total	$25,000	NA

2. **Units-of-production method**

   Depreciation per unit = $\frac{\$25,000}{125,000}$ = $0.20

Year	Annual depreciation	Book value
Begin	—	$32,000
1	35,000 miles × $0.20 = **$7,000**	$25,000
2	32,000 miles × $0.20 = **$6,400**	$18,600
3	28,000 miles × $0.20 = **$5,600**	$13,000
4	25,000 miles × $0.20 = **$5,000**	$ 8,000
5	18,000 miles × $0.20 = $3,600; limited to **$1,000**	$ 7,000
Total	$25,000	NA

   Book value cannot go below $7,000 salvage value

3. **Declining-balance method**

Year 1 depreciation is based on $32,000; ignores salvage value

Rate: $\frac{150\%}{5} = 30\%$

Year	Annual depreciation	Book value
Begin	—	$32,000
1	32,000 × 30% = **$9,600**	$22,400
2	22,400 × 30% = **$6,720**	$15,680
3	15,680 × 30% = **$4,704**	$10,976
4	$10,976 × 30% ≈ **$3,293**	$ 7,683
5	$7,683 × 30% ≈ $2,305; limited to **$683**	$ 7,000 ← Book value cannot go below $7,000 salvage value
Total	$25,000	NA

4. Year 1: $\frac{\$25,000}{5} \times \frac{2}{12} \approx \$833$

   Year 2: $\frac{\$25,000}{5} = \$5,000$

5. Year 1: $\$9,600 \times \frac{2}{12} = \$1,600$

   Year 2: $(\$9,600 \times \frac{10}{12}) + (\$6,720 \times \frac{2}{12}) = \$9,120$

   Found in Problem 3

Unit 20.2

1. Because the asset is used for *personal use,* **no depreciation can be taken**.

2. Your opinion of useful life and salvage value has no bearing on MACRS. Illustration 20-3 classifies a desk as a *7-year property*. Using Illustration 20-4, year 1, 7-year column: $1,200 × 14.29% ≈ **$171**

3. Building value: $850,000 × 80% = $680,000. Using Illustration 20-7, August column: $680,000 × 0.938% ≈ **$6,378**

4. $512,000 cost - $500,000 (maximum Section 179 expense deduction for the year 2015) = $12,000
   $12,000 (depreciable basis) × 20% (from Illustration 20-4, 5-year property) = **$2,400**

   Note: You will get a total deduction of $502,400 ($500,000 Section 179 expense deduction + $2,400 depreciation).

Unit 21.1

1. Because taxable income is less than $100,000, we use the tax table (Illustration 21-1). Find range "at least $16,750 but less than $16,800," single taxpayer column: **$2,063**

2. Because taxable income is $100,000 or more, we use the tax rate schedules (Illustration 21-2).
   Step 1 (locate the schedule): For married filing jointly, we use Schedule Y-1
   Step 2 (find the range): "over $73,800 but not over $148,850"
   Step 3 (find difference between taxable income and base amount): $145,666 - $73,800 = $71,866
   Step 4 (multiply by rate): $71,866 × 25% = $17,966.50
   Step 5 (find the tax): $17,966.50 + $10,162.50 = **$28,129**

3. Use the corporate tax rate schedule (Illustration 21-3).
   Step 1 (find the range): "over $100,000 but not over $335,000"
   Step 2 (find difference between taxable income and base amount): $145,666 - $100,000 = $45,666
   Step 3 (multiply by rate): $45,666 × 39% = $17,809.74
   Step 4 (find the tax): $17,809.74 + $22,250 = $40,059.74 = **$40,060** (rounded to the nearest dollar)

Unit 21.2

1. Sales tax from first dealer: $19,300 × 6.75% $ 1,302.75
   Sales tax from second dealer: $19,300 × 6%   - 1,158.00
   Savings $ 144.75

2. Price of new car $41,000
   Less trade-in   - 2,000
   Net price $39,000 × 5.5% = **$2,145**

Unit 21.3

1. $228,000 \times 35\% = \textbf{\$79,800}$

2. Tax rate = $\dfrac{\text{Total budget of the taxing entity}}{\text{Total assessed value within the taxing entity}} = \dfrac{\$14,372,000}{\$4,259,445,120} \approx .0033741 \approx .003375$ ← *Remember to round up, even if next digit is less than 5*

3. Property tax = Assessed value × Total tax rate = $79,800 \times .031764 = \textbf{\$2,534.77}$

4. Property tax = $\dfrac{\text{Assessed value}}{\$100} \times$ Tax rate = $\dfrac{\$150,000}{\$100} \times \$2.925 = \textbf{\$4,387.50}$

5. Property tax = $\dfrac{\text{Assessed value}}{1,000} \times$ Mill levy = $\dfrac{\$115,000}{1,000} \times 14.654 = \textbf{\$1,685.21}$

Unit 22.1

1. Because the policy is based on value (not on replacement cost), you will collect **$2,800** ($3,300 - $500 deductible).

2.
Basic premium (look across the $150,000 row to column 4)	$ 657.00
New home discount: $657 × 12%	- 78.84
	$ 578.16
Smoke alarm discount: $578.16 × 2%	- 11.56
	$ 566.60
Premium for additional liability coverage	+ 85.00
Total annual premium	$ 651.60 (**$652** rounded)

3.
Basic premium: $\dfrac{\$975,000}{\$1,000} \times \$2.20$	$2,145.00
Discount for having $1,000 deductible: $2,145 × 4%	- 85.80
Subtotal	$2,059.20
Additional liability coverage: $\dfrac{\$975,000}{\$1,000} \times \$0.20$	+ 195.00
Total annual premium	$2,254.20 (**$2,254** rounded)

4. The first $10,000 of Bronson's medical expenses are paid by Bronson's insurance company through his no-fault coverage. Brandi's company will pay the next $25,000 through Brandi's 25/**50**/25 liability coverage. Bronson must collect the remaining $11,000 ($46,000 - $10,000 - $25,000) of medical expenses directly from Brandi (through the courts, if Brandi refuses to pay). The $16,000 damage to Bronson's car will be paid by Brandi's company through her 25/50/**25** liability coverage.

Unit 22.2

1. The footnote of Illustration 22-3 indicates that rates for females are approximately those of a male 4 years younger. So we will use the rate for a 28-year old.

   Annual Premium = $\dfrac{\$200,000}{\$1,000} \times \$2.54 = \textbf{\$508}$

2. **Option 1.** Get cash value: $\dfrac{\$125,000}{\$1,000} \times \$264 = \textbf{\$33,000}$

   Option 2. Reduce the coverage: $\dfrac{\$125,000}{\$1,000} \times \$548 = \textbf{\$68,500}$

   Option 3. Keep $125,000 coverage, but for a shorter term: **21 years, 296 days**

Unit 23.1

1. $P = 2(L + W) = 2(1,650 \text{ ft} + 660 \text{ ft}) = 2(2,310 \text{ ft}) = \textbf{4,620 ft}$

2. $d = \dfrac{C}{\pi} \approx \dfrac{25,000 \text{ mi}}{3.14} \approx 7,961.78 \text{ mi}$; $r = \dfrac{d}{2} = \dfrac{7,961.78 \text{ mi}}{2} = \textbf{3,980.89 mi}$

3.
Area of rectangle: $A = LW = (50 \text{ in.})(30 \text{ in.}) =$	1,500.00 sq in.
Less area of circle: $A = \pi r^2 \approx (3.14)(6 \text{ in.})(6 \text{ in.}) \approx$	- 113.04 sq in.
	1,386.96 sq in.

4. $V = \pi r^2 h \approx (3.14)(13 \text{ ft})(13 \text{ ft})(12 \text{ ft}) \approx 6,367.92 \text{ ft}^3 \approx \textbf{6,367.92 cu ft}$

Unit 23.2

1. Office 1: Rent per square foot = $\frac{\text{Rent}}{\text{Number of sq ft}} = \frac{\$525}{18 \text{ ft} \times 30 \text{ ft}} = \frac{\$525}{540 \text{ sq ft}} \approx$ **\$0.97 per sq ft**

   Office 2: Rent per square foot = $\frac{\text{Rent}}{\text{Number of sq ft}} = \frac{\$480}{22 \text{ ft} \times 24 \text{ ft}} = \frac{\$480}{528 \text{ sq ft}} \approx$ **\$0.91 per sq ft**

2. A = LW = (15 ft)(22.5 ft) = 337.5 sq ft = $\left(\frac{337.5}{9}\right)$ sq yd = 37.5 sq yd

   To convert sq ft to sq yd, we divide by 9

   Total cost = Number of units × Unit cost = 37.5 × \$28 = **\$1,050**

Unit 24.1

1. \$45,000 = (45,000 × .50822) pounds = **22,869.90 pounds**

2. 22,869.90 pounds = $\left(\frac{22,869.90}{.58420}\right)$ U.S. dollars = **\$39,147.38**

3. Sold for: 775,000 Canadian dollars = $\left(\frac{775,000}{1.0183}\right)$ U.S. dollars = \$761,072.38

   Purchased for: 850,000 Canadian dollars = $\left(\frac{850,000}{1.1510}\right)$ U.S. dollars = −738,488.27

   Gain   **\$ 22,584.11**

Unit 24.2

1. The symbol for kilo is k and the symbol for grams is g, so 15 kilograms = **15 kg**

2. The c is the symbol for the prefix centi. The m is the symbol for the base unit meter. So, 22 cm is read as 22 centimeters and means $\frac{22}{100}$ of a meter.

3. Start at milli on the line indicator of Illustration 26-3. Move to centi (1 place to the left). Move the decimal point 1 place to the left, getting: 24.8 mm = **2.48 cm**

4. Using the right half of the distance section of Illustration 26-4: 328 mi ≈ (328 × 1.60935) km ≈ **528 km**

5. C = $\frac{5}{9}$(F − 32) = $\frac{5}{9}$(72 − 32) = $\frac{5}{9}$(40) ≈ 22.22 ≈ **22°C**

Unit 25.1

1. Mean = $\frac{\text{Sum of values}}{\text{Number of values}} = \frac{\$1,350 + \$850 + \$1,475 + \$850 + \$3,900 + \$1,100}{6} = \frac{\$9,525}{6} =$ **\$1,587.50**

2. **Step 1 (arrange values)**   **Step 2 (find midpoint)**

   \$3,900   Midpoint = $\frac{\text{Number of values} + 1}{2} = \frac{6+1}{2} = \frac{7}{2} = 3.5$

   \$1,475

   \$1,350   The midpoint is between the third and fourth values:

   \$1,100   (\$1,350 + \$1,100) ÷ 2 = \$2,450 ÷ 2 = **\$1,225**

   \$850

   \$850

3. Because \$850 is listed most often (twice), **\$850** is the mode. For this day, this was the most *popular* model.

4. The mean is distorted by the \$3,900 sale; the mean price (\$1,587.50) doesn't seem to represent the average price. The mode (\$850) is the lowest value and does not represent the average price. For this set of values, **the median (\$1,225) is probably the best indicator.**

Unit 25.2

1.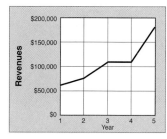

2.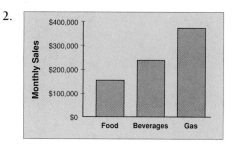

3.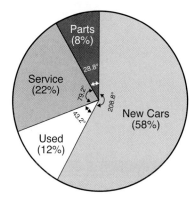

	Calculations		
New cars	.58 × 360°	=	208.80°
Used cars	.12 × 360°	=	43.20°
Service	.22 × 360°	=	79.20°
Parts	.08 × 360°	=	28.80°
	1.00		360.00°
	(100%)		

Unit 25.3

1. Range = 100 (highest value) − 71 (lowest value) = **29**

2. Step 1 Mean = $\frac{\text{Sum of values}}{n}$ = $\frac{100 + 87 + 92 + 71 + 78 + 100}{6}$ = $\frac{528}{6}$ = 88

Step 2 (Subtract Mean)	Step 3 (Square the result)
100 − 88 = 12	(12)(12) = 144
87 − 88 = −1	(−1)(−1) = 1
92 − 88 = 4	(4)(4) = 16
71 − 88 = −17	(−17)(−17) = 289
78 − 88 = −10	(−10)(−10) = 100
100 − 88 = 12	(12)(12) = 144

   Step 4 (add squared deviations): 144 + 1 + 16 + 289 + 100 + 144 = 694

   Step 5 (divide by n): 694 ÷ 6 = 115.67

   Step 6 (square root): The square root of 115.67 ≈ **10.75**

3. First 4 steps are identical to those of Problem 2. Difference is, in Step 5, we divide by (n − 1) instead of by n.

   Step 5 (divide by n − 1): 694 ÷ 5 = 138.80

   Step 6 (square root): The square root of 138.80 ≈ **11.78**

B Answers
Review Problems and Practice Tests

Note: These are the answers to Chapter Review Problems and Practice Tests. Step-by-step solutions are on our website (free of charge). A printed version of solutions is available through college bookstores or through our website.

Chapter 1
Review Problems
1. Three hundred seventeen
2. Eight million, two hundred fifty-seven thousand, one hundred sixteen
3. Two and one tenth
4. Twelve and twelve ten-thousandths
5. 426,000
6. .426
7. 400.026
8. 14,726,111.2
9. 4,800,000,000,000
10. 76.13
11. 123,678,000
12. 23,468
13. 46,000
14. 641
15. 25,442
16. 36,644
17. 115
18. 682
19. 11,628
20. 5,535
21. 82,440
22. 216,000
23. 16
24. 147
25. 212, R32
26. $19,025
27. 2,120 seats
28. 4 over par
29. 288 cans
30. 12 cases
31. $1,700
32. 1,128.509
33. 451.91
34. 24,198.4964
35. 122.23
36. 6.82
37. 12,648.532
38. 236.145
39. 28.0101
40. 114.68964
41. 4.55
42. 51.37
43. 11.84
44. 47,000
45. .0468
46. $652.01
47. $634.48
48. 128.563 acres
49. $41.48
50. $3,059
51. $7.22
52. $1,029.82
53. 84 full gloves
54. 2,428.5 miles
55. 85.8 gal
56. 28.3 mpg
57. $171.32
58. 4,380; 105,120; 38,395,080; 2,687,655,600
59. $41,400
60. $4.26 per sq ft
61. 27 pounds
62. 9 pounds per month
63. $136,800
64. $3,040
65. $4,158.50
66. Staples ($134.00)
67. 155 text messages

Practice Test
1. Eighty-seven thousand, twenty-two and thirty-five hundredths
2. 300.084
3. 26,100,000,000
4. 618.77
5. $29,000
6. 3,275
7. 126
8. 322,000
9. 127.4
10. $11
11. $19,563.50
12. 197.445 acres
13. $5,456.75
14. 19.5 mpg

Chapter 2
Review Problems
1. Numerator: 3 Denominator: 4
2. Proper
3. Mixed
4. Improper
5. Improper
6. $\frac{23}{4}$
7. $\frac{23}{8}$
8. $\frac{17}{6}$
9. $1\frac{1}{2}$
10. $2\frac{2}{3}$
11. 9
12. 35
13. $\frac{2}{3}$
14. $\frac{4}{23}$
15. $\frac{5}{7}$
16. $\frac{2}{5}$
17. $\frac{6}{11}$
18. $\frac{11}{12}$
19. $\frac{17}{15}$
20. $\frac{11}{24}$
21. $\frac{2}{5}$
22. $\frac{3}{10}$
23. $\frac{8}{15}$
24. $\frac{9}{20}$
25. $6\frac{7}{12}$
26. $5\frac{5}{12}$
27. $2\frac{1}{4}$
28. $1\frac{11}{12}$
29. $9\frac{11}{12}$
30. $1\frac{23}{28}$
31. $10\frac{3}{4}$ inches
32. 11 loaves
33. $1\frac{2}{5}$ acres
34. $50,000
35. 120 days
36. $300
37. $\frac{7}{15}$ interest
38. $105
39. 11 ft
40. $33
41. 36 whole shirts
42. $15\frac{11}{50}$
43. $\frac{3}{10}$
44. $\frac{3}{8}$
45. .3125
46. .$\overline{66}$
47. .$\overline{45}$
48. 3.8
49. Problems 45 and 48 are terminating; 46 and 47 are repeating
50. .285 acres
51. $1,760,000
52. Yes. Both fractions can be converted to terminating decimals: .25 + .20 = .45
53. No. $\frac{1}{3}$ cannot be converted to a terminating decimal.
54. $472.50
55. Flour: $5\frac{5}{6}$ cups
    Peanut butter: $1\frac{1}{6}$ cups
    Eggs: 7 eggs
56. $\frac{17}{40}$
57. Housing: $17,100
    Food: $13,680
    Transport.: $8,550
    Other: $29,070

58. 168 acres available
59. 448 homesites
60. $14,000,000
61. $8\frac{1}{8}$ yards
62. 24 suits
63. $125 per suit
64. $320
65. Corner B is the lowest ($60\frac{3}{8}$ inches below builder's level). Point A is $\frac{7}{8}$ inches higher than B; Point C is $2\frac{3}{16}$ inches higher than B; Point D is $\frac{11}{16}$ inches higher than B.

Practice Test
1. $\frac{29}{8}$
2. $4\frac{1}{3}$
3. $\frac{7}{9}$
4. $\frac{17}{22}$
5. $\frac{49}{60}$
6. $2\frac{1}{12}$
7. $3\frac{3}{20}$
8. $1\frac{11}{12}$
9. $\frac{5}{8}$
10. 4.6875
11. $4\frac{3}{4}$ inches
12. $719.20

Chapter 3
Review Problems
1. False
2. 7×12; $7 \cdot 12$; $7(12)$
3. False
4. Yes; No; Yes
5. 7^5
6. 243
7. 14
8. 121
9. 17
10. 18
11. 10
12. 12
13. -7
14. -288
15. 6
16. $2m + 2n$
17. $15a + 10b$
18. $y + 2$

19. $4m + 8$
20. Cannot simplify
21. (b) The other 2 are expressions (no equal sign)
22. $x = 35$
23. $y = 6$
24. $a = 5$
25. $t = 24$
26. $y = \frac{21}{2}$
27. $b = 18$
28. $m = 5$
29. $p = -4$
30. $x = 2$
31. $14 = 14$
32. $608.33
33. $PV = \frac{FV}{(1+i)^n}$
34. $4m$
35. $x + 12$ or $12 + x$
36. $a - 8$
37. $2(x + y + z)$
38. $y = x + 4$
39. $r + 2 = t + 4$
40. $\frac{n}{3} = 18$
41. Britney: $28,500
    Megan: $36,500
42. Warehouse: 3,200 sq ft
    Showroom: 1,600 sq ft
43. $80,000
44. Wife: $150,000
    Each child: $100,000
45. Trucks: 34   Cars: 204
46. $87
47. Water: 400 lb
    Sand: 2,000 lb
    Cement: 800 lb
    Gravel: 2,800 lb
48. Total: $209,000
49. Keep guessing an amount until total coverage is $198,000.
50. Sales tax: $234.86
51. Cashews: 4 oz
    Almonds: 12 oz
    Macadamia: 2 oz
52. $187,416.88
53. 650 customers
54. 26 customers per day

Practice Test
1. False
2. 64
3. 34
4. 29

5. -3
6. $-3a + 13$
7. $m = 40$
8. $y = 35$
9. $p = 4$
10. $p = \frac{5}{3}$
11. $m + 4 = n + 3$
12. Brandy: $12,500
    Carlos: $17,500
13. 106,667 copies

Chapter 4
Review Problems
1. 7.9%
2. 135%
3. .521
4. .083
5. 1.375
6. .00625
7. 87.5%
8. 125%
9. $\frac{9}{25}$
10. $\frac{5}{8}$
11. $40
12. 87.5
13. 150
14. 320
15. 50%
16. 130%
17. $11,500
18. 88.9%
19. Matt: $25,620
    Robbie: $17,080
20. 5 questions
21. $2.80
22. $63
23. $85.71
24. $480,000
25. 57.4%
26. $65.48; $1,035.48
27. $845.84
28. $15.07
29. 81,522 batteries
30. $530
31. 452 sq ft
32. 9.1%
33. 11.7%
34. 7.2%
35. 11.1%
36. 15.6%
37. 32.9%

38. 36.4%
39. 45.6%
40. $6,909
41. $5,509.14
42. 7.1%
43. $67,065
44. $67.68
45. $1,500
46. 163.3%
47. $4,447,000
48. $1,714.29
49. Is, in fact, 64% off
50. Is, in fact, 17.88%
51. Is, in fact, 83%
52. $650.50. This is because Volatile always increased 20% from lower prices and dropped 20% from higher prices.

Practice Test
1. 6.5%
2. .875
3. 31.25%
4. $\frac{1}{8}$
5. $42,000
6. $9,000
7. 87.5%
8. $802.50
9. 21,875 tires
10. 1.2%

Chapter 5
Review Problems
1. $360; $840
2. $175; $525
3. $840
4. $525
5. Answers are the same
6. $3,888
7. 39.25%
8. It means that a 39.25% single discount is identical to a 25/10/10 series discount.
9. $3,888
10. $596.00
11. $7.20; $232.80; Oct. 27; Nov. 21
12. $74.45
13. Aug. 7; Sep. 6
14. Sep. 10; Sep. 30

15. May 15
16. $10,309.28
17. 116.49%
18. Cash discount
19. True
20. False
21. Company B ($2,088)
22. $420; $411.60
23. $252; $231.84
24. $302.81; $290.70
25. $341.25
26. October 18
27. $331.01
28. November 17
29. 37.63%
30. $2,748.75
    $586.50
    $839.52
31. No. Sleeping bag net price = $445.74
32. $3,498.36
33. Mar. 28; Apr. 27
34. $3,398.87
35. $12.54
36. $12.54 − $3.76 = $8.78

Practice Test

1. $615
2. $15.84
3. 35.4%
4. November 17
5. $602.70
6. $12,105.26
7. 63.48%

Chapter 6

Review Problems

1. $3,250
2. $2.07
3. $70
4. $300
5. $0.00
6. False
7. $840
8. $300
9. $175
10. $240
11. $21.60
12. $17.50
13. $24; 50%; 33.3%
14. 28.6%
15. 20%
16. 42.9%
17. 33.3%
18. $24
19. $64
20. 37.5%
21. $24
22. False
23. $200
24. $765
25. $783
26. Dependable ($765)
27. $300
28. 13.2%
29. $1.02 each
30. Total proceeds = $150.60
31. 1.70
32. $1.19 each
33. $496
34. $719.20
35. $634.88
36. $75.12 profit
37. $19.88 operating loss
38. $56 absolute loss
39. 127 cutting boards
40. $6,473.50
41. $520; $1,820
42. 97.2%; $175; 49.3%
43. $2,550; $850
44. $40.71
45. $3,913.04; $586.96; 13.0%
46. 16.7%
47. 150%
48. $70
49. 73.7%
50. 42.4%
51. $100.98
52. $5.98
53. 6.3%
54. $64.02
55. 38.8%
56. 292%
57. The 100% markup is based on the $20 cost. The 50% markdown is based on the $40 retail price.
58. $268.58

Practice Test

1. $840
2. $20
3. $120
4. 40%
5. 28.6%
6. $4,455
7. 35%
8. $0.57 per pound
9. 1.75
10. (b) operating loss
11. 122,750 copies

Chapter 7

Review Problems

1. True
2. (c) bank statement
3. (a) debit memo
4. (c) bank statement
5. (b) credit memo
6. $2,924.00
7. False
8. (b) August
9. B−
10. C−
11. C−
12. C−
13. None
14. None
15. B−
16. B+
17. C−
18. C+
19. C−
20. $12,385.25
21. $18,885.18
22. $700; $550; $374; $2,174; $852; $524.75; $2,324.75
23. Balance is $843.57
24. $2,316.32
25. $9 must be added to reflect correct amt of ck 102; Oct. interest of $11.32 must be added; ck printing of $28.75 must be deducted.
26. $2,316.32

Practice Test

1. (a) debit memo
2. $1,159.56
3. $5,286.35
4. False
5. Add $9.22 for March interest; deduct $48.25 for check printing fees.

Chapter 8

Review Problems

1. False
2. True
3. **Don:** 46.5; 40; 6.5; $12; $320; $78; $398
   Joy: 48; 40; 8; $12.375; $330; $99; $429
   Bo: 40; 40; 0; $10.875; $290; $0; $290
   Thu: 38; 38; 0; $12.375; $313.50; $0; $313.50
4. Brad ($16,163.40)
5. $1,200
6. $268
7. $699
8. $1,296.24
9. $2,947
10. (b) is true
11. False
12. **Dan:** $1,275; $1,275; $79.05; $18.49; $137.22; $63.75; $348.51; $926.49
    Ashlie: $810; $810; $50.22; $11.75; $94.47; $40.50; $196.94; $613.06
    Ian: $1,140; $1,140; $70.68; $16.53; $93.90; $57; $238.11; $901.89
    Totals: $84,830; $3,225; $3,225; $3,225; $199.95; $46.77; $325.59; $161.25; $50; $783.56; $2,441.44
13. Dario: $270
    Maria: None
    Actual tax: $252
14. Soc. Sec.: $93.00
    Medicare: $37.70
15. True
16. False
17. $199.95
18. $46.77
19. FUT: $3.00
    SUT: $39.00
20. $4,071.72
21. True
22. True
23. $18,443
24. $35,654
25. Refund of $346

26. $460
27. $11.50 per hour
28. $155; $36.25; $232.84; $162.50
29. $1,838.41
30. $155; $36.25; $12; $50
31. Owe $927

Practice Test

1. $448.50
2. $42,754.80
3. $457.50
4. $98.25
5. $92.97
6. False
7. $3.60
8. $14,864
9. Refund of $498

Chapter 9

Review Problems

1. $10,000
2. 1 year
3. Oct. 1, 2018
4. $800
5. $10,800
6. $10,533.33
7. $10,933.33
8. False
9. False
10. 290 days
11. 223 days
12. 96 days
13. Jul. 14, 2017
14. Jan. 29, 2018
15. Apr. 17, 2016 (leap year)
16. $487.50
17. $480.82
18. False
19. False
20. True
21. $945.21
22. $701.03
23. **Day 24:** $189.04; $7,810.96; $17,189.04
    Day 89: $17,541.06; $352.02; $17,189.04
    Totals: $25,541.06; $541.06; $25,000
24. $945.21; $701.03; $541.06
25. $P = \frac{I}{RT}$; $R = \frac{I}{PT}$; $T = \frac{I}{PR}$

26. $320.83
27. $4,500
28. 16.75%
29. 15 months (1.25 yrs)
30. $2,800
31. 151 days
32. 8.33%
33. 13.32%
34. 13.18%
35. 417.14%
36. 15.60%
37. 4%
38. 1.75%
39. .625%
40. $805
41. $810.34
42. $811.79
43. George Lavin (Problem 42) ended up with most
44. Bank (6.22% APY vs. 6.17% APY)
45. 5.83%
46. $292.59
47. 76.04%
48. 121.67%
49. $43.07
50. $50.71
51. $939.01
52. 26.13%
53. First bond (8.52% APY vs. 8.5%)
54. $1,534.50; $1,534.49

Practice Test

1. False
2. $12,760
3. Oct. 20
4. $40.32
5. $12,081.37
6. 21.33%
7. 14.68%
8. $562.75
9. 7.28%

Chapter 10

Review Problems

1. 12
2. 1.5%
3. $1,000
4. $50
5. $1,847.68
6. False

7. $1,600 is not a TVM variable
8. $6,000
9. $33,030.64
10. $226,566.42
11. $22,046.72
12. $956,673.97
13. $962,653.18
14. $880,033.18
15. 35: $17,308.48
    45: $52,092.66
    55: $121,997.09
    65: $262,481.31
16. $41,761,132.86
17. $6,136.88
18. About 565 elephants
19. $3,720.47
20. 8,478,758.43 euros
21. $234,000
22. No; need to find PV
23. $128,171.43
24. No; $128,171.43 value less than $150,000 cost.
25. $70,000
26. $54,979.85
27. $840.17
28. Because the 6% rate is less than the 8% prevailing rate.
29. $214.55
30. $4,122.61
31. $9,786.03
32. $3,442.50
33. $6,885
34. $1,721.25
35. $1,480,390.69
36. $3,062,600.87
37. $615,881.98
38. $3,355,040.70
39. $7,243,281.23
40. $311,289.69
41. $420,000
42. No; must find PV of Michael's offer.
43. $230,781.55
44. Ishiro's

Practice Test

1. 20
2. $420
3. $144,501.09
4. $496,875.02
5. $7,698.10

6. $214.55
7. $70,252.22

Chapter 11

Review Problems

1. $29,878.96
2. $1,484.96
3. $2,083.91
4. £5,190,000
5. £1,890,216.06
6. £7,080,216.06
7. 73.63 years old
8. $2,812.50
9. $3,016.78
10. $3,242.99
11. $3,224.85
12. $208,598.64
13. $462.27
14. $5,783.44
15. $46.25
16. 15-yr: $1,369.29
    30-yr: $1,048.82
17. $320.47
18. 15-yr: $96,472.20
    30-yr: $227,575.20
19. $131,103
20. $2,383.71
21. 268.00 months
22. 2.46%
23. 7.03%
24. 2.28%, 6.10%, 2.76%, 3.17%
25. 59.83%
26. No; salary increased only 3.29%
27. 13.58% compounded annually
28. $3,250
29. It will increase
30. $1,147,872.69
31. 529.13 months
32. $6,888.24
33. $247.83
34. $161.48
35. 7.42%
36. $169,596.55
37. $234.14
38. $621,661.20
39. $3,047.30

Practice Test

1. $89.91
2. 35.38 months

3. $1,580.17
4. $320.15
5. $320,390.40
6. 4.33%

Chapter 12
Review Problems
1. 12
2. 1.5%
3. $1,000
4. $50
5. $1,847.68
6. False
7. $1,600 is not a TVM variable
8. $6,000
9. Clear if new problem; do not clear if a variation.
10. Never have to change periods per year setting.
11. False
12. False
13. 3
14. True
15. False
16. $33,030.64
17. $226,566.42
18. $22,046.72
19. $956,673.97
20. $962,653.18
21. $880,033.18
22. 10 yr: $17,308.48
    20 yr: $52,092.67
    30 yr: $121,997.10
    40 yr: $262,481.34
23. $41,761,132.86
24. $6,136.88
25. About 565 elephants
26. $3,720.47
27. 8,478,758.43 euros
28. $234,000
29. No; need to find PV of money saved.
30. $128,171.43
31. No; $128,171.43 value is less than the $150,000 cost.
32. $70,000
33. $54,979.85
34. $840.17
35. Because the 6% rate is less than the 8% prevailing rate.
36. $214.55
37. $4,122.61
38. $9,786.03
39. $3,442.50
40. $6,885
41. $1,721.25
42. $1,480,390.69
43. $3,062,600.87
44. $615,881.98
45. $3,355,040.70
46. $7,243,281.23
47. $311,289.69

Practice Test
1. 20
2. $420
3. $144,501.09
4. $496,875.02
5. $7,698.10
6. $214.55
7. $70,252.22

Chapter 13
Review Problems
1. $29,878.96
2. $1,484.96
3. $1,251.38
4. $2,083.91
5. £5,190,000
6. £1,890,216.06
7. £7,080,216.06
8. 73 years old
9. $2,812.50
10. $3,016.78
11. $3,242.99
12. 290.14 mo (24.18 yrs)
13. It will increase
14. $587,608.96
15. $208,598.64
16. $462.27
17. $5,783.44
18. $46.25
19. 15-yr: $1,369.29
    30-yr: $1,048.82
20. $320.47
21. 15-yr: $96,472.20
    30-yr: $227,575.20
22. $131,103
23. $2,383.71
24. 268 months
25. 261.22 months; 215.03 months
26. $486,661.16
27. $20,735.00
28. 165.34 months
29. 61.02 months
30. No; the extra $5 applies entirely to principal
31. 54 months
32. Save 4.13 months
33. Rebate: $451.36
    2.9%: $457.07
34. $172,530.35
35. $234.14
36. $621,661.20
37. $3,047.31

Practice Test
1. $89.91
2. 35.38 months
3. $1,580.17
4. $320.15
5. $1,138.56
6. $372,676.80

Chapter 14
Review Problems
1. (c) greater than $177.08
2. (b) greater than 6.5%
3. $27,500
4. $4,716.16
5. $34,916.16
6. $7,144.32
7. False
8. False
9. (d)
10. 34 days
11. $6.66;$248.05;$751.95
    $5.93;$248.78;$503.17
    $3.60;$251.11;$252.06
    $254.24;$2.18;$252.06
12. $2,203.63
13. 1.083333%;0.035616%
14. 15.9% rate is lower
15. $410.67
16. $5.13
17. $361.91
18. $8,200
19. $763.96
20. $9,613.96
21. 1: $34.60;$213.01;
       $7,986.99
    2: $42.12;$257.88;
       $7,729.11
22. $419.80

Practice Test
1. $26,899.60
2. 33 days
3. $2,318.41
4. $1,492.13
5. $648.45

Chapter 15
Review Problems
1. False
2. True
3. First: $123,200
   Second: $16,800
4. First: $123,200
   Second: $24,400
   Nash: $7,400
5. False
6. $1,231.42
7. $236,863.20
8. $191.67
9. $1,266.29
10. Yes; if tax or insurance change, TI portion will change.
11. 1: $968.75; $105.87; $149,894.13
    2: $968.07; $106.55; $149,787.58
12. True
13. False
14. $167,700
15. Mo Pmt: $719.46
    Int #1: $600.00
    Prin #1: $119.46
    Bal: $119,880.54
    Int #18: $4,783.10
    Bal Pmt 102:
      $104,155.45
    Int #1-360:
      $139,006.67
    Final Pmt: $720.53
16. Yr 1 Int: $14,926.14
    Prin: $1,285.56
    Bal: $348,714.44
    Yr 2 Int: $35,590.23
    Prin: $3,317.85
    Bal: $345,396.59
    Yr 3 Int: $35,233.70
    Prin: $3,674.38
    Bal: $341,722.21
17. $804.62
18. $189,663.20
19. $189,667.92; $4.72

20. Difference of $4.72. Answer to Problem 19 is correct answer.
21. $79,331.49
22. Balance goes down slower during the first part of a loan because interest is figured on unpaid balance.
23. 83.98 months
24. 276 months (about 23 years)
25. 6.50%
26. It increases
27. $2,762.50
28. $340,000
29. $225,212.50
30. $26,550
31. True
32. $8,750
33. $7,185
34. True
35. $813.92
36. $962.12
37. $813.92
38. $836.98
39. $178.31
40. $114,956.18
41. $11,119
42. First lender gets $116,100; second lender gets $18,400.
43. $54,066

Practice Test
1. $1,319.33
2. $104,905.08
3. $1,042.13
4. $12,345.93
5. 6.5%
6. $36,400
7. $4,107.50

Chapter 16

Review Problems
1. False
2. False
3. $37.50
4. False
5. False
6. True
7. a. $92.13
   b. $78.25
   c. $86.56
   d. Decreased $0.63
   e. 35,200 shares
   f. 1.62% is correct
   g. 27 is correct
8. $3,930
9. $4,480
10. 8.00; 11.00; 29.28
11. Someone willing to pay $65 for a share of stock would be paying about $8 for each $1 of annual earnings.
12. Company A
13. Investors feel Company C has a better future than is indicated by current earnings.
14. True
15. True
16. False
17. True
18. (c) Premium
19. (b) Discount
20. 8.625%
21. 2026
22. 30 bonds
23. $1,267.65
24. The prevailing rate for new bonds is less than the coupon rate for this bond.
25. Decreased $5.83
26. 6.80%
27. $20,010.94
28. True
29. $24.20;$15.79;$95.02
30. True
31. True
32. Stock
33. Stock
34. Bond
35. Both
36. Bond
37. (b) municipal bond
38. The bond paying 7.5% compounded semiannually.

Practice Test
1. $180
2. a. $51.38
   b. 161,300 shares
   c. 60¢ per share
3. $5,737.50
4. 38
5. $1,252.58
6. $83.75
7. (a) less than coupon rate
8. $22,506.25
9. $10.32

Chapter 17

Review Problems
1. 7.77%
2. 17.92%
3. Borrow from credit union at 11.75%; friend is charging 13.12% APR.
4. 17.96%
5. 31.54%
6. 7.07%
7. 7.21%
8. More
9. 7.89%
10. 7.82%
11. 6.875% loan (APR=7.82%)
12. 10.77%
13. Yes, unless you expect rates to drop.
14. 7.03%
15. 2.28%, 6.10%, 2.76%, 3.17%
16. No (3.29%)
17. 2.64%
18. 7.42%
19. 8.84%
20. 8.05%
21. Prevailing rate greater than 7% coupon rate.
22. Able to buy at a discount.
23. 10.71%
24. Able to sell at a premium.
25. True
26. False
27. 23.51% comp annually
28. -4.45% comp annually
29. 59.83% comp annually
30. $123,000
31. 9.52% comp monthly
32. 14.04% comp annually
33. $173,400
34. $84,240.19
35. b and d
36. 3.33% comp annually
37. 5.15% comp annually
38. 5.28% comp annually
39. 2.46%
40. (b) municipal bond
41. $86,350
42. 7.47% comp monthly
43. Less than $55,000
44. $52,010.73
45. 7.5% semiannually (APY=7.64%)

Practice Test
1. 41.54%
2. 7.48%
3. 4.38%
4. 7.88% comp semiannually
5. 9.95% comp quarterly
6. $84,446.54

Chapter 18

Review Problems
1. (a) net income
2. (b) over a given period of time
3. False
4. $80,000
5. $130,000
6. $69,000
7. $783,900
8. $251,600
9. $532,300
10. $161,000
11. A
12. E
13. B
14. G
15. A
16. C
17. D
18. E and F
19. B
20. G
21. $110,900
22. False
23. $63,000
24. $148,000
25. $219,000
26. False

27. True
28. False
29. True
30. A few check figures are given:
    Gross sales:
    101.1%; 100.5%
    ($18,700); (5.1%)
    Net sales:
    100.0%; 100.0%
    ($20,800); (5.7%)
    Total expenses:
    51.9%; 42.2%
    $24,300; 15.8%
    Net income, after taxes:
    2.2%; 10.8%
    ($31,500); (80.6%)
    Total current assets:
    94.6%; 95.2%
    ($31,800); (20.5%)
    Total assets:
    100.0%; 100.0%
    ($32,600); (20.0%)
    Stockholders' equity:
    86.2%; 88.4%
    ($31,600); (21.9%)
31. Sales decreased 5.1%; cost of goods sold increased 3.0%, even though sales decreased; expenses increased 15.8%; total stockholders' equity decreased $31,600.
32. 6.9; for each dollar of current liabilities, BBB has about $6.90 of current assets.
33. 3.6; for each dollar of current liabilities, BBB has about $3.60 of highly liquid assets.
34. 13.8%; for each dollar of assets, BBB owes 13.8¢.
35. 2.3; inventory sold 2.3 times during the year.
36. 44.7%; BBB's goods cost 44.7% of what they sold for.
37. 3.4%; BBB's profit is 3.4% of net sales.
38. 6.7%; BBB's profit is 6.7% of stockholders' equity.
39. (b) Worse
40. Increase profits, increase long-term financing, reduce dividends, and sell additional stock.
41. (a) High
42. Do more advertising, improve sales staff, and reduce inventory.
43. Sole proprietorship and partnership
44. Partnership and corporation
45. Corporation
46. Corporation
47. Sole proprietorship and corporation
48. (c)
49. 57.1%
50. A few check figures:
    Net sales: $1,510,100
    Net purchases: $903,700
    Cost of goods sold: $881,200
    Net income, after taxes $222,300
51. A few check figures:
    Current assets: $65,800
    Total assets: $97,300
    Stockholders' equity: $54,200
    Retained earnings: $34,200

Practice Test
1. An income statement is for a period of time, not a certain date.
2. $216,500; $142,000; $74,500; $44,500
3. $168,000
4. 27.6%
5. Cash: $4,000; 17.4% A/R: ($6,000); (10.3%)
6. (a) 1.7; for each dollar of current liabilities, the company has about $1.70 of current assets.
   (b) 53.6%; for each dollar of assets, the company owes about 53.6¢.
   (c) 2.2; inventory was sold 2.2 times during the year.

Chapter 19
Review Problems
1. True
2. 77 hammers; $919.89
3. $84.88
4. $83.65
5. $87.29
6. $79.45
7. $835.01; $836.24; $832.60; $840.44
8. FIFO
9. FIFO
10. False
11. $12,800; $14,800; $37,400
12. $10,471; $9,355; $20,174
13. $1,010; $1,560; $4,530
14. $4,552; $4,268; $9,390
15. $1,510.44; $1,560; $1,440

Practice Test
1. $1,545.76; $1,600; $1,440
2. $11,510; $64,640
3. (c) Monthly sales per department
4. $3,405.25

Chapter 20
Review Problems
1. False
2. $1,300
3. 5 years
4. $150
5. $1,150
6. $690
7. $610
8. False
9. False
10. $400
11. Dep Exp: $400 each yr
    Accum dep: $400; $800; $1,200; $1,600; $2,000
    Book value: $2,400; $2,000; $1,600; $1,200; $800; $400
12. $428; $448; $376; $480; $268
13. $960; $576; $346; $118; $0
14. 6 months
15. $100; $200
16. True
17. False
18. 5 years
19. 5 years
20. 39 years
21. 7 years
22. $500
23. $593
24. $256
25. $3,001
26. $24,871
27. $24,250
28. $300; $480; $288; $173; $173; $86
29. You get only half a year's depreciation in year 1.
30. $2,122; $7,272; $7,272
31. Get 11.5 months depreciation in year 1
32. $500,000; $10,289
33. $3,150; $5,400; $5,400
34. $8,167; $10,733; $6,440
35. $7,000; $11,200; $6,720
36. 200% declining balance ($25,340)

Practice Test
1. $30,000; 5 years; $5,000; $25,000; $10,000; $20,000
2. $1,564; $1,306
3. $313; $264
4. $78; $301
5. $286; $490
6. $11,336; $24,725
7. $500,000; $1,143

Chapter 21
Review Problems
1. False
2. (a) Tax tables
3. $2,018
4. $25,063
5. $32,719
6. Tom: $6,363
   Shauna: $27,684
7. Tom: $6,363
   Shauna: $26,888

8. Least: Married filing joint ($32,719) Greatest: Married filing separately ($34,047)
9. $4,283,750
10. False
11. $21.72
12. $21.72
13. $1,033.50
14. $19,915.50; $19,626.75
15. (b) state and local govt.
16. $175,000
17. .006586
18. Rounded up to ensure adequate revenues.
19. $4,303.78
20. $4,291
21. $4,604.12
22. $15,367.68
23. $9,716
24. $9,716
25. Same
26. Probably because tax tables are easier to use
27. 15%
28. For each additional dollar of taxable income, they must pay 15% to the IRS
29. 13.72%
30. $2,552.20

Practice Test
1. $6,813
2. $38,344 (rounded)
3. $12,568,878
4. $7,259
5. $2,765
6. .008665
7. $11,826

Chapter 22
Review Problems
1. False
2. $750
3. $600
4. $250
5. $112.77
6. False
7. $775 ($775.35)
8. False
9. $4,328 ($4,327.60)
10. False
11. False
12. False
13. Decreasing term
14. Whole-life
15. Universal life
16. Term insurance
17. $532
18. $532
19. $1,316
20. $1,926
21. $1,926
22. $847.20
23. True
24. $9,600
25. $25,800
26. 18 years, 74 days
27. False
28. 63.57%
29. 6.15%
30. 4.82%

Practice Test
1. $150
2. $373.70
3. $532 ($531.61)
4. $2,706 ($2,706.20)
5. None are true.
6. True
7. With term, we pay for insurance only; with whole-life, we pay for insurance plus savings.
8. $517.30
9. $109,600

Chapter 23
Review Problems
1. 90 degrees
2. True
3. 75 ft
4. 55.32 in.
5. 120 ft
6. 1,980 ft
7. r, d, c
8. 150.72 in.
9. 14.01 ft
10. 1,245 sq in.
11. 678.24 sq in.
12. 1,875 sq ft
13. 7,850 sq mi
14. 3,375 cu in.
15. 6,000 cu ft
16. 785 cu in.
17. 259 tickets
18. 9,231.60 cu ft
19. 5,832 cu yd
20. 68-oz (1.75 cents per oz)
21. $665
22. $26,364
23. $1,044.36
24. $225,000
25. 20.13 pounds
26. $860
27. $133,333.33
28. 1.85 mi
29. 120 days
30. 2,288,897 revolutions
31. 26,256 mi
32. $164.75
33. 2,683.33 cu yd
34. 1,498,464 sq ft
35. 21.50%
36. 4.67 mi
37. $519.44
38. 108 sq ft
39. 19.5 mph
40. 18.83 in.

Practice Test
1. 3,600 ft
2. 10.03 in.
3. 24,000 sq ft
4. 301.44 sq ft
5. 120,000 cu yd
6. 20,347.20 cu ft
7. Yes; $104.31 per sq ft
8. 20 acres

Chapter 24
Review Problems
1. False
2. 2,070.14 euros
3. 1,498.66 pounds
4. 276,621.00 yen
5. $16,036.98
6. $1,496,339.72
7. $66.60
8. 195,161.60 francs
9. $141,196.35
10. $116,556.14
11. True
12. False
13. $5,042,816.37
14. $4,746,698.89
15. Loss of $296,117.48
16. False
17. (b) 200 g
18. (a) 2 m
19. (b) 650 km
20. (a) 65 ℓ
21. 112 km
22. 25 mg
23. 82 ℓ
24. cm
25. km
26. kg
27. 85 cm
28. 120,000 cg
29. 1.3 ℓ
30. 52.91 lb
31. 109.36 yd
32. 16.38 gal
33. 44.45 cm
34. 29.05 m³
35. 402.56 g
36. 21.59 cm × 27.94 cm
37. 1,701 g
38. Rome was warmer (38°C)
39. 37°C
40. -51.1°C
41. 13.608 t
42. $1,558.25
43. $21,204.67
44. 9.63 m
45. 6 hr
46. $5.05 per gal
47. The Washington High record-holder ran the fastest (9.14 m/sec)

Practice Test
1. 388,930 pesos
2. Made $86,563.13
3. 25 km
4. .00105 g
5. 354 g
6. 86°F

Chapter 25
Review Problems
1. 85

2. 87
3. 94
4. $185,500
5. $140,000
6. $88,000
7. The median
8. $6,525
9. $6,286.49
10. 3.31
11. *See below*
12. *See below*
13. Nile
14. About 3,900 mi
15. About 300 mi
16. Sleep: 115.7°
    Job: 57.9°
    Family care: 30.0°
    Personal care: 49.3°
    Leisure: 107.1°
17. *See below*
18. *See below*
19. (c)
20. $4,000 to $5,999.99
21. 7 cars
22. 3 cars
23. 13 hours
24. 4.24
25. 4.74
26. $580
27. 94
28. 3.01

Practice Test

1. $528,000
2. $159,000
3. $120,000
4. The median
5. $759.21
6. *See below*
7. 103.3°
8. 5.48

Ch. 25, RP 11

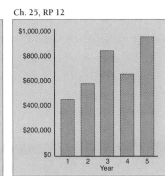

Ch. 25, RP 12

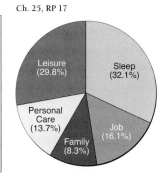

Ch. 25, RP 17

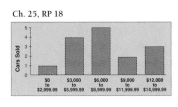

Ch. 25, RP 18

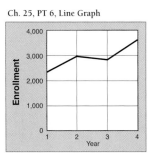

Ch. 25, PT 6, Line Graph

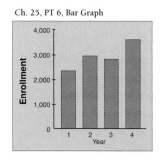

Ch. 25, PT 6, Bar Graph

C Calculator—Quick Start

The text is not a text on how to use calculators. Instead, calculators are used only as a tool to solve certain problems. Calculator keystrokes are shown as the appropriate topic is introduced in the text; however, some calculator features are important for all types of problems and are explained here for the HP 10BII+ and TI BAII PLUS. In addition to reviewing what's in Appendix C, please take the time to watch a video we have created that introduces basic features of the HP 10BII, HP 10BII+ and TI BAII PLUS calculators. To view the video, go to our website (**www.webbertext.com**), click Calculator Videos, enter the access code provided by your instructor, and then click Video #1 (Getting Started) for your calculator. In Chapter 12 you will be prompted to watch Video #2 (Solving TVM Problems) and in Chapter 17 you will be prompted to watch Video #3 (Amortization and Cash Flow Registers).

We have created keystrokes for several other popular calculators. If you are using the TI-30Xa, TI 30X IIS, TI-83 PLUS, TI-84 PLUS, HP 10B, HP 12C, HP 17BII, HP 39gs, Casio 9750G PLUS, or LeWorld Financial, you can request keystrokes by e-mailing *studentsupport@olympuspub.com*.

Arithmetic

Adding, subtracting, multiplying, and dividing is done in the same order as we say it. For example, to multiply 1,222 by 32.8:

HP 10BII+	TI BAII PLUS
1,222 ⨉ 32.8 = 40,081.60	1,222 ⨉ 32.8 = 40,081.60

Notice, when keying in 1,222 we did not key in a comma (there is no comma key). The comma is shown in keystrokes for clarity and appears in the calculator display. Also, notice that we did not key in the decimal point when entering 1,222; the calculator presumes there is a decimal point at the far right.

Calculator Registers

HP 10BII+ Many of the keys have a second function (in gold/orange) on the bottom half of the key. To access the second function, press the gold shift key (▼) first. The symbols above keys 4 through 9 (in blue) are for statistical data. To access this data, press the blue shift key first.

TI BAII PLUS Many of the keys have a second function appearing in color above the key. To access the second function, press the shift key (2ND). The TI BAII PLUS has two modes of operation: the standard-calculator mode and the worksheet mode (designed to guide us through special applications). There are 12 worksheets. To access a worksheet, press the key(s) to select the worksheet. For example, to access the amortization worksheet, press 2ND AMORT; to return to the standard-calculator mode, press 2ND QUIT.

Correcting Entries

If we enter a number incorrectly, we can correct our mistake without having to start the problem over again. Pressing the backspace key (← on the HP 10BII; → on the TI BAII PLUS) gobbles up the last digit. Pressing the clear key (C on the HP 10BII+; CE/C on the TI BAII PLUS) clears the entire displayed number.

Changing Sign

The sign of a displayed number can be changed by pressing the +/- key.

Setting the Decimal

We can select a certain decimal setting, depending on how many digits we want to appear to the right of the decimal point.

HP 10BII+ To set the decimal at, say, 8 places, press ▼ DISP 8. To change to 2 places, press ▼ DISP 2. For a floating decimal (in which trailing zeros are dropped), press ▼ DISP .

TI BAII PLUS To set the decimal at, say, 8 places, press 2ND FORMAT 8 ENTER 2ND QUIT. To change to 2 places, press 2ND FORMAT 2 ENTER 2ND QUIT. For a floating decimal (in which trailing zeros are dropped), set the decimal at 9 places. If we get an answer in the display but want to view more digits than the current decimal setting will allow, we must first store the displayed number by pressing STO 1, then change the decimal setting as outlined above, and finally recall the number by pressing RCL 1.

For both calculators, chain calculations use the internal, more accurate, number, not the displayed number; if we want to use the displayed number rather than the internal number, we "round" the internal number to match the displayed number (for the HP 10BII+, press ▼ RND ; for the TI BAII PLUS, press 2ND ROUND).

Time-Saving Registers

Suppose we want to calculate the total monthly rent on a 72-unit apartment building in which 36 units rent for $850 each, 24 rent for $900 each, and 12 rent for $925 each. One approach would be to write down subtotals and then add subtotals.

```
36 × $850 =    $30,600
24 × $900 =     21,600
12 × $925 =     11,100
Total          $63,300
```

We could instead use time-saving features of our calculators. A few are shown.

HP 10BII+		TI BAII PLUS	
use storage registers		*use storage registers*	
36 × 850 = ▼ STO 1	30,600.00	36 × 850 = STO 1	30,600.00
24 × 900 = ▼ STO 2	21,600.00	24 × 900 = STO 2	21,600.00
12 × 925 =	11,100.00	12 × 925 =	11,100.00
+ RCL 1	30,600.00	+ RCL 1	30,600.00
+ RCL 2	21,600.00	+ RCL 2	21,600.00
=	63,300.00	=	63,300.00
use memory registers		*use parentheses*	
36 × 850 = →M	30,600.00	36 × 850 =	30,600.00
24 × 900 = M+	21,600.00	+ (24 × 900)	21,600.00
12 × 925 = M+	11,100.00	+ (12 × 925)	11,100.00
RM	63,300.00	=	63,300.00

Exponent (Power) Keys

23 × 23 can be written as 23^2, and is read as "twenty three to the second power" or "twenty three squared." 4 × 4 × 4 × 4 × 4 can be written as 4^5, and is read as "four to the fifth power." Calculators have exponent (power) keys that can be used to short-cut the arithmetic. Let's find the value of: **(a)** 23^2 **(b)** 4^5.

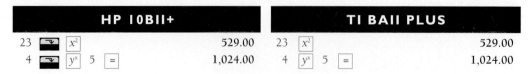

HP 10BII+		TI BAII PLUS	
23 ▼ x^2	529.00	23 x^2	529.00
4 ▼ y^x 5 =	1,024.00	4 y^x 5 =	1,024.00

Compound Interest Formulas

Using a calculator properly is essential in working with the compound interest formulas of Illustration 10-1. Calculator keystrokes for the HP 10BII+ and TI BAII PLUS are provided for each of the 8 formulas: Formula 1A, 1B, 2A, 2B, 3, 4A, 4B, and 5. Before starting, here are a few things worth noting:

- Try your own keystrokes before looking at ours. If your approach makes sense, use it because it will be easier to remember. If you have difficulty, then review our suggested keystrokes.
- The keystrokes shown may, in some cases, be longer than another method but are used because the method is considered to be more conceptually sound and easier to remember.
- The displayed values shown in the keystrokes, in most cases, have 2 decimal places. Having our decimal set at more or less places will not affect the final answer, provided we use chain calculations (remember that chain calculations use the internal, more accurate value, not the displayed value).
- If you are using the TI-30Xa, TI 30X IIS, TI-83 PLUS, TI-84 PLUS, HP 10B, HP 10BII, HP 12C, HP 17BII, HP 39gs, Casio 9750G PLUS, or LeWorld Financial, you can request keystrokes by e-mailing *studentsupport@olympuspub.com*.

Formula 1A (Example 1 of Unit 10.2)

You get an income tax refund of $1,700 and deposit the money in a savings plan for 6 years, earning 6% compounded quarterly. Find the ending balance using compound interest formulas.

$$FV = PV(1 + i)^n = \$1{,}700\,(1.015)^{24} = \$2{,}430.15$$

HP 10BII+		TI BAII PLUS	
1.015 [▼] y^x 24 [=]	1.43	1.015 y^x 24 [=]	1.43
[×] 1,700 [=]	2,430.15	[×] 1,700 [=]	2,430.15

Formula 1A (Example 2 of Unit 10.2)

Suppose a "wise man" had deposited $1 in a savings account 2,000 years ago and the account earned interest at 2% compounded annually. If the money in the account today were evenly divided among the world's population, how much would each person receive, based on a world population of 7 billion?

$$FV = PV(1 + i)^n = \$1(1.02)^{2000} \qquad \text{Then divide by } 7{,}000{,}000{,}000.$$

HP 10BII+		TI BAII PLUS	
[▼] DISP 9	?.????????	2ND FORMAT 8 ENTER 2ND QUIT	0.00000000
1.02 [▼] y^x 2,000 [=]	1.58614733 E17*	1.02 y^x 2,000 [=]	1.586147 17*
[÷] 7,000,000,000 [=]	22,659,247.5371	[÷] 7,000,000,000 [=]	22,659,247.54
[▼] DISP 2	22,659,247.54	2ND FORMAT 2 ENTER 2ND QUIT	0.00

*Note: The number is too large to fit in the display, so it is written in scientific notation: $1.58614733 \times 10^{17}$. In simple language, this means to move the decimal 17 places to the right, resulting in a number of approximately $158,614,733,000,000,000.

Formula 1B (Example 4, Unit 10.2)

You deposit $100 at the end of each year for 4 years, earning 6% compounded annually. Use compound interest formulas to find the balance in 4 years.

$$FV = PMT\left[\frac{(1+i)^n - 1}{i}\right] = \$100\left[\frac{(1.06)^4 - 1}{.06}\right] = \$437.46$$

HP 10BII+		TI BAII PLUS	
1.06 [▼] y^x 4 [=] [−] 1 [=]	0.26	1.06 y^x 4 [=] [−] 1 [=]	0.26
[÷] .06 [=]	4.37	[÷] .06 [=]	4.37
[×] 100 [=]	437.46	[×] 100 [=]	437.46

Formula 2A (Example 1 of Unit 10.3)

Your aunt says she will give you $2,430.15 in 6 years. Assuming that you can earn 6% compounded quarterly, what is the real value of her promise, in today's dollars?

$$PV = \frac{FV}{(1+i)^n} = \frac{\$2,430.15}{(1.015)^{24}} = \$1,700.00$$

HP 10BII+		TI BAII PLUS	
get value of 1.015^{24}		*get value of* 1.015^{24}	
1.015 [▼] [y^x] 24 [=]	1.43	1.015 [y^x] 24 [=]	1.43
store the result in Register 1		*store the result in Register 1*	
[▼] [STO] 1	1.43	[STO] 1	1.43
divide the numerator by what is stored		*divide the numerator by what is stored*	
2,430.15 [÷] [RCL] 1	1.43	2,430.15 [÷] [RCL] 1	1.43
[=]	1,700.00	[=]	1,700.00

Formula 2B (Example 2 of Unit 10.3)

You are selling a valuable coin. You have two offers. The first offer is for $5,500 cash. With the second offer, the buyer will pay you $2,000 at the end of each year for 3 years. Assuming that you can earn 8% compounded annually on your money, which offer is better?

$$PV = PMT \left[\frac{1 - \frac{1}{(1+i)^n}}{i} \right] = \$2,000 \left[\frac{1 - \frac{1}{(1.08)^3}}{.08} \right] = \$5,154.19$$

HP 10BII+		TI BAII PLUS	
determine value of $(1.08)^3$		*determine value of* $(1.08)^3$	
1.08 [▼] [y^x] 3 [=]	1.26	1.08 [y^x] 3 [=]	1.26
get reciprocal		*get reciprocal*	
[▼] [1/x]	0.79	[1/x]	0.79
change sign		*change sign*	
[+/-]	-0.79	[+/-]	-0.79
add 1		*add 1*	
[+] 1 [=]	0.21	[+] 1 [=]	0.21
divide by .08 and multiply by $2,000		*divide by .08 and multiply by $2,000*	
[÷] .08 [×] 2,000 [=]	5,154.19	[÷] .08 [×] 2,000 [=]	5,154.19

Formula 3 (Example 1 of Unit 11.4)

Dale bought a rare baseball card 3 years ago for $1,500. He just sold the card for $2,000 to get some money for his college tuition. What interest rate, compounded annually, did Dale earn on the investment?

$$i = \left(\frac{FV}{PV}\right)^{\frac{1}{n}} - 1 = \left(\frac{\$2,000}{\$1,500}\right)^{\frac{1}{3}} - 1 = .100642 \approx \mathbf{10.0642\%} \quad \text{(with 4 decimal places)}$$

HP 10BII+		TI BAII PLUS	
set decimal at 6 places		*set decimal at 6 places*	
▼ DISP 6	?.??????	2ND FORMAT 6 ENTER 2ND QUIT	0.000000
divide $2,000 by $1,500		*divide $2,000 by $1,500*	
2,000 ÷ 1,500 =	1.333333	2,000 ÷ 1,500 =	1.333333
raise to the 1/3 power *		*raise to the 1/3 power* *	
▼ y^x 3 ▼ 1/x =	1.100642	y^x 3 1/x =	1.100642
subtract 1		*subtract 1*	
- 1 =	**0.100642**	- 1 =	**0.100642**
▼ DISP 2	0.10	2ND FORMAT 2 ENTER 2ND QUIT	0.00

*Note: Raising a value to the 1/3 power is the same as finding the 3rd root of a number. We are asking what value, multiplied 3 times, results in 1.333333. That value is 1.100642 (1.100642 × 1.100642 × 1.100642 ≈ 1.33333).

Formula 4A (Example 2 of Unit 11.1)

You want to accumulate $200,000 for retirement in 40 years. You can earn 6.75% compounded monthly. What amount must you deposit at the end of each month in order to accumulate $200,000 in 40 years?

$$PMT = \frac{FV(i)}{(1+i)^n - 1} = \frac{\$200,000(.005625)}{(1.005625)^{480} - 1} = \$81.71$$

HP 10BII+		TI BAII PLUS	
get value of denominator		*get value of denominator*	
1.005625 ▼ y^x 480 = - 1 =	13.77	1.005625 y^x 480 = - 1 =	13.77
store in register 1		*store in register 1*	
▼ STO 1	13.77	STO 1	13.77
get value of numerator		*get value of numerator*	
200,000 × .005625 =	1,125.00	200,000 × .005625 =	1,125.00
divide by stored number		*divide by stored number*	
÷ RCL 1	13.77	÷ RCL 1	13.77
=	**81.71**	=	**81.71**

C-5

Formula 4B (Example 2 of Unit 11.2)

Suppose you have accumulated $500,000, perhaps from many years of savings or from an inheritance. You put the money in a savings plan earning 6% compounded monthly. You want the plan to last 40 years. How much can you withdraw at the end of each month?

$$\text{PMT} = \frac{PV(i)}{1 - \dfrac{1}{(1+i)^n}} = \frac{\$500{,}000\,(.005)}{1 - \dfrac{1}{(1.005)^{480}}} = \$2{,}751.07$$

HP 10BII+		TI BAII PLUS	
find value of $(1.005)^{480}$		*find value of* $(1.005)^{480}$	
1.005 ▼ y^x 480 =	10.96	1.005 y^x 480 =	10.96
find reciprocal		*find reciprocal*	
▼ $1/x$	0.09	$1/x$	0.09
change sign and add 1		*change sign and add 1*	
+/− + 1 =	0.91	+/− + 1 =	0.91
store this value (the denominator)		*store this value (the denominator)*	
▼ STO 1	0.91	STO 1	0.91
find value of numerator		*find value of numerator*	
500,000 × .005 =	2,500.00	500,000 × .005 =	2,500.00
divide by the denominator		*divide by the denominator*	
÷ RCL 1	0.91	÷ RCL 1	0.91
=	2,751.07	=	2,751.07

Formula 5 (Example 3 of Unit 11.1)

You want to start a restaurant business and estimate it will take $28,000 to get started. You currently have $3,000 and can deposit an additional $425 at the end of each month. If your savings will earn 9% compounded monthly, in how many months can you start your business?

For Formula 5 we must use proper sign convention for PV, FV, and PMT:

PV = negative $3,000 (negative because you pay this amount into a savings plan)
FV = $28,000 (positive because you will get this amount back from the savings plan)
PMT = negative $425 (negative because you pay this amount into a savings plan)

$$n = \frac{-\ln\left[\dfrac{PV + \left(\frac{PMT}{i}\right)}{\frac{PMT}{i} - FV}\right]}{\ln(1+i)} = \frac{-\ln\left[\dfrac{-\$3{,}000 + \left(\frac{-\$425}{.0075}\right)}{\frac{-\$425}{.0075} - \$28{,}000}\right]}{\ln(1.0075)} = 46.83 \text{ months}$$

HP 10BII+

compute and store (-$425 over .0075)

425 [+/-] [÷] .0075 [=]	-56,666.67
[▼] [STO] 1	-56,666.67

compute and store bottom half of numerator

[-] 28,000 [=] [▼] [STO] 2	-84,666.67

compute and store the entire numerator

[RCL] 1	-56,666.67
[-] 3,000 [=]	-59,666.67
[÷] [RCL] 2	-84,666.67
[=]	0.70
[▼] [LN]	-0.35
[+/-] [▼] [STO] 3	0.35

compute and store the main denominator

1.0075 [▼] [LN]	0.0075
[▼] [STO] 4	0.0075

finally: get answer

[RCL] 3	0.35
[÷] [RCL] 4	0.0075
[=]	46.83

TI BAII PLUS

compute and store (-$425 over .0075)

425 [+/-] [÷] .0075 [=]	-56,666.67
[STO] 1	-56,666.67

compute and store bottom half of numerator

[-] 28,000 [=] [STO] 2	-84,666.67

compute and store the entire numerator

[RCL] 1	-56,666.67
[-] 3,000 [=]	-59,666.67
[÷] [RCL] 2	-84,666.67
[=]	0.70
[LN]	-0.35
[+/-] [STO] 3	0.35

compute and store the main denominator

1.0075 [LN]	0.01
[STO] 4	0.01

finally: get answer

[RCL] 3	0.35
[÷] [RCL] 4	0.01
[=]	46.83

D Day-of-the-Year Calendar

(Day Number for Each Day; Adjust for Leap Year*)

Day of Month	(31) Jan	(28*) Feb	(31) Mar	(30) Apr	(31) May	(30) June	(31) July	(31) Aug	(30) Sept	(31) Oct	(30) Nov	(31) Dec
1	1	32	60	91	121	152	182	213	244	274	305	335
2	2	33	61	92	122	153	183	214	245	275	306	336
3	3	34	62	93	123	154	184	215	246	276	307	337
4	4	35	63	94	124	155	185	216	247	277	308	338
5	5	36	64	95	125	156	186	217	248	278	309	339
6	6	37	65	96	126	157	187	218	249	279	310	340
7	7	38	66	97	127	158	188	219	250	280	311	341
8	8	39	67	98	128	159	189	220	251	281	312	342
9	9	40	68	99	129	160	190	221	252	282	313	343
10	10	41	69	100	130	161	191	222	253	283	314	344
11	11	42	70	101	131	162	192	223	254	284	315	345
12	12	43	71	102	132	163	193	224	255	285	316	346
13	13	44	72	103	133	164	194	225	256	286	317	347
14	14	45	73	104	134	165	195	226	257	287	318	348
15	15	46	74	105	135	166	196	227	258	288	319	349
16	16	47	75	106	136	167	197	228	259	289	320	350
17	17	48	76	107	137	168	198	229	260	290	321	351
18	18	49	77	108	138	169	199	230	261	291	322	352
19	19	50	78	109	139	170	200	231	262	292	323	353
20	20	51	79	110	140	171	201	232	263	293	324	354
21	21	52	80	111	141	172	202	233	264	294	325	355
22	22	53	81	112	142	173	203	234	265	295	326	356
23	23	54	82	113	143	174	204	235	266	296	327	357
24	24	55	83	114	144	175	205	236	267	297	328	358
25	25	56	84	115	145	176	206	237	268	298	329	359
26	26	57	85	116	146	177	207	238	269	299	330	360
27	27	58	86	117	147	178	208	239	270	300	331	361
28	28	59	87	118	148	179	209	240	271	301	332	362
29	29	—*	88	119	149	180	210	241	272	302	333	363
30	30	—	89	120	150	181	211	242	273	303	334	364
31	31	—	90	—	151	—	212	243	—	304	—	365

*In leap years, February has 29 days; when using the day-of-the-year calendar, add 1 to each day after February 28. Here is why we have leap years. The earth makes one complete revolution around the sun in 365 days, 5 hours, 48 minutes, and 46 seconds, slightly less than 365.25 days. To keep the seasons uniform over the centuries, a day is added almost every fourth year. *As a general rule, leap years are evenly divisible by 4* (such as 2016 and 2020; these happen to be years of U.S. presidential elections). Having a leap year *every* fourth year gives slightly too much time to maintain the seasons, so an adjustment is made by not having a leap year in century years unless evenly divisible by 400; so the years 1900 and 2100 are not leap years, but the year 2000 is a leap year.

Optional Method for Counting Days

With this method, referred to as the *Days-in-a-Month Method,* we remember how many days each month has. Some people remember how many days in each month by reciting this little ditty:

Thirty days has September, April, June, and November;
All the rest have 31, except February, which has 28.

As pointed out in the footnote to the Day-of-the-Year Calendar, February has 29 days in leap years. Some people like to remember how many days in each month by using knuckles on their hands. Knuckles represent months with 31 days; valleys between knuckles represent 30-day months (except February, which has 28 days—29 in leap years).

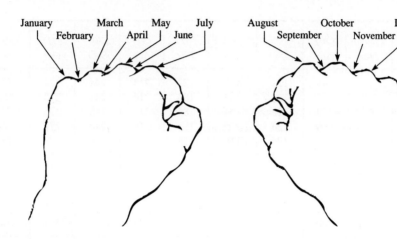

Examples—finding the number of days between two dates

1. Days between Nov. 12, 2013, and Mar. 15, 2014?

Days in November: 30 - 12 =	18
Days in December	31
Days in January	31
Days in February (non-leap-year)	28
Days in March	+15
Total	**123**

2. Days between Nov. 12, 2015, and Mar. 15, 2016?

Days in November: 30 - 12 =	18
Days in December	31
Days in January	31
Days in February (leap-year)	29
Days in March	+15
Total	**124**

Examples—finding the date that is a certain number of days past a given date

3. Date that is 120 days past November 19, 2013?

Days left in November: 30 - 19 =	11
Days in December	+31
Subtotal	42
Days in January	+31
Subtotal	73
Days in February (non leap-year)	+28
Subtotal	101
Days in March: 120 - 101 =	+19
Total	120

   Date is **March 19**

4. Date that is 120 days past November 19, 2015?

Days left in November: 30 - 19 =	11
Days in December	+31
Subtotal	42
Days in January	+31
Subtotal	73
Days in February (leap-year)	+29
Subtotal	102
Days in March: 120 - 102 =	+18
Total	120

   Date is **March 18**

Excel: Solving TVM Problems

In Chapters 10 and 11, we solve time-value-of-money (TVM) problems with compound interest formulas. In Chapters 12 and 13, we use financial calculators. Here in Appendix E, we solve those same problems using Excel®.

When used to solve TVM problems, Excel relies on the compound interest formulas (see Illustration 10-1 of Chapter 10). We provide the values for the TVM variables (i, n, PV, PMT, and FV) and the Excel program does the arithmetic. If you are not quite sure what each TVM variable represents, refer to Unit 12.1 of the text. Remember, using Excel to solve TVM problems does *not* alleviate the need for common sense; it is only a *tool* in solving problems.

Excel has a format for each variable, shown in the following table. (*Note*: We have substituted our standard terminology for some Excel terms.) There are 5 formats, one for each TVM variable.

> ### using Excel to solve TVM problems
>
> **Step 1** Select the Excel format that represents the unknown value:
>
> | If solving for | Excel format |
> | --- | --- |
> | n | =NPER(i, PMT, PV, FV, Mode) |
> | i | =RATE(n, PMT, PV, FV, Mode, Guess) |
> | PV | =PV(i, n, PMT, FV, Mode) |
> | PMT | =PMT(i, n, PV, FV, Mode) |
> | FV | =FV(i, n, PMT, PV, Mode) |
>
> n = total number of periods (such as 48 or 4*12); i = interest rate per period (such as 9%/12 or .09/12); PV = present value; PMT = periodic payment; FV = future value; Guess = estimated periodic rate; Mode = 0 if periodic payments start after one period has lapsed (*end* mode); Mode = 1 if periodic payments start immediately (*begin* mode).
>
> **Step 2** Go to any cell on an Excel spreadsheet. Type the format, substituting known values inside the parentheses. Don't use dollar signs. Use commas only to separate values. Enter dollar amounts as positives if the money is received or negatives if the money is paid.
>
> **Step 3** Press ENTER; the answer will appear. A negative value is shown in parentheses.

Example 1 Sebastian Xavier is a soda pop "addict" and wonders how much money he could accumulate if he stopped drinking soda pop and deposited the $150 per month he spends on the stuff into a savings plan. Sebastian just turned 20. If his savings plan earns 6% compounded monthly and his first deposit is a month from now, what amount would he have at retirement, 40 years from now?

If Sebastian earned no interest, he would end up with $72,000 (480 × $150). Because he is earning interest, he will end up with more than that. Let's use Excel to find the amount. We are solving for FV (the amount at the end of the last period), so.

Step 1 Select format for FV	=FV(i, n, PMT, PV, Mode)
Step 2 Type the format, substituting known values	=FV(6%/12, 40*12, -150, 0, 0)
Step 3 Press ENTER	**$298,723.61**

Sebastian will end up with $298,723.61! He would earn interest of $226,723.61 ($298,723.61 ending balance - $72,000 deposited).

Example 2 You have the chance to buy a promissory note, in which you would receive 28 quarterly payments of $500, starting 3 months from now. If you buy the note, you would receive a total of $14,000 (28 × $500). If you want to earn 8% compounded quarterly, what price should you pay for the note?

We are solving for the amount you should pay at the beginning of the first period (PV), so:

Step 1 Select format for PV	=PV(i, n, PMT, FV, Mode)
Step 2 Type the format, substituting known values	=PV(8%/4, 28, 500, 0, 0)
Step 3 Press ENTER	**($10,640.64)**

By paying $10,640.64 you will earn 8% compounded quarterly.

The answer of Example 2 is shown in parentheses, indicating the answer is a *negative* $10,640.64; it's negative because you will *pay* that amount.

You may wonder if an Excel answer can be relied upon. After all, you are not doing the arithmetic, a machine is. One way to feel more comfortable about an answer is to determine if the answer seems reasonable. In Example 2, you will receive a total of $14,000 (28 payments of $500 = $14,000). If you paid $14,000 for the note, you would earn no interest. In order to earn interest, you must pay less than $14,000, so the answer of $10,640.64 seems reasonable.

When using Excel to solve TVM problems, the Excel program is doing the arithmetic for us, based on the values we provide. Remember the saying

GARBAGE IN, GARBAGE OUT

As implied, if we make a mistake by providing wrong values, the answer will be wrong. Here are a few tips to use when inputting data into an Excel format:

> **TIP** — a few ideas to help things go smoother
>
> **Tip 1** Enter dollar amounts as positives if the money is received, or negatives if the money is paid. Each problem will have at least one positive dollar amount and at least one negative dollar amount.
>
> **Tip 2** Don't use dollar signs ($) and commas when entering amounts; commas are used only to separate values. To enter $200,000 type 200000—not $200,000, $200000, or 200,000.
>
> **Tip 3** A periodic rate can be entered as a percent or as a decimal number. For example, 8% compounded quarterly can be entered as 8%/4, .08/4, 2%, or .02, but *not as* 8/4 or 2.

If you will be using Excel a lot, it will be helpful to create an Excel page that is reserved solely for solving TVM problems. One way to do that is to open up a blank Excel spreadsheet, widen Column A to accommodate about 70 characters, and then make it look like the one below. Reserve Cells A2, A5, A8, A11, and A14 for substituting values. Then, save the file (perhaps as "TVM Problems").

	A	B
1	Solve for n: =NPER(i, PMT, PV, FV, Mode)	
2		
3		
4	Solve for i: =RATE(n, PMT, PV, FV, Mode, Guess)	
5		
6		
7	Solve for PV: =PV(i, n, PMT, FV, Mode)	
8		
9		
10	Solve for PMT: =PMT(i, n, PV, FV, Mode)	
11		
12		
13	Solve for FV: =FV(i, n, PMT, PV, Mode)	
14		
15		

Let's redo Example 1, using the Excel spreadsheet we created. After substituting the known values in Cell A14, the spreadsheet will look like this:

	A	B
13	Solve for FV: =FV(i, n, PMT, PV, Mode)	
14	=FV(6%/12, 40*12, -150, 0, 0)	

After pressing ENTER, the spreadsheet will look like this:

	A	B
13	Solve for FV: =FV(i, n, PMT, PV, Mode)	
14		$298,723.61

Note: For the remainder of Appendix E, we will follow the concepts and examples of Chapters 12, 13, 15, and 17. Excel solutions will be shown in place of financial calculator solutions.

Unit 12.1 Time-value-of-money terminology

The concepts, examples, and solutions are identical to those shown in Unit 12.1.

Unit 12.2

We have already solved Examples 1 and 2.

Unit 12.3 Future value

Example 1	Step 1	Select format for FV	=FV(i, n, PMT, PV, Mode)
	Step 2	In Cell A14, type the format, with known values	=FV(5%, 3, 0, -400, 0)
	Step 3	Press ENTER	$463.05
Example 2	Step 1	Select format for FV	=FV(i, n, PMT, PV, Mode)
	Step 2	In Cell A14, type the format, with known values	=FV(2%, 2000, 0, -1, 0)
	Step 3	Press ENTER to find the account balance	$158,614,732,760,369,000.00
	Then	Find the amount per person:	
		In Cell A15, type: =A14/7000000000 Then, press ENTER	$22,659,247.54
Example 3	Step 1	Select format for FV	=FV(i, n, PMT, PV, Mode)
	Step 2	In Cell A14, type the format, with known values	=FV(4%, 15, 0, -4800, 0)
	Step 3	Press ENTER	$8,644.53
Example 4	Step 1	Select format for FV	=FV(i, n, PMT, PV, Mode)
	Step 2	In Cell A14, type the format, with known values	=FV(6%, 4, -100, 0, 0)
	Step 3	Press ENTER	$437.46
Example 5	Step 1	Select format for FV	=FV(i, n, PMT, PV, Mode)
	Step 2	In Cell A14, type the format, with known values	=FV(6%, 4, -100, 0, 1)
	Step 3	Press ENTER	$463.71

Note: For future problems, solutions will be given on one line.

Example 6 **Kristen:** =FV(i, n, PMT, PV, Mode) → =FV(6%/12, 50*12, -50, 0, 1) → $190,306.35
Erica: =FV(i, n, PMT, PV, Mode) → =FV(6%/12, 25*12, -100, 0, 1) → $69,645.89

Unit 12.4 Present value

Example 1 =PV(i, n, PMT, FV, Mode) → =PV(5%, 3, 0, 463.05, 0) → ($400.00)
Example 2 =PV(i, n, PMT, FV, Mode) → =PV(8%, 3, 2000, 0, 0) → ($5,154.19)
Example 3 =PV(i, n, PMT, FV, Mode) → =PV(8%/2, 12*2, 30, 1000, 0) → ($847.53)
Example 4 =PV(i, n, PMT, FV, Mode) → =PV(10.25%/12, 15*12, 900, 7000, 0) → ($84,086.80)

Unit 13.1 Sinking funds

Example 1 =PV(i, n, PMT, FV, Mode) → =PV(6.75%/12, 40*12, 0, 200000, 0) → ($13,543.18)
Example 2 =PMT(i, n, PV, FV, Mode) → =PMT(6.75%/12, 40*12, 0, 200000, 0) → ($81.71)
Example 3 =PMT(i, n, PV, FV, Mode) → =PMT(6.75%/12, 40*12, -3000, 200000, 0) → ($63.61)
Example 4 =NPER(i, PMT, PV, FV, Mode) → =NPER(9%/12, -425, -3000, 28000, 0) → 46.83 mo
Example 5 3%: =PMT(i, n, PV, FV, Mode) → =PMT(3%/12, 65*12, 0, 1000000, 0) → ($415.86)
  9%: =PMT(i, n, PV, FV, Mode) → =PMT(9%/12, 65*12, 0, 1000000, 0) → ($22.14)
  15%: =PMT(i, n, PV, FV, Mode) → =PMT(15%/12, 65*12, 0, 1000000, 0) → ($0.77)

Unit 13.2 Annuities

Example 1 $I = PRT = \$500{,}000 \times 6\% \times \frac{1}{12} = \$2{,}500$
Example 2 =PMT(i, n, PV, FV, Mode) → =PMT(6%/12, 40*12, -500000, 0, 0) → $2,751.07
Example 3 =NPER(i, PMT, PV, FV, Mode) → =NPER(6%/12, 4000, -500000, 0, 0) → 196.66 mo
Example 4 =FV(i, n, PMT, PV, Mode) → =FV(6%/12, 20*12, 2000, -500000, 0) → $731,020.45

Unit 13.3 Loan Payments

Example 1 =PMT(i, n, PV, FV, Mode) → =PMT(7.5%/12, 5*12, 13500, 0, 0) → **($270.51)**
Example 2 **30-yr loan:** =PMT(i, n, PV, FV, Mode) → =PMT(7.75%/12, 30*12, 160000, 0, 0) → **($1,146.26)**
 15-yr loan: =PMT(i, n, PV, FV, Mode) → =PMT(7.25%/12, 15*12, 160000, 0, 0) → **($1,460.58)**
Example 3 Solution is the same one shown in Example 3 of unit 13.3 of the text.
Example 4 =NPER(i, PMT, PV, FV, Mode) → =NPER(7.75%/12, -1460.58, 160000, 0, 0) → **190.95 mo**

Unit 15.3 Amortization

As of the printing of this text, Excel does not have an amortization program that is precise. In fact, your author has attempted to get corrections made, to no avail. As a result, we will skip this unit of the text using Excel. In Example 6 of Unit 17.2, we will use the =FV format to *approximate* an unpaid balance. Following Example 6, we will review how to find the interest and principal portion of payments.

Unit 17.1 Solving for interest rate paid

In this unit we will be solving for a rate. Notice the Excel format is: =RATE(n, PMT, PV, FV, Mode, Guess). Here are a few things to keep in mind when solving for *i*:

> **when solving for *i* using Excel**
>
> - A "guess" is required because Excel uses an iterative (guess and check) method for calculating the rate. Using our guess for the periodic rate, the program cycles through the calculation until a rate is accurate to within 0.00001%; if the program can't find a result within 20 tries, the "#NUM!" error is returned, in which case we must enter a better guess. For consistency, our first guess will be based on an annual rate of 12% (so a monthly periodic guess would be 1%, a quarterly periodic guess would be 3%, and so forth).
> - The answer is shown as a percent. To see more digits to the right of the decimal point, right click on the cell, click Format Cells, highlight Percentage, and then adjust the decimal setting.
> - If the answer is not an *annual* rate, multiply by the number of periods per year to get the *annual* rate.

Example 1 I = PRT = $6,000 × 8% × 3 = $1,440; $6,000 + $1,440 = $7,440; $7,440 ÷ 36 = $206.67

 Using our Excel page reserved for solving TVM problems:

 Select format for *i* =RATE(n, PMT, PV, FV, Mode, Guess)
 Type format in Cell A5, substituting known values =RATE(3*12, -206.67, 6000, 0, 0, 1%)
 Press ENTER 1.21% (*This is the interest rate per period*)
 In Cell A6, type =A5*12
 Press ENTER **14.55%** (*This is the annual rate*)

Example 2 Don't forget, payments start immediately (*begin mode*), so Mode = 1:

 =RATE(n, PMT, PV, FV, Mode, Guess) → =RATE(6, -87, 480, 0, 1, 1%) → 3.48 × 12 = **41.79%**

In solving for an APR, we first calculate the payment, and then calculate the APR by substituting *net proceeds* (the amount the borrower has use of) for PV.

Example 3 =PMT(i, n, PV, FV, Mode) → =PMT(7.5%/12, 5*12, 13500, 0, 0) → **($270.51)**
 =RATE(n, PMT, PV, FV, Mode, Guess) → =RATE(5*12, -270.51, 13400, 0, 0, 1%) → 0.65 × 12 = **7.81%**

> **TIP converting periodic rate to annual rate**
>
> In Example 3, you may have used a calculator to multiply the periodic rate (0.65) by 12, getting 7.80 (instead of 7.81%). By doing so, you lost a bit of accuracy. To maintain accuracy, either use more digits for the periodic rate (.651135) or follow the procedure used in Example 1 (use Cell A6 to multiply the value in Cell A5 by 12).

Example 4 =PMT(i, n, PV, FV, Mode) → =PMT(7.25%/12, 15*12, 160000, 0, 0) → ($1,460.58)
           =RATE(n, PMT, PV, FV, Mode, Guess) → =RATE(15*12, -1460.58, 153440, 0, 0, 1%) → 0.66 × 12 = **7.93%**
Example 5 =PMT(i, n, PV, FV, Mode) → =PMT(7.25%/12, 15*12, 160000, 0, 0) → ($1,460.58)
           =RATE(n, PMT, PV, FV, Mode, Guess) → =RATE(15*12, -1460.58, 151940, 0, 0, 1%) → 0.67 × 12 = **8.10%**

In the next example, we must find Tara's unpaid balance after payment 84. As mentioned, there is not an Excel program (as of the printing of this text) that will amortize precisely. With financial calculators we find that balance is $106,158.81. In Example 6, we will *approximate* an amount ($106,158.79) using the =FV format. Notice, the difference is only 2¢; in most cases, the difference will be substantially greater.

Example 6 **Step 1 (calculate payment):**
           =PMT(i, n, PV, FV, Mode) → =PMT(7.25%/12, 15*12, 160000, 0, 0) → ($1,460.58)
           Step 2 (approximate unpaid balance after payment 84):
           =FV(i, n, PMT, PV, Mode) → =FV(7.25%/12, 84, -1460.58, 160000, 0) → ($106,158.79)
           Step 3 (calculate APR, reflecting the early payoff):
           =RATE(n, PMT, PV, FV, Mode, Guess) → =RATE(84, -1460.58, 151940, -106158.79, 0, 1%)
           → 0.70 × 12 = **8.35%**

In Example 6, we found the approximate unpaid balance ($106,158.79) after payment 84. We can find the interest and principal for any series of payments (payments 1 through 84, in this case), as shown below:

Total paid: 84 × $1,460.58 $122,688.72
Principal portion: $160,000 balance at start of that series - $106,158.79 balance at end   - 53,841.21
Interest portion $ 68,847.51

Example 7 We calculated Tara's real APR, reflecting the early payoff, in Example 6: 8.35%. Because the APR on the contemplated loan is greater than the note rate of the existing loan (8.25%), Tara should not refinance.

Unit 17.2 Growth rates

Please pay special attention to the KEY box of Unit 19.3. The same principle applies to Excel.

Example 1 =RATE(n, PMT, PV, FV, Mode, Guess) → =RATE(4, 0, -8570, 11677, 0, 12%) → **8.04%**
Example 2 =RATE(n, PMT, PV, FV, Mode, Guess) → =RATE(107, 0, -49.11, 11577.51, 0, 12%) → **5.24%**

Unit 17.3 Solving for interest rate earned

Example 1 =RATE(n, PMT, PV, FV, Mode, Guess) → =RATE(3, 0, -1500, 2000, 0, 12%) → **10.0642%**
Example 2 =RATE(n, PMT, PV, FV, Mode, Guess) → =RATE(5*4, 25, -1700, 2100, 0, 3%) → 2.40 × 4 = **9.60%**
Example 3 =RATE(n, PMT, PV, FV, Mode, Guess) → =RATE(18*2, 35, -1050, 1000, 0, 6%) → 3.26 × 2 = **6.52%**
Example 4 =RATE(n, PMT, PV, FV, Mode, Guess) → =RATE(12*2, 35, -1050, 930, 0, 6%) → 3.00 × 2 = **6.00%**
Example 5 Don't forget, the $50 payments start today (begin mode), so Mode = 1:
           =RATE(n, PMT, PV, FV, Mode, Guess) → =RATE(3*12, -50, 0, 1650, 1, 1%) → -0.48 × 12 = **-5.71%**
Example 6 =RATE(n, PMT, PV, FV, Mode, Guess) → =RATE(168, 1550.60, -150000, 0, 0, 1%) → 0.73 × 12 = **8.74**

Unit 17.4 Cash flow problems

A problem in which the periodic payment changes is known as a **cash flow problem**. For cash flow problems, we refer to the interest rate as an **internal rate of return** (or **IRR**), and we refer to the present value as **net present value** (or **NPV**). We can use Excel to solve cash flow problems. First, let's create an Excel spreadsheet reserved for solving cash flow problems:

> **setting up an Excel spreadsheet for solving cash flow problems**
>
> **Step 1** Open a blank Excel spreadsheet.
> **Step 2** In Cell A1, type **Solve for IRR: =IRR(B1:B?, Guess)** *(Cell A2 is reserved for substituting known values)*
> **Step 3** In Cell A4, type **Solve for NPV: =NPV(i, B2:B?)+B1** *(Cell A5 is reserved for substituting known values)*
> **Step 4** Save the spreadsheet (perhaps as "Cash Flow Problems").

Now that we have a spreadsheet template, here are a few steps that we can use to solve cash flow problems:

> ### solving cash flow problems with Excel
>
> **Step 1** Enter the initial cash flow in Cell B1. Don't use dollar signs or commas. Enter dollar amounts as positives if the money is received or negatives if the money is paid.
> **Step 2** Enter the remaining cash flows in Column B. If more than one cash flow occurs at the same time, combine before entering. Clear cells under the last cell used.
> **Step 3** Move the cursor to the cell reserved for the unknown value (Cell A2 if solving for IRR, or Cell A5 if solving for NPV). Type the format, substituting known values.
> **Step 4** Press Enter. The answer will appear.

Example 1 **Step 1** Enter the initial cash flow in Cell B1: -2000
Step 2 Enter the remaining cash flows in Column B: 100, 150, 0, 2825 (remember to combine the two cash flows that occurred in year 4). Last cell is B5; clear cells under B5.
Step 3 Move the cursor to Cell A2. Type: =IRR(B1:B5, 12%)

After Step 3, the Excel spreadsheet should look like this:

	A	B
1	Solve for IRR: =IRR(B1:B?, Guess)	-2000
2	=IRR(B1:B5, 12%)	100
3		150
4	Solve for NPV: =NPV(i, B2:B?)+B1	0
5		2825

Step 4 Press ENTER. The answer will appear in Cell A2: **12.06%** (with appropriate decimal setting)

In Example 1, we found the IRR for a problem where the payment changes. Next, we will find NPV when the payment changes. In Example 2, we will do it the old-fashioned way: using the TVM format for PV. In Example 3, we will try it using the cash flow format for NPV.

Example 2 **Step 1** PV of the first stream of payments (120 payments of $2,000)
=PV(i, n, PMT, FV, Mode) → =PV(8.5%/12, 120, 2000, 0, 0) → (161,308.94)
Step 2 PV of the second stream of payments (60 payments of $3,000)
=PV(i, n, PMT, FV, Mode) → =PV(8.5%/12, 60, 3000, 0, 0) → (146,223.55)
Step 3 The value in Step 2 ($146,223.55) is the value at the *beginning* of that stream of payments (120 months from now), so the present value *today* is:
=PV(i, n, PMT, FV, Mode) → =PV(8.5%/12, 120, 0, 146223.55, 0) → (62,685.67)
Step 4 Find total PV
PV of first stream of payments (from Step 1) $161,308.94
PV of second stream of payments (from Step 3)   + 62,685.67
Total PV   **$223,994.61**

Example 3 **Step 1** Enter the initial cash flow in Cell B1; in this problem it is 0.
Step 2 Enter the 2000 cash flow in the next 120 cells (B2 through B121); to do so, enter 2000 in Cell B2, and then copy and paste in the remaining cells. Enter the 3000 cash flow in the next 60 cells (B122 through B181). Last cell is B181; clear cells under B181.
Step 3 Move the cursor to Cell A5. Type: =NPV(8.5%/12, B2:B181)+B1
Step 4 Press ENTER. The answer will appear: **223,994.61**

Notice, we got the same answer as in Example 2.

> ### TIP — keep track of cell numbers
>
> In Example 3, it is easy to get cell numbers confused. Here's one approach to stay on track:
>
> First cash flow in Cell B1
> Next 120 cash flows: B2 through B121 (1 + 120 = 121)
> Final 60 cash flows: B122 through B181 (121 + 60 = 181)

F Formulas: Concepts in Using Compound Interest Formulas

In Chapters 10 and 11, we solve time-value-of-money (TVM) problems with compound interest formulas. A formula for each variable (PV, FV, i, PMT, and n) is shown in Illustration 10-1 (Chapter 10). Pay special attention to the footnotes. Notice that i represents the periodic rate, in decimal form. Also notice that the right-hand column of Illustration 10-1 provides for an adjustment if the periodic payment is made at the beginning of each period; adjustments are not required in Formulas 1A, 2A, and 3 because there is no periodic payment.

If you are wondering where the formulas came from, you are in luck; you can request the derivations at *studentsupport@olympuspub.com*.

Using the formulas requires a basic understanding of calculator keystrokes, exponents, order of operations, chain calculations, reciprocals, and logarithms. A brief explanation of each follows.

Calculators

Knowing how to use calculators is essential in using the compound interest formulas. Keystrokes for the HP 10BII+ and TI BAII PLUS are included in the text. Appendix C includes some basic features of these two calculators, as well as specific keystrokes for each of the compound interest formulas. We have created keystrokes for several other popular calculators: TI-30Xa, TI-30X IIS, TI-83 PLUS, TI-84 PLUS, HP 10B, HP 10BII, HP 12C, HP 17BII, Casio 9750G PLUS, and LeWorld Financial. If you are using one of these calculators and would like a set of keystrokes (including keystroke examples for each of the compound interest formulas), e-mail us at *studentsupport@olympuspub.com*.

Exponents

To save space, repeated multiplication is often written with an exponent. For example (1.03) (1.03) (1.03) (1.03) could be written as $(1.03)^4$, read as "1.03 to the fourth power" and results in 1.125508810. Most calculators have exponent keys (such as y^x or ^) to shortcut the arithmetic.

Order of Operations

So that people worldwide can get identical answers to mathematical problems, a universal order of operations is used; refer to Unit 3.1 of the text. Some expressions contain more than one set of parentheses, in which case we use parentheses ( ), brackets [ ], and braces { } to distinguish each set. *We always do calculations within the innermost set first.* Here is an example of the order of operations:

$$\$50,000 \left[\frac{(1+.03)^4 - 1}{.03}\right] = \$50,000 \left[\frac{(1.03)^4 - 1}{.03}\right] = \$50,000 \left[\frac{1.125508810 - 1}{.03}\right]$$

$$= \$50,000 \left[\frac{.125508810}{.03}\right] = \$50,000\, [4.1836270] = \$209,181.35$$

Notice the set of parentheses inside the brackets. We must first simplify inside the parentheses, using the order of operations. Because the exponent 4 is outside the parentheses we ignore the exponent until we are through simplifying inside the parentheses. We add 1 + .03 to get 1.03. Next, we simplify inside the brackets, using the order of operations. The first step is to apply the exponent: 1.03^4 = (1.03)(1.03)(1.03)(1.03) = 1.125508810. Next we simplify the numerator: 1.125508810 - 1 = .125508810. Next, .125508810 ÷ .03 = 4.1836270. We have now simplified inside the brackets. Finally, $50,000 × 4.1836270 = $209,181.35.

Chain Calculations

In some solutions, like the one above, each successive step depends on a previous value. A common mistake is to write an intermediate result as a rounded value with only a few decimal places. By doing so, we lose accuracy. Rounding should take place only for the final answer. Let's see what would have happened in the previous problem if we had written each intermediate result with two decimal places:

$$\$50{,}000 \left[\frac{(1+.03)^4 - 1}{.03}\right] = \$50{,}000 \left[\frac{(1.03)^4 - 1}{.03}\right] = \$50{,}000 \left[\frac{(1.13) - 1}{.03}\right] = \$50{,}000 \left[\frac{.13}{.03}\right] = \$50{,}000\,[4.33] = \$216{,}500$$

By rounding each intermediate result to two decimal places, we got an answer of $216,500 instead of the correct answer of $209,181.35—we're off by more than $7,300! Here are three methods we can use to avoid rounding intermediate results:

Method 1. When using a calculator, do chain calculations if possible.

Method 2. For some problems the arithmetic cannot be done with chain calculations. Many calculators have storage registers, allowing us to store intermediate results. We can recall the numbers later.

Method 3. If we cannot use chain calculations and our calculator does not have storage registers to store the intermediate results, we should write the intermediate results with as many decimal places as possible.

Worth Noting

The formulas use periodic rates, in decimal form. For a rate of 7.5% compounded monthly, the periodic rate, in decimal form, is $.075 \div 12 = .00625$. For a rate of 8.5% compounded monthly, the periodic rate, in decimal form, is $.085 \div 12 \approx .007083333$; notice the result is a repeating decimal, with the 3s continuing forever. *The solutions in this supplement use 9 decimal places for periodic rates that are repeating decimals.* As a result of rounding the rate to 9 decimal places, a few final answers may vary slightly from what the answer would be if we had used more decimal places in the periodic rate. Some calculators will accept more digits to the right of the decimal point; by entering repeating decimals with as many digits as you can, any error in the final answer will be minimized. To eliminate error in the final answer, we could enter the rate as a chain calculation; for a rate of 8.5% compounded monthly, for example, we could enter $(1 + i)$ as $(1 + \frac{.085}{12})$.

Reciprocals

Two values whose product is 1 are reciprocals. The reciprocal of a fraction is found by switching the numerator and denominator. For example, the reciprocal of $\frac{2}{3}$ is $\frac{3}{2}$; notice, $\frac{2}{3} \times \frac{3}{2} = 1$ (that is the definition of a reciprocal). A whole number can be written as a fraction. For example, 4 can be written as $\frac{4}{1}$. So the reciprocal of 4 (or $\frac{4}{1}$) is $\frac{1}{4}$.

The reciprocal of a decimal number is found by dividing 1 by the number. For example, the reciprocal of 1.10 is $1 \div 1.10 \approx .90909090$. Notice that the answer is a repeating decimal (the digits keep repeating forever), so we use the symbol $\approx$ to show that the value is approximate.

Many calculators have a key that will find the reciprocal of a number. Look at your calculator. If it has a reciprocal key (such as 1/x), find the reciprocal of 1.10 (it should match the answer shown above, to your decimal setting).

Logarithms

A logarithm (or log, for short) is a number that represents an exponent. To illustrate, we know that $3^2 = 9$. We might ask "to what power must we raise 3 to get 9?" Using logarithms, we would say, What is the log base 3 of 9 (written as $\log_3 9$)? The answer is 2.

Using an exponential equation	Using a logarithmic equation
$3^2 = 9$	$\log_3 9 = 2$

In the above two equations, "3" is the base, "2" is the exponent, and "9" is the result. Many problems that occur in nature and business require the use of logarithms in which the base is a certain value, symbolized by the letter e. The value e is defined as the value that the expression

$$\left(1 + \frac{1}{n}\right)^n$$

approaches as n approaches infinity (∞). The following table shows what happens as n becomes larger and larger.

n	$\frac{1}{n}$	$1 + \frac{1}{n}$	$\left(1 + \frac{1}{n}\right)^n$
1	1	2	2
5	0.2	1.2	2.48832
10	0.1	1.1	2.59374246
1,000	0.001	1.001	2.716923932
1,000,000	0.000001	1.000001	2.718280469
1,000,000,000	0.000000001	1.000000001	2.718281827
10,000,000,000	0.0000000001	1.0000000001	2.718281828

As you can see, the values in the right-hand column increase less and less each time the *n*-value increases. The last value in the right-hand column is the *e*-value (to 9 decimal places): 2.718281828. This application occurs so often that it is given a special name: natural logarithm, identified by the symbol "ln" (from Latin, *logarithmus naturalis*). Using Formula 5 of Illustration 10-1 requires finding the natural logarithm of a number (see the symbol "ln" included in the formula). For example, we may be asked to find the natural logarithm of the value 3.25. This could be written in logarithmic form as:

$$\log_e 3.25 \quad \text{or} \quad \ln 3.25$$

Another way to ask for "ln 3.25" is to ask To what power must the value *e* (approximately 2.718281828) be raised to get 3.25? If we raise 2.718281828 to the first power we, of course, get 2.718281828 (lower than the target value of 3.25). If we raise 2.718182828 to the second power, we get approximately 7.388517886 (greater than the target value of 3.25). The answer, therefore, is somewhere between 1 and 2, but closer to 1. We could guess exponents and check them until we end up with 3.25. We can also get the answer on our calculators by using the "natural log" key (LN). The answer comes out 1.178654996.

G Glossary

Absolute Loss   A loss that occurs when merchandise is sold for less than cost.

Accelerated Depreciation   Any depreciation method that results in greater amounts of depreciation expense in the early years of an asset's life and lesser amounts in later years.

Accountant   A person who summarizes data into financial reports.

Accounting Equation   Assets = Liabilities + Owner's Equity.

Accumulated Depreciation   A running total of depreciation expense to date.

Acid-Test Ratio   A business ratio found by dividing cash plus accounts receivable by current liabilities.

Addend   A number being added. For 4 + 5 = 9, 4 and 5 are addends.

Add-On Method   A method used to calculate a loan payment in which interest is figured in advance on the full loan amount.

Adjustable Rate Mortgage (ARM)   A mortgage loan in which the interest rate is adjusted at set intervals, based on a specified interest rate index.

Adjusted Basis   Basis (cost) of an asset minus accumulated depreciation.

Advance   *See* Draw.

Amortization Schedule   A loan payment schedule that shows the interest and principal portion of each payment, as well as the unpaid balance.

Amortized Loan   A loan repaid with periodic payments of equal amount.

Angle   The figure formed by two lines diverging from a common point.

Annual Percentage Rate (APR)   The "real" annual rate paid for borrowed money, the disclosure of which is required by the Truth in Lending Act. The APR is designed to help consumers compare interest rates.

Annual Percentage Yield (APY)   The true annual rate that is paid to depositors. For 5% compounded quarterly, the APY is approximately 5.09%.

Annual Rate   The stated annual rate of interest.

Annuity   A repetitive, uniform withdrawal of funds.

Annuity Due   A series of regular payments in which the payments ar made at the beginning of each period.

Assessed Value   Property value (often computed as a certain percent of fair market value) that is used to calculate property tax.

Asset   Something of value owned by an individual or business.

Automatic Teller Machine (ATM)   A machine that allows customers of a banking institution to make deposits, withdrawals, and transfers of money.

Average Daily Balance   Sum of the daily balances divided by the number of days in the period.

Back-End Load   The transaction fee on a mutual fund paid when shares are sold. *See also* Front-end Load.

Back-End Ratio   *See* Debt-to-Income Ratio.

Bad Check   A check that is not honored by the bank, because of nonsufficient funds in the account.

Balance Sheet   A financial report showing a company's financial position on a certain date. It shows assets, liabilities, and resulting equity of the business.

Balloon Payment   A single, often large, payment on a loan at an agreed-upon time that pays whatever balance is still owed.

Bank Discount Method   *See* Discount Method.

Banker's Interest   *See* Ordinary Interest.

Bank Reconciliation   A process of comparing the bank statement balance with the checkbook balance to verify that they are both correct.

Bank Statement   A report sent by a bank to a customer showing the beginning balance, transactions, and ending balance (all according to the bank's records).

Bar Graph   A graphical presentation using bars to represent data.

Base   A value upon which a percent is applied. For 4% of 200 = 8, the base is 200.

Basis   The cost of an asset.

Bear Market   Situation in which investors are pessimistic about the overall economy and stock market. *See also* Bull Market.

Beneficiary   The person to whom life insurance proceeds are paid.

Bond   A written promise of a business or governmental agency to repay a specified sum on a certain date, usually with periodic interest during the term.

Bondholder   An investor who owns a bond.

Bond Report   A report prepared by a private company, designed to help investors evaluate the quality of a particular corporate or municipal bond.

Bookkeeper   A person who records transactions for a business.

Book Value   *See* Adjusted Basis.

Bounced Check   A check that is not honored by the bank, because of nonsufficient funds in the account. It is returned to the payee unpaid.

Break-Even Price   The exact selling price that covers all of the sellers expenses, providing no profit and no loss.

Bull Market   Situation in which investors are optimistic about the overall economy and stock market. *See also* Bear Market.

Capital Budgeting   The evaluation of a long-term project, such as whether to invest in plant and equipment assets.

Capital Gain   Profit from the sale of an investment.

Cash Discount   A discount (in dollars) given for paying an invoice promptly (within the discount period).

Cash Discount Rate The percent of discount (such as 2%) a buyer gets for paying an invoice within the discount period.

Cash Flow Problem A situation in which the cash flows change from period to period.

Cash Value The cash reserve portion of all life insurance policies except term that may be borrowed against or may be received in cash if a policy is canceled.

Celsius A scale used to measure temperature. 0° Celsius represents the temperature at which water freezes, and 100° Celsius represents the temperature at which water boils.

Centi A prefix in the metric system denoting $\frac{1}{100}$.

Centigrade The previous name for Celsius, used to measure temperature. *See* Celsius.

Certificate of Deposit (CD) A special savings account in which the depositor agrees to leave money for an agreed-upon period of time.

Chain Discount *See* Series Discount.

Check Written, signed instructions from a checking account customer directing the bank to pay a specified sum of money to a particular person or company.

Circle Graph A graphical presentation using a circle to present the data; the circle (representing the whole) is divided into parts.

Circumference The distance around a circle.

COD Abbreviation for "cash on delivery."

Closed-End Fund A mutual fund that sells no more shares after the initial offering. *See also* Open-End Fund.

Coefficient A number that multiplies a variable. For $3y^2$, the coefficient is 3.

Collateral An item of value (such as furniture, a car, or a home) that is pledged by a borrower. If the borrower defaults on the loan, the lender can sell the collateral and use the proceeds to repay the loan.

Combining Like Terms Combining constants and variables of a mathematical expression.

Commission A fee paid for completing a business task or performing a service.

Common Expense *See* Overhead.

Common Stock Ordinary stock in a corporation, with no guaranteed dividends but typically with voting rights. *See also* Preferred Stock.

Comparative Statement Financial statements from two or more successive accounting periods placed on the same report.

Complement What is required to make up a "whole" (or 100%). For example, the complement of 25% is 75%, because they add up to 100%.

Compound Interest Interest calculated on principal plus previous interest.

Compound Interest Formula A special formula designed to solve time-value-of-money problems.

Compound Interest Table A special table of decimal values designed to help solve time-value-of-money problems.

Compounding Period The amount of time that occurs between interest calculations. For a savings plan that pays interest quarterly, the compounding period is three months.

Condominium Unit Owner's Insurance Insurance purchased by a condo owner to protect belongings and to provide liability protection.

Confirmed Letter of Credit A guarantee by the payee's bank, in addition to the letter of credit issued by the payor's bank. *See also* Letter of Credit.

Constant The known value in a mathematical expression. For $3a + 5$, 5 is a constant.

Consumer The ultimate user of a product or service.

Consumer Loan A loan for personal, family, or household purposes.

Contingency A provision in an agreement that allows the buyer or seller to void the agreement if certain conditions are not met.

Conventional Loan The basic type of mortgage loan.

Corporate Bond A written promise of a corporation to repay a specified sum on a certain date, usually with periodic interest during the term.

Corporate Stock *See* Stock.

Corporation A business entity that sells shares of stock to investors who become owners of the corporation. A corporation is like a person, able to buy assets, borrow money, and perform other activities that sole proprietors and partners perform.

Cost of Goods Sold (COGS) The amount paid by a business for the goods sold during the period of time covered by the income statement: COGS = beginning inventory + cost of goods purchased - ending inventory.

Coupon Rate The annual rate, printed on the face of a bond, that is used to calculate interest.

Credit Card A small plastic card that identifies the person who has been approved for open-end credit.

Credit Memo Written notice by a bank notifying a customer that the bank has increased the account balance.

Credit Period The total amount of time a buyer has to pay an invoice before it is declared overdue and subject to late charges.

Cross-Canceling A process used in multiplying fractions, based on switching denominators and reducing fractions before multiplying.

Current Asset An asset that can be converted into cash or consumed within 1 year (or one operating cycle, whichever is longer).

Current Liability A debt that must be paid within 1 year (or one operating cycle, whichever is longer).

Current Ratio The relation of a company's current assets to its current liabilities: Current Assets ÷ Current Liabilities.

Cylinder A three-dimensional object whose base is a circle, whose diameter is the same from top to bottom, and whose sides are perpendicular to its base.

Day-of-the-Year Calendar A special table that assigns a number to each day of the year. This table can be used to determine maturity dates, due dates, or the number of days between two dates. See Appendix D of the text.

Debit Card A card, similar to a credit card, except the amount charged is deducted immediately from the checking account.

Debit Memo Written notice by a bank notifying the customer that the bank has reduced the account balance.

Debt Ratio A business ratio found by dividing total liabilities by total assets.

Debt-to-Income Ratio A ratio used by mortgage lenders to qualify a borrower: monthly housing costs ÷ monthly income.

Deci Prefix in the metric system denoting $\frac{1}{10}$.

Declining-Balance Depreciation   An accelerated depreciation method where a constant percent is multiplied by the adjusted basis.

Decreasing Term   A form of term life insurance, in which coverage decreases over the life of the policy.

Deductible   For insurance purposes, the amount the insured must pay before the insurance company pays.

Default   A condition that exists when a borrower fails to fulfill his or her obligations (for example, if the borrower is late on a payments or fails to maintain adequate insurance).

Deficiency   A shortage of funds. A deficiency exists when the proceeds of a foreclosure sale are not sufficient to pay a lender.

Deficiency Judgement   A court-ordered decree in which a borrower is directed to pay an amount still due a lender after proceeds of a foreclosure sale are applied.

Deka   Prefix in the metric system denoting 10.

Denominator   The number below the division line of a common fraction. For the fraction $\frac{3}{4}$, the denominator is 4.

Deposit Receipt   A receipt given by a bank to its customer, verifying a deposit of money.

Depreciable Basis   The portion of an asset's cost that can be depreciated over its useful life: cost - salvage value (or land value).

Depreciation Expense   The amount claimed as an expense because of an asset's loss of usefulness. Depreciation expense is only a "paper" entry, not a cash outlay.

Diameter   The distance from one side of a circle to the other side, passing through the center; stated another way, the diameter is twice the radius.

Difference   The result in subtraction. For 8 - 3 = 5, 5 is the difference.

Differential Piece Rate   A sliding-scale piecework rate in which the rate per item increases as the number of items produced increases.

Disclosure Statement   A written disclosure required by the Truth in Lending Act, in which lenders must inform borrowers of total finance charges and the APR.

Discount   A term used for bonds, denoting that the price paid by an investor is less than the face value. *See also* Par and Premium.

Discount Method   A method used to calculate interest for simple interest loans, in which interest is calculated on the maturity value and a 360-day year is used.

Discount Period   The first part of a credit period, during which the buyer is entitled to a cash discount.

Discounting Notes   The process of buying/selling a promissory note to produce a desired yield; because the notes are generally sold for less than the note balance (at a discount), the process is referred to as discounting the note.

Distributive Rule   Rule stating that the product of the sum of numbers equals the sum of the individual products. For example $2(a + b) = 2a + 2b$.

Diversification   Investing in a variety of things rather than putting too much money in a single investment.

Dividend   (1) In division, a number that is being divided. For $8 \div 2 = 4$, $\frac{8}{2} = 4$, and $2\overline{)8} = 4$, the dividend is 8. (2) For corporate stock, a distribution of corporate profits to stockholders.

Divisor   A number that is being divided into another. For $8 \div 2 = 4$, $\frac{8}{2} = 4$, and $2\overline{)8} = 4$, the divisor is 2.

Dollar Markdown   Price reduction, in dollars.

Double-Declining-Balance Depreciation   A accelerated method of depreciation using twice (200% of) the straight-line rate.

Double Taxation   A situation in which earnings are taxed twice. For example, corporate profits are taxed; then any remainder that is distributed to stockholders is taxed again.

Double Time   Double pay, received by some employees for working Sundays and holidays.

Dow Jones Industrial Average   A well-known index that monitors the price changes of 30 carefully selected stocks.

Draw   An amount paid to salespeople at regular intervals, often deducted from earned commissions.

Due Date   *See* Maturity Date.

Earnings per Share   A corporation's annual earnings (net income, after tax) divided by number of shares outstanding.

Electronic Funds Transfer (ETF)   A transaction that transfers funds electronically.

Employee   A person who works for a wage or salary.

Employee's Withholding Allowance Certificate   *See* Form W-4.

Employer   A person or business that employs people for a wage or salary.

End of Month (EOM)   A cash discount method in which the credit period does not start until the end of the month in which the invoice is dated.

Equation   Two mathematical expressions separated by an equal (=) sign. For example, $2y - 2 = 8$ is an equation; $2y - 8$ by itself is not.

Equity   Assets minus liabilities. For a home, the value minus mortgage balance(s).

Equivalent Fraction   Two or more fractions that have an identical value like $\frac{6}{12}$ and $\frac{1}{2}$.

Equivalent Single Discount Rate   The single trade discount rate that results in the same dollar amount of discount as the series discount from which it was derived.

Escrow Account   An account maintained with a lender for payment of property taxes and/or insurance.

Estimated Payments   Income tax payments, often made quarterly, that apply against tax liability.

Exact Interest   Simple interest, based on a 365- or 366-day year. *See also* Ordinary Interest.

Exponent   A superscript that indicates how many times a base is to be multiplied. For 5^3, the exponent is 3 and means (5) (5) (5), or 125.

Export   To send products (or services) to another country.

Extended Coverage   An additional package of insurance that provides protection against hazards not covered by a basic policy.

Extra (ex, or X)   A term used for cash discount purposes, in which the cash discount period is extended. Example: 3/10-80 extra.

Face Value   (1) For bonds, the amount printed on the face of the bond; the maturity value. (2) For insurance policies, the amount of insurance, printed on the face of the policy.

Factor   A value used in multiplication. For $3 \times 8 = 24$, 3 and 8 are factors.

Fahrenheit   A scale used to measure temperature. Water freezes at 32° Fahrenheit and boils at 212° Fahrenheit.

Fair Labor Standards Act   A federal law that establishes work conditions, minimum hourly pay, and standards of employee treatment.

Fair Market Value The price for which a property can reasonably be expected to sell.

Federal Insurance Contribution Act (FICA) A Federal act that requires most nongovernmental employers to deduct certain taxes from employees' paychecks.

Federal Unemployment Tax (FUT) A federal tax paid by employers. The money is used to administer state unemployment agencies.

FHA loan A mortgage loan in which the lender is insured against loss by the Federal Housing Administration (FHA).

Finance Charge The extra amount of money (in addition to the principal) a borrower pays for borrowed money. Finance charges include interest, points, and loan fees.

First-In, First-Out (FIFO) An inventory valuation method that assumes that the first goods purchased are the first to be sold; the present inventory therefore consists of goods most recently purchased.

First-to-Die Insurance Insures more than one person, but the death benefit is paid when the first dies.

First Mortgage A mortgage loan held by a lender who is "first in line" in event of default. *See also* Second Mortgage.

Fixed Costs Costs of a business that do not change with a change in sales volume.

FOB Destination Means the seller pays all freight to the buyer's place of business. "FOB" stands for "free on board."

FOB Shipping Point Means that the buyer pays for freight.

Formula A rule or principle expressed as an algebraic equation.

Form W-2 (Wage and Tax Statement) A wage and tax statement given to employees each year by the employer.

Form W-4 (Employee's Withholding Allowance Certificate) A federal form completed by an employee that is used by the employer in determining how much federal income tax to withhold from the employee's pay.

Fraction Part of a whole. The fraction $\frac{3}{4}$ indicates 3 parts out of 4.

Front-End Load The transaction fee on a mutual fund paid at the time of purchase. *See also* Back-End Load.

Front-End Ratio *See* Housing Ratio.

Future Value The value of something at a specified time in the future (at the end of the last "period"). For savings plans, future value represents what a deposit or series of deposits will accumulate to over time. For investments, it is the value at the time the investment is liquidated.

General Partnership A partnership in which all partners are liable for the debts of the partnership.

Good Faith Estimate An estimate of closing costs that lenders are required to provide to buyers before the loan closing date.

Grade-Point Average (GPA) An average grade per credit hour.

Graduated Equity Mortgage (GEM) A mortgage loan in which the payments change at set intervals.

Graph A visual representation of data.

Graveyard Shift A work shift during the early morning hours, such as midnight to 8 AM.

Greatest Common Divisor (GCD) The largest value that will divide evenly into both the numerator and denominator. For the fraction $\frac{6}{8}$, the GCD is 2.

Gross Earnings *See* Gross Pay.

Gross Loss *See* Absolute Loss.

Gross Pay The total amount of compensation received by an employee before any deductions are made.

Hazard A danger or peril for which people buy insurance.

Hecto Prefix in the metric system denoting 100.

Home-Equity Credit Line Open-end credit in which the borrower pledges equity in a home as collateral.

Homeowner's Insurance Insurance for an owner-occupied single-family home.

Horizontal Analysis A method of analyzing the change (from one year to another) for each component of a balance sheet or income statement.

Housing Ratio A ratio used by mortgage lenders to qualify a borrower: (monthly housing costs + monthly consumer debt) ÷ monthly income.

Import To bring products or services in from another country.

Impound Account *See* Escrow Account.

Improper Fraction A fraction whose numerator is larger than the denominator. $\frac{7}{2}$ is an improper fraction.

Income Statement A financial report that shows the revenues and expenses of a business for a given period of time. It shows how profitable the business is. Also called a profit and loss statement or an *operating statement*.

Installment Loan Borrowed money that is paid back with equal payments.

Insured A person who is insured.

Insurer An insurance company.

Intangible Asset An asset having no physical existence but having value because of the rights conferred as a result of its ownership and possession (such as a patent or trademark).

Interest Money paid for the use of borrowed money.

Interest Rate *See* Rate of Interest.

Interest Rate per Period *See* Periodic Rate.

Internal Rate of Return (IRR) An interest rate earned; it considers the dollar amount and timing of each cash flow.

Inventory Goods on hand for sale.

Inventory-Turnover The number of times a company's average inventory is sold during an accounting period.

Investment Asset For balance sheet purposes, an asset held for future use or to sell at a profit in the future, such as investment land, stocks, or bonds.

Invoice Document used for recording a sales transaction.

Junk Bond A bond that has minimal safety.

Kilo Prefix in the metric system denoting 1,000.

Last Day of the Credit Period The last day an invoice can be paid before an invoice is declared overdue and late charges are assessed.

Last Day of the Discount Period The last day an invoice can be paid to get a cash discount.

Last-In, First-Out (LIFO) An inventory valuation method that assumes the last goods purchased are the first to be sold; the present inventory therefore consists of the oldest items.

Letter of Credit A guarantee by a bank that payment will be made. If certain conditions are satisfied, and the party responsible for payment fails to pay, the bank will pay.

Liability Money owed to a creditor.

Life Insurance Insurance used to provide compensation to families following the death of someone they depend on for income.

Limited Liability Company (LLC) A special type of business ownership that limits the personal liability of its owners.

Limited Partner A type of partner in a limited partnership who is not actively involved in the business or personally responsible for the partnership debts.

Limited Partnership A type of partnership in which some of the partners (called "limited partners") take no active role in the business and are not personally responsible for the partnership debts.

Line Graph A graphical presentation with lines, ideal for presenting trends over time.

Line of Credit Pre-approved credit, up to a certain limit. *See* Open-End Credit.

List Price The original price of merchandise before any trade discount is given. The list price may be an arbitrary figure, or it may be the suggested retail price.

Loan-to-Value (LTV) Ratio The loan amount divided by the value of the property, generally expressed as a percent.

Long-Term Liability A debt that is not a current liability.

Loss A situation that occurs when business costs exceed revenues.

Lowest Common Denominator (LCD) The smallest value that all other given denominators can be evenly divided into. For the fractions $\frac{1}{4}$ and $\frac{1}{6}$, the LCD is 12.

Maker A checking account term, referring to the person who writes a check.

Manufacturer A person or business who assembles component parts or finished products.

Markdown Price reduction (in dollars).

Markup Selling price minus cost.

Maturity Date The date a loan (or bond) is due.

Maturity Value (1) For a simple interest note, the total amount (principal and interest) that must be repaid on the maturity date. (2) For a bond, the principal amount which must be repaid to the investor on the maturity date.

Mean The arithmetic average, found by dividing the sum of values by the number of values.

Median The value at the midpoint of a series of numbers, arranged from high to low.

Merit-Rating System A system used by many state unemployment agencies to determine how much state unemployment tax an employer must pay.

Metric Line Indicator A line graph showing metric prefixes, helpful in converting from one metric measurement to another.

Metric System A decimal system of measurements, used in most of the world. The basic units are meters, liters, and grams.

Mill One-tenth of a cent (or one-thousandth of a dollar). Mills are one type of property tax rate, multiplied by each $1,000 of assessed value to determine property tax.

Milli A prefix in the metric system denoting $\frac{1}{1,000}$.

Minuend A number from which another number is subtracted. For 8 - 3 = 5, 8 is the minuend.

Mixed Number A value composed of a whole number and a fraction. For example, $12\frac{1}{4}$ is a mixed number.

Mode The value that occurs most often in a set of numbers.

Modified Accelerated Cost Recovery System (MACRS) The method of depreciation required on all federal income tax returns for property placed in service after 1986.

Money Market Account A savings account similar to a passbook account, except a minimum balance must be maintained and the account generally has check-writing privileges.

Mortgage Insurance A guarantee by a private company or governmental agency that insures a lender for an agreed-upon sum in the event a loan is not repaid.

Mortgage Loan A loan secured by real estate.

Multiplicand In multiplication, the first or top number being multiplied.

Multiplier In multiplication, the second or bottom number doing the multiplying.

Municipal Bond A bond issued by a state or local government.

Mutual Fund An investment fund in which numerous people contribute; the money in the fund is then invested in specific investments on behalf of the group of investors.

Net Amount Due Net price minus cash discount. This is the actual amount the buyer owes the seller on an invoice, after trade and cash discounts.

Net Asset Value (NAV) For mutual funds, the value of one share, found by dividing the fund's net assets by the number of shares issued.

Net Income *See* Profit.

Net Pay Gross pay minus deductions. This is the dollar amount of an employee's paycheck.

Net Present Value (NPV) The present value of future cash flows for a cash flow problem (one in which the cash flows change from period to period).

Net Price The actual price a business pays for merchandise, after trade discounts but before cash discounts.

Net Proceeds Proceeds from a loan after deducting front-end loan costs.

Net Worth The equity for a personal financial statement.

New York Stock Exchange The largest stock exchange in the United States, located on Wall Street in New York City.

No-Fault Insurance Motor vehicle insurance that reimburses for bodily injury (up to a certain dollar limit) without regard to who was at fault.

No-Load Mutual Fund A mutual fund in which shares are purchased directly from the mutual fund company, without a transaction fee.

Nominal Rate The stated annual rate of interest.

Nonforfeiture Options The options available to the policyholder on termination of a life insurance policy that has a cash value.

Nonsufficient Funds Check A check without adequate funds in the checking account. Also called a *bad check* or *bounced check* if not honored by the bank.

Note Balance The current, unpaid balance on a promissory note.

Note Rate The interest rate stated on a promissory note.

Numerator The number above the division line of a common fraction. For the fraction $\frac{3}{4}$, the numerator is 3.

Odd Lot   Less than 100 shares of stock.

Online Banking   A system that allows individuals to perform banking activities on the Internet.

Open-End Credit   Privilege of borrowing up to an approved credit limit.

Open-End Fund   A mutual fund that continues selling shares after the initial offering. *See also* Closed-End Fund.

Operating Loss   A loss that occurs when the selling price of merchandise is greater than cost but not high enough to cover operating expenses.

Operating Statement   *See* Income Statement.

Ordinary Annuity   A series of regular payments in which the payments are made at the end of each period.

Ordinary Dating Method   The most common method used for cash discounts. For example, 2/10, n/30 means the buyer gets a 2% discount if the invoice is paid within 10 days of the invoice date.

Ordinary Interest   Simple interest, based on a 360-day year.

Ordinary Life Insurance   *See* Whole Life Insurance.

Original Marked Price   The price of an item before it is marked down.

Origination Fee   For mortgage loans, this is a one-time front-end fee charged by the lender (often about 1% of the loan amount).

Outstanding Check   A check written but not yet deducted from the bank's balance.

Outstanding Deposit   A deposit made but not yet added to the bank's balance.

Overhead   A business expense not directly associated with a specific department or product.

Overtime Pay   The pay for working more than 40 hours per week.

Owner's Equity   The net value of a business to the owner, found by subtracting liabilities from assets.

Par   A term for bonds, in which the price an investor pays is equal to the face value. *See also* Premium and Discount.

Parallel   A condition in which two lines travel in the same direction (and therefore never cross).

Partial Payment   A payment that is less than the total balance owed.

Partial Product   In multiplication, the result of each individual step of multiplication.

Participating Policy   A life insurance policy in which the policyholder shares in the profits of the company.

Partnership   A type of business, other than a corporation, that has two or more owners.

Partnership Agreement   An agreement between the individual owners of a partnership, spelling out each partner's rights and responsibilities.

Par Value   *See* Face Value.

Passbook Savings Account   A savings account used for daily deposits and withdrawals. The depositor generally earns interest on the average daily balance.

Payday Loan   A loan in which a person who receives a regular paycheck can get a loan, similar to an advance on their pay.

Payee   A checking account term, referring to the person to whom a check is made payable.

Payment   *See* Periodic Payment.

Payoff Amount   The amount of money needed to pay off a loan, including interest to the date of payoff.

Payor   The person who writes a check.

Payroll Register   A multicolumn form used to record a company's payroll for each pay period.

Percent   Means hundredths. For example, 5% means five hundredths, $\frac{5}{100}$, or .05, denoting five parts out of a hundred.

Percentage Method   A method employers can use in determining how much federal income tax to withhold from an employee's pay.

Percent Markdown   Markdown divided by original marked price, expressed as a percent.

Percent Markup on Cost   Markup divided by cost, expressed as a percent.

Percent Markup on Selling Price   Markup divided by selling price, expressed as a percent.

Perimeter   The distance around a figure.

Period   *See* Compounding Period.

Periodic Inventory   An inventory determined by taking a physical count of merchandise at regular intervals.

Periodic Payment   The amount of money that is paid or received each "period" on a regular basis.

Periodic Rate   The interest rate per period. For an annual rate of 15%, the monthly periodic rate is 1.25%.

Perpendicular   Intersecting by forming a right angle (90°).

Perpetual Inventory   An inventory that is continuously updated by recording the purchase and sale of each item.

Personal Financial Statement   A "balance sheet" for individuals, listing the assets and liabilities of the individual (or couple), as well as the resulting net worth.

Personal Identification Number (PIN)   A private code used to authorize a transaction on a debit card or ATM machine.

Personal Property   Property other than real property, such as cars, business inventory, clothing, and money.

Piecework Rate   Compensation based on how many items are produced or completed.

Pie Chart   *See* Circle Graph.

Plant and Equipment   Long-lived tangible assets that are held for use in the production or sale of other assets or services.

Points   A one-time front-end loan fee for getting a loan with a rate lower than the prevailing rate. Each point is 1% of the loan amount.

Population Study   A statistical study that gathers data on each member of an entire group. *See also* Sample Study.

Portion   Product obtained by multiplying the base by the rate. For 4% of 200 = 8, the portion is 8.

Preferred Stock   A type of corporate stock for which dividends are paid (often in fixed amounts) before dividends are paid on common stock.

Premium   (1) For bonds, a term denoting that the price paid by an investor is greater than the face value. *See also* Par and Discount. (2) For insurance, the fee collected from the insured.

Prepayment Penalty   A special fee on some loans for paying the loan off early.

Present Value   In a time-value-of-money problem, the value of something at the beginning of the first period. For savings plans, present value is the initial one-time deposit. For investments, it is the initial investment. For loans, it is the loan amount. Present value can also be the discounted value (in today's dollars) of amounts to be received in the future.

Price/Cost Ratio The relation between selling price and cost (selling price ÷ cost).

Price–Earnings (PE) Ratio The relation between the price of stock and the corporation's most recent annual profit per share: price per share ÷ annual earnings per share.

Principal The amount of money that is originally loaned or borrowed; also the portion of a loan payment that reduces the loan balance.

Proceeds For simple interest loans that use the discount method, proceeds are the maturity value minus interest. This is the amount given to the borrower. The borrower then repays the maturity value.

Product The result in multiplication. For 3 × 8 = 24, 24 is the product.

Profit The excess of revenues over expenses.

Profit and Loss Statement *See* Income Statement.

Profit Margin, before Tax A business ratio found by dividing net income (before tax) by net sales.

Promissory Note A written promise to repay a loan.

Proper Fraction A fraction whose numerator is smaller than the denominator. $\frac{3}{4}$ is a proper fraction.

Property Tax A tax levied on real and personal property by local governments. The money is used for education, streets, police and fire protection, and other local services.

Property Tax Rate The rate that is applied to the assessed value to determine property tax. Property tax rate = Total budget ÷ Total assessed value within the entity.

Prospectus A document that explains a stock or mutual fund offering.

Prox *See* End of Month.

Quotient The result in division. For 8 ÷ 2 = 4, $\frac{8}{2} = 4$, and $2\overline{)8} = 4$, the quotient is 4.

Radius The distance from the center of a circle to the outside.

Range The difference between the highest and lowest values in a set of data.

Rate Percent that is applied to the base. For 4% of 200 = 8, the rate is 4%.

Rate of Interest Percent used to calculate the dollar amount of interest.

Rate of Return A rate earned on invested money.

Ratio A comparison of two numbers, such as 15 to 12, $\frac{15}{12}$, 15:12, or the equivalent 1.25:1 that is used in most business applications.

Real APR The APR from the borrower's standpoint. In some cases (especially real estate loans), the borrower's real APR is even higher than the reportable APR because certain loan costs are not used in calculating the reportable APR.

Real Estate *See* Real Property.

Real Estate Appraiser A person who can assist in estimating the value of real estate.

Real Estate Broker A person who can assist in buying and selling real estate.

Real Property Land, buildings, and other improvements attached to land.

Receipt of Goods (ROG) For cash discount purposes, an indication that the credit period begins the date goods are received, not the date of the invoice. Example: 2/10, n/30 ROG.

Reciprocal Two values whose product is 1 are reciprocals. The reciprocal of a value is found by switching the numerator and denominator. The reciprocal of $\frac{5}{7}$ is $\frac{7}{5}$; the reciprocal of 4 is $\frac{1}{4}$.

Recovery Period For federal income tax purposes, the length of time (in years) over which an asset can be depreciated.

Rectangle A two-dimensional figure having four sides and four 90° angles.

Rectangular Solid A three-dimensional object, whose base and sides are all rectangles.

Reduced Price The price at which a product is sold, after any markdown.

Reducing the Fraction Creating a new fraction with a smaller denominator, without changing the value. For example the fraction $\frac{6}{8}$ can be reduced to $\frac{3}{4}$.

Refinance To get a new loan, in which all or part of the proceeds are used to pay off an old loan.

Regulation Z *See* Truth In Lending Act.

Remainder In division, the left over amount.

Renter's Insurance Insurance purchased by a tenant to protect the tenant's belongings and to provide liability protection.

Repeating Decimal A decimal number with repeating digits (such as .09090909 . . .).

Replacement Cost The cost to replace damaged or lost property.

Reportable APR The APR that a lender must report to a borrower in accordance with the Truth in Lending Act. *See also* Real APR.

Reserve Account *See* Escrow Account.

Retailer A business that sells goods directly to consumers.

Retained Earnings Portion of corporate earnings (profits) that is not distributed to stockholders.

Return on Equity A business ratio, found by dividing net income (after tax) by equity.

Revolving Credit *See* Open-end Credit.

Rider An attachment to an insurance policy that provides additional benefits. A rider, of course, results in additional premium.

Right Angle A 90° angle.

Rule of 78 A method used in some states to calculate interest. With this method, extra interest is applied to the early part of a loan and less to the latter part of a loan.

Salary A fixed amount of money each pay period.

Sales Tax A tax levied on sales to the final consumer. The tax is collected by state and local governments.

Sales Tax Rate The rate that is used to calculate sales tax.

Sales Tax Table A table showing various price ranges and the resulting sales tax. The table requires no calculations.

Salvage Value The projected value of an asset at the end of its useful life.

Sample Study A statistical study in which data is gathered on a sample group rather than from an entire population. *See also* Population Study.

S Corporation A special type of business entity that has the tax treatment of a partnership and the liability benefits of a corporation.

Second Mortgage   A mortgage loan held by a lender who is "second in line" in the event of a default.

Second-to-Die Insurance   Insures two people, but the death benefit is paid only after both have died.

Section 179 Expense Deduction   A special federal income tax deduction allowed on capital expenditures of certain income-producing property.

Security   *See* Collateral.

Self-Employed   People who work for themselves, rather than for someone else (as an employee).

Series Discount   Two or more individual trade discounts taken one after the other (such as 25/15/10).

Simple Interest   Interest calculated only on principal. Compound interest, on the other hand, is calculated on principal plus previous interest.

Simplifying an Expression   Rewriting a mathematical expression so it is easier to understand.

Sinking Fund   A fund set up to accumulate a certain sum on a specified future date.

Sliding Scale (Variable) Commission   A commission that varies with sales volume. As sales volume increases, so does the commission rate.

Sliding Scale Discount   A type of cash discount in which the discount rate decreases over time (such as 4/10, 2/30, n/60).

Sole Proprietorship   A type of business that has only one owner.

Specific Identification   An inventory valuation method in which each inventory item is identified (by tagging or other mark). Value of the total inventory is established by adding the actual cost of each individual item.

Square   A rectangle with all four sides having equal length.

Stacked Bar Graph   A bar graph in which two or more bars are stacked together.

Standard Deviation   A statistical measurement that shows how data are spread around the mean.

State Unemployment Tax (SUT)   A state tax paid by employers, used to aid unemployed workers.

Statistics   The process of collecting, organizing, tabulating, interpreting, and presenting numerical data.

Stock   Ownership in a corporation.

Stockbrokerage Firm   A company that belongs to a stock exchange and can therefore represent investors there.

Stock Exchange   A place where stockbrokerage firms meet to buy and sell stocks and other securities for their investors.

Stockholder   An investor who purchases stock in a corporation.

Straight Life Insurance   *See* Whole Life Insurance.

Straight-Line Depreciation   A depreciation method that assumes the asset loses an equal amount of usefulness during each year.

Subtrahend   A number being subtracted from another. For 8 − 3 = 5, 3 is the subtrahend.

Sum   The result in addition. For 4 + 5 = 9, 9 is the sum.

Swing Shift   A work shift between the day and night shift, lasting from about 4 PM to midnight.

Taxable Income   The income upon which income tax is calculated.

Tax Assessor   A person who establishes the value of property for property tax purposes.

Tax Bracket   For income taxes, this is the rate that is applied to the *highest dollar* of taxable income.

Tax Rate Schedules   Schedules used to calculate income tax; for federal income tax, tax rate schedules are used by people with taxable income of $100,000 or more.

Tax Table   A table used to calculate income tax; for federal income tax, tax tables are used by people with taxable income less than $100,000.

Term   The length of time for a loan or an investment, generally stated in months or years.

Terminating Decimal   A decimal number with trailing zeros (such as .2500).

Term Insurance   A type of life insurance that provides protection for a given period of time.

Time   For simple interest loans, the length of time for the loan, stated in years.

Time-Value-of-Money Problem   A financial problem based on the principal that money earns interest over time.

Total Tax Rate   For property tax, the sum of property tax rates from each taxing entity.

Trade Discount   A discount off the list price.

Trade Discount Amount   A discount, in dollars, off the list price.

Trade Discount Rate   The rate (such as 25%) that is multiplied by list price to determine the trade discount amount.

Trend Analysis   Comparing financial statements from two or more successive accounting periods.

Truth in Lending Act   A federal law that requires lenders to inform certain borrowers, in writing, of finance charges and the annual percentage rate (APR).

Unit Cost   The cost per unit, such as the cost per ounce or per square foot.

Units-of-Production Depreciation   A depreciation method that bases depreciation on usage.

Universal Life   A form of life insurance in which the policyholder can increase, decrease, or suspend premiums.

Useful Life   Estimated number of years an asset will be useful.

U.S. Rule   A rule used to calculate interest. With the U.S. Rule, interest is calculated to the date payment is received, and a 365-day year is used. The remainder of each payment is treated as principal, reducing the loan balance.

U.S. Securities   Various types of bonds issued by the U.S. government, including T-bills, Treasury notes, Treasury bonds, and savings bonds.

Usury Law   A state law that sets a maximum interest rate.

VA loan   A mortgage loan in which the lender is partially insured against loss by the Veterans Administration (VA). The borrower must be a qualified veteran.

Value   *See* Fair Market Value.

Variable   A symbol (usually a letter of the alphabet) that represents an unknown number.

Variable Costs   Costs of a business that change with a change in sales volume.

Variable Life   A type of life insurance in which the policyholder can instruct the company how to invest the cash reserves (with limitations).

Vertical Analysis A method of analyzing a financial report where the amount for each component is compared to a total.

Wage Bracket Method A method an employer can use in determining how much federal income tax to withhold from an employee's pay.

Weighted Average (1) For inventory valuation, a method in which the value for each item is the average cost of goods available for sale during the accounting period. (2) For statistics, *See* Weighted Mean.

Weighted Mean A mean (average) for data where values each have a different relative importance.

Whole-Life Insurance A type of life insurance in which the insured pays a constant premium until death. Unlike term insurance, this type of policy builds up a cash value.

Whole Number Any number that is 0 or larger and doesn't contain a decimal or fraction. 3 and 308 are whole numbers; -2, 4.12, and $\frac{2}{5}$ are not whole numbers.

Wholesaler A middleman in the distribution process who purchases from manufacturers or other wholesalers.

Wire Transfer An electronic transmission of money.

Withholding Allowance The number of exemptions claimed by an employee on Form W-4.

Yield An investors rate of return, such as with bonds.

Yield During Ownership An investor's yield on a bond, assuming that the bond is sold before maturity.

Yield to Maturity (YTM) An investor's yield on a bond if the bond is held to maturity.

Zero-Coupon Bond A type of bond that pays no periodic interest; instead, the bondholder buys the bond at a discount and receives the face value at maturity.

Index

Absolute loss, 127
Accelerated depreciation, 428
Accountant, 387
Accounting equation, 393
Acid-test ratio, 399
Addend, 7
Addition
    of decimals, 15–16
    of fractions, 33–34, 36
    of whole numbers, 7–8
Additional Medicare tax, 161, 165, 167
Add-on method, 360
Adjustable rate mortgage (ARM), 324, 325
Adjusted basis, 426
Advance, 160
Allocating overhead, 416
Amortization, 321
    calculator registers for, 321
    calendar-year, 322
    negative, 324, 325
    schedule, 319, 323
Angle, 484
Annual percentage rate (APR), 183, 293, 327, 360
    comparing, 186–87, 364–65
    effect of loan costs on, 186, 361–64
    for a mortgage loan, 362–65
    in deciding whether to refinance, 365
    real, 363
    reportable, 362–63
    with add-on method, 360
Annual percentage yield (APY), 191–92
Annual rate, 192
Annuity, 230–31, 276–77
    insurance, 475
Annuity due, 212, 231, 259
Appraisal of real estate, 313
Area, 486–88
    of circle, 487
    of rectangle, 487
    of triangle, 487
Assessed value, 453
Asset, 392
    current, 392
    types of, 392
Auto mileage, 18
Automatic teller machine (ATM), 142
Average daily balance, 299

Back-end load, 350
Back-end ratio, 314–16
Bad check, 141
Balance sheet, 392–95
Balloon payment, 324
Bank discount method, 188

Banker's interest, 183
Bank reconciliation, 144–48
    follow up to, 147–48
Bank statement, 144–45
Bar graph, 524
Base, 76
    solving for, 78
Basis, 426
    adjusted, 426
    depreciable, 426
Bear market, 343
Beneficiary, 471
Bondholder, 346
Bonds, 346–48
    brokerage fees for, 348
    corporate, 346
    interest rate for, 346
    investing in, 346–48
    junk, 347
    municipal, 346
    quotes, 347–48
    rate of return for, 368–69
    reports, 347
    risk for, 347
    U.S., 346, 348
    values, 215–16, 262
    zero-coupon, 346
Bookkeeper, 387
Book value, 426
Bounced check, 141
Break-even price, 127–28
Bull market, 343
Business entities, 388, 391, 395

Capital gain, 350
Capital budgeting, 216, 262
Car loan, 232, 278, 292–97, 361–62
Cash discount, 97, 102–08
    effect on an income statement, 390
    end of month (EOM), 105–06
    extra, 106
    for partial payments, 106–07
    involving freight and returned goods, 102
    measuring the benefit of, 107–08
    ordinary dating method, 103–04
    rate, 102
    receipt of goods (ROG), 105
    sliding-scale, 104
    terms, 101–06
Cash flow problem, 370
Cash flow registers, 371
Cash value, 472, 474
Celsius, 509–10
Centi, 506, 508

Centigrade, 509
Chain discount, 100
Check, 141
    register, 142, 144
    stubs, 143
Checking account balance, 144
Circle, 484
    area of, 487
    circumference of, 486
Circle graph, 525
Circumference, 486
Closed-end fund, 350
COD, 102
Coefficient, 50
Collateral, 294, 313
Combining like terms, 53–54
Commission, 160
    sliding scale (variable), 160
Common denominator, 34
Common expense, 416
Common stock, 342 (*See also* stock)
Comparative statement, 396, 397–98
Complement, 99
Compounding period, 206, 250
Compound interest, 179, 189–92
    formulas, 208, 209
Condominium, 468
Constant, 50
Consumer, 97
    loan, 183
    price index (CPI), 242, 380
Contingency, 316
Converting fractions, decimal numbers, and Percents, 38–40, 74–75
Converting measurements
    metric to metric, 508
    metric to U.S., 508–09
    U.S. to U.S., 491–93
Corporation, 342, 388
    income tax return for, 391
    S Corporation, 395
Cost of goods sold (COGS), 390, 391, 414–15
Counting days, 103–06, 181–82, 296
Coupon rate, 346
Credit, 298
Credit cards, 298–300
Credit memo, 143
Credit period, 102
    last day of, 103
Cross-canceling, 35
Current asset, 392
Current liability, 392
Current ratio, 399
Cur yld for a bond, 347–48

I-1

Cylinder, 489

Day-of-the-year calendar, 103, 181, 296, Appendix D
Debit card, 142
Debit memo, 143
Debt-to-income ratio, 314–15
Debt ratio, 399
Deci, 506–08
Decimal
   changing to words, 4–5
   repeating, 39
   system, 4
   terminating, 39
Declining balance depreciation, 428–29
   for partial year, 429–30
Deductible, 466
Default, 312
Deficiency, 297, 312
Deka, 506, 508
Denominator, 30
Deposit receipt, 145
Depreciable basis, 426
Depreciation
   accumulated, 426
   declining balance, 428–29
   expense, 426
   for federal income tax, 431–35
   for financial accounting, 426–30
   for partial years, 429–30
   for rental real estate, 431–34
   straight-line, 427
   terminology, 426
   units-of-production, 427–28
Diameter, 485, 486
Difference, 8
Differential piece rate, 160
Disclosure statement
   for a car loan, 294
   for a mortgage loan, 327
Discount
   bank, 188
   cash, 97, 102–08
   chain, 100
   method, 188
   note
      in which payments do not change, 215, 254, 261–62
      in which payments change, 372–73
   period, 102
      last day of, 103
   series, 100
   trade, 97, 98–101
Distributive rule, 53
Diversification, 349
Dividend
   for division, 10–11
   for corporate stock, 342, 343, 348, 395
Division
   of decimal numbers, 17–19
   of fractions, 34, 35, 37
   of whole numbers, 10–11
Divisor, 10
Double-declining-balance depreciation, 428

Double taxation, 395
Double time, 158
Dow Jones Industrial Average, 343
Draw on pay, 160
Due date, 180

Earnings per share, 345
Electronic funds transfer, 142
Emergency fund, 188
Employee, 157
Employee's Withholding Allowance Certificate (Form W-4), 162
Employee taxes, 161–65
Employer, 157
Employer taxes, 165–66
End of month (EOM) dating, 105–06
Equation, 54
   balancing scales concept, 54–55
   expression vs, 54
   procedure for solving, 54–57
Equipment, evaluating purchase of, 216, 262
Equity
   in a home, 320
   owner's, 393
   partner's, 393
   stockholders', 393
Equivalent fractions, 31–32
Equivalent single discount rate, 101
Escrow account, 317
Estimated payments, 168
Estimating, 14–15
Exact interest, 183
Excel, TVM Problems, Appendix E
Exchange rates, 504
Exemptions, 162, 447
Expense, 388
Exponents, 50, 210
Export, 503
Extra (ex, or X) dating, 106

Face value, 346, 468
Factor, 9
Fahrenheit, 509–10
Fair Labor Standard's Act, 158
Fair market value, 453
Federal income tax
   for businesses, 450–51
   for individuals, 446–50
   itemized deductions, 447
   liability, 167–68
   rates
      for corporations, 450
      for individuals, 449
   standard deduction, 447
   withholding, 162–64, 168
Federal Insurance Contribution's Act (See FICA tax)
Federal unemployment tax (FUT), 166
FHA loan, 313
FICA tax, 161
   for employees, 161
   for employers, 165
   for self-employed, 166–67
FIFO, 413–14

Finance charge, 183, 293, 360
Financial calculators, 252
   problem-solving strategy for, 252–55
First-in-first-out (FIFO), 413–14
Fixed costs, 128
FOB, 102
Foreclosure sale, 312–13
Formulas, 57
   for area, 486–88
   for circumference, 486
   for percent, 76
   for perimeter, 484–85
   for volume, 488–89
Fraction, 30
   adding and subtracting, 33–34, 36
   converting, 30–32, 38–40, 75
   dividing, 35–37
   equivalent, 31–33
   improper, 30
   multiplying, 35, 37
   proper, 30
   reducing, 32–33
Freight, 102
Front-end load, 350
Front-end ratio, 314
Future value, 206, 207–213, 250, 255-59

General partnership, 395
Good faith estimate, 326
Grade-point average (GPA), 521
Graduated equity mortgage (GEM), 325
Gram, 506, 507, 508
Graph
   abuse, 524
   bar, 524
      stacked, 525
   circle, 525
   for presenting data, 523–26
   line, 523
Graveyard shift, 158
Greatest common divisor (GCD), 32–33
Gross earnings, 158
Gross loss, 127
Gross pay, 158
Gross profit, 390–91
Grouped data, 526
Growth rate, 366
Guess and check method
   with compound interest formulas, 235–36
   with word problems, 61

Half-year convention, 433
Hazard insurance, 466
Hecto, 506, 508
Home equity credit line, 298, 300, 325
Home ownership, 312
Homeowner's insurance, 467–68
Horizontal analysis, 396–98
Housing ratio, 314–15

Import, 503
Impound account (See Escrow account)
Improper fraction, 30
Income statement, 388

abbreviated, 389
expanded, 390
for merchandising company, 389, 390
for service company, 389
Income tax (*See* Federal income tax)
Inflation, 242, 380
Installment loan, 232, 278, 292–97
Paying off, 295–97
Insurance (*See also* Life insurance)
auto, 469–71
business property, 469
cancellation, 467
condominium, 468
coverage, 466
deductibles, 466
extended coverage, 467
hazard, 466
homeowner's, 467–68
life, 471–75
no-fault, 470
premiums, 465, 466, 468, 469
property, 466–69
renter's, 468
Insured, 465
Insurer, 465
Intangible asset, 392
Interest
banker's, 183
exact, 183
for bonds, 347
for partial payments, 184
in simple interest formula, 180
ordinary, 183
portion of each payment, 184, 296, 318–19
rate, 206, 250
per period, 190, 206, 250
using Rule of 78, 297
using U.S. Rule, 183, 293, 295
Internal rate of return (IRR), 370–71
Inventory, 412
methods, 412–15
periodic, 412
perpetual, 412
turnover, 399
Investment asset, 392
Invoice, 102
filing, 108
IRR (*See* Internal rate of return)
Itemized deduction, 447

Junk bond, 347

Keogh, 91–92
Kilo, 506, 508

Last-in-first-out (LIFO), 414
LCD, 34
Leasehold interest, 223, 270
Length, 484
Letter of credit, 505
confirmed, 505
Liability, 392
current, 392

insurance, 467, 468, 469
long-term, 392
Life insurance
annuity, 475
beneficiary, 471
cash value, 472
decreasing term, 471
first-to-die, 472
ordinary, 472
second-to-die, 472
riders, 473
straight, 472
term, 471, 472
universal life, 472
variable life, 472
various types of, 471–72
whole life, 472, 473
LIFO, 414
Limited liability company (LLC), 391, 395
Limited partner, 395
Limited partnership, 395
Line
graph, 523
parallel, 484
perpendicular, 484
Line of credit, 298
Liquidity, 398, 399
List price, 98
Liter, 506, 507, 508
Loan
amortized, 318
car, 232, 278, 292–95, 361–62
conventional, 313
finding the length of, 280
foreclosure, 312-13
installment, 292–97
mortgage, 312, 313–20, 324–27
secured, 294, 313
Loan-to-value (LTV) ratio, 314
Loss
absolute, 127
business, 388
gross, 127
operating, 127
Lowest common denominator (LCD), 34

MACRS, 431–35
Maker, 141
Manufacturer, 97
Margin, 118 (*See also* markup)
Markdown, 117
as a percent, 123–24
in dollars, 123–24
series, 123
Mark-on (*See* Markup)
Markup, 117
formulas, 118, 121
for services, 120
percent, 121
on cost, 118–19
on cost vs on selling price, 122
on selling price, 119–20
MasterCard, 298
Mathematical symbols, 50
Maturity date, 180, 181, 346

Maturity value
for bonds, 346
for simple interest notes, 180–81
Mean, 520
calculating, 520
weighted, 520
Measurements, 483
Measures of dispersion, 527–29
Median, 521–22
Medicare tax, 161, 165-67
Additional Medicare, 161, 165-67
Merit-rating system, 166
Meter, 506, 507, 508, 509
Metric system
converting
metric to metric, 508
to U.S. measurements, 508–09
line indicator, 508
rules for writing, 507
Mid-quarter convention, 433
Miles per gallon (mpg), 18
Mill, 455
Milli, 506, 508
Minimum hourly wage, 158
Minuend, 8
Mixed number, 30, 36–37
Mode, 522
Modified Accelerated Cost Recovery System (*See* MACRS)
Monetary exchange rates, 504–06
effect on foreign investments, 505–06
effect on foreign invoices, 504–05
Moody's, 347
Mortgage, 232–33, 279, 312
alternatives for financing, 324–26
conventional, 313
default on, 312–13
escrow account, 317
fees and costs, 326–27
first vs second, 312–13
FHA, 313
insurance, 326
reverse, 325
VA, 313
with different term, 233, 279, 317
Multiplicand, 9
Multiplication
of decimal numbers, 16–17
of fractions, 34–35, 37
of whole numbers, 9–10
Multiplier, 9
Municipal bond, 346
Mutual funds, 349–50

Negative amortization, 324, 325
Net amount due, 102
Net asset value (NAV), 349
Net income, 166, 388, 389, 390, 391
Net pay, 164
Net present value, 370, 372
Net price, 98, 99
comparing, 100
Net proceeds, 362, 363
Net sales, 389, 390
Net worth, 394

I-3

New York Stock Exchange, 342
No-fault insurance, 470
No-load mutual fund, 350
Nominal rate, 192, 298
Nonforfeiture option, 474
Nonsufficient funds check, 141
Note
    balance, 215, 261
    discounting, 215
    promissory, 215, 261
    rate, 361
Number of days, 103–05, 181–82, 296
Numerator, 30

Onine banking, 142
Open-end credit, 298–300
Open-end fund, 350
Operating cycle, 392
Operating loss, 127
Operating statement, 388
Order of operations, 51–52
Ordinary annuity, 212, 231, 259, 279
Ordinary dating method, 103–04
Ordinary interest, 183
Original marked price, 123
    with anticipated markdown, 124–26
Origination fee, 326
Outstanding check, 145
Outstanding deposit, 145
Overhead, allocation of, 416–18
Overinsured, 467
Overtime pay, 158
Owner's equity, 393

Par
    for a bond, 346
    value, for a bond, 346
Parallel, 484
Partial payment
    for an invoice, 106–07
    for a simple interest loan, 184
Partial product, 9
Participating policy, 473
Partnership, 388
    agreement for, 388
    general, 395
    income tax return, 391
    limited, 395
Par value, 346
Pay
    gross, 158
    net, 164
Payday loan, 187
Payee, 141
Payoff amount for a loan, 184, 297
Payor, 141
Payroll register, 164–65
Percent, 74
    conversions, 74–75
    formulas, 76
    markdown, 123
    markup on cost, 118–19
    markup on selling price, 119–20
    solving problems involving, 76–79
Percentage increase and decrease, 80–84

Percentage method, 163–64
Perimeter, 484–85
Period (See Compounding period)
Periodic inventory, 412
Periodic rate, 190, 206, 250, 298
Perpendicular, 484
Perpetual inventory, 412
Personal financial statement, 394
Personal identification number (PIN), 142
Personal property, 315, 453
Piecework rate, 159–60
Pie chart, 525
Pizza, cost per square inch, 491
Plant and equipment, 392
Points for a loan, 326
Polygon, 484
Population study, 527, 528
Portion, 76
    solving for, 77
Preferred stock, 342
Prepayment penalty, 183, 327
Pre-qualified, 314
Present value, 206, 213–17, 250, 260–63
    for a series of uneven payments, 370, 372–73
Price/cost ratio, 126
Price earnings (PE) ratio, 345
Pricing strategy, 124–26
Principal, 180
    portion of a periodic payment, 184
Product, 9
Profit, 388
    gross, 390
Profit and loss statement (See Income statement)
Profit margin, before tax, 399
Proper fraction, 30
Property tax, 317, 453–55
    assessed value, 453
    rate, 453–55
Prospectus, 350
Prox (See End of month dating)

Quotient, 10

Radius, 485, 486
Range, 527
Rate
    annual percentage (APR), 183, 293, 327, 360
    growth, 366
    nominal, 192, 298
    periodic, 190, 206, 250, 298
    solving for, in percent formula, 78–79
    solving for, in simple interest formula, 186–88
Rate of return
    internal, 370, 371–72
    on a bond, 368
    on a mutual fund, 369
    on a promissory note, 369
    on a stock investment, 367
Ratio, 398
    acid-test, 399
    back-end, 314

    business, 398
    current, 399
    debt, 399
    debt-to-income, 314
    front end, 314
    housing, 314
    inventory turnover, 399
    price earnings, 345
Real estate, 312, 453
    appraiser, 313
    broker, 313
Real property (See Real estate)
Receipt of goods (ROG) dating, 105
Reciprocal, 35
Reconciling a bank statement, 144–48
Recovery period, 431
Rectangle, 484
    area of, 487
    perimeter of, 485
    volume of solid, 488–89
Reduced price, 123
Reducing a fraction, 32–33
Refinance, 363
Regulation Z (See Truth in Lending Act)
Remainder, in division, 11
Repeating decimal, 39
Replacement cost, 466
Reserve account (See Escrow account)
Retailer, 97
Retained earnings, 394
Returned goods, 102, 390
Return on equity, 399
Revenue, 388
Reverse mortgage, 325
Revolving credit (See Open-end credit)
Right angle, 484
Rounding, 6–7
Rule of 72, 282
Rule of 78, 297

Salary, 158
Sales tax, 451–52
Salvage value, 426
Sample study, 528–29
Savings bonds, 346
S Corporation, 395
Section 179 Expense Deduction, 434–35
Security (See Collateral)
Securities and Exchange Commission (SEC), 344
Self employed, 166
    FICA tax for, 166–67
    taxes for, 166–68
Series discount, 100
Service company, 388–89
Signed numbers
    addition and subtraction of, 52
    multiplication and division of, 52
Simple interest, 179
    formulas, 180, 185
    vs compound interest, 189–90
Sinking fund, 228–30, 274–76
Sliding scale commission, 160
Sliding scale discount, 104
Social security tax, 161–62, 165, 166–67

Sole proprietorship, 388
Solving equations, 54–57
Specific identification method, 412–13
Square, 484
Standard & Poors, 347
Stacked bar graph, 524–25
Standard deduction, 447
Standard deviation, 527–29
State unemployment tax, 166
Statistics, 519
Stock
    brokerage firm, 342
        fees, 344
    common, 342
    corporate, 342
    dividend, 342
    exchange, 342
    index, 343
    investing in, 344
    preferred, 342
    price, 343
    quotes in a newspaper, 343–44
    rate of return on, 367
    selecting, 345
Stockholder, 342, 388
Stockholders' equity, 393
Story problem (*See* Word problem)
Straight line depreciation, 427
    for partial year, 429–30
Subtraction
    of decimal numbers, 16
    of fractions, 34, 36
    of whole numbers, 8–9
Subtrahend, 8
Sum, 7
Swing shift, 158
Symbols, 50

Tax
    Additional Medicare, 161, 165, 167
    assessor, 453
    bracket, 450
    FICA, 161
    income, 446–51
    Medicare, 161, 165
    property, 453–55
    rate schedules, 447, 449
    sales, 451–52
    self-employed FICA, 166–67
    social security, 161, 165
    tables, 447, 448
    withholdings, 161–64, 165
Taxable income, 446–47
Temperature conversions, 509–10
Terminating decimal, 39
Terms
    combining, 53–54
    like, 53
Time, 180, 185–86
Time-value-of-money problem, 205, 249
Trade discount, 97, 98–101
    amount, 98
    chain, 100
    rate, 98
    series, 100
    single, 98–99
Treasury
    bill, 346
    bond, 346
    note, 346, 348
Trend and ratio analysis, 395-99
Triangle, 484, 487
Truth in lending act, 183, 294, 360

Underinsured, 467, 470
Uninsured motor vehicle, 470

Unit cost, 490–91
Units of production depreciation, 427–28
    for partial year, 430
Useful life, 426
U.S. Rule, 183, 293
U.S. Securities, 346
Usury law, 187

VA loan, 313
Valuation of inventory, 412–15
Value (*See* Fair market value)
Variable, 50
Variable commission, 160
Variable costs, 128
Vertical analysis, 396
VISA, 298
Volume, 483, 488–89
    cylinder, 489
    rectangular solid, 488–89

W-2 Form, 167
W-4 Form, 162
Wage bracket method, 163
Weighted average inventory method, 413
Weighted mean, 520
Whole number, 4, 7–11
Wholesaler, 97
Wire transfer, 505
Withholding allowance, 162
Word problem, 12, 58
    strategy for solving, 12–15, 58–61

Yield, on a bond, 368–69

Zero-coupon bond, 346